Manning the Race

SEXUAL CULTURES: New Directions from the Center for
Lesbian and Gay Studies
General Editors: José Esteban Muñoz and Ann Pellegrini

Times Square Red, Times Square Blue
Samuel R. Delany

Private Affairs: *Critical Ventures in the Culture of Social Relations*
Phillip Brian Harper

In Your Face: *9 Sexual Studies*
Mandy Merck

Tropics of Desire: *Interventions from Queer Latino America*
José Quiroga

Murdering Masculinities: *Fantasies of Gender and Violence
in the American Crime Novel*
Greg Forter

Our Monica, Ourselves: *The Clinton Affair and the National Interest*
Edited by Lauren Berlant and Lisa Duggan

Black Gay Man: *Essays*
Robert Reid-Pharr *Foreword by Samuel R. Delany*

Passing: *Identity and Interpretation in Sexuality, Race, and Religion*
Edited by María Carla Sánchez and Linda Schlossberg

The Queerest Art: *Essays on Lesbian and Gay Theater*
Edited by Alisa Solomon and Framji Minwalla

Queer Globalizations: *Citizenship and the Afterlife of Colonialism*
Edited by Arnaldo Cruz-Malavé and Martin F. Manalansan IV

Queer *Latinidad*: *Identity Practices, Discursive Spaces*
Juana María Rodríguez

Love the Sin: *Sexual Regulation and the Limits of Religious Tolerance*
Janet R. Jakobsen and Ann Pellegrini

Manning the Race: *Reforming Black Men in the Jim Crow Era*
Marlon B. Ross

Manning the Race

Reforming Black Men in the Jim Crow Era

MARLON B. ROSS

NEW YORK UNIVERSITY PRESS

New York and London

NEW YORK UNIVERSITY PRESS
New York and London
www.nyupress.org

Library of Congress Cataloging-in-Publication Data
Ross, Marlon Bryan, 1956–
Manning the race : reforming Black men in the Jim Crow era / Marlon B. Ross.
p. cm. — (Sexual cultures)
Includes bibliographical references and index.
ISBN 0–8147–7562–4 (cloth : acid-free paper) —
ISBN 0–8147–7563–2 (pbk. : acid-free paper)
1. African American men—Social conditions—20th century.
2. African American men—Race identity.   3. African American men—
Sexual behavior.   4. Masculinity—United States—History—20th century.
5. Homosexuality—Social aspects—United States—History—20th century.
6. Sex role—United States—History—20th century.   7. American literature—
African American authors—History and criticism.   8. African American men
in literature.   9. Masculinity in literature.   10. Homosexuality in literature.
I. Title.   II. Series.
E185.86.R77   2004
305.38'896073'009—dc22   2003025044

New York University Press books are printed on acid-free paper,
and their binding materials are chosen for strength and durability.

Manufactured in the United States of America

c 10 9 8 7 6 5 4 3 2 1
p 10 9 8 7 6 5 4 3 2 1

In memory of Sara Elaine Bryan Ross (1923–1994)

Acknowledgments

For a project that has spanned so many years and pages, it is hardly surprising that millions of incalculable debts—intellectual, institutional, collegial, and personal—have been accrued. This project was conceived and initiated during a fellowship leave made possible by the generosity of the John Simon Guggenheim Foundation. I wish also to thank the Department of English; the Center for Afroamerican and African Studies; the Rackham School of Graduate Studies; the College of Literature, Science, and Arts; and the Office of the Vice President for Research at the University of Michigan, for various sorts of institutional support. Thanks to the College of Arts and Sciences, Department of English, and Carter G. Woodson Institute for Afro-American and African Studies at the University of Virginia for a much-needed leave in the final lap of revision. I'm grateful to staff, students, and colleagues at the California Institute of Technology, and particularly Kevin Gilmartin, for their hospitality during the spring of 1996. I would be remiss not to mention the support of students, staff, and colleagues at Michigan's Center for Afroamerican and African Studies—especially James Jackson, Don Sims, Elizabeth James, and Camille Spencer.

I am grateful to colleagues, programs, and audience participants at universities across the country and over the ocean who gave me an opportunity to engage in dialogue about the direction of this project, including the works-in-progress seminar at Yale University's African American Studies program, particularly Cathy Cohen; the William Bennett Munro Memorial Seminar Lecture at the California Institute of Technology; the Distinguished Lecture Series of the Humanities Institute and the masculinities workshop at University of California at Davis; the cultural property conference at St. John's College, Oxford University, especially Ron Bush and Elazar Barkan; the English Department at University of California at Santa Barbara, especially Julie Carlson; the University of Detroit's Symposium on African American Manhood, especially Roy E. Finkenbine; the State University of New York College at Geneseo, especially Laura Doan; the English Department at the University of Massachusetts, especially Christine Cooper; the Claud Howard Visiting Scholar Lectureship at Southwestern University, particularly Walt Herbert and David Gaines; and Michigan's Institute for Research on Women and Gender. My research assistants over the years—Scott Heath, Doris Dixon, Jennifer Hughes, and Michael Lewis—have been models of precision. I'm grateful to all the graduate and undergraduate students at Michigan who enthusiastically agreed to be subjected to courses broaching the topics of this book.

As to the many other intellectual obligations, it must suffice to allow the citations to name the vast majority of them. The members of Michigan's faculty/graduate student seminar on gender in African American Life and Culture—especially Elsa Barkley Brown, Michael Awkward, and Michelle Wright—continue to stimulate me through their work. There are other colleagues who have expressed their confidence in my work—even when I wasn't sure of what I was doing—through spirited conversations, among them: Anne Herrmann, Veronica Gregg, Sandra Gunning, Arlene Keizer, Deborah McDowell, Sharon Holland, Jennifer DeVere Brody, Sally Robinson, Alan Wald, Stacey Olster, Elyse Blankley, Patsy Yaeger, Alan Nadel, and the late Lem Johnson. The anonymous press reviewers provided invaluable advice that helped to sharpen the argument, and Eric Zinner, Despina Papazoglou Gimbel, and Emily Park adeptly guided a ragged manuscript toward bookdom.

For my family—Daddy, Sandra, Regina, Marcia, Ron, Enola, Lance, and Mother, to whose memory this book is dedicated—thank you for believing that if I'm determined to do it, it must be important. And, of course, my biggest thanks to Ian, for putting up with my daily kvetching, and for intellectual inspiration, good humor, Yoga, serenades, and home grounding in the best and worst of times.

Manning the Race

Introduction

Manning the Race: Reforming Black Men in the Jim Crow Era explores how men of African descent were marketed, embodied, socialized, and imaged for the purposes of political, professional, and cultural advancement during the early decades of the twentieth century. By foregrounding black manhood as a culturally contested arena, the study probes the changing meanings and enactments of race, gender, nation, and sexuality in modern America. It examines how black men have attempted to formulate and re-form their experiences, roles, and self-concepts as men in a variety of genres, media, and social practices, as well as how the construction of black manhood has been articulated and negotiated in relation to interested others—particularly black women and white reformers concerned with tutoring, managing, civilizing, and disciplining "the black man" for the benefit of domestic prosperity, racial uplift, and national progress. As this task of black manhood reform is carried out amid and against the entrenched system of Jim Crow, the study investigates the diverse and often conflicting strategies exploited to contest and defeat this system. From the castrating violence of lynching to political and legal disenfranchisement; from discriminatory employment practices to exclusionary patterns of white male socializing; from derogatory racial/sexual typing in science and popular media to strictures on sexual, romantic, and companionate liaisons; from patronizing forms of address and social interaction to systemic modes of social segregation—all have conspired to unman, and thus discredit, black men as influential leaders of the race, within the nation and on the world stage.

The Jim Crow regime poses an impossible paradox for those endeavoring to build an efficacious black manhood. On the one hand, the Jim Crow system insists that men of African descent are not fully men—in effect, that they are not capable of being *normal* men—as a justification for excluding them from those rights, rites, networks, and entitlements that endow middle-class white men with their proper claims as proprietors and entrepreneurs within the economy, fathers and defenders of the state, heads of families and households, inseminators and creators of civilization, inventors and discoverers of scientific progress, and empowered citizens of the nation and the world. On the other hand, while Jim Crow insists on black men's natural deficiency as men, it necessarily also demands that they adhere and aspire to the social codes established for the conduct of men. The Jim Crow regime exploits the ideology of black male deficiency to justify and administer an entrenched color line through violence, intimidation, coercion, and the sadistic manipulation of the courts, schools, public transport, and other instruments of public interest. As it does so, it unwittingly exposes the arbitrariness of the gender line that is supposed to separate all men from women as a natural division in culture. In managing the color line effectively, the Jim Crow regime finds itself attempting to guard a sexual fault line that not only tries to segregate black men from white women but also—and less frequently analyzed—tries to segregate white men from black men, except in those scenarios where the white man's authority over black men is institutionally and structurally staged and reinforced: for instance, the southern planter in charge of his black sharecroppers, the northern industrialist supervising laborers at the bottom of the factory system, the white railroad trainmen bossing around servile black porters, the white businessman standing over the "shine" who polishes his shoes, the white military officer commanding black troops, and the armed white mob lynching defenseless black men.

In her study *Gender and Jim Crow,* Glenda Gilmore has explained how this system sought to subordinate African American women, who resisted Jim Crow using the same gendered resources that were supposed to disqualify them from acting on their own behalf. I would take this idea further by indicating how the Jim Crow regime itself is a *sexual* system of oppression. Demonstrating that Jim Crow is as much a regime of sexual classification as it is a form of racial imposition, *Manning the Race* spotlights this constant interplay between, on the one hand, race as a contested gender line of demarcation bifurcating the category "man" into superior versus inferior males and, on the other hand, gender as a racially contested line of demarcation dividing the category of "race" into manly versus unmanly groups of men. As we shall see throughout this study, and in the discussions of chapters 4 and 5 especially, even in those biracial institutions established to fight the worst offenses of the Jim Crow regime—the NAACP, the Urban League, and other cross-racial patronage agencies—an internal color/gender line is quietly reproduced to protect the white founders and directors from competing directly with black men *and women.* Because the Jim Crow regime insists on a gender norm that is already impossible for African Americans to fulfill, one strategy of attacking the regime entails resistance to masculine normalization itself, a project that casts black men in different roles across a range of institutions, practices, media, genres, and discourses. Showing how these ideological struggles over gender and sexual norms have shaped and been shaped by particular genres, cultural formations, political activities, and social practices, *Manning the Race* pursues the racial and sexual logic operating in rival modes of gendered interaction between white and black, male and female, husband and wife, token leader and folk masses, patron and protégé, activist and artist, heterosexual and homosexual, as well as between blacks and whites in triangulated relations with other racialized or ethnic groups such as Europeans, American Indians, Africans, Irish immigrants, West Indians, and working-class whites.

By interrogating the interstices between such identity categories, *Manning the Race* seeks to advance recent theories of the social construction of identity while challenging some of the most common assumptions—in both scholarship and popular discourse—concerning the placement of black manhood as an ongoing subject of political and cultural debate. This study has been particularly influenced by four interdisciplinary fields: black feminist theory, race theory, masculinity studies, and sexuality and queer studies. From the work of black feminist theorists such as Barbara Christian, Hortense Spillers, Deborah McDowell, Mae Henderson, Cheryl Wall, Claudia Tate, Valerie Smith, Gloria Hull, Angela Davis, Hazel Carby, and Ann duCille, this study understands the social practices, literature, and other cultural materials associated with African Americans to constitute not only a rich cultural tradition but also a theoretical intervention in itself.[1] Black feminist theory has obvious bearing for understanding black manhood, as it has been attuned from the outset to the necessity of exploring the interplay between "femininity" and "masculinity" as supplementary categories conditioning the notion of a black race by excluding black women from "femininity" as a privileged, if subordinating, quality of white womanhood, and by doubly excluding black women, as well as black men, from the highest values of full human agency and citizenship endowed by "masculinity."

As Hazel Carby has asked in her move from examining black womanhood to black manhood, can the theories honed in the study of black women's traditions be deployed to understand black manhood?[2] The answer to this question is most definitely yes.[3] As Carby has suggested, however, the pressure on black manhood entitles it to a racial representativeness not accorded to black womanhood, such that it is possible to discuss the condition of "the race" as though that condition could be equated solely with the crisis of black manhood (*Race Men* 9–41). Keeping the theoretical lessons of black feminism uppermost in mind, I have resisted any attempt to segregate the experiences, writing, structures, and practices of African American men from those of black women—or indeed from those of other identity groups. Yet, at the same time, this study argues that black manhood should be understood as a peculiarly instituted identity formation with a particular history of its own. My attempt to balance this historically particular cultural peculiarity with the interrelational nature of cultural identification has led me to examine black women's role in the construction of black manhood at strategic moments in the argument, including, for instance, the work of Fannie Barrier Williams, Ida B. Wells-Barnett, Jessie Fauset, and Nella Larsen.

Manning the Race also seeks to advance race theory, in particular with regard to the task of moving beyond exclusive attention to the black body—collective and individualized—as the sole stigmatized object of racial and sexual subordination. Spillers's work and Lindon Barrett's book *Blackness and Value: Seeing Double* have been especially instructive in this effort. Without a doubt, we must continue to attend to the body, as it is assumed to operate as the sole carrier of identity in dominant discourses on sex and race. However, as Barrett and Spillers have theorized in different ways, more attention needs to be brought to the borders, boundaries, and gaps that determine how bodies are constituted and how cultural identities are conceived and administered, repelled and opposed.[4] Based in the notion that bodies occupy unequal binary categories, black versus white and male versus female being foundational, the logic of race and the logic of sexual anatomy bolster each other in what Robyn Wiegman calls "economies of visibility" as she traces the analogous thinking that led Western science to locate economies of unequal identity *inside* the flesh.[5]

Certainly, the black male body itself becomes one visible stamp of Jim Crow exclusion. Hoping to push beyond the visible body as abstract object, however, I suggest here the need to analyze the body in motion or arrested at a threshold: migrating across the Mason-Dixon line or across an invisible line separating civilization from frontier; remigrating from city to city and neighborhood to neighborhood across tenuous class lines within black communities; arrested at the door of a Jim Crow car, the margin of a white male social network, or the front door of a colleague's house. I argue that the body in motion gets us closer to the sense of Jim Crow violence, coercion, and exclusion, as well as to the sense of black manhood as a moving target that cannot be situated in only one static place, behavior, or image. This study also demonstrates how the body out of place or arrested in place—the body poised to transgress the color line, for instance—has also been turned into a personal weapon of racial and sexual confrontation and trespassing at a particular historical juncture, when those schooled for racial uplift in egalitarian post-emancipation Negro institutions find their individual ambitions thwarted by the newly erected strictures of racial segregation at the turn of the nineteenth century.

I am also concerned to flesh out the techniques and structures of observing in-motion bodies—as in, for instance, photography, Darwinist evolutionary narratives, the use of empirical science in race polemics, artistic sketching, allegorical catalog, personalized narratives, sociological ethnography, institutional networking and tokenism, cross- and intraracial patronage uplift mechanisms, and the fictionalization of intimate contacts within the race. In addition to techniques for observing the body in motion and arrested, the focus particularly of Part 1, *Manning the Race* foregrounds notions of taboo social contact and circulation, the body touching other bodies—African American, Native American, Jewish American, queer—as a way of disturbing the color/gender line of Jim Crow. Part 2 focuses on such contacts in the institutional settings of biracial patronage organizations, and Part 3 focuses on such contacts in the indigenous settings of African American institutions and neighborhoods as they are depicted in urban folk fiction of the 1920s and 1930s. Thus, in chapter 1 we see W.E.B. Du Bois distancing the emancipated slave from the Jew through scapegoating, and in chapter 5 we see him distancing his own person from that of a black subordinate at the NAACP who has become embroiled in homosexual scandal.

Like Barrett, I am interested in showing how other sense perceptions—sound and smell in addition to touch—simultaneously supplement and disturb the attempt visually to classify bodies by sex and race in order to segregate and degrade them in the Jim Crow regime. Thus, included here are discussions of how encounters with black men's voices reveal the gender competition at stake among men in the establishment of New Negro patronage institutions. For instance, in chapter 2 we examine Carl Van Vechten's attempt both to mystify and to type the high tenor voice of Taylor Gordon in order to patronize him as a primitive in need of cultural mediation. In chapter 5 we consider Claude McKay's slighting of Alain Locke's prissy voice in order to diminish Locke's role as a manly leader of the New Negro cultural movement. Similarly, in chapter 4 I call attention to Du Bois's and Mary White Ovington's obsessions with physical touch—ambivalently de-eroticized—across race and gender as a radical act destabilizing Jim Crow assumptions. Ironically, given the hegemony of sight as a scientific technique for controlled observation in sociological ethnography, in chapter 3 we see how the smell of black workers on nonsegregated streetcars erupts into—and potentially disrupts—the neutral voice of Charles S. Johnson's policy study on the Chicago race riot of 1919. We begin to understand the invasive potential of even the most seemingly passive bodies when odor is taken into account as a hidden cause of racial rioting. In chapter 7, we come to see how racial self-loathing can be incited by the smallest ephemera of an assaulting smell. Such is the case when the odors of the black underclass on the segregated train sicken Nella Larsen's heroine in *Quicksand*.

This study argues that bodies are always in motion, changing their cultural-historical placement by struggling against the terms of their stigmatization even when arrested—for instance, when stopped from entering a Jim Crow train car. And it further argues that in-motion bodies are always collectively determined, even when represented as isolated by exceptional cunning, daring, talent, alertness, education, or some other quality of individual achievement. In chapter 2, I argue that the New Negro personal narrative—autobiographies and novels written by the first generation not to experience slavery directly—intentionally isolates the narrator-hero as a way of establishing a manly agency that can out maneuver Jim Crow restraints. Throughout the study, I track the myriad ways in which Jim Crow imposes the notion of collective obligation to a consolidated racial group, while also demonstrating how individualism and exceptionalism, characteristics claimed exclusively by white middle-class masculinity, are exploited with varying degrees of success to attack this racial/sexual imposition.

Speaking of chattel enslavement, Spillers theorizes that the African American subject is illegitimately "twice-fathered," first by the biological African father and symbolically by the white slave master as the patriarch of the plantation and the nation or vice versa.[6] The black race, then, is constructed as an il/legitimate family line from the start (as we see Du Bois lamenting in *Souls of Black Folk*), a family always under the shadow of bastardy, crisis, subjection, and dismemberment. But this natural il/legitimacy need not be viewed merely as a negative condition. As the oxymoron of "natural illegitimacy" indicates, the twice-fathering reveals an opportune lapse in racial/sexual logic. Issues of paternal il/legitimacy function in a variety of cultural practices that impinge on efforts to reform black manhood. For instance, in chapter 1 we examine William Pickens's attempts to man the race by writing a revisionist history of the Darwinist competition among the races, and we see Charles Chesnutt slyly insinuating that illegitimacy plagues all racial lines, such that the only scientific solution is systematic miscegenation to create a single American race. The il/legitimacy of racial paternity shows up in surprising places; we find, in chapter 2, Walter White interrogating the il/legitimacy of medicine, high art, and political machinery as patriarchal institutions closed to a black man skilled at all three, and in chapter 3, sociologists struggling to keep middle-class Negro neighborhoods—and their family legacies of racial exceptionalism—distinct from those of the black masses migrating to the cities. In chapter 5 we find the adherents of the Negro Renaissance resorting to the curiously confused racial/gender imagery of the black male as midwife and the white woman as godmother of black renaissance talent. As we see in chapters 6 and 7, the writers of the Harlem Renaissance urban folk novel obsess on paternal il/legitimacy as well, but as a subversive resource that potentially liberates black urban migrants from the arbitrary strictures of conventionally gendered domesticity and labor. As Dorothy Roberts has suggested in her study of how U.S. social policy seeks to control black women's reproductivity, *Killing the Black Body,* this is more than a matter of the reproduction of individual bodies as sexed, raced, and classed beings. The question of il/legitimacy brings attention to the naturalized attributes imposed on collective groups in constantly changing ways, helping to determine their physical mobility and social circulation by restricting access to the material resources, social contacts, and political and psychic benefits of full citizenship.

Manning the Race is also indebted to various works in the emerging field of masculinity studies, especially the essays in *Engendering Men,* edited by Joseph Boone and Michael Cadden, Gail Bederman's *Manliness and Civilization,* Michael Kimmel's *Manhood in America,* E. Anthony Rotundo's *American Manhood,* Kaja Silverman's *Male Subjectivity at the Margins,* and Sally Robinson's *Marked Men.* While influenced by the substance and methods of these studies, *Manning the Race* seeks to overcome the tendency in this field to view black manhood either as a reactive identity overdetermined by the hegemony of white masculinity or as a parallel, if marginalized, cultural formation mimetically patterned on white masculinity.[7] Given the primary objective of these studies to explain white masculinity as the dominating cultural discourse, it is understandable that black manhood identity frequently gets thinned out to the extreme polar cases of hypermasculinity (as black men's overidentification with the white masculine norm) or metaphorical emasculation (as black men's total abjection from that norm). For certain, both of these extremes help explain the cultural history of black manhood, but neither satisfactorily adjudicates the complex maneuverings entailed in the ever-changing project of black manhood reform as historically situated through enslavement, Jim Crow, Civil Rights, Black Power, and other political-cultural movements.

As the analysis of Walter White's hero in *Fire in the Flint* and other works reveals, unlike in dominant discourses on (white) manhood, where emasculation becomes the metaphorical sign of a Freudian crisis within the hegemonic structure of masculinity, in African American culture emasculation bespeaks an actual threat of castration in acts of racial violence such as lynching.[8] This significant difference—between emasculation as metaphorical threat in a crisis of domination versus castration as actual threat in a crisis of ongoing oppression—reveals to what extent the study of black manhood cannot simply be collapsed into masculinity studies any more than a study of black male identity could overlook the crucial insights provided by key works in this emergent field. Fortunately, the case for distinguishing black manhood from the larger field of masculinity studies has already been capably made in a handful of cultural studies books, the most notable among them being Carby's *Race Men;* Phillip Brian Harper's *Are We Not Men?;* the collection of essays entitled *Representing Black Men,* edited by Marcellus Blount and George P. Cunningham; and, most recently, Maurice Wallace's superb book *Constructing the Black Masculine,* as well as David L. Dudley's literary-critical study *My Father's Shadow.* Building on the insights of these previous studies, I hope to further the objective of characterizing the particular diversities evident in conceptions of black manhood, theorizing and historicizing the cultural differences *within* this identity by bringing attention to struggles around socioeconomic class, immigrant and migrant status, education, region, religion, color, gender-role conformity, political affiliation, cross-racial attraction, and sexual orientation.

Most of the work on black manhood tends to focus on particular individual literary figures, especially on their autobiographies, or on controversial topics that explode into current events in popular culture. Both the more literary approach, spotlighting the celebrated figures of self-making autobiography (represented by Dudley's excellent study), and the cultural-studies approach deconstructing the flashpoints of black male controversy (most influentially represented by Harper's work), have shaped my thinking here. Self-making autobiography must be central to understanding black manhood identity, and the ongoing debate over black male models, mentors, and tokens ensures that the analysis of prominent figures will always be needed. Because the ideology of the self-made man is crucial to the notion of manhood reform, *Manning the Race* constitutes an intellectual history of a wide range of individual men who have served—controversially—as models and foils for black masculine competence, including famous figures such as Booker T. Washington, W.E.B. Du Bois, Charles Chesnutt, Walter White, Charles S. Johnson, Alain Locke, Langston Hughes, Claude McKay, E. Franklin Frazier, and Wallace Thurman, as well as lesser-known ones such as activist William Pickens, educator Robert Russa Moton, artist John Henry Adams, singer Taylor Gordon, sociologist George Edmund Haynes, novelist Rudolph Fisher, social critic Gustavus Adolphus Steward, and literary historian Benjamin Brawley, among others. Rather than making these individuals the primary subject of analysis, however, the book concentrates on the cultural practices, social structures, and political activities that shape black manhood as a collectively contested identity that is repeatedly espoused through exceptionally individualized and prominently self-making men.

Just as literary analysis of self-making autobiography is still a useful tool, so mass cultural studies is well suited to unpacking the dominant discourse surrounding the ongoing black male crisis. In the hands of adept cultural critics such as Harper, Wallace, Carby, and Michael Awkward, these topics do the work not only of contemporary cultural critique but also historical edification.[9] I hope that *Manning the Race* can shed some light on these phenomena. Instead of a strictly mass cultural studies approach, however, I have focused on black manhood as a long, layered, and often self-conflicting process of cultural-historical transformation.[10] Although I am concerned to show how black manhood has been shaped by a hegemonic discourse of race and masculinity, evident in how African American men have imagined and imaged themselves, I am also concerned to show how struggles to reform the notion of black manhood—in terms of citizenship, patriarchy, patronage, companionship, romance, militance, and male entitlement—have constantly worried, disrupted, and altered the dominant discourse on race and masculinity. Taking African American writing and activism as crucial sites of self-conscious theorizing on the concept of manhood, *Manning the Race* seeks to frame black manhood as a dialectical process in which black men themselves—as intellectuals, activists, academic sociologists, artists, novelists, teachers, bureaucrats, laborers, and members of families, cohorts, buddy networks, and sexual relationships—have constantly upset the Jim Crow regime simply by working through their own and others' efforts to identify, discipline, subject, and re-form their sense of their manliness. Accordingly, *Manning the Race* analyzes a succession of social, political, and cultural movements for racial reform. Instead of following one temporal sequence across the decades from the 1890s through the 1930s, the study is organized around the political debates, social interactions, and reworkings of literary and other cultural forms occurring within and across particular sites, genres, forms, institutions, and practices at different moments of the Jim Crow era.

Another way in which this study takes an approach different from previous cultural studies work on black manhood concerns the central place of sociology as a major institution involved in the legitimation of black men's gender formation. I argue here that sociology as a discipline was early and fast in constructing black manhood as an object of study appropriate for black men during the Jim Crow regime, and crucial to their professionalization as cultural authorities on the condition of the race as a whole. Early urban sociology (1890s–1940s) is especially instructive because it was so dominated by white and black men cooperating and competing for authority over the social policy on the race question, as we see in the work of the black male sociologists examined in chapter 3 and in the sexual rivalries of biracial organizations discussed in chapter 4. Just as literary and cultural critics have tended to overlook the importance of the sociology of black manhood, so, with the exception of Anthony J. Lemelle Jr.'s *Black Male Deviance,* sociological treatments of the black male problem have tended to overlook the influence of literary and cultural critique on their constructions of black manhood identity.[11] More recent sociological black manhood studies—for instance, Elliot Liebow's *Tally's Corner: A Study of Negro Streetcorner Men* (1967), Dan Rose's *Black American Street Life* (1987), Elijah Anderson's *Streetwise: Race, Class, and Change in an Urban Community* (1990), and Mitchell Duneier's *Slim's Table: Race, Respectability, and Masculinity* (1992)—participate in a long national tradition of local surveillance of black male life as a way of discovering, each time as though it had not been discovered before, the relative deviance or ordinariness of black men's gender conduct. Although such studies exploit the same narrative techniques evident in fictionalized accounts of black male urban migration and settlement dating back to the turn of the nineteenth century, they have rarely been analyzed in relation to this fiction.[12] Early black men's sociology is also especially revealing in that the three most influential early black male sociologists—Du Bois, Charles S. Johnson, and Frazier—displayed an interest in literary composition as a mode of manhood reform. As we shall see, their work is informed and influenced by the New Negro autobiographies, novels, and race polemics being composed by others—when they are not themselves composing such—and in turn, their sociological demeanor, method, and authority become thematized in black urban folk fiction of the 1920s and 1930s in both serious and satirical takes on ethnography as a mode of racial slumming, voyeurism, and surveillance. Whereas sociology still tends to treat black manhood identity largely in terms of the sociosexual binary of respectability versus deviance, *Manning the Race,* building on previous black manhood studies, attempts to get beneath this binary by exploring the political and cultural imperatives for perpetuating it.

The new field of sexuality/queer studies has also been instrumental in shaping this aspect of *Manning the Race.* Although I have been influenced by the two most common ways of talking about sexual identity in queer/sexuality theory—sexuality as social discourse and sexuality as performance of a cultural script—this study does not fully accord with these approaches. Because I am concerned to understand black manhood reform as a collective process of cultural revision and transformation not only for African American men but for others interested in the disciplining of black men's desires, discursive formation and performative sexuality are not always helpful concepts, emphasizing, as they do, the subjection or reiteration of individuals as representatives of groups, rather than the way groups collectively struggle to change their cultural formations even against the grain of their prescripted social identities. Curiously, the most influential queer theorists have had little to say about the relationship between race and sexuality with regard to men of African descent, and when they have addressed the subject, they have limited discussion to a binary of predictable ideas: either the question of black men's homophobia (usually referring to Frantz Fanon and black nationalism as quintessential cases) or the question of black gay men's alienation from both black and queer communities (invariably taking Baldwin as the quintessential case).[13]

I try to avoid queer theory's tendency to recognize black male same-gender desire only when it is legitimated by being either ostracized by black male homophobia or salvaged by its connection to white queerness. I hope to move beyond this binary of black male homophobia supplemented by black male homosexuality as alienation from blackness by placing black male same-gender desire in the larger cultural perspective of black male sexuality, and in turn placing black male sexuality in the larger cultural perspective of black manhood identity. In doing so, we begin to get a more historically and culturally nuanced sense of the complicated, sometimes conflicting experience and representation of same-sexuality in African American writing, institutions, politics, and social networks. This is not to deny that black homosexuality has an important relationship to the expression of homosexuality in dominant U.S. culture. Indeed, it would be impossible to separate one from the other. Challenging previous work in gender and race studies, which tends to lament the *absence* of images of homosexuality, the book illustrates the prominence and importance of same-sexuality in black men's writing and social practices by examining the representation of sissies, sweet men, sweetbacks, dandies, aesthetes, roustabouts, boys, wolves, punks, freaks, dinges, faggots, daggers, and men-loving men in the construction of racial identity and community across the Jim Crow era.

African American literary writers have employed sex (sexual desire, sexual intercourse, sexual orientation, the gendering of sex) self-consciously as a lever for prying underneath the dominant notion of race in African American texts since at least the mid–nineteenth century.[14] In European-descended discourses, sex and sexuality have been organized predominantly on the site of women's bodies as an intrinsic lack of control within them. Thus, this universal hierarchy—abstractly and categorically placing all men above all women—could be based in the idea of men's superior capacity for sexual and other kinds of self-discipline.[15] In the establishment of a racial hierarchy, a naturalized exception had to be made for men of African descent; otherwise there could be no justification for the division into, and the systematic subordination of, one group of men as distinguished from another group.[16] When African American men were exempted from full citizenship over the course of the 1880s and 1890s, a peculiar discourse exempting emancipated African American males from the principle of universal male emancipation had to be legally systematized, a discourse that settled, at its most basic level, on the sexual deviance and consequent social irresponsibility of black men's desires and ambitions—equating or analogizing the unreliable passions and uncountable impulses of men of African descent to the unaccountable mysteries of women as legitimately disenfranchised creatures. Of course, the discourse connecting the African to a regressive animality was in place long before the rise of Jim Crow.[17] Just as upper-class Anglo-Saxon women were seen as needing protection by their fathers, husbands, brothers, and sons due to the natural frailty of their flesh, so African American men were conceptualized as needing to be guarded and preempted from the masculine privileges of social, political, and economic rule due to the natural savagery of their desires.

Placing the question of black men's sexual deviance in a fuller cultural context, this study also attends to the seldom analyzed problem of competitive, professional, fraternal, erotic, and sexual relations between men as a racialized phenomenon. Borrowing from Eve Sedgwick, this book explores the relevance of homosocial theory for African American men without assuming the universal application of the theory for all men.[18] Although African American men can desire and aspire to a homosocial relationship, unequal racial status presents gender, sexual, and social impediments. I have coined the term *homoracial* to indicate the different dynamics that result from the pressures of a gendered hierarchy of the races—indicating how in United States culture homosociality historically relies on the systematic exclusion of black men, as well as the central targeting of women as sexual objects and homosexual men as scapegoats. The theory of homoraciality is explained more fully in chapter 1, where Pickens's polemical race history provides a perfect example of its operation, and is elaborated in succeeding chapters. Although much of this study emphasizes how black men's sexual identity is publicly staged in an agenda of racial reform, I have learned from the work of Elsa Barkley Brown how important it is not to reduce black men's experiences and self-representations to gender enactments in the public sphere, and I have learned from the work of K. Ian Grandison how to look behind the public facade that African Americans present in negotiating Jim Crow to discover private spaces not only embattled by racial violence but also nurtured by a degree of racial separation and autonomy proffered by all-black institutions and communities.[19] Especially in chapters 4 through 7, this study analyzes men's internal *companionate relations* as a crucial dynamic operating in the agendas of black manhood reform.[20] In some instances, such relations seem to be studiously avoided. Both Washington and Pickens, for example, represent their closest ties as being with *white* men—Washington as a companionate disciple, Pickens as an adversary—or with women. The male writers of the New Negro Renaissance, however, explore companionate relations between black men in a variety of forms that erect male companionship as a foundation of their new urban colonies in the North.[21] Manly companionship shades over indistinguishably into homoeroticism, as homoeroticism shades over imperceptibly into same-sexuality. As discussed in chapters 4 through 7, I do not assume that sexual expression between African American men in the context of black cultural experience is necessarily "homosexual" or "gay." I argue that same-sexuality takes a variety of forms in black men's conduct and writing, and that it is often exploited as a way of understanding the role of dominant masculinity in racial oppression.

The study is organized around three kinds of racial/sexual movement: (1) the individual and collective migratory body in motion across color lines and gender lines; (2) the black male person in social circulation within biracial institutions and patronage networks; and (3) the "footloose" mass migrant restlessly seeking community amid the changing racial and class affiliations and sexual boundaries of the northern city. Part 1 examines the New Negro body in migratory motion in narratives and visual scenes of civilizational advance. Part 2 focuses on how black men maneuver newly organized biracial institutions and social networks established to fight Jim Crow. If Part 1 shows the black male body in movement through "open" spatial vistas such as world civilization, geographic migration, the frontier, and the fast-moving transport of trains, Part 2 zones in on claustrophobic scenarios within political organizations and social networks where black and white, male and female, come into literal touch with one another. Although this touching is supposed to disrupt the segregationist logic of the Jim Crow regime, we discover that progressive biracial touching has its own racial and sexual restraints, frequently benefiting white patrons as it appears patronizingly to uplift black wards. Just as narratives and scenes of civilizational advance necessarily create a sexual undertow in which New Negroes must decide how to represent the sexual demeanor of the race—as aggressive or neutered—so these progressive social contacts raise issues of cross-racial intimacy between the sexes and among men, as well as gendered rivalry among men within and across racial and sexual boundaries.

Part 3 returns to the migratory black body, but this time within the indigenous social networks of the emerging black urban neighborhoods in northern cities. The same migratory masses whose "footloose" restlessness worries the black male sociologists of Part 1 inspire the urban folk novelists of Part 3. Giving us a glimpse of life from the threshold between upwardly aspiring middle-class New Negroes and the lateral movements characteristic of the "underworld" of the folk masses, these novels cast suspicion on all the devices of upward mobility analyzed in the previous chapters: the race of civilization, individualized heroic narrative, sociological surveillance, biracial uplift organizing, and artistic patronage networks. In effect, the urban folk novel stands as a critique of any New Negro whose notion of progress or upward ascent relies on a straight and narrow path through the American system of Jim Crow.

The diverse efforts at black manhood reform detailed in this study indicate to what extent this historical juncture shapes and is shaped by a particular ideology of black manhood identity. After a brief respite when black men's manhood rights are tenuously asserted under the policies of "radical" Reconstruction, the Jim Crow regime is extended and intensified nationally from the 1890s through the 1930s.

Black men discover that to have won "emancipation" is not to have won the gendered entitlements granted to white men upon reaching the age of twenty-one, that magical age of manhood emancipation. For black men, the obvious disconnect between these two meanings of emancipation conditions their identity as racial and gendered beings seeking a vehicle through which they can assert historical agency. Every major racial reform institution or movement organized to assail this regime is riddled with the question of what it means to be a black male without access to the naturalized entitlements endowing manhood in dominant culture: citizen, head of household, founder of the nation, leader of a race, victor over the frontier, scientific inventor, captain of industry, commander on the field of battle, and patron of advancing civilization. At the same time, the effort to reform black manhood against the strictures of Jim Crow has been an ongoing struggle to move beyond the dominant conventions of masculinity as they have been coded and enacted in the ideology of white male supremacy.

Part I Trespassing the Color Line

Aggressive Mobility, Sexual Transgression, and Racial Consolidation in New Negro Movements

The new spirit which has produced the New Negro bids fair to transform the whole race. America faces a new race that has awakened, and in the realization of its strength has girt its loins to run the race with other men.

—E. Franklin Frazier ("New Currents of Thought
among the Colored People of America" 71)

It is still true of the Negro in America, as it once was of the serfs in Europe, that city air makes men free, and this is true in more ways than are ordinarily conceived of. The great cities are now what the frontier and the wilderness once was, the refuge of the footloose, the disinherited, and all those possessed by the undefined *malaise* we call social unrest.

—Robert E. Park ("Politics and 'the Man Farthest Down,'"
in *Race and Culture* 168)

It may be said that great nations produce great men, but, with equal truth, great men make great nations. . . . The history of any nation is embodied in the history of its great men.

—Charles Chesnutt (quoted in William L. Andrews,
The Literary Career of Charles W. Chesnutt 87)

Confronted by a seemingly intractable system of Jim Crow, African American leaders at the turn of the nineteenth century were presented with the problem of how to exploit the newness of the century to advocate for a new paradigm of race relations. For African American men, this problem was inextricable from the peculiar question of how to lay claim to the manly charge of leading the race into modernity while being denied both the prerogatives of normal manhood entitlement and the attributes of entrepreneurial self-making and scientific discovery associated with a modernizing racial temperament. If the condition of the black race itself defined social backwardness, economic dependence, and biological regression in the spheres of both progressive political governance and dominant scientific research, then how could African American men launch their race into modernity by positioning themselves as a new breed of black male leaders exempt from or transcending this definitive racial condition? With a flurry of polemical tracts and visual aids, autobiographical and fictive writing, anthologizing, political action, and social research aimed at exploiting the newness of the century to organize and advertise a new order of Negro leadership, black men, sometimes in league with black women and sometimes at odds with them, struggled to formulate and articulate the character of a new figure whom they called "the New Negro." The emergence of this exceptional figure not only betokened what they saw as an unprecedented leap forward toward modern civilization for a race barely two generations before benighted by enslavement, illiteracy, and familial and social disorganization. It also embodied and represented the newness of a race quickly modernizing itself from top to bottom, or sometimes even from bottom to top.

The newness of the Negro was proclaimed, advocated, demonstrated, and illustrated in a variety of political campaigns, writing enterprises, research studies, and mass media interventions, often with conflicting ideological agendas. The work of modernizing the Negro was dominated by three "genres," or authoritative modes of expression: new-century race treatises and anthologies (race tracts and albums), New Negro personal narratives (autobiographical and fictional), and professional sociological studies. At one extreme, the work of accelerated race modernization appeared to be highly and self-consciously partisan, flagrantly presenting the New Negro as new exactly because he was eager to do battle on behalf of the race like a newly armed, forward-looking man. Ready to designate friends and foes among the dominant race, this polemical mode tended to see those within the race as either new incarnations of Negrohood or outright barriers to self-modernization. At the other extreme, the making of a New Negro entailed not racial partisanship but objective, neutral methods of scientific investigation, policy making, and social management based in the newest principles of social-scientific thought and practice.

On one side, new-century race treatises tended to take their cues from the tradition of polemical race writing and social protest going back to the struggle over abolition but infused with the newness of racial autonomy by eschewing old forms of white patronage and exploiting every available means of mass media, including a burgeoning black press. On the other side, black male sociology looked solely to the nonpartisan objectivity of empirical science as the future arbiter of modern authority. As the New Negro personal narrative—fictional and autobiographical— makes apparent, this opposition between polemics and science was falsely binary across all three genres. The personal narratives flirt with the authoritativeness of social science, both thematically by often including figurations of the scientific investigator as characters and formally by adopting the realistic narrative pose of a cool-headed participant-observer relaying ethnographically accurate knowledge of the social system called Jim Crow. At the same time, these personal narratives invest supreme value in the subjective nature of racial contests—positing exceptional individuality as the leading edge of racial modernization and staging race leadership as a spectacle of solitary personal risks and confrontations on the part of black manhood. Furthermore, race polemics and professional sociology, each in its own way, bent the norms set up by their respective social and rhetorical practices. While it looks to hard-hitting political advocacy, the competitiveness of market forces, and mass media controversies as the proper arena for racial self-empowerment, the polemical race tract is self-conflicted, also erecting its sense of racial authority on the objectivity of ethnology and Darwinian science. Similarly, while black sociology clings to empiricist protocols, voiceless prose, collaborative research, and bureaucratic reporting of results through appointed committees, it nonetheless is wrenched from normative social science by eruptions of racial invective and protest and by internecine jockeying for professional credentials to validate racial leadership beneath the studied temperament of disinterested analysis.

All three New Negro expressive modes demonstrate the self-legitimating behaviors carried out in the interest of claiming normal masculine capacities for taking charge of the racial household, but not without embroiling male New Negroes in activities of social and sexual transgression. Frequently, this transgression occurred through the process of taking charge of physical mobility itself. In one way or another, New Negro ideology depends on a self-congratulatory awareness of the individual leader's insistence on the manly freedom of mobility—movement across racial lines, into urban enclaves, up the social ladder, and ultimately toward civilized sophistication. At the same time, the New Negro spokesman manifests a nervous self-consciousness concerning the intensified mobility of the Negro mass, whose ensuing migration cityward and northward enfolds him into a mass movement as just another migrant, rather than as an exceptional leader breaking race barriers single-handedly. Without this anticipation of the Great Migration, any formulation of the New Negro would be impossible, just as polemics, personal narrative, and professionalization could not occur without the mobile masses upon whom race leaders ground their activist authority as racial spokesmen, test their exceptionality as individual adventurers, and base their social-scientific theorems about the race problem and how to solve it expertly.

The New Negro's nervousness amid the black mass bespeaks his plight as a modernizing subject. To be beholden to the mass is potentially to fall into a manic, vagrant cycle of footloose trafficking from neighborhood to neighborhood, city to city, region to region—signaling loose morals. The black masses may seem aimlessly migratory without race leaders self-proclaimed and verified by ruling white men. Likewise, New Negroes could seem incapable of controlling this migratory motion if they identified too closely with the folk, whose identity is still burdened with a primitive, enchained backwardness too clumsy for most white men to call their spontaneous migration a form of self-modernization. According to New Negro ideology, it is up to the black male leader to straighten this circular, vagrant motion into a linear trajectory that can be recognized as progress. Ironically, the black mass could at the same time seem too careless in their mobility, racing toward fast-paced cities before they have had time to adjust their slow slave minds to modernity's speed. In this sense, the black mass may appear too forward, rather than too lagging and lethargic, and it is up to the New Negro manfully to corral, police, and manage the risks presented by a maladjusted, overly energetic mass racial body.

Whether the mass is too slow or too fast, the New Negro leader must jeopardize his own bid to being seen as a specimen of modern Negro identity on account of the social and sexual taboos associated with a people both trapped in the primitive behaviors of the plantation and snared by the degenerate impulses of the urban fast track. The New Negro must maneuver around these traps and snares of social and sexual deviance even while needing to deviate from the strict Jim Crow path in order to prove his mettle for modern leadership.

Race polemics, personal narrative, and professional sociology compelled new-century black men to trespass that very color line (either tacitly or ostentatiously) that was drawn to police black men's place outside the modernizing opportunities of a male-governed U.S. culture. The first three chapters comprising Part 1 of this study examine the rhetoric, format, context, psychology, and politics of each New Negro genre—race tract and album, personal narrative, and sociological study—to understand how and why the formations of black manhood relied so heavily on modes of mobility in New Negro ideology in the first decades of the twentieth century. The manly charge of New Negro identity, we discover, is self-conflicted in different ways for each of these genres, not only as a racial agenda but also as a sexualized vehicle for racial advancement. At stake in what I call "the race of the races" toward civilization are questions of racial/sexual identity played out in different ways in each genre. Across these genres, however, these chapters are concerned to interrogate several especially vexing theoretical problems of racial/sexual identification. One concerns the role of mobility, broadly defined, as one of the crucial ideological components of New Negro progress. Complementing a more familiar discussion of the North-South migration axis, I lay across this pattern the less-discussed East-West axis and suggest that both axes must be viewed in the complicated give-and-take of racial movements strongly invested in cosmopolitanizing the New Negro into a figure I call "the New World Negro." In other words, New Negro treatises, personal narratives, and social science constantly offer a critique of the parochialism of U.S. racial supremacy by appealing to the international context in which the race of the races necessarily is conducted. The potential of mobility is manifested in a variety of other forms and modes—from the polemical notion of black men collectively racing toward modernity to the explosive image of a black hero aggressing against Jim Crow by stepping boldly into a segregated railcar; from the idea that black men have proceeded up the social ladder at an accelerated pace to the black middle-class ambivalence expressed over the "footloose" masses. By bringing attention to physical mobility, geographic migratoriness, mental alertness, social circulation, and swift cultural advancement, New Negroes intend to give momentum and motive to the collective black body as an agency seeking, and quickly discovering, its own moorings.

The second theoretical problem of identity relates closely to the staging of a New World Negro in that it draws attention to the tendency of these writers and activists to triangulate New World Negro identification along the axis of other racialized/sexualized groups. Particularly vital here is the rhetorical and ideological role that American Indians play in these strategies of comparative race racing, as engagement with the East-West axis necessarily raises questions of the ideological cost connected to narratives of black Manifest Destiny and to New Negro narrators who claim a frontier/cowboy assertiveness in fighting Jim Crow. Finally, although Part 1—and the larger study as well—has used recent theories of identity performance and mimicry to understand the ideological agendas of racial advancement, I have rejected some of the pivotal components of these influential approaches to racial/sexual identity formation. Most important, I suggest that to rely on performativity alone as the theoretical ground for racial and sexual identity is to overlook the ways in which collective identification is historically shaped by particular social, political, economic, and cultural changes-sometimes self-consciously pursued by those performing or challenging the cultural roles determined by their identity. Identity performance explains part of the psychology at work when individuals identify collectively, but it fails to account not only for the self-conscious political uses of identity to bring about social change but also for the fact that identity formation is itself enacted in ways that are constantly transformed by the historical circumstances of individuals and groups.

1   Un/Sexing the Race

Modernizing and Marketing the New World Negro

> The vogue of the New Negro, then, had all of the character of a public rela-
> tions promotion. The Negro had to be "sold" to the public in terms they
> could understand. Not the least important target in the campaign was the
> Negro himself; he had to be convinced of his worth.
>
> —Nathan Irvin Huggins (*The Harlem Renaissance* 64)

> In the history of nearly all other races and peoples the doctrine preached at
> such crises has been that manly self-respect is worth more than lands and
> houses, and that a people who voluntarily surrender such respect, or cease
> striving for it, are not worth civilizing.
>
> —W.E.B. Du Bois (*Souls of Black Folk* 43)

Instead of looking back with bitterness and regret at the dire circumstances dealt the race in the waning years of the nineteenth century, many African American thinkers greeted the prospect of the twentieth century with excitement and optimism, evident in a spate of turn-of-the-century publications that determined to capitalize on the new century to forecast better things to come. These black leaders charged the race and themselves with keeping track of the progress made and to be made in the new century as documentary proof of the race's well-timed pace toward modernity. Having recently acquired both literacy and their own educational institutions, these New Negroes, as they called themselves, were intent on documenting not only their steady ascent as a race but also their sense of competence in being able to judge and measure their own progress for themselves. These new-century works—both published texts and the activities, agendas, and institutions that pressured the texts to be written—were constructed contrarily as objective documentation of the race's progress and as partisan marketing vehicles for self-consciously advertising the race's ongoing achievements. As in the case of Booker T. Washington's Tuskegee project, the efforts were sometimes aimed at procuring monetary and political support for particular race agendas and institutions; at other times the profit reaped was more abstract and indirect, such as propaganda geared toward effecting a change in racial attitude not only in whites but also among African Americans themselves. New-century race marketers self-consciously set about fostering attention to the energetic mobility of blacks as a sign of the race's modernization and as a spectacular instance of the race's rapid progress despite the severe handicap posed by segregation, anti-black violence, disenfranchisement, unequal economic opportunity, and other barriers erected by the Jim Crow regime. The image of the handicap was a popular one, as it exploited the notion of the race's agile mobility in multiple senses, including epoch-shaping urban migration, self-willed sociopolitical movement, self-tutored educational progress, a quick ascent up the socioeconomic ladder, and a swift race through the stages of civilization to reach the advance guard of modernity in what leaders pointed to as an unprecedented leap from primitive enslavement to self-motivated racial agency. In emphasizing not only the accelerated mobility but also the handicapping circumstances, new-century activists hoped to reconceptualize radically the worth, status, and iconography of the race.[1] By investigating how African Americans positioned the race as a spectacular instance of fast-paced self-modernization, we can begin to see how they helped set the terms by which their role in the new century would be interpreted.

In popular culture as well as in scholarship, the increasing curiosity about black culture among the white elite—a curiosity that peaked in the 1920s "Negro Renaissance"—has been regarded largely as a phenomenon motivated by whites themselves, particularly by their prurient interest in exciting new artistic expressions such as sexually charged jazz. The fascination with all things Negro during the 1920s and afterward was inspired in large part by the prolific work of race marketers who set out systematically to recast the race's relation to modernity, to U.S. national identity, to cosmopolitan culture, and to entrenched notions of advancing civilization. The unprecedented interest in Negro American culture was not something that inevitably happened as a by-product of white Americans' adoption of a modernist sensibility or of black Americans' serendipitous arrival in northern urban centers; it was a happening self-consciously prepared for and painstakingly cultivated by a steady stream of race reflections and advertisements composed by African Americans around the turn of the nineteenth century *to stage the progress of the race* according to the agendas of often-competing ideological camps.

New-century race workers were certainly concerned to rewrite the script through which Negroness was identifiable and performable to a white audience that was invested in sustaining racial difference, although this was not their overriding concern. Identification with a racial group "cannot be understood outside a process of iterability, a regularized and constrained repetition of norms," to use Judith Butler's apt phrasing.[2] To identify with a racial group is to perform or reenact—partly unconsciously—the norms established to delimit such racial belonging. The race workers to some extent were performing their affiliation with Negroness even as they were attempting to impart a new structure and substance to what it meant to be a Negro.

The theory of racial performance, however, fails to explain the extent to which these race promoters—and African Americans more generally—selfconsciously attacked the norms and stigmas through which their collective identification was oppressively reinforced. In this sense, racial identification was not so much a reiterative norm unselfconsciously performed as it was a self-conscious ideological struggle in which the script was being revised in response to insufferable circumstances and in anticipation of new historical opportunities.[3] Race promoters' obsession with advertising their self-modernization should therefore not be seen primarily as a performance of racial/sexual identity enacted for the consumption of white patrons and sympathizers. It was, more accurately, a self-conscious ideological struggle to stage the reform of the race in order to achieve collective agency—and ultimately the entitlements of citizenship—in the face of a Jim Crow regime bent on reducing the race to a material and ideological condition of political dependency, economic servitude, social marginality, sociological dysfunction, cultural backwardness, sexual contamination, and physically violated victimization. Thus, when I speak of "staging the race," I am referring to the reenactment of a racial/sexual performance of identity only secondarily. Most crucially, I emphasize how new-century race advocates wanted to clock the advanced stage of civilization achieved by African Americans at this particular moment, and how they did so by resorting to discursive and iconographic techniques that spotlighted the collective interests of the race in various public forums suited to the delivery of polemics, propaganda, advertisement, portraiture, and scientific observation.

To understand the new-century promoters as involved in collective self-transformation that stages their own development as a quickly advancing race is also to consider this juncture of the turn of the nineteenth century in a different cultural-historical perspective. By focusing on group and individual mobility, and the gender and sexual implications of these, I hope to reframe the importance of the period's migratory movement by placing it in the ideological and material context of arguments over the proper place of the Negro along the axis of civilization. Migration and remigration account for just one aspect of mobility as a figure for collective movement, racial progress, socioeconomic ascent, and the freedom of movement as an embodiment of emancipation. In other words, the white supremacist argument that Negroes should "stay in their place" is not just a figure of speech. It means that they should literally stay put. That they should not move around geographically is also an injunction that they not move forward into modernity. For new-century race promoters, therefore, the direction of geographic movement—south to north, east to west, countryside to city, from north back to south, or from west back to east—was not so important in and of itself. Such directions did, however, have ideological implications; how could they not, given the African American cultural promise betokened by northward movement as freedom, or the American cultural baggage of westward movement as Manifest Destiny?[4] More important than this directionality, however, was the *fact* of constant movement, the material reality of constantly claiming the right to pick up and move as a right to advance according to the needs and whims of a group that could transform itself by thinking through its feet. Transit, then, is key to understanding the imperatives of staging the race.

The cultural, legal, political, and economic arrangements of the Jim Crow regime insisted on a binary black/white logic to manage anxieties over and threats to white supremacy, and our understanding of this post-Reconstruction period has largely accepted this binary as determinative in the political, social, and literary works of the period. When we examine these race tracts and albums, however, we find that new-century race workers constantly foregrounded the plurality of racial identifications, in the United States and globally, as a way of attacking this oppressive binary logic. Repeatedly, New Negroes pointed to Irish Americans, Jewish Americans, Native Americans, and native Africans not merely in passing but as crucial to the argumentative and/or visual structure for staging racial progress. New-century works sometimes exploited these racialized others to leverage the New Negro's stage of racial development as superior. As frequently, however, they spotlighted these other groups to topple the white supremacist assumption that racial hierarchy is fixed, stable, and immutable to individual and collective historical intervention.

This chapter also demonstrates how both race workers and racial modernization were intrinsically bound up with assumptions about, and controversies over, gender and sexual dispositions. Deciding how to stage the race always hinged on either explicit or implicit notions of the race's sexual identification and gender-role performance. Likewise, in measuring the race's advance along a scale of civilization that originates with savagery and culminates at an ever-receding finish line of modernity, gender/sexual conformity was a crucial indicator of modernization, although what constitutes conformity is sometimes fiercely contested. While some new-century race promoters struggle to *unsex* the race (that is, to reverse the weight of sexual abuse and mutilation historically heaped upon the race throughout enslavement and Jim Crow), others more modestly attempt to *desex* the race—to repress, suppress, or bracket for the moment any sexual connotations pertaining to the race in particular and to notions of race reversion and progress more generally. Yet others more boldly believe that the race can claim the modern advance guard only by asserting an aggressively sexualized identity, at least for leading men within the race, and thus set out to *resex* the race. Sometimes a race promoter, even in a single work, exploits more than one of these strategies, as we see Washington and Alain Locke doing, and the attitudes of male New Negro promoters tend to be quite different when it comes to the sexual composition of black women.

Whether unsexing, desexing, or resexing the race, these new-century race marketers grapple with the ways in which a race among the races toward modernity presupposes the sexual basis of racial progress. At the crudest level, the flourishing of a racial group depends on sex in the sense of both successful procreation strategies and productive intragender (among men) and cross-gender (between men and women) interaction.[5] As we shall see, the un/de/re/sexing that occurs in new-century texts constantly alludes to, and confuses, biological and cultural justifications for the race's modernizing imperative, whereby either procreative sex or gender interaction may be either biologically or culturally determined. Similarly, these texts proffer quite different scenarios for cross-racial gender exchange: some silently consent to sexual modesty as the proper restraint on black men in the presence of white men and women in compliance with Jim Crow strictures, whereas others flagrantly advocate black men's sexual assertiveness amid whites as proof of their Darwinian procreative competitiveness and competence. Defining themselves as "New Negroes"—a phrase whose sexual ramifications are myriad and complex—these race promoters perform deft rhetorical and iconographic maneuvers to match their claims to a newly modern mobility, which in turn they insist characterizes the race as a whole.

The charge to stage the race as ready to compete in the new century is carried out in various kinds of texts that manage the problem of the race's sexuality in different ways. While the argumentative *race tract* focuses on agile verbal discursiveness as a sign of the Negro's readiness for the newly modern century, the *race album* achieves a similar effect by focusing on the immediate impact of a visual display accompanied by brief verbal descriptions of the black subjects' achievements. Despite the chosen format, all these works rely on the narrative of a competitive race among the races in the search for racial survival, progress, and prosperity. The verbal gymnastics of a treatise couch the argument in narrative histories that tell the story of an age-old contest among the races moving toward an ending yet to be determined. The race album tends to subordinate the larger Darwinian narrative in order to frame smaller rags-to-riches biographies, highlighting the careers of individual black men ascending to the peak of their powers. These divergent genres of race promotion implicitly depend on each other in the same way that a picture is answered by a caption or a caption can be seen to tell the story of its accompanying picture. The choice of medium, however, can tell us much about the rhetorical strategy, ideological orientation, and gender stance of its author's staging scheme. Whereas the polemical tract tends to announce the sexual aggression of the writer as betokening the fierce competitiveness of the race, the race album shies away from such sexual aggression on the surface, instead visualizing the race as a congenial masculine club whose leading (male) members have leagued *with* one another for mutual benefit and uplift of the race rather than *against* any other racial group who may happen to be ahead of or behind them in the race toward modern civilization. The ideology and rhetoric of the race of the races help structure a wide array of new-century efforts and also structure the claim to a Negro Renaissance in the 1920s. While it helps enable an enunciation of self-modernizing African American agency, particularly for black male leaders, the concept of the race of the races also imposes limits on the kind of black manhood agency—and thus the kind of subjectivity—that can be staged and activated, in published works and organized sociopolitical efforts alike.

Migratory Mobility and the Sexually Assertive Race Tract: Chesnutt and Pickens

The hope and anxiety issuing from these promotional works are leavened by African Americans' newfound mobility, evidenced especially in the onset of the Great Migration. Motivated by a desire for greater social and economic opportunity, the mass migration necessarily raises in the mind of dominant society the specter of a black mass unloosed from the social and sexual restraints enforced by Jim Crow through modes of sexualized racial intimidation and torture that frequently culminated in lynching. This mobility of the race always threatens to elicit a sexual reaction, whether the mobility is more circumscribed, such as Booker T. Washington's advocacy of material upward mobility within the confines of the Black Belt rural South, or more geographically expansive, such as William Pickens's advocacy of cosmopolitan travel around and across national boundaries. As Hazel V. Carby has suggested, "black migrants came to be regarded as easily victimized subjects who quickly succumbed to the forces of vice and degradation."[6] Carby demonstrates how the emergence of black women migrants in particular creates a "moral panic" in response to which both individuals and institutions set out to correct "the behavior of black female migrants [which] was characterized as sexually degenerate and, therefore, socially dangerous" (23). Black male migrants create a similar kind of panic among middle-class observers, both black and white, but as Carby indicates, the gender implications of this anxiety over black mobility differ for men and women. As opposed to the errors of prostitution for women, the Great Migration produces anxiety over black men's sexually explosive behavior not only against women (cross-sexual) but also in relation to other men (same-gender).

In some new-century race tracts, however, black men's migratory movement elicits not so much anxiety and the call for individual discipline and institutional surveillance as the promise of a more sexually competitive and competent, and thus a more modern, racial identity. Perhaps because they are written in the early stages of the Great Migration, these sexually assertive tracts attempt to resex the race away from commonly denigrated perceptions of the Negro male's sexual nature, not so much by denying the race's sexuality as by foregrounding the positive aspects of black men's robust sexual appetite as a motivating factor in a healthful, prosperous racial progress. This section focuses on two such tracts, one by Charles Chesnutt, published toward the end of his writing career, and another by William Pickens, who is just beginning his career in tandem with the onset of the Great Migration.

When Chesnutt arrives in Cleveland in 1883, African Americans are, as in all northern cities, a negligible percentage of the population, with only 2,500 living there. But with each census that population multiplies in great leaps, from 8,448 in 1910 to 34,451 in 1920 and more than doubling in the next decade. Although black inhabitants are still outnumbered by foreign immigrants, who make up 35 percent of the Cleveland population in 1910, the rising tide of black migrants cannot be overlooked.[7] Like the other black migrants, Chesnutt arrives in the hopes of escaping the worsening Jim Crow conditions in the South and seeking political, social, and economic dreams made palpable by the rising fortunes of the industrial leadership centered in northern cities.

Born to free mulatto parents in Cleveland in 1858, Chesnutt went South with his parents to their home state of North Carolina in 1866, where the family joined others who hoped to benefit from the opportunities of Reconstruction. This post–Civil War migration reminds us of blacks' ongoing investment in relocation as a strategy for race uplift, but it likewise points out the barriers that can be placed on promising narratives of black mobility—a lesson evident in Chesnutt's own take on the pitfalls and potentials of remigration. Nursing his ambition as a writer but making a living as a teacher, Chesnutt experienced frustration with the South and with his status as a mulatto there—a frustration that seems to have increased after his marriage in 1878 and with the prospect of raising children under such circumstances. After teaching and serving as a principal in the freedmen's school that he himself had attended, Chesnutt, fed up with the increasing discrimination of the North Carolina Jim Crow establishment, returns to Cleveland in 1883, where he is able to study law and to secure a comfortable middle-class living for his family. On the side, Chesnutt pursues a writing career, publishing stories in the *Atlantic Monthly* and eventually getting two short-story collections published in 1899. Although he is able get three novels printed through major publishing houses from 1901 to 1905, he gives up on a writing career in annoyance with the kinds of constraints placed on discussing race issues during the post-Reconstruction period. Occasionally active in local and regional politics and in the National Association for the Advancement of Colored People (NAACP), as well as in local literary and social societies, Chesnutt finally gains greater recognition as an important example for and influence on the Negro Renaissance when he is awarded the NAACP's Spingarn medal in 1928, four years before his death.

Chesnutt's own remigration experience, his frustration in his chosen career, his relative financial comfort but social marginality in Cleveland society, and his identity as a light-skinned mulatto help shape his outlook on race progress, as expressed obliquely in his fiction and outright in his new-century race tract. By examining the fictional race tract that Chesnutt places in the mouth of a minor short-story character, we can get a sense of the turmoil just beneath the surface of his optimism in the tract that he authored in 1900.

Published in his 1899 collection *The Wife of His Youth,* Chesnutt's short story "Uncle Wellington's Wives" explores the sexual dilemmas attending the seemingly liberating mobility enabled by remigration. Although in one sense the story is a parable about respecting the marriage bond, more subtly it explores the sexual license enabled by black male migration as both an opportune opening toward upward social movement and a selfish opportunism endangering the race's collective mobility. Uncle Wellington Braboy, the protagonist, has begun to feel that his wife, Milly, impinges on his sense of emancipation with her constant nagging for good middle-class husbandry. In question is whether a marriage made during enslavement can effect a social advance, or whether manly emancipation must include liberation from obligations enforced during slavery. Uncle Wellington's situation represents the larger condition of the race during and after Reconstruction, as African Americans are still tied down by historical obligations made during slavery but desire a greater expanse for action and ascent that might be effected by nullifying such obligations, even a bond supposedly as intimate and binding as marriage. What is the role of sexual liberation in the individual and collective search for racial progress?

Uncle Wellington's dissatisfaction with his marital bond is brought home to him in a lodge meeting, when a gentleman from up north reminds him of what's possible now that he's free:

> On this particular occasion the club had been addressed by a visiting brother from the North, Professor Patterson, a tall, well-formed mulatto, who wore a perfectly fitting suit of broadcloth, a shiny silk hat, and linen of dazzling whiteness,—in short, a gentleman of such distinguished appearance that the doors and windows of the offices and stores on Front Street were filled with curious observers as he passed through that thoroughfare in the early part of the day. (203)

Professor Patterson represents the kind of New Negro whom Uncle Wellington has failed to become—a failure marked by the difference between *uncle,* an honorary but emasculating slave term for any older black man, and *professor,* an honorific term used by turn-of-the-century African Americans to indicate a male who had achieved such a high degree of learning (largely informal) that he deserved to be treated with the authority granted to formally educated scholars.[8] By representing Patterson's speech before the male audience of a lodge meeting, Chesnutt provides us a signal instance of the cultural complications that accompany any attempt to stage the advance of the race. Patterson stages the performance of his racial identity in the sense that he speaks as a self-educated colored gentleman who resists his racial/sexual subordination by attempting to mimic the dress, address, and bearing of an educated white man. Beyond this racial/gender performance, however, his speech enlists a specific intended audience, the aspiring colored men of the lodge, in a specific social agenda: the remaking of the manhood of the race by focusing their aspirations on the business, educational, and conjugal opportunities available through northward migration. The speech also has intended consequences for how these men conceive of their racial agency, encouraging them to pick up and move north.

Professor Patterson's lecture on "The Mental, Moral, Physical, Political, Social, and Financial Improvement of the Negro Race in America" represents the sort of race tract common during the time, and which Chesnutt himself would publish only one year after the short story. But here Chesnutt treats Patterson's tract with mild satire, indicated by the inflated, all-inclusive title and the pretentious manner in which the speech is delivered. The tract contains matter that Uncle Wellington has heard before, including rumors about the liberties afforded a man of color in the North. "The professor waxed eloquent with the development of his theme, and, as a finishing touch to an alluring picture, assured the excited audience that the intermarriage of the races was common, and that he himself had espoused a white woman" (205). Providing himself as an object lesson, Patterson stages not only his own personal progress from an "uncle" to a "professor" but, more important, the progress of the race as a whole, presumptuously equated with the male would-be leaders of the race. The particular historical formation of the fraternal lodge, established during enslavement by free men of color and enlarged by the more respectable former slaves after emancipation, provides the perfect forum for Patterson to make his case. As Maurice Wallace and Corey Walker have indicated in different ways, the fraternal lodge is a crucial site for the construction of an actively "free" black manhood identity both for free men of color in the early years of the American republic and for freed male slaves in the years after emancipation.[9] This secret lodge protects these men from the prying eyes of whites and women as they seek rituals for claiming an effective manhood identity. Professor Patterson's speech, then, can be seen as one such instance of manhood reform, in which Patterson himself is the manly model for the lodge brothers.

As Patterson's "alluring picture" excites the audience, we recognize that Chesnutt himself is implicating a crude sexual excitement in the noble narrative of racial progress, so that we cannot fail to see the irony of emancipated black men spurred to carry forth the progress of the race through intermarriage with women outside the race. Uncle Wellington attends to the orator not so much because his words are fresh or enticing as because his clothes and bearing validate them. "Any lingering doubts uncle Wellington may have felt were entirely dispelled by the courtly bow and cordial grasp of the hand with which the visiting brother acknowledged the congratulations showered upon him by the audience at the close of his address" (206). Uncle Wellington and his lodge brothers correctly base emancipation on liberties, especially the license to marry whomever one wants, and thus on the freedom of being the kind of patriarchs powerful white men seem to be. Whether this linkage is enough to achieve true emancipation for the race is another matter. Chesnutt emphasizes throughout the story the "brotherliness" of race struggle and advancement, implying the familial basis of the race's condition. If black men are all blood brothers in the struggle, then what would it mean for them to choose wives not based in that blood relation? The fraternal bond does not here reciprocate in a sense that black brothers owe an obligation to black sisters. In fact, the passion of the lodge brothers for white women implies that sexual deviance lurks in the familial logic of brotherhood: If all black men are brothers, then shouldn't they *not* be marrying their black sisters? Patterson's example creates a triple charge for manly mobility: (1) to move more freely in the North; (2) to signal this freer movement by taking a white woman to bed; and (3) to move up the social ladder in having taken a white woman as wife.

When Wellington goes north and calculates his chances of social ascent through hard work, he works as hard as Milly does in the South. Ironically, he ends up having to support his new "white" wife at a subsistence level through laundering, the same vocation that Milly has been banking on as a gradual progress by fastidiously saving the little money it provides. Chesnutt here is satirizing the popular idea, embodied most in Booker T. Washington, that hard work, thrift, cleanliness, and sexual circumspection will necessarily lead to racial progress.[10] Having apparently achieved all his desires in the North, especially a "white" wife, Wellington realizes that he has been tripped by another sort of color/sexual line: the only sort of woman that he has access to is an immigrant Irish working-class housekeeper almost as socially tenuous as he.[11] When Wellington's Irish wife discovers that her own ambitions for upward mobility and assimilation are thwarted rather than carried forward by her marriage to a black man, she leaves him for a white man whom she claims to be her long-lost first husband.[12] The liberty beyond race that Wellington seeks through geographic and social mobility turns out to be merely sexual license, as his identity as an emancipated man relies overmuch on overcoming the sexual restrictions placed on him as a black man.

Characteristically, Chesnutt concludes the story with a happy ending that verges on the formulaic. Wellington returns to Milly in the nick of time, as she is being proposed to by a preacher, and having learned the powers and limits of his mobility, he can adjust his personal desires to the needs of the race. When Wellington does act on his motivations by going north and then returning south, he seems to rebalance the gender/sexual dissonances impeding his marital progress, and by extension impeding his racial progress. Professor Patterson's race tract is especially instructive, for the story's cautious moralistic closure seems to issue a warning to those who are eager to prognosticate a sunny future for the race through the proliferation of jocular tracts.

Significantly, Patterson's speech contradicts the most famous new-century race tract, Booker T. Washington's 1895 Atlanta Exposition speech. Washington insists that Negroes should resist the desire to become footloose and instead "cast down your bucket where you are." For Washington, this means settling down to work not only in the rural Black Belt South at the bottom of society but also—a part of the injunction frequently overlooked—in the larger world, in which Negroes are to be found jowl to jowl with people of other races: "[C]ast it down in making friends in every *manly* way of the people of all races by whom we are surrounded" (*Up from Slavery* 219, italics added). Whereas Washington enjoins African American men in particular to find friendly terms for interacting beneficially with those who have Jim Crowed them, Patterson demands that Negro men should abandon their southern homes and ways for northern liberties. Chesnutt parodies Washington's famous speech when he has Patterson convert the great accommodator's lesson in "manly" cooperation with all races into a lusty wooing of the women of the superior race—an alarming conversion that puts the most dangerous spin on Washington's demand for racial circumspection by remaining "[i]n all things that are purely social . . . as separate as the fingers" (221–222). Furthermore, whereas Washington's speech was, crucially, delivered foremost to a white male upper-class audience of his former masters, and secondarily to Northerners and Southerners, blacks and whites, men and women, at the event that was to celebrate the rise of the New South, Patterson's speech is delivered to an all-black, all-male lodge under the assumption that the South is unsalvageable, that New Negro and New South are inimical concepts.[13] Finally, Washington entreats the Negroes in his audience to resist any inclination toward what might be perceived as "uppity" behavior by whites, just as he urges them elsewhere in *Up from Slavery* to avoid "what was called the educated Negro, with high hat, imitation gold eye-glasses, a showy walking-stick, kid gloves, fancy boots, and what not—in a word, a man who was determined to live by his wits" (119). Patterson, the image of a man determined to live by his wits, models and extols exactly what Washington attacks. As stagings of the proper approach to advance the race, Washington and Patterson could not be more at odds. However, Washington's performance before the white-controlled exposition is really aimed at milking white male superiority to curry resources for building the best-funded Negro institutions up to that time (not only Tuskegee Institute but also agricultural and business enterprises and political spoils networks), whereas Patterson's seemingly more aggressive approach is based in narrowly individualistic behaviors of cross-racial desire. By the story's closure, Chesnutt seems to side with Washington's accommodating injunction to "cast down your bucket where you are." Patterson's new-century agenda fails as Uncle Wellington returns to his wife, to his place in the South, and to his wife's Bookerite determination to rise slowly upward toward social respectability through menial hard work, cleanliness, frugality, and domestic circumspection.

If in "Uncle Wellington's Wives," Chesnutt chastises Patterson's optimistic attitude by siding with Washington's cautious accommodationism, in his own new-century race tract he counters Washington's jocular belief in good works with a program so radical that it seems to verge on either total utopianism or wholesale mockery of the boosterish attitude endemic to these tracts. Chesnutt seems to abandon the hope of racial uplift through autonomous acts of institutional race building and instead rests his case for a modern Negro with the drastic possibility of erasing the black presence (and thus the white) altogether through geographic dispersal and eventual assimilation into an amalgamated American race. He advocates this stance in a trilogy of articles titled "The Future American," published by the *Boston Evening Transcript* in 1900. In the first article, "What the Race Is Likely to Become in the Process of Time," Chesnutt points out that the notion of the future American has become a "popular theme" for essayists:

> The popular theory is that the future American race will consist of a harmonious fusion of the various European elements which now make up our heterogeneous population. The result is to be something infinitely superior to the best of the component elements. This perfection of type . . . is to be brought about by a

combination of all the best characteristics of the different European races, and the elimination, by some strange alchemy, of all their undesirable traits—for even a good American will admit that European races, now and then, have some undesirable traits when they first come over.[14]

Silently buttressing this idea of amalgamation are two important historical understandings sardonically insinuated in the essay: (1) the feasibility of a steady trickle of black migrants to the northern cities and (2) the reality of cross-racial mixing that has occurred in the South under circumstances that seem most uncongenial to such intermixing. Given the relatively progressive and integrated conditions of black migrants in cities like Cleveland, Chesnutt has some reason to hope that this trickle of African American migrants will, over a long period of time, become scattered and absorbed within the larger population, rather than concentrated and huddled in consolidated, segregated ghettos. Against the dominant tendency of projecting onto African Americans irregular sexual and marital relations, Chesnutt looks to the reality of racial intermixing in the South as an indication that, under freer conditions in the North, miscegenation may become much more common and also wholly lose its stigma.

Pursuing and exploiting the logic used by white progressive writers who have attempted to turn anxiety over southern and eastern European immigration into a benefit by promising the immigrants' assimilation into a perfect American union, Chesnutt wants to extend this idea to the two most maligned and marginal groups, American Indians and Negroes. He takes advantage of confusion within race discourse itself (in which the European is sometimes figured as a single race and sometimes as various races based on national, linguistic, or class identifications) to argue for the unqualified benefit of total national miscegenation.[15] If native Anglo-Saxons can learn to absorb and intermarry with the "race" of Irish who crowd into United States cities in the middle and latter parts of the nineteenth century, then why wouldn't they eventually be able to absorb a trickle of native colored migrants, most of whom are part European in the first place? Chesnutt strategically uses the anxiety over "dark" European immigrants to make a case for the closer consanguinity of native white and colored Americans.[16] This scenario can work only if Indians and Negroes are perceived as having positive racial qualities to contribute as well as negative qualities to be eliminated. As SallyAnn H. Ferguson rightly points out, it might appear that Chesnutt is willing to abandon the vast majority of black people trapped in the rural areas of the Deep South, given the unlikelihood of the darkest former slaves ever being able to enjoy this type of assimilation, as opposed to descendants of free mulattos like Chesnutt. Or is he, as Arlene A. Elder suggests, making a radical move to obliterate race altogether, and thus risking an ideal for all people classified as Negro?[17] Another way of thinking about this notion, however, indicates to what extent Chesnutt's vision relies on mass migration, urbanization, and cross-racial contact in modes that go far beyond white men's backdoor sexual exploitation of black women.

Writing four hundred years after the first missionary explorers to Africa and America expressed outrage at natives' perverse sexuality, Chesnutt can reclaim the right of these colonized groups to the progress of civilization only by resorting to a sexual solution.[18] If Chesnutt's ambivalently sardonic tone befits a mulatto whose sense of birthright is trumped by his racial il/legitimacy, it is also fitting that his new-century tract intermingles with this tone a strain of scientific authority issuing forth a biological solution to the cultural dilemma of race. What justifies his theory of total amalgamation is an idea that he puts forward as a newly documented biological fact. Sex between the races produces not the monstrous half-breeds of legend and fantasy but instead productive individuals, like himself, who possess the best characteristics of the combined races and ensure the amplified diversity of the American species. In other words, Chesnutt implicitly claims cross-racial sex—during the time viewed as religiously, morally, socially, and legally deviant—as a biological imperative and thus as a social norm providing the grounds for national progress.

> There are no natural obstacles to such an amalgamation. The unity of the race is not only conceded but demonstrated by actual crossing. Any theory of sterility due to race crossing may as well be abandoned: it is founded mainly on prejudice and cannot be proved by the facts. . . . My own observation is that in a majority of cases people of mixed blood are very prolific and very long-lived. . . .
>
> By modern research this unity of the human race has been proved . . . , and the differentiation of races by selection and environment has been so stated as to prove itself. ("The Future American: What the Race Is Likely to Become" 20)

Notice how he moves from "race" in the second sentence as a unity of all humans in a single species, to "race" in the third sentence as a category separating humans into disparate groups, and then back again in the first sentence of the succeeding paragraph to "race" as a unity and "races" as a differentiation among groups. In this see sawing between the conflicting meanings of race, cross-racial sex becomes the natural imperative of modernity, bolstered by the most up-to-date research. Arguing from biological fact to cultural inference, Chesnutt is suggesting that within mixed blood resides a unifying potential that necessitates such intermingling: "There can manifestly be no such thing as peaceful and progressive civilization in a nation divided by two warring races, and homogeneity of type, at least in externals, is a necessary condition of harmonious social progress" ("The Future American: A Complete Race-Amalgamation Likely to Occur" 24). Chesnutt clearly alludes here to the Civil War and Reconstruction, a moment of national crisis when the myth of a master white race was fractured by bloody battles among various white groups proclaiming irreconcilable versions of the myth. Chesnutt reminds his fellow citizens that this violence can erupt in any moment, turning a seemingly secure racial subordination into interracial and intraracial warfare. In his visionary future, the past violent aggression of white men against Indians and Africans is transformed into a peaceful intermixing that literally erases any physical hint of racial difference among Americans. The conquest of Indians and the enslavement of Africans are necessarily accompanied by sexual contamination on the part of frontiersmen and slave masters, resulting in the mulatto and "mixed breed." Chesnutt exploits this contamination as the potential for an advanced mode of cross-racial sex that moves beyond the primitive violence of historical white male aggression.[19]

Exploiting the lapse in patriarchy that Hortense Spillers alludes to when she points out the illogic of "twice-fathering" that occurs under enslavement, Chesnutt must keep before his readers' eyes the unsavory reality that Europeans have repeatedly gone against law and custom to mate with and force themselves on Africans. He makes this history of sexual deviation the sole subject of his second "Future American" article, whose subtitle is "A Stream of Dark Blood in the Veins of Southern Whites." In this essay he unsexes the black race by reversing the dominant logic of racial crossbreeding: against the social and legal notion that any person with any discernable degree of African inheritance must be Negro, Chesnutt speaks of "white Southerners" with African blood coursing through their veins. This framing of racial hybridity totally subverts the logic of the Supreme Court 1896 *Plessy v. Ferguson* decision, as Chesnutt himself well understands. In a speech titled "The Courts and the Negro," Chesnutt uses the language of lynching to describe how the Supreme Court mangles the symbolic body of Reconstruction in *Plessy,* which codifies the policies of Jim Crow by insisting that whiteness is a pure value contaminable by Negro blood: "And then the Court stabbed in the back, and to death, this ideal presentment of rights, and threw its bleeding corpse to the Negro,—the comprehensive Negro, black, brown, yellow, and white."[20] Chesnutt points to the hybridity of "races" within the Negro identity as a way of also asserting the multiplicity of races within each race and the impossibility of attempting to manage or purify any one race by subordinating the others. The *Plessy* decision itself, however, indicates to what great cost—considering the economic inefficiency of separate facilities—white Americans would go to retain the legality of racial supremacy. As Saidiya Hartman points out, "[t]he 'reasonableness' of race as a legal classification was animated by anxieties about equality, bodily integrity, and degrading contact," and "in some respects these anxieties were particular to the postemancipation context" (*Scenes of Subjection* 197). Coming as it does upon the heels of *Plessy,* Chesnutt's appeal to the most intimate form of social contact as a solution to the most violent panic over cross-racial contamination seems perversely absurd.

Given Chesnutt's own Caucasian features, his ability to pass, and his flight to a more integrated, progressive northern city where black people are scattered and few, it is understandable how he can reach such a solution as amalgamation, even if tongue-in-cheek.[21] With each decade, however, the great black migration makes the idea of racial dispersal seem more like fantasy or delusion. By the 1920s, dispersal, assimilation, and amalgamation into a racially undifferentiated nationalism are countered by the inescapable bodily presence of the new black urban mass. Rather than assimilating blackness, and therefore whiteness, out of existence, the Great Migration helps refigure the body of the black race, which in turn refigures notions of black masculinity and sexuality. In a sense Chesnutt's solution represents a dead end for new-century race workers, for whatever its subtle ironies and scientific certainties, it too boldly advocates racial erasure, which during the time necessarily conjures notions of racial suicide and extinction—notions that seem consonant with white supremacists who are claiming as a biological fact the black race's eventual disappearance due to its inability to adapt to the rigors of the on-coming modern era. Against Chesnutt, other race promoters seek ways of staging this mass migratory experience toward America's financial, industrial, and intel-lectual centers to make the case for an impending uplift of the race through an un-precedented racial consolidation within the heart of modernity.

If Chesnutt's trilogy "The Future American" occupies an extreme in which race promotion turns into its opposite, race extinction, then William Pickens's *The New Negro: His Political, Civil and Mental Status, and Related Essays* (1916) embodies the most expansive, exemplary, and synthetic instance of a race promotion tract, one that borrows from various arguments only to subordinate them all to an overar-ching narrative of the competition among the races in the race toward modernity. Influential in the early history of the NAACP, Pickens (1881–1954) is now largely, and unfortunately, forgotten in the annals of African American and U.S. history. As the national field secretary for the NAACP, Pickens has been credited with help-ing enlarge the membership of the organization through his exceptional oratori-cal skills. In addition to publishing *The New Negro,* two autobiographical volumes, and a novella/short-story collection called *Vengeance of the Gods, and Three Other Stories of Real American Color Line Life* (1922), he was a popular syndicated colum-nist for black newspapers at the height of the black press's influence. His first major publication, *The New Negro* signals his contest with Washington, who had pub-lished a book with a similar title in 1900, and assertively pushes a self-image and a collective racial image directly at odds with Washington's accommodationist strat-egy. Pickens's own migratory experience across the country—from South to West to North to East to South and East again—so much influences his sense of the power of geographic mobility that he forges an evolutionary theory of race progress that hinges on the physical movement of peoples across continents. The race that is most mobile—most cosmopolitan—is the one that can dominate for the duration.

The New Negro reveals to what extent the New Negro agenda of assimilation through consolidation rests on an ambivalently gendered paradigm of masculine competition, warfare, and potential peacemaking among the races.[22] Pickens's col-lection of essays pursues its self-divided agenda by trumpeting both the distinctive racial heritage of Africa and the history of indiscriminate racial mixing that char-acterizes world populations. "In the dawn of civilization there were no hard and fast lines among the colors of the human race," he writes, "but it is certain that the darker groups matured more quickly and took the lead" (9). Early on, then, this tract suggests an ambivalent attitude toward color and race, implying on the one hand the naturalness of interracial promiscuity, on the other hand an inevitable race rivalry, the rise of the fittest to dominate the other races. While racial identity seems a historically unstable affair, the fixity of race seems the *raison d'être* mobilizing all historical change. According to Pickens, as the original great civilization, Egypt is ruled by a rainbow of groups, excluding only the uncivilized Caucasians. "Milleniums before the wolf suckled Romulus," Pickens writes, "many centuries before Homer sung, the black and brown and yellowish peoples ruled in Egypt, overran the civilized and known world, and brought and wrought the usual changes of civilization before Greece and Rome were even names in the earth" (9). Pickens uses a predictable Darwinist understanding common in this period, but in his unusual scenario, the dawn of history witnesses racial coalition (sexual intermixing) among black, brown, and yellow, who dominate over the white race. This potential for coalition anticipates the possibility of future alliances developing out of even the fiercest competition in the modern era—that between warring black and white tribes in the early-twentieth-century United States. Pickens distills early world history to a bare outline of warring race-tribes of men, alternately invading and invaded, mixing and unmixing, rising and declining as (in)discrete racial groupings. Africa's darker group at first takes the lead but then falls behind. Just as the "energetic" Europeans have advanced by assimilating Egyptian civilization, however, so the darker groups are now rising again as a result of having assimilated European civilization in the New World.

Contrary to the dominant view of civilization as an unfolding progress of races ordered by stable hierarchy across history, Pickens stresses a dynamism at the heart of this process, and it is this that constitutes his bid for representing a New Negro generation. This dynamism characterizes not only his polemic on the New Negro but also his self-characterization in his autobiographies, where both his highly mobile body and his highly active, alert mind signify the claim to renewal and newness. Civilized progress in this sense becomes not just the graduated trajectory of a race's slow "struggle upward," as he claims that "New Negroes" of the previous generation would have it, but the sign of an aggressive, versatile, prolific, energetic, jazzy, remigratory momentum best characterized as the idea of restless modernity, a desire for new discoveries so intense that the subject cannot sit still. Pickens quickens the pace of upward mobility and racial uplift by insisting on the essentially volatile, aggressive nature of progress itself. Henry Louis Gates Jr. pinpoints the way in which this claim to being a New Negro must be constantly repeated throughout African American history. In effect, each generation repudiates the name, political strategy, persona, and bodily self-representation of the previous one in a bid to claim a certain kind of progress. "It is a bold and audacious act of language," Gates writes, "signifying the will to power, to dare to recreate a race by renaming it, despite the dubiousness of the venture" ("Trope of the New Negro" 132). Gates makes the mistake, however, of viewing the race-staging procedure as purely "rhetorical," in the pejorative sense of that word. To the contrary, according to Pickens the body itself must be, in some way, put at risk—and must be displayed at risk—in staking this claim to racial advancement. When Pickens tries to wrench this "new" epithet from the hands of the previous generation, he is displaying the risks he has taken, and would be willing to take, to deserve the appellation. For instance, becoming an active and visible member of the NAACP in the heart of the Deep South while teaching at a school run by missionary whites constitutes a new twist on the long-established modes of political action. Surely Pickens knows that to engage in such activity is to risk losing his livelihood, if not his life. And if he does not anticipate Washington's having him dismissed from the faculty of Talladega College in 1914, he surely understands the dire warnings issued by the white president and the American Missionary Association (AMA) officials responsible for the college.[23] However dubious a wholly new identity for the self or the race must be, the break with Washington is real enough, and so is the reoriented attitude toward racial accommodation and educational strategy that this break betokens and from which it results.

Gates is right, nonetheless, to point to the kind of linguistic inflation and reiteration that the label "new" and the experience of historical breakage necessarily entail. The history in Pickens's *The New Negro* is racially static; despite his claim of constant mixing of blood, the racial colors of various groups in his story continue to persist. The dynamism occurs instead in terms of the status of the races, which is constantly changing. Such is the case, he argues, for the diasporan scattering of the African race, whose handicap in one historical moment can become a benefit in another. Another way in which the continuity of history and racial identification work against Pickens's claim to historical breakage and a wholly "new" identity is the discrepancy between his idealized self-image and the documentable actions that he takes. To stage a progress, he represents himself as always possessing, or at least as always having been destined for, the psychological and historical reorientation that he claims he represents and embodies. It seems, however, that Pickens starts out much closer to Washington, perhaps even as a Bookerite disciple. Sheldon Avery provides evidence of this in Pickens's 1903 Yale oratory contest speech, titled "Misrule in Hayti." Speaking to his white audience at Yale, Pickens claims that the American Negro is "'centuries ahead of his Haytian brother' because of the 'special blessing' of white, Christian civilizing influences" (quoted in Avery, *Up from Washington* 16). Thus, when he advocates for the "subjugation of the island by America" as "an act of kindness" (16), he is implicitly agreeing with Washington's rhetoric in *Up from Slavery*, where the temporary enslavement of the American Negro is characterized as a blessing in disguise. No doubt, for Pickens to "rise to higher things," such as the ability to attend Yale, he needs "the power of a stronger hand" to help him along the way. He seeks and receives such patronage throughout his career from white and black alike, but during his radical decades, he conditions his new identity as a Negro on a model of manly self-sufficiency that is supposed to be a break with Washington's rhetoric.

Unfortunately for Pickens, winning the oratory contest brings attention as well from Washington's greatest African American adversary, William Monroe Trotter, militant editor of the Boston *Guardian*. Accusing Pickens of being a Bookerite disciple, Trotter also charges him with the kind of gender and racial treachery that Du Bois charges Washington with in *The Souls of Black Folk*. Calling Pickens "uncouth and provincial," Trotter suggests that he is the first Negro to win the coveted prize only because of his "surrendering his self-respect, sacrificing his pride, emasculating his manhood, and throwing down his race" (quoted in Avery, *Up from Washington* 17, 16). Washington's attempt to exploit Pickens in a libel suit against Trotter must have been a quick and dirty lesson for the young college man, not only in the entanglements of Realpolitik but also in the dangers of accommodationist ingratiation. Pickens's aspirations at Yale represent exactly the desire to rise above the perception of being "uncouth and provincial." For Pickens's generation, as Trotter well knows, these are the stereotypical characteristics of a rural Southerner, and being a *black* rural Southerner, in the eyes of newer Negroes like Trotter, is tantamount to being an "uncle," an antiquated Negro with a slave mentality. When Pickens places his bets on the NAACP, even though still in the South, he also casts his lot with the putative sophistication and cosmopolitanism, the aggressive consolidation and invasive cross-racial contact, of the urban North, as the only sustainable version of newer Negrohood.

By writing *The New Negro,* Pickens is, in effect, affirming and displaying his New Negro manhood against Trotter's charge of racial emasculation and "uncleness." Although his tract appears to be about a global history of tribal race wars, it is really about the national politics of advance-guard civilization being mediated in America's northern urban centers.[24] Not surprisingly, then, barely beneath the surface of this text is its logic of masculine insemination as the promiscuous scattering of seed in a cosmopolitan context. The "contact" and "scattering" of the race resulting from slavery thereby turn out to be the long arm of providence at work in history, for the race is now situated ideally for its renaissance. Like Chesnutt's optimistic amalgamation, Pickens's tract insists on the fortuitous outcome of race contacts in the new century: "But whatever his condition, a providence has given him the widest contact, has scattered his scions in all the earth and is making him one of the most versatile races of modern history. He stands to-day on the threshold of a renaissance of civilization and culture after four hundred years of interruption by captivity, slavery and oppression" (*New Negro* 14). A race reaches its peak through its ability to inseminate but ironically falls into its nadir for the same reason—its narcissistic containment of its potency once it reaches the top (see *New Negro* 11). In other words, the power of racial supremacy, once achieved, becomes the impotence of racial segregation as a striving for purity. Pickens's conflation of biological intermixing of races and a cultural "confluence of many streams" grounds the tract in current scientific thought and thus gives it a sense of cutting-edge authority.

At work in his history are competing metaphors of fluent amalgamation, always suggesting the dispersal of race and color altogether, and rigid belligerence, suggesting instead world history as an ongoing battle scene of perpetual invasions and conquests. "And they are now awakening to the truth that they must advance along all lines to make their advancement secure," he says about American Negroes, "that they must 'straighten out their front,' as they say in the European war" (15). We see this bellicose metaphor of race invasion, penetrating urban white neighborhoods, repeatedly conflated with cultural integration and biological miscegenation across a range of New Negro discourses, especially in the urban folk novel, discussed in Part 3. Driving these conflicting metaphors are ambivalences about both the meaning of race as a sign of advancing culture and the posture of masculine aggression as a sign of race solidarity. What should not be overlooked here is the implicit valuation of two sexual characteristics normally seen as regressive: promiscuous miscegenation and the gendering of race as an unstable sexual (com)position. Pickens celebrates indiscriminate sexual mixing as a subtle metaphor for racial cosmopolitanism, as he casts the gender status of a race as historically unstable. At one moment the African race is the manly ravisher, penetrating and inseminating the passive Europeans; at another moment the Europeans become the sexual aggressors, having their way with pacified Africans. A race is not permanently typed as masculine or unmasculine, aggressive or passive, inseminating or inseminated; instead, its position as top or bottom and its composition as manly invader or unmanned boy are constantly renegotiated in the give-and-take of history. In an odd way, all races are figured as male for Pickens, but they are males at different stages of development at different moments. In being invaded and pacified, then, a race is not exactly feminized or emasculated but, more precisely, stripped *temporarily* of manhood, a process and state for which we do not have a satisfactory vocabulary. The closest analogy would seem to be the sexual practices of Athenians in the classical age, where part of the definition of civilized manhood entails sexual domination of an adolescent boy, but one who possesses the potential to assert his own manhood and citizenship by sexually dominating another boy.[25] By no means has Pickens, in deviating from the standard account of social Darwinist racial competition, toppled the masculine structures and values that enable this narrative of world civilization to cohere. Ironically, he exploits gender deviation figuratively, and perhaps unwittingly, to enable a future in which the African race (at least in its New World incarnation), through the manly powers of unpredictable insemination, can be on top again.

At the heart of Pickens's book we find his eloquent advocacy for urbanization of the Negro as the basis for his progress toward newness. His book is directed against racial spokesmen, especially Bookerite disciples such as Robert Russa Moton (1867–1940), who make the case for the South as the best place for African Americans. Speaking as a voice of moderation in his own 1929 race tract, *What the Negro Thinks,* Moton echoes Washington's anti-urban, anti-migration preachments at the peak of the Great Migration. The migrant moved north, "where he was assured he would be snubbed and spurned, even mobbed; be cheated by exorbitant prices; be crowded into unsanitary tenements; and finally die of cold and disease; only to be buried in the warm welcoming soil of the sad, forsaken South" (*What the Negro Thinks* 59). Moton's image of the North perpetuates the one fostered in southern newspapers by whites who had become alarmed over the number of African Americans willing to abandon the South. Such newspapers spread "the persistent rumor . . . that blacks would freeze to death in the North."[26] Moton reinforces the idea that it is only in the South, and only through Bookerite agricultural and entrepreneurial pursuits, that the race can achieve its renaissance.[27] Countering such Bookerite notions, Pickens writes, "Some say that the education of the Negro tends to pull him away from the farm and deranges the economic system of the South, and that the city Negro is not worth as much to the (white) South as is the rural Negro. These views consider the Negro in his relation to white people only as a commodity" (*New Negro* 161). Against the idea that blacks should consolidate for economic development in the "wastelands" of the rural South, turning those wasted fields into industrial might, Pickens's faith in the renaissance of African civilization is lodged in the scattered contact and consolidated massing that can be achieved only in cities.[28]

The process of transforming the Negro from an agrarian commodity (the victim of sharecropping) to an agent of his own interest also requires that the race take control of the media on which modern civilization thrives. In the "whiter light of the centers of civilization," black people come under heightened scrutiny, but closer attention does not guarantee a more accurate intention (see *New Negro* 161). Although Pickens associates urbane civilization with whiteness here, he significantly relativizes this association by using the comparative "whiter." In the urban context, all boundaries—between white and black, between urbanity and primitivism, between power and dispossession—become relative, unstable, up for grabs. The unsophisticated flaws within a newly arrived black migrant may stand out more in the "whiter light" of finer judgment enabled by cosmopolitan media, but to remain huddled in the shadows of southern obscurity preempts enlightenment in the first place. What Pickens proposes and enacts in *The New Negro,* then, is a modern advertising campaign in which the Negro becomes new through gaining control of the circulation of his own image in the publishing houses, magazines, newspapers, and advertising concerns of the urban centers. In addition to actual physical mobility, both as geographic migration and as invasions into white centers of power, rapid racial progress is based in the efficient circulation of New Negro imagery in modern media.

In the foreword to his 1922 novella, *The Vengeance of the Gods,* Pickens spells out how the need of each race to invent and reproduce its self-image grows out of a sort of Darwinian competition for survival and superiority among the races:

> People do not present another race as beautiful and heroic, unless that race is far removed from them in time or space; or unless, as in the case of the white man and the American Indian, the stronger race has killed off the weaker and removed it as a rival. . . .

> If the Negro wants to be idealized in a world where the Negro is a considerable potential factor, he must idealize himself,—or else he must expect a sorry role in every tale. . . . It is not simply that the white story teller *will not* do full justice to the humanity of the black race; he *cannot*. A race must present its own case and ennoble its own ideals. (7)

Whereas Chesnutt needs the American Indian as the ultranative other who can confirm the short-sightedness of racial exclusion in misbegotten narratives of future American nativity, Pickens needs the American Indian to sound a warning about the eventual outcome of a lost race rivalry with white men. If the New Negro does not rise to the occasion to stage the race's progress according to its own terms, like the Indian the Negro will be doomed to "a sorry role" in some other group's narrative of racial advancement. As we see in the next chapter, this use of Native Americans accords with Pickens's overall reliance on a frontier ethos to ground his staging of racial advancement. If the New Negro is to win racial self-respect and citizenship rights, he can do so only by wresting away from white men their exclusive claim to Manifest Destiny.

The cultural campaign for racial self-interest that Pickens theorizes is enacted historically in a variety of ways through a variety of genres and media, from the public relations work done by biracial organizations such as the NAACP and National Urban League to the establishment of black urban sociology as the dominant scientific discourse on the identity of the black race, from new-century race albums that visualize the collective identity of the race to personal narratives of singular racial trespassing, from Negro Renaissance modernist experiments in visual iconography focused on the Talented Tenth to new novelistic forms that spotlight the urban folk masses as the wellspring of modern mobility. Across these, we can see the same gender contradictions and cross-racial tensions at work that characterize Chesnutt's and Pickens's race tracts.

Staging the Race: Verbal Display in Du Bois and Washington

A strong influence on Pickens's and other New Negro projects is the eighteenth-century concept of the "great chain of being," a European Enlightenment notion in which the universe was seen as ordered into a stable hierarchy of graduated states of being, from inanimate modes on the lowest rungs to God on the highest.[29] Under the influence of Darwin, by the late nineteenth century this chain of being had been temporized into the concept of a hierarchy of races relatively fixed in their place in relation to each other, but each moving forward at its own pace toward greater civilization, although "primitive races" were sometimes seen as static, forever left behind in this quick race toward perfected culture. As is evident in Pickens's formulation of the rise and fall of competing race tribes, this race of races, or race racing, is usually expressed in narrative form. The persistent linearity of Pickens's prolific narrative types, however confused, communicates his striving after a procreative line of patrimonial lineage, even to the extent that women are virtually absent. In *The New Negro,* Pickens forcefully subordinates description and visual imagery in his commitment to a fast-paced narrative driven toward the decisive conclusion of unswerving New Negro advancement in the New World. Other new-century works resist the flagrant aggression implicated in Pickens's fiercely patrilineal structures, opting for more cautious displays of racial ambition, as indicated by the interchange between narrative thrust and pictorial arrest. In many works, this takes the form of actual pictures—sketches or photographs—whose visual impact so overshadows the competition embedded in the race-racing narrative that they become eidetic albums to be admiringly eyed rather than fast-paced stories of aggressive social mobility.[30] In the most influential instance of the race album, Booker T. Washington's *A New Negro for a New Century* (1900), in addition to slowing down the story of Negro drive to an almost static visual proof of the current stage of racial progress, the pictorial display tends to soften the blow of the competitive challenge being engaged *against* the white race in favor of a cooperative, often fraternal enterprise between black and white male leaders of each race.

Even without actual pictures, however, the new-century race promoter can effect an arresting display by exploiting the technique of *ekphrasis,* the attempt to render a visual picture through descriptive language, whether through the extended description of a literal person or scene or through the showy array of fixed allegorical figures. The interaction between discursive and visual forms, between narrative and picture, enables the author to *stage* the race in two senses: (1) to mark and document the particular stage that the race has reached in the race toward modernity; and, simultaneously, (2) to place a visual embodiment of the race on a metaphorical stage in which characters are cast as racial specimen, scenes are set to provide the sociohistorical context, and a performance is mimed to illustrate the momentary status and ongoing prospects of the race.

At stake in these various narrative and visual strategies is the question of how best to represent the situation of the race at a particular moment to a particular audience for a particular agenda. Narrative drive and visual representations provide different benefits and disincentives depending on the context, and depending crucially on the author's judgment concerning how best to treat the problem of un/de/re/sexing the race. Both Du Bois and Washington are fond of exploiting ekphrastic displays in their writing, though they use different techniques inspired by contrary political orientations. Du Bois favors the highly allegorized mode of the historical pageant, a dialectical procession of pictorial scenes that interrupt the narrative or argument in order to represent visually abstract crises and personages shaping grand events in history. Washington favors more earthy cross-racial portraits of individuals engaged together in quotidian self-help activities, offering visual proof of his pragmatically empiricist approach to racial advancement. Du Bois struggles with this question of how to stage the race from his earliest publications to his last, as he experiments with various intersections of verbal and visual representation.[31] As we see in this section, *The Souls of Black Folk* (1903) shares a close kinship with Washington's assumptions about race racing, evident in Washington's portraiture of the "wild" Indian students brought under his tutelage at Hampton Institute's experimental Indian school. In *Souls*, Du Bois accepts the idea of cross-racial patronage in which the best of the white race lends a helping hand to the best of the black race, the Talented Tenth, who in turn lend a hand to the black folk masses and, implicitly, also to white Southerners who are as lagging in as feudal a past as the former slaves. This formulation of race racing is also similar to that found in Pickens's "Misrule in Hayti" speech. Washington's wild American Indians, Pickens's childlike Haitians, and Du Bois's debased Southerners perform a similar part in staging the advanced status of the Negro race. "I freely acknowledge that it is possible, and sometimes best," Du Bois writes, "that a partially undeveloped people should be ruled by the best of their stronger and better neighbors for their own good, until such time as they can start and fight the world's battles alone" (*Souls* 143–144).

Like Chesnutt's "Future American," Du Bois's new-century race tract expresses and elicits a strong sense of disillusionment with the current condition of race relations amid the rollicking optimism displayed in works like Washington's and Pickens's; but Du Bois's lamentation, unlike Chesnutt's, is also framed by an idealizing retrospect in which past race relations offer hope for recovery and recuperation. Du Bois is deeply aware of the contradiction inherent in the notion of race racing when applied to Negroes at the turn into the twentieth century. No matter how strongly one may assert that the race is racing toward equality, inclusion, and modernity, its material conditions seem to contradict that assertion, for increasingly across the land, Negroes—new and old—are immobilized, both literally and figuratively. As their social, political, and economic mobility is cut off in venue after venue, so their ability to go wherever they please physically is increasingly curtailed by Jim Crow policies supported by the supreme law of the land. As the most graphic display of the physically arrested black body, lynching is especially at the forefront of these New Negroes' efforts to reanimate the inevitableness of black mobility and progress. By interrupting his race-racing narrative with arresting verbal pictures, Du Bois attempts to acknowledge this situation while retaining hope for a quickened pace in the future.

Du Bois's longtime intellectual investment in allegorical and ekphrastic iconography is evident in his interest in historical pageantry. He composed and produced *The Star of Ethiopia*, which Claudia Tate describes as "a spectacle with a cast of 1,200 that dazzled audiences in New York (1915), Washington (1916), and Philadelphia and Los Angeles (1924)." Du Bois employs the pageant form to portray in his own words "'the history of the Negro race and its work and sufferings and triumphs in the world' by combining 'historic accuracy and symbolic truth.'"[32] On the occasion of the convocation tribute held in honor of Du Bois's seventieth birthday, the honoree himself addressed the audience with an autobiography casting his life as "A

Pageant in Seven Decades: 1868–1938."[33] Du Bois is attracted to the form because of its capacity to embody for a mass audience a collective history made passionately empowering through a procession of visual display. Also, the pageant is seductive for him because he tends to view history as an Hegelian march of abstract principles and personages making their way through crisis toward, or being hindered from, a triumphant ideal made manifest in human movement. The pageant is an essentially allegorical mode in which individual persons perform the roles of world-historical personages who mime the grand crises and advances of a regional, national, or global celebratory histoy. When Du Bois employs the pageant form in his writing, he complicates the live theatrical medium by investing passionate historical dilemmas with intellectual rigor and historical critique.

In *Souls*, Du Bois allegorically stages a hopeful future for the race, ironically by looking backward to the white patronage of abolitionists and Reconstruction radicals like the Yankee schoolmarms, whose almost sanctified acts of patronage indicate their advanced status beyond other whites. These portraits of white patrons—idealized through a rhetoric of pure ethereality unmarred by bodily, material, monetary, or sexual appetite—serve as allegorical models for the black Talented Tenth, as well as for the old plantation aristocracy, New South white capitalists, and Yankee industrialists whose opportunistic interest in blacks is currently smeared by a crude and crippling materialism, both monetary and sexual in nature. Typical of many new-century stagings of the race, Du Bois's *Souls* subdivides the white and black races so that in each can be detected advanced and lagging groups—almost to the extent that they become four mutually intersected races (white patrons, black Talented Tenth, white laggards, black laggards) instead of bilaterally opposed enemies. Du Bois's phrase "partially undeveloped people" refers to those black and white laggards in need of a helping hand. Rejecting the notion that only the Negro exists "in his race-childhood" (66) or that all Negroes exist only at that stage, Du Bois instead creates stunning visual scenarios capturing the past, current, and potential interactions among these four racial subgroups.

Appealing to "the best of both races in close contact and sympathy" (136), his injunction throughout *Souls* is for the advanced black and white *men*, in particular, to reform themselves by joining hands to lift the lagging black and white Southerners, taking the actions of the interracial coalition of abolitionists and radical Reconstructionists of the 1850s through the 1870s as the model. This eloquent plea is made through a discursive range that runs the narrative gamut from autobiographical anecdote to national history, from military history to allegorical redemption parable, and from sociological case study to fictional short story; but it is Du Bois's pageantry in *Souls* that is calculated to tug the heartstrings and thus to prick the conscience of the advanced camps of blacks and whites. "Progress in human affairs is more often a pull than a push," Du Bois writes, "surging forward of the exceptional man, and the lifting of his duller brethren slowly and painfully to his vantage-ground" (79). The imagery of narrative driving motion ("surging forward") complemented by a stationary stance of upward lifting ("vantage-ground") is repeated in a variety of scenarios suggesting this redemptive ideal of a steady, concerted, cooperative, self-sacrificing—indeed, almost sacrificially eschatological—progress. The rhythm of Du Bois's race tract replicates this idea of fast-paced narrative motion constantly interrupted by long pauses for visually idealized observation and contemplation.

Although there are myriad instances of such pageantial scenes in *Souls*, perhaps the most arresting can be found in his description of the Yankee schoolmarms who go southward during radical Reconstruction to staff the fledgling missionary and freedmen's schools. New England *feminine* philanthropy of the 1860s and 1870s comes to represent the ideal of cross-racial, cross-class patronage for contemporary males. He situates this New England motherland as the nurturing resource of past benevolence and present source of melancholic failure and grievous loss. Although he attacks the New England of his present (and especially the *male* Yankee industrialists) for failing the standard previously set, he positions its past action as the standard against which all future patronage must be judged. An idealized New England represents the capacity for generous sacrifice without the desire for compensation—the spirit of gift giving—as opposed to both slavery and capitalist commerce as systems of profiteering exchange:

> This was the gift of New England to the freed Negro: not alms, but a friend; not cash, but character. It was not and is not money these seething millions want, but love and sympathy, the pulse of hearts beating with red blood;—a gift which to-day only their own kindred and race can bring to the masses, but which once saintly souls brought to their favored children in the crusade of the sixties, that finest thing in American history, and one of the few things untainted by sordid greed and cheap vainglory. The teachers in these institutions came not to keep the Negroes in their place, but to raise them out of the defilement of the places where slavery had wallowed them. (*Souls* 83–84)

Calling this educational uplift experiment of the northern missionaries for the freed Africans "the contact of living souls," Du Bois promotes this moment as eliciting the true meaning of patronage. This patronage is hands-on, not a sort of proxy philanthropy in which the patron sends money to do the work of charity. Monetary charity—the kind being practiced by Northerners in the post-Reconstruction period in league with Washington's brand of black self-help—is too easily confused with monetary exchange, in which motives of profit and vainglory can easily slip into the process. The Reconstruction teachers put their *bodies*, their *lives*, on the line—not their money. Black male patronage should reform itself on that soulful Reconstruction experience, not on Washington's Tuskegee patronage spoils system, with its exchange of economic and political privileges for deferred political and social rights.[34]

Appealing to the popular urban settlement house and other social and moral reform movements of the Progressive Era, Du Bois emphasizes humanistic and humanitarian acts that require actual cross-racial touching.[35] "The colleges they founded were social settlements; homes where the best of the sons of freedmen came in close and sympathetic touch with the best traditions of New England. They lived and ate together, studied and worked, hoped and harkened in the dawning light" (*Souls* 84). In contrast to Chesnutt's and Pickens's resexing of race relations by insisting on the procreative basis of modernization, Du Bois's notion of "close and sympathetic touch" operates to desex race relations by suppressing the taboo of intimate physical touching—erotic and otherwise—between whites and blacks, while ironically basing the cross-racial patronage effort on this figure of actual physical proximity. The physical closeness of blacks and whites, their eating and living together, enables the success of the educational experiment after emancipation, and this ideal cooperation between an advanced and a lagging race can be set before us, he insists, *without* erupting into fears over the implications of black people being touched by whites or, more alarmingly, of black men touching white women. Du Bois insists on the high-minded soulfulness of this cross-racial touching, a bond so pure that the physicality of the body itself—and its wayward desires—is sacrificed on the altar of social equality and intellectual idealism.[36]

Having been influenced strongly in his education by the Hegelian teachers at Fisk and Harvard, the young Du Bois not surprisingly places the primary cause for uplift in the realm of an idealized notion of soul, immanent within the strivings of those social leaders who seek to guide the folk beyond a primitive condition.[37] According to this way of thinking, individual motives ("love and sympathy") operate through donated institutions (missionary schools) to overcome the unfairness embedded in economic structures and political systems. Cross-racial friendship is worth more than alms, character more powerful than cash. The human touch transcends institutional ideologies. The formal consequence of Du Bois's reliance on individual motives and soulful sacrifice is his deployment of arrestingly purified portraits of actual and imagined persons reaching out to touch debased others. Du Bois's Yankee schoolmarm sets forth a visual display that focuses on the actively but calmingly still bodies of the matrons, whose soulful missions to the war-torn South interrupt, and thus contrast sharply with, the masculine migrations of Civil War soldiers, capitalist interlopers, and disinherited southern planters and white workers:

> The annals of this Ninth Crusade are yet to be written,—the tale of a mission that seemed to our age far more quixotic than the quest of St. Louis seemed to his. Behind the mists of ruin and rapine waved the calico dresses of women who dared, and after the hoarse mouthings of the field guns rang the rhythm of the alphabet. Rich and poor they were, serious and curious. Bereaved now of a father, now of a brother, now of more than these, they came seeking a life work in planting New England schoolhouses among the white and black of the South. They did their work well. In that first year they taught one hundred thousand souls, and more. (22–23)

This passage contains the structural logic of benign migration and studied arrest that characterizes notions of proper mobility in *Souls of Black Folk*. The good intentions of the Civil War and Reconstruction are brought to fruition by these daring women, whose accomplishments, ironically, overshadow the government's masculine efforts in war and peace. It is not so much that the Civil War and Reconstruction are historical mistakes for Du Bois as that they are contaminated and thus weakened endeavors. As opposed to these epic events, which resemble too closely the activities of the Rebels and post-Confederate white councils, the agency of gentlewomen's schoolteaching can be made to appear purely motivated, especially in retrospect. Whatever soldiers, politicians, and capitalists had to gain from warfare and Reconstruction, Yankee women, innocent of worldly bloodshed and politics and saddled with no worldly thing to gain, can be represented as icons of unblemished self-sacrifice. In a mission purer than that of the chivalrous Crusaders to the Holy Land seven centuries previous, these women risk ill repute and assault, figured as the "ruin and rapine" that accompany even the holiest of wars. And it is "souls" (undetectable as white or black) that they teach, not merely hands, hearts, or heads (the trilogy that Washington borrowed from Puritan ideology and made famous through his Tuskegee experiment).[38] Du Bois casts a doubtful eye on invasive migration narratives that imply or threaten interracial warfare and sexual conquest and instead shifts our attention to the becalming, stabilizing picture of feminine teachers ministering to the degraded poor. Such cross-racial, cross-class touching modernizes the race in a way that attempts not only to erase the dangers of interracial sexuality but also to diminish the contaminating threat of a vulgar marketing campaign, with all of its debasing associations with money, capitalist profiteering, and prostituting consumption.

In this way Du Bois hopes also to resolve a second and third contradiction inherent to his advocacy of race racing in the post-Reconstruction moment. How can he insist on the "sympathetic touch" as the basis for race uplift while still holding to the Darwinian view of evolution as motivated by fierce competition among races? How can he distance himself and his program from the competitive implications of a race-marketing campaign while engaging in exactly that through his racial polemics? Du Bois uses verbal portraiture to deploy an ambivalent strategy of segregating the material aspects of racial marketing from the spiritual aspects of racial modernization—a canny usage that Alain Locke will intensify in his New Negro project a generation later. While highlighting the purely spiritual and cooperative, Du Bois cannot ignore the divisively competitive realities of his Jim Crow moment. He acknowledges this through negative verbal pictures that serve as an antithesis to an idealized cooperative past. If one dialectical phase of his procession spotlights the idealized image of a past moment of feminine patronage, other scenes in the procession depict the messiness of Du Bois's contemporary moment, in which the cross-racial touch is soiled by greed and lust. By forcing us to dwell momentarily in the negating present, Du Bois knowingly risks our reversion and degradation toward the worst aspects of a war-torn history. He is counting on his readers, however, to achieve some distance from the present as it is frozen in an allegorized visual scene, and thus to judge the present morass rather than be trapped in it.

Against the idealized feminine portraits of surging forward and lifting up Du Bois paints invidious portraits of those who seek to push backward and pull down, and these debasing figures are as mercilessly racialized and sexualized as the cooperative saintly band of "the best of both races" is deraced and desexed. In contrast to the Yankee schoolmarms, whose feet seem barely to touch the ground as they quest southward, Du Bois presents an array of sordid migrants currently impeding the steady progress of all racial groups: Yankee interlopers, disinherited southern planters, upstart New South capitalists, distressed white industrial workers, aimless former slaves, Ku Klux Klan lynchers, "vagrant" criminals of both races, fallen black women turned to shiftless prostitutes, and money-grubbing Jews. These groups agitating and marauding across the land, inciting rapine and ruin through their greed, present the foreboding collective image of a nation on the verge of apocalypse—the most radical form of narrative arrest, representing in the Christian tradition the final pageant that brings an end to time itself. Speaking in particular of the retaliatory behaviors spawned by racial violence against Negroes, Du Bois warns: "I insist that the question of the future is how best to keep these millions from brooding over the wrongs of the past and the difficulties of the present, so that all their energies may be bent toward a cheerful striving and co-operation with their white neighbors toward a larger, juster, and fuller future" (89). This narrative of national catastrophe spurred by sectional exploitation, violent reprisal, and racial factionalism gets fixed in various scenes, all fixated on the corrupting influence of material—bodily, sexual, and monetary—appetite. For instance, Du Bois provides this dire picture of the malingering consequences of Civil War:

> The rod of empire that passed from the hands of Southern gentlemen in 1865, partly by force, partly by their own petulance, has never returned to them. Rather it has passed to those men who have come to take charge of the industrial exploitation of the New South,—the sons of poor whites fired with a new thirst for wealth and power, thrifty and avaricious Yankees, shrewd and unscrupulous Jews. Into the hands of these men the Southern laborers, white and black, have fallen; and this to their sorrow. (138)

Notice how the corrupting image of the phallic "rod of empire" passing from one masculine set of hands to another contradicts the purifying image of gentle feminine hands lifting up the oppressed to a higher vantage-ground through the teaching of the alphabet. If the hands of white male patrons and Talented Tenth Negroes are not seen as exactly feminine (because Du Bois insists on a manly patronage as well as a pure and gentle one), they are so influenced by the chaste Yankee school matrons that they are noticeably softened. There is no doubt, however, about the negatively virile effects of the "rod of empire." As is often the case when sacrificial redemption is promised, the anti-Semitic, scapegoating icon of the moneyed Jew seals the promise. The progressive future of black allied to white is cemented through this Jewish scapegoat, whose presence ushers in a whole series of vengeful bloodletting, flesh-dealing scenarios of criminality. Although, unfortunately, the series of evils culminates with the "unscrupulous Jews," at least they are not singled out racially but instead conjoined with other racialized groups debasing, and debased by, the current system of political spoils and economic greed.

Du Bois also depicts dispossessed whites carrying out their avarice and lust on their ignorant former slaves, who in turn become murderous and prostituted by a wayward, lynching justice as they are "swept in moments of passion beyond law, reason, and decency." "Such a situation is bound to increase crime, and has increased it," Du Bois exclaims. "To natural viciousness and vagrancy are being daily added motives of revolt and revenge which stir up all the latent savagery of both races and made peaceful attention to economic development often impossible" (146). Through such pageantial portraits, Du Bois pictures racial *reversion* occurring at this moment, before our very eyes. The opposite of race progress, this reversion, too, is a kind of race racing—a racing backward. This movement is captured in the manic migrations of myriad groups from North to South or from war-torn South to homesteading West in search of a quick buck; it is likewise captured in quick ascents and falls, as the former planter class becomes impoverished and northern Jews, industrialists, and opportunistic middle-brow white Southerners quickly rise to power during Reconstruction.[39] As the social and biological sciences of the time purported to prove, criminality signals the degeneracy of a race, its backward movement toward a jungle savagery. Du Bois attempts here to wrest this criminology from a divisive racial logic whereby the Negro is biologically predisposed to criminality, rape, and prostitution and any whites who engage in such acts literally can be seen to display apish African body features. Du Bois insists that this potential for savage reversion is equally "latent" in both races.

Because the racial narrative is transformed into a moral struggle between good and evil *souls,* rather than a war between white and black *bodies,* Du Bois's visual strategy likewise foregrounds a moral allegory whose interpretation depends on spiritual *insight* rather than mere material *sight.* As we shall see Locke doing, Du Bois presents figurative bodies whose bodily attributes of race and sex become either transcended through a progress into modernity or debased through reversion to savage appetite. Against the purifying ideal of the Yankee schoolmarms, Du Bois represents a web of warped physical/sexual entanglements so enchaining that the most powerful, the gentleman slaveholder, and most victimized, his slave concubine, are trapped together in a murderous embrace of mutual hatred (see *Souls* 26). Rather than being emulative models, these are counterexamples, inspiring pity and remorse instead of love and sympathy and trapping us in doubling self-division and eternally recurring recriminations. In viewing them, we are blinded with tumultuous, enervating physical lust, rather than purified and activated with a sweet vision of soulful active service. The scene is meticulously structured as doubling.

The enslaved woman seems to mimic her master. Just as he comes from a lineage of manly men, she has an "awful face black with the mists of centuries." Appropriately, her lineage is darkened both by her severance from her own obscure past in Africa and by the theft, rape, and bastardization of her (male) children. She does not give in passively, for she "had aforetime quailed at the white master's command." Her "quailing" indicates her drawing back from him not only in fear but also in resistance to his sexual demands. But like him, she bows to slavery, as she "had bent in love over the cradles of his sons and daughters." The most static scene in all of *Souls,* this is the complete antithesis of racial advancement—a scene so replete with negative passion that it threatens to forestall any motivation for racial progress because just our glimpse of it traps us in its cycle of divisive recriminations and reiterations of past wrongs. Slave master and concubine "ever stand" opposed and together—like Hegel's moment of recognition between lord and bondsman—fanning the fires of hatred, violence, and death.[40]

In the pictorial strategy of *Souls,* Du Bois builds a dream of racial uplift on the Yankee woman's ability to transcend her body, while he chains our vision of dark womanhood to this cycle of bodily ruin and rapine embodied in the black female concubine/mammy. Paul Gilroy positions Du Bois's representation of black women in his nonfiction works in a different way. "This integral racial culture is something that Du Bois consistently figured in the feminine gender," Gilroy writes. "[S]uccessive images of the female form embody the harmony, mutuality, and freedom that can be acquired by dissolving individuality into the tides of racial identity."[41] This is not the case with the concubine, who instead represents the indelible stain of a bastardized racial lineage. However, as in the case of a backwoods Tennessee schoolgirl, Josie, later in the text, black womanhood does sometimes represent for Du Bois this aspiration toward racial refinement and wholeness, but in a different way from black manhood. Figures of dark womanhood are not given the idealized uplift agency portrayed primarily for Yankee schoolmarms and Talented Tenth black men.[42]

Du Bois is not suggesting that individual white men and black women cannot transcend the historical wreckage of slavery, the Civil War, and Reconstruction. He seems to imply instead that the tutelage of a historical transracial consciousness depends on contemplation and sublimation of a purer bond, supposedly uncontaminated and immune to the infections of past hatreds and present disappointments. Because *Souls of Black Folk* operates allegorically, represented individuals allude to larger and deeper cultural conflicts and "symbolic truth"—in the very way that the gray slaveholder and dark concubine stand for reciprocal hatreds that lock lord and bonds(wo)man in a destructive history. Contemplating either the paternalistic master as a potential patron or the "mother-like" slave woman as a potential matron can only repeat what Du Bois calls "the red stain of bastardy" (9), an illegitimate line of descent and thus an impure future action. Just as the slave master, no matter how benevolent, must always be a perversion of fatherhood, so the slave concubine always perverts motherhood into an impure mammified condition. In the scenes and narratives of the text, it is solely the black (male) patron who is imaged as bringing about racial modernization through contemplation of the temporarily lost ideal of the Yankee schoolmarm touching her black wards. By portraying white femininity and black manliness cross-racially in such ways, Du Bois hopes to invert the meaning of social Darwinist accounts of racial survival, displacing bloody and hasty competition between the leading men of the races with a pacifying, steadying rapprochement. "It is, then, the strife of all honorable men of the twentieth century," Du Bois writes, "to see that in the future competition of races the survival of the fittest shall mean the triumph of the good, the beautiful, and the true" (134). The "beautiful" here is a third term mediating two others in this Neoplatonic dialectic in a manner similar to how Du Bois's chaste schoolmarms mediate between good black men and true white men. In sharp contrast to Pickens's internecine race of the races, what Du Bois advocates in the end as the best preparation for modernization is the cultivation of "a few white men and a few black men of broad culture, catholic tolerance, and trained ability, joining hands to other hands, and giving to this squabble of the Races a decent and dignified peace" (72).

Du Bois's stance on race racing is not static, however, even as he continues to exploit tactics of allegorical pageantry to explore its contradictions. In a much later race tract published in 1940, *Dusk of Dawn: An Essay toward an Autobiography of a Race Concept,* Du Bois repudiates not so much the spirit and method of *Souls* as its basic ideological assumption about the temporal situation of the races. He records his repudiation as a vivid scene of revelation, occurring to him when he "first set foot on African soil." Reflecting on his intellectual struggle with the concept of race, he writes that since the time of one of his first pamphlets, *The Conservation of Races* (1897), "the concept of race has so changed and presented so much of contradiction that as I face Africa I ask myself: what is it between us that constitutes a tie which I can feel better than I can explain?" (*Dusk of Dawn* 117). Du Bois then ponders how "efficiency and happiness do not go together in modern culture" (125). In a scene that explicitly rejects the drive toward modernization, which gives to the white race a significant lead in the "swift foot-race" of civilization, Du Bois also unsettles the idea of the race of the races:

And there and elsewhere in two long months I began to learn: primitive men are not following us afar, frantically waving and seeking our goals; primitive men are not behind us in some swift foot-race. They are abreast, and in places ahead of us; in others behind. But all their curving advance line is contemporary, not prehistoric. They have used other paths and these paths have led them by scenes sometimes fairer, sometimes uglier than ours but always toward the Pools of Happiness. Or, to put it otherwise, these folk have the leisure of true aristocracy—leisure for thought and courtesy, leisure for sleep and laughter. They have time for their children—such well-trained, beautiful children with perfect, unhidden bodies. Have you ever met a crowd of children in the east of London or New York, or even on the Avenue at Forty-second or One Hundred and Forty-second Street, and fled to avoid their impudence and utter ignorance of courtesy? Come to Africa, and see well-bred and courteous children, playing happily and never sniffling and whining. (*Dusk of Dawn* 127)

Despite his assertion of a bond between himself and Africa, here he places himself with the efficient moderns of Europe and America, not with "the leisure of true aristocracy" that he sees around him in Liberia. And although Du Bois has not abandoned the race of the races totally, he manages here to dislodge the stable hierarchy, the temporized chain of being, that assumes "primitive men" to be "behind," "frantically waving and seeking [the] goals" already determined by the white West. The possibility of other goals and "other paths" within civilization comes close to jettisoning civilization itself as an illusion of racial ideology: If "primitive men have already arrived," then whence, exactly, are European Americans so busily racing, and where exactly is it that ever-newer Negroes seek to go? Positing the villages of Liberia as an advance guard of modernity—"all their curving advance line is contemporary, not prehistoric"—Du Bois presents his African idyll as a challenge to the civilizing meccas of London and New York, whether the downtown cultural enterprises and pace setters of the white United States around Times Square ("the Avenue at Forty-second") or the uptown centers of New Negro culture in Harlem ("the Avenue at . . . One Hundred and Forty-second").

To carry his point, Du Bois cannot avoid the issue of Africans' "primitive" sexuality, which European culture has taken as a signal of a lagging status remaindered by civilization. Notice, however, how he attempts to resex the image of the race by emphasizing that "primitive" sexuality can also connote an earthy, uncontaminated, Edenic sense of native purity:

I have read everywhere that Africa means sexual license. Perhaps it does. Most folk who talk sex frantically have all too seldom revealed their source material. I was in West Africa only two months, but with both eyes wide. I saw children quite naked and women usually naked to the waist—with bare bosom and limbs. And in those sixty days I saw less of sex dalliance and appeal than I see daily on Fifth Avenue. (127–128)

Du Bois needs to separate nakedness from sexuality, the body's presentation from the person's respectability, in the same way that he has to work through the confusion between the body's color and the person's racial heritage. (Although uplift is aimed at transcending the body as a racialized object, new-century race workers find themselves, in different ways, returning to the exposed black body as material evidence of black capacity.) Du Bois further implies that the naked African body is in concert with an open, frank, clean sexuality, as opposed to the European ethnographers who "talk sex frantically" but leave obscure their evidence. He turns on its head the idea that clothes are a sign of respectable higher civilization because they cover the nasty sexual organs: the modern European cloaks his frantic obsession with "sex dalliance and appeal" beneath his respectable clothes. It is Europe (including America), not Africa, that "means sexual license," for whereas Africans dress as though they have nothing to hide, Europeans hide their illicit desires behind their civilized clothes.

Like Chesnutt and Pickens, Du Bois is able to rewrite the competition of the races so as to provide different paths where the black race can prosper on its own terms. The racial renewal that occurs from this revelation—the conversion he experiences when he sets foot on African soil for the first time—still leaves him preferring the cosmopolitan West, New York, and seeking to reimage the African in the eyes of the West through modernizing communication. "Wherefore shall we all take to the Big Bush?" Du Bois asks. "No. I prefer New York. But my point is that New York and London and Paris must learn of West Africa and may learn" (128). Du Bois's portrait of the idyllic naked Africans performs an argumentative service similar to that played by the American Indians in Chesnutt's "Future American" trilogy. By triangulating American Negroes with another group who can represent an alternative civilizing advance to that of white men, the new-century race advocate attempts to short-circuit the entrenched ideology that places white men far ahead in the civilizing race.

Washington's account of serving as headmaster of the experimental Indian school at Hampton is just as concerned with the purified black body as Du Bois's Liberian idyll, and he uses American Indians similarly to the way Du Bois uses Africans or Pickens uses American Indians. For Washington, race racing is intimately bound to the binaries of clean versus dirty work and proper clothes versus primitive nakedness, binaries that can be visualized in arresting scenes. It is not a simple movement, however, from dirty work to clean labor and from tattered hand-me-down clothes that expose to genteel ones that fully cover the body. On the one hand, he glorifies manual labor; on the other hand, he desires to rise above such labor to "white-collar" brain work. His determination to gain literacy is motivated by a "dread" of the soot that clings to the skin as a result of coal mining, as he relates in *Up from Slavery*: "Work in the coal-mine I always dreaded. One reason for this was that any one who worked in a coal-mine was always unclean, at least while at work, and it was a very hard job to get one's skin clean after the day's work was over" (38). Though mining represents the sort of labor Washington venerates as the cure to the backwardness of the former slaves, it is exactly the desire to leave behind toil in the dirt, the second skin of blackness made by the soot, that leads him to become a house servant for Mrs. Ruffner, the strict white woman who provides him with work when he is a boy.[43] Despite what he learns about the true industry of laundering from Mrs. Ruffner, he still desires to move beyond it to make his living. In each instance, he has to dirty himself to prove his capacity for keeping himself clean. For whites like Ruffner and Samuel Armstrong, his white mentor and head of Hampton Institute, he repeatedly performs this ritual of housekeeping, which, on the one hand, confirms his patrons' association between his darker skin and the need for dirty labor and, on the other, proves his special capacity to keep the dirt from further sullying his skin. As head of Tuskegee, he finds himself promulgating in his teachers and student-disciples a commitment to the same ritual of dirtying to clean up. To teach his black wards not to be embarrassed by besmirching labor, "each afternoon after school I took my axe and led the way to the woods" (*Up from Slavery* 131).

The paradox of his situation is captured in the pair of chapters at the heart of the autobiography, "Making Bricks without Straw" and "Making Their Beds before They Could Lie on Them." In the former, his students are reminded of the upward movement of the race through hard work, which rightly binds them to the soil—or in this case, the mud pits—until the race can prove itself worthy of a more advanced status. "It was not a pleasant task for one to stand in the mud-pit for hours, with the mud up to his knees. More than one man became disgusted and left the school" (151). The latter chapter, while referring to teaching the skill of carpentry by having the students make the school's furniture, also alludes to the students' learning to make their beds and keep their linens as well scrubbed as their bodies. "Over and over again the students were reminded in those first years—and are reminded now—that people would excuse us for our poverty, for our lack of comforts and conveniences, but that they would not excuse us for dirt" (174). Paradoxically, dirtying up and keeping clean inculcate obverse aspects of the value of race advancement. Whereas the ritual of dirty labor teaches self-conscious humility regarding the race's degraded status, the ritual of cleaning up teaches respect for the uplifting direction of the race and the need to be ever vigilant in purifying the literal soot that symbolically contaminates black skin. Washington, then, presents himself as an object lesson in racial uplift to both whites and blacks, as when he writes, "I have always in some way sought my daily bath" (58). His clean mulatto skin precedes him, announces him, displays him, represents who he is—clean enough for whites to deal with as a racial intermediary, dirty enough for blacks to follow as the leading racial patron.

In the same way, in the age that perfected the system of United States political patronage, Washington learns that he has to be adept at working both ends of the system if he is to enable the race to race ahead. He has to become both the ultimate passive recipient of political spoils, those leftovers of power brokered for him by more powerful white men, and the ultimate political boss, a dispenser of spoils among his own black political wards. A nagging question confronting any would-be black patron of the time was whether a black leader could gain the respect of the masses, or whether the conditions necessarily bred a disrespect deriving from the insight that any black leader, in order to achieve tangible results, had to depend on handouts and hand-me-downs from white political leaders, given the disenfranchisement, economic deprivation, and educational disadvantage of the race. "I have heard it stated more than once, both in the North and in the South, that coloured people would not obey and respect each other when one member of the race is placed in a position of authority over others" (168). Washington is, of course, eager to dispel this notion, as it serves to justify the position of those who would prevent black leadership. Nonetheless, he faces a real dilemma. To obtain political favors under the present circumstances, Washington has no choice but to act as a corrupt political boss, especially given the erosion of black voting power after the 1890s. But political bosses maintain their power through the use and abuse of dependent voting blocs, to which Washington has no access. Thus, any accomplishment he manages looks like both the power of the masses he represents and the impotence of a man totally dependent on the begrudging kindnesses of others. Washington's despotic mastery of his own wards—the teachers and students of Tuskegee as well as the political appointees answerable to him across the nation—communicates successfully his capacity to command obeisance from the masses. His success at Tuskegee alerts those in power, gaining him the ear of presidents. Against the negative consequence of the political obsequiousness publicly demanded from a man with no votes to offer in exchange for the favors he receives, Washington gains something more intangible and more influential: the image of a black man handling, if not wielding, national political clout.

Washington's tutelage under Armstrong has prepared him well for performing this sort of symbolic political exchange in order to gain obvious, visible spoils—"making bricks without straw." It is important to remember that during this period reformers were still heavily engaged in trying to clean up government through advocating a civil service system that could get rid of the favoritism, nepotism, ballot stuffing, corporate bribery, and other corruptions of the public trust now seen as negative aspects of political patronage; nonetheless, patronage remained a tried and true formula in local and national politics throughout Washington's lifetime.[44] Somehow Washington must learn to get down and dirty by practicing patronage politics while enhancing his clean image as a chaste, nonpolitical race leader. Alan Trachtenberg explains that the struggle over political patronage also acquires a gender bearing, with nonpartisan, high-minded, pristine reformers becoming associated with a prissy, effeminate culture, while party stalwarts picture themselves as hard-knuckled, competitive, real-world men:

> Not surprisingly, reformers and genteel intellectuals who stood above party battles invited the scorn of the regulars, a scorn couched frequently in images fusing anger at feminizing culture with sexual innuendo, the manly braggadocio of the stalwart: "political hermaphrodite," miss-Nancys," "manmilliners." Nonpartisans were a "third sex," "the neuter gender not popular either in nature or society." In the images of both sides, reform above parties and loyalty within parties, the issue seemed to join culture versus politics, the realm of the feminine against the realm of the aggressive masculine. (*Incorporation of America* 163)

Ironically, the racial compromise that restricts the would-be black leader from attempting to participate in institutional governance may serve to protect Washington from being classed in dominant culture among the political sissies, political hermaphrodites, and sexually perverted "Miss Nancys."[45] White America honors him as a strong, mature leader *because* he eschews public politics and prefers to concentrate on "softer" concerns such as higher education and agricultural, financial, and social associations devoted to bringing order, industriousness, cleanliness, moral virtue, and discipline to an African American population imaged as the opposite of these. Northern black critics like Du Bois, however, are prone to attack Washington for playing hard-knuckled party boss of the race behind doors, on the one hand, and for injuring the "manhood" of the race by refusing to step into the ring for the public political bouts against Jim Crow, lynching, and other racial maladies infecting the United States political system, on the other. Despite such gender-inflected criticism from members of his own race and incredible strictures from the white rulers, Washington is able to conduct messy patronage politics while usually retaining his reputation as a clean nonpartisan, nonpolitical leader of the black people.

Armstrong's Hampton Institute, the freedmen's school on which Tuskegee is modeled, presents an important arena in which Washington is able to learn this balancing act between macho politics and "Miss Nancy" racial caretaking. When Armstrong asks him in 1880 to take charge of an experiment in managing the education of "wild" reservation Indians at the normal school, Washington handles the racial nitty-gritty of the job, as he will later master the minefield of big-time patronage politics. In this scenario, the Indians represent the "spoils" that Washington must manage, and when he does so with finesse, it pays off in Armstrong's recommending the young man to head the new school to be established at Tuskegee.

> [Armstrong] secured from the reservations in the Western states over one hundred wild and for the most part perfectly ignorant Indians, the greater proportion of whom were young men. The special work which the General desired me to do was to be a sort of "house father" to the Indian young men—that is, I was to live in the building with them and have the charge of their discipline, clothing, rooms, and so on. (*Up from Slavery* 97)

In his experiment as a "house father" to Indians, we find the perfect figure for Washington's overall plight as an aspiring race leader. It is one thing to be the father of a race or nation, like George Washington, quite another to be a "house father," which implies a proximity to menial chores, hygiene, and the basics of refining parlor conduct. Furthermore, Washington's charges are not from his own "race" or "nation"—literally, given that the reservations are supposed to be semi-autonomous sovereign states—but instead from a race whose status in relation to African Americans is fraught with ambiguity. In such instances as this, we see the import of the failure to get the Supreme Court in *Plessy v. Ferguson* to recognize the confusing multiplicity of "races" as an admission of the legal absurdity of Jim Crow. If white patronage spoils will be allocated based on a binary logic of hand-to-hand contest between two naturally opposed races, then the only recourse, it might seem, is to make sure that the black race remains that sole other race against which whites define themselves. Washington's reasoning seems to be this: if Jim Crow reduces the South to two races separate and hardly equal, then the only option blacks have in this game is to make sure that others falling outside the black/white binary are exploited to advance, rather than to upset, blacks' role as the race next in line.

African Americans and Indians were bound together so tightly both ideologically and by "blood" that, as Jack D. Forbes points out, it is sometimes impossible to know in early colonial records whether terms such as *colored, negro, mulatto,* and *mestizo* indicate a person of African descent, a Native American, or some intermix of both.[46]

As with his fluid gender relations, in which he accepts a domesticated version of racial fathering, Washington can transfigure the anomaly of being a "primitive" in charge of "savages" into an heuristic scene modeling the race's advance by, on the one hand, taking supremacy over filthy, naked Indians and, on the other hand, subtly identifying with their resistance to assimilation, and thus complete extinction as a distinctive cultural group posing an alternative to the racial aggressions of white "civilization." To place Washington in charge of disciplining and civilizing Indians is to test to what extent he himself has disciplined his racial nature into a civilizing object for others' instruction. As Donal F. Lindsey remarks in his history of the Hampton Indian project, "Contrary to the stated beliefs of Hampton whites, [Washington] was convinced that the task of civilizing Indians would be more difficult for a black than a white man." This may have been the case, but in his *Southern Workman* propaganda Washington had to position himself as a self-confident man in full charge of his wards. As Lindsey points out, placing blacks in charge of Indians was as much a matter of keeping black instructors at the lower rungs of the institutional ladder as it was an attempt by white administrators to reduce any racial tension between Negroes and Indians by "deliberately intensifying association" between the two groups.[47]

> I knew that the average Indian felt himself above the white man, and, of course, he felt himself far above the Negro, largely on account of the fact of the Negro having submitted to slavery—a thing which the Indian would never do. The Indians, in the Indian Territory, owned a large number of slaves during the days of slavery. Aside from this, there was a general feeling that the attempt to educate and civilize the red men at Hampton would be a failure. (*Up from Slavery* 98)

Even as Washington emplots a narrative of cross-racial affiliation and human common interest with the Indians, he positions his own race ahead in the patronage rivalry. The distance black people have traveled from slavery toward civilization outpaces the Indians in their territorial strongholds, where some of them once lorded over black slaves.

Nowhere is this one-upmanship more apparent than in Washington's series of articles on the progress of his Native American charges, which he wrote for Hampton's propaganda periodical *The Southern Workman*.[48] Taking on the persona of an explorer-colonizer writing back to the metropole about the natives, or an anthropologist doing participant-observer fieldwork on primitive people, Washington assumes the alienation between his "American" audience and his charges. As the mediator between the two, he plays out in a more extreme form that position he takes between his white patrons and the Black Belt folk.

> Ask the average American what he knows of the characteristics of the ancient Angles and Saxons, or the Romans, and he would not hesitate for an answer. Ask him what he knows of the real character of the American Indian, and he is confounded. To show the public that the Indian is a man, that he thinks, does wrong, does right, has a mind and body capable of improvement, is the object of these "incidents." (*Booker T. Washington Papers* 2:78)

Pointing to the irony of what the "American" knows about people so distant in time and geography compared to what they know about the American Indian, Washington could be (and is) metonymically talking about African Americans as well. However, his position enables him to speak as though white Americans *do* know about African Americans, given that he, a black man, serves as a trusted, educated medium through whom they can go to understand the civilizing potential of what is conceptualized as a singular Indian race. "Has the Indian any of the tender feelings?" he asks, rhetorically for those in the know. He answers with the arresting portrait of a meeting between uncle and nephew after two years apart. "For five minutes they stood clasping each other's hands, unable to speak a word, and weeping as though their hearts would break, but with joy instead of sorrow" (2:79).

Washington makes the most of each displayed incident as a lesson not only about the progress of the Indians but, more important, about the Negro's already secured place in civilization in comparison to the Indian. In "New Arrivals" he recounts:

> Some of the actions of the new boys, before they get initiated into the habits of civilized life, are quite amusing to the old boys, who forget that it has been but a few months since they acted in the same way. Their fun began when one little fellow, who evidently meant to begin his life at Hampton by doing his work well at the table, for that purpose, left his coat in his room. (2:82)

This scandal of appearing without his coat could almost be a joke on the detailed and meaningless rituals of etiquette in "civilization." It serves instead, however, to demonstrate Washington's mastery over both civilization and his playful, uncivilized charges. "Things went on in this way for several mornings without improvement, and I had to turn the joke on the old boys by making them take the new boys for roommates and teach them to keep house. Now, the smoothness of their beds and the neatness of their rooms would teach a lesson to some lady housekeepers" (2:83). This is the perfect position for Washington, for it enables him to construct his "Miss Nancy" housekeeping role. At the same time, he is also constructing the pliability of that role by showing how his mastery of it can be used to launch him into the contrary role of a leading patron for others of an inferior race. In effect, the position he occupies in relation to the "wild Indians" is analogous to the position his mentor, Armstrong, occupies in relation to the primitive former slaves.

Like the United States elite who go in search of a degraded other to raise up as a display of their worthiness for global power brokering and modeling civilization, Washington patronizes the Indians as a display of black Americans' potential model citizenship. "I found that they were about like any other human beings," Washington writes in looking back on the experience in *Up from Slavery*—an obvious understatement of his equal humanity in relation to putatively superior whites. "I had their love and respect." Thus, in the Indian experiment Washington both indicts the white Americans for not treating Indians with human respect and exploits them in order to demonstrate his own higher level of civilization. In several articles in the *Southern Workman,* he emphasizes the generosity of the colored students toward their less fortunate Indian colleagues (see *Booker T. Washington Papers* 2:85–86). He then takes the subtle indictment of white Americans one more step: "The introduction of the Indian here will at least show that the colored man has learned enough to know that it is his duty to help the unfortunate wherever he finds them, whether clothed in black, white or red skins" (2:86). To speak of skin as clothing points up the irony of many white Americans' less evident generosity and lack of prejudice toward the less fortunate races. Skin color is merely a matter of clothing, he suggests, and can be put on or taken off like the clothes of civilization or savagery, rather than being a matter of native colors indelibly dyed into unchanging racial mentalities.

In *Up from Slavery,* when Washington observes that the Indians' resistance to European customs proves the most difficult problem, it occasions an unusual outburst of sardonic satire: "[B]ut no white American ever thinks that any other race is wholly civilized until he wears the white man's clothes, eats the white man's food, speaks the white man's language, and professes the white man's religion" (98). Topping this sharp irony aimed against whites, Washington again exploits his civilizing test and converts the potential feud between black and red clients into a visualized object lesson *to whites:*

> There were a few of the coloured students who felt that the Indians ought not to be admitted to Hampton, but these were in the minority. Whenever they were asked to do so, the Negro students gladly took the Indians as room-mates, in order that they might teach them to speak English and to acquire civilized habits.

I have often wondered if there was a white institution in this country whose students would have welcomed the incoming of more than a hundred companions of another race in the cordial way that these black students at Hampton welcomed the red ones. How often I have wanted to say to white students that they lift themselves up in proportion as they help to lift others, and the more unfortunate the race, and the lower in the scale of civilization, the more does one raise one's self by giving the assistance. (99)

In this lesson Washington precisely phrases the ideology of patronage as racial uplift, with its underlying current of "proportionate" uplift for the patron race. According to this nonthreatening scenario, the races in front always stay ahead, and the more they reach back to pull the lagging races forward, the more they speed ahead of the races they help. Clearly, Washington's specific aim is to suggest that the white elite should welcome hundreds of black Americans into their institutions as a generous act of (self-)patronage. Like the system of patronage politics, with its voting wards determined by urban ethnic rivalries, such a vision of racial patronage would turn the vicious racial divisions bloodying the U.S. soil into an affiliating system of benign racial spoils.

As is discussed in chapter 4, this system of national spoils based on racial patronage is also intimately tied to United States imperialist exploits abroad. The motivations that cause Armstrong to put Washington in charge of the Indian education experiment at Hampton also cause the federal agency in charge of the colonies to contract with Tuskegee to educate Cubans and Puerto Ricans after the Spanish-American War. Though Washington's experiment with these imperial spoils in the shape of colonial bodies seems to have been less successful than his civilization of the Indians, it is the political opportunity and its empirical visual display that are important: seeing the foreign students from far-flung U.S. colonies trekking to Tuskegee to become civilized and learn the latest applied sciences makes the black institution a central site of American civilization and modernity.[49] Recognizing that first-class citizenship is defined by the power to patronize the imperial others who come under your rule as a heightening of that rule, Washington impersonates the position of the colonizer in making room at Tuskegee for the less fortunate Cubans and Puerto Ricans. By generously taking on the burden of civilizing the master's colonial and territorial exotics, Washington stakes a claim to full citizenship for America's internally colonized race, the African Americans.

Washington's success or failure as a racial patron can never be a settled question, because despite the tangible results of his career—most notably the justly celebrated institution at Tuskegee—what Washington most intimately engaged and achieved is symbolic and intangible in nature: the spectacle of all "races" in the country being forced to imagine, if not believe, that a black man could be a national leader. His visual set pieces of his relationship to his Indian charges may take a tone (more jocular) and visual technique (empiricist rather than idealist) different from Du Bois's race tracts, but the two rely on a similar strategy of racial triangulation. The ambivalence that Du Bois displays toward the naked Africans works in the same way as Washington's ambivalence toward his naked Indians; in both cases, the new-century race leader stakes a claim to advanced status closer to white men while lobbing an attack at white men for not respecting the greater cultural integrity represented by these triangulated racial others.

The Arrested Gaze:
The Race Album and the Fraternal Look of the New World Negro

That a thinker like Du Bois has such a difficult time abandoning the concept of global race racing even in 1940, when he records his first setting foot on African soil in *Dusk of Dawn,* indicates to what extent this notion dominates the thinking of new-century race promoters of the late nineteenth and early twentieth centuries at least up to World War II. Calling into question Paul Gilroy's notion of African Americans' historical relationship to cosmopolitanism, the new-century race works insistently place New Negro identity on the stage of world history. Gilroy tends to equate a cosmopolitan outlook with black writers' emigration to Europe after World War II, effectively erasing the importance of the West Indies, Africa, Latin America, as well as Europe, to the race work of previous black American intellectuals and activists.[50] Gilroy also tends to equate cosmopolitanism with European *travel* in particular, as though visiting a place necessarily enlarges a person's identity—a common assumption embedded in the word *cosmopolitan,* which culturally derives from the experience of aristocratic continental travel in the form of the eighteenth-century British "Grand Tour." As Pickens remarks in his autobiography, *Bursting Bonds,* many wealthy white Americans made a point of traveling to Europe, but this seems to have had no impact on their nationalist prejudices.[51]

Although most African American new-century race workers did travel to Europe in the cause of their race advocacy, this act is not in and of itself the source of their insistence on placing New Negro identity in a global perspective. Following through with Pickens's logic, it is also the case that one can possess a politically sophisticated global identity without having the financial means of world travel. As we have seen in the cases of Chesnutt, Pickens, Du Bois, and Washington, and as we shall see later with Locke, Walter White, Ida B. Wells-Barnett, James Weldon Johnson, Claude McKay, Langston Hughes, Nella Larsen, and others, the New Negro concept of race racing is necessarily embroiled in a globalized vision of the Negro's modernizing role. The New Negro is thus always also the New World Negro. These race leaders tend to see their modernity as an aspect of their destiny in the "New World" of the Americas, and they also understand the geopolitics pitting the New against the Old World, the "tropical" against the temperate zones, the "primitives" against the "civilized." The problem of how to claim civilizing modernity necessitates their investment in a comparative—and often critical—approach to questions of cultural advancement and backwardness.

Even as these race workers advocate on behalf of the Negro's entry into full national citizenship, their nationalist agenda either implicitly or explicitly appeals to and borrows from notions of cosmopolitanism and instructs the New Negro, and his racial counterparts, to cosmopolitanize the race. Just as Pickens attempts to energize a race-tribe of black men by mobilizing an unstable racial hierarchy across global history, so global race racing frames Washington's *A New Negro for a New Century* in even more determinative ways. As "AN ACCURATE AND UP-TO-DATE RECORD OF THE UPWARD STRUGGLES OF THE NEGRO RACE," Washington's anthology, like Du Bois's idealized verbal pageantry, presents an image of the race not at war with other races, and certainly not at war with the top race, but working in concert with the top race to bring about a common modernity advantageous to all. Unlike Du Bois, however, this new-century race album represses, as much as possible, catastrophic hauntings by past or current interracial conflicts. Instead, the volume insists on a fraternal league of cooperative masculine ventures protected by patriarchal householding rights—self-congratulatory, bullish on capitalist self-marketing, and enamored of modern communication techniques such as photography as engines for a fast but steady racial progress. If the narrative of *A New Negro* presents the black race as lagging, the photographic display presents it as catching up with every step. While basing its ideology, narrative structure, historiography, and iconography on the global race of the races, *A New Negro for a New Century* ironically also attempts to invert race racing from a contest between European and African to a marathon relay in which black and white run together, their race leaders passing the baton of civilization back and forth.

A New Negro is as much focused on manly warfare as Pickens's *The New Negro*, but its militarism is aimed at gathering black and white men into a single, cooperative fighting unit whose bonds are intensified by the mutual dangers of the battlefield. In this scenario, global races do not involve inevitable adversaries in an ongoing race war; instead, the antagonists are Old versus New World, the old racial rivalries from the Old World pitted against racial coalitions in the New. Gates brings attention to the volume's "militaristic emphasis" ("Trope of a New Negro" 138), with seven of its eighteen chapters devoted to black men's roles in United States wars from the Revolution to the Spanish-American War, which occurred just two years before its publication. As Glenda Elizabeth Gilmore has pointed out, the Spanish-American War represented for many African American men an opportunity to prove their manhood on a global scale. However, conscious of the implications of having black men in uniform, advocates of Jim Crow, like the southern Democrats, found ways of countering black men's claim to manhood through military prowess (*Gender and Jim Crow* 81). Not only did white Southerners attempt to diminish the black soldiers' role in the war, but leading white northern men also exploited images of black men's childlike nature to advance themselves as true men and national saviors spreading the empire of United States democracy. The most important white man to engage in such anti–black manhood propaganda was none other than the acclaimed hero of the Spanish-Cuban-American war, Theodore Roosevelt.

The first five chapters of *A New Negro* are devoted to justifying and celebrating the heroism of the Spanish-American War largely, if not solely, as a way of vindicating black men's courage against Teddy Roosevelt's spurious claims of their cowardice. The anthologists quote offending passages from Roosevelt's 1899 *Scribner's* magazine article, where he describes himself as halting the defection of the black soldiers through a commanding show of Anglo-Saxon mastery:

> This I could not allow, as it was depleting my line, so I jumped up, and, walking a few yards to the rear, drew my revolver, halted the retreating soldiers, and called out to them that I appreciated the gallantry with which they had fought and would be sorry to hurt them, but that I should shoot the first man who, on any pretense whatever, went to the rear. . . . This ended the trouble. (Quoted in *A New Negro* 54)

Roosevelt's claims of the black soldiers' retreat insinuate how black men are unsuited for modern warfare across the seas, and thus for modern citizenship on the global stage. This constitutes an image of racial regression—black soldiers in need of a manly reform so radical that its possibility is doubtful. Characteristically, Roosevelt establishes his own manliness through his absolute mastery of the black soldiers dependent on him. His representation of the colored Rough Riders strikes at the very heart of Washington's New World Negro agenda, which advocates an emulative self-reliance and self-discipline for the race in conjunction with exemplary patronage—not discipline—from powerful white men until the race has caught up. By attacking the powerful image of the black infantryman, Roosevelt also threatens Washington's empiricist strategy of providing incontrovertible proof of New World Negro progress through *visual evidence* that can be grasped immediately, *at a glance.*

The anthologists of *A New Negro* need to point out Roosevelt's lies without antagonizing the war hero about to become president or damaging their larger campaign of presenting the Negro as a force for national unity and global progress. Optimistically proclaiming "sectionalism" no longer a problem, the introduction tries to implant the image of a nation no longer disunited over "the Negro problem," and thus the image of a black race consolidated across regions and fully allied with the country's progress as a whole. "The cries of an enthralled and afflicted people have been answered and humanity has been redeemed," the introduction proclaims (3). "Redemption" is the euphemism for the "New" South's restoration of (white) self-governance, negotiated after Reconstruction as the sacrifice of black Southerners' political rights. The introduction in effect embraces Washington's own negotiation of redemption and the New South in his Atlanta Exposition speech of 1895. It is the "mutual progress," separate yet interconnected, evoked in the Atlanta speech that *A New Negro for a New Century* is devoted to effecting and enacting.

By making Spain the villainous aggressor and the United States a noble savior in the cause of Cuban independence (a debatable take on the Spanish-Cuban-American war), the anthology strategically revises the global history of European conquest. The anthology writes a new history in which the old racial rivalries of Old World Europe, Africa, and Asia are pitted against the new progressive racial alliances for freedom in the New World. According to *A New Negro*, the war against Spain represents the renewed unity of the Union:

> But the declaration of war with Spain was responded to with a fervor and enthusiasm in every State of the Union, among all the race elements of the population, that put at rest forever any lingering suspicion that the Republic would be divided in sentiment in the face of a foreign foe. Nowhere in the country was more enthusiasm displayed than in the Southern States. The old flag, the stars and stripes, for the first time since 1860 was displayed everywhere in the Southern States. (23–24)

Just as Washington would eagerly take charge of Hampton's experiment in civilizing Native Americans from the reservations, just as he would later eagerly enroll at Tuskegee students from United States imperial territories, including Cuba, so the anthology exploits the Spanish-Cuban-American war to prove the world-class leadership competence of post-Reconstruction Negro men, a capacity determined as much by their manly self-discipline and self-reliance in consolidating the race for progress as by their commitment to a truce concerning all unresolved racial issues. White Southerners rally around the stars and stripes to fight for Cuba despite the fact "that of the total Cuban population of 1,631,687, 528,998 are classed as negroes and mulattoes, and that these latter, in all the revolutions in Cuba, have been, for the most part, the inspiration in council and backbone in the field" (24). While the anthology acknowledges the politics of patronage and patriotism operating to ignite the enthusiasm of the southern whites for the Cuban cause, it resists reading in a cynical way either the domestic political machinations or the imperialist-racist implications of the war.[52]

The image of black and white American and black and white Cuban soldiers joining in a common cause against the Old World aggressor also provides a perfect opportunity for creating a *homoracial* context for New World Negro uplift. As Eve Sedgwick has pointed out, patriarchal power in the West is conventionally based in heterosexual male rivalry and bonding, which excludes not only sexual others (women and homosexuals) from the construction of power but also racial others.[53] By using the term *homoracial* I highlight the ways in which African American men, and men of other oppressed races, sometimes engage in homosocial bonding *with white men*, as well as with one another, in an attempt to raise themselves to the status of ruling men in the dominant race. The "mutual progress" of the New World Negro does not mean that racial coalition extends in all cases to all races; it is an opportunistic coalition. In chapter 14 of *A New Negro*, "Exodus and Settlement in the North and West," we discover how this New World Negro discourse adopts the rhetoric of Manifest Destiny as a way of lifting the Negro up to the standards of European civilization on the backs of American Indians. Race racing always implies "just deserts," a matter of which client race deserves greater rewards from the dominant race. When a lagging race shows the energetic self-reliance to sally forth into the American wilderness without aid of the dominant race, it should be duly recognized and rewarded.

> Not one dollar of public funds soever, national, state, or municipal, was used in buying land or furnishing supplies for these poverty-stricken black imigrants [*sic*]. . . . Congress could, without the slightest qualms of conscience, vote away millions of acres of the richest lands to railroad monopolies. The government could appropriate millions of acres of land and millions of dollars in money to support the wild Indians, many of them drinking, gambling, and living a life of idleness, vagrancy, and crime. (289)

All the pathologies targeted at African American life—especially at black migration to the northern cities—are here attributed to "wild Indians" on the reservations. The Native Americans become undeserving of the land and money appropriated by the government, as opposed to the black western pioneer, who has "spent two and one-half centuries in unpaid toil to enrich the South, from which he is now forced to flee empty-handed and almost naked" (289), and who risks his own minuscule fortune on the frontier without support of the government. Classing the Native Americans with the villains of the Progressive Era—railroad magnates, factory kings, and commodity trusts—the chapter must sacrifice another racial group in order to claim a right to Manifest Destiny, and does so without the more astute ambivalence displayed in Washington's presentation of his Hampton Indian experiment.

This need to put "lower" races in place to ensure a faster pace for one's own race continues with a vengeance in the succeeding chapter, "Kentucky's Hospitality," which records the achievements of captives under the "milder" mode of enslavement in the border states and celebrates the cooperation between heroic Negroes and white pioneers in making the frontier safe for civilization. Recalling Washington's *Up from Slavery* description of how the male slaves protected the old and young mistresses when the masters are away during the Civil War, the chapter tells stories of faithful slaves protecting the master's wives and daughters from massacring Indians. Because the Kentucky masters were small farmers, pioneers who understand firsthand the rigors of hard work (unlike the Deep South aristocratic planters), they treated their slaves more sympathetically and work the land beside them. This portrait of pioneer enslavement as a more racially cooperative venture logically concludes with an idyllic verbal portrait of post–Civil War settlement in Kentucky: "In the Blue Grass Region, most of the Negroes have settled in little villages of their own, around the large towns. Here the more thrifty of them own their homes, and others can rent on reasonable terms." Characteristically for this anthology, a distinction is made between contributions of black men and women. "There are no better farm laborers in America than those Kentucky black men. The women, however, are not inclined to be as industrious" (332). The idyll of homoracial harmony must exclude women's contribution. What to do with black women in this vision of homoracial uplift is a difficult problem for *A New Negro*.

The verbal aspect of *A New Negro* cannot help but become entangled in its own confusions as it attempts to narrate the Negro's racial progress while minimizing the damaging impact of past enslavement and current Jim Crow practices—as indicated by the above passage complaining of the unrewarded labor of slavery. These confusions are everywhere evident but especially salient in the westward migration narrative. *A New Negro* embraces the idea that *Dusk of Dawn* struggles against. One cannot have an image of black progress as long as blacks are doomed to inhabit the tropics. One cannot have Manifest Destiny, the United States version of (white) civilized progress, without migration west or north, or wherever a free man chooses. Thus, we see Washington in 1900 putting his imprimatur on a volume that seems to advocate what he elsewhere seems to regret and preach against: the Negro's abandonment of the South for greater opportunities elsewhere. The narrative confusions of the anthology are further evident in its implicit use of gender polarities as a gauge of race progress.

In the chapters that celebrate "Heroes and Martyrs" (chapter 11) and "Fathers to the Race" (chapter 16), the anthology reveals its conflicted agenda through homoracial and heterosexual imaging. The four heroes and martyrs of chapter 11 are men who have given up something substantial, two of them their lives, for the progress of the black race. While the chapter acknowledges the crucial historical role of white patrons such as John Brown and William Lloyd Garrison, the structure and pictorial politics of the volume as a whole insist on the *self-reliance* of New Negro (male) leadership. Alongside the imagery of homoracial coalition in international enterprises such as wars, imperialist ventures, settling the frontier, taming Indians, fighting slavery, and establishing "progressive" world-class educational institutions,[54] the volume embodies the aspiration of ruling African American men, in all things essential to the good order of the household of the race, to tend to their own affairs. This is why the predominantly white chapter on "Heroes and Martyrs" is balanced later by "Fathers to the Race," which commemorates the earliest African American race leaders. "Fathers to the Race" serves as a transitional chapter into the final two on the colored women's club movement. Though *A New Negro* opens by reaffirming the homoracial heroism of Teddy Roosevelt's black and white Rough Riders, it closes with a nod to black women's race work, gendered as refining community service and social work. Thus, in the end, despite its advocacy of black and white men's homoracial connectedness and cooperation, the race album emphasizes a proper sexual bond between black men and black women, displayed as conventionally gendered heterosexual marriage. In "Fathers to the Race," two male race "fathers" (Frederick Douglass and Toussaint L'Ouverture) are paired with two female race "fathers" (Phillis Wheatley and Sojourner Truth), a gender (a)symmetry that unintentionally defamiliarizes the metaphor that constitutes male leaders and founders as "fathers," while also uncovering the awkwardness of attempting to commemorate women's leading roles within this patriarchal, husbanding paradigm. Nonetheless, until the last two chapters, the volume remains pictorially a black man's preserve, parading before our eyes upright male soldiers, pioneers, businessmen, and educators.

The limit on the gender bond is represented powerfully in the visual register by the asymmetrical segregation of all the photographs of female New Negroes to the last two chapters.[55] Gates says that the final chapters demonstrate "an urge to displace racial heritage with an ideal of sexual bonding" ("Trope of a New Negro" 139). It is not so much a shift from racial heritage to sexual bonding, however, as a shift from homoracial bonding with white men to heterosexual bonding with black women, primarily as handmaidens and spouses. "Racial heritage" is constituted as such *through* "an ideal of sexual bonding," for it is through the subordinated addition of the women that the leading men can represent themselves as perpetuating that heritage as a line of proper heterosexual reproductive descent. Fannie Barrier Williams initiates her chapter on the women's club movement by pointing to the relative lack of gender differentiation within African American historical experience. "[I]t ought to be borne in mind," she writes, "that such social differentiations as 'women's interests, children's interests, and men's interests' that are so finely worked out in the social development of the more favored races are but recent recognitions in the progressive life of the negro race" (*A New Negro* 378). The final chapters serve, then, to claim this recent gender differentiation, for without the apparent difference between men's and women's roles, there can be no New Negro patronage to lift the black masses. A cruder but perhaps more accurate way of putting this is that the women's presence in the volume classifies the men as elite leaders of the race—indeed, it *classes* them as elite men. According to Williams, it is within the middle-class woman's sphere of refined service and culture that elite black women must operate and aim their desires: "[B]ut colored women as mothers, as home-makers, as the center and source of the social life of the race have received little or no attention. These women have been left to grope their way unassisted toward a realization of those domestic virtues, moral impulses and standards of family and social life that are the badges of race respectability" (379, 382). As the final chapters represent the advancement toward women's "domestic virtues," they also serve to represent black men's ability for self-reform, to improve a situation where there has been "no protection against the libelous attacks upon their [black women's] characters, and no chivalry generous enough to guarantee their safety against man's inhumanity to woman" (382).

The women's visible aspiration to feminine refinement—captured in their photos—completes the picture of the men's aspiration toward manly leadership. Predictably, the women represented in this gallery of photos virtually all come from a couple of traditional feminine professions, mainly teachers and heads of service

Figure 1.1. Mrs. Hart, Jacksonville, Fla., Promoter of a Monument to Commemorate the Valor of Black Soldiers in the Spanish-American War; from *A New Negro for a New Century*.

organizations.[56] Mrs. Hart's photo seems especially important in the sexual iconography of the volume, as her effort to have a monument erected to commemorate the "Valor of Black Soldiers in the Spanish-American War" presents a gratifying feminine complement to the photos of male veterans of this war (409; see Figure 1.1).

The anthologists perhaps see their strongest evidence for the rise of a New World Negro in this visual proof, the photographs selected for admiration and emulation. In the post-Reconstruction period, photography itself becomes a battle-ground, as New Negroes attempt to exploit its technology for the purposes of displaying the successes of the race. According to Kevin Gaines, "Because photography was crucial in transmitting stereotypes, African Americans found the medium well suited for trying to refute negrophobic caricatures. In addition, black painters, illustrators, and sculptors, along with writers of fiction, produced antiracist narratives and iconography featuring ideal types of bourgeois black manhood and womanhood" (*Uplifting the Race* 68). The visual evidence of these Jim Crowed New Negro books indicates that great care is taken in selecting the "ideal types" for photographic subjects, and some attention is also paid to the placement of photographs in the volumes. Gates points out, "Booker T. Washington's portrait forms the frontispiece of the volume, while Mrs. Washington's portrait concludes the book, thus standing as framing symbols of the idea of progress" ("Trope of a New Negro" 138). This symbolism of Booker T. Washington and Mrs. Booker T. Washington (frontispiece and 425; see Figures 1.2 and 1.3) also embodies the demand

Figure 1.2. Booker T. Washington; from *A New Negro for a New Century.*

Figure 1.3. Mrs. Booker T. Washington; from *A New Negro for a New Century.*

for the New Negro patriarch to take care of his own racial household in league with a strong matriarch. Furthermore, it enacts Washington's belief that the best proof of black people's progress and growing acceptance as United States citizens will be the evidence of the senses, the external display of respectability through material commodities, bodily cleanliness, and transparent self-discipline.[57]

The photographs provide such evidence of the senses in the clothes, postures, and physiognomy of the black countenances displayed. In the chapters on the war, black American and Cuban officers are pictured: the photo of Charles E. Young, an officer in Cuba during the Spanish-Cuban-American War, is the first after Washington's portrait (13; see Figure 1.4). This stands out as the only photograph to present a full-body view: Lieutenant Young is in full dress uniform, with cape, hat, gloves, and ceremonial saber. Such a dashing display, bordering on a dandy figure, is exactly the kind of appearance that New World Negro men need to assert but that could easily, under the wrong circumstances, provoke a violent reaction from white onlookers. All the other photos and sketches are bust shots, almost all frontal—suggesting the integrity of character that comes with directness and that can be read phrenologically by the shape of the head. In this way, the race album attempts to avoid the insinuations associated with the display of the black body as the embodiment of backward savagery. These black countenances are supposed to present self-evident proof against those who display black physiques to illustrate the physical, intellectual, and moral inferiority of African peoples. However, it is the "outer" covering of clothing, grooming, hairstyles, and facial expressions that really communicates the newness of these Negro figures. The "interior" character represented by the dignified heads can always be too easily read as racially regressive, simply because they *are* "Negroid" heads, or at least identified as such by their inclusion in this volume on the New Negro.

The racial implications of the hyperformality in the photos can easily get lost in history if we forget that this style of portraiture is not "natural" but evolves as a "realistic" way of portraying the authority and respectability of solidly middle class late Victorian patriarchs. This realistic style of photography asserts class and gender norms so quietly and yet so forcefully that we can easily overlook how historically fabricated is the masculine attire of dark suit, white shirt, and simple cravat—no less a uniform than the ones worn by the military officers—and how culturally situated is the posture of spine stiffened, shoulders broadened, chin slightly tilted up, eyes locked, face absolutely sober. The choice of isolated, individual portraits might also easily go unnoticed because it is so familiar to us. Except for the portrait of Anna J. Cooper (385) in a conventional pose at her desk, all the photos are abstract and contextless. They do not bespeak the subjects' success by relating them to their houses, parlors, families, places of work, or instruments of their profession. The abstract, autonomous individualism connoted in their isolation from context, however, seems contradicted by the uniformity of their social representation.[58] Unlike Du Bois's densely symbolic array of pictorial allegories, each of which needs detailed contemplation and interpretation, *A New Negro*'s photographs present them-

Figure 1.4. Chas. E. Young, First Lieutenant of Regular Army, Graduate of West Point Academy, and Major of Volunteers in Cuba; from *A New Negro in a New Century.*

selves as self-evident narratives of racial modernity that can be captured and understood without deliberation.

In a pair of 1904 essays for *Voice of the Negro,* artist John Henry Adams Jr. provides an even more revealing race album through "rough sketches" of the "the New Negro Man" and "a study of the features of the New Negro Woman." The articles are intended not only to model the physical characteristics that signal a new black elite but also to advertise the talents of these men and women in captions beneath the sketches. If Washington's photographs are intended to indicate the New Negro's mastery of photographic technology as immediate proof of the New Negro's fast track toward modernity, and if Du Bois's erudite allegories are supposed to prove his mastery of the learned knowledge of civilized Europe as a credential for modernizing patronage, then Adams's sketches are supposed to reveal his facility with the high traditions of European art, on the one hand, and his professional

Figure 1.5. Professor John Henry Adams Jr. of Morris Brown College; from "Rough Sketches: The New Negro Man." Sketch by John Henry Adams Jr. Photo courtesy of the Library of Congress.

training as an alert and practical businessman, on the other. The caption beneath Adams's self-sketch reads: "Prof. John Henry Adams, Jr., of Morris Brown College. He is considered the rising negro Artist of the South. The Atlanta Constitution pronounces him 'nothing short of a genius' and says that 'he may some day startle the world with his paintings'" ("Rough Sketches: The New Negro Man" 447; see Figure 1.5).[59] Adams does not trust his sketches of New Negroes to speak for themselves. Unlike the at-a-glance photographs from *A New Negro*, his sketches all receive ample explanation, so that the heuristic pedagogy of the visual imagery is not lost on the reader/viewer. In other words, the captions beneath the figures become heuristic legends, thumbnail verbal sketches narrating the stories of great or soon-to-be great men. Like Du Bois's allegories, these sketches and their narratives are intended not just to be looked at but to be contemplated—gazed at and studied, gazed at again and restudied, like great works of art. Thus, the sketch of Jesse Max Barber, the only one that covers a full page in the article, displays the impeccable formality of his clothing as he is seated at a desk peering down into an open book (451; see Figure 1.6). However, rather than focusing on the style that makes a man a New World Negro, the legend seeks to capture the man who makes the clothes: "The above sketch shows Editor Jesse Max Barber in his characteristic attitude while engaged in study in what he calls his 'Sanctum Sanctorum.' Mr. Barber is a very close student of current economic and sociological questions, as his narrations of current events in 'Our Monthly Review' will show" (351). Barber's studious attitude is encoded in the visual cue of his attention being directed totally on his book. The representation of his seriousness and talent as an analyst of current events is embodied in this relation to the book, so that the visual and verbal sketch confirm each other.

In an even more exaggerated fashion than *A New Negro,* the "Rough Sketches" articles focus as race albums on a chivalric standard for differentiating the roles of male and female New Negroes—a resexing of the best specimens of the race from stereotypes of savagery to refined chivalry. As indicated by its subtitle, the article on the New Negro woman emphasizes her facial features, rather than her accomplishments, whereas the legends for the New Negro men emphasize astonishing accomplishments for men so young. The caption for one of the female sketches reads: "This beautiful eyed girl is the result of careful home training and steady schooling. There is an unusual promise of intelligence and character rising out of her strong individuality. A model girl, a college president's daughter, is Lorainetta" ("Rough Sketches: A Study of the Features of the New Negro Woman" 324; see Figure 1.7). Linking feminine beauty to a sort of finishing-school education, Adams suggests that it is a matter not of innate biological features but instead of careful breeding that can place the black woman on the same pedestal with her European

Figure 1.6. Jesse Max Barber; from "Rough Sketches: The New Negro Man." Sketch by John Henry Adams Jr. Photo courtesy of the Library of Congress.

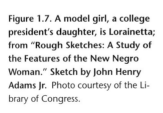

Figure 1.7. A model girl, a college president's daughter, is Lorainetta; from "Rough Sketches: A Study of the Features of the New Negro Woman." Sketch by John Henry Adams Jr. Photo courtesy of the Library of Congress.

counterparts. Another caption reads: "You cannot avoid the motion of this digni-fied countenance. College training makes her look so" (324). As opposed to the focus on "attitude," which signifies an aspiring mental stance of engagement with the world, worthy of being acted on, Adams's verbal and visual sketches of New Negro women emphasize their "look," which signals an inspiring physical deport-ment worthy of being gazed upon. As with *A New Negro,* the problem presented to Adams is how to instill in his readers/viewers the message *beneath* the skin, so that the color of the skin can code upward mobility instead of an embodiment of the "lower"—whether lower class, lower civilization, lower intelligence, lower achieve-ment, lower physical refinement, or lower impulses. His sketches of the female New Negro present a soft, delicate, refined facade that betokens inner purity, seren-ity, and depth. Although each portrait achieves this romance of the feminine in a slightly different way, he projects this onto Lorainetta through the dark shading that covers half her face: Lorainetta is not easily possessed by the viewer; despite her softness, she is distant and reserved. Adams is able to combine feminine mys-tery—almost *sensuous* (bordering on, but stoutly resisting, a *sensual*) allurement—with the ideal of chastity. The purpose of these refined, romantic women is to up-hold and hold out a standard of feminine purity that cannot be touched by the lower impulses normally imputed to them by the dominant race.

Even more than Washington's race album, Adams's pair of articles demote nar-rative and polemic in favor of arresting modes of visual illustration, even in the verbal portions of the text. "The New Negro Woman" article begins with Adams and another young black gentleman, Alford, observing the unusual sight of two ladies—one black, one white—"engaged in a happy, spirited conversation" as they ride in a carriage through downtown Atlanta. The sight halts the men momentarily, and Adams puts the question of which woman is more beautiful. When Alford answers without pause that the colored lady is more beautiful, Adams reasons: "Alford saw beneath the first skin surface down to the last layer of race greatness,—the preserving and honoring of race identity and distinction" (323–324). Using the language of southern chivalry to its fullest, the article's purpose is twofold: to get black men to "appreciate" the rising beauty of black women and to get all men to appreciate feminine refinement in both races. Adams says that this conversation with Alford motivates him to search the world for black feminine beauty and then to capture it in the sketches: "Look upon her, ye worlds! And, since there is none better, swear by her. If there is none purer, none nobler, which have stamped pre-eminence in the very countenance of man, woman and child, cast your glittering swords, and sheaths, and armor, at her untarnished feet and pledge the very life that you enjoy to the defense of her life" (325). The archaic chivalric language, more ornate than Du Bois's, indicates to what extent Adams relies on high-cultural European standards, even as he ambivalently wants to claim the refined black woman as the sole possession of black men: "This beauty which you have used to tame your generations shall be yours no more, and this person that has served your rawest purposes shall not enter again into your halls" (324). The forceful "you" in such sentences reveals to what extent these verbal and visual sketches are aimed as much at white men as at an African American audience. Not only do they constitute an accusation against white men; they also serve as a warning that the purity of these colored beauties cannot be soiled, both because the women transcend the "lower" and because they will be chivalrously protected by black men. At the same time, however, this project of forcing all men to recognize the beauty in black women serves to claim this beauty as the measure of civilization achieved and achievable by the black race *as a whole* through the recognition of black men's equality with white men, signaled by both group of men's desire to defend pure womanhood: "There is an inseparable linking between mother and mother, be one white and one black: and the final triumph of civilization shall be when womanhood is a unit in all things for good and when manhood is a common factor in her defence" (324–325). Thus, white men glancing at these sketches must be made to recognize that they desire these women, recognizing their beauty, while also made *not* to desire them lasciviously, as though they are mere flesh to be exploited as concubines and prostitutes.

Accordingly, while providing black women the importance of being schooled for refinement and inspiring white men to respect and defend the black woman and her race, the album is also a visual training manual that seeks to reform black men by teaching them the language, demeanor, and behavior of worldly gentlemen. One caption reads: "We want more men who have the proper sense of appreciation of deserving women and who are deserving themselves. This is a death-knell to the dude and the well-dressed run-around" (325). Just as the sketches of the New Negro woman show how refined dress and manners are not enough, so it is not enough for the New Negro man to wear the clothes and manners of a gentleman. Adams understands that it is relatively easy for the new urbanites to acquire some of the physical trappings of the gentleman, for—as we see in succeeding chapters—the black dude and the dandy are becoming a new stereotype for black men in the early decades of the century. Negro men, already represented as "fresh from the plantations," are newly stereotyped as donning fancy urbane apparel without the status, education, and "attitude" required to wear these emblems of status. The objective of Adams's New Negro woman is to embody the men's rightful aspiration of this symbolic status, to symbolize through her physical demeanor the rising status of the race. The job of the New Negro man is quite different, requiring actual action in the world. New Negro men must associate only with one another, exorcising the dudes, dandies, and "well-dressed run-arounds" from their network. This idea of "contact" extends Washington's notion in relation to white mentors. It indicates a new world of self-promoting opportunity within the upper echelon of the race through manly vocations such as architecture, Christian social work, dentistry, government service, and journalism.[60] The New Negro will be a builder—better, a designer—of a new civilization through the purity of both his manly camaraderie and his feminine companionship.

The sketches reproduce all the markers of a middle-class demeanor and posture observed in the Victorian photographic portraits of *A New Negro for a New Century,* but they do so through this notion of chivalrous contact, which seems a bit alien to Washington's celebration of skilled labor, dirtying up to clean up, and Black Belt entrepreneurship literally in touch with the lowest of men. These injunctions to chivalry may seem quaint and harmless from this side of history. Nothing could be further from the truth, however, as the editors of *Voice of the Negro* discover when they barely escape a lynching for their adoption of chivalrous postures. Although Adams and his fraternity of New Negro men could banish the barbaric danger of lynching from their high-toned articles on the New Negro, they could not banish this danger from their lives.

The incentive of photography or sketches in presenting evidence of the senses *at a glance* ironically has the distinct disadvantage of immobilizing the image of the New Negro *over a period of time*. Portraiture, whether visual or verbal, halts the narrative of progress by fixing the image in a specific historical moment. Washington's gallery in *A New Negro* attaches Negro achievement to a particular aesthetic in a particular moment of time; it cannot capture the actual progress signaled by the adjective *new*. The sober solidity of Washington's photographs, while gesturing the stability of racial achievement, might be seen to work against the idea of social mobility—the guiding principle of the race's perpetual struggle, renewal, and upward climb. This difference between Washington's 1900 version of the New Negro and Pickens's 1916 version is dramatic. Both in *The New Negro* and in his autobiography, Pickens downplays visual and verbal portraiture for the rush of narrative mobility itself. We see in the next chapter how the structure of New Negro autobiography and fiction tends to emphasize energy and mobility toward self-determined goals. This is an explicit rejection of the race-album notion of displaying a step-by-step training manual, a visualizable map, that not only tells how members of the New World Negro fraternity should get there but also pictures what they should look like once they have arrived.

The Inner Genius of New Negrodom:
The Aesthetics of Modernity in Locke's *New Negro*

Pickens's race modernization has much in common with Alain Locke's most famous 1925 version of New Negro marketing. In *The New Negro: An Interpretation*, Locke, too, repudiates the iconographic tradition fixed in realistic, dour Victorian portraiture by Washington and his colleagues. Unlike Washington, Du Bois, or Pickens, Locke spent his adult life studying and teaching in academe, rather than engaging in the larger world of uplift and race politics.[61] This is not to suggest that Locke came to the concept of the New Negro without a political orientation, only that his orientation was shaped by his commitment to the life of the mind as a political objective in itself.

Locke's redirection of race modernization can be glimpsed both in the contents of his contributions to the anthology and in the volume's visual structure. He repackages the New Negro to show that "[s]eparate as it may be in color and substance, the culture of the Negro is of a pattern integral with the times and with its cultural setting" (x). Reminiscent of Washington's famous accommodationist dictum, Locke claims integration and racial integrity as simultaneous objectives of New Negro cultural uplift. For Locke, New Negro culture is quintessentially modern—not in Washington's sense of quickly progressing apparatuses of modern industry and enterprise but instead in the sense of spiritual, psychological, emotional, and artistic modernity. "Each generation . . . will have its creed, and that of the present is the belief in the efficacy of collective effort, in race co-operation" ("New Negro" 11). Locke values change itself, and the bias toward youth that change favors. As editor, adviser, and patron, Locke sees his role, and that of the other adherents of the New Negro Renaissance, as to pursue and reveal what he calls "a renewed race-spirit" (foreword to *New Negro* xi). Given that Locke represents his movement as one that has already achieved a geographic and social home—the northern urban centers—it is not surprising that he revises Pickens's focus on the drive toward energetic mobility back to a sort of Bookerite assumption on stability and solidity of place and status, despite his focus on youthful change. Against Washington, though, Locke turns the discourse of New World Negrodom away from the evidence of the senses, away from an accumulative display of material and physical endowments, and toward the concept of "the race-gift as a vast spiritual endowment from which our best developments have come and must come" ("Negro Youth Speaks" 47). Thus, he explicitly associates the New World

Negro with the artistic experimentation of high modernism, with its tendency to value abstraction and artistic expressionism over figurative or photographic realism, to emphasize Freudian creative and Jungian collective un/consciousness, and to search the globe for aesthetic riches in heretofore overlooked cultures.[62] Given his belief that Africa's traditional culture, correctly interpreted, represents a level of sophistication so high that Europe must borrow from it to modernize itself, it might be said that the American Negro must "go back" in order to go forward to his already-awaiting modernity. Like Du Bois, Locke is suggesting that Africans have, in some aspects, already won the race of the races; but his heavy reliance on European taste as the basis for determining levels of civilized culture contradicts his gesture toward an African-inspired apperception of genius. In tone and form, if not in format, perhaps Locke's race modernization is most similar to Du Bois's *Souls* in that both rely heavily on the symbolic value of an *internal* contest of the New Negro spirit, or what Locke calls "the race genius" ("Negro Spirituals" 199), rather than on the material (economic, procreative, sexual) competition with whiteness.

Like other new-century race marketers, Locke theorizes a "New World Negro." Part 2 of his *The New Negro* comprises a series of essays celebrating African Americans' coming of age in the urban North, situating the race as the leading representative of New World aspiration at the opportune moment of the United States's emerging cultural ascendancy. In describing Harlem as the "race capital" of the New Negro, Locke lauds the urban diversity that others frequently see as a threat to the social, moral, and sexual development of the race (see "New Negro" 6–7). Appealing to concepts of "race contact" popular among progressive social scientists during the time, he sees the cultural diversity of the city as a "laboratory," but unlike them, he does not see the city as a vast, amorphous, impersonal assimilating organism.[63] Locke is *not* forecasting a Negro culture assimilated into European "civilization." His "great race-welding" seems instead an antidote to the "melting pot" that was the object of sociological theory since Israel Zangwill's 1908 play of that title. Locke celebrates the prolific diversity *within* the race more than the diversity of races in the city. By introverting the race-contacts theory, exploring it from the *inside* of black culture, Locke can suggest that "race contacts" refers as much to contacts among various classes, ethnicities, and nationalities within the race as to contacts among biologically or culturally differentiated races. As opposed to losing cultural identity, the "race genius" discovers its milieu within this urban demography, as the Negro's spirit transforms, and is transformed by, these conditions.

Locke himself transforms the physically constraining political realities of "prejudice and proscription" into "a common area of contact and interaction" in a single sentence—suggesting how the New Negro's spiritual genius recasts the seemingly ironclad "terms of segregation" by remolding them into "the laboratory of a great race-welding." Fusing metaphors of scientific innovation with those of artistic experimentation, Locke makes Jim Crow seem like a transitory phase out of which the old Negro willfully, dialectically improvises and thus transubstantiates the New.

This also means that African Americans will soon no longer need patronage from the dominant race, because not material but spiritual resources are at stake. "It is a social disservice to blunt the fact that the Negro of the Northern centers has reached a stage where tutelage, even of the most interested and well-intentioned sort, must give place to new relationships, where positive self-direction must be reckoned with in ever increasing measure" ("New Negro" 8). This break with the rhetoric of cross-racial patronage is enacted in the anthology through the integration of European and white American contributors who write about the race genius *without* attention necessarily being brought to their own racial identification. Locke even goes so far as to include an essay by Melville J. Herskovits, "The Negro's Americanism," which contradicts the basic premise of Locke's theory of race genius by suggesting there is absolutely no difference—biological or cultural—between black and white Americans.[64] It is as if Locke, by including this essay, is signaling the New Negro's capacity for standing his own ground alongside and against white authorities on race. Because they have "broken with the old epoch of philanthropic guidance, sentimental appeal and protest," New World Negroes are not threatened by or sensitive to others' theories about them, for "[t]here is a growing realization that in social effort the co-operative basis must supplant long-distance philanthropy, and that the only safeguard for mass relations in the future must be provided in the carefully maintained contacts of the enlightened minorities of both race groups" ("New Negro" 7, 9).[65]

Washington's image of newness set up a patriarchal family romance in which the various generations of New Negroes are harmonized and ordered by procreative lineage and by the hierarchical structure of the legitimate paternity and metaphorical household of the race. By taking the New Negro movement out of the proper household, Locke attempts to place it in the streets, in the midst of the hustle and bustle of the masses. But his project is hemmed in by a discernible ambivalence about the masses themselves. As Johnny Washington notes, "On the one hand, he maintained that the aesthetic tastes of the Black masses lacked refinement and, on the other, he insisted that the Black masses were the repository of cultural and spiritual energy, from which the artist must draw in order to produce culture."[66] Locke's ambivalence is captured in this statement: "No sane observer, however sympathetic to the new trend, would contend that the great masses are articulate as yet, but they stir, they move, they are more than physically restless" ("New Negro" 7). This restlessness, like Pickens's "bursting bonds," locates New Negro aspiration in the uncontainable vitality of the black mass, a far cry from the dominant image during Washington's era of a lethargic, passive folk waiting for incentives, discipline, and strong leadership from above. That Locke emphasizes the term *masses* itself indicates an ideological shift. "In a real sense it is the rank and file who are leading, and the leaders who are following," Locke suggests in describing how the preacher finds himself "following his errant flock, the physician or lawyer trailing his clients" to the urban North. "A transformed and transforming psychology permeates the masses" ("New Negro" 7).

As the masses lead their social superiors, so youth lead their elders in this new phenomenon, for like the masses they have this "physically restless" rush to the future. "What stirs inarticulately in the masses," he writes, "is already vocal upon the lips of the talented few, and the future listens, however the present may shut its ears" ("Negro Youth Speaks" 47). Another feature that makes youth the bearer of newness is a sort of T. S. Eliot–like objectivity that marks not only their racial advance but also their artistic modernity. "The younger generation has thus achieved an objective attitude toward life. Race for them is but an idiom of experience, a sort of added enriching adventure and discipline." Having achieved this modern objectivity, Negro youth can let go of "all those pathetic over-compensations of a group inferiority complex which our social dilemmas inflicted upon several unhappy generations" ("Negro Youth Speaks" 48).

If we link these "over-compensations" to Washington's focus on the evidence of the senses as material/physical display of arrival, we can see how Locke's assertion of Negro youth's unselfconscious objectivity also determines an internalization of New Negro valuation. No longer an external matter of demonstrating technical mimicry, the New Negro claims modernity by resisting the surface issues arising from controversies of skin-color, dialect, and physiognomy. "The artistic problem of the Young Negro has not been so much that of acquiring an outer mastery of form and technique as that of achieving an inner mastery of mood and spirit" ("Negro Youth Speaks" 48). It is the inner life of the Negro that measures advancement, and only by representing this innerness can the New World Negro be glimpsed. Locke's *New Negro* takes this problem of internal versus external representation of the race quite literally. No photographs offer visual proof that the Negroes contributing to the volume look the part of success. The capacity for material success must be taken for granted. "There is ample evidence of a New Negro in the latest phases of social change and progress," he says, "but still more in the internal world of the Negro mind and spirit" (see foreword to *New Negro* ix). Throughout his essay "The New Negro," Locke puns on these notions of visual representation as a way of suggesting that a focus on what the Negro looks like—whether in terms of whites' minstrel caricatures or blacks' impersonation of white bourgeois poses in front of the camera—can no longer be tolerated. "[T]rue social portraiture" has nothing to do with physical appearances or the "watch and guard of statistics" that "[t]he Sociologist, the Philanthropist, the Race-leader" use in trying to capture an image of the race from "the external view" ("New Negro" 3). These tabulators of the Negro "are at a loss to account for him" because "[h]e simply cannot be swathed in their formulae" (3). This "new figure on the national canvas" can be revealed only through "artistic self-expression," a "self-portraiture" of the spirit and mind. "[V]ibrant with a new psychology," the New Negro rejects the "stock figure perpetuated as an historical fiction" and also refuses to contribute to this "creature of moral debate and historical controversy" by trying to protest it. "The Negro himself has contributed his share to this through a sort of protective social mimicry forced upon him by the adverse circumstances of dependence" (3). In this critique, Locke is suggesting that New Negrodom is an "iconoclastic" movement (10) that not only blasts the stereotypical images of African Americans but, more radically, disrupts the cycle whereby African Americans try to present themselves as acceptable either by mimicking those stereotypes or by overcompensating with painfully respectable bourgeois portraits.

In rejecting the bourgeois realism of photography for the iconoclastic inwardness of modernist art, Locke sees himself as pushing New Negro representation forward to "the legacy of the ancestral arts." His essay of this name makes an interesting maneuver, similar to that of Pickens and Du Bois, when it indicates that Africans have preceded Europeans in the race toward civilization. He takes the idea a step further by suggesting that in being brought to the New World, African Americans lost the advanced sophistication of their ancestral arts:

> The characteristic African art expressions are rigid, controlled, disciplined, abstract, heavily conventionalized; those of the Aframerican,—free, exuberant, emotional, sentimental and human. Only by misinterpretation of the African spirit, can one claim any emotional kinship between them—for the spirit of African expression, by and large, is disciplined, sophisticated, laconic and fatalistic. The emotional temper of the American Negro is exactly opposite. What we have thought primitive in the American Negro—his naïveté, his sentimentalism, his exuberance and his improvizing [sic] spontaneity are then neither characteristically African nor to be explained as an ancestral heritage. They are the result of his peculiar experience in America and the emotional upheaval of its trials and ordeals. ("Legacy of the Ancestral Arts" 254–255)

Locke uproots the stereotype of African culture by throwing it fully onto the African American. The cultural backwardness of the Negro, then, is a result of American experience as history, not African blood as biology. Like the Old World European, the Old World African possesses a high civilization, represented by the achievement of his art: disciplined, abstract, laconic, fatalistic, and thus sophisticated. The modernity of African culture—as opposed to the lagging aspect of African American (and thus also American) culture—is indicated by a prescient modernist *aesthetic* in African arts. As Locke characterizes the African aesthetic, it counters everything we associate with middle-class showy material accumulation—the Victorian bric-a-brac advocated by Washington[67]—emphasizing instead emotional, spiritual, formal, and material restraint. The circumstances of enslavement and second-class citizenship, Locke argues, have alienated African Americans from this disciplined ancestral aesthetic; this African prescience, however, lays ground for the emergence of African Americans themselves into the spotlight of American and global modernity. African Americans can now lay claim to a New World spirit, as long as they lodge it in the sophisticated, formal attributes of Old World African civilization.

Locke does not abandon pictorial representation in this flight from a Bookerite materialist ethos. Interwoven with the verbal narratives of race arrival and race welding is his own race album, one transformed from a Bookerite patriarchal family album into a diversified montage by modernist aesthetics. Alongside the abstract art deco–like design by the German artist Winold Reiss and the expressionist "symbolic sketches" by Reiss's African American student, Aaron Douglas, the artistic portraits in *The New Negro* are as crucial as the realistic photographs in the earlier race albums. Like Adams's rough sketches of New Negro men and women, these sketches and designs are supposed to open up a fresh interpretation and iconoclastic vision of the beauty in African American forms and countenances. The volume also evinces what Locke calls "cultural reciprocity," which we might define as the demand for an ideal "equivalence" (Locke's word) in the inevitable exchange of values and practices that occurs wherever distinct cultural groups meet.[68] In Locke's essay "The Legacy of the Ancestral Arts," the gallery of African ceremonial masks and sculptures brings the countenance of the African back into sight, not through the brutality of the clumsy camera lasciviously eyeing the muscular forms and "homely" features of a putatively apish African race in anthropological texts of the time.[69] The bronze sculpture from Benin (265; see Figure 1.8) captures the kind of aesthetic that Locke wants African American artists to emulate. What makes the Benin sculpture of a head different from the distorting minstrel mask forced onto African Americans on the stage, in literary and filmic representation, and sometimes in everyday life of Jim Crow is the historical presence of Africa's continuous traditions, despite colonialism, that underlies its aesthetic unity. It is the absence of this cultural-historical continuity that haunts the African American artist. The self-expression found in these African arts indicates the sophisticated objectivity the artists possess in interpreting their own figures and also provides an objective position from which to view African physiognomy for African American artists, whose visions have been clouded by generations of internalized self-loathing and externalized masking. "The Negro physiognomy must be freshly and objectively conceived on its own patterns if it is ever to be seriously and importantly interpreted," he writes. "Art must discover and reveal the beauty which prejudice and caricature have overlaid. And all vital art discovers beauty and opens our eyes to that which previously we could not see" (264). The African countenance, presented through the stylized race genius of Africa's self-expression, becomes a sight of civilized beauty. For the African, the dignified face set in bronze is a continuous (ancestral) lineage; for the European, European American, and African American, it is "iconoclastic," a break with the stilted past.

Houston A. Baker Jr. persuasively points to the combination of "marronage, masses, and modernism" coming together in Locke's anthology "in a striking, even an aggressive manner" (*Modernism and the Harlem Renaissance* 79). This combination, Baker suggests, leads to a powerful reconstitution of race discourse through the graphics. In highlighting this revolutionary potential *within* Locke's New Negro aesthetic, Baker reminds us of an aspect of the volume that could eas-

Figure 1.8. Bronze sculpture from Benin; from Locke, *The New Negro*. Permission granted by the Berlin Ethnological Museum, Germany.

ily be overlooked, given both the hyping and debunking of the period that has transpired from Locke's time to our own. As "subversive," iconoclastic, or revolutionary as Locke's advocacy of an African-inspired aesthetic may be, however, it is riddled with myriad ambivalences, issuing from not only the verbal articulations but also the graphic aspect itself. One of the most instructive instances is the startling disparity between the visual and verbal components of "The Legacy of the Ancestral Arts." All the figures depict African art objects, but all the art-historical detail is focused not on discussing these representative pieces but instead on European artists' avant-garde borrowing from, and thus validation of, African art. The irony is that Locke has come to see validity of the African arts and the beauty of African physiognomy afresh through the mediation of Europe's interest in African "exotica." After quoting the influential British modernist art critic Roger Fry on the sophistication of African art, Locke comments, "The most authoritative contemporary Continental criticism quite thoroughly agrees with this verdict and estimate" (261). Ironically, it is an Old World coalition—Europe restocking its depleted culture through African images—that comes to the rescue of a provincial, stagnant New World aesthetic (see 264). This appreciation of European artists' contribution to "discovering" an African aesthetic helps explain why Locke chose the European artist Winold Reiss for the New World Negro portraits in the volume.[70]

Figure 1.9. Alain Locke; from Locke, *The New Negro.* **Portrait by Winold Reiss.** Courtesy of the National Portrait Gallery, Washington, D.C.

Perhaps what attracts Locke to Reiss's New Negro portraits is a combination of "naturalistic accuracy and individuality" associated with realistic photographic portraiture. Setting off this realism, though, is a highly stylized figuration, which seems to comment on the constructed nature of the familiar photographic-artistic portrait. We can see this fusion (or tension) at work in Reiss's portrait of Alain Locke, the one that comes first in the volume (facing page 6 in *The New Negro;* see Figure 1.9). Just as Washington and Moton preside over the earlier New Negro anthologies, so Locke presides over this one.[71] In all the Reiss portraits, the head and hands of the subjects are in stark color, whereas the rest of the drawing—the clothes being most prominent—is in delicate black and white. On the one hand, the physical features, head and hand, appear photographically realistic, as if a montage has been created with the three-dimensional photograph of face and hands mounted onto the two-dimensional drawing of the clothed body. On the other hand, the portrait is highly stylized in that the face and hands float upon the white canvass almost surrealistically. Inverting the Bookerite logic of the earlier race albums, where urbane clothing marks the rise of true men, here it is not the clothing that makes the man but the man that makes the clothing—pushing the logic of Adams's sketches further. Nevertheless, as it seems to suggest the reality of the person or personality—what Locke calls the "individuality" and the "psychology"—above the facade of the clothing, the portrait also highlights the texture and coloring of the skin. As surely as the picture says this is a man to be respected and admired equally with white men, the portrait also seems to bespeak Reiss's interest in this *Negro* man. It is the vibrancy of the color (the luscious brown of the skin and muted red of the lips) that brings vitality to the portrait against the unreal black and white of the Western costume. What Jeffrey Stewart notes of the Paul Robeson portrait is equally true of the others: "[I]t seems as if Robeson is emerging from whiteness wearing white culture in the form of Western clothing" (*To Color America* 49). Or it could be the other way around: the face and hands become the mask and gloves of minstrelsy, ironically shining out in living color—the exotic against a field of drab black-and-white western clothing.

The portrait of Roland Hayes (facing 208 in *New Negro;* see Figure 1.10) even more clearly announces the idea that a racial type is being studied by a patron from another civilization.[72] The head floats on a white canvas detached from any body. It looks like a death mask, except that the eyes are open and penetrating. It also looks like an African ceremonial mask, except that the head's features are realistically (almost surrealistically) rendered, not abstract in any sense.[73] Despite the modernity announced by his respect for his black subjects and by his experimental, stylized treatment of forms and color, Reiss's portraits of New World Negroes present an overall impression of racial type that reveals a fascination with the tension between the subjects' exotic, primordial black skin and their fashionable Western attire.

Whereas Bookerite photographic realism asserts that the subjects are Negro in color and social consolidation only, for in every other way they are quickly rising

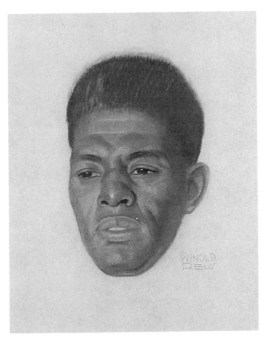

Figure 1.10. Roland Hayes; from Locke, *The New Negro.* Portrait by Winold Reiss. Courtesy of the National Portrait Gallery, Washington, D.C.

United States moderns, Locke's *in*sight into the New World Negro not only raises the unintended question of whether the soul—the genius of the race—itself possesses racial attributes but also posits gender attributes to the notion of racial progress.[74] Despite his attempt to keep racial identity (and its manifestation in art) fluidly diverse, he repeatedly expresses racial progress in terms of a process of (masculine) maturation. Even as Locke embraces the new proletarian poetry of the 1930s and 1940s as vital to racial progress in art, he cannot wholly give up his appreciation of the aesthetic, a province culturally associated with the bourgeois feminine and rejected by proletarian poets partly for this reason. This tension between his attraction to the feminine aesthetic and his desire for a masculine progress is evident in his 1936 essay "Propaganda—or Poetry," in which he tries to steer a middle ground between "decadence" and the "doctrinaire":

> Right here we may profitably take account of an unfortunate insistence of proletarian poetry on being drab, prosy and inartistic, as though the regard for style were a bourgeois taint and an act of social treason. Granted that virtuosity is a symptom of decadence, and preciosity a sign of cultural snobbishness, the radical poet need not disavow artistry, for that is a hallmark of all great folk-art. (73)[75]

As we see in Part 2 of this study, Locke's dismissal of decadence and snobbery in cultural expression constitutes a rear-guard defensive maneuver, for Hughes and McKay—two of the New Negro writers he tries to midwife most forcefully—turn against him by accusing him of displaying exactly these faults.

Despite Locke's ongoing celebration of race genius as a sort of democratically diverse endowment borne within the aesthetic, he scripts racial progress in masculine terms. In his retrospective reviews and other essays, he continues to present himself as a sort of Socratic midwife, capable of bringing forth the genius awaiting in each newer Negro generation.[76] Indeed, almost invariably in these essays, Locke prefers the best of the newer writers to the best of the older ones, indicating his desire to see the sons outstrip their fathers with each generation.[77] This sort of progress, as I have argued elsewhere, is based in patrilineal assumptions.[78] The writer must inherit the father's estate but go beyond it, outgrowing the forefathers' discipline aggressively to assert his own authority in a mastering text that stakes a claim to his "coming of age." We can see this idea clearly in Locke's celebration of Wright's *Uncle Tom's Children*: "[B]y this simple but profound discovery, Richard Wright has found a key to mass interpretation through symbolic individual instances which many have been fumbling for this long while. With this, our Negro fiction of social interpretation comes of age" ("The Negro: 'New' or Newer" 8). The language of adolescence, coming of age, and maturity here is not merely cliché. It signals Locke's investment in vigorous, virile (male) youth as the hope of continuing progress, and it makes his reception of older writers into a constant denouement. Implicitly, the social Darwinist narrative of the race among the races provides the logic for such thinking, and although the sort of bellicose version of this race progress adopted by Pickens and Chesnutt has dropped out, sexualizing assumptions about racial procreation silently frame Locke's assertions. Every second novel or volume of poems by a promising new writer becomes almost necessarily a disappointment. How could anyone both continue to develop and start afresh at the same time? Yet Locke's aesthetic seems to court exactly such a paradigm of progress. As well as within the career of an individual author, across history itself he sets up this expectation of continuity coupled with an ever-new capacity for outstripping previous efforts. By 1952, in his retrospective essay "From *Native Son* to *Invisible Man*," he has begun to trace a canonical patrilineage along the male axis from Jean Toomer to Richard Wright to Ralph Ellison as coming-of-age touchstones in African American fiction.

As a New Negro project, the gender politics of Locke's 1925 anthology and his later reviews may seem at first glance like an advance over the Bookerite *A New Negro*, for Locke does not repeat the earlier volume's overcoded visual display of the heterosexualized racial household. Nonetheless, as Cheryl Wall has noted, there is a masculine appeal at work in Locke's language in *The New Negro*.[79] In his later essay "The Negro: 'New' or Newer?" such masculinist language is even more apparent:

> And so we have only to march forward instead of to counter-march; only to broaden the phalanx and flatten out the opposition salients that threaten divided ranks. Today we pivot on a sociological front with our novelists, dramatists and social analysts in deployed formation. But for vision and morale we have to thank the spiritual surge and aesthetic inspiration of the first generation artists of the renaissance decade. (7)

Locke mixes spiritual and martial metaphors, perhaps appropriately for the militant, didactic bent of much 1930s proletarian writing that he is appraising in the essay; however, it is not clear how the militancy of the 1930s surges or marches out of the "aesthetic inspiration" of the 1920s, rather than contradicting and counteracting the earlier decade. The martial language seems alien to other aspects of his vision of cultural reciprocity, fluidity, and pluralism, and seems instead to return to Pickens's bellicose vision of race modernization.

Just as *The New Negro* anthology gives the visual impression of racial typology even as it celebrates an iconoclastic break with old Negro stereotypes, so it also gives an impression of gender typing even as it moves away from the model of Washington's patriarchal household, Du Bois's gentle but manly Talented Tenth patronage, Adams's chivalric sketching, and Pickens's conquering race-tribes. The gender preference of the anthology is written in the visual images as well as in Locke's, and others', words. The "Brown Madonna" (frontispiece; see Figure 1.11) highlights the feminine allegory of spirituality purified of suggestive sensuality—a project in line with Du Bois's unsexed Yankee matrons and Adams's sketches of chaste but alluring New Negro women. While offering an iconoclastic break with the predominant disrespectful racial image of the black woman—converting the mammy into a madonna—this secular rendering of the ultimate maternal icon nonetheless is *not* a break with the more general sexualized/spiritualized dichotomy familiar in European traditions that allegorize women in high, religious, monumental, and state-sponsored (not to mention nationalist and fascist) art. The "Brown Madonna" presides over the volume because she represents Locke's conviction that the realm of the aesthetic—beauty, style, purity, form, idealism, spirituality—provides access to the psyche (the soul) through the sensuousness of embodied forms, in this case, the resexing of the Madonna's absent sensuality.

In addition to "Brown Madonna" and "Ancestral: A Type Study" (facing 242), all the anonymous type studies depict women—including "From the Tropic Isles" (facing 342), "The Librarian" (facing 394), "The School Teachers" (facing 410)—whereas all the men's portraits are singular studies of named individuals. The double portrait titled "The School Teachers," for instance, presents two anonymous young women physically and emotionally bonded and bending over an open book (Figure 1.12). Instead of looking down, their sad, pensive large eyes stare out at us. Not exactly inviting us into their world, their faces possess instead the look of startled, virginal innocence, unaware of the dangers that lurk beyond the idealizing dreams of the page. Reiss's personality or celebrity studies include five men and only two women.[80] In European iconographic traditions, the feminine images are

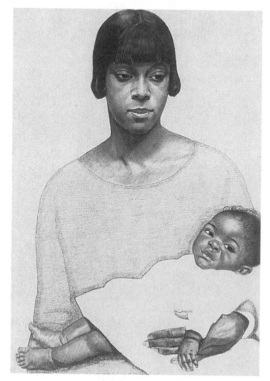

Figure 1.11. The Brown Madonna: A Genre Study; from Locke, *The New Negro*. Portrait by Winold Reiss. Courtesy of the Fisk University Galleries.

Figure 1.12. The School Teachers;
from Locke, *The New Negro*. Portrait
by Winold Reiss. Courtesy of the Fisk
University Galleries.

frequently used to embody allegorically such abstract ideals as beauty, virtue, justice, patriotism, and the soul. Such iconography, however, seems out of sync with
the West African "ancestral arts" that Locke celebrates, and in particular with the
specific pieces he chooses for illustrating his "Ancestral Arts" essay (where all except one of the African sculptures identify male or nongendered images). As Naomi
Schor has argued, the European notion of the aesthetic is often represented as a
realm of the feminine, but the feminine at work in the interest of a desire for masculine mastery and transcendence of the material body (*Reading in Detail* 11–22).
By insisting on the objectivity of the aesthetic to provide insight into the New
Negro spirit beyond the Negroid body, Locke exploits the feminine aesthetic in a
similar manner.

But Locke's gender/sexual negotiation is even more complicated than this. As
we see in chapter 5, we should not overlook the impression of Locke's own body in
his attempt to aestheticize the New Negro agenda for political ends. As an effete academic with marked "sissy" mannerisms, Locke's own gender embodiment and
sexual orientation operate in the reception of his aesthetic theory among those he
seeks to patronize. In the end, Locke cannot transcend the external gender/sexual
impressions made by his own body any more than his aesthetic theory is able to
transcend the cultural and racial implications of women's sexuality and gender in
his own time.

2 The Cool Pose of Racial Trespassing

New Negro Personal Narrative as Jim Crow Realism

> I have learned the uplifting lesson that the real heart of humanity appreciates manhood above things.
>
> —William Pickens (*The Heir of Slaves: An Autobiography* 138)

Alain Locke represents race modernization as a relatively peaceful, biracial, collective effort based in the potentially effete site of politically indirect aesthetics. For the Locke of 1925, the realities of Jim Crow need not continue to command a hard-hitting, head-on response but instead can be dealt with on the sly, through progressively sophisticated artistic forms and materials that reveal the inner truth and beauty of modern Negro identification. Locke can take such a stance largely because of his formalization of the race anthology—a collection of multiauthored essays and graphics that represent the identity of the race as both hybrid and coherent, both uniquely distinctive and reciprocally pluralistic. While other new-century race albums focus on collective histories and individual careers of the best specimens of the race, Locke's race anthology attempts to capture the diversity, fluidity, and migratory change inherent in any group demarcated as culturally distinct.

On the opposite side of the spectrum from Locke, other New Negro promoters attempt through highly personalized narratives (autobiography and autobiographically tinged fiction) to reshape the collective identity of the race. Such narratives tend to represent the New Negro subject as a rugged individual who puts the realities of Jim Crow existence up front not to lament, grieve, or curse the race's double consciousness and "red stain of bastardy," as Du Bois's *Souls* would have it, but to boast their individual hand-to-hand duels in overcoming the enemy known as Jim Crow. These are figures who celebrate their victory over the roughest adventures of American racial discrimination, segregation, and violence—in the primitive South, in the Wild West, and in the grueling urban North—to become manly commandos in the politics of racial uplift. Their adventuring into every region of the country and their actual and imaginative forays into Europe identify them as New World Negroes ready to do combat with Jim Crow in its various regional and global manifestations. Because they take their black bodies with them as they move around, they also take the color line with them—or, more precisely, others project the color line onto them even as they themselves refuse to be defined by its conscriptions. Whereas Locke's *The New Negro* insists on an inner experience so transformative that it can transcend the black body's historically encrusted bondage within the Jim Crow context, these personal narratives seek to stage the necessarily violent confrontation between the New Negro subject, an alert mind in control of an active body, and the Jim Crow environment it en/counters. Agreeing with Locke that New Negro subjectivity is constituted by an impregnable inner sanctuary of willful self-making, these narratives take this to mean that such subjects must become engaged in potentially bloody shoot-outs and showdowns when Jim Crow "prejudice and proscription" try to block their energetic movement forward through self-determining modernity. Authors of New Negro personal narratives tend to value trenchant realism when it comes to recognizing the intractable nature of Jim Crow, and they measure the giant size of their heroism in overcoming it accordingly. Like the polemical tracts that seek to market a modernizing image of the race, the personal narratives tend to insist on a partisan—frequently even antagonistic—subject position for the New Negro amid the harshest realities of Jim Crow. Unlike the race tracts, however, the autobiographical and fictive stories self-consciously and intensely *individualize* the New Negro, even as they are ultimately concerned with the *collective* image of the race. Given the investment in autobiographical subjectivity and heroic individualism evident in these tales, we have to ask how so individualized an identity can at the same time claim ownership in, and demand commitment to, a racial collectivity.

This chapter explores this conundrum first by examining the autobiography of William Pickens, whose personal narrative can be taken as normative in the sense that he strongly leans on dominant United States gender norms to construct his New Negro identity, and in the sense that this formation of racial belonging comes to represent the ideal of manliness—in African American culture over the course of the twentieth century. In the paradigm that Pickens extols, New Negro narrative should achieve its political end through its uniquely masculine stance, which manages a cool attitude toward the precarious balancing act of being an "insider" within dominant gender norms and also being the "outsider" most prone to undermine the normalizing force of race. On the one hand, the New Negro hero is constantly on the verge of falling into a pleasingly indifferent passivity, a macho coolness represented especially in the figures of the shoot-from-the-hip cowboy, the cool-headed laborer, the traveling trickster, and insouciant sweetback. On the other hand, the same figure, pushed slightly further in the same direction, falls into a fiercely bullish anger, which often erupts into bar fights ("black on black" violence or lashing out at white supremacy). This tradition of New Negro aggression enacts what Ross Chambers has aptly defined as "oppositional behavior," "the rule of using the characteristics of power against the power and for one's own purposes" (*Room for Maneuver* 10). Chambers explains how this kind of narrative falls short of outright revolutionary resistance, even though it encourages the reader to take positions that oppose the power structure in local, piecemeal, ad hoc ways. He aptly characterizes oppositional behavior as a "disguise" that "can be worn completely unconsciously (it can be second nature) or quite consciously, or with all the degrees of partial awareness that lie in between" (9). The "straight-up" coolness that Pickens advocates constitutes just such a disguise, not because it is *not* felt as "second nature" but because it is a pose conditioned as authentic as much by the racial circumstances he confronts as by the cultural assumptions about masculinity he has adopted.

Richard Majors and Janet Mancini Billson have identified the "cool pose" as a major "survival value" and "coping strategy" among contemporary African American men. "Cool pose is the black man's last-ditch effort for masculine self-control," they write (*Cool Pose* 29). Although Majors and Billson trace the concept of cool back to West Africa (55–58) and understand the pose to be a form of "masking" that can be traced back to enslavement (5–8, 27–28), ultimately they associate the cool pose with the poverty, dislocation, "anomie," and "street life" deriving from urban (primarily northern) "ghetto" conditions in the twentieth century. Even though the same masculine attributes define manly heroism in dominant United States culture, sociologists tend to view them as a form of "deviant," extreme masculinity that must be brought under control in the context of black urban culture. Majors and Billson overstate the potential for cool pose to serve as a cause for an astonishing range of social problems, for if cool possesses similar characteristics to the romanticized ideal of masculinity in dominant culture and is seen as the cause for success in white male leaders, then how can it result in such a plethora of pathologies among African American men?

Pickens exploits the cool pose to mark him as participating in what is considered *normal* American manhood. He knows that when white men perform such behaviors, their masculinity is reaffirmed as normative. To defeat the notion of black men's lagging, servile, accommodating "inherited" nature—an inheritance dramatically reimposed in each act of lynching—Pickens has to overemphasize aggressive behaviors and claim them as normative also for black men. In exaggerating such behaviors to *normalize* African American maleness, he ironically risks making black manhood seem overly aggressive and thus *ab*normal. But this is a risk he is more than willing to take, for he believes that the racial immobility resulting from resignation and retreat is far worse than an overcompensating aggression. Pickens therefore boldly represents himself in terms of "straight-up" practices we immediately recognize in celebrated romances of manliness associated with the American frontier, the muscular working class, soldiering, athleticism, and heroic national leadership like that of George Washington, Andrew Jackson, and Teddy Roosevelt.

In examining Pickens and these other New World Negro narrators, we can see how the solitary cowboy pose—with its celebration of violence, territoriality as

Manifest Destiny, sexual independence (and sometimes outright hostility to women), rugged individualism, and compulsory masculinity—accords with United States standards as the heart of manly success. Moreover, reducing the cool pose to one particular kind of masculine behavior, without recognizing its historical variations and internal contradictions, ignores to what extent African American representations of cool have embraced a range of behaviors. Cool should not be simply equated with Pickens's normalizing riffs on the solitary cowboy, the fearless warrior, the muscular worker, and the national leader who combines civilizing progress with natural machismo, any more than it should be reduced to a distortion or exaggeration of normal (i.e., white) masculinity as a sort of "hypermasculinity."[1] If Pickens uses the pose to broadcast his claim to masculine normalcy, with all the entitlements this should bring, other New Negro narrators demonstrate how the cool pose can be manipulated toward other, not-so-conventional ends. Ida B. Wells proves how a black woman's unusual relation to the gender line—considered not quite a lady because of her race and yet still marginalized as a woman—can sometimes be exploited against the color line, and vice versa. Walter White asks us to consider what a sissy New Negro might look like as a way of interrogating conventional masculinity as the anchor of New Negro leadership. And Taylor Gordon's narrative takes the logic of the cool New Negro trespasser to its logical extreme, flirting with the notion that his aggressive individualism enables him to transcend the race and its handicaps altogether.

These confrontational New Negroes have in common an individual claim to exceptionality as the basis for their tactical assault on the color line, yet their antagonistic attitudes are shaped by a shared historical situation: they are the first generation of black autobiographers born after emancipation, and thus without a firsthand experience of enslavement. They are the generation reared as young people under the tutelage of Reconstruction ideals, only to come into adulthood under the iron claws of violent segregation. Pickens, Wells, and White are all trained in liberal post-emancipation institutions where they are nurtured in not only their obligation to the race but also their own sense of social equality. Taught the abolitionist Yankee creed that intelligence, courage, principle, and character are rewarded without regard to race, their personal expectations collide head-on with a Jim Crow regime set on teaching them their inferior place. Those educated in the same institutions a generation later would be more acclimated to the harsh realities of Jim Crow, for the triumph of Washington's vocational pedagogy and Jim Crow's violent reign would be more self-evident. Taylor Gordon's claim to an exceptional relation to Jim Crow involves his upbringing in Montana, where because of the relative lack of color lines he conceives himself more a wide-open westerner than a Negro. In all these cases, however, we find that an exceptional claim to the attributes of American manliness places pressure on the race collectively to stand in the gap of the racial divide and spit straight in the face of Jim Crow. The personal narratives of this generation are composed under the looming shadow of

Washington's celebrated *Up from Slavery,* and each struggles to resist the Bookerite compromise with Jim Crow while coming to terms with Washington's upbeat tone concerning the race's drive toward modernity.

Defending Manhood as New Negro Weapon: Pickens's *Bursting Bonds*

Pickens's title change, updating his 1911 autobiography, *The Heir of Slaves,* into the 1923 *Bursting Bonds: The Autobiography of a "New Negro,"* indicates the militancy that intensifies as he expands the narrative over the course of a decade. As William Andrews has pointed out in his introduction to Pickens's memoir, the narrator views all of life as a masculine "*con*test in which he could assert himself as a man only by competing literally head-to-head with any and all challengers" (xix). Pickens structures his life as a series of battles royal, in which both his physical strength and mental skills are unfairly tested and unequivocally proved. In contrast to Washington's *Up from Slavery,* which flexibly genders his stance to position him as master disciple and disciplined patron, Pickens emphasizes his rivalrous encounters with others who always have an advantage, especially savagely cruel white southern men from the bottom to the top of the class scale. His most formative experiences come, like Washington's, in learning to work for and with whites at menial tasks; but unlike Washington, Pickens focuses on "uncivilized" outdoor tests with rough men rather than the cooperative housekeeping lessons of a civilizing northern culture. What Pickens self-consciously does is bring the African American men's autobiography out into Teddy Roosevelt's rough-riding frontier country.

Even though Pickens thinks he is headed for command of a black college in Washington's footsteps, his representation of his ascent to such a position—and ultimately his rejection of the black college administrator position as too effeminate—differs markedly from that of the Wizard of Tuskegee.[2] For Pickens, the civilizing mission of teaching the heirs of slaves has little to do with object lessons in body scrubbing and housekeeping. Instead, it entails, on the one hand, standing one's ground in hand-to-hand combat with those who seek to impede the progress of the race and, on the other hand, overt political organizing, using the most modern advocacy techniques. In both cases, a kind of directness is being celebrated— in the former, the boldness of primitive manly aggression; in the latter, the self-boostering posture of one who flagrantly uses mass media for self-promotion. Contrary to the strategy in which Chesnutt, Du Bois, and Washington identify, however ambivalently, with the naked "primitiveness" of native Africans and American Indians, Pickens identifies unrelentingly with the rugged frontier myth, partly to prove that he has mastered the wilderness and is more than ready to conquer civilization itself.

As Gail Bederman has shown, early-twentieth-century nationalist-imperialist leaders in the United States desired to retain a primitive masculine power while casting civilization as the act of moving beyond and ruling over "primitive" behavior. This paradox fueled much of the anxiety over a loss of national manhood during the Progressive Era.[3] Like "whiter" race leaders of his time, Pickens has to balance virility as the source of progressive power against refinement as the consequence of civilizing progress, but his racial situation further complicates this logic. Like the whiter race leaders, the New Negro must base his cultural strength in mythic masculine attributes such as physical stamina, the cunning of hunter and hunted, and territoriality, but must do so without reverting to the uncivilized brutality that supposedly defines the bottoms (Negroes and white industrial workers) and margins (Indians and Africans) of civilization: the brutal Deep South, the Wild West frontier, and the big-city factory. Otherwise, his drawing on native instinct as a manly resource will simply resex his image as a black raping beast. Beyond reaffirmation of the kinds of masculine claims being made by ruling whiter men, Pickens has the further task of legitimating the black race's (meaning the black *man's*) right to claim a place in the struggle over civilization. Pickens concocts a strategically brilliant New Negro mobility in which he is able to retain his bond with the rugged machismo associated with the hard labor of factory and railroad workers and the wildly aggressive freedom associated with cowboys and Indians while advancing to the discipline, self-discipline, and bureaucratic management considered to be the proper purview of formally educated, urbane, office-bound white ruling men.

Bursting Bonds charts Pickens's rise as a New World Negro through homoracial rivalries with whiter men who unwittingly toughen him and prepare him for self-reform. He sees the fierce contests that take place as rites of passage that shape the muscularity and street smarts of the young man destined for militant leadership. In early industrialization, before the legalization of labor unions, competition for unskilled, manual labor could make the factory floor seem like an arena of ceaseless competition, engaged in by those at the bottom of society in an attempt to survive the degradations and uncertainties of a migratory urban existence. Moving from job to job, frequently from city to city, the early industrial laborers had only their strength, native wit, luck, and occasionally one another to count on when attempting to get and keep a wage-earning position, as the fresh migrants from Europe and the South repeatedly discovered.[4] Pickens exploits this harrowing view of factory labor to emphasize both his own rise above it and the almost instinctual attributes of animal cunning required to survive it.

When working at a stave factory as a teenager, Pickens is confronted by a whiter fellow worker named "Dink" Jeter, who is responsible for tossing up to Pickens huge boards for stacking. Jeter constantly tries to catch the younger man off guard and hit him with the boards. Pickens's description of his rival makes it clear that Jeter represents the epitome of physical fitness matched with a moral abjection that results from grueling unskilled labor: "This man was hard as iron in face and heart; stout as an ox in frame; tireless as a machine in action. His wickedness was simple, straightforward; the only good phase of his character was his honest disclaimer of all goodness" (*Bursting Bonds* 21). Jeter is defined in terms of brute animality and rote machinery, indicating the ironic potential for savage reversion that can result from modern factory labor. In this sense, Jeter's white working-class identity is related to the machinery of the black body, merely a piece of property honed for long stretches of burdensome labor relieved by occasional bouts of animal inactivity and appetite. Although Jeter helps literally to construct the city's emerging modernity through his repetitive manual labor, he is still perceived as marginal to that modernity, almost as much as any plantation Negro. Jeter instinctively understands that being cooped up in the factory with a black boy risks downing him to the level of a "nigger," and thus he is intent on literally knocking the black boy off his perch to claim his right to white masculinity as a superior identity.

"Usually if a man tries constantly to hurt you and you constantly prevent him," Pickens writes, "he helps you, advances you in the world, the damages which nature assesses in your favor for the unjust attacks upon your life and character" (21). The heir of slaves must compete on the turf of these brutish machine-men, but always with a keen sense of self-awareness, or what Pickens calls "eternal vigilance," as though he is watching himself from a higher, more advanced point in the future of his own career—and in the future of the race itself. Secure in his identity, he can safely identify *with* the competing whiter men as much as *against* them, an identification that enables him to do battle with them on their level, using their wiles and weapons, without becoming one of them. It is an identification that will eventually command the respect of the black masses, even as he moves beyond them. Substituting Jeter for Washington's Samuel Chapman Armstrong as a mentor from whom the black leader loathes to part, Pickens tears the civilized mask from the face of the strong whiter man's patronage. When Pickens meets Jeter years later, he can bond cross-racially (homoracially) with him because he has moved on to bigger enemies and bigger prizes: "This chance meeting with 'Dink' Jeter was a test for the sentiment which I had expressed years before, when I thought he was dead: that I could never feel hatred or resentment toward the man, and that as I looked back, he seemed to be one of my appointed teachers who trained me in the art of vigilant self-defense" (72). Because he has had to survive on the bottom and at the margins, Pickens can aggressively anticipate the worst savagery that whiter male competition at the top has to offer. He cannot blame Jeter, for beneath the cover of racist behavior lies the Darwinian struggle of savage existence in which the poor of all races are forced to engage.

When Pickens journeys to the frontier to do railroad work with his father, to get money to attend Talladega College, he again proves his mettle against older, more savage, whiter men. This stint on the southern frontier confirms his Darwinian worldview: "There was no law in that wilderness but the law of the jungle. I had seen the foreman chasing white men with a revolver, as one might chase rabbits" (29). As in all the autobiography's episodes, the narrator's mettle is duly recognized by a white man who helps deliver him from that phase of the struggle:

> On my first day at concrete-mixing the men laughed and swore that I could not last till noon, but would "white-eye." That term was applied to the actions of the sufferer because his eyeballs rolled in a peculiar manner, showing the white, when

he became overheated and fell upon the ground. I did last till noon; and then the foreman, a stocky German of the coarsest possible nature who had kept a half amused eye on me all the morning, expecting to have some fun when I should "white-eye," was so touched by the determination with which I stuck till noon that he gave me lighter work. (28)

Pickens's refusal to "white-eye," or faint, may be taken as a pun, indicating as well the stereotype of the black man whose eyes bulge in a moment of fear or anxiety. In either case, the white-eye jeopardizes Pickens's claim to manly directness and modern openness. To "white-eye" is to lose sight of one's situation in the game of hunter and hunted. It is to lose the agility of always being aware of the potential danger in one's jungle surroundings. By retaining his self-aware gaze, Pickens also assures that the whiter eye of his boss will be impressed when gazing upon him. His "evident intelligence" wins for him "a little better position from the good-natured, coarse spoken German," as he is placed "to assist the cook and keeper of the commissary boat" (28). In the figure of the German foreman, we see that the wild frontier contains the whole world in microcosm. In learning to conquer the respect of the German, Pickens is also preparing for the New World Negro's global footing. Despite his coarseness, or perhaps because of it, the foreman can see in Pickens a true man, and this transcendent manliness forges an unspoken, perhaps unspeakable bond between them beyond color, race, social status, social aspiration, nationality, and geographic origin.

Ironically, Pickens's "better position" takes him away from the more masculine tasks that have supposedly served to bring out and strengthen his manliness. The upward move from hard labor on the construction crew to lighter labor in the kitchen, both capsulizes and threatens to capsize the larger irony of Pickens's illustration of New Negro manhood. The goal is to get to the less coarsely masculine place in culture—the seat of learning, the furnished parlor, the executive's office—and yet making it there depends on how well one can compete on the turf of the coarsely masculine.

As Pickens moves from the frontier to the big city, the quality of his homoracial contacts indicates his quickly rising status above those with whom he labors. At the ironworks in Chicago, he impresses the Polish immigrants:

I was a "helper," supposed to assist the workmen wherever my services were needed. I was an apparently unwelcome object to the Poles until they found out that I could speak German with them. These members of the Catholic faith were much entertained and amused at my repetitions of German and mediaeval Latin poems to the swinging of my iron sledge. They sought my company and conversation at noon. (35)

Like John Henry, the legendary railroad worker of African American folklore, Pickens awes the other workers, not merely with his strength but, more important, with his cosmopolitan learning. Giving the lie to Washington's notion that a black boy studying a French primer in a lowly cabin—or in this case, medieval Latin poetry amid the Chicago ironworks—is absurd (see *Up from Slavery* 122), Pickens wants to demonstrate that the world is much larger than the bottomlands of Alabama or the wilds of the Arkansas frontier; a broad worldly education prepares one to meet modern global realities in a basic way that industrial skills alone cannot.

Pickens wants to make the further point that a "great city" opens gates not accessible to an old-fashioned, parochial Negro, who supposedly merely knows his local place in the narrow scheme of things. Yet the New World Negro cannot afford to leave behind the muscular virtues of hard physical labor associated with the accommodated rural past. "[T]he ironwork gave me superior physical strength, which is a good part of any preparation for college. At night I read Carlyle and Emerson, Latin and German, in anticipation of work at Yale" (*Bursting Bonds* 35–36). In addition to providing exercise for his intellectual muscles, a great city beckons the New World Negro to lose his place, for he finds himself jostled and pinned with people from around the world who are also alienated and in search of community. Pickens indicates that being out of one's place in the city means aggressively taking opportunities in places where black people are not expected—foreseeing a potential for the race's self-empowerment as a massive consolidation *out of place*. Being vigilant in one's self-defense requires constantly invading the enemy's turf and turning him into an ally, as Pickens does with the Polish ironworkers. This invasion of supposedly white turf is a form of racial trespassing, a more aggressive kind of racial passing: crossing over as though one belongs, as though one will blend into the white crowd. As opposed to the passing person, however, the trespasser knows, and to some extent desires, spectacular confrontation rather than invisibility. Ironically, then, Pickens's New World Negro, desiring racial consolidation out of place, desiring to join the black mass in a freer northern setting, also ends up having to make occasions for solitary trespassing, for being out of place alone. "I redoubled my determination and easily passed by all the huge temptations of a great city. On Sundays I attended Moody's church and the city Young Men's Christian Association. It appeared strange to me that out of 40,000 Negroes I saw no other one at this Young Men's Christian Association during the whole summer" (36). Rather than assume the color line can determine where he doesn't belong, Pickens exploits the anonymity, alienation, and hordes of the great city to test and contest racial limits, always aware that he may have to defend his right to be where he is.

Through the emplotment of his life, Pickens hopes to forge past, present, and future; Washington, Du Bois, and Locke; rural folk, urbane Talented Tenth, and urban mass; muscular industry, relentless propaganda, and cosmopolitan learning—all into a narrative both synoptic and synthetic, whereby each previous black man's autobiography is subsumed, internalized, and transcended by his own in the decisive motion of New World Negro progress. His disposition to anticipate his competition takes the form of triple preparation: clean living and Yankee Christian temperance in the Bookerite mold are bonded to physical duration and mental cunning from the folk mass, then the two together are enhanced by Du Boisian and Lockean concentration on arrogant mastery of the highest classics of European learning. Despite his rigidly normalized gender location, to represent black (male) success Pickens, like Washington, Du Bois, and Locke, must construct a fluid persona in relation to subject positions routinely stratified in dominant culture. Instead of choosing between low and high, between the rural folk (Washington) and the northern elite (Du Bois and Locke), and between the city's emerging folk mass and the urbane Talented Tenth, he represents the New Negro as synthesizing these parts as a project of cultural heritage that reaches back to the first assimilative, multiracial Egyptian civilization that he commemorated in *The New Negro.*

Against Bookerite humility and Du Boisian anguished passion and regret, Pickens's New World Negro preempts the arrogance of the privileged whiter man and turns it into the New Negro notion of cool. He knows that he will offend simply by being out of place, competing with his supposed superiors, so he ups the ante by assuming first place and then by brashly advertising his presumptuousness. This strategy constitutes a sort of passive-aggression. Washington had segregated his two faces, the accommodating house servant for the race in public and the ruthless power broker of black interest in private; Du Bois in his early writing had theorized this doubleness not as a calculated political compromise but rather as a deeply felt, genuine angst of psychic dislocation. Pickens publicizes the relationship between his unbridled individual ambition and his binding service to the race as a badge of arrival. He makes it appear as though he does not go looking for a fight (the passive part), but repeatedly he puts himself out of place, above his place, knowing full well that someone will take offense and call his stance a mere bluff (the aggression). When confronted with an imposition, he does not back down, no matter how big the opponent. His bravura is intended to set him apart not only from the dominant black male image of the previous generations but also from those potential whiter patrons who might mistake him for an old-fashioned Negro rather than a New Man.

When a whiter patron does make such a mistake, Pickens merely meets the passive-aggression of the would-be patron with his own brand, mirroring and thus preempting the masculine tactics of his foe:

Among the best and seemingly sincerest of my Yale friends were some boys from the South, especially the freedom-loving hills of the border states. But there was one fellow from the same state school of my own state [Alabama]. We entered Yale together and he, knowing me to be a Southern Negro fighting for my very existence, was at first very, very patronizing. He would "hello" me a block away, inquire with a half amused, half good-natured smile "how I was making it?" and make every effort of bland superiority. I uniformly and politely accepted all his good advances, never seeking them. Soon my classmates began to talk on the campus about my work. He became less friendly—I had to be nearer to him than the distance of a block to get a "hello." (*Bursting Bonds* 40)

As the southern whiter boy's patronage gradually turns into stony hostility with each new success of his black rival, Pickens retains his cool, indifferent pose. Just as he could measure his growing strength by the increasing intensity of Jeter's determination to knock him from his perch in the stave factory, so he measures his achievement at Yale through this rival's diminishing pretense of goodwill. In effect, the stage management advertised in the book serves as a basic training manual for the new crop of young black Southerners seeking an education in elite northern universities.

This image of uncompromised, unswerving, solitary race warrior seems to deny the extent to which any individual would need political, social, and economic alliances to survive the indignities and impediments of Jim Crow. While the narrative rehearses in detail the brutalizing restrictions of a Jim Crow reality, it also necessarily evades the ideological confusions and traps awaiting the ambitious New Negro. It would be impossible to achieve personal uplift without joining one of the ideological camps that controlled the patronage of institutions and individuals. By silently overstepping this political reality, Pickens dubiously portrays himself as a self-sufficient agent who wins the Yale oratory prize and other accolades on the strength of his own voice alone.

At the heart of this break is a disavowal of blacks' "imitative faculty." Washington's public persona based black progress on a process of self-apparent mimicry: his mimicry of his white mentor Armstrong and the black race's mimicry of Washington. After acknowledging the devotion of missionary founders, administrators, and teachers, Pickens distances himself from the kind of hero worship Washington engages in toward his white mentors:

> The truth ought to be told bravely, if anything is told. Because of the peculiar genius which has been developed in the white-and-black relationship in America, even the good, conscientious, missionary white people are likely to find a really straight-out, straight-up, manly and self-respecting Negro coworker inconvenient at times, to say the least. . . . Life forced upon me, or developed within me, the habit of thinking for myself, so that I have never been afraid to stand alone,—too little afraid perhaps. I have never had a disposition to imitate any authority, either in writing an essay, making a speech, getting a lesson into a pupil,—or sketching an autobiography. (49–50)

Resting his claim to an authentic self on his achievement of an authentic masculinity, Pickens calls into question not only the manliness of his white superiors and coworkers but also the genuineness of the whole missionary movement that Du Bois made the touchstone of a new-century worldly Negro identity. Pickens's claim to a unique masculine stance is ironic, given how relentlessly his narrative tracks his own pursuit of the prizes doled out by patriarchal high culture, such as the Yale oratory contest, and given his mimicry of popular Wild West scenarios and clichéd strenuous-life anecdotes as a way of measuring his achievement. Of course, this is the irony haunting *all* self-made-man stories: success is based on the uniqueness of the man who makes himself, and yet the only reason we recognize that success as characteristically unique is because the structure of the story is formulaic; it mimics all other such stories.

Pickens's persona relies on some blunt debt accounting and credit taking. The white Yankee schoolmarms who are almost universally sanctified in black post-Reconstruction writing get weeded out in the autobiography.[5] Baldly comparing the black missionary schools to Harvard and Yale, Pickens lashes out at "absentee control," which is also a criticism of white control of black education. Just as he has viewed his rise as a contest of manly strife and competition, he sizes up the white and black men who so frequently take the reins of power in missionary schools in terms of his southern bottomland—urban jungle—wild frontier ethos. "One of the greatest drawbacks to these missionary enterprises is the absentee control," he writes, "and the consequent necessity for dealing with the whole situation through one man, sometimes, by accident, a very little man." As much as the debilitating racial condition fostered by this arrangement, Pickens is protesting its gender abnormality, whereby a little artificial man is supposed to command a bigger real one. "An arrangement wherein a narrow and small-minded man is put in a position of authority over larger-spirited and broader-minded men, is one of the most annoying things in this world—*for the little man in charge*. The bigger men can stand to be under him much better than he can stand to be over them" (48). Whereas Washington portrays himself as content to accept a mediated relationship between himself and Armstrong, Pickens demands hand-to-hand, eye-to-eye, man-to-man contact. He wants to look his rival in the eye, size him up, and have it out. As long as money greases the mediated relationship between Washington and his patrons, he is satisfied to let them think that they can control him. Pickens rejects the mediating justification of money. He doesn't care that the absent landlords are providing the cash that keeps the college running; such mediated contact cannot substitute for actual presence. The narrative repeatedly emphasizes that money can be effective only when it is manhandled, only when the individual fairly competes for it through hard work, ingenuity, demanding his just deserts, and advertising his muscular achievements.

This is why so much of *Bursting Bonds* focuses on metaphorical shoot-outs and literal showdowns between Pickens and whiter bad men while enabling him to retain more sympathy for whiter men who are degraded by the system than for black "stool pigeons" or the vast majority of rural black folk, who are simply down and out. In an episode at Wiley College, he describes in great detail how he stands up to the bluff of a white man who owes him money but tries to cheat him out of it. Despite the white man's manipulation of a black messenger boy in an effort to accuse Pickens of double-dealing, Pickens meets him eye to eye, without blinking:

Then a ludicrous thing happened, which almost made me laugh out, in spite of the situation. The white man leaned over toward me and said under his breath, with a threatening gleam in his eye: "Well, don't you talk so loud!" Why did he say that? Because by that time all the colored people around had come as near as they dared—to listen. And a Texas white man, of all disgraces, was most ashamed for colored people, whom he had bullied often before, to hear some new-comer Negro talking back to him defiantly. (63–64)

By characterizing the episode as "ludicrous" and emphasizing the white man's self-conscious stage movement, Pickens both inhabits the myth and gains distance from it. We want to laugh with him at the absurdity of this Texas showdown, to ridicule the childishness of masculine bravado and egotism, but the stakes riding on this game are too high. Pickens cannot *not* afford to play along, for his only other option would enact yet another absurd mythic melodrama, the black man white-eyeing and bowing to a white boss-man at the slightest threat of violence. Pickens's dilemma excludes any conception of courage and self-respect not already determined by the dominant binary of competitive macho versus cowardly emasculation—a binary Washington attempted to evade by linking his gender identity with the proper household and domesticity. Accepting the binary limits of the dilemma, it becomes impossible to define a courageous act in the face of racial violence in any terms outside of these Wild West rituals. At least Pickens is able to reverse the terms, if not to overturn them. Instead of the black man being cast as a desperate impersonator of manhood, the whiter man is revealed as a desperate bully, staging for a black audience a scene he knows to be a lie.

In all the showdowns, Pickens portrays himself as alone against a stronger foe or against several men with the authority of law and the force of weapons and numbers on their side. In this way, he follows minutely the structure of the Wild West myth, at the expense of the racial consolidation he theorizes in his book *The New Negro*. To stand together with other black men and women would seem to diminish his manhood by undermining his territorial claims of never imitating any authority beyond the virile self. But because the New Negro is always also a representative of his race, a man who seeks to bind his race in a common agenda, Pickens is very much aware of the need for black others to legitimate his actions. This is why all his showdowns are staged before a live audience. These others in need of his protection become spectators to the showdown, in sympathy either with him or ironically with his enemy, but they cannot act *with* him or *for* themselves. Their paralysis is his heroism. This is clearly depicted in the Wiley College incident, where the colored onlookers "had come as near as they dared—to listen." They cannot act, no matter what the outcome, for they have been "bullied often before" (64).

Pickens's coolly realistic narrative revises Bookerite exceptionality, which recognizes that there can be only one supreme accommodator. If another leader aspires to the role simultaneously, as William Councill attempts to do as president of Alabama Agricultural and Mechanical, then the whole strategy falls apart.[6] The exceptionality justified by this strategy can be seen in the authorized biography

Booker T. Washington: Builder of a Civilization (1916), coauthored by Emmett J. Scott and Lyman Beecher Stowe. Primarily written by Scott (Washington's devoted secretary and right-hand man for sixteen years), the biography was intended, the year after Washington's death, to seal his legacy and strategy for history (hence the coauthorship with the grandson of Harriet Beecher Stowe), and the book reads as one long propaganda sheet for Washington's claim to being the sole builder of African American "civilization." Thus, Scott portrays Washington's black adversaries as little men who do not keep their word and are out of touch with the black folk mass. In contrast to Pickens's confrontational Pullman car account, where he represents himself as sleeping with his hand on his gun after refusing to enter the Jim Crow car, Scott emphasizes how Washington regularly rode in Pullman cars without incident: "The conductors, brakemen, and other trainmen, as a rule, treated him with great respect and consideration and oftentimes offered him a compartment in place of the berth which he had purchased" (100). Because "Pullman cars in the South are not as a rule open to members of the Negro race," Scott and Stowe write, "[i]t is only under more or less unusual conditions that a black man is able to secure Pullman accommodations" (100). It is not because Washington was seeking "social equality" with whites that this exception to Jim Crow was consistently and eagerly made but because of his unique status as "leader of his race": "The work he was compelled to do, however, in constantly travelling from place to place, and dictating letters while travelling, made it necessary that he conserve his strength as much as possible. He never believed that he was defying Southern traditions in seeking the comfort essential to his work" (101). There is ironic tension between the biography's depiction of Washington's total self-sacrifice and the necessity that he be pampered in the Pullman cars. Only the singular leader of the race, because of his unique martyrdom, can afford to evade Jim Crow restrictions as an essential comfort of his self-sacrificing service.

Pickens's cool realism eschews such a visible double standard and demands equal treatment for all deserving men. As proof that black men are generally deserving, the strategy entails the need for more than one supreme cowboy if the exception is not to become an anomaly. The New Negro's brave, cool demeanor is supposed to be contagious; this is a crucial reason why it must constantly be advertised and updated. The more exceptional individuals engage in daring acts, the more visible the fighting spirit of the New Negro will become—hence, the better the chances for consolidating the folk mass behind these exceptional fighters. And yet, the more individuals there are behaving in such ways, the less exceptional the behavior becomes. This contradiction haunts Pickens's narrative without being fully dealt with, whereas other New Negro personal narratives take it up as a central concern. In *Bursting Bonds* the contradiction is especially pronounced in Pickens's ambivalence toward the folk mass for whom he is supposed to serve as a New Negro model. We should not overlook the lingering resonances between Washington's and Pickens's placement of the consolidated folk mass. While both search for viable bonds to a people depicted as largely paralyzed at the bottoms and margins, both also advertise their worthiness for leadership of the race through ridicule of the people they seek to consolidate.

Scott's official biography best captures the studied ambivalence of Washington's attachment to and satirizing distancing from the black folk mass. "Mr. Washington was the kind of leader who kept very close to the plain people. He knew their every-day lives, their weaknesses, their temptations. To use a slang phrase, he knew exactly what they 'were up against' whether they lived in the country or city" (26). It is important for Scott and Stowe to emphasize how Washington could "[w]ithin a comparatively short period" address both the rural folk and the urban mass: "two audiences as widely separated by distance and environment as the farmers gathered together for the first Negro Fair of southwestern Georgia . . . and five thousand Negro residents of New York City assembled in the Harlem Casino" (26–27). Likewise, he could as easily "alternately address himself to" an auditorium containing "several hundred whites on one side of the centre aisle and twice as many blacks on the other" (28). This kind of versatility matches Washington's chameleon, gender-bending roles. Washington's biographers acknowledge no contradiction between his closeness to the folk mass and his exceptionality. In fact, "[l]argely because of his intimate knowledge of the plain people," they claim, he "appealed to the great of the earth" (150). Scott and Stowe appropriately use the fable of a giant touching soil to characterize the leader's unique status as one of the soil without being dirtied by it:

> He kept in constant and intimate touch with the masses of his people, particularly with those of the soil. Like the giant in the fable who doubled his strength every time he touched the ground, Booker Washington seemed to renew his strength every time he came in contact with the plain people of his race, particularly the farmers. No matter how pressed and driven by multifarious affairs, he could always find time for a rambling talk, apparently quite at random, with an old, uneducated, ante-bellum black farmer. (135)

As evidence of Washington's versatile social range, the biography duplicates verbatim snippets of conversation with many lower-class individuals, black and white, reminding us of how Washington would also slip into black dialect to tell a joke about Black Belt people, always toward the end of making a specific point, and make others feel comfortable with his greatness. These folksy jokes, as they ridiculed such fabled foibles as old-time blacks' tendency to steal chickens, also served to ingratiate and humiliate him before whites. At the same time, he points to "a profound respect for the wisdom" (135) of an ignorant people, intertwined with their foolishness, as a way of claiming his own nonthreatening wisdom to whites.

Pickens, too, spices his autobiography with folksy anecdotes about the ignorance, susceptibility, folly, and childishness of old-time black people. One telling example focuses on the supposed gullibility of an illiterate, superstitious Black Belt population. In explaining why his family was prone to move so eagerly from state to state and jumped at the opportunity to move to Arkansas sight unseen, he writes: "The agent said that Arkansas was a tropical country of soft and balmy air, where cocoanuts, oranges, lemons and bananas grew. Ordinary things like corn and cotton, with little cultivation, grew an enormous yield" (8). But the closer they got to their destination, the colder it became:

> We were hauled many miles through cypress "brakes" and snow and ice suffi-ciently thick to support the teams. The older people, I suppose, had by this time comprehended the situation, but we children were constantly peering out from under our quilts and coverings, trying to discover a cocoanut or an orange blos-som, while the drivers swore at the mules for slipping on the solid ice. Perhaps nothing could equal this disappointment unless it be the chagrin of those igno-rant Negroes who had been induced to go to Africa under the persuasion that bread trees grew there right on the brink of molasses ponds, and wild hogs with knives and forks sticking in their backs trotted around ready baked! (9)

While this anecdotal explanation makes the narrator superior to his childhood self and to the people he has left behind, it also sustains his attachment to them. Like Washington, Pickens is a man of the people, unspoiled by high education, not be-cause he is humble and knows his place but because he retains his commitment to, native understanding of, and affection for the folk.

Such ambivalent bonding characterizes New Negro personal narrative more than it does the tracts and albums, where, as in the case of Chesnutt or W.E.B. Du Bois's early work, the author does not see his higher educational and social status as an impediment to leadership but instead as a natural badge. For New Negro per-sonal narrative, class division threatens the ideal synecdochic relation of leader to folk to an extent that Talented Tenth status becomes deeply problematic. It is the harsh reality of the rural downtrodden folk, after all, that structures the narrative as brutally realistic about southern Jim Crow horrors. Whether through Washing-ton's gender-bending domesticating hygiene or Pickens's gun-toting muscularity, the folk must be nudged along into a modernizing mass without losing their posi-tive, down-to-earth qualities. In rejecting Washington's consolidation in place, these New Negro personal narratives, while posing out-of-placeness as an advance, must grapple with the urbane pretense, anonymity, alienation, and desperate hord-ing that haunt urban dislocation and threaten to propel the mass into either self-alienated, frustrated passivity or self-destructive, anarchic rage.

Sissy Heroics: Walter White's *Fire in the Flint*

One year after the publication of *Bursting Bonds,* another New Negro migrant and NAACP officer published his first novel, *Fire in the Flint.* Pale, blue-eyed, blond Wal-ter White (1895–1955) called himself a "volunteer" Negro, a label that puts a new spin on New Negro identity. However, as he elaborates in his autobiography, *A Man Called White* (1948), his African American inheritance is reinforced through his experiences of Jim Crow in early-twentieth-century Atlanta. At the age of thirteen, he observed firsthand mob violence against blacks during the 1906 riots, when he and his father kept watch in their home with guns in hand. White was instrumental in founding the Atlanta chapter of the NAACP, through which work he became acquainted with James Weldon Johnson, then the field secretary of the organization. White gave up a comparatively lucrative job in a life insurance company to join the fledgling, financially strapped organization in 1918, himself becoming an assistant field secretary. Like Pickens, White risked his life to investigate lynchings and race riots. Exploiting his capacity to pass, he was able to gather information from the perpetrators of these crimes that would never have been given to a person visibly of African descent. Succeeding Johnson in 1932, White was the second African American to head the NAACP as executive secretary. The relationship between Pickens and White, his boss at the NAACP, was stormy, with each man sporadically appealing to the largely white board of directors—though Pickens more characteristically would appeal directly to the court of public opinion in his news columns.[7]

Part of the difference in outlook between Pickens's and White's New World Negro ideologies probably stems from the two men's quite different backgrounds. Avery describes White as "close to being the quintessential organization man," who "worked in closer harmony with the NAACP board," "rarely challenged a policy once it had been adopted," and politically was less radical than Pickens (*Up from Washington* 90). Just as class and color no doubt played a role in White's fast track and Pickens's frustration at the NAACP, these cultural identifications cannot be overlooked as influences on their representations of the New World Negro in personalized narratives. Whereas Pickens constructs a militant who must battle his way into prominence, White, who has a plush job waiting for him once he graduates from Atlanta University, is concerned with retaining the cultured worldly sensibility and humanistic sensitivity of the New World Negro as a courageous patron of the downtrodden black masses.

White's concept of patronage led him to be deeply suspicious of Pickens's ideal of the confrontational, macho warrior. Whereas Pickens spent most of his time on the road either making speeches to mass audiences or doing NAACP fieldwork, White developed close contacts with the white patronage elite in New York. Through these contacts, especially H. L. Mencken and Mary White Ovington, White was encouraged to write his first novel, *Fire in the Flint,* which he claimed, he had never before considered doing. The very idea for the novel arose out of White's peculiar racial position. Mencken and James Weldon Johnson, he writes, "tried to convince me that the variety of experiences which my appearance made possible by permitting me to talk with white people as a white man and with my own people as a Negro gave me a unique vantage point" (*A Man Called White* 65)— a vantage point that looks suspiciously similar to Washington's ability to comfort two opposed audiences simultaneously.

As a central player in the Harlem Renaissance, in which he was both a patron and an early star,[8] White, more than Pickens, engaged the sphere of the aesthetic as a potential site for uplift and thus created a position closer to Locke's.[9] Examining the gendering of the aesthetic in White's novel, we are able to see more clearly how Locke's reliance on the aesthetic raises questions of masculine conformity that are subliminal in his writings and anthology, *The New Negro*. We can also see how White's color, social rank, intimate contact with the New York elite, and investment in gentlemanly refinement contribute to a more ambivalent masculinity not usually associated with the notion of cool pose, but whose identity would be impossible without its mediation. As Locke and White identify with the realm of the aesthetic as a high European site that can validate their cultural authority as black men, they also risk distancing themselves from the masculine authority that can be derived from identifying with "straight-up" feats on the frontier and among factory labor. White especially, who links his pale skin to a genteel inheritance of voluntary racial patronage, pits artistic sensitivity, intellect, and cosmopolitanism against the frontier brutality, materialism, and provinciality of the American race struggle, especially in the rural Deep South. It is not that White equates Old World Europe or whiteness with the positive values of an intellectual, cosmopolitan, artistic outlook—his dark-skinned hero in *Fire in the Flint* exemplifies just such an outlook—but that the racial struggle itself reduces both black and white to a materialistic, provincial, jingoistic, warmongering savagery that White links to the thoughtless aggressions of conventional masculine conquest. Although intellect, beauty, and sensitivity are not fully equated with whiteness in and of itself, by implication they *are* linked to a failure to conform with white masculinity, and thus a potential failure to achieve a heroic stance.

Like Pickens, White proposes that if the new black leader is already out of place in Washington's Black Belt, then at least being out of place in the urban North brings advantages for racial uplift that can never be realized in the backwards nether region. Ironically, White makes this point by portraying a hero bent on following Washington's impossible example of returning south to serve those who need him most while retaining a Du Boisian respect for cosmopolitan high culture—the same synthesis explored by Pickens.[10] By suggesting the impossibility of follow-through in a Bookerite mode, White proposes that there can be no viable heir to Washington. Likewise, by raising the question of how a black (male) leader can be enamored by high culture and still connect with the backwards rural folk he serves, White explores the limits of cultural high-mindedness as a repression of political reality, especially represented in the brutal racial violence enacted by those white men who are threatened not only by black "uppityness" but also by anything seemingly "foreign" or "deviant." By rewriting a tragic end to Pickens's narrative, White challenges the idea that a solitary cowboy can rescue the race, and he goes much deeper to question to what extent a solitary race warrior can exist at all, given the self-doubt that must afflict any African American living under Jim Crow and the dubious affiliation between this figure and the white supremacist mobsters who also identify with—and base their actions on—the mythology of the warrior.

White's hero, Dr. Kenneth B. Harper, has received the best education available in the North and returns south in the idealistic mission of establishing a Washington-inspired black hospital.[11] Dr. Harper attempts to stay clear of politics, for he understands that his success as a healer of physical and racial ills depends on his ability to accommodate himself to southern racial strictures. His father's final advice to him sets the ideal toward and against which Kenneth struggles when he returns from medical school, the Great War in Europe, and New York City:

> What was the exact way in which his father had put his philosophy of life in the South during that last talk they had had together? It had run like this: Any Negro can get along without trouble in the South if he only attends to his own business. It was unfortunate, mighty unpleasant and uncomfortable at times, that coloured people, no matter what their standing, had to ride in Jim Crow cars, couldn't vote, couldn't use the public libraries and all those other things. Lynching, too, was bad. But only bad Negroes ever got lynched. And, after all, those things weren't all of life. Booker Washington was right. And the others who were always howling about rights were wrong. . . . Do something! Be somebody! And then, when enough Negroes had reached that stage, the ballot and all the other things now denied them would come. (*Fire in the Flint* 17–18)

Dr. Harper's father's attitude toward the central inflammatory images of racial hatred in the age—the Jim Crow car and the lynch mob—signals his antiquated opinion (and a popular caricature) of Washington's strategy. The doctor's memory of his father's advice indicates to what extent he has not managed to invent a stance and a strategy of his own. The hero finds himself at odds both with his younger brother, Bob, a Pickens-like straight-shooter who is eager to move north, and the doctor's sweetheart, Jane Phillips, a woman possessing innovative, courageous New Negro ideas and spirit but without the gender status commensurate with the will to act on them. Unlike Pickens's autobiographical narrator, Dr. Harper is portrayed at the center of a network of other African Americans who pull and tug him in conflicting but self-revealing directions, and who explicitly make his heroism im/possible.

Despite his attempt to follow his father's advice, Dr. Harper finds himself embroiled in racial controversies and called on to lead black sharecroppers in their search for economic independence. Even his medical practice becomes a politicized activity, as he seeks to persuade his potential black clients that a black man can possess medical knowledge equal, even superior, to that of white doctors. Despite his efforts at cultivating the patronage of moderate Southerners from the old elite planter class and to set up a farmers' forum (clearly modeled on Washington's nonpolitical Annual Farmers' Conference), he is unable to stay above the political fray. Kenneth Harper is unable to choose the cool demeanor fully developed in other New Negro personal narratives, though his studied attempt at a neutral nonchalance above the fray allies his character with a crucial aspect of coolness. By characterizing his hero as self-consciously seeking pacifist detachment from the issues that affect him most passionately, White presents an off-center, square aloofness that can serve as a critique of New Negro masculine self-control. Gravitating toward opposing positions, Dr. Harper honors the high values of honesty, integrity, professional competence, and idealism. While pursuing the double vision of a Bookerite-Du Boisian compromise, he overlooks the internal doubleness crucial to each mentor's stance. He confuses Bookerite humility with a schoolmarmish, undevious integrity, causing him to take half-measures in adopting behind-the-scenes strategies. This infuriates Jane. He similarly confuses Du Boisian cultivated intellect with a stoic aesthetic distance from the nuts-and-bolts activism implied in Du Bois's embattled prose. This infuriates Bob, his younger brother.

Ironically, Kenneth Harper's tortured imbalance is caused partly by his World War I experience. Differing attitudes toward warfare are also reflected in the political strategies of Pickens and White before the United States entered World War II. Whereas White tended to be more pacifist and saw the potential entry into the war as taking attention away from domestic race problems, Pickens urged entry into the war early on as a way to link fascism to American racism and to prove the manly citizenship of African American soldiers. (Significantly, Oswald Garrison Villard, one of the white founders and most influential patrons of the NAACP, was also strongly committed to pacifism even during World War II. It was over this issue that White had Pickens ousted from the NAACP.) Against Pickens's celebration of military values, White poignantly makes his hero a pacifist war veteran who despises the belligerent Darwinian contest that is supposed to teach the toughest manly values: "The worse [sic] night had been when the Germans made that sudden attack at the Meuse. For five days they had been fighting and working. That night he had almost broken down. How he had cursed war! And those who made war. And the civilization that permitted war—even made it necessary. Never again for him!" (19). Kenneth's revulsion at warfare is directly connected to his desire to avoid political controversy in the South, where he sees the same hyping of suspect values at work. Warfare, politics, and mass media (all Pickens's favored venues) are conjoined in Kenneth's mind in such a way that they represent the worst competitive impulses of parochial power-hungry men, as opposed to an ethos of community service, devotion to a vocation as a form of caretaking, and appreciation of transcendent beauty and life beyond the confines of the local. Kenneth's suspicion is expressed early in the novel through his reflections on his war experience:

During the early months of 1917, when through every available means propaganda was being used to whip into being America's war spirit, one of the most powerful arguments heard was that of the beneficial effect army life would have on the men who entered the service. Newspapers and magazines were filled with it, orators in church and theatre and hall shouted it, every signboard thrust it into the faces of Americans. Alluring pictures were painted of the growth, physical and mental, that would certainly follow enlistment "to make the world safe for democracy." (42)

Using Kenneth as a self-consciously flawed mouthpiece, White is able to question Pickens's notion about mass media serving as the fulcrum for civilizing progress. In Kenneth's mind, manipulative modern media are closely allied with the savage "war spirit" that runs amok on the actual battlefields abroad and on the metaphorical battlefields of anti-black, anti-alien riotings at home. White's relation to modern mass media must necessarily be complicated, however, by his own role in the NAACP, which thrives on exactly such media.

Through Kenneth's retrospection on the war, White mounts a critique not only of the myth that internecine competition creates beneficial manliness but also of the illusion that parochial boys will accrue a broadened perspective on the world—a cosmopolitan schooling—from their war experience:

> Their lives had been too largely confined to the narrow ways to enable them to realize the immensity of the event into which they had been so suddenly plunged. . . . The old narrow life began again with but occasional revolts against the monotony of it all, against the blasting of the high hopes held when the war was being fought. (42–43)

White contrasts the blasted hopes of parochial white men with the much more fundamental disillusionment of black soldiers who had gone to war "not to fight for an abstract thing like world democracy, but because they were a race oppressed" (43). The implication is that the violent contest of warfare has ratcheted up these white men's ambitions without broadening their minds or creating a constructive outlet for expression, resulting in occasional "spasmodic revolts" in postwar America—such as the mass riots that victimized black people, foreigners, and labor radicals during and immediately after the war. For White, defining manhood as the result of violent contestation and territoriality dooms both black and white, men and women, to endless rounds of scapegoating, reprisal, and death. This cycle threatens most those who are racially oppressed in the backwaters, where disillusioned white veterans return to nurse enlarged masculine egos cramped by narrow minds in narrow lives. Training white men to the ways of expert violence can only result in their turning that expertise against an internal, domestic enemy, once the external enemy has been removed as a target for intensified masculine bullying. What we see in White's novel, then, is an unusual critique of manly warfare not from the standpoint of the direct violence it visits during battle but instead from the vantage of its aftereffects on society.

White explicitly connects parochialism with a failure to appreciate the finer, gentler arts and associates this failure with the macho frontier values on which Pickens bases his uplift agenda. Anglo-American soldiers return to a "typical Southern town," he writes, "reasonably rich . . . —amazingly ignorant in the finer things of life. Noisy, unreflective, their wants but few and those easily satisfied. The men, self-made, with all that that distinctly American term implies. The women concerned only with their petty household affairs and more petty gossip and social intercourse. But, beyond these, life was and is a closed book. Or, more, a book that never was written or printed" (39). Contrary to dominant values, White does not see United States culture feminized by the influence of bourgeois "household affairs" as a sign of upward mobility. Instead, the separate spheres of manly frontier and household affairs reflect each other's values perfectly, enabling each to support and supplement the other's narrow view of the whole, and making the superficially gentle women as coarse and belligerent in their conformity as the self-made men. The overall effect is settled complacency and fiercely monitored conformity.

The image of the closed book in the passage above is intended literally, for White is suggesting through Kenneth the notion that in such a closed society, worldly knowledge gained through reading is held suspect. And the suspicion of such learning is directly connected to jingoism, sexism, and heterosexism.

> The companionship and inspiration of books was unknown. Music, even with the omnipresent Victrola, meant only the latest bit of cheap jazz or a Yiddish or Negro dialect song. Art, in its many forms was considered solely for decadent, effete "furriners." Hostility would have met the woman of the town's upper class who attempted to exhibit any knowledge of art. Her friends would have felt that she was trying "to put something over on them." As for any man of the town, at best he would have been considered a "little queer in the head," at the worst suspected of moral turpitude or perversion. (39)

Even as the passage suggests Kenneth's own brand of internalized xenophobia (his attitude toward jazz and other "ethnic" music), it demarcates the rigid gender strictures that caution both women and men to tread a narrow path, giving the lie to the myth of self-making. Kenneth is conscious of how high art is associated with "furriners" (foreigners), the foreign, the decadent, the effete, moral turpitude and perversion, and thus his own reading habits and interests must remain a closeted form of solitary escape if he is to be perceived as a respectable mediator between the black folk and the bourgeois white rulers of Central City. His catalog of deviances climaxes with perversion, implying same-sexuality and indicating to what extent he fears that his cosmopolitan interests might cast suspicion on his own gender/sexual conformity. The same attitudes that keep Kenneth locked in racial strictures also keep the townspeople locked in their parochial gender and sexual roles. Kenneth then identifies alcohol and sex as the "two releases from the commonplace, monotonous life" of these supposedly "self-made men" (39), and he sees both as having deleterious, deadly effects on the "Darktown" community, the bottom or tenderloin, where poor blacks are forced to live and to give vent to white men's frustrations with their own narrow lives. In the novel, alcohol and illicit sex represent respectively the mob violence and rape perpetrated by white men drunk on their own masculine power. These twin horrors ruin the lives of the oppressed blacks of Darktown on a daily basis and, more immediately, ruin the lives of the Harper family by the end of the novel.

For White, the parochial hinterland is irredeemable; but, unlike Pickens, White questions whether the masculine values supposedly best taught in these training fields are not as obsolete, oppressive, and culturally destructive as the hinterland itself. The novel implies that as long as this rough-riding masculinity remains the ideal for all men in the United States, they will rule and commandeer even the largest, most cosmopolitan cities in line with parochial mores.[12] The liberating North that haunts Kenneth's—and Bob's—dreams and beckons beyond the plot of the novel is itself an escapist illusion. It is just as well that Bob has decided, just before he is lynched, to follow in Kenneth's footsteps in going north for education only to return south for service to the race. The North of Bob's dream is make-believe because he has never been there. The North of Kenneth's reminiscences is no less make-believe because it tends to dope him into nostalgic, escapist reverie about a transcendent "whiter" civilization.

Instead of presenting Kenneth's resistance to bold political activism as either sissy cowardice or impotent naïveté, as both Jane and Bob at first fear, White encourages us to consider Kenneth as being intrigued by the potential for redefining manhood in terms of community service, professional caretaking, and an appreciation for the transcendent beauty and sanctity of life—attributes conventionally associated with upper-class white women's role in dominant culture and that could cast suspicion on him as being effete, morally contaminated, and sexually perverted. E. Anthony Rotundo argues that in the nineteenth-century North two professions, ministry and medicine, "conducted their activities away from concentrations of men and power, and they directed their activities as much at nurture as at competition" (*American Manhood* 205):

> [A] doctor interacted less with men than with women. The female sex played the dominant role in the physical care of the family, and—especially in the households that could best afford the attentions of a doctor—women were far more likely than their husbands to be present when a physician visited the home. (207)

This situation closely describes Kenneth's position as a doctor in the early-twentieth-century rural South. By making Kenneth a doctor, White is able to exploit the traditional association of medicine with a special caretaking role, exempt from competitive masculinity (before the modern hospital becomes a common feature of the rural habitat). The novel draws attention to this ambivalent gender status of doctors' work in relation to other masculine vocations of the competitive marketplace and wild frontier. Kenneth is most frequently in the company of women, whether his mother and sister at home, where his clinic is located, or the women he attempts to educate in modern medical practices as a result of their obligation to do the nursing and caretaking for their families. Thus, when he is catapulted into the rough-andtumble politics of the farmers' cooperatives, he seems out of place and lost. His attitude and demeanor identify him with a "softer," more self-doubting, self-deprecating mode of community service. And yet, medicine is also figured as the symbol of aggressive modernity. It is only in the urban North that Kenneth could have received such up-to-date scientific knowledge, and when a serious operation must be performed, it is to the New South city of Atlanta that he must take his patient. Medicine serves as a perfect figure for Kenneth's predicament, as he resides on the cusp between feminine and masculine, and as he, through the most modern of sciences, seeks to lead a folk identified with backwardness, superstition, and a feudal slave past.

His devotion to reading the classics likewise produces an ambivalent potential. On the one hand, such reading represents the overcoming of the parochialism that plagues the hinterland. On the other hand, reading becomes escapist fantasy for Kenneth, a solitary concentration away from political reality instead of racial consolidation out of place, in unity with the folk mass. "To Kenneth, when work grew wearisome or when memories would not down, there came relaxation in literature, an opiate for which he would never cease being grateful to Professor Fuller, his old teacher at Atlanta" (*Fire in the Flint* 44). Opium signifies both the curative quality of medicine that enables a patient to endure unthinkable suffering and the pacifying, doping quality reflected in Marx's famous statement to the effect that religion is the opiate of the people. Atlanta University, long the base of Du Bois, embodies the hope of liberal education over the priority of vocational training, represented here by Kenneth's pragmatic medical practice among the poor. As both hands-on vocation and higher art, medicine and reading contain simultaneous imperatives toward solidarity and isolation, political pragmatism and apolitical narcissism. And yet, by making one the opiate for the other, and both a palliative escapism, White seems to cancel both out. Instead of the synthesizing dialectic suggested by Pickens, these contraries seem paralyzing and thus insufficient to the task. Describing Kenneth's reading habits over several pages, White culminates with the young doctor's appreciation of Du Bois, whose writing he admired "perhaps best of all." But he reads Du Bois's "fiery, burning philippics . . . with a curious sort of detachment— as being something which touched him in a more or less remote way but not as a factor in forming his own opinions as a Negro in a land where democracy often stopped dead at the colour line" (46–47). This mixing of supposed opposites demonstrates how "high" reading can easily devolve into a matter of style, and how service to the people can devolve into a narrow attention to professional detail.

Just as Du Bois's fiery prose gets inverted into a nonpolitical detachment, Kenneth's vision of racial caretaking threatens to sink to the level of jockeying for patronage: "His office completed, Kenneth began the making of those contacts he needed to secure the patients he knew were coming. . . . It was a simple matter for Kenneth to renew acquaintances broken when he had left for school in the North. He joined local lodges of the Grand United Order of Heavenly Reapers and the Exalted Knights of Damon" (47). While these fraternal orders seem like parodies of the parochial masculinity that Kenneth despises in the frustrated white rulers, they are also important organizations where racial solidarity and fraternal self-educa-tion are forged, as we saw in the case of Chesnutt's Uncle Wellington Braboy. Such organizations are as ambiguous as Kenneth's own classical reading and medical practice. Even as they reproduce separate gender spheres and ideologies of social sexual conformity and social status climbing, they also counter the dominant cul-ture's insistence on black marginality, disorganization, and social inferiority. They, too, contain the doubleness of high-culture aspiration and pragmatic service, of so-cial elitism and populist solidarity, that is so frequently imagined as impossibly split into warring Bookerite and Du Boisian camps. White's portrait of a Bookerite-Du Boisian hero pivots the invention of a New Negro personality on the ability to move beyond this parochial masculine feud. At the same time, White worries whether the abandonment of that feud might also mean that the New Negro will fall into the kind of impotent docility each camp has imagined and projected as the worst possible legacy of the rival's policies.

One major way that White experiments with unblocking this impasse is to re-cast the role of romance in the making of the would-be black leader. For one critic of *Fire in the Flint*, the romance element seems so much out of place that it "is in-credibly naïve and more fitting a sentimental novel than a novel of protest."[13] Just as White elicits our suspicion of manly contests, he also questions to what extent the romance/marital courtship plot reaffirms or subverts the Pyrrhic dilemma of choosing self-humbling caretaking service or persistent invasion of high (whiter) culture, as either option can be imaged as sissy retreat or bullying confrontation. White images Kenneth's plight as a self-defeating argument between these two selves: "Kenneth usually ended these arguments with himself with a feeling of complete impotence, of travelling around like a squirrel in a circular cage. No mat-ter where he started or how fast or how far he traveled, he always wound up at the same point and with the same sense of blind defeat" (93). As the combined metaphors of caged squirrel and Sisyphean traveler indicate, an undercurrent of dark doubt bubbles beneath the New World Negro belief in the liberating agency of mobility: What if New Negroes are moving fast toward nowhere, rather than running toward some progressive goal of civilized uplift?

In different ways, Bob and Jane bring an unsettled, almost vacuous hero to a more even keel and provide him with a focused objective. Through this triangu-lated construction of a hero, White reminds us of the familial, gender, and sexual bonds that operate in complicated ways to produce the illusion of the singular, courageous historical (male) agent in the image of the "manhood of the race." As a rebellious younger brother, Bob starts out representing Locke's and Pickens's youth-ful, restless New Negro hungry for the urban street. Bob poses the question of whether Kenneth's off-center, cautious, suspect masculinity can serve as a model for other young men. In the structure of the novel, the issue comes down to a sim-ple question that Pickens would surely appreciate: Who's going to protect the women? When Bob in a rage goes after the white rapists who have assaulted his sister, only to end up lynched by them, we are left to wonder what Kenneth would have counseled at that moment of crisis. The plot takes Kenneth away on a mission in Atlanta to perform both a medical operation on an old woman superstitious about modern surgical techniques and a political operation in scoping out some suspicious white leaders who claim to be interested in helping his sharecroppers' cooperative. These dual operations give him cause for optimism in the future of his leadership, and thus his manhood, just at the moment when his sister and brother back home are being raped and lynched, respectively. The necessity for geographic distance in order to administer higher aid—the image of New Negro cityward migration to save the folk from the South—intensifies the dilemma of the New Negro's choice between long-term uplift from a distance and short-term staying behind to protect women and youth from the immediate dangers of rape and lynching.

Kenneth's optimism in Atlanta in this preclimactic moment also issues from having finally won Jane's hand. Fully half the novel is devoted to the romance plot, but to divide the romance from the political reform elements is misleading, for each is so intertwined with the other that White makes Jane's capacity to fall in love with the hero a result of her ability to reform him into her image of an activist, Pickens-like New Negro. If Bob's presence asks who will protect the women and youth, then Jane's presence makes that question seem at once fleshly palpable and much too abstract. Jane demands more (or less) than protection, and through her intelligence and determined agency, she proves that men need protecting from their own masculinity as much as black women need protection from the assaults of white men. By refusing to allow Bob and Jane to become alter egos for the hero, White initiates a rethinking of both the masculinist bases for heroism and the sexual/gender conformity that underpins so many representations of racial leadership and solidarity, from the origins of anti-slavery protest in black America to White's own time. Kenneth would not be a hero without the implicitly interconnected intercessions of his brother and sweetheart—which is to say that Kenneth is no (conventional) hero, even though he occupies that position in the narrative.

Kenneth's awkwardness as a lover is intended to unsettle a variety of cultural assumptions regarding urbanized modern black men. By moderating Kenneth's masculinity, White is able to do more than blast an emerging stereotype that projects a citified sweetback lurking beneath every apparently shy country black boy—the stereotype we see in Pickens, as well as in Van Vechten's influential male figures from *Nigger Heaven,* in the sexual anxieties of urban sociology, and in Taylor Gordon's autobiography, *Born to Be.* White more fundamentally connects Kenneth's reluctant heroism to an introspective questioning of the limits of conventional masculine poses. Kenneth's cautious, self-conscious lovemaking seems to result naturally from his solitary devotion to books, medicine, art, women's power, and humble service to the race. He is the opposite of cool, and it is exactly his gender deviance that makes him so seemingly uncool.

Kenneth is unsure how and whether to express his aching passion for Jane, given the way he has already subordinated any personal desires to an overreaching, diffuse idealism. And because Jane is stronger, more driven, more self-directed, more systematic, more self-confident, more logical, more worldly, more sexually determined than he—more "self-made" and more "manly"—she complicates any notion he or we may innocently hold of her passion being supplementary, mysterious, and coy. As Jane sizes Kenneth up, she realizes that she must take matters into her own hands, and this entails giving him a good sense of his own limits. In taking the lead, she makes a man of him in the eyes of the public, even as we come to recognize that such categories are insufficient barometers of the gender climate.

Jane's description of her experience on the Jim Crow car aptly summarizes her firm, vigilant approach to life. She is coming back to her hometown after teaching school in North Carolina, and Kenneth, meeting her at the station, had "let his thoughts run riot while she had been away." The irony in Kenneth's thoughts cannot be overlooked, for it is exactly his refusal to participate in actually running riot—warmongering, racial violence, taking vengeance on a vulnerable white girl—that makes his masculinity suspect. Kenneth is too unsure of himself to pursue any more intimate line of questioning than asking whether Jane's trip was pleasant.

> "Ugh, it was horrible!" she replied, shuddering at the memory of it. "I had a Pullman as far as Atlanta, but there I had to change to that dirty old Jim Crow car. There was a crowd of Negroes who had three or four quarts of cheap liquor. They were horrible. Why, they even had the nerve to offer me a drink! And the conductor must have told everybody on the train that I was up front, because all night long there was a constant procession of white men passing up and down the coach looking at me in a way that made my blood boil. I didn't dare go to sleep, because I didn't know what might happen. It was awful!" (136)

Jane's self-assurance and contained rage match that of Pickens's narrator in *Bursting Bonds,* as do her vigilance and determined dignity in the face of multiple indignities and physical threats. The difference in male and female vulnerabilities seems almost irrelevant, given the similar outcomes and mental frames required to meet the racial and class hostilities head on. Though Jane does not sleep coolly with her hand caressing a hidden gun, like Pickens's persona, she stays awake with the same calm reserve, the same cool, ready for whatever action she may have to take—though exactly what she could or would do remains unarticulated. Jane's situation even looks like Pickens's in how both stand out from other, lesser African Americans (the "crowd of Negroes who had three or four quarts of cheap liquor"), indicating the exceptional cool quality of mental alertness, self-confidence, and class aspiration that separates these figures from the rest.

Throughout the dialogue, Jane's "straight-up" firmness and go-to-it-ness tend to accentuate Kenneth's befuddled, circuitous, self-deprecating introspection. His self-consciousness does not result in the vigilant self-awareness that Jane deploys in anticipating racial danger but instead serves to shelter and hide him from what needs to be seen and done. This is why her barrage of words about the Jim Crow experience seems to leave him vulnerable and impotent. Before her description, he had already given in to doubt about his worthiness to court her. "As he followed her to his car, he turned over in his mind just what it was that disappointed him so in her greeting. He couldn't put his finger on it exactly, but she would have greeted Bob or any other man just as warmly and he would not have felt jealous at all" (135). Can he be a leader of the race if he is such a follower of women and doubter of his own sexual power? "He waited for an invitation to come in, but in the excitement of seeing her mother and father again, she forgot all about Kenneth" (136). On the one hand, readers desire, as Jane does, for him to take charge, to dispel the horrors hanging around the Jim Crow car by protecting her from them. On the other hand, like Jane we are attracted to his deference, to his intuitive respect for her capacity to look out for herself.

When Jane confronts him about his timidity in approaching the race problem, she is also chastising his timidity in love. When he attempts to defend his manhood against her castigating tirade, she overpowers him again with her words: "Without pausing for a reply, she went on, her words pouring out in a flood that made Kenneth feel as he did as a boy when spanked by his mother" (138). This inversion of the gender hierarchy expresses itself to Kenneth as the mother's physical power over a naughty son. White insists on the normality of Jane's berating of her timid lover, attempting to empty it of any sexual connotation by reference to the socializing maternal image. Jane is correcting and improving through punishment for the sake of a normative end. Kenneth's only defense rests in reestablishing his gender superiority against Jane's ignorance of how hard it is to be a man: "He was resentful—what did women know about the practical problems and difficulties of life, anyway?" (140). Acknowledging that she has "touched [his] masculine vanity," Jane proceeds to offer a practical course of action for solving the problem at hand in the idea of sharecroppers' cooperatives. When she insists on Kenneth presenting the idea to the farmers as his own, White is able to make an explicit commentary on the illusion of black (male) heroism from the viewpoint of a woman who sacrifices a bid to such heroism for the sake of the race:

> Like all women, coloured women, she realized that most of the spirit of revolt against the wrongs inflicted on her race had been born in the breasts of coloured women. She knew, and in that knowledge was content, that most of the work of churches and societies and other organizations which had done so much towards welding the Negro into a racial unit had been done by women. It was amusing to see men, vain creatures that they are, preen themselves on what they had done. It was not so amusing when they, in their pride, sought to belittle what the women had done and take all the credit to themselves. Oh, well, what did it matter? The end was the all important thing—not the means. (167)

This is a rare moment when White breaks the narrative point of view, providing Jane's perspective instead of the male hero's. The soliloquy unintentionally reveals the limits of White's own critique of the relation between gender conformity and racial solidarity. Jane's refusal to become resentful for her background role, while it places a high value on the larger cause, also reduces the question of sexual equality to a matter of subordinating immediate means to an all-important end. By rerouting Jane's gender dissonance into a resonant romance solution, whereby she achieves her larger end of racial activism by accepting the hand of the man she has reformed into an activist, White halts the powerful dismantling of compulsory masculinity he has been seeking to perform.

Kenneth fails racial consolidation in the end not because of how he has conformed to parochial gender expectations (or has failed to do so) but because he violates United States racial strictures forbidding black men access to white women, although he does so innocently and unwittingly. He is literally in the wrong place, the rural South, at the wrong time, the emergence of the modern Negro. The tragedy of his lynching portends the racial/sexual waste that is expended in his efforts under such circumstances, as his mother is left sonless, his sister raped and "ruined," his fiancée widowed before married, his younger brother's life cut off by a white mob. The penultimate scene of missing men and mourning women reverberates with the melancholic disjunctions of Du Bois's *Souls of Black Folk*, even as it attempts to propel the race toward a necessary future.

White makes Kenneth's medical skill and compassion the immediate cause for his tragic end. After having learned of his sister's rape and his brother's lynching, he is called on to nurse the daughter of a white man who has left for Atlanta. In the end, Kenneth finds himself cloistered with the white man's wife and sick daughter in the white man's house, surrounded by a mob intent on seeing his mission of mercy as a sexual assault. Braving the mob to nurse a sick white girl in his own grief seems the ultimate welding of conventional masculine heroism and unconventional male self-sacrifice through caretaking of the enemy's women and children; in manly warfare, even women and children cannot always be spared. On the one hand, Kenneth's act looks as though it confirms Washington's claim about the fidelity of black male slaves in protecting the old and young white mistresses while the master and his sons are fighting in the Civil War. On the other hand, it looks like Pickens's confrontational strategy of refusing the color line whatever the danger. In the end, however, it is neither.

In the last moments of the novel, Kenneth careens violently between "primal" instinctual rage and desperate resort to high principle. When told of the fate of his siblings, he goes "wild":

He sprang to his feet. A fierce, unrelenting, ungovernable hatred blazed in his eyes. He had passed through the most bitter five minutes of his life. Denuded of all the superficial trappings of civilization, he stood there—the primal man—the wild beast, cornered, wounded, determined to fight—fight—fight! . . . He would demand and take the last ounce of flesh—he would exact the last drop of blood from his enemies with all the cruelty he could invent! (268–269)

This climactic moment is pivotal in New Negro personal narrative. It is the moment in which the narrative strips "whiter" civilization, the progress on which the New Negro has based his own ambition, in order to discover the necessity of "primal man." If civilization is a mask to the black man whose condition disables a gentle embrace of higher, finer things, even more is civilization a superficial mask for the white mob, who set the preconditions inhibiting black people and themselves from progressing toward an ideal civilized state. Instead of tearing the mask away, Kenneth sinks down to the floor, "exhausted by the fierceness of his rage" (272), and falls into a stupor: "His soul was even as the body of a woman in travail" (274). This most feared state is where the hero has been headed from the outset: a paralytic stupor implied in his escapist reading, his timid lovemaking, his self-annihilating caretaking. He crosses over the line that Du Bois only toys with in mourning the firstborn son in *Souls* (see 169–175). Whereas Du Bois projects his own "feminine" hysterical mourning for the dead son onto the mother-wife, in order to protect his own more aggressive stance as a man, White's mourning man becomes a fainting, hysterical woman, whose body is too weak for the wild grief that careens through it.

This stalemate between masculine aggression and feminine indecision, between the fight for survival and commitment to high principle, is temporarily resolved in the house of the Ewings, the white upper-class family who call for Kenneth's help in a moment of medical crisis. In the Ewings' house, Kenneth moves back and forth wildly between watching the daughter die while pretending to treat her and seeking to save her life as a sign of his own superior civilization and modernity in the midst of white men's savage violence. When principle wins out over the instinct for revenge, White intends for Kenneth's heroism to be enhanced. "Feverishly he worked. He called to his aid every artifice known to him. Valiantly, eagerly, desperately he toiled" (293). Kenneth's decision seems reaffirmed when Mrs. Ewing reveals that her husband has left the house not in revulsion over having a black doctor lay hands on his daughter but to risk warning Kenneth against returning and to request the governor to send protection for the black doctor. Once Kenneth has saved the white girl, he must face the mob surrounding the house. His final contest is a decision both to fight the mob unto death and to escape with his life, both an act of revenge and an act of self-defense, both manly charge and sissy flight: "With superhuman strength born of hatred, bitterness, and despair, he lunged at the speaker. Almost at the same time that his fist landed in the man's face, his foot went into his stomach with a vengeance. He put into the blow and the kick all the repressed hatred and passion the day's revelations had brought forth" (297–298). Immediately afterward, "Kenneth stepped over the body of the one who had just gone down before him, and, like an expert half-back running in a broken field, darted out to the sidewalk. Fifty—forty—thirty—twenty—ten—five more yards and he'd be in his car and away!" (298). Irresolute even in death, Kenneth's heroism waffles between confrontation and retreat, between frontier violence and escape to a more civilized space. He conflates the archetypal male hero—the football star running for the touchdown—and the archetypal sissy—the vulnerable man who chooses survival on the fringe over the masculine pride of going down fighting.

Whether Kenneth has protected or wasted his manhood also seems an unresolved question for White. The novel closes with an Associated Press report of Kenneth's lynching that goes across the country. Agreeing with Pickens's focus on the mediation of the black image, White implies that until the rest of the country has direct knowledge of men like Kenneth, their actions will go up with the flames that sear their bodies. Of course, the novel itself becomes an act of such mediation. By recording Dr. Kenneth Harper's indecisive failure, White hopes to create a public space in mass media for the New World Negro's emergence as a warfare of the civilized pen over the savage sword.

Whatever Kenneth's indecisions, we cannot imagine a more conventionally gendered ending for Jane, as she bears a "grief too deep for tears" (299) and yet breaks down into an uncontrollable weeping. The tragic closure depends on our forgetting that the resources, ideas, fiery spirit, and flinty nerve resided more in Jane than in her lost lover. For Jane to remain defiantly active would seem to mitigate the tragedy of Kenneth's death. Instead, her loss seems total and absolute, given that it is only through Kenneth, a special man reformed in her image, that she can act. The "work of the churches and the societies and other organizations which had done so much towards welding the Negro into a racial unit" may have "been done by women," but in light of the flames from Kenneth's lynching pyre, such institutions seem small and ephemeral. The question is whether highlighting the danger to women, exposed as they were to Jim Crow indignities and the fires of the mobs, necessarily diminishes black men's claims to an honorable manhood, as Pickens and White differently seem to imply.

The Black Body as Uplift Instrument: The Personal Narratives of Ida B. Wells and Taylor Gordon

As scholars have recently pointed out, black women are subject not only to sexual assault under Jim Crow strictures but to outrages of mob violence and lynching usually associated primarily with black men.[14] The defense of the race is just as dangerous an affair for black women, and in this period the defense of the race, the defense of black manhood, and the defense of black women are tightly interwoven with the problem of an individual's literal self-defense. Whereas White makes anxiety over female exposure to such violence a basis for discriminating between masculine and feminine heroism in *Fire in the Flint*, Ida B. Wells-Barnett (1862–1931) goes in the other direction in her autobiography, *Crusade for Justice: The Autobiography of Ida B. Wells.*[15] Wells portrays her self-defense as the natural outgrowth of her individual strength and her uplift obligation through and beyond her gender, for in an atmosphere where women are as subjected to racial violence as men, women must be equally prepared for self-defense. While she is cognizant of the ways United States culture attempts to situate women differently in relation to strength, violence, and self-making individualism, she insists on a narrative paradigm that equates women's capacity for self-defense with men's. As Sandra Gunning notes, "the very conduct of Wells's life seems to fly in the face of any kind of conventional genteel feminism" (*Race, Rape, and Lynching* 81). "Clearly Wells had dramatically redefined virtuous black womanhood," Gunning continues, "in order to claim access to all topics without regard to community judgment, even when that judgment threatened to defeminize her" (83). Wells's unfinished autobiography shows how persuasively a black woman can plot her life according to the "self-made man" narrative normally reserved for men seeking a claim to cultural influence *as men.*

In placing Wells amid the male writers, we can observe how their "masculine" performance can be manipulated effectively by a woman. Reproducing the protocols of Pickens's lone cowboy narrative, with its cool demeanor, Wells forces us to rethink the hidden logic of masculinity in such a narrative simply by making herself, a black woman, its hero. In doing so, she also preempts the migration narrative—pointing to how it is enmeshed in the mythology of American Manifest Destiny. If adventurous white men go west in search of self-made manly fortune, and oppressed black men go north in search of a self-made modernization of their racial manhood, then where exactly do women go in attempting to escape and oppose their oppression? Such a question presents a challenge not only to Wells as a New Negro woman who insists on her own right of self-defense but also to New Negro men, who are being called on to reform themselves based on the mutual needs of black women.

In the concluding paragraph of the introduction to her mother's autobiography, Alfreda M. Duster exploits the language typical of masculine self-making narratives while pointing out the disjunction between her mother's accomplishments and historical notoriety in 1970. "The most remarkable thing about Ida B. Wells-Barnett is not that she fought lynching and other forms of barbarianism," Duster writes. "It is rather that she fought a lonely and almost single-handed fight, with the single-mindedness of a crusader, long before men or women of any race entered the arena; and the measure of success she achieved goes far beyond the credit she has been given in the history of the country" (*Crusade for Justice* xxxii). Fortunately, since the posthumous publication of the autobiography, Wells has begun to receive more of the credit she deserves. The question of credit cannot be disentangled either from the race leader's gender or from the bold form and tone of the narrative itself. Wells was instrumental in getting the anti-lynching agenda into the international spotlight, as she helped generate the modern media campaign that Pickens referred to in *The New Negro* and that both he and White enacted in their narratives. Using the methods of social science, journalism, and public relations, Wells could be seen as a living example of the modern race leader Pickens proposed.[16]

Although Wells's situation in its early phase is uncannily similar to Olivia Davidson's, lady principal of Tuskegee, she is eager to remove any hint of the kind of feminine martyrdom that Washington's narrative predicated for his second wife.[17] Davidson is projected to us as a feminine icon whose object lesson serves to refine the coarse social, sexual, dress, and work habits of rural southern black women by melding race work with an impeccably refined ladylike demeanor. Like Davidson, Wells is called on to corral any ambition into three decidedly feminine activities: uplift homemaking without adequate resources, nursing without becoming contaminated physically and metaphorically by those whom she touches, and teaching without becoming arrogantly authoritative. Unlike Davidson, she fails miserably at all three. It is not a failure of ability, however, but a refusal of will—a sort of diversion from conventional norms by insisting on her *natural* bent for a more aggressive leadership role as race reformist. Her narrative, instead of following Davidson's into a fatal diminution of the flesh in total feminine sacrifice to the great man who represents the manhood of the race, depicts a life that looks similar to Pickens's macho version of New Negro progress. Her husband becomes the peripheral, domesticated spouse required in such narratives, and her homemaking another arena for seminal self-making.[18]

Yet Wells presents a complicated picture of one catapulted into greatness as much by coincidence or unintended diversion as by the strength of her own courage. She constantly reminds us of the many people, black and white, southern and northern, women and men, U.S. citizens and British, who seek to help or hinder the cause she represents. She is isolated on the stage of fame because she must speak first, distinctly, and uniquely in her own voice, but she is also joined on that stage by many others who make her heroism possible. The image of her protest of the lynching of black men and women, provided in chapter 10, perfectly captures this paradox: "The leading colored women . . . were all there on the platform, a solid array behind a lonely, homesick girl who was an exile because she had tried to defend the manhood of her race" (*Crusade for Justice* 79). In contrast to Pickens's self-portrayal, in which the opportunity itself is a matter of self-making, Wells represents herself as being called to lead by a force or community beyond the self, diverting her from a mere middle-class feminine role. Like the Old Testament prophets, she is at first disoriented and humbled by this choice, but then, as she finds her voice and her audience, she becomes self-directed and emboldened. While she encounters this opportunity by chance, circumstance, or providence, the important thing is how she responds to it.

In this scene she describes how she transforms the initial act of stumbling into a lifelong crusade of self-making and race reform. Making her speech before this array of leading colored women, "a feeling of loneliness and homesickness for the days and the friends that were gone came over me and I felt the tears coming" (79). The old life is being left behind as the community of women ordain her for a life of leadership. On the one hand, she remains irritated at herself over this "breakdown": "After all these years I still have a feeling of chagrin over that exhibition of weakness. Whatever my feelings, I am not given to public demonstrations. And only once before in all my life had I given way to woman's weakness in public" (80). On the other hand, this public display is a virtue: "But the women didn't feel that I had spoiled things by my breakdown. They seemed to think that it had made an impression on the audience favorable to the cause and to me" (80). As Wells recognizes, such an impression, however favorable, undercuts her cool strategy of race leadership even as it enhances her right to feminine leadership for the audience. Once she overcomes this display of "woman's weakness," which identifies her as possessing the deep sentiment needed to feel for and lead the whole race, she never looks back. This womanly sentiment must be taken for granted, for in the future she cannot afford to display it.

If nothing is accidental in Pickens's narrative of Manifest Destiny, in Wells's the world is full of unpredictable occasions that confirm the need to pluck success out of happenstance. As Pickens goes in search of adventures that will enable him to grow through racial trespassing and self-making, Wells finds herself constantly caught in the middle of unbearable crises that call for decisive action. When she is left orphaned at fourteen, the oldest of six surviving children, she demands, against the elders of the community, that the family be kept together with her as the head. "Of course they scoffed at the idea of a butterfly fourteen-year-old schoolgirl who had never had to care for herself trying to do what it had taken the combined effort of father and mother to do" (16). Characteristically, Wells represents herself physically as a conventional female—vulnerable, flighty, delicate like a butterfly. Beneath this feminine exterior, however, are a (wo)manly spirit and nerves of steel. Attempting to support herself and fulfill her new parental obligation through the expected vocation of teaching, she finds herself constantly at odds with her peers and her supervisors. Finding that she has a knack for journalism, she begins to moonlight as a reporter while teaching, but this immediately gets her into trouble: she cannot help but "protest against the few and utterly inadequate buildings for colored children. I also spoke of the poor teachers given us, whose mental and moral character was not of the best. It had been charged that some of these teachers had little to recommend them save an illicit friendship with members of the school board" (36). Placing her job in jeopardy, she chooses principle over domestic security, an act that helps her find her calling as a journalist, and one that recalls Pickens's refusal to submit to the "little men" in charge of Talladega.

This formative event also sets up her (wo)manly charge: her own "mental and moral character" is above reproach. She will not allow us to confuse her strength with sexual looseness—the typical charge made against women, especially black women, who insist on defending themselves against inequities and oppression. As Gunning points out, Wells is blunt in addressing the sexual hypocrisies of those in power, and as Joy James suggests, in order to do so, Wells had to reject "the discourse of civility" for an "abrasive militancy" that "distanced her from those who maintained the importance of conciliatory rhetoric" (*Transcending the Talented*

Tenth 81). This bluntness dismisses the idea that proper women should be squeamish over talking about sex. It is not truth telling about sex that is scandalous but the unprincipled sexual behavior that white men engage in with black women in the dark. Part of Wells's agenda is to put the spotlight on this behavior, breaking the taboo not only of ladies' silence on matters of sex but also of black people's silence on the true causes of lynching and rape in the South. About one of her peer teachers she writes: "This beautiful young girl carried on her clandestine love affair with this young white man, growing bolder as time went on" (*Crusade for Justice* 36). Just as Pickens attacks those weak black men who become "stool pigeons" in seeking success through intimacy with powerful white men, so Wells is not afraid to criticize the occasional weak black woman seduced by white men's wiles, and boldly to attack white men for their lascivious, clandestine practices.

Wells is pushed out in the process of protecting the schoolchildren, her own high principles, and the reputation of black womanhood as a whole. Teaching represents in the autobiography the prostitution of the mind and flesh that black women must make to survive and get ahead. Because she refuses such compromises of spirit and flesh, she serendipitously finds her home in journalism instead, an unconventional woman's profession. There she does not have to submit to authority, especially as she is able to buy a controlling interest in her own newspaper. The opposition between teaching and journalism is exactly the opposition between the sacrifice of her ambition and the discovery of an empowered self: "The confinement and monotony of the primary work [of teaching] began to grow distasteful. The correspondence I had built up in newspaper work gave me an outlet through which to express the real 'me' and I enjoyed my work to the utmost" (31).

Unlike White's Dr. Harper, but like Pickens, Wells expresses no doubt about the capacity of a vocation to do both the work of self-making and the work of racial uplift. Even reading can provide a space for dreaming while also preparing her for a great future in the world. "I could forget my troubles in no other way. I used to sit before the blazing wood fire with a book in my lap during the long winter evenings and read by firelight" (21). This "voracious" reading comes in the context of deciding to sue the railroad for Jim Crow practices. If she is not a conventional lady, it is because white racists refuse to let her play that role. Again and again, she comes to the defense of the black race because no one else—no black *man*—seems to be in exactly her place at a time when a right needs protecting. This is another way of saying that her racial oppression ironically opens up an opportunity for her to act against and above gender strictures through racial trespassing, which for her necessarily also implies gender trespassing. In the dramatic encounter on the Jim Crow car, we see her take this opportunity. In one of the most memorable passages, Wells narrates her unladylike physical resistance in a "straight-up," matter-of-fact tone that belies the danger into which she has been catapulted:

> In a little while when he [the conductor] finished taking tickets, he came back and
> told me I would have to go in the other car. I refused, saying that the forward car

was a smoker, and as I was in the ladies' car I proposed to stay. He tried to drag me out of the seat, but the moment he caught hold of my arm I fastened my teeth in the back of his hand. (18)

Notably, Wells is mustering such unladylike behavior for the sake of asserting her status as lady. She insists on staying in the "[white] ladies' car," where she belongs, not in the smoky colored car, where all classes and sexes are jostled together. In asserting her right to be a gentlelady, her body ironically becomes a weapon. The very thing—her sexed black body—that marks her oppression by enabling the conductor to spot her trespassing in the (white) ladies' car also becomes the vehicle of her militant resistance.

Like Pickens, Wells highlights the *spectacular* nature of her resistance, the way in which the mere assertion of a basic right attracts a complicit audience, who become witnesses to her heroism against their wills. Joanne Braxton notes how "early in *Crusade,* Wells reveals her established pattern of forming her identity through public conflict" (*Black Women Writing Autobiography* 115). The way Wells describes her behavior on the Jim Crow car is the perfect example of this. Three white men ganging up on a lone black woman should garner the sympathy of the white gentlemen and ladies, but instead their gaze proves that she alone is worthy of the title of lady: "They were encouraged to do this by the attitude of the white ladies and gentlemen in the car; some of them even stood on the seats so that they could get a good view and continued applauding the conductor for his brave stand" (*Crusade for Justice* 19). Such passages, common in New Negro personal narratives based in Jim Crow realism, express the psychological warfare entailed in being constantly subjected to surveillance because of the automatically transgressive visibility of one's skin.

Charles Johnson attempts through phenomenology to describe this experience of being reduced to an external body defined by the surface of the skin, or what he calls epidermalization: "If I am the sort of 'Negro' brought up to be a 'credit to the race,' I must forever be on guard against my body betraying me in public; I must suppress the profile that their frozen intentionality brings forth—I police my actions, and take precautions against myself so the myth of stain, evil, and physicality . . . does not appear in me."[19] New Negro discourses are motivated by a self-conscious resistance to this familiar experience, for in resisting it lies the hope for progress as a reclamation of fuller agency and total humanity. Johnson lists three common responses to epidermalization: (1) "use this invisibility of my interior to deceive, and thus to win survival"; (2) "display my eloquence, culture, and my charm to demonstrate to the Other that I, despite my stained skin, do indeed have an inside"; (3) "seize the situation at its root by reversing the negative meaning of the body and, therefore, the black-as-body" ("Phenomenology of the Black Body" 130–131). The New Negro personal narratives also devise a fourth option overlooked by Johnson: to turn the spectacle of the surveyed body into a staged drama between an original self and white (and sometimes black) spectators, who become inauthentic others subject to readers' judgments. These narratives turn the act of policing the black body into a confrontation in which the black person's agency belies the attempt to reduce the person to the stain of skin color. This spectacle puts epidermalization into crisis.

In perfecting this tactic, Pickens and Wells claim that the real danger to the body is worth the risk in order to preserve the authentic interior self. For Wells, this danger is complicated by the perception of a woman's greater vulnerability, indicated in the episode by the tearing of her ladylike clothes: "[A]lthough the sleeves of my linen duster had been torn out and I had been pretty roughly handled, I had not been hurt physically" (*Crusade for Justice* 19). The point of such spectacles in the literature of the Jim Crow era is to psychologize, as well as to politicize, the individual and collective behavior of black people. Acting coolly in this manner, regardless of what is felt on the inside, establishes and sustains a "new" self, forging in turn a "new" race through which the psychology of self-esteem will take care of itself.

Although Wells's capacity to take care of herself may be taken as a comment on the New Negro's and the New Woman's strength, it must also be taken as an implicit criticism of both women and black men who have failed to conduct themselves accordingly. In case we miss the criticism, she makes it explicit: "None of my people had ever seemed to feel that it was a race matter and that they should help me with the fight" (21). Wells follows up her criticism with bold action. "I went back to Memphis and engaged a colored lawyer to bring suit against the railroad for me. After months of delay I found he had been bought off by the road, and as he was the only colored lawyer in town I had to get a white one. This man . . . kept his pledge with me and the case was finally brought to trial in the circuit court" (19). Wells's autobiography is full of situations where other African Americans fail to defend the race, but it also celebrates many moments when race cooperation, either among women or between men and women, wins the day. Rather than suggesting the weakness or unmanliness of black men for failing to protect her womanhood, in such passages Wells demonstrates that she can protect herself—her right to a chaste woman's body—in the process of defending the race. The failure of the colored lawyer is an individual flaw, not a group indictment. This distinction between individual culpability and collective obligation to the group is crucial to the narrative structure and sexual politics of Wells's story.

Much of the story is devoted to naming names, sometimes famous ones. Wells spends a great deal of time explaining the controversy that exploded in England when she reported in an interview that Frances E. Willard, the president of the Women's Christian Temperance Union, made public comments condoning lynching (see chapter 25 in *Crusade for Justice*). Likewise, she credits Susan B. Anthony for her insight into racial issues while carefully recording Anthony's failure in her willingness to sacrifice racial equality in favor of white women's suffrage (229–230). This concern with credit and culpability goes beyond an autobiographical desire to set the record straight. It is an integral part of Wells's revision of the self-making strategy: individuals should receive credit for their *individual* gumption but should likewise receive blame in proportion to their culpability in failing their *collective* obligation. However self-made they may be, individuals are responsible for and answerable to larger communities on which their individual welfare ultimately depends.

For instance, in the public dispute between Willard and Wells over the cause of lynching, a London newspaper prints a misleading interview with the American temperance leader "to guard Miss Willard's reputation." Rather than being silenced by this tactic, Wells responds: "With me it is not myself nor my reputation, but the life of my people which is at stake" (209). Wells puts the African American practice of testifying to use in modern propaganda, as she is able to exploit the London press to do damage to Willard's "reputation," that ephemeral value most dear to a lady. At the same time, she puts the significance of reputation as a womanly value in its place. Like a proper lady, Willard uses her English connections to make her case delicately, to guard her reputation through innuendo and gossip. No doubt to Willard's surprise, Wells strikes back in a straight-out manner, with the bluntness of political warfare, reminding the English spectators that because real people's lives are at stake, she does not have the luxury of innuendo and doublespeak. As with Pickens's lone cowboy persona, Wells's strategy resides in all-out directness, regardless of the effect on reputation. Whereas Pickens's racial trespassing implies a sexual aggression, Wells's trespassing makes boldly explicit the sexual transgression at stake in such actions. She cannot behave the way a proper lady is supposed to, but the values of womanly uprightness turn out to be more in line with her chastity, moral principle, and self-respect—all deeper values associated with being a lady.

Because she is not a devotee of reputation (in its customary sense when applied to ladies), Wells makes it clear that she is not afraid, under certain circumstances, of being associated with others' cross-racial sexual transgressions. She comes to the defense of Frederick Douglass and his second wife: "I, too, would have preferred that Mr. Douglass had chosen one of the beautiful, charming colored women of my race for his second wife (see *Crusade for Justice* 73). Against Pickens's identification with Jack Johnson in *Bursting Bonds* (55), Wells implicitly makes a distinction between the famous abolitionist and the famous boxer, based in Douglass's authenticity as a person whose commitment to uplift suggests a sincere love for a woman who happens to be white, as opposed to Jack Johnson's purely self-serving attachment to white women, whom he desires because they are white. Johnson's "weakness" reveals itself in his failure to exploit his status and wealth for the benefit of the race (see 359). Wells's critique of Jack Johnson indicates how she wants to establish "reputation" on her own terms. By no means is she willing to embrace the perverse sexual "underworld" that figures like Jack Johnson, Claude McKay, Rudolph Fisher, Taylor Gordon, Wallace Thurman, and many later African American men of the Jim Crow era flagrantly wrote into their narratives. This limit on how far she is willing to extend the embrace of "reputation" results partly from her social milieu and aspiration as a bourgeois woman responsible for the moral life of Chicago's black citizens and for leading the race into modernity and the nation into a more civilized sexual behavior. However, given these particular circumstances, it is noteworthy that she boldly extends the line of sexual tolerance as far as she does, which is much farther than the respectable white women reformers of her time.

Nowhere is Wells's own cowboy persona more apparent than in her response to the 1892 Memphis lynchings and riots:

> I had bought a pistol the first thing after Tom Moss was lynched, because I expected some cowardly retaliation from the lynchers. I felt that one had better die fighting against injustice than to die like a dog or a rat in a trap. I had already determined to sell my life as dearly as possible if attacked. I felt if I could take one lyncher with me, this would even up the score a little bit. (62)

Perhaps Wells here alludes to Claude McKay's popular sonnet "If We Must Die," which served as the New Negro anthem for militant self-defense against mob violence since its publication in 1919. But Wells revises focus on gender-specific manliness as the definition of militant courage, as evident in the concluding couplet: "Like men we'll face the murderous, cowardly pack, / Pressed to the wall, dying, but fighting back!"[20] Wells has to keep before her readers' eyes her own determination against the dominant assumptions about women's vulnerable reputation, just as McKay's sonnet seeks to imprint a manly image against the propaganda about black men's passivity. Unlike McKay and Pickens, who seem to revel in the potential violence of the showdown that finally proves their manhood, Wells is careful to offer a critique of the recklessness that can result from overzealous cowboying, a tendency to forget the primary collective goal by putting one's own and others' lives needlessly at risk. When her newspaper office is destroyed, she is on a business trip in New York:

> In due time telegrams and letters came . . . begging me not to return. My friends declared that the trains and my home were being watched by white men who promised to kill me on sight. They also told me that colored men were organized to protect me if I should return. They said it would mean more bloodshed, more widows and orphans if I came back, and now that I was out of it all, to stay away where I would be safe from harm.
>
> Because I saw the chance to be of more service to the cause by staying in New York than by returning to Memphis, I accepted their advice, took a position on the New York Age, and continued my fight against lynching and lynchers. (62)

Working in concert with the black men of Memphis, Wells creates a montage in which her solitary crusade serves as the foreground of a collective effort that must reach across gender, race, and nationality. That she is a self-determined, self-made woman does not make her so foolhardy as to ignore the good advice of friends.

In her chapter "A Divided Duty," Wells treats directly the sexual politics of motherhood. Admitting the difficulty of fulfilling both motherly duties and the obligation of her race work, she nonetheless provides a conciliatory image: "It was because I had to nurse him [her oldest child] that I carried him with me when I went over the state making political speeches" (249). Braxton has shown how Wells's autobiography shifts toward issues of domesticity in the second half without diminishing the importance of her role as activist (*Black Women Writing Autobiography* 134). Wells's most compelling resolution of this conflict between domesticity and political activism comes late in the narrative, when her husband, a lawyer, asks her over family dinner to go downstate to Cairo, Illinois, to collect facts about a lynching. "I objected very strongly because I had already been accused by some of our men of jumping in ahead of them and doing work without giving them a chance" (*Crusade for Justice* 311). Once her husband has given up, it is her oldest child who persuades her: "I looked at my child standing there by the bed reminding me of my duty, and I thought of that passage of Scripture which tells of the wisdom from the mouths of babes and sucklings" (311–312). Against "some of our men," Wells presents the powerful image of her husband and children urging her on to lead the crusade: "Next morning all four of my children accompanied my husband and me to the station and saw me start on the journey. They were intensely interested and for the first time were willing to see me leave home" (312). As in the beginning, in the end she is both a solitary warrior, doing work that no other (man) can do, and a woman whose self-making depends on the kindness, support, advice, and collaboration of significant others.

Wells goes to great lengths to make her juggling of homemaking and political activism seem a rare feat of the time. According to historian Stephanie J. Shaw, however, this balancing act was the norm for African American women of Wells's generation and rising professional social status. Shaw concludes that these women do not fit the stereotype frequently applied to all women of this time in that their families and social networks placed great emphasis on their succeeding professionally as a natural extension of their homemaking role.[21] In many ways, Wells's career fits this pattern, with one crucial exception. Unlike the women in Shaw's history, all of whom achieve status in traditionally feminine professions, Wells is able to invent a career in masculine-identified activities. In *Crusade for Justice*, Wells embraces many of the assumptions of Pickens's coolly realistic New Negro paradigm. Although she enlarges and revises it to make room for a woman's race leadership, she, like most black male writers of the time, exploits self-making ideology to assert the inevitability of racial progress as a consequence of the actions of exceptional race leaders. As indicated in her attacks on Willard and Jack Johnson, and her willingness to pass public judgment on Frederick Douglass, Wells understands that an essential part of her own self-making in defending the "manhood of the race" entails the reform of others' sexual, as well as racial, attitudes. This means that Wells must already be secure in her own identity as a black woman, even as she trespasses both racial and gender strictures intended to define that identity in lesser terms.

Pickens and Wells do not exactly narrate a search for an appropriate racial identity through transformed sexual roles. Instead, they force us to assume the naturalness of their sexual selves as issuing from the bedrock of a secure racial identity. However, the necessarily exaggerated nature of this claim to racial and gender self-security has a tendency to cause the New Negro narrator to identify too thoroughly with a sort of cowboy/frontier ethos based in a racialized Manifest Destiny, with its genocidal implications for American Indians. In this regard, when White suggests that the American frontier mentality constitutes a violent force for racial and gender conformity, he offers up a critique of Wells's kind of gender-revised self-making narrative as much as Pickens's more conventionally gendered narrative. Even more profoundly and disturbingly, the celebration of the New Negro's mobility as a form of freedom cannot withstand this critique. Migration in the United States is never fully liberating, for it is necessarily contaminated by the ideology that seeks to sacrifice the native peoples of the continent for the sake of those immigrants who desire an "empty" land to move across and conquer.

In his autobiography *Born to Be,* Taylor Gordon (1893–1971) offers a challenge to Pickens's and Wells's crucial claim to racial self-security as the foundation for New Negro identity, but he does so without in the least disturbing their blindness toward the larger racial/gender implications of a frontier/cowboy ethos. In fact, he exaggerates the equation of western frontiersmanship with racial freedom. By borrowing the New Negro migration plot, he literalizes the idea of fashioning a new race out of a consolidated racial condition. For Gordon, racial identity is not the already-known cause that motivates and justifies a racial progress; it is the unknown variable that draws him toward (dis)identification with a race attempting to discover itself in an act of American self-making. His autobiography takes New Negro self-making narrative so far that it falls in on itself, becoming almost its opposite, a narrative that plots racial consolidation as a loss of destined individuality, innocence, and idealism. The more Gordon's narrator learns about his racial heritage, the more unmanned he becomes, because this association threatens to rob him of the cowboy values he learned while a young boy out west. The very racial ties that enable Pickens and Wells to find their gun-toting heroism and straight-up boldness tend to jeopardize Gordon, roping him into a race left behind by modernity and beset by passivity, superstition, petty divisiveness, bad reputation, and all sorts of devious, unbusinesslike dealings, including aberrant sexuality. In such a scenario, blackness is at best an ambivalent discovery and at worst an unbearable burden. Although *Born to Be* may take this anxiety of black massing to an extreme, it reveals how the paradigmatic New Negro migration plot contains its antithesis within itself.

Born to Be was published one month before the 1929 Stock Market crash, the event that Langston Hughes identified as bringing to an end the high hopes of the

New Negro Renaissance itself. Appropriately, Gordon's autobiography comes at the end of the decade that promised to place African Americans in the vanguard of modernity. Having experienced a brief stint of fame as a singer of Negro songs, Gordon quickly sank back into obscurity not long after his autobiography was published. His participation in the Negro Renaissance indicates to what extent individual ambition could exploit its opportunities without necessarily identifying with its ultimate goal of collective racial progress through reform of the sexualized self.

Not aware that his own opportunity for fame and fortune would crash along with the economic downturn, in his autobiography Gordon moves toward an ironic closure, in which his race's hopeless backwardness serves as a backdrop for his optimism about his own future.[22] That optimism is based solely in the exceptional notion that as a man born and bred in the wide-open spaces of the West, away from the black folk down South or the black urban mass in the Northeast, his future is not tied to that of other black people. The broad-minded West, with no history, has prepared him for modern success in a way not open to black people pathetically trapped in the racial quagmire of history. By alluding in his closure to black people's supposed obsession with the "next world," a religiosity that prevents them from embracing science and other features of modernity in the here and now, Gordon turns the spiritual and blues ethos inside out. He can celebrate his fate in life, rather than bemoan its harsh unfairness. "Thanks to Fate for teaching me the fundamental laws that I may live within this world and enjoy all the milk and honey I can get," he concludes. "Ho! Ho! . . . I wonder what I was born to be?" (*Born to Be* 235). Not born black regionally, nor destined to become black psychologically, regardless of his growing awareness of how others in the East and South identify him with blackness through phenotype, he holds sure to the bigger American dream of being able to invent himself in whatever successful image he desires.

Against the United States notion of modernity as the transcendence of history through its obliteration and the self's reinvention in an infinite westward frontier adventure, we witness Gordon's own eastward pull, back to the corrupted past, back to the black folk mass, and ultimately back to the Old Country. Although going East in European American culture represents a search for sophistication, cultural authority, and Old World legitimacy—as we see in writers as diverse as Henry James, Ernest Hemingway, Gertrude Stein, Theodore Dreiser, and Carl Van Vechten—this movement is still a backward trek, a potential rejection of New World openness that comes at great cost to the adventurer. When Van Vechten, for instance, makes a bid for leading the cultural avant-garde, he follows a familiar trajectory from bourgeois midwestern town to Chicago, from Chicago to New York, from New York to Paris. As he returns to New York with greater confidence in his own capacity for cultural leadership, he positions himself as the most visible mediator not only between the new jazz culture of African Americans and the encrusted white United States establishment but also between the sophistication of a more broad-minded (and potentially deviant) European scene and parochial United States interests. Van Vechten's race, class, economic and social resources, and regional origin protect his public reputation from the corruptions he seeks to enjoy and to insinuate into dominant American culture.

Gordon's narrative attempts to follow this Van Vechtenian pattern of western origins protecting the innocent while they seek to exploit the corruptions of encrusted eastern power. This should not be surprising, given Van Vechten's patronage of Gordon and of *Born to Be*. In his foreword to the original edition, Van Vechten, whom Gordon calls "the Abraham Lincoln of negro art" (185), emphasizes the newness of *Born to Be*—its blues idiom, its embrace of both the Wild West and the European nobility, its "doubtless justified" criticism of the backwardness of "the Negro."[23] But amid these supposedly unfamiliar signs of a fresh modernity, he also wants to link Gordon to the prototypical western naïf, Huckleberry Finn:

> I suspect that a new kind of personality has succeeded in expressing itself. It is a type of personality that many writers have tried to express—one of the earliest examples perhaps is Mark Twain's Huckleberry Finn—but no one has been entirely successful until Taylor Gordon somehow got himself on paper, lanky six-feet, falsetto voice, molasses laugh, and all the rest of him, including a brain that functions and an eye that can see. The result is probably a "human document" of the first order, to be studied by sociologists and Freudians for years to come. (v)

"Taylor Gordon somehow got himself on paper" thanks in no small part to his rich white patrons: Muriel Draper, who edited the book and writes a terribly condescending introduction, and Van Vechten, who "midwifed" it into print and wrote a supercilious preface. This appeal to Gordon as a more successful Huck Finn keeps Gordon the perennial naive Westerner, an inverted image of Van Vechten's own sophisticated westernness, while acknowledging that the black man singing his primordial spirituals and blues has become the ultimate sign of urbane modernity, with its power both to bewitch and to shock. While the blues serves to authenticate Gordon's identity for Van Vechten and the audience, Van Vechten diverts our attention away from the oppressive racial lament intoned by the blues. Instead Van Vechten's interest is fixed on Gordon's "falsetto voice"—"from the first tone the boy produced" (xlvii)—and the utterly "amusing" nature of the book that issues from that voice. Given that Gordon himself in no way emphasizes the high pitch of his own voice—an association that would immediately be linked to gender/sexual deviation and opera castrati[24]—it seems significant that Van Vechten wants to highlight this characteristic. As high priest of the avant-garde, Van Vechten situates his found object between scientific modernity (the probing social scientists and Freudians) and another more ephemeral notion of the modern: the primeval voice magically captured in modern print. The modern-primeval voice of the Negro singer for Van Vechten contains an implicit gender-bending quality, a deviation from the complacent American sexual norm.

The eastward bent of Gordon's frontier narrative reminds us of the contrary direction African Americans normally take in their Jim Crow–era migration tales, and of their alternative take on modernity. In the New Negro period, African Americans tend to write against the grain of the familiar U.S. mythology that a frontier can protect one from the horrors of inequality, poverty, Old World corruption, murdering greed, and genocide. It is not East/West that provides the most compelling axis of escape and self-invention but South/North; yet this South/North axis is always for African Americans implicated in manipulations of inequality, corruption, deprivation, and genocide—captured in the popular phrase labeling the North "up South."[25] The extent to which Gordon rejects identification with blackness can be measured by his rejection of the characteristic African American critique of the United States mythology of the East/West axis.[26] Even as Pickens and Wells exploit the myth of the West to set up their cowboy poses, they make it clear that northward urban migration is the *only* direction imaginable for race leaders, not the westward frontier. Wells, for instance, makes a trip to Oklahoma to report the truth firsthand, and in doing so, she begins to ponder moving there herself. In characteristic fashion, however, she accidentally ends up in the Northeast instead, to "give the East a lookover before I decided where I would cast my lot" (*Crusade for Justice* 58). It is in the Northeast that she meets the "big guns" engaged in their deliberations, but "was not very favorably impressed by what I did see" (59). It is clear, however, that her destiny lies in the Northeast, as a leader among these "big guns," rather than on the Oklahoma frontier, where so many of the friends, acquaintances, and readers from her hometown cast their lot based on her advice.

Taylor Gordon's decision to move East, too, results from an attraction to established power, but in a way more similar to Van Vechten than to Wells. He envisions himself consummated by eastern authority, rather than reforming it toward an aim of racial parity and uplift. He sees how the governor of Montana—who was the equivalent of "six men, he was so hot"—is willing to wait over three hours to meet with John Ringling, who was slumbering comfortably in his private railroad car all the while. This incident "showed me very plainly that Easterners were people of power and conviction any time they had money. . . . I made up my mind then that the West was fine, but I wanted to be an Easterner" (*Born to Be* 55). At the heart of Gordon's motivation to move East is a naive identification with eastern power, money, "conviction," and whiteness. Gordon's myth of the West follows the dominant United States pattern at the risk of his own denial of a racial bond. His idyllic depiction of growing up in Montana enlists a number of themes dear to the national consciousness; but even in the midst of rehearsing these myths, he finds himself claiming racial exceptionality:

> I fitted right in the network perfectly on account of the pigment of my skin. I was accepted both high and low, never questioned why or what I was doing in conspicuous places. My alibi could be mother sending laundry home, or a city sheik sending a note to his sweetie. . . . But generally my face was a passport stamped in full. I was even admitted into the saloons long before boys of my age were. (17)

In Gordon's (anti–)New Negro narrative, then, we find the most extreme manifestation of the blindness infecting the American frontier mentality. When he claims that the West is innocent of racial history, he erases the racial oppression of the American Indians more thoroughly than does Pickens or Wells. To suggest that the West is open and free of racial impositions is to deny the barbaric violence perpetrated on Native Americans to "win" the West. Touting this myth of western freedom, Gordon celebrates his ability to move among the polar extremes of social life, from the bawdy houses to the big houses of wealthy men. Against his own claim that race is not a factor on the frontier, he pinpoints his skin color as the passport that allows him to travel across the social spectrum and up and down the hierarchy without suspicion or restriction. Denying any experience of epidermalization, he wants the West to represent absolute freedom of movement without imputation or assault—a pure fantasy of physical movement without sociopolitical restraint. Gordon inverts the usual formula, suggesting that the pigment of his skin provides this freedom of movement, instead of its being the marker that curtails that movement across color lines.

The upshot of this passage, however, is that the young Gordon is doing the secret bidding of the respectable white citizens. In a sense, then, it is true that his race is a "passport," but ironically, it is a passport exactly because whites do not question the morality of having a young black boy in whorehouses and saloons at such an early age. Despite his later distaste for black men's lethargic acceptance of pimping and sweetbacking as the only allowable profitable vocations open to them, the young Gordon is, from the beginning, literally a go-between for the white race's whores and pimps. Whether Gordon is trying to deny it or bringing surreptitious attention to it, his racial role in the West is to carry the dirty secrets of respectable white citizens' deviant liaisons, just as part of his mother's role is to clean their dirty laundry. In contrast to the obligatory Jim Crow train scene we find in the other New Negro personal narratives, where the black body itself must be transformed from an obstacle into a weapon of defense in creating both a physical and a psychic space of freedom for the migratory New Negro, Gordon's black skin is supposed to open doors across illusory lines of color. This is indeed a form of racial trespassing, but one denying the oppressive realities of Jim Crow that are exhibited in the racial realism of other New Negro personal narratives.

It is Gordon's black face that gives him a passport to become briefly a famous singer of blues and spirituals in the United States and Europe during the period when patronage of blacks is in vogue. For his face to be "stamped in full," however, it must also be stained in full. To turn that stain into a stamp of approval from high society, Gordon must separate the race from the face, the racial character from the dream of the West. He wants freedom and uplift not because he is black; instead, he wants it because he has purportedly already experienced it beyond race as a Westerner. Like Teddy Roosevelt, Gordon pins his manhood on his rough riding in the West. Like Roosevelt, he attributes his overcoming of crippling childhood illness to initiation into western cowboying:

When my pins got good again [leg braces put on to correct his diptherial paraly-
sis], I had reached the point in life where all boys wanted to be men. I acted as
much so as possible. I got high-heeled boots, a six-horse-roll on my pants, leather
cuffs, Stetson hat, with a package of Bull Durham tobacco in my breast pocket and
let the tag hang out, always chewing a match in company. I used to rig myself out
this way for a dance. (42)

To what extent such meticulous mimicry of the cowboy myth indicates racial self-
consciousness and overcompensation is difficult to discern.[27] We can definitely say,
however, that this cowboy myth serves to compensate for his anxieties over coming into contact with other black people as he moves eastward. Supplementing this
cowboy pose is a repertoire of other United States self-made features: scientific inventiveness, a paradoxically casual but obsessive concern with making a fortune,
and a similarly paradoxical relation to romance, sex, and women. Many New Negro
trespassing narratives tend to emphasize a moment of revelation, a fall from grace,
when race hits the individual and forever changes his or her life.[28] For Gordon's
narrator, this revelation comes not once but repeatedly. This is appropriate, given
that his apparent stance is a bewilderment that comes from dissociation from the
abject black object, with which others, black and white, insist on identifying him.

Significantly, his first lesson comes only after he has left the open West. In Minneapolis, when a waiter rejects his money, he experiences the impact of race for the
first time (67–68). That his face could be a passport in Sulphur Springs, Montana,
but his money a bar in Minneapolis sets up the contradiction against which the narrative struggles. For Gordon, money represents racially transcendent power, but
true wealth cannot be gained within the limits of the Bookerite puritan hard labor,
humble commerce, and gradual accumulation. The kind of wealth Gordon needs to
reaffirm his identity beyond race can be gained, according to American myth, only
from a magical combination of exceptional talent, good luck, and intuitive risk taking—a combination represented in the autobiography by tinkering invention. Because *Born to Be* insists on retaining the pure capacity of money to signal United
States masculine freedom and success, Gordon must keep his narrator optimistically naive about how money is obtained in the first place through tight networks
of white homosocial privilege and exclusion. If only African American men would
be more like John Ringling, they, too, could travel unrestrictedly across the country
on their own railroads, metaphorical or literal. This dream of freedom is, then, the
inverse of that represented by Scott and Stowe, as they picture Washington gratefully taking rides without restriction across the country on other (white) men's Jim
Crow railroad cars. The railcar as unconstrained freedom and wealth is intended to
erase the trenchant realism embodied in the Jim Crow railcar confrontation scenes
that serve as the climax of so many New Negro personal narratives.

In the Minneapolis restaurant, Gordon's response to racial discrimination emphasizes how the West both salvages and unmakes his manhood in this moment
of being put in his colored place:

"Get to hell out of here. Don't you understand? Niggers can't eat in here."

Even at that I couldn't get it through my head why he [the waiter] should be mad at me. I hadn't done anything, but I knew he was hot. My right hand automatically fell to my left hip where old Betty always hung when I was alone. She wasn't there! I can't describe the lonely feeling that came over me. I have never felt like it since. It seemed as though everyone whom I knew had died at once. (68)

That Gordon has money to pay in no way opens his access to the Jim Crow restaurant. When the money as the equalizing currency fails him, he goes for another vehicle in the equalizing myth. Automatically reaching for his gun (aptly imaged as a female), reaching for his cowboy sense of manhood, he comes up empty exactly at the moment he needs that phallic symbol most. Without a gun, the white waiter is able to kill off everyone in Gordon's universe. The gun itself becomes an empty, useless weapon in any case, for no gun can heal the wound inflicted by this act of racial emasculation. Gordon would never again be able to reclaim his innocence, his manhood, his West, or his raceless face as belonging fully and unselfconsciously to himself.

It is this incident that sends him in search of a reformed racial identity, an adventure comprising the narrative's main interest and at the same time adventitious to it. He sets out to be rich and powerful like John Ringling but gets waylaid by the deviousness of racial politics. He ends up discovering his fame and fortune not by inventing a new contraption to reduce friction on the railroads but instead from being overheard while singing to himself during his portering on Ringling's private railcar. Importantly, though, it is not a Negro spiritual he is singing when he is discovered but opera, along with Caruso on a Victrola. Rather than traveling a straight-shooting path to "American" self-made success, Gordon finds himself exploring the devious paths an African American man must take, and at every step, he finds himself relying on the whims of rich, powerful white men, especially the same circus impresario who initiated his drive to become an "Easterner."

As he begins to learn about race from the whores, pimps, and sweetbacks of Minneapolis, he experiences his first acknowledged doubt about his own implication in this game:

In bed, I began to take myself serious. All the grand things I had planned to be were pipe-dreams. They couldn't be done! Then all my nicknames came to me— Snowball, Zip and Blacky. But they called Jimmy Keen "Blacky" too, and really the only thing black about him was his hair. Besides, with all my nicknames, none of them made any difference about where I ate or slept. It baffled me to think that the mask that aided me so much at home, was all against me in the cities I dreamed of. (76–77)

Gordon's projection of his self-denial in the narrative is nowhere more poignant, even pathetic. His face that once signified "a passport stamped in full" now becomes a "mask," recalling Paul Laurence Dunbar's poem "We Wear the Mask": "We wear the mask that grins and lies, / It hides our cheeks and shades our eyes,— / This debt we pay to human guile." Dunbar scripts the African American face in a tragic mode as a "debt" to "human guile," which we must pay in order to survive. "With torn and bleeding hearts we smile, / And mouth with myriad subtleties."[29] If the black face under white supremacy must necessarily mouth "myriad subtleties," then Gordon's desire to mask his own racial reality participates in the deviousness of racial politics that he claims to stand above as a raceless Westerner. The fact that so much rests on his nicknames not being racially generated indicates to what extent his skin color, if not race itself, has subliminally allowed him to accept those names without resistance. If this "mask" of blackness has "aided [him] so much" out West, then it has been a determining element of who he was born to be all along. To see this would be to bring his identity as a raceless Westerner crashing onto his head—which is what happens in any case, given that no person of identifiable African descent could remain in this pipe dream for long.

That he toys with the idea of sweetbacking logically follows on this threat to his raceless western identity. What he has suffered is an assault on his desire to have the United States frontier represent the quintessence of westernness in its larger sense, the "West" as the imperialist center of scientific progress, political freedom, advanced civilization, and futuristic modernity. In this double meaning of the West (U.S. frontier exceptionalism as well as the whole of the white Euro-American world made rich by imperialist plunder), the privilege of being American can be taken for granted only if the privilege of being white precedes it. Gordon's newfound black buddies tell him that he has three choices: go home, be a railroad porter, or become a sweetback and gambler. Notably, only the first choice is never a true option. The West that supposedly breeds him a free, raceless man has no attraction to him in the revelation of his being a Jim Crowed black man. He tries his hand at portering, but this, too, despite its semblance of free physical movement, reminds him of his servile inheritance. As he becomes a private porter for John Ringling, he remains so close and yet so far from the source of eastern power. Unlike its role in other New Negro narratives—where railroad portering represents the ceaseless, circular, predetermined wandering dictated by life on preset tracks—Gordon's railroad is a symbol for conquest over the frontier of one's biggest dreams. This is why throughout the narrative he makes so much of his private knowledge of Ringling as the master of his own railroading dynasty.

As Gordon comes to reap success unexpectedly through his Negro inheritance—his "natural" singing and entertaining ability—he must distance himself not only from the minstrel stereotype of that heritage but also from its actual history. To succeed as a New Negro renaissance artist he needs both his racial bond and its denial. We find him, like that other circus impresario, Van Vechten, driven to learn all about these queer black people but ever conscious of his patronizing upper hand: "But there was something in their earthy dances and jokes that told me I must learn all about niggahs, because I was one of them, and to be one and not know something about them would be bad" (98). This is as close as Gordon comes to suggesting consolidation out of place, but even here the fact that he comes to blackness as a naive, resigned student indicates how blackness itself must be out of place for a true raceless Westerner like himself. "In all and all, I convinced myself that my people were as hard to figure out as perpetual motion" (173). This ingenious, ingenuous statement initiates chapter 16, titled simply "My People." The irony of that phrase captures its similar use as the title of chapter 12, "My People! My People!" of Zora Neale Hurston's 1942 autobiography, *Dust Tracks on a Road*. Both Hurston and Gordon set themselves up above "the race" by being able to castigate it. Unlike Hurston, however, Gordon is totally mystified (or pretends to be) as to why African Americans remain, in his view, so thoroughly unreformed and unmodern. "With all the opportunities they have had since the Civil War, if they were a noble people, there is no way to convince me they would stay in the South under the most trying conditions and leave the millions of acres of unsettled land west of the Mississippi lie dormant" (*Born to Be* 173). Although this chapter reduces to the absurd the logic undergirding New Negro migration narratives as a bid for modernity, it also bespeaks an impatience with the folk mass that resonates with many African American texts of the period.

Out of this dilemma grows Gordon's ambivalent critique of Negro deviousness, superstition, and passivity, and his notion that it is not he who needs to be reformed into a New Negro man but all other Negroes who are in need of reform. "Being that the white man classes all niggahs alike, though he treats 'em different, the mystery to me is why they don't join together as one big tribe. I have white people tell me they will soon, but I don't think this generation will witness it, unless the white people have it up their sleeves that they are soon going to send all negroes to Africa or some-other place" (173). Identifying against and surreptitiously with the Negro, Gordon must go to white people in order to understand the mystifying behavior of his kind. We cannot fail to see the humor in this, especially since he imputes the greater deviousness of white people in charging black people with such a sin; the mystery of black people's divisiveness metonymically jumps over to the mystery of "why the white man classes all niggahs alike, though he treats 'em different." But white deviousness in no way diminishes Gordon's distancing himself from black deviousness. It only makes him saner than either race. Even Christianity turns out to be a great con game: "The main reason for accepting it now is because they [black people] think they are getting something for nothing." Instead of fussing with religion, "[e]very Negro should know why there are not large perpetual motion machines that could fly from here to Europe and back without stopping, or from here to Mars: if they did, they wouldn't be so pious. They would realize that if there is a God he is a scientific God" (174).

Gordon's contrast of the perpetual-motion machine to African American religiosity indicates the backwardness of his people while setting forth his own modernity. Commenting on Ralph Ellison's concept of the "thinker-tinker," Herman

Beavers points out the role that this kind of inventiveness plays in Ellison's critique of African American culture: "Ford, Edison, and Franklin each offer a unique combination of mechanical know-how, persistence, and public presence, which they employ in dilemmas of a technical or scientific sort. Their skill at negotiation, as the forces of disorganization swirl around, marks their passage into the ranks of self-made men."[30] In his appeal to the perpetual-motion machine, Gordon is working toward a similar strategy. The idea of perpetual motion, infinite resourcefulness, comes to represent his perpetual capacity for self-making reformation above the politics and divisiveness of race. The machine, a source of energy through frictionless materiality, is the perfect image for Gordon's desiring a frictionless body that can move through American society without racial tensions or intentions. He idolizes and wants to be counted among what Beavers aptly calls "figures of resourcefulness" (12); unlike Ellison's invisible man, however, Gordon figures blackness as a foil to such resourcefulness, rather than its ground. Even as he exploits the African American musical tradition to achieve fame and fortune by singing spirituals and blues, he wants to separate the spiritual resourcefulness of African American music from the material, and materialist, resourcefulness of the "know-how" of both the global and the national West.

Gordon summarizes his sense of the relation between black and white in an analogy: "To me the white and colored people are like man and wife—can fight all they please with each other, but let some one else step in and they both will hop on them, Teeth and Claws" (173). This feminization and domestication of the black race as wife contradicts the impact of the image, which makes both races equally fierce and equally devious. In the end, however, it is African Americans who apparently must take the blame for racial self-consciousness. Thus, Gordon moves toward closure by severing the tie that seems to jeopardize his manhood freedom. Better to be the "man" than the "wife" where equal fighters are concerned. The African American pimps and sweetbacks he discusses pervert this manly entitlement by taking money for sex. Thus African American racial deviousness falls into sexual deviance, each implied in the other.

But Gordon wants it both ways. His association with the race highlights his cosmopolitan, cutting-edge urbanity. He can cut a trendy and profitable figure in the New Negro Renaissance only through his alliance with racial exoticism and the race's sexual deviance:

> If I had a movie-tone of my actions on the road I have travelled so far, I would be willing to go back to the mountains, surround myself with wine, women and song, and spend the rest of my days. But I haven't got it, and I'm still a poor man, so I must keep on, with the world's greatest celebrities, artists, musicians, writers, bull-dikers, hoboes, faggots, bankers, sweetbacks, hotpots, and royalty, who have framed my mind so that life goes on for me, one thrill after another—too many to mention. (235)

Figure 2.1. On the Job; sketch by Miguel Covarrubias for Gordon, *Born to Be.*

Just as his face serves as a passport to move among high and low, respectable and deviant, rich and poor in his frontier hometown, so now he stakes his future on this full stamp. However, unlike Van Vechten, who could go slumming and practice "deviant" sexual acts with African American men clandestinely without losing his status—indeed, enhancing it through his association with deviant black masculinity—Gordon is merely a face in this pageantry. He can elbow faggots, dikes, hotpots, and hoboes because he, sporting a black mask, belongs on the margins of society with them. It is only the curious alchemy of the 1920s that makes royalty and celebrities desire the company of one like him. This ambivalence toward deviance recapitulates his duplicitous denial of race's import in his life. "No wonder the Race Question has never been the big ghost in my life," he exclaims (234). The race question is, in fact, the biggest ghost in his narrative, making him an eerie "mask" in his own autobiography.

Gordon's racialized encounters haunt his autobiographical intention to deny the impact of the color line on his identity. Even more haunting to his claim of having achieved a raceless mobility, the book is illustrated through a series of ten sketches that Miguel Covarrubias was commissioned to compose for the volume. In these we see the logic of the New Negro new-century album turned on its head. If Washington, Adams, Locke, and others sought ways to promote the Negro's newness through visual proof of his rapid progress into the advance guard of modernity, the publishers, editors, and patrons of Gordon's autobiography exploit visual sketching to rescript his narrative as fully determined by the color line. In the same way that Muriel Draper and Van Vechten transfix Gordon's identity as a Negro ward who needs their superior patronage to bring his narrative into print, so Covarrubias's series of cartoons visually arrest the fast-paced narrative by reminding Gordon and his readers of the Negro's proper racial place. The sketches show Gordon or other Negroes frozen in a static pose, as white bodies in motion define the energetic action of the scene. In the colorful frontispiece, Covarrubias's cartoon "On the Job" freezes Gordon in his servile role as porter (Figure 2.1). As fleshy, wealthy whites luxuriate in the jazz age—listening to the new music, dancing and drinking with abandon—Gordon is excluded from these titillating pleasures. He stands at the ready with his tray of drinks, both marginal (the silent, invisible servant boy) and central (the black presence from whose body emanate the vicarious pleasures of "primitive" Negro culture). If Gordon's narrative wants to claim that he is a full-fledged agent in the national experiment in modernity, Covarrubias's frontispiece reminds us on which side of the color line the narrator properly belongs.

Each of Covarrubias's sketches repeats this notion in a different way. In "Stakes Up" (facing page 32), we see three lanky white cowpokes in a bowling alley (Figure 2.2). As one cowboy bowls his black ball down the alley, scattering the pins with

Figure 2.2. Stakes Up; sketch by Miguel Covarrubias for Gordon, *Born to Be.*

the ball's blast, we observe a little black boy, the young Gordon, whose face is as round as the black bowling balls. He sits next to the alley, waiting to perform his job of rearranging the fallen pins, scrunching his body to avoid being hit by the pins. The active, forward thrust of the white cowboy only intensifies the immobilized pose of the Negro boy at the far end of our gaze. The sketch seems to be a parody of a Wild West showdown, but instead of Gordon occupying one end as a proper cowboy, he is an unarmed black boy, a marginal target for whatever ball or pin the true white cowboy may shoot in his direction. The sketch contradicts Gordon's own notion of his raceless mobility as a budding young cowboy on the western frontier.

Nowhere is this tendency to freeze Gordon's identity as an old-style Negro more clearly glimpsed than in Covarrubias's final cartoon, "Singin' for Royalty" (Figure 2.3; facing page 208). The sketch is supposed to capture Gordon's fast-paced, self-made success as a singer, but instead it positions him as the curious, exotic object of the sophisticated gazes of European royalty—no different from the "Noble Savage" Indian chiefs and Venus Hottentots who historically were brought to Europe to entertain the modernizing elite. On the right side of the sketch, Gordon stands in formal dress with his hands folded in front of his crotch, his eyes shut, and his mouth wide open in song. On the other side of the sketch sit the peering profiles of three snooty white aristocrats, one glaring directly at Gordon (and at us) through her opera glasses. Gordon's human face disappears into a singing mask, an open black hole. By allowing himself to be represented in his own autobiography in such a way—in effect, as a blackface minstrel—Gordon becomes complicit in the con game that pretends he can be identified as Negro and not be constrained by Jim Crow. The autobiography itself becomes a minstrel dance, as Gordon, claiming a raceless identity, wants to say that his black face is just a mask that hides a raceless soul, yet in order to rise above his servile position as a porter, he must sing darky songs like a black man. Gordon seems not to understand what other New Negro narratives know from the outset: in the moment of a Negro's speaking—whether singing spirituals or writing an autobiography—if he fails to make the spectacle a racial confrontation that turns the tables on those surveying him, then he will become merely a spectacle in color. As Gordon opens his mouth to sing, as the cartoon portrays him, he is trapped in that minstrel pose against his will, an open mouth without an authentic voice. We would like to think that Gordon understood the duplicity of his situation, but the problem with his pretending *not* to understand his race is exactly the difficulty of seeing the narrator's self-knowledge through the minstrel's mask.

The reviews of Gordon's book in the two leading magazines of the time indicate that his black male contemporaries were also disturbed by a perception of minstrelsy, and thus an Old Negro mentality rather than a fast-paced New Negro mobilization of black manhood. In his *Opportunity* review, Eugene Gordon writes, "*Born to Be* is a funny book. It is funny because the author takes himself

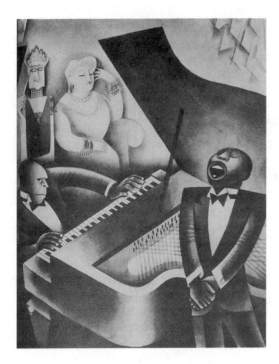

Figure 2.3. Singin' for Royalty; sketch by Miguel Covarrubias for Gordon, *Born to Be.*

very seriously. It is funny in the sense that a pompous person is funny; that is, without being aware of it" (22). Du Bois's review in the *Crisis* is even more damning:

> Taylor Gordon's autobiography is another product of the Van Vechten school of Negro literature. . . . I may be wrong, but in this book I get the impression that Taylor is "cutting up" for the white folk. I can see Carl and Muriel splitting their sides with laughter, while he jiggs and "jah-jahs!" But of life, of real life, in the drab western town, there must have been poignant tragedy as well as screaming farce. I would like to hear a little more of the inner life of that dark mother and of the other wandering children. . . . Covarrubias has illustrated the book. . . . I am frank to say . . . that I think I could exist quite happily if Covarrubias had never been born. ("Browsing Reader" 129)

Gordon's topic calls for "serious" treatment, but the Van Vechten mode prevents it.

Can we call Gordon's persona in *Born to Be* a New Negro? Even if many of his actions seem to emulate the racial trespassing behavior we have identified as a mark of the coolly realistic New Negro, the overall effect of his book seems to contradict this persona. On the one hand, it is inevitable that someone should eventually exploit an extreme mobilization of the concept of the New Negro, taking manhood reform as racial trespassing to its logical outcome in the claim to a raceless identity as a self-making American man. On the other hand, it is ironic that Gordon's white patrons are so easily able to exploit the New Negro technique of visual proof against him. It is further ironic that Gordon's raceless New Negro identity should resemble so closely the old Negro face of minstrelsy, which is the obstacle that New Negrodom desires to overcome in the first place.

3 New Negro Social Science

Sexual Deviance, Black Male Professionalization, and the Sociology of Containment

> But alas! While sociologists gleefully count his bastards and his prostitutes, the very soul of the toiling, sweating black man is darkened by the shadow of a vast despair.—W.E.B. Du Bois (*Souls of Black Folk* 9)

> It should be kept in mind that racism tended to equate expertness with [white] skin color. The label "expert" was applied only to those blacks who were white certified.
> —Butler A. Jones ("Tradition of Sociology Teaching in Black Colleges" 130)

> To trace the black man in American sociology is tantamount to tracing the history of American sociology itself.
> —Stanford M. Lyman (*Black American in Sociological Thought* 15)

> Encouraging him to apply his talents in the constructive field of research has a value, I think, in that he will be less likely to become simply an agitator.
> —Will Alexander (quoted in Anthony M. Platt, *E. Franklin Frazier Reconsidered* 86)[1]

In post-Reconstruction discourse, the city poses a threat to racial consolidation and uplift, as we have seen in Bookerite rhetoric on migration northward. Even though Cleveland embodies an escape for Charles Chesnutt in his personal life, in his fiction northward migration could be much more troubled and troubling. His character Uncle Wellington makes the mistake of confusing a degree of sexual license—his freedom to marry an Irish immigrant—with increased socioeconomic influence. When he returns south, he returns to a "normal" marriage arrangement in the sense of both monogamy and sexual bonding within the race. Similarly, in Paul Laurence Dunbar's *Sport of the Gods* (1902) and Pauline E. Hopkins's *Contending Forces* (1900), the freer atmosphere of the northern city only increases the seductiveness of moral/sexual license without effecting any concomitant political, economic, or social reform. As Bernard W. Bell points out, African American fiction after Reconstruction tends to be "[c]aught up in the white nationalist and agrarian ideological snares" of Anglo-American literature of the time, resulting in a stance that is "at best ambivalent about the rural South and the migration of blacks to the cities" (*Afro-American Novel and Its Tradition* 74). Building on Bell's work, Kevin Gaines explains that this ambivalence toward urbanization results from intense class anxieties embedded in the uplift ideology of black leaders and intellectuals. "Like many bourgeois whites, they associated tenements and slums with social and cultural decay. For blacks, social change also meant challenges to religious traditions of black leadership and authority by new secular pastimes and attractions" (*Uplifting the Race* 179). Fearful that lower-class southern migrants would erode their attempts to present a progressive image of the race, most black leaders of the time mirror the views of their white counterparts. "To many elite blacks . . . the movement to the North had worsened the black elite's already considerable sense of dislocation. Themselves illequipped to assist the migrants, they were largely incapable of viewing the migration positively," Gaines writes. "Their outlook, rooted in the philosophy of industrial education, often characterized blacks as disorderly, unfit for citizenship, superstitious, criminal, lazy, immoral, and needing to be compelled to work" (180). As Gaines demonstrates, even the early work of Du Bois shares some of these fears and anxieties (see 152–178).

Yet many of these leaders, being migrants themselves, could not help but express some empathy for those perceived as socially beneath them, and given the physical constraints of segregation and the ideological restraints of the uplift concept, they could not totally dissociate themselves from the liberating impulse of the migration. The fear of a people demoralized by licentious urban conditions nevertheless clouds the consolidating aspects of the uplift agenda, hinting toward some nostalgia for the purer, simpler rural life even as migration away from these rural backwaters is figured as necessary to survival; whatever moral safeguard the rural South may harbor for the assaulted black race it more than takes away through the immoral menace of strict Jim Crow. For Pickens, White, and Wells, migratory dislocation disrupts familiar racial patterns, presenting new opportunities for racial trespassing as much as new challenges. New Negro personal narratives such as theirs saw the northern city as a stage where racial resistance could be most effectively enacted by exceptional leaders and the common people whom they led. For these activist writers, morality meant the courage of one's convictions in the face of a white mob, a morality higher and deeper than the sociomoral conventions upon which racial supremacy justified lynching, Jim Crow, and cross-racial sexual strictures.

Pickens's call for a mass media campaign to redirect public discourse concerning black urbanity was answered in a variety of ways after World War I, but one crucial effort appeared in the highly visible field of urban sociology, which became virtually synonymous with the study of race in the United States—and was sometimes analogized to the ethnological studies conducted by anthropologists on "primitive" cultures in "tropical" locales. Urban sociology not only became fertile ground for the effort to redirect black discourse concerning the adaptability of African Americans to modern civilization. It also became a central site for the construction of a modern professional cadre of African American men (despite the fact that the work of black and white women preceded and spurred it on).[2] Through this professional discourse, the black male proponents of urban sociology hoped to situate the future of the race at the heart of modernity—making the race modern by granting it the status of the most systematically studied group in the country, according to the most up-to-date social scientific methods. While these urban sociologists wanted to modernize African American society by making black people total *objects* of modern study, their studies helped constitute the sociologists themselves as thoroughly modern *subjects,* capable of engaging the most recent techniques of a cutting-edge science. In their distinctly modern studies, however, we can detect a constant resistance to their own "neutral" methods, which sought to objectify, categorize, and map every observable aspect of urban African American life. By literally mapping the social and physical boundaries of black masses in northern cities, the black male sociologists not only expressed their anxiety over black migrants' unruliness but also demonstrated their own ability to serve as responsible managers of the masses—or at least, to develop the expertise required for such management. The question of sexual reform, and black manhood reform in particular, was pivotal to this tension between objective methods and a propagandistic agenda of self-imaging, between turning the urban mass into sociological objects and insisting on the sociologists' own fully active scientific and historical agency as leading black men.

By reading these social-scientific texts as cultural narratives, we discover how their authors used urban ethnography to construct their own masculinity as normal, their sexuality as self-disciplined, and their social status as professional—that of men deserving managerial responsibility for the black urban mass. In a sense, the black male sociologists from the turn of the century to the 1940s embody the most prominent, consistent, far-reaching manifestation of New Negro ideology, though expressed in an impersonal, restrained mode, almost opposite to the trespassing "cool" narratives examined in chapter 2. At the same time, the injunction for neutrality, dispassion, and scientific distance constitutive of the emergence of sociology as a science might be connected to both the harsh realism and the cool perspective employed by New Negro personal narratives. Just as the narratives insist on mastering the dire realities of Jim Crow through a sustained sense of personal transcendence, so the black male sociologists exploit the protocol of scientific objectivity as a sort of "cool" mastery of the volatile racial condition they are supposed to be dispassionately studying.

In the half century of peak migration, from W.E.B. Du Bois's 1899 *Philadelphia Negro,* to Kenneth Clark's 1963 *Dark Ghetto,* scholars repeatedly turned to sexual conformity and deviance within black communities in an attempt to understand the broader causes and effects of northward migration and resettlement, of cultural stagnation and advancement.[3] Microscopically scrutinizing the sex lives of the migrants, these scholars discern apparent differences in familial and sexual re-lations between the racial majority and the black masses but hope to dislodge the dominant discourse claiming blacks' natural looseness, partly through their own self-discipline in social-scientific method. The black sociologists' ability to manip-ulate dispassionate language, hard numbers, case studies, ethnographic participant observation, and rational explanation of black sexual behavior serves to prove the falsity of the stereotype of black sexual deviance even as the sociologists grapple with a population whose diverse sexual habits might be seen to affirm the stereo-type.[4]

Like the static techniques of photography employed in New Negro albums, these social-science studies hinge on a discourse of numbering and mapping of groups whose mobility and instability present a constant challenge to the demo-graphic charts and maps employed in the new science. As quickly as a neighbor-hood had been surveyed and enumerated, the statistics could become obsolete, given the scope of the migration and the constant movement of unsettled migrants between one city and another, in and around various parts of a city, and back and forth between North and South. The urban sociologist started with the empiricist assumption that an accurate assessment of a group's character, material needs, and cultural resources could be measured through ethnographic and demographic studies, and though numbering attempts to repress the subjective element at stake in racial imaging, these projects are saturated with the subjective political agenda of racial imaging. Like Pickens, the social scientists were interested in forging an image of this new urban population—one in need of constant tracking and updat-ing—that could reflect their racial potential for a modernizing nation-state. The urban studies focus on a cluster of topics that attempt to chart to what degree the black migrants are contained by and in their new environs: What is the actual number of these migrants? What are the actual geographic boundaries of these set-tlers' communities? How do they group together or apart, how far away from or close to nonblack neighborhoods? How adequate is their shelter for keeping them off the streets and out of trouble? How far from their homes do they have to travel in order to find work? Which social classes do they fit into, and what resources do the relatively scarce upper-class members have for maintaining control of the lower classes? What sort of organizations and leisure activities do they engage in? Do they settle inside or outside normal families? Are they sexually promiscuous?

All these questions revolve around the concerns of the dominant race, who feared that black migration might be an unmanageable process that would create a new racial creature, the New Negro, not containable by or in the systems put in place to police race and class relations in the industrializing United States. As Nell Painter notes, "White southerners migrated North in far greater numbers than blacks, but their migration did not attract the same notice or violence" (*Standing at Armageddon* 337). Although sociologists were eager to exploit the black migration as an object for professionalizing their own image and modernizing the image of the race, they also recognized the double bind presented by bringing further attention, however positively formulated, to this phenomenon. As a sociology of containment, these studies are also concerned, therefore, with challenging the idea that black people, especially black *men,* cannot police their own sexual desires and social ambitions. The double bind was that toward whichever direction the sociologists might take the racial image, they risked provoking negative reactions from the "whiter light of civilization." To image a race in control of itself might suggest a laissez-faire attitude toward these migrants, who the sociologists already believed were in need of various forms of "whiter" patronage in order to adapt to the city. To image a race out of control might suggest that the dominant society must take a militant approach to black migration—similar to the violence perpetrated against African Americans around 1917, and the anti-immigration and seditious alien acts passed around the same time—rather than make benevolent gestures of economic aid and civil and social reform.[5] Hence, these writers promulgated a sociology of containment not only in the restrained methods they employed in their search for apparently unbiased means for tracking their subjects' habitats, desires, and physical movement but also in their attempt to control and direct the potentially volatile responses of their whiter readers. As in the more self-consciously assembled narratives of the Harlem Renaissance novelists, examined in chapter 6, these sociologists were seeking an activist narrative that could contain an objective portrait of the race while motivating influential groups to act on behalf of the black mass. Unlike New Negro novelists, however, the sociologists did not profess openly any liberating potential in deviating from social/sexual norms.

The Migratory Nether World:
The "Submerged Tenth" in Du Bois's Sociology of Surveillance

Considered the first black sociological text, Du Bois's *The Philadelphia Negro: A Social Study* sets the rhetorical, thematic, formal, and ideological patterns that most others follow, regardless of his later distancing himself from this kind of sociological discourse, and despite the fact that sociological theories and methods change over this fifty-year period. According to Herbert Aptheker, "A generation later, Du Bois was to criticize his *Philadelphia* book, for it suffered, he thought, from a certain 'provincialism' and tended to examine the realities of the oppression of Black people 'from the point of view of religion, humanity and sentiment' rather than from the point of view of socio-economic realities and class alignments" (*Literary Legacy of W.E.B. Du Bois* 37). Even in the study itself, however, Du Bois voices some hesitation about the limitations of social science. He initiates *The Philadelphia Negro* by questioning the credibility of his methods—statistical analysis informed by surveys and interviews and historical analysis bolstered by direct observation and cautious generalization:

> [T]hey are liable to error from the seemingly ineradicable faults of the statistical method, to even greater error from the methods of general observation, and,

above all, he [the researcher] must ever tremble lest some personal bias, some moral conviction or some unconscious trend of thought due to previous training, has to a degree distorted the picture in his view. Convictions on all great matters of human interest one must have to a greater or less degree, and they will enter to some extent into the most cold-blooded scientific research as a disturbing factor. (3)

Due to entrenched racial stereotypes, "convictions" about African American people can appear in sociological research as much because of an attempt to correct some prejudice as because of the prejudice itself. At the turn of the nineteenth century, racial prejudice, after all, is still validated by "cold-blooded" science. The metaphor is used in a calculated way here. Du Bois is all too aware of how a claim to cool dispassion for one's objects of study can turn into cold-blooded contempt. To forbid the moral precepts of sentiment, compassion, and empathy—key principles undergirding the work of abolitionists, whom he elsewhere sets up as a model for social action—might be to banish the very conduits of human benevolence enabling uplift in favor of mechanisms akin to the profit machines of industry and commerce. For Du Bois the cold-blooded metaphor also conjures the dangers of Darwinian assumptions concerning the survival or extinction of racial species ill fit for their environs. He is alarmed at the prejudice of many biological and social scientists, who were suggesting that the naturally hot-blooded temperament of the black migrants would not allow them to survive the cold climate of the North, just as their hot sexual passions would unfit them for the modernity of the urban environment. The cold-blooded "neutrality" of these racist assumptions—the absence of any humanizing sympathy—enables white scientists to devalue the humanity of their African American objects of study.

On the one hand, the ability to neutralize convictions and to discipline emotions proves one's capacity for professional reward, modern citizenship, and racial leadership; on the other hand, Du Bois defines an authentically full humanity as the ability to include "the human interest" at the heart of human problems—a definition that seems at odds with his social-scientific method, which demands that interest's elimination on the part of both author and reader. Likewise, the black sociologist needs to *neutralize* the whiter audience—to enable them to see the Negro problem with the cold objectivity of science—while simultaneously attempting to *humanize* that audience—to make them experience the humanity of the race through a "warm," felt connection to it. As Keith E. Byerman has pointed out, Du Bois's self-conflicted approach must take for granted the rooting of racial prejudice in simple human ignorance, rather than in some more systematic ideology:

He largely ignores the irrational basis of prejudice. But this neglect is inherent in the nature of the project. To affirm that prejudice has psychological depths too deep to plumb scientifically would be to deny the possibility of intelligent and "practical" reform. His book's raison d'être would be destroyed. He in fact continually returned to this problem, always refusing to believe that it was outside the discourse of reason and yet also displaying an apocalyptic sensibility that suggested despair if reason could not name and resolve the problem. (*Seizing the Word* 59)

As sociological methods provide Du Bois a basis for hope, an intellectual program, and a productive mode of indirect action as social reform, they also provide a putatively race-blind discourse that explicitly bars the relevance of his color to the outcome of his work, and thus the discourse promises a dialogue beyond racial prejudice. Would this aim of a race-neutral discourse jeopardize the larger goal of racial reform by erasing from his voice the potential contribution of his personal knowledge of the social implications of race prejudice? I agree with Shamoon Zamir: "Du Bois's adoption of the stance of objective observer and analyst in his historiography and sociology pushes him toward the centrist positions of liberal and professional consensus in the midst of his social critique" (*Dark Voices* 94).

Greater than Du Bois's anxiety over the potential distortions in the methods themselves is his anxiety over the dangers of regression, disruption, and downward mobility represented by the bottom of the black social scale, or what he calls the "submerged tenth" (*Philadelphia Negro* 311). Among this class he claims that "signs of idleness, shiftlessness, dissoluteness and crime are more conspicuous than those of poverty" (59). Whether this group is salvageable remains an open question in *The Philadelphia Negro*. While Du Bois frames the study as participating in "a battle for humanity and human culture" that cannot afford to underestimate the potential in any human being, he also passes harsh judgments on the "submerged tenth" that seem to cut them off from this redemptive ideal. When he abandons the determination of social class as a division made "almost entirely according to income" for a division that "brings in moral considerations and questions of expenditure," he develops a classificatory analysis that "reflects more largely the personal judgment of the investigator" (311). This judgment, based in his own moral and class biases, casts the lowest social rank into a "sinister" group of "wily" conspirators whose crimes are incomprehensible to the rational scientist:

> Many people have failed to notice the significant change which has come over these slums in recent years; the squalor and misery and dumb suffering of 1840 has passed, and in its place have come more baffling and sinister phenomena: shrewd laziness, shameless lewdness, cunning crime. The loafers who line the curbs in these places are no fools, but sharp, wily men who often outwit both the Police Department and the Department of Charities. Their nucleus consists of a class of professional criminals, who do not work, figure in the rogues' galleries of a half-dozen cities, and migrate here and there. . . . The headquarters of all these are usually the political clubs and pool-rooms; they stand ready to entrap the unwary and tempt the weak. Their organization, tacit or recognized, is very effective,

and no one can long watch their actions without seeing that they keep in close touch with the authorities in some way. (312)

Du Bois posits a group of "professional criminals" who are the dark double of his own professionalism in bringing things to scientific light. Their nefarious expertise constitutes the barrier to the agenda of his sociological project of total knowledge and *bourgeois* control. Du Bois piles up the adjectives to characterize these men as dissembling conspirators who operate clandestinely to entrap innocent African Americans, but whose actions implicate the white authorities. These men literally block the capacity for total surveillance that this method implies. He can detect their corruption of the authorities, and the authorities' corruption of them, but his observation is limited to what he can *openly* observe.

One could say that this submerged tenth is the nether limit of Du Bois's own sociological practice. They block his powers of observation not only through their constant physical movement from place to place, difficult for the social scientist to track, but also through their nefarious dealings in dark, secret places unsafe for the social scientist to enter. Furthermore, because these criminals are in league with corrupt police and other municipal officials, and because they devote themselves to careers of crime expertly honed with each experience, they begin to mirror Du Bois's own professional ambition, even to the extent that he, like them, must compromise himself by accepting the complicitous conditions placed on his research by the philanthropic bureaucrats, municipal authorities, and academic institution (the University of Pennsylvania) funding it. The kind of charitable intention for which he is conducting this research is outwitted by these "submerged" men, and ironically, his description of their actions seems to acknowledge defeat beforehand in the Department of Charities'—and his own—attempt to provide answers for how better to observe and control them.

Du Bois characterizes this class as a hard core that brings down individuals from the grade of energetic and thrifty poor above it. He implies that the venality of this group cannot be fully explained by the history of enslavement, present conditions of poverty, or racial segregation. It seems that once an individual slips into or is entrapped by this lumpen social class, there is no return. In other words, this core of criminals at the very bottom of society represents the liminal point beyond which redemption is impossible. Though individuals within this bottommost social group inhabit the nation-state, for all practical purposes they live outside its rules and obligations, and thus outside the rights and privileges of social, political, and economic citizenship. To fall into this pit almost certainly means being lost to manhood reform permanently. This hard core presents a risk to others, as it constantly feeds on the larger group of poor African Americans who inhabit the same sections of the city, and to whom the criminal element's members are related as blood family, as well as by racial identification. This implication of guilt by association shows up in Du Bois's description of another group of criminals who surround the core of "more desperate" ones (312), as the bottommost threaten to pull down the whole race, rank by rank, into this quagmire of social and moral marginality:

> The size of the more desperate class of criminals and their shrewd abettors is of course comparatively small, but it is large enough to characterize the slum districts. Around this central body lies a large crowd of satellites and feeders: young idlers attracted by excitement, shiftless and lazy ne'er-do-wells, who have sunk from better things, and a rough crowd of pleasure seekers and libertines. . . . They are usually far more ignorant than their leaders, and rapidly die out from disease and excess. Proper measures for rescue and reform might save many of this class. Usually they are not natives of the city, but immigrants who have wandered from the small towns of the South to Richmond and Washington and thence to Philadelphia. Their environment in this city makes it easier for them to live by crime or the results of crime than by work, and being without ambition—or perhaps having lost ambition and grown bitter with the world—they drift with the stream. (312–313)

Creating ranks within the class of criminals, Du Bois distinguishes between more innocent victims and the absolutely guilty. Partly what defines the innocent criminal class is their migration from the rural South, where enslavement and harsher economic and social conditions can more easily explain their backwardness. The irredeemable hard core, however, migrates from city to city in search of fresh conning grounds. If "[p]roper measures for rescue and reform *might* save many" soft-core criminals (emphasis added), the hard-core ones must be truly lost. The distinction between redeemable and irredeemable criminals indicates to what extent Du Bois must flirt with the cold-blooded attitudes of the racist scientists he is trying to attack. That the softer criminals "rapidly die out from disease and excess" seems almost a tonic, a natural cure of a Darwinian kind. Their weakness as individual specimens—their lack of ambition—dooms them to extinction in the harsh jungle of the modern city. Du Bois's own sociological ambition, evidenced in his ability to track and measure the decline of the weak migrants, presents itself silently as a New Negro foil to their unfitness.

By focusing on criminality as the definitive measure of social status, Du Bois bases class on a scale of moral worthiness and social conformity that links ever-lower rank with ever-increasing deviance. Not only does the lowest rank become thoroughly depraved, but the highest becomes the moral, sexual, and social norm. "Thus we have in these four grades the criminals, the poor, the laborers, and the well-to-do. The last class represents the ordinary middle-class folk of most *modern* countries, and contains the germs of other social classes which the Negro has not yet clearly differentiated" (310, italics added). With each "grade," the risk of criminality—and thus of marginality—becomes more certain: each rank is a step down in terms of not only social and economic status but also moral and sexual depravity. Du Bois's analysis of class in the Seventh Ward in Philadelphia might be summarized thus:

modern, normal, saved settled proper citizens	Top grade: the well-to-do Talented Tenth	11.5%
	2nd grade: the working class aspiring but short-sighted and lagging	56%
	3rd grade: the underemployed poor recent migrants from the South: satellites and feeders	30.5%
savage, deviant, damned footloose criminals	4th grade: submerged tenth, hard-core bottom	5.8%?

With each grade downward, the risk of irreversible marginality becomes greater; but the negative influence of the bottommost is spread even to the top grade, as the United States construction of race binds even the most talented Negro citizen to the most abject black criminal. Likewise, with each step down there is greater instability, just as each grade is literally defined by its increasing tendency toward unsettled migration. The Talented Tenth is defined as such largely because its members have been settled in the urban North and in the same stable neighborhoods over generations, whereas individuals in the second grade are not so much stable as sluggish and "lagging." The third grade have recently moved to the North and thus are geographically unsettled, morally confused, and socially disorganized, while those in the hard-core bottom continue to move feverishly from city to city, from neighborhood to neighborhood, apparently without plan or discernible pattern. Whereas the top grade remain stable by socializing with one another in a tight network that keeps them literally in one place, the lowest grade nefariously mix out of group indiscriminately, moving up and down the social scale promiscuously, and even mixing surreptitiously with white authorities in secret, dark corners all over the city, thus doing harm up and down the social scale by their instability. From top to bottom, it is also increasingly difficult to document the exact numbers and behaviors of each rank, due to their increasing physical mobility. While the habits and numbers of the top grade can be determined with the greatest certainty because of their settled state of affairs in established networks and institutions, the bottommost are the most undetectable due to their clandestine criminal habits and their restless movement, no doubt in part to further hide those anti-social activities. About the bottom rung Du Bois writes: "This would include between five and six hundred individuals. Perhaps this number reaches 1000 if the facts were known, but the evidence at hand furnished only the number stated. In the whole city the number may reach 3000, although there is little data for an estimate" (314). The footloose habits of the bottommost present a challenge to the empirical basis of Du Bois's sociological method, though, ironically, it is exactly such footloose behavior that is supposed to be contained and corrected by the deployment of this method. The sort of energetic migratory movement celebrated in the personal New Negro narratives of the previous chapter is here denounced as both sign and cause of the race's downward mobility.

Just as the "third social grade," the poor, tend to fall into criminality "partly because of the poverty, more because of the poor home life" (315), so the second grade, the laborers, *should* tend to rise, or at least have the moral training to do so. Instead, however, most of them remain in this grade. Their lagging status is attributed as much to their moral limits as to their limited ability and opportunities: "They are hard-working people, proverbially good-natured; lacking a little in foresight and forehandedness, and in 'push.' They are honest and faithful, of fair and improving morals, and beginning to accumulate property" (315). In his remarkable book *Sweet Home,* Charles Scruggs points to Du Bois's class ambivalence in relation to the black lower middle class, meaning the two middle grades:

> Du Bois's attitude toward the middle class reveals a crucial ambivalence. He understands that the economic insecurity of its members makes them cling to an image of respectability because of the suspicion that the color line that binds all will be drawn even more tightly around them. Yet this fear, understandable in itself, is death to the idea of community. . . . The masses recoil from an aristocracy who should lead them, because of that aristocracy's snobbishness; and the aristocrats reject fraternity, fleeing contact with those who threaten to drag them down into the barrel of crabs. . . . Du Bois shows a real fear of falling into that barrel himself, associating its bottom with the streets and not the home, which should be, he argues, "the centre of social life and moral guardianship." (22–23)

On the one hand, Du Bois seems to suggest that the middle grades have reason for complaint; on the other, he feels that they belong at their lower status. "Most of them are probably best fitted for the work they are doing, but a large percentage deserve better ways to display their talent, and better remuneration. The whole class deserves credit for its bold advance in the midst of discouragements, and for the distinct moral improvement in their family life during the last quarter century" (*Philadelphia Negro* 316). The moral self-restraint of the upper ranks qualifies them for their fitness in a "modern" environment, as it also mirrors the cool restraint of the social scientist, whose morality is supposed to be excluded from his method even as it frames his superior point of view. Being on top means being able to see down to the lower levels and thus having an obligation to survey and judge the moral, social, and work skills of those beneath.

Although Du Bois calls the members of the second rank of honest, hard-working laborers "the representative Negroes" (315)—perhaps because he estimates them as a majority of 56 percent (316)—it is the well-to-do rank that he claims should be taken to represent the race as a whole. The laborers are the majority, but the well-to-do represent the true norm:

> Finally we come to the 277 families, 11.5 per cent of those of the Seventh Ward, and including perhaps 3,000 Negroes in the city, who form the aristocracy of the Negro population in education, wealth, and general social efficiency. In many respects it is right and proper to judge a people by its best classes rather than by its worst classes or middle ranks. The highest class of any group represents its possibilities rather than its exceptions, as is so often assumed in regard to the Negro. The colored people are seldom judged by their best classes, and often the very existence of classes among them is ignored. (316)

Du Bois's question of which rank best represents the race suppresses the larger question of how any race can be represented by any individual or group identified with it. Associating the top class with modernity as well as with normative morality, he makes clear that progressive reform and progress can occur only in and through this group. In celebrating this Talented Tenth, historically we have often forgotten that the concept strongly calls for its monstrous other, the submerged tenth. On the shoulders of this elite group falls the greatest responsibility for uplift, even though they are much smaller in number than the second rank. Ironically, as Du Bois exploits the detachment and objectivity of social-scientific discourse to try to discourage prejudice—literally prejudgment—of African Americans, he simultaneously encourages a facile moral judgment of individuals based on their social rank, and of the race as a whole based on the perceived accomplishments and potential of the highest rank.

It is also ironic that Du Bois's social division according to sociomoral conformity undermines his goal of racial consolidation through what he calls "the art of social organized life":

> Looking back over the field which we have thus reviewed—the churches, societies, unions, attempts at business co-operation, institutions and newspapers—it is apparent that the largest hope for the ultimate rise of the Negro lies in this mastery of the art of social organized life. To be sure, compared with his neighbors, he has as yet advanced but a short distance; we are apt to condemn this lack of unity, the absence of carefully planned and laboriously executed effort among these people, as a voluntary omission—a bit of carelessness. It is far more than this, it is lack of social education, of group training, and the lack can only be supplied by a long, slow process of growth. (233)

Du Bois links professionalization of the race—its training in social organization and institution building—to the need for racial unity, and yet his approach reveals how much such professionalization relies on racial division through the proliferation of sociologically observable social classes. Although the top- and bottommost grades are essentially pure and undivided, the middle groups are further divided into subgroups, due not only to their unpredictable capacity for rising or falling but also to Du Bois's ambivalence about this unpredictability. Much of the study's logic depends on the strict delineation and separation of social ranks, including Du Bois's own capacity to speak as a well-educated, morally disciplined, socially conforming authority who can comprehend the moral failures of each rank. When he speaks of the exasperation experienced by the "better class of Negroes" concerning "this tendency to ignore utterly their existence," he is also speaking of himself, as is evident in his need to "fix with some definiteness the different social classes which are clearly enough defined among Negroes to deserve attention" (310). He writes that "if the foregoing statistics have emphasized any one fact it is that wide variations in antecedents, wealth, intelligence and general efficiency have already been differentiated within this group [the race]" (309).

Because Du Bois wants to separate African Americans into distinct social classes to use the highest as a model of morality and "social efficiency" for the others, he seems disturbed by the intermixing of social classes in physical space due to racial segregation: "On small streets . . . is a curious mingling of respectable working people and some of a better class, with recent immigrations of the semi-criminal class from the slums" (61). In "one of the best Negro residence sections of the city," Du Bois observes, "[s]ome undesirable elements have crept in" (61). He is concerned about containing these elements in order to protect the "quiet, respectable families, who own their own homes and live well" (62), just as the white patrons who have funded the study are concerned about containing the Negro elements of the city to protect the white communities. This ineradicable tension between the desire for racial consolidation and the desire to separate from the "undesirable elements" is evident in the spatial demography of the Seventh Ward, which Du Bois takes great care to illustrate in language and graphics. Just as white supremacy demands stereotyping African Americans as one homogenous, morally flawed underclass, so segregation demands the intermixing of good and bad elements in the same physical space. The analysis that results from his objective sociological observation determines residential *race integration* in the city to be an objective to be desired, but residential *class integration* in the race to be an evil to be corrected.

Just as the best elements among the Negroes try to enforce class segregation street by street, so Du Bois attempts to separate the good from the bad for his white patrons, literally street by street. The various street-scale maps of the Seventh Ward make graphic this "grading" surveillance, putting into proper ranks the inhabitants of each street and thus the rank of each street, as though the streets themselves are not liminal spaces where constant racial and class trespasses occur (Figure 3.1). The static nature of the sociological map, its fixing in print and visual image the rank of each family and each street, contradicts Du Bois's hope that individuals, families, and streets *should* naturally progress and rise. By the time his report is published, some individuals, families, and streets will have sunk, others perhaps will have risen, but most will remain unclassifiable as the contest between rich and poor, good and evil, continues unabated with each new mass of migrants. Like the

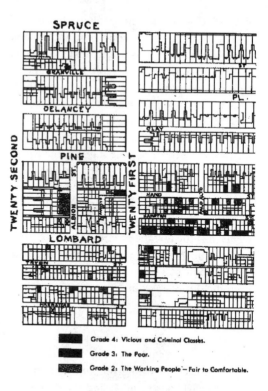

Figure 3.1. Excerpt from "The Seventh Ward of Philadelphia, the Distribution of Negro Inhabitants throughout the Ward, and Their Social Condition," from Du Bois, *The Philadelphia Negro.* Courtesy of the Albert and Shirley Small Special Collections Library, the University of Virginia.

realistic photographs of Washington's new-century race album, these sociological maps, as a technique of marking black manhood leadership, make a bid to objective modernity by arresting forward movement, constant change, and unpredictable mobility—those attributes of the mass that social thinkers such as Chesnutt, Pickens, Wells, and Locke theorize as the very basis of New Negro modernity.

As Du Bois insinuates that the purity of the Negro "aristocracy" requires physical distance from the seductive contaminating influences of the bottom 10 percent, he ironically also advocates a hands-on role for the top 10 percent in bringing the race up by keeping it under control. The proximity of the upper and lower classes seems to breed mutual contempt instead of patronage: "[T]he first impulse of the best, the wisest and richest is to segregate themselves from the mass. This action, however, causes more of dislike and jealousy on the part of the masses than usual, because those masses look to the whites for ideals and largely for leadership" (317). This is natural for the Negro lower class under such circumstances, Du Bois remarks. Furthermore,

> it is just as natural for the well-educated and well-to-do Negroes to feel themselves far above the criminals and prostitutes . . . , and even above the servant girls and porters of the middle class of workers. So far they are justified; but they make their

mistake in failing to recognize that, however, laudable an ambition to rise may be, the first duty of an upper class is to serve the lowest classes. (317)

Being good patrons to the lower classes means being above them, clearly superior to them and separated from them, yet willing to go among them to work on their behalf. Unlike white patrons, who need not fear being confused with those they seek to aid, black patrons must fear being confused with, or even becoming, their less fortunate wards. "Instead then of social classes held together by strong ties of mutual interest we have in the case of the Negroes, classes who have much to keep them apart, and only community of blood and color prejudice to bind them to-gether" (317). Just as the necessity of a Talented Tenth class breeds for Du Bois the necessity of a "submerged tenth," so the relation between top and bottom must necessarily be constituted by a twinning opposition. The submerged tenth is the darker monstrous double that on the one hand keeps the Talented Tenth distinctly at the top of a demarcated hierarchy but on the other hand also threatens to top-ple them. Racial ideology dictates that whites must potentially confuse one group for the other or not be able to see any difference between the two. Racial segrega-tion dictates that the two groups be forced into the same neighborhoods. And this threat of contamination moving from the submerged into the Talented Tenth is most perfectly embodied in the figure of sexual incontinence.

Like many later urban sociologists, Du Bois focuses on "sexual looseness" as the core of the "Negro problem" and the "monogamic ideal" as its solution (72). "There can be no doubt but what sexual looseness is to-day the prevailing sin of the mass of the Negro population, and that its prevalence can be traced to bad home life in most cases" (72). Although those who engage in deviant sexual be-havior constitute "a very small percentage," "[t]hey are the dregs which indicate the former history and the dangerous tendencies of the masses" (193). As *Souls of Black Folk* will later try to reclaim the race from its heritage of il/legitimate paternity by mourning broken families and shattered dreams, *Philadelphia Negro* tries to con-tain the contaminating influences of sexual looseness, which in turn represents the threat of a racial group not keeping to its proper social and physical boundaries. But just as the colored upper class cannot risk association with its loose lowest grade without being classified at that level, so Du Bois cannot avoid the advocacy, conviction, and emotion that accompany the "first duty" of a black patron. While separating his self-disciplined scientific voice from the loose behaviors of his wards, in the end he binds himself to them with an emotional outburst that explodes the boundaries he has worked so assiduously to demarcate. He momentarily abandons the cold-blooded tone of an objective observer and lets loose with a tirade that re-figures *all* African Americans together as the "helpless" victims of white civiliza-tion's criminal acts of theft, debauchery, and genocide:

The problems are difficult, extremely difficult, but they are such as the world has conquered before and can conquer again. Moreover the battle involves more than a mere altruistic interest in an alien people. It is a battle for humanity and human culture. If in the hey-dey of the greatest of the world's civilizations, it is possible for one people ruthlessly to steal another, drag them helpless across the water, enslave them, debauch them, and then slowly murder them by economic and social exclusion until they disappear from the face of the earth—if the consummation of such a crime be possible in the twentieth century, then our civilization is vain and the republic is a mockery and a farce. (388)

Reminding his readers that they are on the verge of the twentieth century, he welds modernity to the Negro problem, as he will do again later in *Souls of Black Folk* by identifying the most pressing issue of the new century as the problem of the color line, and more specifically by tying modernity to the desire to bring about a scientific solution for racism.

This pitting of white criminal against black victim in *Philadelphia Negro* gets quickly replaced, however, with a call for mutual trust and cooperation. Just as Du Bois wants to contain "dangerous tendencies" of the Negro to the lowest rung of the social scale, he also needs to contain his own impulse toward disgust and attack of white racist criminality. His whole project is anchored on such self-restraint. Such manly discipline explicitly entails *sexual* self-restraint of the upper-class New Negroes, as he suggests that there is little danger of sexual contamination when the best among the black and white mingle for patronage purposes: "Natural pride of race, strong on one side and growing on the other, may be trusted to ward off such [sexual] mingling as might in this stage of development prove disastrous to both races" (394). He emphasizes the need for the white and black upper classes to work together:

[I]n their efforts for the uplifting of the Negro the people of Philadelphia must recognize the existence of the better class of Negroes and must gain their active aid and co-operation by generous and polite conduct. Social sympathy must exist between what is best in both races and there must no longer be the feeling that the Negro who makes the best of himself is of least account to the city of Philadelphia, while the vagabond is to be helped and pitied. (396)

To understand this vision of upper-class cross-racial cooperation, we must remind ourselves of how Du Bois defines the bottommost criminals largely through their indiscriminate mixing with white authorities. Mixing between white men at the top and black men at the bottom is necessarily dangerous, nefarious, instable. It is a topsy-turvy mirror image of proper race relations, in which white authorities rely on physical contact with the Talented Tenth—and them alone—in seeking remedies to the Negro problem. His vision of upper-class racial cooperation, later to be modeled in the NAACP, accepts momentarily the physical boundaries set up between the races, but to do so, Du Bois must make it clear that cooperation across these boundaries does not require living in the same neighborhoods or intermarrying—at least not at this stage of each race's development. "The little decencies of daily intercourse can go on, the courtesies of life be exchanged even across the color line without any danger to the supremacy of the Anglo-Saxon or the social ambition of the Negro," he states in the penultimate paragraph (397). Just as geographic footlooseness—moving around from city to city, neighborhood to neighborhood, class to class, and across racial groups—indicates a danger zone to be avoided exactly because it blurs the proper norms set up by class, racial, and gender boundaries, so the geographic stability of black and white upper classes guarantees mutual progress. Upper-class blacks and whites know their proper place—know how to stay in their proper locales—even as they intermingle politically to work together on the race problem. Blacks in the lower classes, however, cannot be trusted to lead in this sort of interracial work because of their geographic and social-status instability. Because they are so footloose physically, socially, and morally—because they do not know their proper places—they cannot know how to conduct themselves as proper citizens among whites. Most significant, *black men* from the lower grades cannot be expected to know how to conduct themselves among the *white women,* who are the ones most frequently engaged with hands-on race work from their side of the color line. Contact between black men and white women, already figured as the greatest danger zone in United States race relations, must be managed with the utmost delicacy, discrimination, self-restraint, and gentlemanly sure-footedness, all characteristics that Du Bois identifies as *not* belonging to the lower-grade blacks.

The Philadelphia Negro here enacts what it preaches. According to David Levering Lewis, the study was "for the times, a unique interracial collaboration" between Du Bois and the white feminist sociologist Isabel Eaton, whose study of Negro domestic service in the Seventh Ward was appended to the text (*W.E.B. Du Bois: Biography of a Race* 191). Lewis notes that the more conservative white male leaders of the College Settlements Association (CSA), which sponsored the study, "urged that a promising young African-American scholar, a male, be given the direction of the Seventh Ward study, instead of one of [the white] feminists" from the CSA (188). If Du Bois needs the funding and validation of the CSA in order to conduct his sociological study, likewise the CSA needs him to moderate the perceived dangers lurking within the race. Relying on the black man to delve among the hard-core professional criminals, the male CSA patrons also offer some protection to Isabel Eaton, who, like Mary White Ovington and some other white female founders of social work, was beginning to display some curiosity about ministering to the poor black migrants. By accepting Du Bois's expertise, and later the expert credentials of other black men sociologists, the white patronage organization could better mediate between the demands of a progressive patronage among the city's black population and the fears of invasion and assault that this population's presence represented to the patrons themselves and to their wives, sisters, and daughters.

We can see, then, that Du Bois's sociological method of delineating fixed social ranks within the race is more than a matter of scientific protocol. Beyond the desire to survey and thus stabilize the feverish motions of the migrant masses, this division into social ranks ensures the stability of the black male sociologist himself. It gives him a secure social class—the Talented Tenth—as a physical base, and implicit ideological justification for his trustworthiness as a gentleman of color among elite white women. The more secure and stable the Talented Tenth can be seen to be in Philadelphia and in *The Philadelphia Negro,* the more at ease Du Bois's white male patrons can feel not only about him as an individual sociologist but also about the whole class of black male sociologists needed as intermediaries between a footloose race of migrants and the white race, whose settled status at the top of United States society must be protected even in the midst of liberal racial reform.

The Black Male Sociologist as Chivalrous Christian Mediator: George Edmund Haynes

If Du Bois's emotional restraint implicitly helped validate his findings for the liberal white patrons who funded his project, the work of George Edmund Haynes (1880–1960) represents an even more explicit instance of how objective social science could promote the ideological interests of white patrons through the professional rise of the black male sociologist as a chivalrous mediator between the footloose black migrants and white middle-class female social workers. By placing the well-known work of Du Bois next to that of Haynes, now largely forgotten, we can gain a clearer sense of how sociology operates as a gendering mechanism for black men's sexual self-reform at the turn into the twentieth century. A Southerner by birth, Haynes adhered more to the principles of Washington than to those of Du Bois, but like the latter man, he was trained at the most prestigious black and white institutions. After graduating from Fisk, Haynes studied at Yale, the New York School of Philanthropy, and the University of Chicago, and he further was the first African American to be awarded a Ph.D. from Columbia. Having studied social science at the two leading centers, Chicago and Columbia, Haynes was considered the first black professionally trained sociologist. For two years he was a fellow at the New York Bureau of Social Research, where he conducted studies on black migration and social conditions in the North, from which emerged the subject of his dissertation, "The Negro at Work in the City of New York: A Study in Economic Progress" (1912). In 1910, Haynes was appointed the organizer and first head of the Fisk Department of Social Science, which during the 1930s, under the tutelage of Charles S. Johnson, replaced Atlanta University as the leading center for sociological research in the South. Before he left for Fisk in 1910, Ruth Standish Baldwin invited Haynes to join with her in founding what became the National Urban League. (Ruth Baldwin and her husband, William Henry Baldwin Jr., son of abolitionists and a railroad magnate, became two of the biggest patrons of Tuskegee.)[6] In addition to working closely with Mrs. Baldwin in his capacity as educational secretary for the Urban League, Haynes held positions in the YMCA and the Interworld Church Movement and during World War I became director of Negro Economics for the United States Department of Labor.

As evident in Haynes's career trajectory, the black male sociologist constituted his professional credentials not only through institutions, governmental and private, whose segregationist and economically exploitative interest in the Negro migrant must be suspect. The validity of his credentials also depended on an implicit *gendering* of racial reform, in which he could be trusted to work with white female social workers and philanthropic matrons without presenting a threat to the sexual order of Jim Crow. Moral markers such as an explicit adherence to puritanical missionary Christianity and its chivalrous gender values, however contradictory to scientific method, assisted in arming some black male sociologists against suspicion of their social and sexual circumspection. The black male sociologist was to protect the white female social workers from the hot temperaments of the volatile masses as he projected a model of self-restraint countering the notion that *all* Negroes must degenerate into sexual license amid the temptations of the modern city. Furthermore, he must also segregate his professional purpose from that of black women reformers, who by the first decade of the twentieth century were much better organized for social action on a national scale. Rather than uniting with black women's social work in institutional ways, black male sociology sought to distinguish the role of professional black men from that of both white and black women.

Conducted for and published by the Home Missions Council in 1918, Haynes's study *Negro Newcomers in Detroit, Michigan: A Challenge to Christian Statesmanship,* while it aspires to rational objectivity in its social analysis, simultaneously promulgates Christian faith as the solution to the urban Negro problem, as indicated by the title. Like most of the social reform discourse of the time, the study mixes the zeal of a Christian missionary with the putatively neutral methods and tone of the new social science to create a cultural mediator, the black Christian social scientist-reformer, who can bring elite blacks and whites together to aid (and monitor) the moral and work discipline of the new black masses. Like Du Bois, Haynes occasionally stumbles into an emotional outburst that belies both his neutral tone and the Christian dogma of long-suffering patience:

> People will endure being poorly paid, half fed, poorly clad; living in poor houses; having poor schools for their children; being limited in many of the other opportunities of life when they believe they can do no better. But when they believe they see opportunities to get better wages, better food, better clothes, better houses, better schools for their children, greater freedom, they may be mistaken in what they think they will get, they may blunder in trying to get it, but they know what they want and will seek it. (*Negro Newcomers in Detroit* 7)

Like the southern migrants who burst the bounds of Jim Crow strictures by pushing into the crowded tenements of the North, the syntax of this passage breaks out of the passive, impersonal constructions of scientific prose. In most of the pamphlet Haynes follows the logic of sociological objectivity by keeping a strict distance between the black migrants as his objects of study and himself and his readers as rational agents responsible for understanding and reforming these objects. Racing toward the climax of African Americans' desire and agency, however, this passage enacts the inevitability of black migration, given the unbearable conditions of southern life, and thus counteracts the tendency in the study to conceptualize the migrants as immobile masses in need of external direction and management. While the study presents the migration to Detroit as a phenomenon that "has created far-reaching community problems" (8), by starting the study with an explanation of why they are migrating, Haynes implicitly and temporarily creates an empathetic relation with his investigative objects that stresses their right to Christian compassion and systematic benevolence.

Like Du Bois, Haynes creates social classes based on degrees of moral conformity in order to justify reforming the inhumane conditions under which the migrants live. Haynes can gain the cooperation of his white patrons and matrons in changing these conditions only by focusing on the moral reform of the individuals suffering under them. To support the idea of interracial cooperation, he must furthermore keep distinct a moral line separating those African Americans capable of cooperation, himself included, from those who need socioeconomic uplift through moral discipline. Just as longtime residents often see themselves as superior to any newcomers, Haynes characterizes the longtime black residents of Detroit as a social, moral, and intellectual elite. "For many years preceding 1915, Detroit had a small Negro population. It consisted mainly of families of a high grade both in intelligence and well-being. They lived in various parts of the city, self-respecting and respected for their intelligence and moral character" (8). The moral, social, and financial respectability of these families is indicated by their integration within the city. It is only when "Negroes of the undesirable type" come from other large cities to follow the race tracks across the international border into Windsor, Canada, that a Negro ghetto is created in Detroit. Such an explanation, while it does not erase racism as the cause for segregation, provides a rational explanation for white people's desire to separate themselves from African Americans. As the number of Negroes increases, the bad ones begin to outweigh the good. Haynes presents the problems of segregation and overcrowded housing as being as much a question of moral danger as a matter of inhumane living conditions. "The 'buffet flat,'" he writes, "is a sort of high-class combination of a gambling parlor, a 'blind tiger' and an apartment of prostitution. It is especially dangerous because it is usually in a private house in a neighborhood of homes, is run with all signs of respectability and caters especially to the youthful and unwary" (21). The habit of renting out rooms in homes in order to compensate for the exorbitant rents he calls "the lodger evil" (22).[7]

The newcomers' lack of discipline, a behavior developed in the South, threatens their ability to succeed in the factories. Haynes surveys the manufacturers, rather than the workers, for an understanding of the migrants' difficulties in the factories, and he quotes one employer who says that "nine-tenths of the complaints of employers against the Negro is that he is too slow. He does not make the speed that the routine of efficient industry demands" (17). Ironically, while the migrant masses are too energetic and footloose when it comes to their patterns of migration and neighborhood settlement, they are too slow when it comes to learning the routines of industrial labor. This paradox is similar to Du Bois's assessment that the third grade of workers are prone to instability and thus downward mobility because they are not farsighted and ambitious enough. Their physical mobility in one sphere helps explain their physical sluggishness in another.

Haynes's solution to all these problems is "supervision" in matters large and small by the Detroit Urban League, the employers, and the churches, black and white. This includes manufacturers building houses for the migrants in the shadow of the factory, which to some employees might be reminiscent of the plantation shacks behind the master's big house. Even in matters of recreation the migrants must be managed. "The large number of heavily attended pool-rooms call for some plan of organized supervision" (27). Similar to Washington's use of education, hygiene, and moral training as utilitarian vehicles for racial uplift, Haynes views the church as a tool for modeling industrial efficiency in the Negro. "First, the type of Negro workman who is attracted to the church is likely to be the type that is sober, industrious and reliable. Second, church attendance helps to make most workmen into such a type" (30). Given that he views the church as an instrument of control to rear Negroes out of southern work habits, it is not surprising that Haynes is suspicious of the shouting Christianity usually practiced by the migrants: "[T]he less intelligent type will probably be led into forms of religious fervor toward religious results that do not connect with the active ethics and pressing problems of the day" (31).

Haynes's industrial gospel translates the Christian ethic into an instrument of mass control and racial uplift within the constraints of industrial capitalism. His plan takes advantage of what he calls the "highest expression of both individual and group life of Negroes," the church (28). At the heart of Haynes's plan is the need for a black professional sociologist who can work with the white Christian patrons and matrons to manage, monitor, and educate the migrants. The study concludes with this question: "Would it not be a strategic step to put a man in Detroit?"

The Detroit forces might be increased now by putting a colored man in the field to help carry the heavy work such as a co-operative church and community organization would necessarily be called upon to do. If sent, he should not be independent of any existing staff of colored social workers, but might be a regular part of it. He might be given every opportunity to move slowly and be of help,

not a hindrance through acts taken on half knowledge of the church and community conditions. He might be sent to Detroit in the spirit of Christian service
to do a constructive, co-operative work. (39–40)

Haynes situates the black male sociologist as the most logical person to combine
social science, Christian service, self-service, and service to the race. We can take
his call for a "*man* in Detroit" quite literally, for, as in the case of the CSA's desire
for a colored *man* to shield white female social reformers, Haynes's notion of a
"Christian states*man*" views this work in the black ghetto as a crusade into morally
(i.e., sexually) dangerous territory that might too easily be seen as placing the black
professional woman as much at risk as the white female reformer. At least according to the logic we saw in John Henry Adams's New Negro woman essay, it would
be a great moral, social, and racial error to put a black woman in such a position,
for it would imply her lesser status as a refined lady needing gentlemen's protection. As a statesman, the male sociologist can draw on his more clearly defined
civic privilege and civil right when dealing with church patriarchs, captains of industry, and city fathers. Although middle-class African American women had already organized themselves on a national basis by the mid-1890s (the National Association of Colored Women was founded in 1896) to do exactly the kind of work
for which Haynes claims a man is needed, his study seems to overlook their work.
We might go so far as to say that his own reforming credentials require the erasure
of black women's organization.

The Social Accommodations of Chicago Sociology in
Charles S. Johnson and E. Franklin Frazier

As we move into the post–World War I era of academic sociology, more clearly articulated and delineated away from social work, philanthropy, political progres-
sivism, and missionary Christianity, the construction of the black sociologist is still
based on the kinds of methodological, class, and ideological tensions that surround
the black professional's moral superiority and agency over the investigative object's
problematic social, moral, and sexual status. By the 1920s, the theories of sociology practiced at the University of Chicago dominated the profession, especially in
the fields of race relations and urban sociology. As the department that had (and
still has) produced the greatest number and the most influential black sociologists,
the Chicago School had become synonymous with the study of the black ghetto,
just as the South Side of Chicago, where the university fearfully resides, had become the most researched object of study. In "Black Sociologists and Social
Protest," Charles U. Smith and Lewis Killian suggest provocatively that the philosophy of Chicago sociology—especially through one of its cofounders, Robert E.
Park—is indelibly influenced by the accommodationist tenets of Booker T. Washington.[8] It might also be pointed out that some of the white men who supported
Park—notably Julius Rosenwald—were important patrons of Tuskegee, and later of

Fisk during the 1930s through the mid-1950s, when Johnson, first as chair of sociology and then as president, would develop his "Fisk Machine." Whatever the degree of Bookerite influence, the point does highlight how one of the major tenets of the Chicago School accords with Washington's notion of uplift. According to this tenet, the task of the sociologist is to use objective methods to measure in material terms (condition of housing, boundaries of neighborhood, cleanliness of laborers) the extent to which the Negro mass has adjusted to the moral, social, and economic habits of the dominant culture.

Ernest W. Burgess, a junior colleague of Park's and himself an important contributor to Chicago sociology, has described Park's attitude toward training graduate sociology students to do race research:

> Park set about preparing young men for research in this field. The task was none too easy. Students attracted to this area, whether white or Negro, generally held strong sentiments against racial discrimination and for Negro rights. They were predisposed to fight valiantly for them. Park told them flatly that the world was full of crusaders. Their role instead was to be that of the calm detached scientist who investigates race relations with the same objectivity and detachment with which the zoologist dissects the potato bug. They must prepare themselves to be social scientists if understanding and factual knowledge were to be achieved.[9]

As has frequently been pointed out about anthropological discourse, the objectivity of the investigator serves to hide to what extent he or she influences and is influenced by the culture being examined.[10] More specifically, the ethnographic methods of the Chicago approach, strongly beholden to concepts of participant observation developed in anthropology, tend to hide the ideological limits of the dominant culture while obscuring the extent to which the sociologists are operating as a moral barometer to gauge for the dominant culture the potential for African American civilization. In a sense, like Washington, the objective black sociologist becomes an object lesson, proving the race's capacity for equality by displaying the sociologist's mastery of the scientific temper. Against this background of the black male sociologist's self-discipline and scientific caution is foregrounded the ambiguous nature of the black mass. As the black sociologist's credentials are being implicitly affirmed through the neutrality of the discourse, the capacity of the black mass to achieve such a status of self-mastery, civil productivity, and social normality is being probed and measured.

In his classic text of African American and Chicago School sociology, *The Negro Family in the United States* (1939), E. Franklin Frazier refers to this assimilative task of the professional sociologist when he locates his book as updating W.E.B. Du Bois's "pioneer series of monographs devoted to the application of objective methods to the study of the Negro's adjustment to modern civilization" (xix). As with Pickens and other New Negro advocates, the Chicago sociologists are concerned with a need to update continually the Negro's progress toward modernity (equated with urbanity), but instead of a race among the races, Chicago sociology sees this progress as a process of "adjustment" to modernity that all groups are undergoing in different ways, according to their particular cultural situations. Unlike the tendency in the anti-Bookerite New Negro agendas of Du Bois, Locke, Pickens, and Wells, in which African Americans or African culture is seen as a resource for revitalization and progress, the New Negro sociologists tend to see the dominant culture as providing the resources and standards according to which African American social practices must adjust. Adjustment occurs through what Park calls "race contacts," the breakdown of particular cultural inheritances into the anonymity and constant change that result from daily encounters with myriad other cultural groups experienced in the great cities, where the immigrant populations far outnumbered Anglo-Saxon native-born citizens before World War II. Although the sociological theory of race contacts has a rhetorical effect different from the cool aggressions of anti-Bookerite New Negro racial trespassing, they have in common the vital aspect of trust in shoulder-to-shoulder contact of the races, as opposed to any acceptance of racial segregation as the strategic response to racial subordination and oppression. The black Chicago sociologist's "cool" resides in his scientific distance from a problem that he passionately wants to solve through the power of his leadership credentials as a black man highly educated in prestigious northern institutions. Unlike the combatively aggressive New Negroes, however, the Chicago sociologists must subordinate their strong-willed personalities and self-promoting individualism to the collective, anonymous, colorless voice of scientific method— or at least, they must pretend to do so when they write *as* professional sociologists.

In defending Charles S. Johnson (1893–1956) as the foremost black sociologist of his generation, August Meier must rely on what Johnson does *not* publish as a measure of his greatness: "The fact was that Johnson seldom published his most thoughtful and original ideas. Instead he tended to limit himself to empirical description, to keep abreast of the most recent research in the field, but—acting cautiously—not to move beyond it" ("Black Sociologists in White America" 264).[11] In Johnson's case, this subordination of voice for the sake of sociological neutrality happened quite literally through what he refused to publish. It also happened methodically and rhetorically in his first major sociological contribution, which is not even attributable to his name. With the 1922 publication of *The Negro in Chicago: A Study of Race Relations and a Race Riot in 1919,* Johnson's contribution was altogether swallowed by the biracial patronage organization, the Chicago Commission on Race Relations, that sponsored the study. In *The Slum and the Ghetto,* T. L. Philpott writes: "The men who directed the staff's research and drafted the text of *The Negro in Chicago* were . . . Graham Romeyn Taylor, a social worker and a respected analyst of urban problems, and Charles S. Johnson, the pioneer black sociologist. . . . So free is the volume of overt anti-Negro bias that some historians believe it to be not a collaboration but 'Johnson's work'" (211).[12] However, Philpott points out that "*The Negro in Chicago* is not the book that Charles S. Johnson would have written on his own, but his scholarship informed the text and made it a sociological classic," adding further that "Johnson educated and influenced his collaborator Taylor and the white commissioners, and he strengthened the black commissioners in their effort to wrest every concession they could from their white counterparts" (228).

Like Du Bois's *Philadelphia Negro* and Haynes's *Negro Newcomers in Detroit,* Johnson's study indicates the kinds of ideological compromises necessary for the black professional sociologist if he is to gain work, accrue a reputation, and enact his brand of New Negro reform of the race and of himself. Johnson's contribution in *The Negro in Chicago* goes further along this path because of its bureaucratic process and collaborative scientific nature. Given the circumstances of Johnson's report—working under Taylor and directly for a commission whose white members ultimately dominated the report's objectives—the question of cool concerns the pressure to become a good team player while rubbing shoulders with white patrons and coworkers when one's own power is less than equal.[13] In addition to Johnson's being directly accountable to Taylor and the white commissioners, the commission itself operated on a shoestring budget that makes the attached patronage strings very apparent. According to Martin Bulmer, even though the commission was appointed by the governor of Illinois, no state support was forthcoming, and the commission had to rely on loans from Rosenwald. "These financial problems, as well as the orientation of its members, pushed the commission to adopt a more academic approach," Bulmer writes, "rather than a political one, to the problems of race relations in the city" ("Charles S. Johnson" 292).

Actually, the "academic" approach—Chicago sociology—is "political," if by this we mean advocating a particular ideological stance with consequences to structural power, social organization, institutions of governance, and economic opportunities. In the more narrow sense of the political—attention to local and state political institutions and politicians—*The Negro in Chicago* is revealingly silent.[14] The sociological nature of the project, its scientific or academic rather than political objective, helps enforce the subordination of the African American voices—of the black commissioners and interviewees, as well as Johnson's—despite the focus on ethnographic observation, demographic mapping, interviews, and case studies promoted in Chicago method. Just as any dispute that Johnson might harbor with the outcome of the research must be self-filtered in order for him to cooperate with his white colleagues and sponsors, so part of his job has to be to filter any material in the interviews that seems to oppose the final objectives of the report. A report aimed at bringing about racial reconciliation can hardly focus on airing black resentment, vengefulness, and animosity among those directly and indirectly hurt by the riots and, more generally, by residential segregation and racism.

Johnson quickly gained an accommodating reputation, similar to Washington's. According to Meier, Johnson even liked to think of himself as "the most powerful Negro in America," a phrase borrowed from Washington. His capacity for "detachment" is what gave Johnson his influence as a sociologist and a patron. As late as 1981, Bulmer is still celebrating Johnson's "detachment":

> The lasting value of the report lies not in its white reform orientation, which is long *passé*, but in its demonstration of the relevance of social science to policy issues. This was achieved not only by comprehensive inquiry and empirical documentation, much of it novel by standards of social science at that time, but also by a very high degree of scientific detachment from the emotional subject-matter it was dealing with. Both Johnson and Park developed this detachment to a very high degree.[15]

Contrary to Bulmer's attempt to separate scientific detachment from white patronage and racial compromises, the two are inextricable. Johnson's mastery of this detached demeanor must be based on his willingness to subordinate his own voice and agenda—whatever they may be—to the demands of biracial "cooperation" and academic teamwork in the scientific vein. Ironically, this demeanor does not come without other sorts of controversy. "His colored friends scold him for being a calm student rather than a rabid reformer. White people get mad at his presumption in understanding them and their customs better than they do themselves."[16] In other words, like Du Bois's and Haynes's passionate outbursts in the midst of studied neutral prose, Johnson's cool detachment comes back round to a less apparent form of racial trespassing. His mastery of himself to present an "objective" picture of the riots (in which many more African Americans were killed and harmed than whites) presupposes his sociological mastery of white society as well. Concerning the erasure of race in the body of the report, Waskow comments that "the writing is so effectively detached that neither a Negro nor a white seems to be writing (and in a sense this was the case, since the writing was done by Negroes and whites in close collaboration)."[17] Instead of representing himself as leading the charge into white territory, as Wells and Pickens do in their autobiographies, Johnson tiptoes into that contested space of power by masking his self-will and historical-political agency from the process and product resulting in *The Negro in Chicago*.

In the final analysis, the absence of a racial identification in *The Negro in Chicago* is no more a guarantee of "objectivity" than its presence would necessarily be. In this case, the apparent racelessness of the report obscures the ways in which the leading commissioners were ideologically committed to an agenda of noninterference in both capitalist affairs (even though job and real estate discrimination were clearly causes of the uprisings) and governmental affairs (even though police negligence and harassment were also a concern). Although it was not until later that Johnson's crucial role in *The Negro in Chicago* was fully credited, his work on the report helped him secure soon thereafter the position of educational secretary at the New York headquarters of the Urban League, where he became the editor of *Opportunity*, the organization's magazine, and thus a major patron in the New Negro Renaissance.

Amid a massive pile of statistical analyses, surveys, interviews, archival research, case histories, empiricist generalizations, and passive bureaucratic language, *The Negro in Chicago* affirms the familiar and familial compulsions that determine modern normality: "The normal family is generally recognized as consisting of five per-sons—two parents and three children. Properly they should make up a single group and live by themselves. The 274 families studied were chosen as follows. . . . " (154). In this kind of empiricist sociology, the norm silently slips from indicating a prac-tice engaged in by a numerical majority of individuals, and thus verifiable by sta-tistics, to mean that which is "proper" morally and socially—a subjective matter that can never be gleaned from empirical method, no matter how neutral it seems to be. In New Negro sociology, an anxiety develops especially around "unattached" individuals, who, as we have seen in Du Bois and Haynes, are represented as cru-cial destabilizing figures in the movement toward African American adjustment to the norm. In their classic 1945 study of Chicago, St. Clair Drake and Horace H. Cay-ton, for instance, lament the "notorious and widespread wandering" that they point out results from "primarily a search for better or supplementary jobs." Such roving creates a problem because it keeps "normal" families from being organized. "The roving of masses of Negro men has been an important factor during the eighty years since slavery, in preventing the formation of stable, conventional, family units. It has shifted the responsibility for the maintenance of household units to the women of the lower class" (*Black Metropolis* 583). Contrary to the role of mobility in New Negro trespassing narratives, in male New Negro sociological discourse the mobility of individual men (and sometimes women, depending on the particular anxiety being expressed) becomes a threat to the sociological project of counting bodies and normalizing ways of life. The constant shifting back and forth between South and North, between city and city, is represented as abnormal and self-destructive rather than as a pragmatic subversion of the Jim Crow and sharecropping regimes, in which the curtailment of black people's movement em-powered the white political, police, and plantation establishment. Likewise, in *The Negro in Chicago* these roving individuals not only fail to create normative families themselves but also jeopardize potentially normal families by interjecting them-selves into them. "[T]he migration brought to the city many unattached men and women who could find no other place to live except in families," Johnson writes. "Not only do lodgers constitute a social problem for the family, but, having little or no interest in the appearance and condition of the property, they are in many instances careless and irresponsible and contribute to the rapid deterioration of the buildings" (158).

The Chicago sociologists carry forth the Bookerite notion of the proof of the senses, as they tabulate in minutest detail such matters as the percentage of indi-viduals observed in "normal" families, the size and conditions of houses, whether homes are owned or rented, the conditions of hygiene among laborers, and the lit-eral proximity of black and white families. The ideological implications of these standards of measurement are lost in their role as scientific techniques. Because of the vulnerable status of more recent European immigrants and the confusion con-cerning their racial status in relation to native-born Anglo-Americans, comparative analysis also plays a large role in these studies. The object of study almost as much as African Americans, the immigrant ghettos serve for the black sociologists to remind white patrons of the potential for Negro assimilation. Thus, this comparative commentary also provides opportunities for countering the notion of racial inferiority as an explanation for circumstantial differences in populations.

> The fact that in the main Chicago Negroes live in more rooms per dwelling than immigrants, whose standard of living has not yet risen, does not necessarily mean that the Negroes have a greater appreciation of a house with more rooms. The explanation in many cases is that the Negroes take whatever living quarters happen to be available, which often are large residences abandoned by well-to-do whites, and then adapt their mode of living to the circumstances. (*Negro in Chicago* 161)

As race is used as a marker for all measurements, it becomes a reliable gauge for sociological truth about the status of all individuals identified with the group; but as it is constantly contested by the inability of such measurements to provide an accurate "explanation in many cases," it is undermined as a reliable gauge.

Park's idea of race contacts becomes a central aspect of measuring the level of the race's adjustment to civilization. Chapter 6 of *The Negro in Chicago* surveys every imaginable space in which encounters between the races can occur, from the interracial cabarets of Bronzeville to the high-culture institutions of the downtown Loop. The black sociologist must be cognizant of the smallest detail operating to stall a progressive image of the race from the viewpoint of dominant culture. By observing relationships in these public and private spaces, the riot commissioners are able to rationalize behaviors that otherwise would remain merely a matter of racial assumption and prejudice, and thus to present a case for overcoming white fears of black invasion. Their description of the contacts on public transportation is an especially apt example of this. "[C]ontacts of Negroes and whites on street cars provoked little discussion until the migration of Negroes from the South began to be felt," the commissioners write. "The great majority of the migrants are laborers. Many of them are ignorant and rough mannered, entirely unfamiliar with standards of conduct in northern cities" (301). When the commissioners explain the tendency of some African Americans to "sit all over the car" as resulting from a lack of adjustment to an urban environment outside Jim Crow, they also explain away much of the racial animosity operating among whites and blacks in their discomfort with these "noisy" migrants. "Few white people realized how uncertain the southern Negro felt about making use of his new privilege of sitting anywhere in the car, instead of being 'Jim Crowed'" (301). Instead of an aggressive act of Negro invasion, the behavior of both blacks and whites becomes unintentional, a result of ignorance that can be rectified with the accurate knowledge provided by the sociologist's observations. Even as it relies heavily on the crude senses of sight, sound, smell, and touch, the study must pretend *not* to be about such sensuous experiences but instead about the statistically hard numbers of an empirically verifiable science.

Like Washington, Johnson picks up on matters of hygiene as one way of reducing an objectionable sight/smell/sound/touch of the race as aggressively encroaching on white people. "Soiled and ill-smelling clothes were a large factor in making Negro workingmen objectionable to many whites even of the same working class" (303). Johnson points out that black male workers, because they live farther away from the factories and stockyards and have no access to baths, must take public transportation in their smelly work clothes and bodies. Providing ample evidence from the Negro press that sophisticated members of the race are as aware of the problem as white riders, he demonstrates the capacity of race leaders to discipline themselves: "The Negro press of Chicago tried to make the migration Negro realize how the odor attaching to his clothes was affecting public opinion" (304).[18] Note here how the report emphasizes the smell of the black male worker's *clothes*, not his person. Beneath the white commuters' complaint must be a notion, however, that the sweat from black male bodies smells different from that from white bodies. By emphasizing that the complaints come from whites who are "even of the same working class," the report slyly reminds its readers that white working-class bodies smell the same way and for the same reason, and that complaints against black commuters must have a rational explanation beyond the irrational bigotry that projects a different odor onto black bodies, whether sweaty or not.

Johnson's narrative of these incidents of race contacts, despite the horrors of the 1919 riot, displays an unceasing optimism about the future of the urbanized race. The capacity for maintaining such optimism depends implicitly on the notion that social science can detect, explain, and remedy the migrants' missteps, rather than on the reality of whites' mistaken prejudices about the race. It is evidently easier to set up a program for reforming black male workers' misbehavior than it is to change white people's beliefs about—and putative sense experiences of—black bodies.

> Most of the difficulties in transportation contacts reported and generally complained of seem to have centered around the first blundering efforts of migrants to adjust themselves to northern city life. The efforts of agencies interested in assisting this adjustment, together with the Negro press, and the intimate criticisms and suggestion for proper conduct of Chicago Negroes, have smoothed down many of the roughnesses of the migrants, and as a result friction from contact in transportation seems to have lessened materially. (309)

As we saw with the cool New Negro narrators from the previous chapter, public transportation has represented historically to African Americans the front line of the race war—and a way of powerfully imaging race relations as a war in which the color line embodies the front line of battle. As Robin D. G. Kelley has suggested, concerning skirmishes between blacks and whites on buses in Birmingham between the wars, "loud talking," sitting all over the car, and invading white space represent intentional forms of racial resistance.[19] The numerous streetcar encounters recorded in *The Negro in Chicago* could easily be viewed as similar modes of racial trespassing and aggression, even if only subliminal on the part of migrants eager to test their new-won freedoms in the big city. The commission's tendency to explain such trespassing behavior in terms of nervousness, roughness, ignorance, and lack of adjustment to modernity indicates the ideological invest-ment of its methods in the notion of the race's backwardness and its need of as-similation to the urban North's more civilized culture.

The logic that always lurks behind the notion of race contacts involves an anx-iety over interracial sex as a deviant practice according to dominant values. Given that interracial sex had been legalized in Chicago at the time of the study, cases of what the report calls "accidental contact" (308) had the potential to turn into more intimate and intentional contacts, even between respectable individuals. Because the final objective of Chicago sociology was the socioeconomic assimilation of African Americans into normative United States life, the taboo surrounding inti-mate race contacts always threatened to jeopardize peaceful (nonsexual) interracial bonding. Consequently, these studies tend to focus on the improper cross-racial in-timacy that goes on in red-light districts and tenderloins as a counterimage to proper assimilation. Because these unrespectable spaces of intimate race contact are normally situated within the Black Belts of northern cities, they are also seen as shedding an unfair shadow over the race as a whole. Johnson attempts to untan-gle these unrespectable, deviantly sexualized places associated with interracial cou-pling from a morally respectable interracial intimacy beyond the underworld vice dens:

> The habitués of these resorts are usually an irresponsible type of pleasure seekers, and frequently they are vicious and immoral. Newspapers and several of the civic agencies have violently criticized these places as a menace, but in their attacks the emphasis has usually been shifted from the menace to morals to that of arousing sentiment against the mingling of races. (323)

To separate these taboo places from the taboo of mixed coupling would be a step in clarifying how they constitute a danger to "morals and established law and order, and a nuisance to the neighborhoods in which they are located" (323). The need to purify Negro communities of these "black and tan resorts" is equated with the need to cleanse African American families from all deviations from the United States norm.

Johnson's accommodation through "objective," collaborative sociology results, ironically, in a voice even more muted than Washington's accommodationist mode. Washington's strategic embrace of segregation enables him a great deal of gender fluidity, propagandizing of an individualized personality, and under-the-table maneuvering within the rhetorical and activist constraints put in place by Jim Crow. Compared to Johnson, Washington does not look like much of an "organi-zation man" after all. Johnson loses all three tactical possibilities in his commission participation. He ends up with the shared authority of a scientist and organization man, but without the public authority of either a compelling personality beyond the commission or the benefit of a compelling capacity for public dissent (which we shall see Frazier retaining) within the constraints of the commission and its report. Hence, it should not be surprising that in the more recent reception of Johnson's work and career in black sociological theory since the 1970s, there is a need to defend Johnson against charges of his being indirect, evasive, timid, and passive. Richard Robbins tries to make the case in favor of Johnson in the midst of this move toward radical sociology: "This 'indirection' did not spring from any kind of timidity," he argues, "but from disciplined belief, from conviction. When a time came for advocacy, Johnson did not hold back. He was the sole Negro college president to come publicly to the defense of Du Bois in 1951" ("Charles S. Johnson" 63–64). The same charge of a sort of unmanly cowardice that has accompanied Washington's legacy haunts Johnson's reputation, such that apologists must seek to distance him from its aura.[20]

The defense applied to Johnson could be, and has been, used in trying to contextualize and resuscitate the image of Washington as well. Public accusations of unmanliness have been thrown sporadically at the most highly visible black male writers—including Washington, Du Bois, Trotter, Pickens, White, and Locke—even though these men took care to delineate radically different approaches to the role of manhood reform in race uplift. There is no certain shield against such a charge, given that making the charge itself operates in, and indeed helps constitute, racial discourse as a way of competing within, attacking, and policing the parameters of black manhood in interpreting the past and struggling for an empowered future. In other words, the task of reforming the race necessarily involves a question of individual black men's capacity for manly leadership, a question that quickly leads to suspicion, innuendo, and accusation concerning the virility of rival men. As racial intermediaries, black male sociologists of the Jim Crow era are especially vulnerable to the charge of an emasculating compromise. In contrast to Pickens's self-promotion as a hard-hitting, highly mobile subject, the black male sociologist must nurture an image of masculine self-restraint, submission to scientific protocol, and the submergence of manly individualism to larger institutional and bureaucratic demands.

Johnson's assimilative approach is not limited to his collaboration on the Chicago riots report, but at least we get to hear one of his voices when he begins to publish under his own name. When he takes over *Opportunity* and rises as a New Negro patron in New York, he continues to express a cautious, conservative, humanist point of view even in matters of artistic culture. His most visible product of these New Negro Renaissance years is perhaps *Ebony and Topaz: A Collectanea*, published in 1927, a rival to Locke's *New Negro*. Comparing this volume briefly with Locke's, we can gain a better sense of how Johnson situates himself as a reformed black man deserving of leadership in the reform of other men. A biracial collection of poetry, fiction, sociology, and artwork, the format of *Ebony and Topaz* looks very similar to *The New Negro,* with one crucial exception: whereas Locke spotlights his own contributions through various introductory essays, Johnson limits his presence to a three-page introduction.

The first paragraph of the introduction clears the ground by insisting on a lack of any political, ideological, or theoretical purpose:

> It is only fair to rid this volume, at the beginning, of some of the usual pretensions, which have the effect of distorting normal values, most often with results as unfortunate as they are unfair. This volume, strangely enough, does not set forth to prove a thesis, nor to plead a cause, nor, stranger still, to offer a progress report on the state of Negro letters. It is a venture in expression, shared, with the slightest editorial suggestion, by a number of persons who are here much less interested in their audience than in what they are trying to say, and the life they are trying to portray. This measurable freedom from the usual burden of proof has been an aid to spontaneity, and to this quality the collection makes its most serious claim. (*Ebony and Topaz* 11)

Johnson's cautious humanism makes Locke's theorizing look downright politically radical. The "slightest editorial suggestion" implicitly serves as a critique of Locke's more fulsome theoretical systematizing in the earlier anthology, with its "usual pretensions." Johnson's appeal to "spontaneity," "expression," "freedom," and lack of attention to audience situates him in a long tradition of romantic ideology, in which the romance itself enjoins spontaneous expression as a freedom *from* ideology. There is no "burden of proof" or pressure to "plead a cause" or report on the progress of the New Negro. As such, even the general political frame of Locke's call for African American solidarity and cultural revisioning becomes a burden too heavy to place on the shoulders of budding artists and scholars in search of spontaneous self-expression. But Johnson quickly contradicts—and thus reveals—himself in the very next paragraph, as he addresses the very audiences about which he says his contributors should not be concerned: "It is not improbable that some of our white readers will arch their brows or perhaps knit them soberly at some point before the end. But this is a response not infrequently met with outside the pages of books" (11). Johnson's introduction is also aimed against Du Bois's attempt to discourage low images of the Negro: "Some of our Negro readers will doubtless quarrel with certain of the Negro characters who move in these pages. But it is also true that in life some Negroes are distasteful to other Negroes" (11).

Johnson's assimilative ideology still grounds this romantic appeal to real life as an unarticulated standard for art. On the surface, this looks similar to Locke's demand for exploring the variety of African American life, and there is certainly some overlap. Locke's demand is based in a difference that consolidates for the purpose of group uplift; as Houston Baker suggests in *Modernism and the Harlem Renaissance,* there is a nationalist program beneath his theorizing. Johnson, by contrast, expresses a primary interest in differentiation within the group in order to assimilate to bourgeois white norms. In the very first sentence, he displays his concern for the "effect of distorting normal values." The normalizing function of his volume is carried out ironically through the same sort of art that Locke wants to see as iconoclastic, blasting through encrusted racial norms:

> Following the familiar patterns, we are accustomed to think of Negroes as one ethnic unit, and of whites as many,—the Nordics, Mediterraneans; or Germans, Irish, Swedes; or brachycephalics and dolichocephalics, depending upon our school of politics or anthropology. The significance of the difference is not so much that Negroes in America actually represent different races among themselves, as that there is the same ground, in dissimilar customs and culture patterns, which are the really valid distinctions between the races, for viewing Negroes differently among themselves. (11)

Johnson brings attention to the arbitrariness of racial constructions by pointing to the conflicting ways of categorizing whiteness in geography, ethnology, and measurement of skull, yet without articulating the solidity of whiteness as a political category of racial supremacy. Whites *are* one race when it matters to those who support the racist system. Neither proliferation of races in whiteness nor in blackness can unbalance the color line of racial difference. That line exists not because people cannot see differences among the groups but because these differences are authorized as normative categories in the first place. Johnson cannot solve the race problem by trying to make black variation look just like white variation, because variation within groups does not, in the end, dissolve dissimilarities across the divide, dissimilarities normalized as racial difference. Thus, unlike Locke, he misses the vital link between artistic variety and racial consolidation as a necessary, perhaps temporary, political strategy for even the most aesthetically inclined New Negro project.

I do not want to overemphasize the differences Johnson creates to supercede Locke as a newer or anti–New Negro. He borrows from Locke as much as he spars with him. This is especially the case where Johnson spotlights "self-criticism" as a crucial part of progressive movement:

> The Negro writers, removed by two generations from slavery, are now much less self-conscious, less interested in proving that they are just like white people, and, in their excursions into the fields of letters and art, seem to care less about what white people think, or are likely to think about the race. Relief from the stifling consciousness of being a problem has brought a certain superiority to it. There is more candor, even in discussion of themselves, about weaknesses, and on the very sound reasoning that unless they are truthful about their faults, they will not be believed when they choose to speak about their virtues. A sense of humor is present. The taboos and racial ritual are less strict; there is more overt self-criticism, less of bitterness and appeals to sympathy. The sensitiveness, which a brief

decade ago, denied the existence of any but educated Negroes, bitterly opposing Negro dialect, folk songs, and anything that revived the memory of slavery, is shading off into a sensitiveness to the hidden beauties of this life and a frank joy and pride in it. The return of the Negro writers to folk materials has proved a new emancipation. (12)

This passage could have come straight out of Locke. And so we find that Johnson is an emancipated New Negro, despite himself. Johnson's focus on candor, self-criticism, and humor indicate to what extent he is concerned about what white readers, critics, and reformers say, for one of their major accusations, as we see in chapter 4, concerns the supposed oversensitivity of the educated Negro. By describing this shared agenda that he culls from the contributions, Johnson falls away from the claim to sheer spontaneity, expression, variation, and freedom, but he returns to it as he moves toward conclusion. "Those seeking set patterns of Negro literature will in all likelihood be disappointed for there is no set pattern of Negro life," he repeats toward the end. "If there is anything implicit in the attitude toward life revealing itself, it is acceptance of the fact of race and difference on the same casual gesture that denies that the difference means anything" (13). Although this is a fanciful statement for a noted sociologist to be making, it refreshingly reaffirms the duplicity in Johnson's voice. Johnson's sociological works—and those by others selected in the volume—assume a set, organized pattern for Negro life. As we have seen with the other New Negro sociologists, however, the code of sociological discourse may demand that he speak one way as he searches out that pattern, but speaking outside or between the lines of that discourse, he must always tell a slightly different story.

Unlike Johnson, E. Franklin Frazier (1894–1962), almost Johnson's exact contemporary, is accused of overstepping the racial boundaries, including his positions at Tuskegee, the Atlanta School of Social Work (where he was director from 1922 to 1927), Fisk University (under Johnson, with whom he had a difficult relationship), in the commission on the Harlem Riot of 1935, and at Howard University.[21] If for Johnson the authority lay in the compromise that brought practical influence, for E. Franklin Frazier it lay in the ability to be direct and uncompromised, in whatever medium.[22] Frazier deployed a hot tone alongside his sociologically neutral one throughout his career, whether as a student at Howard, a social work administrator, a graduate student at Chicago, or the director of a riot commission. Unlike Johnson and to a greater extent than even Du Bois, Frazier wrestled with his own sociological protocols by raising his voice to an angry pitch in those critical moments when sociology failed, or more precisely, when he wanted to make the limits of the sociological compact self-evident. By raising his voice, by writing controversially—provocatively even—Frazier insisted that sociology is only one tone among many, one mode of truth among competing discourses. In "The Pathology of Race Prejudice" (1927), he argued that the kind of race prejudice familiar in the South constituted a pathology that needed a cure. The essay stirred up the Atlanta newspapers and ultimately prompted a threat of mob violence against him. In 1935, he published a caustic essay, "The Du Bois Program in the Present Crisis," for the first issue of the journal *Race,* in which he attacked Du Bois for being "an aristocrat in bearing and in sympathies": "He has only an occasional romantic interest in the Negro as a distinct race. Nothing would be more unendurable for him than to live within a Black Ghetto or within a black nation—unless perhaps he were king, and then probably he would attempt to unite the whites and blacks through marriage of the royal families" (12–13). The year before he died, he published in *Negro Digest* an essay titled "The Failure of the Negro Intellectual," a tirade against the conformity of African American intellectuals that ends with a prophetic warning: "It may turn out that in the distant future Negroes will disappear physically from American society. If this is our fate, let us disappear with dignity and let us leave a worthwhile memorial—in science, in art, in literature, in sculpture, in music—of our having been here" (36). It is the submission to sociology's stake in assimilation while refusing to be tamed by sociological rationalism that characterizes Frazier's identity as a male sociologist in particular and as a New Negro more generally.

With the publication of his family-life studies in the 1930s, Frazier became the most influential African American sociologist; he was elected in 1948 as the first black president of the American Sociological Association. Like Johnson, Frazier was born in the South, educated at first at a black college (Howard), then at northern white institutions (Clark University in Massachusetts and the University of Chicago). But Frazier never achieved quite the status ease of Johnson, who quickly found his niche in the National Urban League, then as chair of sociology at Fisk and later president of the university. In his institutional roles at the Urban League and then at Fisk (which at the time was one of the most heavily endowed black colleges), Johnson wielded the sort of social and financial access and patronage influence that neither Du Bois nor Frazier ever achieved, for the latter men lacked the racial tact and willingness to become the kind of "organization men"—to borrow from Houston Baker's analysis (*Long Black Song* 92–94)—that Washington had made the hallmark of black male leadership at the beginning of the century. Despite Frazier's rise to eminence among the most respected sociologists in the country, during his career he never had easy access to research funding, leave time, and other forms of institutional support enabled by intense interest of wealthy private foundations in the Negro problem. In *E. Franklin Frazier Reconsidered,* Anthony M. Platt makes a persuasive case for Frazier's ambivalent relationship to the academic and social work institutions on which he depended for an income. (A similar ambivalence emerges in his marriage: though an ardent feminist, Frazier did not want his wife, who came from the colored elite and was herself formally educated, to work outside the home.) When teaching at Tuskegee, Frazier took a bale of hay into the classroom as a visual satire on the institution's industrial focus. At the Atlanta School of Social Work, where in his capacity as director he had the delicate task of supervising a white woman, he battled against the South's racial strictures and ended in controversy for his stance and his writing. After graduate work at Chicago, he went to Fisk, where again he ended up challenging Johnson and Jim Crow. Even if Platt's biography has an investment in revising the institutional view of Frazier so that he looks more similar to Du Bois, we can see the validity of Platt's picture in Frazier's writing itself.

Although Frazier's polemical essays in journals such as *Opportunity* and *Race* are usually segregated from his academic sociological writing, when we view the two in relation to each other and in the context of Frazier's New Negro reform inheritance, we can begin to understand better the interrelations between New Negro polemics and New Negro male sociology.[23] Although Frazier showed interest in imaginative literature—he focused on classical liberal arts at Howard and wrote fiction—his intellectual tendencies seem almost the obverse of Locke's desire to piece together an objective portrait of the Negro through aesthetic media. In many ways, Frazier seems like an incongruous personality for a conviction in objectivity, but in a sense, his resorting to sociology represents as much a resistance to objectivity as giving in to its seductive power. Like Locke, Frazier sees his sociology as one piece of a story, and aware that the other, less "objective" pieces are not separate, he allows them to peep through the deliberate, calm, neutral prose of his sociological writing. In some works, such as *The Black Bourgeoisie,* he seems to combine satire and sociology so seamlessly that scholars still argue about the book's authentic classification. In other words, Frazier is the consummate New Negro sociologist. He borrows sociology—the most authoritative sociology of the time—to credential himself and writes confidently, as though sociology as a field scientifically secures his own insider status; otherwise, he would not feel secure enough occasionally to slice through the discourse with the sharp edge of his tongue. When he writes as a polemicist on New Negroes themselves (the urban, educated elite of which he becomes a member), he poses as an outsider trespassing, like a white (or alienated black) sociologist viewing the African American ghetto.

Nowhere is the contrast between Frazier and Johnson so stark as in the fates of their respective riot reports. Frazier's report on the 1935 Harlem uprising, titled "The Negro in Harlem," was never officially published, and though there are a handful of sociological analyses of the report, it has not gone down in history as one of the seminal sociological texts. As a defiant gesture to Mayor F. H. LaGuardia, who commissioned the report but refused to publish it, the *Amsterdam News,* Harlem's most popular black newspaper, published it in full for the 18 July 1936 issue. The newspaper's response to the report is the best evidence of its radical nature. The report itself veers away from accepted sociological protocols, taking sides with the black community, calling the white police camped in Harlem the "enemy," and urging that specific governmental actions be taken to correct the problems. In other words, the "riot" committee, composed of eminent African Americans and whites from the community, took the report as an occasion to set the record straight on discrimination, health, jobs, housing, crime, police brutality, and all the ills brought on not by the African American residents but by racial oppression.[24]

The banner, front-page headline for the *Amsterdam News* issue is "COMPLETE RIOT REPORT BARED." In the middle column of the front page, the editors target the fact that this is the first time the complete report is available to the public:

> More than the complete report, the Amsterdam News is here making public for the first time the original chapter of conclusions—Chapter IX—which was considered too hot, too caustic, too critical, too unfavorable by the Mayor, and was allegedly revamped by the commission to make it more to his liking. The Chapter Nine in the official report in the Mayor's hands is the softer, less biting chapter. ("Complete Riot Report Bared" 1, 6)

The editors point out that "the findings of the Commission will be found to be nothing new—no facts that Harlemites and New Yorkers have not known, or could not have known long before the riots of March 19" (6). However, "these conditions are reviewed and uttered by a commission having the sanction of the head of the City government, and conclusions are made not only by the social workers and reformers, but by the 'salt of the earth,' the man in the street, the men and women who feel most the rigors of starvation; the spiked heels of the police, and the crushing load of high rents and discrimination in employment most" (6). Although the newspaper's prose is more purple than the report's, its description of the report's findings and point of view is accurate.

Frazier used the academic structure of Chicago sociology to determine the causes of the uprisings—the type of effort pioneered by Johnson's *The Negro in Chicago*—but he exploited that structure differently. The "salt of the earth" become not native informants to be studied so that reformers can find out what's wrong with them but complainants presenting their case to the mayor and the city. After a brief history of the uprisings (chapter 1) and a description of the hearings held (chapter 2), chapter 3 details "The Negro Community in Harlem," the obligatory "ecological" approach of providing social-historical, demographic, economic, and geographic context. Instead of assuming a supposedly neutral point of view—more precisely, the point of view of the white governance and business reform leaders— the report takes on the voice of the oppressed. For instance, in discussing job discrimination in public utilities, the report reads, under the subheading "Utilities' Reasons Only Rationalization":

> The reasons offered by the officials of the public utilities are on the whole merely rationalizations of policies and practices which have no basis in reason or fact. Undoubtedly, tradition and custom have played a part in the almost total exclusions of the Negro from all but the most menial positions. But in a large cosmopolitan community like New York City where all races of the globe are engaged in

its competitive life, custom and tradition do not present insuperable obstacles to the employment of Negroes as they would in a small community.

Negroes, contrary to traditional and customary ideas regarding their economic status, occupy positions of authority requiring intelligence and character in federal, state and municipal agencies. What peculiar circumstances, one may ask, exist in the public utilities which make it necessary to exclude the Negro or keep him in menial jobs? (Frazier, "Negro in Harlem" 7)

The question tagging this series of charges verges on the sardonic, a tone to which Frazier is partial in his polemical essays. While Frazier uses the conventional techniques to gather data for the report, again he turns the technique against "objectivity" as a matter of not taking sides. The report validates the concerns of the Harlemites as though the job of the commission is to voice those concerns; the logic of the people becomes the logic of the report. For instance, connecting the lack of jobs to the uprising, the report, after discussing groups of workers who have spoken during the hearings, concludes: "The outburst on March 19 expressed the pent-up resentment of the Negro against exclusion from all but the most menial jobs in the establishments which he supported to a large extent" (7). One of the most incendiary aspects of the report entails the recommendations for how to handle and discipline the police, including a recommendation for a biracial citizens' committee to which African Americans can directly make complaints of police harassment and brutality. The excited and supportive response of the *Amsterdam News* to the report indicates to what extent it addressed the concerns of the community without fear of reprisals from the white power structure. What in conventional social-science terms may look like slanted invective the report takes as simple, direct truth telling, thus pointing up the limited conceptualization of conventional sociological truth as the primary effect of absolute neutrality.

Frazier received no professional advancement for directing this report, but in printing photographs of the chairman of the commission, the secretary, and Frazier as director (all three African American), the *Amsterdam News* clearly desires to laud the commissioners for their forthrightness. By turning academic sociology into a tool of and for black people's protest, Frazier turns the black male sociologist's role of muted mediator into a weapon of racial self-empowerment. His photograph encased within the report indicates a different political relationship to African American community from the anonymity of Johnson's role, and likewise a more aggressive gender relationship to white authorities. Frazier becomes a "race man," a black male leader who has stood up to the white power structure and has stood by the assaulted black masses in order to man the front line of the race war.

Frazier's report on the 1935 Harlem riot displays the sociologist's blending of science and polemics in the most blatant terms. The report trespasses the line separating them so systematically that, in effect, Frazier insists there is no theoretical or methodological contradiction between them. The conduct of New Negro trespassing in his Negro family studies—more conventionally academic and scientific—is subtler. There Frazier takes the logic of sociological causation as far as it can go. For Frazier, African American culture is engaged historically in a struggle between the anarchy spreading from an unregulated sexual impulse and the order provided by conformity to the sexual norm of respectable United States family life. This struggle was initiated when captives were first brought to colonies and relegated to the status of property. In *The Negro Family in the United States,* Frazier writes: "When the sexual impulses of the males were no longer controlled by African customs and mores, they became subject only to the periodic urge of sexual hunger. Under such circumstances the males, as is generally true, seized upon the woman who happened to be at hand and with whom they had been thrown into closest contact" (26). This controversial idea that African Americans were robbed of all cultural values and practices upon being enslaved has the effect of turning the captives into the animals that white slavers and slaveholders insisted they already were. His theory relegates the captives—especially the men—to a cultural vacuum in which they are reduced to the most primitive biological and sexual urges. The only way of escaping this cultural vacuum is to adopt the normative sexual practices of the dominant race. Ironically, this drive to adopt the respectable behavior of the dominant race leads to a slavish, superficial mimicry of the worst aspects of white bourgeois life, especially among the small black middle class—a pattern that Frazier describes in chapter 20, "The Brown Middle Class," and that he castigates with merciless rigor in his 1957 book, *Black Bourgeoisie: The Rise of a New Middle Class.* These almost satirical swipes at the colored middle class reveal his deep disappointment in the group to which he himself belongs and, paradoxically, the highly subjective class analysis motivating the most celebrated black practitioner of the empiricist, ethnographic Chicago School.

Frazier's work nonetheless has been celebrated for its objectivity and technical mastery.[25] It is not his mastery of the disciplinary protocols that causes controversy over his work, but instead the conclusions he reaches. Frazier layers his conclusions so authoritatively within the contours of the protocols that his occasional sardonic flashes can be easily missed by a reader more attentive to substance than to tone and style. His roasting of the middle class reaches fever pitch in the brilliant final chapters of *Black Bourgeoisie.* Speaking of the vacuousness of the Negro press and its tendency toward "wish-fulfillment," Frazier zaps these professionals as a "mouthpiece" for the middle class: "From the stories which appear in *Ebony* it seems that rich Negroes are appearing faster than they are dying" (*Black Bourgeoisie* 186). We cannot miss the irony in his use of the term *mouthpiece* to describe the professional activity of black media, and cannot help wondering to what extent he wants to suppress any fear that his own activity resembles theirs, especially given his professional investment in normalizing the family structure of the black masses.

In chapter 9, "'Society': Status without Substance," Frazier reduces the middle class to a group whose understanding of their function derives from the misplaced mimicry of rich whites at leisure:

After emancipation they continued in the role of personal servants, and therefore saw the white man only in his home or when he was engaged in recreation. They never saw the white man at work in the shop or factory and when he engaged in the serious matter of business. As a consequence they devoted much time and much of their meager resources to attempting to carry on a form of "social" life similar to the whites'. (*Black Bourgeoisie* 203)

His indictment of the class can be characteristically summed up in one trenchant sentence: "Playing, then, has become the one activity which the Negro may take seriously" (205). The hint of irony and frustration underneath the scientific prose of his earlier family studies eddies up in full force in *Black Bourgeoisie*. This aggressive satire, interestingly, situates Frazier on the other side of the same coin that posits the male race leader as professional sociologist. The same authority that gives the sociologist his capacity to assess scientifically the condition of the race also gives him the right to judge the failure of the race, even when this means airing dirty laundry for all the world to see. The fact that the American Sociological Association awarded Frazier its most coveted prize for *Black Bourgeoisie* indicates to what extent the dominant race enjoyed inspecting that dirty laundry. In this last of his studies, he becomes the courageous solitary social crusader, willing to use his sword to cut through the "masks" of black social life, willing to risk antagonizing friends and associates within his own group, in order to bring sanity, productivity, and truth to a people whose lives, once they "attain middle-class status, . . . generally lose both content and significance" (238). By holding on to both, Frazier presents his own lone voice crying in the black wilderness as a model of productive, substantive, courageous race leadership.

Although Frazier saves the poison in his pen for his own social group, his frustration is hardly less evident in his discussion of other classes, their historical formation, and the history of the race as a whole. According to Frazier, if one polar extreme experienced in African American history and culture is slavish normality without substance, the other tends toward an anarchic deviance, expressed especially through the sexuality of the lower strata. This sexual deviance arises from recurring historical crises that in different ways cut off African Americans from normative United States life:

The mobility of the Negro population after emancipation was bound to create disorder and produce widespread demoralization. Thousands of Negroes flocked to the army camps where they created problems of discipline as well as of health. Some wandered about without any destination; others were attracted to the towns and cities. When the yoke of slavery was lifted, the drifting masses were left without any restraint upon their vagrant impulses and wild desires. The old intimacy between master and slave, upon which the moral order under the slave regime had rested, was destroyed forever. (*Negro Family in the United States* 96)

The transforming mobility of the race that is variously celebrated in the New Negro literature of Pickens, Wells, White, Locke, Gordon, and others becomes in Frazier a catastrophic phenomenon. Doubtless Frazier, with his proven sense of the ironic, recognizes the tragic paradox of attributing a "moral order" to the "slave regime," but he wants to emphasize the irony of disorder attending the mass migrations of the race in their quest for freedom. As blacks have to remake themselves at every turn of history, their mobility—both physical and social—inevitably creates "disorder," "widespread demoralization," and "problems of discipline." Their "vagrant impulses and wild desires" seem to mock their constant migrations, ending in a sort of moral/sexual vagrancy: "Promiscuous sexual relations and constant changing of spouses became the rule with the demoralized elements in the freed Negro population" (97).

Frazier's anarchic interpretation of the emancipation and Reconstruction moment, which in most New Negro thinking represents a high point in African American and United States history, downplays the myriad organizations and social movements embarked on by the freed people, such as their introduction of public education to the South. When Frazier does acknowledge successes, he tends to individualize them: "The success which attended the Negro's first efforts to get established as a free man depended, of course, to a large extent upon his character, intelligence, and efficiency, which in turn reflected his schooling during slavery" (101). This odd statement underestimates the capacity of the freed people to discipline and collectively to organize themselves without the "schooling" provided by external forces. Frazier goes so far as to attribute whatever stability and discipline he finds in African American communities to the presence of non-African blood.

> What, then, have been the contributions of those families of mixed blood that have fused with the Negro to the development of Negro family life? First among these contributions was their part in strengthening patriarchal traditions. In all these hybrid communities where it has been possible to trace family traditions, male progenitors were reported as the founders of the family lines. This was a natural consequence of the fact that these family lines were established in most instances by pioneer settlers. . . . The founders of these families migrated during the pioneer days of America across the mountains into the wilderness and there laid out communities. Consequently, these families have had a long history of industry and thrift and a sturdiness of character that differentiate them from the mass of the Negro population. (244)

Partaking of the myth of the West that we saw promulgated by Taylor Gordon, Frazier attempts to discriminate between "pioneer" migration into unsettled territory, which he sees as socially and sexually assimilative, and crowding mass migrations that tend to settle African Americans in established cities. The pioneer sort is positive because it is familial, more precisely patriarchal in character, whereas the urban mass migration promotes the mobility of unattached men and women, female-headed households, so-called extended families, and groups that cluster in unas-similated ghettos.[26]

The children of mixed-blood families, Frazier suggests, "generally exhibit the re-straint and self-discipline which have distinguished their forebears" (244–245). Their religion is "free from the extreme emotionalism of the Negro masses," and they "have often been regarded as queer by the general run of Negroes because they exhibited a firmness of character and a selfsufficiency unknown to their more pli-able and sociable Negro associates" (245). Relying on this idea of mixed blood, Fra-zier seems to confirm, against the grain of his environmental sociological ap-proach, the nineteenth-century notion that poverty results from inheritable char-acteristics of laziness, lack of intelligence, and licentiousness.[27] Frazier's hope for the black masses is that they will become disciplined by the industrial labor already familiar to the white proletariat (see 447–475). His focus on economic productiv-ity—whether as an intellectual or industrial capitalist value—assures that he will view the middle class as a moral, social, and economic wasteland and the Negro masses not yet engaged in industrial labor as an undisciplined, illegitimate under-class. It is only through an "adjustment" to the patriarchal norm that this situation of "poverty and cultural backwardness" (374) can be rectified.

Between the Lines of Drake and Cayton's *Black Metropolis*

In another classic Chicago sociology text, *Black Metropolis: A Study of Negro Life in a Northern City* (1945), by St. Clair Drake and Horace R. Cayton, the agenda of nor-malization is less prescriptively encoded, as the study keeps much closer to the pro-tocols of objectivity, neutrality, passive observation, and a stylistic monotone.[28] Drake and Cayton cleverly exploit the empiricist protocols of trained interviews and case studies in the attempt to reflect the points of view of the various levels of African American society, but this strategy also serves to screen where they them-selves are placed and what they believe. As a result of this screening process, they are able to present an amazingly coherent picture of the race as a group highly dif-ferentiated by class, political opinion, vocation, and mood, and yet also highly co-gent as a single, singular group. This masterful screening—I am tempted to call it a masking[29]—seems to cast the authors as disinterested observers, whereas they must have a personal stake in marshalling momentum for social, political, and economic reform.

In this passage taken from the chapter "The World of the Lower Class," the au-thors skillfully import vernacular language into their scientific discourse to give us a flavor of what they consider lower-class behavior:

Lower-class people will *publicly* drink and play cards in places where people of higher status would lose their "reputations"—in the rear of poolrooms, in the backrooms of taverns, in "buffet-flats," and sometimes on street corners and in alleys. They will "dance on the dime" and "grind" around the juke-box in taverns and joints, or "cut a tug" at the larger public dance halls. They will "clown" on a street corner or in public parks. It is this *public* behavior that outrages the sensibilities of Bronzeville's "dicties." "It gives The Race a bad name," they are quick to announce. (610)

As the writing slips into the language of the people and back and forth between lower- and upper-class phrases, we lose track of how it actually orients itself much more within the mental frame of the upper class. The first sentence is clearly expressed from the upper-class zone of experience, if not from their point of view, though it is an upper class talking privately among themselves. If we read between its lines, we understand that the upper class are not above playing cards and drinking *in private;* what galls them is that the lower class, not concerned about "reputation," do so flagrantly in public. *Reputation* is an upper-class word in this context, but by putting quotation marks around it, Drake and Cayton reaffirm their neutrality, on the one hand, by suggesting that neither their word nor their moral judgment is at stake. On the other hand, this use of quoted phrases gleaned from interviews obscures how the paragraph—and the study—defines the lower class relative to the upper class. This description of lower-class behavior as *too* public expresses the upper class's anxiety more than providing an explanation of why the lower class might take pleasure in such behavior, despite the berating of their superiors. The authors' subject orientation is further clarified by the fact that the chapter on the upper class concludes with excerpts "abstracted from a mass of interviews" concerning "the pattern of lower-class life as defined by the upper class" (559), which includes judgments from the mouths of the upper class: "full of slang about gates, cats, and other jive talk" (560); "family life very loose" (560); "dirty homes—dirty children—dirty people" (560); "immorality is one of the criteria of lower-class behavior" (560); "they are boisterous in public" (561); "orgies in the home" (561); "they are emotionally unstable" (562). Such assessments of the migrant mass could have been heard issuing from the mouths of the Chicago sociologists themselves. The two chapters on lower-class life contain no counterpart identifying how the lower class define the black upper class. Thus, when Drake and Cayton seem to move into the lower-class frame of mind by employing their "slang," they do not have the power to compensate for the class bias already set up. With use of the term *dicties* we come close to a lower-class point of view, but as all lower-class slang is likely to be used by the upper class privately among themselves, the term reveals as much about upper-class ambivalence as about lower-class observations of the elite.[30]

Expanding on Johnson's and Frazier's use of case histories, *Black Metropolis* creates illustrative narratives about individuals whose stories embody general trends within the race. In fact, Drake and Cayton use storytelling so deftly that some of the case histories read like plots from the sort of New Negro personal narratives examined in chapter 2. Drake and Cayton's chapter "Lower Class: Sex and Family" begins like a fictional story: "It was Christmas Eve, 1938. Dr. Maguire had just finished a hard day. Now for a highball, and then to bed. The doctor stepped back and admired the electric star at the top of the Christmas tree and the gifts neatly stacked beneath it" (564). The story that follows shares an uncanny resemblance to Walter White's characterization of Dr. Kenneth Harper's life and his relationship to his patients in *Fire in the Flint*. When Dr. Maguire is called away to attend a man who has been stabbed by his common-law wife in the slums, Drake and Cayton fictionalize his thoughts:

> For a moment, Dr. Maguire felt sick at his stomach. "Are these my people?" he thought. "What in the hell do I have in common with them? This is 'The Race' we're always spouting about being proud of." He had a little trick for getting back on an even keel when such doubts assailed him: he just let his mind run back over the "Uncle Tomming" he had to do when he was a Pullman porter; the turndown he got when he wanted to intern at the University of Chicago hospital; the letter from the American Medical Association rejecting his application for membership; the paper he wrote for a white doctor to read at a Mississippi medical conference which no Negroes could attend. Such thoughts always restored his sense of solidarity with "The Race." "Yeah, I'm just a nigger, too," he mumbled bitterly.
>
> Then he forgot everything—squalor, race prejudice, his own little tricks of psychological adjustment. He was a doctor treating a patient, swiftly, competently, and with composure. (566)

This fictionalized factual story of a Chicago doctor initiates the study of family and sex in the lower class. Its point is to contrast concretely Dr. Maguire's family life with the emotionality, instability, and lack of discipline in the lower class. Maguire occupies the conventional heroic position, and it is his professional competence especially that is figured as heroic. His commitment to the race indicates that he is a "race man," a "New Negro," as Drake and Cayton define these terms extensively in the final chapters. His wife, Sylvia, provides the support for this New Negro heroism: "She was that way, always ready to protect him and conserve his strength. What would he be without her?" Dr. Maguire wonders (565). The story contrasts Sylvia, who nags Maguire about not being paid by his lower-class patients, with her husband, and thus pits his idealistic race consciousness against her practical concern for the family's economic and social status in a way highly reminiscent of White's depiction of Dr. Harper and his fiancée, Jane Phillips.

The fantasy of Dr. Maguire's internal dialogue reveals more about Drake and Cayton than about the lower-class family and sex, as it focuses on the hardships of being a professional man under circumstances of racial oppression. When we move from Dr. Maguire's story to the story about the troubled lower-class couple whom he has come to see, we cannot attend to their dialogue without screening what they say through the viewpoint of Maguire and his story of professional frustration and racial heroism. This use of fiction disturbs Drake and Cayton enough that they feel compelled to provide a footnote at the bottom of the chapter's first page:

> This account of a doctor's Christmas experience is based on an actual incident witnessed by one of the authors, when he was a participant-observer in a group of lower-class households for six months, and on interviews with the physician involved and his wife. The principal characters' inner thoughts are obviously fictionalized. But the other quoted material in this chapter, as throughout the book, has been selected from interview-documents gathered by trained interviewers and has not been subjected to imaginative recasting. (564)

Taking the demands made in Chicago sociology to their logical conclusion, *Black Metropolis* surveys the innermost detail of African American life by binding the interview/case study to the daydream that cannot be monitored inside the head of the subject under surveillance. In the lingo of the people they study, the sociologists are doing what they suggest is habitual among all African Americans—"taking it out in talk":

> Negroes of all class levels have a habit of "taking it out in talk." If we examine the random comments, the unprompted conversations, the discussions and arguments, that go on among Bronzeville's lower class, we will find that they, no less than the more literate higher status groups, are not satisfied with things as they are. (718)

Black sociologists engage in this practice no less than their subjects, though in a more systematic and directed way. The discourse allows them to air the complaints, miseries, and injustices of African American life, even to place the blame with some claim to accuracy. "A newspaper headline, a radio comment, a chance remark or gesture, can convert a gambling den into a forum on the race problem, or a group of street-corner jitterbugs into a conspiracy of verbal revolt" (718). Like their objects of study, Drake and Clayton turn sociology into "a forum on the race problem." By providing an ecological understanding of race in its myriad contexts, then, the sociologists can also be understood to be operating as ceaselessly reforming New Negroes.

In a section titled "The New Negro Mentality," Drake and Cayton define—and implicitly argue for—a radical new way of race thinking that results from African Americans' engagement in the international politics developing from World War II:

> The change in the Negro's mentality came about so rapidly that few people, even Negroes, realized its extent. It often took the form of continued and intensified demands for better housing, better schools, and health programs. More

fundamentally, it was expressed in the Negro's refusal to accept segregation without complaint. . . . But underneath all this was the Negro's determination to become a full citizen, to plan and think for himself regardless of past friends and old
leaders. (763)

In such passages, the authors actually use their social science to codify what previous writers have been claiming through more subjective means: the arrival of a totally new Negro on the urban scene. Once the "change in the Negro's mentality"
is statistically tabulated and validated by social-scientific method, the phenomenon of the New Negro is no longer merely a matter of accommodation, protest politics, modernist aesthetics, or special pleading by race men and women. The subjects that Drake and Cayton describe so objectively are the authors themselves, the
New Negroes offering new policies in a more self-confident language. The assertion
of radical breakage from the past that Gates has identified as the New Negro phenomenon, then, can be seen as a hidden foundation of the science that claims an
objective knowledge of African American people. All the policies mentioned in the
above passage are at the heart of the analyses and policies put forward by the black
sociologists in a discourse where they can expertly "plan and think" for themselves. "In trying to assess the situation, white people did not realize that in measuring 'gains' for the Negro they were using an obsolete yardstick. At a time when
entire peoples were being liquidated or given equality over night, the theory of
'gradual gains' for Negroes had little meaning" (763). Like Du Bois's passionate plea
bursting through his prose at the end of *The Philadelphia Negro,* Drake and Cayton's
prose here almost breaks into advocacy, identifying them with the New Negro demands that they are describing as the latest phase of African American thought in
1945.

Black Metropolis's resort to "imaginative recasting" and near advocacy exemplifies how these sociological studies—despite their professional distancing maneuvers—are deeply entangled in the contradictions of masculine self-making that we
examined in the New Negro personal narratives. In *Black Bourgeoisie,* Frazier identifies a pattern in black middle-class men that we might apply to the sociologists
themselves:

These discriminations cause frustrations in Negro men because they are not allowed to play the "masculine role" as defined by American culture. They can not
assert themselves or exercise power as white men do. When they protest against
racial discrimination there is always the threat that they will be punished by the
white world. In spite of the movement toward the wider integration of the Negro
into the general stream of American life, middle-class Negroes are still threatened
with the loss of positions and earning power if they insist upon their rights. (220)

The masculine role of the black male sociologist allows for a discourse of complaint
without the sociologist being unduly punished by the white world, and sometimes

even allowing for him to be rewarded for it. Whereas the narratives of Pickens, Wells, and White define their protagonists' New Negro leadership through overt confrontation, self-conscious involvement, and racial trespassing, the professional sociologists achieve a similar leadership role by screening their personal stake in the racial war and distancing their involvement through the neutrality of science. Speaking of Du Bois's Atlanta studies, Elliott Rudwick points out that the rise in black sociology has another effect: "[T]his picture of Negroes as social scientists, and as individuals interested in the findings of social science, represented a view which was very far from the traditional racial stereotypes" (*W.E.B. Du Bois* 52). The reality, of course, is that their authoritative status as experts of and on the race no less enacts racial trespassing, evidenced most forcefully by the fact that they are trained in the most prestigious white universities of the cosmopolitan North. By identifying urban sociology so closely with the issues of race contacts, these masterful sociologists invade the well-guarded intellectual territory of the dominant race and stake their claim to scientific modernity, efficient leadership, and systematic self-patronage.

Part II   Negotiating Racial Uplift

Gender Rivalry and Erotic Longing in the Making of New Negro Patronage

> But it is not so much the educational development of the Negro under enormous difficulties that constitutes the outstanding feature of his artistic accomplishment as it is his marvelous adaptability to Caucasian civilization.
>
> —Fred De Armond ("Note on the Sociology of Negro Literature" 369)

> Thus the new frontier of Negro life is flung out in a jagged, uneven but progressive pattern. For a group historically retarded and not readily assimilated, contact with its surrounding culture breeds quite uneven results. There is no fixed racial level of culture. The lines cut both vertically and horizontally. There are as great differences, with reference to culture, education, sophistication, among Negroes as between the races.
>
> —Charles S. Johnson ("New Frontage on American Life" 297)

> But these nice modern faddists—they give me a feeling of white lice crawling on black bodies.   —Claude McKay (*Long Way from Home* 337)

The so-called New Negro Renaissance represents one of the best arenas in which to investigate the individual and institutional dynamics constructing black manhood identity in the early twentieth century. The gender and sexual patterns of racial identification among black men are variously worked out in race patronage and its contradictions during this period. New modes of black manhood identity—noticeably interdependent with old ones—are formulated in the biracial patronage organizations that emerge in and around the New Negro Renaissance, when writers, black and white, male and female, experiment with literary and artistic culture as a means of cross-racial engagement for African American uplift and national progress. Following through with the New Negro ideology of urbanizing and making cosmopolitan the black masses for the task of race racing, the New Negro Renaissance writers ambivalently saw themselves as setting a pattern for future cultural work. Hope for a Negro Renaissance grew out of the mass migration from around World War I through World War II (though largely dashed along with the economy of the Great Depression), when the question looming over the migration focused on whether African Americans would "adapt" or "regress," words with obvious social Darwinist implications. As Charles S. Johnson indicates in his essay from Locke's *The New Negro,* these migrants were considered culturally "retarded" and not "readily assimilable" into "sophisticated" modern civilization. For many African American male middle-class leaders—some of whom had been educated in the North, like Johnson, or had lived there a long time—and their Euro-American patrons, the fear was that the race would regress into a fate worse than that experienced in the backwaters of the southern Black Belt. Just as palpable as this fear, however, was the excitement expressed by white patrons and black writers who latched onto the migratory experience as a prophetic sign that "[t]here is no fixed racial level of culture" (Johnson, "New Frontage on American Life" 297).

For white patrons the migration presented a rare opportunity in which social-scientific, political, literary, and artistic experimentation could be carried out to test the adaptability and usefulness of black folk culture—frequently still viewed as a primitive, superstitious slave culture—when tossed into the midst of the most modern New World cities. For black male leaders, some of whom had made the migration themselves, this was no less an opportunity to disprove the wisdom of Jim Crow white supremacy, whose systematic enforcement had gripped the whole country since the 1890s, and to prove the adaptable modernity of a people worthy of joining the uneven, jagged mix of urban civilization, with all of its rising cultural amenities and influences in the nation and the world. If social segregation, political disenfranchisement, and economic deprivation were the true causes of black people's "retarded" status in United States civilization, then what better place to prove this than in these northern cities, where some of those liabilities were lessened, if not removed? Posing the question this way, black and white sociologists, philanthropists, and artists searched for signs of the future direction of the race in its new environs, while black writers predicted, celebrated, satirized, and denied—sometimes all at the same time—the feasibility and effectiveness of cultural "renaissance" in the first place, as they considered the miserable economic circumstances of most migrants in their new urban "colonies."

The two chapters of Part 2 of this study examine the sexual/racial/class entanglements of patronage that ensue when white patrons, fascinated with and disturbed by the black invasion, and black clients, hyped and ready for a new racial scene, come together in these new cross-racial cultural projects aimed at defeating Jim Crow. I mean the word *sexual* in both the sense of (1) gender roles based on cultural assumptions about anatomical sex and (2) the gender bonds, binds, and rivalries constituting sexual attraction, courtship, intimacy, and intercourse in early-twentieth-century United States culture. This kind of personal race philanthropy assumes or assigns specific gender roles to the civilizing acts of patrons (white and black), based on their anatomical sex, as it also assumes or assigns peculiar gender roles to the lucky black beneficiaries. The beneficiary's recipient act of dependence carries its own gender implications, placing black men, for instance, in a position of childlike need in relation to both male and female patrons. In this sense of sex as the socially negotiated process of maintaining racial status through normalizing gender hierarchies, similar issues of gender dominance and subordination arise within intraracial patronage, in which African American men usually command more immediate and better access to the resources of patronage, as donor or client, and in which middle-class African Americans possess analogous leverage over those among the working class and disemployed poor as white patrons exert over their black clients.

Complicating the enforcement of these sex/gender norms is the other meaning of sex operating in race patronage. The implications of cross-racial fascination and attraction are frequently at work in, or projected onto, intimate cross-racial contact in a period when social proximity outside of an employer-employee relation is strictly taboo, even in the more racially relaxed urban North. Although cross-racial patronage need not harbor either repressed erotic or openly sexual desire, always at stake in such civilizing acts are the kinds of psychic want and gratification that arise in enacting the desire for power, beneficent as it may be, over others' careers, social identities, and lives, based on a difference in social, economic, and racial rank. I suggest in these chapters that patronage desire gets structured along libidinal lines as though it were a mode of sexual desire. Patrons and donors—black and white, male and female—repeatedly exploit the language of erotic courtship and sexual desire when speaking of racial patronage in letters, memoirs, political tracts, sociological writings, and literary texts, so much so that the eroticized structure of patronage relations becomes as naturalized and familiar as the racial and class hierarchy on which patronage is based. Furthermore, this eroticized structure can be observed in the social and institutional—indeed, almost ritually formulaic—practices that emerge to signal and perform the generosity and goodwill of patronage as an activity of racial uplift. These ritual acts are collectively symbolic insofar as they announce to the world a beneficent interest in the lagging race as a group and the commitment to labor in potentially stigmatized social groupings, such as "nigger-loving" institutions, bringing black and white, male and female together.

Repeatedly, we see that the collectively symbolic rituals of patronage can be expressed only through highly personalized *individual* gestures that spotlight the unique contribution or genius of the generous patron and likewise the unique potential or genius of the fortunate protégé. On the one hand, only this particular patron could do this particular act for this particular protégé. On the other hand, what this particular donor does is no different from what any other donor does for any other client. Despite constant claims of originality and uniqueness on the part of the donor in acting presciently on behalf of an individual Negro client, whose talents would be invisible and untapped without the donor's sage powers of artistic detection and cultural prognosis, the actual patronage is always ritualistically formulaic, and the patron-protégé bond predictably scripted to behave like all others. The language of attraction, wooing, adoration, and devotion so familiar from the cultural ideology of courtship and romance serves to enhance and intensify the idea that patronage relations are deeply personal, beneficently intended, perhaps even destined or fated. By the same token, the social, political, and cultural institutions created to carry out these rituals demand individual relations between donor and client be endowed with the power and constraint of collective identifications, ironically reinforcing racial, gender, sexual, class, regional, and national identities while claiming to bridge, even eradicate such social divisions. As a result, just as the individual intimacies lovingly fostered in a donor-client relation tend to bear out the social divisions necessitated by institutional hierarchies, so the institutional work of race patronage emanates from, and often gets reduced to, the individual dynamics of a lover's spat. In the end, race patronage cannot avoid or overcome socioeconomic motives and forms, for just as patronage institutions still operate through economic mechanisms of employer and employee, advisory board and laboring staff, trustee and entrusted, so intimately personal bonds negotiated between patron and protégé are necessarily haunted by the capitalist economy of profit, scarcity, and competition.

Indeed, the rhetoric of both personal and institutional patronage is indebted to humanistic ideals of gift-giving generosity, sacrifice, reciprocation, and devoted gratitude in the feudal mode of noblesse oblige and fidelity, protector and ward, lord and master. In this sense, United States race patronage is patterned on the European *ancien régime* in which the aristocratic court was supposed to foster a romantic devotion between the patron and his courtier—the truest meaning of courtship. Such courtliness (and the romance structure that it encourages), however, merely masks the profit economy and nationalist ideology at stake in United States race patronage. Race patronage during the New Negro Renaissance helps work through and work out the terms of United States internationalist ascendancy through domestic interracial romance. As beneficent donors to their black wards, the white American cultural elite can signal and enact their readiness to become a donor civilization on a global scale. No longer merely the crass recipients and imitators of a high cultural standard set by their European betters, the United States cultural elite can now lay claim to their own high civilization, uniquely American but universally imitable, evinced through the higher culture that they generously endow and donate to their degraded black clients, who must gratefully emulate their white cultural benefactors in no less a way than the white United States elite have emulated European aristocrats and other high-cultural arbiters.

Finally, given the entanglement of high-cultural renaissance patronage with a lower kind of patronage as monetary exchange in the jazz age, it would be misleading to try to separate high cultural aspiration from low sexual impulse. Thus, in these chapters we continue the exploration of the dual meaning of patronage begun in Part 1, where we examined Washington's and Du Bois's negotiations of patronage as a pure charitable act, potentially sullied by the touch of money and the logic of profitable exchange; Locke's, Pickens's, Wells's, White's, and Gordon's rejection of materialist Bookerite patronage for versions of racial and self-autonomy that rely on the internalized integrity and competitive determination of the individual race leader; and the conduct of uplift professionalization as an act that entrusted black male sociologists to the empiricist protocols, political compromises, and competitive gender performances characteristic of the emergence of sociology as a masculine institution capable of fashioning national policy on the urban race problem. In the jazz age, the white "seekers after new sensations," to use James Weldon Johnson's words, go slumming in the Negro districts and visit the sexually taboo "black and tan resorts" (*Black Manhattan* 160). These seekers of the exotic and lewd in "primitive" black folk culture are properly also called "patrons" by the renaissance writers. Instead of generously donating their money for the cause of art, uplift, and modernizing civilization, these other patrons gratify their lower, deviant passions by purchasing the excitement of social taboos: illegal alcohol, on-the-spot lessons in Negro dance and sexually suggestive blues and jazz (considered salacious in upright, middlebrow national culture), sexual flirtation with black people, as well as cross-racial sex itself through the availability of black prostitutes, female and male. These two modes of patronage—high and low, giving and buying, the refined court and the vulgar market, the altruistic and the exotic, modern experimentation and primitive lust, progressive civilizing management and recessive letting go—are kept distinct in the rhetoric of high-minded cross-racial public institutions, political organizations, literary competitions, award ceremonies, and journals such as *The Crisis* and *Opportunity*—all of which help promote the idea of a racial renaissance. It is impossible, however, to keep them apart in the ideological reality of patronage rituals. The vicious patrons seeking new sensations are not only psychologically and "temperamentally" related to the highbrow patrons; they are frequently the same individuals. The sexual entanglements of New Negro patronage provide black male writers and uplifters an opportunity for attempting to remold the face of black manhood as the vanguard of progressive culture, but at the same time race patronage, with its attendant sexual bases, tends to reinforce the compulsory modes of dominant masculinity that script African American manhood as a sign of masculine deviance, marginality, and cultural backwardness.

To understand the status of black manhood as a ward of white patronage, we need to examine not only the rhetoric, imagery, and conduct of black male clients and their black female rivals for patronage but also the psychology and practice of patronage as negotiated by white benefactors, male and female. Furthermore, we need to understand how the emergence of Harlem Renaissance cultural arts patronage, such as poetry and fiction prizes, is intimately related to and assumes a structure similar to emergent biracial political-social reform organizations, which are also based in eroticized acts of racial patronage. Politics and aesthetics conventionally have been viewed as different, if not contrary, strains of uplift in the New Negro period, even when the same individuals have been involved in both activities at once. By exposing the patronage structure at work in both modes of uplift, we can better grasp the benefits and costs of political reform patronage as a cultural act (the focus on chapter 4) and cultural arts patronage as a political act (the focus of chapter 5). Both political reform and cultural arts during this period are enmeshed with a cardinal assumption of the time among racial liberals: that cross-racial cooperation depends on physical intimacy. Because the Jim Crow regime dictated absolute separation of the races in all things "purely" social (to rephrase Washington), liberal institutions and individuals devoted to uplift could combat the mythology and ideology of Jim Crow only by insisting on close physical contact. The intimate biracial bond of the arts donor to her or his protégé and of the social reformer to his or her client serves to symbolize how Negroes and whites can work closely together to benefit the nation without falling into the cross-racial sexual deviations that Jim Crow advocates insist must inevitably result from such taboo touching. Of course, given the implications of any such physical contact across race during this era, it is not surprising that explosive issues arise between white patrons and their clients, as well as among black clients competing with one another to become leading patrons of the race.

Bringing into the gambit of cultural Negro Renaissance patronage European American figures such as Oswald Garrison Villard and Mary White Ovington, who have been solely associated with the NAACP, National Urban League, and other social reform movements, helps highlight the racial and sexual entanglements that operate across the struggles in politics and aesthetics. As different as biracial civil rights organizing and Harlem Renaissance patronage may have looked on the surface, they shared important features, not the least of which was the historical structure of patronage itself. Such modern professional race organizations as the NAACP constituted the predominant way in which men like Du Bois, White, James Weldon Johnson, and Charles S. Johnson were put in opportune positions to become black male race patrons during the New Negro Renaissance—Du Bois, James Weldon Johnson, and White as executive officers at the NAACP, Charles S. Johnson as an officer in the Urban League. Fortunately, some scholarly work has already been done—notably by Cheryl Wall, Gloria Hull, Deborah McDowell, and Thadious Davis—to explain the obstacles confronted by Harlem Renaissance black women writers attempting to capitalize on the new patronage gestures of the period, and I rely heavily on their theoretical and literary-historical scholarship here. Little has been done to probe the patronage circumstances embroiling black women involved in biracial social reform institutions, however. By focusing on Ida B. Wells's struggle to participate in the founding of the NAACP, chapter 4 brings attention to the gender discord erupting between not only black men and women but also black and white women, all of whom are disadvantaged in different ways in attempting to enact the highest racial patronage roles, normally reserved for ruling white men. Wells is especially revealing because, given her tendency bluntly to identify the sexual dynamic at work in American race relations, she is not afraid to expose the erotic entanglements that influence activities putatively pure of such implications. These chapters thus place patronized black manhood in a dense network of social, psychic, economic, and sexual relations, demonstrating how its construction is constituted as much by how others (white men, black and white women) construe their intimate relations to it as by how black men themselves articulate and sublimate their experiences of their own identity.

While chapter 4 emphasizes the personal patronage rituals beneath the surface of biracial, bi-gendered political reform organizing during the New Negro period, chapter 5 turns our attention to the politics of patronage at work in the artistic claims of the New Negro Renaissance, as it investigates both the high cultural aspirations and low sexual implications of black male clients' relationships with their patrons, black and white, male and female. Through this dense network of patronage relations, we come to understand not only how leading black men must necessarily become sexual objects to more powerful white arbiters of culture but also how black men attempted to reposition themselves as patrons and creators of culture, prolific progenitors whose sexual identity cannot be reduced to sexual-object status.

4 Civilizing Acts

The Sexual Appeals of Patronage
in New Negro Political Organizing

> But philanthropy on the psychological level is often guilt-motivated, even when most unconscious.
> —Ralph Ellison ("*An American Dilemma:* A Review," in *Collected Essays* 331)

> But the Negro is on trial, and witnesses are continually called to tell of his failures and successes. We have seen that both in the attitude of the world about him, and in his own untutored self, there are many obstacles to prevent his advance; and his natural sensitiveness adds to these difficulties.
> —Mary White Ovington (*Half a Man* 193)

> [A]fter I had grown tired of books, and while I was looking about for something more thrilling than a logical formula, I discovered a new interest in the study of the Negro and the race problem.
> —Robert E. Park (*Race and Culture* vii)

Looking back on the early years of the NAACP, from 1908 to 1927, in the autobiography that he drafted in 1958–1960, W.E.B. Du Bois reviews and laments some of his initial difficulties in dealing with one of the white founders of the organization, Oswald Garrison Villard (1872–1949):

> To a white philanthropist like Villard, a Negro was quite naturally expected to be humble and thankful or certainly not assertive and aggressive; this Villard resented. I knew Villard's mother, who was Garrison's favorite child, and I liked her very much. His uncles were cordial and sympathetic. There was much that I liked in Villard himself, but one thing despite all my effort kept us far apart. He had married a wife from Georgia, a former slave State, and consequently I could never step foot in his house as a guest, nor could any other of his colored associates. Indeed I doubt if any of his Jewish co-workers were ever invited. I knew the reasons for this discrimination, but I could hardly be expected to be happy over them or to be his close friend. (*Autobiography of W.E.B. Du Bois* 256–257)

As a political organization aimed at desegregating the United States through legal redress, legislative lobbying, and protest agitation, the NAACP embodied the most progressive agency to bring together blacks and whites, men and women, Jews and Gentiles, upper and lower classes in the pursuit of racial reform. The tactics of the NAACP required coalition building not only to forge a mass consensus but also to model for the nation the salutary effects of close racial contact. Perhaps the only organization where the politically restless Du Bois could find a base from which to mold his peculiar praxis of racial self-help and relentless integrationism, the NAACP nonetheless constantly forced him into a politically compromised position. This is nowhere more evident than in his initial status as the only Negro on its governing board.

This solitary status saddled Du Bois with what, in another context, Kobena Mercer calls "the burden of representation," the contemporary notion that works of art produced by minority artists must "stand in" for the whole racial group identified with the artist (*Welcome to the Jungle* 234). Du Bois's position on the NAACP board is in many ways analogous to the contemporary situation that Mercer describes. However, whereas the artwork takes on the representative burden, in Du Bois's case his *person* carried the burden. His presence on the board was supposed to stand in for the inclusion of the black community as a whole. As Mercer points out, racial ideology structures the burden of representation through a cultural assumption of scarcity. Instead of making audible the heterogeneous voices in a particular racialized community through processes of accessible dialogue, representation serves to highlight the community's exclusion by rationing its inclusion through benevolent token gestures. "In such a political economy of racial representation where the part stands in for the whole," Mercer writes, "the visibility of a few token black public figures serves to legitimate, and reproduce, the invisibility, and lack of access to public discourse, of the community as a whole." In other words, "in a situation where racism rations access to resources, questions of structure are displaced by a voluntaristic emphasis on individual agency" (240). Du Bois's position on the NAACP board perfectly embodies this type of displacement, as his token representative voice tends to hide the larger patronage dynamic in which the structure of the early NAACP often excluded those whom it set out to aid exactly through the act of granting a voice to a few exceptional volunteers as competent representatives of the whole oppressed group. This structure of assumed scarcity operates at many levels to suggest that capable individuals are scarce within the race, and hence only particular ones can volunteer to represent it, while it actually rations access to the resources of the new organization on the principle that those resources are themselves scarce. Early-twentieth-century race patronage—in both political organization and artistic philanthropy—operates through this paradigm of scarcity, resulting in the notion that members of the race must compete with other African Americans to prove themselves worthy of the donor's attentions and resources and capable of shouldering the burden of representing the race.

While blacks are required to compete among themselves for the putatively scarce attention and resources of white donors, the patron's status, security, and access to resources are supposed to exempt and protect him from having to compete with his black clients. Race patronage is shaped by the patron's denial of the rivalry that necessarily occurs between the white benefactor and his black protégés. As an act of generosity whereby the patron's material wealth as well as his social and spiritual endowment are sacrificed on behalf of an inferior group, race patronage is supposed to mark the patron's purely beneficent and transcendent motives and objectives in relation to individuals of the subordinate race. Ironically, the same structure that requires the subordinate to prove himself worthy to the patron through intraracial competition begets the subordinate's desire to prove himself equal to—or better than—the patron, demarcating the patronage act as a temporally limited gesture in the long affair of racial cooperation, whose goal is equal access to *all* resources without the mediation of white self-sacrifice through the remediation of black capacity. Whereas the patron's racial identity is forged through the perpetuation of the intermediary role, the client's ambition is to achieve and supercede the patron's superior status, resulting in a cross-racial rivalry that lies just beneath the pacifying surface of racial coalition.

In the early twentieth century, the tenets of Jim Crow constrain the structure and practice of race patronage in peculiar ways. White liberals define their generosity through their willingness to work in close settings with individual blacks against dominant social protocol. The physical closeness of the cross-racial relationship is itself a protest against Jim Crow and an affirmation of a belief in the political equality of the races under law. It is not necessarily, however, an affirmation of blacks' claims to biological, social, or economic equality. In fact, most white patrons of the Jim Crow era define their patronage as an experiment, testing to what degree the black race can move toward the civilized status of modernity identified with a European inheritance. To base white liberal patronage on symbolic gestures of physical contact means, however, that the fundamental logic of Jim Crow is contested. Along with close contact comes a congeries of ramifications that reverberate through the social, psychic, visceral, and bodily experiences of patron and patronized along and across the line of color, including physical attraction and repulsion, emotional friendship and animosity, psychic desire and denial, familial affiliation and distancing, and social identification with and against the racial other.

The ideology of scarcity becomes both productive and enervating in the New Negro era because its structure is expressed through *personal* relationships that are seen to embody or represent race relations as a whole. Du Bois's resentment at Villard's treatment—lingering fifty years after the deed—appears to be personal in nature. Du Bois names his frustration through questions of familiarity and animosity, through bonds to Villard's family, and through the matter of whether or not he is allowed to enter Villard's house. These personal matters, however, embody and exemplify not merely the relationship between a powerful white man and the black man who desires to be his equal but also the relationship between a powerful white race as donor and its oppressed other as disaffiliated client. To assert one's right or aggress against the donor is to be ungrateful for his self-sacrificing benevolence. Resentment, a notoriously personal emotion, characterizes Villard's relationship not only to Du Bois but to *any* Negro who receives the good works of the white man's philanthropic gift. When Du Bois points out that Villard would perhaps not even allow a Jew into his house, he positions the Jew as a member of an affiliated race also experiencing oppression but occupying a middle ground between the Jim Crowed black man and the sacrosanct white patron's household. Because Jewish Americans were prominent in the origins and sustenance of the NAACP as patrons for the black race, Du Bois is able to communicate through his positioning of them the extreme nature of Villard's exclusionary practices. Villard's resentment—and Du Bois's resentment of it—both hides and exposes how the new NAACP mode of race patronage subsumes and sometimes reduces collective political work to a structure of interpersonal relations across race that is itself gendered in peculiar ways.

If Villard's exclusion of Du Bois from his house indicates the limits of the white patron's *political* understanding of race, Du Bois's appeal to his own personal bonds with Villard's family, especially the white patron's elders, indicates the black man's worthiness to be admitted as an equal not only into Villard's household but, more important, into the white man's *political* enclave of power and resources. As male head of the household, Villard has the rightful power to decide whether the doorway to his domicile should be a barrier to or a threshold of cross-racial interaction, just as his inherited status as an arbiter and master of white civilization grants him the power to decide where to draw the color line in United States politics, society, and culture. Villard's decision to exclude even Du Bois from his private network indicates to the black ward that his inclusion on the NAACP board is paradoxically another form of racial and gender exclusion. Du Bois can never be sure whether he is deemed sexually unworthy because he is a *black* man or deemed racially unworthy because he is personally not *man* enough—or not genteel enough—to transcend the handicap of his blackness. These personal rivalries intrinsic to race patronage are as key to understanding early-twentieth-century biracial political work as the manifestos, procedures, meetings, and activities that comprise more apparently the process of political organization and institution building.

Du Bois's sketch of Villard indicates the complex network of patrilineal affiliations and disaffections that constitute this conduct of cross-racial politics. By pointing to the philanthropic behavior of Villard, the grandson of the great abolitionist William Lloyd Garrison, Du Bois as late as the 1960s is still commenting on the failure of the *sons* of abolitionists to live up to the patronage record set by their forebears—a *family* obligation that further personalizes the political commitment. Casting himself as a well-known friend of the Garrison family, Du Bois highlights the effect of the symbolic—and here also literal—marriage between North and South during the Jim Crow era, as the North adopts its segregating ways from the

South and thus authenticates and legitimates racial apartheid as a *national* project. Villard can style himself a leading race patron while consenting to a strict code of racial/ethnic Jim Crow in his own household, *personally* justified by his betrothal to a southern wife but *politically* justified by notions that are transparently illogical to Du Bois. The personal marriage trumps the need for a rational political explanation. Whether Villard is really a friend to the race is borne out by whether he can really be a friend to Du Bois, a test of the white aristocrat's authentic patronage bid that works in both directions: whether Du Bois can become a patron of his own race depends on whether he can entice Villard into a relation of manly fraternity, a masculine equality so far beyond race that it acknowledges a fraternal (that is, a blood) obligation between black and white. As symbolic blood relation, the fraternal bond itself would affirm the black man's rightful citizenship as a true son and potential father within the national family. We could even go so far as to say that the palpable intrusion of the intimately personal in New Negro race patronage is supposed to mark it as a new mode for a new century, a mode based on the capacity of the races to cooperate intimately across the color line.

The Machinery of Patronage

In Du Bois's *Autobiography,* the chapter on the founding of the NAACP follows the chapter on the failed Niagara movement, an organization originally formed by "[f]ifty-nine colored men from 17 different states" to overcome the stranglehold of the "Tuskegee Machine" (248). That the Niagara movement was an all-black affair has frequently been noted, but that it was also initially an all-male affair has rarely been analyzed. David Levering Lewis instructively describes the initial gathering as one as much bound by silent claims of gender exclusivity as motivated by ambitions for racial consolidation:

> The new arrivals at the rambling Erie Beach Hotel were all the more intriguing due to their impressive livery and comportment. They exuded an air of self-assurance and professional success. . . . Something of their self-conscious purpose and the impression they must have made upon Niagara during those four days of ideal July weather was captured in a photo of many of the Fort Erie group members. . . . The falls cascade on a mock background as three rows of men in white Panama hats and Stetsons . . . stare straight ahead—although a debonair Du Bois, obviously pleased with himself, looks off to his right from the second row.[1]

Like the materialist photographs of the Bookerite new-century albums, the 1905 Niagara photograph (Figure 4.1) bespeaks the impulse to codify racial autonomy and strength through masculine uniformity—through the uniforms of upper-middle-class masculine attire. As a fraternal consensus, the Niagara movement was beset by tensions from the outset, among them the issue of whether women should be invited to the second meeting scheduled for the following year in Harper's Ferry,

Figure 4.1. Some members of the first meeting of the Niagara movement, 1905. Photo courtesy of the W.E.B. Du Bois Library, University of Massachusetts, Amherst.

West Virginia. The identification of the movement with John Brown's masculine heroics of self-sacrifice indicates how the members were intent on shaping their agenda in terms of political confrontation, as opposed to Washington's accommodationist rhetoric, and likewise how any white conspirators hoping to aid the movement must take John Brown as their model, not the industrial capitalist patrons endowing Washington's Tuskegee Machine, including Villard. If the Niagara movement was to exemplify the physical, emotional, and mental initiative of black men seeking to capitalize on their own resources in tentative coalition with black women, the emergence of the NAACP as a biracial, bi-gendered organization necessarily calls into question the manly initiative and autonomy of the Niagara movement men. In coming to the aid of the subordinated race, the white men and women who initiated the NAACP in league with black men and women would have to negotiate the terms of cross-racial cooperation as much as they would have to contest the protocols of an ascendant Jim Crow. As much as they might desire to presume the patterns of their patronage as preset by racial hierarchy, they would have to wrestle with black men and women who had different ideas about this new interracial coalition, even as the latter's notions of a cross-gender coalition might be already hemmed in by the sexual tensions of gender hierarchy.

Accordingly, Du Bois's chapter in the *Autobiography* on the NAACP poses the problem of how to work effectively in a cross-racial organization—founded, financed, and directed by whites—without duplicating the patronage model of Tuskegee. Du Bois lays out a compelling economic explanation for the evils of

Progressive Era philanthropy, most of whose money for race projects goes to or is filtered through the Tuskegee Machine:

> Moreover, it must not be forgotten that this Tuskegee Machine was not solely the idea and activity of black folk at Tuskegee. It was largely encouraged and given financial aid through certain white groups and individuals in the North. This Northern group had clear objectives. They were capitalists and employers of labor and yet in most cases sons, relatives, or friends of the Abolitionists who had sent teachers into the new Negro South after the war. These younger men believed that the Negro problem could not remain a matter of philanthropy. It must be a matter of business. (*Autobiography of W.E.B. Du Bois* 239)

Underplaying the agency of Washington in the Tuskegee Machine, Du Bois constructs Tuskegee patronage as the paradigm that the Niagara movement set out to bring down. The image of the "machine" here works in at least three ways: (1) to suggest the corrupt, self-interested insider machinations of turn-of-the-century politicians, who dole out favors to constituents in exchange for political power and financial gain for themselves; (2) to suggest the dominance of capitalist profit and factory-like automation, whereby Tuskegee patronage becomes a profit-making venture by turning black folk into mass factory labor; (3) to suggest the mechanistic impersonality of the patrons as industrial masters in relation to the black wards as laboring machines kept in proper running order by black supervisors like Washington. This impersonality controverts the original patronage of the abolition movement, an irony highlighted by the fact that the current crop of impersonal patrons are personally related to the abolitionists. Implicit in Du Bois's critique is the notion that patronage can be reformed into cross-racial alliance only once the personal aspect of cross-racial contact is restored.

Calling Washington "the political boss of the Negro Race in America"[2] and his enterprise the "Tuskegee Machine," Du Bois associates this mode of patronage with the infamously crooked political operations dominating local and state government, and thus with the corrupt practices that reformers were aiming to bring down in the Progressive Era. "But we are compelled to point out that Washington's large financial responsibilities have made him dependent on the rich charitable public and that, for this reason, he has for years been compelled to tell, not the whole truth, but that part of it which certain powerful interests in America wish to appear as the whole truth." Du Bois quotes an appeal to England and Europe that he wrote at the behest of John Milholland, one of the white NAACP patrons, concerning the statements made by Washington during a 1910 tour of Europe, where he "is giving the impression abroad that the Negro problem in America is in the process of satisfactory solution."[3] Again, we see how important Europe is as a "higher" civilization symbolically situated to arbitrate the race conflict in the United States and, implicitly, the ideological conflict between the Du Bois and Washington camps. As we see later, the white patrons have good reason to be overly sensitive to how Europeans view their handling of the race problem, for their own international standing is at stake at a moment when they are claiming the global authority of American culture. Thus, what appears to be a parochial affair—or at the least an American nationalist one—turns out to possess global sources and consequences.

The Tuskegee paradigm of patronage concentrates influence in one black male leader whose character, demeanor, and apparent ideological accommodation make him, though exceptional, an ideal representative of the interests of the subordinated group. Although Washington develops close relationships with some of his patrons—such as Andrew Carnegie—he himself (or his machine) is also the dispenser of the spoils, helping determine which black schools, libraries, politicians, newspapers, scientific projects, and business enterprises are worthy of this largesse. Based on the logic of Jim Crow separation that Washington rhetorically upheld, such patronage must necessarily result from profitable self-interests of each group, not from any sense of social fraternity, personal friendship, or physical intimacy between white donor and black ward.[4] The Tuskegee Machine is indeed efficient machinery, a great institutional enterprise hinging on Washington's personality but intended for the bureaucratic and ideological control of the conduct and uplift of a whole people and region.

In this way, Tuskegee philanthropy differs significantly from New Negro Renaissance patronage, which focuses more on an ideology of singularity and exceptionality on the part of both patrons and clients—a contrast that can help us understand Du Bois's critique of Washington and his hopes for NAACP political cooperation. Although the cultural focus of Negro Renaissance patronage in the 1920s is administered through journals, awards, and grant agencies such as the Rosenwald Fund, it is more fundamentally conceptualized and enacted in the context of a personal relationship between an individual patron and an individual client for the greater spiritual good of art, beauty, civilization, and race relations. Based in a much more aestheticized sphere than the Tuskegee Machine's decidedly bourgeois vocational, materialist, industrial focus, Negro Renaissance patronage nonetheless usually embraces the larger utilitarian aim of racial advancement. Negro Renaissance patronage mimics the patronage system of the European Renaissance, in which discriminating individuals from a social elite condescendingly lavish money, praise, and attention on rare, talented individuals of lower rank who lack the resources to support their own artistic and scientific careers. Thus, Negro Renaissance patronage seems not to be at all about economic self-interest of the kind that Du Bois attacks. As opposed to the Tuskegee model, in which donors leave their centers of power and gather to take train rides through the backwaters to see how well their money has been spent,[5] the renaissance model requires that the clients and their productivities be always at hand, apparently ready and eager to reciprocate the patron's discriminating judgment and beneficence with reciprocal attention and flattery. In other words, Tuskegee patronage dictates a proper Jim Crow physical distance between the white donors and their black clients, who are supposed to stay put in the Black Belt either of the rural South or of the urban ghetto. New Negro Renaissance patronage, however, dictates physical proximity that bespeaks some sort of simulacral "blood" intimacy, such as that between a father and his *adopted* son. The location of such race patronage is the symbolic court of the urban cultural centers where the elite patrons reside. No doubt, Du Bois is correct when he identifies the corrupting influence of the profit motive on Tuskegee's fashioning of race patronage after Reconstruction; as we shall see, however, Negro Renaissance patronage possesses just as deeply disturbing, though less immediate and apparent, motives of self-interest, as it buttresses the racial, sexual, and class structures that result from the rule of capitalist profit and a myth of Manifest Destiny for United States cultural ascendancy in the world, an ideology that positions the white United States elite as the proper beneficiary inheriting Western civilization from a Europe soon to be overshadowed by America.

The NAACP, with its overt agenda of legal and political reform on matters of race, provided the first major well-funded ideological counterweight to the Tuskegee Machine. But the NAACP patronage structure, with its roster of white financiers and hands-on supporters, must have seemed more like a rival to Tuskegee's system of spoils than a new venture in racial cooperation and revised race patronage, especially given how it superceded a Niagara movement directionless in terms of a practical political program because cash-strapped and barred from adequate political, economic, and social resources. In fact, Du Bois's early role on the Board of Directors and Walter White's later role as executive secretary (director) bear a resemblance to Washington's Jim Crow spoils system. Just as Du Bois rejects Washington's patronage machine despite at least two offers to him to join it, there are prominent instances of black leaders rejecting the emerging NAACP machine because of their perception that it funnels white control through patronage of select black male leaders. Du Bois points out that two of the most radical African American race leaders of the time refuse to join the leadership of the NAACP, despite the new organization's attempt to absorb the black Niagara movement into its structure:

> An impressive number of scientists and social workers attended; friends of wealthy philanthropists were present and many Negroes but few followers of Booker T. Washington. In the end [William Monroe] Trotter, the most radical Negro leader, and Mrs. Ida Wells Barnett who was leading an anti-lynching crusade, refused to join the new organization, being distrustful of white leadership. I myself and most of the Niagara Movement group were willing to join. (*Autobiography of W.E.B. Du Bois* 254)

Du Bois's comment about Wells-Barnett mystifies an already obscure event. When Du Bois is called to read the names of those who have been selected for the Committee of Forty, the interim group that becomes responsible for formulating and overseeing the new organization, Wells-Barnett's name mysteriously has disappeared from the list. By examining this originating event of the NAACP as a moment of sexual exclusion, cross-racial intrigue, and eroticized rivalry, we can better understand the role of physical intimacy and sexual interplay in the formation of the black male patron's identity within anti–Jim Crow cross-racial political organizing.

In her autobiography, Wells-Barnett records her own interpretation of the Committee of Forty controversy. She blames primarily two individuals, Du Bois and Mary White Ovington.[6] Wells-Barnett either observes or imagines in the relationship between Du Bois and Ovington a cross-racial, cross-sexual alliance revolving around an eroticized power move. Speaking of the controversial event, Wells-Barnett remembers: "Those white men had done all they could to rectify the deliberate intention of Dr. Du Bois to ignore me and my work. I was too furiously indignant at him to recognize my obligation to try to hold up their hands" (*Crusade for Justice* 326). She continues: "I cannot resist the conclusion that, had I not been so hurt over the treatment I had received at the hands of the men of my own race and thus blinded to the realization that I should have taken the place which the white men of the committee felt I should have, the NAACP would now be a live, active force in the lives of our people all over this country" (328). Wells-Barnett clearly believes that a sexual rivalry has intervened in the cross-racial founding of the organization. Through her eyes, Du Bois has bonded with Ovington to marginalize the most renowned black female political activist of the era, and Ovington has manipulated Du Bois, the most renowned black male political activist, to achieve this end. Ironically, Wells-Barnett at the same time posits an alliance between herself and the white men of the organization, thus accentuating the implication of cross-racial, cross-sexual rivalry. Although she sees the first black male–white female alliance as abetting a destructive factionalization of the cross-racial agenda, she sees the ensuing black female–white male alliance as an antidote to such destructive behavior, despite the fact that the sexual structure of the latter seems an inverted mirror image of the former.

Perhaps what Wells-Barnett has observed in coming to this conclusion is the kind of "innocent flirtation" that David Levering Lewis describes in the relationship between Du Bois and Ovington: "They would often behave as though they were or wished to become lovers, but, despite Du Bois's considerable tested appeal to intelligent women, they almost certainly never were" (*W.E.B. Du Bois: Biography of a Race* 350). Wells-Barnett's description of Ovington portrays her, in this moment of getting Wells-Barnett excluded from the Committee of Forty, as a woman who has exploited feminine wiles to overthrow a rival: "As I stood on the sidewalk waiting . . . , Miss Mary Ovington, who had taken active part in the deliberations, swept by me with an air of triumph and a very pleased look on her face" (325). Wells-Barnett judges Ovington, and thus the NAACP, harshly as being blinded not only by racial ignorance and regional parochialism but, more important here, by sexual favoritism for black men:

> Thus was launched the movement which now has the national reputation as the NAACP. This movement, which has lasted longer than almost any other

movement of its kind in our country, has fallen far short of the expectations of its founders. The reason is not far to seek. It has kept Miss Mary White Ovington as chairman of the executive committee. Miss Ovington's heart is in this work, but her experience has been confined solely to New York and Brooklyn, and a few minor incidents along the color line.

It is impossible for her to visualize the situation in its entirety and to have the executive ability to seize any of the given situations which have occurred in a truly big way. She has basked in the sunlight of the adoration of the few college-bred Negroes who have surrounded her, but has made little effort to know the soul of the black woman; and to that extent she has fallen far short of helping a race which has suffered as no white woman has ever been called upon to suffer or to understand.[7]

Erotic innuendoes entangle with sexual politics in this passage. It is clear, however, that Wells-Barnett places Ovington in the position of a white lady engaged in race work partly for the sake of gaining "adoration" from African American men, a scenario more familiar from the mid-1960s to early 1970s Black Power movement. This scene of a white patroness centered among black men engaged in erotic longing for her almost rehearses a politically problematic image of black men's desire that Wells-Barnett herself is most instrumental in defeating in her anti-lynching campaign. The image differs, however, from that of the black male rapist in the obvious self-restraint she represents these educated black men displaying in the presence of a desirable white woman. Wells-Barnett also seems to imply a class aspect to this scene of cross-racial adoration in pinpointing "the few college-bred Negroes" who surround Ovington. In displacing the middle-class black woman from this group of middle-class men, Ovington has transformed what should be a unified black front against lynching and Jim Crow into a scene of exceptional black men worshiping (and desiring) the white woman in their midst.

Wells-Barnett is drawing a wide line between Ovington's secondary status as a female of the dominant race and the oppressed status of *all* African Americans—a line that Ovington herself draws quite differently in her discussions of the color line and the need for transracial alliance. As we saw in chapter 2, Wells-Barnett is also suggesting that some African American men are blinded by the sexualization of the race, an ideology that is exacerbated, rather than diminished, in the cross-racial, cross-sexual alliance of the first modern full-fledged civil rights organization. In Wells-Barnett's assessment, the cost of Ovington's eroticized distraction is the effectiveness of the NAACP itself. According to Charles Flint Kellogg, Wells-Barnett expresses concern not only over her own marginalization but also over the role foisted onto Jane Addams:

Mrs. Ida Wells-Barnett felt slighted when Villard called a meeting of the Chicago branch at Hull House without notifying her. She complained that Villard and Du Bois wanted Jane Addams to "mother" the movement, although she had neither the time nor the strength to lead this new crusade. Mrs. Wells-Barnett resented the patronizing assumptions of the academic few who wanted to keep the organization in their own hands.[8]

Wells-Barnett's language here is especially interesting in that Ovington is sometimes referred to as the "Mother of the New Emancipation"—a correspondence indicating a crucial aspect of how women's roles of race patronage tend to get gendered.[9] Wells-Barnett's disappointments with the gender politics of the organization eventually led to her resignation.

Ovington's much briefer account of the Committee of Forty controversy comes almost as an afterthought in the final sentences of her chapter on the founding of the NAACP in her memoirs, *Black and White Sat Down Together*. Wells-Barnett "was a great fighter," she writes, "but we knew that she had to play a lone hand. And if you have too many players of lone hands in your organization, you soon have no game."[10] In other places, Ovington indicates that she has a very high opinion of black women reformers, but she also reveals a suspicion of their ability to be team players. "Negro women enjoy organization," she writes in *The Walls Came Tumbling Down*, her 1947 personal reminiscence of the history of the NAACP. "They are ambitious for power, often jealous, very sensitive. But they get things done" (124). This general assessment seems in accord with Ovington's individual judgment of Wells-Barnett. Earlier in *Black and White*, Ovington indicates that the committee responsible for naming the Committee of Forty ran into trouble over whether to ask Washington to serve, fearing that they would never be able to raise money without him: "The matter was thrashed back and forth, and in the end we made a compromise. If Washington's name was omitted, the radicals agreed to have a few conservative names on the committee and not to include Washington's bitterest enemies" (59). It is not clear, however, whether Wells-Barnett's name was taken off at the last minute because she was perceived as one of those "bitterest enemies." On the one hand, we can see from Ovington's commentary that Wells-Barnett is right when she accuses Ovington of backing the decision to marginalize her. On the other hand, Ovington's characterization of Wells-Barnett as a "lone hand" fits perfectly the lone cowboy persona that Wells-Barnett promulgates in her race work, as we discussed in chapter 2. Nevertheless, we shall see that Wells-Barnett has hit on something important in her charge of a sexual basis for Ovington's race patronage.

Tellingly, in his record of these events Du Bois leaves out—consciously or subliminally—the sexual intrigue and suspicion at work in this political, ideological wrangling. Du Bois's masculine claim to patronage of the race depends as much on his silencing the sexual implications of his status as it does on his voicing loudly his assertion of a right to be included in Villard's household as an intimate. His status as an adored object of Ovington's attention silently makes him a masculine rival to Villard, whose erection of the color line at the threshold of his domicile articulates his rejection of physical (that is, *sexual*) intimacy between the races as the limiting point of his racial generosity. Likewise, Du Bois's siding with Ovington over Wells-Barnett, for whatever *political* reason, necessarily appears to suggest a *personal* (that is, a potentially sexual) motive. It is left to Wells-Barnett to raise this ugly implication, for *she* is the one, as a black woman, who must suffer displacement by a white woman, whose attraction and adoration can serve to enhance the black man's bid to become a rival with, and thus an equal to, the patronizing white man. Thus, we can see that the assumption of scarcity also applies to women's representation in the political organization, and in the case of Wells-Barnett and Ovington, the two women seem exchangeable because they are women even despite their racial difference.

What is crucial about this soap opera is not who did what to whom when but how the grand gesture of a progressive new mode of race patronage to counter the Tuskegee Machine so readily slips into the quicksand of a scandalous sexual melodrama. It would be terribly misleading to focus on this sort of misalliance between Wells-Barnett and Ovington as though the physicality of sexual desire occurs in New Negro cross-race patronage only when powerful women—both feminists at that—enter the conventionally masculine fray of Realpolitik. The interracial and intraracial relations between men also participate in this sexual dynamic in ways that are just as revealing of the black male leader's claim to racial self-patronage. In other words, the rivalrous relations between men also possess gender—and indeed erotic—implications. With Villard as chair of the NAACP Board of Directors and Du Bois the token African American in the inner circle as the only black officer, the power struggle between the two men begins immediately. As we have seen, Du Bois considers Villard a race patron unworthy of his abolitionist ancestors—a perception that could not have been helped by Villard's repeated efforts to bring Washington into the leadership of the NAACP as a way of bridging the two ideological uplift camps. Likewise, it seems that, as Du Bois suspects, Villard resents Du Bois's self-assertion as a black race leader.

Villard presumes that he is heir apparent to his grandfather as leader of the black uplift movement. In his 1939 autobiography, *Fighting Years,* not only does he represent the Negro problem as a part of his patrilineal inheritance; he also casts himself as someone who has learned the character of colored people through the trial of hard, hands-on experience in attempting to uplift them. Growing interested in black education after his 1902 trip south on the Ogden Special, Villard becomes the president of the Board of Directors of the Manassas Industrial School, which he calls "a small, struggling imitation of Hampton [Institute]" (175). In discussing his patronage of the school, he writes, "For twenty-two years I directed the destinies of that little school without any success whatever beyond the raising of considerable sums of money and the modernizing of the physical plant" (175). Villard's insinuation is quite clear: he could do the work necessary to modernize the physical plant, but he cannot modernize the black people, who remain a backward horde inhabiting a modern school built with the generosity of his money. Villard's own language seems to confirm Du Bois's suspicion that Tuskegee-like patronage depends on the machinery of capitalist profit as the white patron's self-motivated investment in a future black factory labor force. For Villard, the failure of the black Southerners is exactly their resistance to becoming factory hands in accordance with the most modern principles of industrial automation.

Villard clearly lays the blame for the failure of the Manassas school on the "shortcomings" of his black clients:

> My work at Manassas was one of my outstanding failures but it gave me so clear an insight into the underlying problems, the weaknesses, and shortcomings of the colored people that I have felt more than compensated for my time and trouble. At least I know why it is that they have been so retarded in achieving the economic or political power in our national life which a solid front of twelve millions of Americans could exercise. I believe that I got more education out of my connection with Manassas than any pupil who sat upon its benches. Finally I resigned because the colored people of the neighboring counties would not do their share in financing the enterprise. (*Fighting Years* 175–176)

Sounding exactly like his ideological predecessor, Samuel Chapman Armstrong, Villard views African Americans as a "retarded" race who should have progressed more, given the kind of "time and trouble" that he and other white "merchant philanthropists," to adopt his own phrase, have expended on them.[11] Accounting for this "failure" as a learning experience on the characteristic "weaknesses" and "shortcomings" of African Americans, Villard suggests that this lesson teaches him exactly what they need and what he needs to do for them.

Villard's assessment of the Manassas experiment reveals the ideological orientation of his patronage attitude. Like 1920s cultural renaissance patrons who picture themselves as learning something crucial about race and humanity in the process of aiding African American artists, Villard acknowledges his compensatory learning only to turn it into a rationale for why his clients desperately need particularly *his* patronage. As much as his patronage is aimed at reforming them, his assumptions about them causes him to imagine the patronage relation as one that goes wholly in one direction: downward from the white patron to the "retarded" race. Villard remains staunchly in the tradition of his father, the railroad and electricity financier and speculator who was, in Michael Wreszin's words, a "liberal capitalist," one with a healthy distrust of aristocratic privilege but trusting in the principles of laissez-faire economics, the aristocracy of individual talent, limited government interference in economic matters, and the moral duty of *noblesse oblige* for the wealthy elite.[12] Proud of the fact that his father left his privileged status in Germany out of a political dispute with his own father, showed up in the United States with twenty dollars in his pocket, and in a matter of years became one of the leading industrialists of the late nineteenth century, Villard makes his father's life into an Horatio Alger story, despite the fact that his father was able to curry access to the wealthy and powerful through his friends. Villard's father was well enough connected, for instance, that he could in 1881 call upon "his friends to loan him $8,000,000 for a certain enterprise which he had in mind, with no other explanation of what the money was to be used for except the simple statement that he would account for it in the following May" (*Fighting Years* 14). Like so many such real-life cases of rags to riches, Villard's father did not leave behind a network of influential people when he left the Old Country.

Clearly, the homosocial bonds that Villard's father possessed with wealthy white men provided him easy access to capital not available to men of African descent, not to mention black women. Incapable of understanding—or unwilling to understand—why African Americans as a group were not able to effect the same sort of bootstraps parable after receiving the largesse of white patrons during the Progressive Era, Villard can only attribute this failure to their flawed racial temperament. Blind to the ways in which his own race patronage excludes black women and men from white male homosocial bonding, Villard can also be blind to the ways in which "self-made" success depends on the social networks of such bonding as a vehicle to capital.

Despite the differences in race patronage among the materialist-profit focus of the Tuskegee Machine, the political-coalition focus of the NAACP, and the cultural-inspiration focus of the Negro Renaissance, all three share this crucial similarity: they reinforce the economic benefits of white male homosocial bonding by preserving white men as the managers of capital while appearing to open the doors of initiative and enterprise to lesser others, particularly black men. In actuality, however, select members of the race—especially "exceptional" black men—are merely made the beneficiaries of others' capitalist spoils without altering the opportunities for African Americans to manage capital itself. Therefore, all of these patronage paradigms promote a rhetoric of political and cultural inclusion—whether based on developing skilled labor (Tuskegee), cross-racial contact through political work (the NAACP), or cultivated artistic talent (the Negro Renaissance)—while fundamentally serving to sustain the system of capital as a set of exclusionary homosocial practices of racial and sexual difference.

The feuds between Ovington and Wells-Barnett and between Villard and Du Bois must be understood also in terms of this *economic* struggle, even though they are represented usually by these participants and in the historical scholarship as social, political, and ideological disputes. Even Du Bois, after being influenced by Marxism, tends to emphasize the social aspect when he tells how he and his rival are two sons of New England old stock, two sons of Harvard, two sons of the liberal tradition, but two men on opposite sides of an ideological color line. Du Bois suspects Villard's racial self-understanding, however much Villard sees himself as having learned all he needs to know about colored people from the Manassas experiment.[13] The feud presents a prototypical instance of homoracial struggle between a white man who thinks he knows what is best for the black race because of his superior social and racial patrilineage and a black man who wants to prove that he knows best because of his racial experience and a claim to advancing modernity, autonomy, equality, and the right to self-patronage for the race.

Villard believed there should be African Americans on the NAACP board, but for a reason that would surely have made the proud Du Bois bristle. In his history of the NAACP, Kellogg explains, "Villard felt that an important function of the association's 'board' would be its ability to educate and train the exceptional Negro and to place him where he could be of the greatest possible service to his people."[14] The feud came to a head with Villard's resignation as chair of the board in 1913, but not before taking a form typical of such homoracial conflicts from the Jim Crow era to the present. As Lewis aptly describes the feud, "The more Du Bois and Villard grew to detest each other, the more their movements became like two boxers elaborately squaring off for a murderous pounding" (*W.E.B. Du Bois: Biography of a Race* 474).[15] The masculine contest is actually expressed through a writing match in which the two men come to metaphorical blows over whose project more authentically represents some aspect of the African American experience.

Ironically, the homoracial writing competition pitting Du Bois against Villard circles around an anti-slavery rebel who gave up his life for the cause of abolition, John Brown, but it is the white grandson of abolitionists who challenges the descendant of Africa over his interpretation of a white martyr.[16] When the NAACP was being founded, each man was racing to complete a biography of John Brown. When Du Bois's book came out in 1909, Villard took the opportunity to publish an unsigned review in *The Nation* and the *New York Evening Post* (which were owned by Villard's family) savaging Du Bois's book. The review begins by reducing Du Bois's book to scholarship "from the point of view of the negro," clearly a limiting term given the ideal of objective historical scholarship being promoted during the time:

> That so gifted a writer as the author of "Souls of Black Folk" should be tempted to write a new life of John Brown from the point of view of the negro is easily understood. . . . So little have the negroes themselves as yet done to honor the memory of John Brown that this book might have taken on a special significance. But Du Bois's work is disappointing in that it betrays no original research and abounds in inaccuracies.[17]

Villard's racial condescension is enacted as a sign of racial generosity, for in stooping to give Du Bois any attention at all as a scholar, Villard bestows on him the sort of gift that can come only from someone who has truly mastered abolitionist history and those white patrons who are the proper agents and benefactors of it. Such racial condescension attempts to preempt Du Bois as a rival historian—that is, as a masculine rival—by turning him into a natural protégé whom Villard himself must assist and position. Villard turns the review into an opportunity to assign Du Bois the status of a black man in need of reform, which only a white man like himself can provide. Framing Du Bois's work as naturally retarded, in other words, Villard can think of the black man's biography only in terms of what African Americans should do to "honor the memory of John Brown." John Brown's sacrificial race patronage places a debt of honor on the black race, as though African Americans must feel honored that a white man should sacrifice his life for them and must repay in eternal gratitude what cannot be paid in any other form.

Furthermore, the review subtly makes it appear that Du Bois can be "gifted" when writing about the "souls of black folk" but falters when striving to write about the soul of the great white abolitionist—as if the black scholar has overextended his racial reach, too far beyond the color line. Metaphorically, Du Bois has made the faux pas of crossing the threshold of Villard's domicile, for John Brown is properly affiliated with the white patron not only through their common whiteness but also through the white martyr's metaphoric affiliation with Villard's abolitionist grandfather. In correcting Du Bois's errors, some of the mistakes Villard highlights concern the racial identity of Brown's followers: "to Jeremiah G. Anderson of Indiana, born of sturdy, white farmer parentage, he [Du Bois] attributes negro blood" ("Harper's Ferry and Gettysburg" 405). As if a contradiction existed between "sturdy" parentage and "negro blood," Villard corrects the record by putting Du Bois and his biographical subjects in their proper racial places. Villard is clearly concerned, according to the protocol of Jim Crow, with keeping black and white bloodlines separate in historical discourse, even if in reality keeping white veins clear of black blood would be impossible, given the secret intimacies forced onto captives over generations.

Villard's review cleared the way for his own best-selling biography published a few months later. Outraged by the review, Du Bois wrote a letter to *The Nation,* but the periodical refused to publish it, and Du Bois's book delivered very poor sales. Du Bois was not able to turn the tables to make the case for the white man's reform by a black man. As late as his 1968 autobiography, Du Bois still claimed the merit of his own book: "In 1909 I published *John Brown,* one of the best written of my books, but one which aroused the unfortunate jealousy of Villard who was also writing a biography of Brown" (*Autobiography of W.E.B. Du Bois* 259). By pointing to "jealousy" as Villard's motive, Du Bois again turns what should be an intellectual matter into a personal one. This is not because he mistakenly reduces the issue to the level of the personal; race is always personal and, as such, is always sexualized in some manner. The sexual aspect here has to do with respecting proper patrilineal legacies: Who has the right to claim as his own intellectual progeny the influence of John Brown? The immediate power struggle between Du Bois and Villard was, to a large extent, tilted in the white man's favor, because he has on his side not only the benefit of white supremacy and a railroad fortune but also the weight of two of the country's most influential periodicals. According to Lewis:

> Villard, the real force behind the Committee of Forty, was accustomed to moving in the world as one whose anointed course was manifest and impervious to cor-

rection. His was the imperiousness of an eleven-year-old who in 1883 had traveled to Montana country with deferring dignitaries from Washington and Europe to watch Henry Villard, his father and president of the German-financed Northern Pacific, hammer home a golden spike linking the northern route across the continent. . . . Since 1902, he had helped raise $150,000 for the Tuskegee endowment fund. (*W.E.B. Du Bois: Biography of a Race* 397)

As the heir to a railroad fortune as well as an abolitionist legacy, it would seem that Villard fits perfectly Du Bois's description of the kind of patron who supported the Tuskegee concept out of economic self-interest.

But perhaps this is not the case. Like the Negro Renaissance patrons, Villard's investment in the Negro problem seems to have been less related to the self-interest of economic profit in the crudest sense. As one of the country's intellectual elite, who in this period were frequently the sons and daughters of the previous generation of robber barons, Villard played an important role in turning *The Nation* and the *Evening Post,* previously a conservative periodical, into two of the nation's leading instruments for sophisticated liberalism. It is this group of modernist intellectuals—Van Vechten being another important instance—who, though still focusing one eye on England and Europe as the repositories of past civilization, kept the other eye steadily focused on the clear promise of the United States as the emerging frontier for progressive modernity. To see Villard's motive as solely *personal* economic self-interest is far too narrow. His motive was, more broadly, the ascendancy of United States economic, social, and cultural hegemony as a world power, whose destiny he could have a hand in shaping.

It should not be surprising, then, that one of Villard's key motivating factors in helping found and lead the NAACP concerned his embarrassment over the befuddled reaction of European intellectuals to the state of race relations in the United States and to the lack of a concerted patronage effort on the part of the country's white elite. In the speech that he gave as the chair of the committee responsible for outlining a charge for the new organization at the National Negro Conference of 1909, Villard wrote: "The enlightened traveller who comes to this country from Europe, whether it be Dr. Barth from Germany, or H. G. Wells or Sir Harry Johnston from England, to study our social and racial conditions, is usually appalled at the prejudice against the negro he encounters."[18] When such men asked him what organizations were focusing on helping the race, he had no good response. Villard scolds himself and his fellow intellectual-social elite for not having any substantial organization to show these eminent Europeans. His commitment to the downtrodden race in his own country underscores his sense of his place in national and world civilization and bears heavily on his sense of identity and privilege as one who has inherited ownership and control of the Negro problem just as he inherited the patrimony of the railroad and electricity stocks. When considering the gender and sexual dynamics of race patronage, therefore, we should not underestimate the social, psychic, and ideological impact of the desire to sustain a place in such patrilineal structures, however much this cathexis toward patrimony may *seem* to contradict the progressive intention of a cooperative cross-racial venture. In having to negotiate Villard's considerable power, formal and informal, over the emerging organization, Du Bois must have been painfully aware, like Trotter and Wells-Barnett, that suspicions would be in order, however much good intentions and a small measure of other people's fortunes were put on the line for black uplift.

Despite his focus on such social, political, and ideological entanglements in his feud with Villard, Du Bois also understood the economic factor in race patronage. To avoid being beholden to the board under Villard, Du Bois says, he devised a plan to keep the new NAACP journal, *The Crisis,* separate fiscally and thus independent ideologically from the board's editorial influence. Initially, Du Bois repeatedly circumvented Villard's attempts to rein in his calls for social equality in the increasingly popular and economically self-supporting periodical. Villard's opposition to Du Bois was not merely a matter of pulling social, racial, and gender rank. It was more substantially an ideological difference resulting from Villard's desire to maintain his superior social, racial, economic, and patrimonial investment as a manifestation of his deeply felt commitment to the race. Expressing conflicting feelings about the social equality of the races, Villard suggested there were two sides to the lynching controversy when he demanded that Du Bois report statistics of black crimes alongside his reports on lynchings. Du Bois's successful dodges of such demands through the fiscal independence of *The Crisis* ultimately diminished Villard's hand in the organization—a remarkable outcome, given Villard's myriad advantages.

Du Bois attributes his success in the early days of the organization to an "anomalous" doubleness that also hinges on a peculiar but symptomatic economic relationship of patronage disemployment. Despite Du Bois's arguments for the *personal* as the proper sphere embodying cross-racial cooperation, we discover that it is in the economic sphere of employer to employee that the struggle against white patronizing practices is most effectively waged:

> I held the rather anomalous position of being both a member of the board and, as executive officer, the board's employee. This was not from any demand which I made, but was due to the inescapable fact that I knew the Negro problem better than any of the white members of the board, and at the same time I was the one colored man whom they could put their hands on to carry out the objects of the organization. My double capacity was repeatedly a matter of discussion, and sometimes dispute; but no answer was forthcoming for 24 years. (*Autobiography of W.E.B. Du Bois* 257)

Du Bois's "double capacity" reminds us of double consciousness, a theory that the scholarship on Du Bois has taken as a way of explaining racial oppression solely in terms of psychological, epistemological, ideological, sociological, and discursive effects. In Du Bois's 1968 *Autobiography,* however, we discover that he applies the theory of doubling to his tenure at the NAACP as an economic cause of racial oppression as well. The theory is useful for understanding his status, and that of other black leaders, as a patron of the race who also must be a gainfully employed protégé of those more capable of being race patrons because of their inherited economic wealth and social status. Du Bois was needed by the board as a token of their intention to deal fairly in bringing African American leaders into the political struggle for their rights, but unlike the other *male* board members, he also needed to be employed by the organization to be able to carry out this political work. The appearance of a single-minded political integrity among the white men could be protected and enhanced by their lack of an *apparent* economic self-interest in helping organize an oppressed people politically—a major difference from the clear economic benefit accruing to captains of industry from their interest in promoting industrial education at black colleges. In fact, the white male NAACP patrons were expending their time, energy, political, social, and economic capital as a sacrifice for this cause without any *direct* economic return, whereas Du Bois—and all other black men employed in executive positions by the NAACP—can more easily be perceived as possessing a prime opportunity for double-dealing and selling out as a result of economic dependence on political work. In this way, Du Bois is no less vulnerable than Washington to the charges of an appearance of financial self-interest that he makes against Washington.

Du Bois's notion that he "was the one colored man whom they could put their hands on to carry out the objects of the organization" may be accurate in some sense, but it is also deeply problematic and part of the economic illusion of scarcity in the structure of race patronage during the Jim Crow era.[19] As long as Du Bois was able to keep *The Crisis* financially independent, he was able to hire black middle-class staff, to take his own editorial line (sometimes in direct conflict with the "parent" organization), to appeal directly to the race in print as well in speeches made on the road, and to claim the journal as a black-controlled institution within the larger white-controlled patronage structure. That he was able to maintain a significant degree of autonomous control over his project by keeping it separate from the NAACP agenda ironically approaches the way that Washington created autonomous control of the black Tuskegee Machine with the backing of a seemingly noninterfering white patronage structure. "For Du Bois, the relationship between the NAACP and *The Crisis* was governed by the otherwise repellent doctrine of separate but equal," Lewis points out, "and the subordination of the former to the latter, if need be" (*W.E.B. Du Bois: Biography of a Race* 472). In other words, given the disincentives of race patronage to grant to black leaders their political—much less economic—due, it was better to negotiate the limitations of a separate, segregated institution within the larger white-controlled structure than to be apparently equal with no autonomy for one's own agenda. Du Bois's explanation of his anomalous *economic* status as a patron is structurally similar to Washington's, despite the two men's ideological skirmish.

The fact is that Du Bois, like Washington and unlike his white male patrons, depended on the spoils of race patronage for a living. He could not afford to work at the NAACP without pay. Villard's capacity to view his race work as literal patronage—as a form of *noblesse oblige*—allowed him to imagine himself as bestowing an honor on the race, an honor whose sacrifice deserved an eternal debt of gratitude. This is a debt that the black race could never repay both because blacks literally could not afford to pay back the rich white capitalist and because it coerced a spiritual debt—an aura of white self-sacrifice—for which there is no adequate mode of reciprocation. The spiritual debt raises the ante, so to speak, of the patron's investment to the level of a permanently unequal exchange, whereas the monetary debt at least presents the promise that the amount dispensed can one day be repaid in full, with interest.

At the same time, the notion of spiritual debt also embeds the obligation of gratitude so deeply in the body and psyche of the black beneficiary that, as we shall see in the case of Langston Hughes, it can be exorcised only through a debilitating physical and psychic illness cured accordingly by vomiting the gifts of the white donor. The spiritual obligation forced by the white donor places the black ward in an impossible position. Like Du Bois, the black male ward must desire physical and emotional proximity to the white patron in order to gain access to the patron's considerable resources of money and capital, social prestige, political clout, homosocial influence, family obligation, and civilizing mastery; at the same time, he must desire his autonomy as an antidote to being infected with the eternal debt and gratitude fostered by such intimacy. Du Bois's status was like that of a vassal suitor who needs to inflame desire in his lordship, but not so much desire that, in being granted his suit, he finds himself in irreparable debt to his superior. Just as the European courtly practices on which United States racial patronage is based infuse political supplication with the language of erotic seduction and vice versa, so racial patronage sublimates the sexual taboos of Jim Crow (that black and white men cannot procreate or inherit the same family line) into the political maneuvers of cross-racial patronage.

For Du Bois to remain "his own man," he had to make *The Crisis* economically self-sufficient, which meant that he also had to justify the provision of his own salary—an unavoidable conflict of interest for virtually all African American race leaders of the period.[20] When *The Crisis* began to lose subscribers during the Depression, Du Bois found himself no longer able to sustain this independence, and he ended up having to part with the organization. Under such circumstances, it seems inevitable that the underlying economic basis for Du Bois's patronage status must eventually undercut the semblance of limited autonomy. The white patrons set up standards to make it appear that only a limited number of African Americans could become central to the organization without damaging its efficiency. This sort of patronage thrives on a capitalist economic logic in which competence is a scarce commodity within the Negro race, a scarcity literally embodied in the exceptional black male leaders at the NAACP and that must be compensated by the excess of competence among white patrons, male and female.[21] Rather than Du Bois being indispensable to the NAACP *as a unique individual,* then, he was indispensable merely as a token value, a representative body who could be exchanged for another deemed of the same kind or of similar worth.[22] In this system of patronage the market demand—the degree of dispensability or worth of Du Bois's talent—is determined by the white patrons whose money makes the political work feasible. Not surprisingly, the white patrons were able to put their hands on another colored man who could carry out the objects of the organization at the same time that Du Bois began to lose the economic independence of *The Crisis.*

Tensions arose between Du Bois and the first African American secretary of the organization, James Weldon Johnson, in the early 1920s, which also played out in a triangulated relationship to Mary White Ovington. In addition to the suppression of the black female as a proper rival and the white male as a claimed rival, the political influence of the black male leader who would be patron is tested in sexualized rivalry with other black men, a test that must be staged before the observing gaze of white patrons, male and female. Although some of the disputes between Johnson and Du Bois were definitely ideological and focused on Du Bois's control of *The Crisis* in ways that could be seen to conflict with the policies of the NAACP, the rivalry of two black men for the attention of a white woman helps to define this ideological difference. Wedin writes:

> Du Bois's resistance [concerning control of *The Crisis*] increased as Johnson's star ascended. They were the same age, and their careers equally distinguished. Johnson excelled in administrative, negotiating, people, and language skills, conversing in French or Spanish on his trips to Haiti or Nicaragua. He was also as black as Du Bois—and that meant the editor lost leverage that he used in conflicts.
>
> With Johnson's rise, the necessity to keep Du Bois on board diminished, and he felt it. He took great offense in 1923 when, from his point of view, he was not asked until the last minute to be on the Kansas City convention program, and then was told by Ovington that they could not pay everyone's way.[23]

Wedin goes on to explain that Du Bois "might well have been jealous on another score: Johnson supplanted him in Mary White Ovington's admiration and affection."[24] Seemingly confirming the validity of Wells-Barnett's depiction of Ovington, the feud between these two leading men of the leading civil rights organization could easily be represented as merely a personal matter of incompatible temperament or as more seriously a problem of how masculine rivalry operates under consequences of racial oppression. However, to cast this rivalry solely in such terms is to overlook the extent to which the ideological limitations and complications of the patronage system encourage such a rivalry. After all, power in dominant society is frequently enacted and symbolized through competition over a desirable woman. Why would a patronage organization founded, funded, and administered by some of the most influential white men in the nation be exempt from such a paradigm? If anything, the logic of black exceptionality—the idea that only one *man* has the right to speak for the race—might tend to intensify this dominant paradigm.

If the rise of Johnson created a rivalrous racial situation, then in 1931, at the outset of the Great Depression when *The Crisis* was losing its customer base, the rise of Walter White, Johnson's handpicked protégé, to the executive directorship boded even worse for Du Bois. White and Du Bois entered into a homoracial skirmish as they became the two most influential black men in the organization, fighting for the support of the predominantly white board. Du Bois's assessment of White's ambition parallels that which he offers of Villard's:

> White could be one of the most charming of men. He was small in stature, appealing in approach, with a ready smile and a sense of humor. Also he was an indefatigable worker, who seemed never to tire. On the other hand, he was absolutely self-centered and egotistical to the point that he was almost unconscious of it. He seemed really to believe that his personal interests and the interest of his race and organization were identical. This led to curious complications, because to attain his objects he was often absolutely unscrupulous. (*Autobiography of W.E.B. Du Bois* 293)

First consider why Du Bois begins his complaint by noting that White is "small in stature." Does this small stature make White less threatening as a black man rubbing shoulders with white men *and white women?* Du Bois seems to think so when he links White's diminutive stature to his being "appealing in approach, with a ready smile and a sense of humor." Subtly, Du Bois is suggesting that a diminutive black man can use his size to diminish his masculine threat. Jack Johnson understood this racial/sexual dynamic of cross-racial male rivalry when he exploited his gigantic size (and exaggerated the size of his penis) to psyche out the less-than-great white hopes in the boxing ring, and in his conquest of white women.[25] Just as white men labeled blacks "uncles" to emasculate them, so they could be more at ease with a little black man, similar to the way that medieval sultans could trust their harems only to eunuchs. We must connect Du Bois's use of the black male physical body to Pickens's tendency to focus on black male leadership as a matter of sizing up the potency of one's rivals. In the same way that Pickens calls the black intermediaries at black colleges "the little men in charge," Du Bois implies that white men place White in charge of the black uplift effort because he is merely a little man. And as we see in the next chapter, this reduction of masculine rivalry to the physical size of a man's body parts also plays a role in Negro Renaissance patronage rivalry, as both Claude McKay and Langston Hughes attempt to diminish the patronage influence of Alain Locke by foregrounding his "small hand," which implies a sissy demeanor that lessens his claim as a racial leader of the New Negro avant-garde.

Du Bois's characterization of White is interesting in light of our discussion of the sissy hero of White's first novel, *Fire in the Flint*. Du Bois's portrait seems the opposite of White's fictionalization of a heroic black aspiring patron. Whereas White's Dr. Harper is ambivalent about his claim to leadership, timid about his command of others, incapable of viewing his private needs as synonymous with his public obligations, and desirous of an undisturbed private life of contemplation, Du Bois portrays White as aggressive and undeviating in his political purposes and as someone ambitious to become the predominant race leader. The danger of White's equating his own interests with the interests of the race is one that it would be difficult to avoid under circumstances in which white patrons hand-select the black men who are to serve as mediators between them and the race. And the "burden of representation" in this equation of White and the black race becomes even more twisted when we remember that White called himself a "volunteer Negro." White's whiteness would, like his small stature, go far in diminishing white men's closeted fears of having to compete head to head with real black men. Unlike his resentment of Villard, Du Bois's rivalry with White is more easily structured as the opposition of equals. In the logic of cross-racial patronage, either man can replace the other in representing the race. From the viewpoint of the homoracial rivalry that Du Bois and White experience, however, each sees the other as the one in need of reform, just as each sees himself as the man best capable of tutoring the other.

When Du Bois describes White as attempting to control what emerges as the leading black uplift organization of the country, he is making an implicit analogy to Washington's machinery. That he sees White as equating his personal ambition with the uplift of the race also indicates this. However, Du Bois's personal control of *The Crisis* was also, on occasion, seen as a sort of political machine by others. According to Lewis, May Childs Nerney, one of the white women who served as NAACP executive secretary in the early years, started referring to *The Crisis* as Du Bois's "personal machine" (*W.E.B. Du Bois: Biography of a Race* 477). Washington himself also implied that Du Bois was attempting to set up a sort of black boss machinery. In a letter to T. Thomas Fortune he charged Du Bois with cowardice, which helps explain his rival's capitulation of the race to white men:

> Du Bois did run away from Atlanta. All the time that the riot was going on, Du Bois was hiding at the Calhoun School in Alabama—a school which I was responsible for establishing some fifteen years ago. He remained there until the riot was over and then came out and wrote a piece of poetry bearing upon those who were killed in the riot.
>
> There are some curious things going on. It seems strange that our friends Villard and John E. Milholland are attempting to run and control the destinies of the Negro race through Du Bois. I think they will have a tough time of it, as in my opinion, the Negro in New York like the Negro everywhere else is going to do his own thinking and own acting and not be second fiddle to a few white men, who

feel that the Negro race belongs to them. I am glad that you went for Du Bois in the way that you did.

Following Washington's instructions in publishing articles that would discredit Du Bois's role in the NAACP, Fortune responded: "When we get done with Dr. Du Bois I am sure that he will have some trouble in handing over the leadership of the race to white men."[26]

Washington impugns Du Bois as a coward by stringing together a series of associations that begins with accusations about his hiding during the Atlanta race riots, his then writing in sympathy with the victims of the riots, and his actions in the NAACP. Reminiscent of the fears of White's hero Dr. Kenneth Harper that his secret enjoyment of belles lettres will put him in a suspect gender position as a black leader, Washington links Du Bois's "piece of poetry" with unmanly illegitimacy and insufficiency. Poetry is opposed here to the masculine world of Realpolitik, just as Du Bois's naive faith in liberal arts is posed as an inadequate tool for the strong-arm power plays required of one who expects to lead the reform of the black masses in an age of robber-baron industrial capitalism. Washington's instruction to Fortune to use hard-hitting, underhanded yellow journalism to discredit Du Bois indicates exactly the kind of real-world tactics that Washington believes a canny—and manly—race patron must be willing to exploit.

Although Washington, Wells-Barnett, Johnson, Du Bois, and White are clearly doing what they think best for the race from their individual points of view, the logistics and economics of cross-racial patronage in this period demand that each be in competition to be leading mediator between white patrons and the mass of the race itself. In this competition, Wells-Barnett is at a tremendous disadvantage due to sex, as her struggle over the Committee of Forty bears out. Her gender presents a complicating factor in that, given the existing suspicions about black leaders' competence to carry out rationally the inflammatory political objects of the organization, her self-confident, demanding personality would even more likely be taken as the temperamental envy of a difficult prima donna. Like the idea that there must be sexual competition between black and white women in the politics of race patronage, the homoracial struggle between white and black and black and black men derives from a sexual ideology that views black men and women as properly lesser rivals in the terrain of white men's homosocial competition and superior *noblesse oblige;* at the same time, black male leaders are seen as beholden to rich white patrons, male *and* female, for their entitlement to mediating leadership as the patriarchal heads of the race. To earn that patrimony of white *noblesse oblige,* one must first have an independent income; one must also be able to identify peremptorily with the advanced civilization of a race that has sped so far ahead of all others that it can afford to look back and toss favors to those left behind.

Mothering the Race: The White Woman as Race Patron

While a black woman like Wells-Barnett had to struggle to be included in the cross-racial political organizing of the early decades of the twentieth century, upper-class white women were presented with other challenges born from possessing high social status without attendant access to political clout, income and capital, and the homosocial cliques of white male privilege. This paradox of white women's highly visible role in the Progressive Era reform movements in general, and in anti–Jim Crow race reform in particular, is embodied in the word *patron* itself. To what extent can a white woman become a patron, as opposed to occupying the status of *matron*, a seemingly less dissonant term given the gender roles circumscribing her within the domestic sphere? As we shall see in the next chapter, this question relates to the habit of applying the term *midwife* to men given credit for originating and managing the Harlem Renaissance. To call a woman a patron or a man a midwife may seem a naive gender-bending gesture, but more is at stake in such terminology than semantics. "Midwife" bespeaks the tendency to view aesthetics and artistic culture as feminine spheres of influence. It would be hard to imagine someone saying that a man had midwifed a war, a new form of government, or a great sports team. The "midwife" label also befits the problematic gender identity of influential black men in United States culture more broadly. To say that a black man *fathered* the Harlem Renaissance seems to give too much potency both to the man's role in United States culture and to the status of the renaissance itself as a bastard child of American culture.

Similarly, women's relation to the term *patron* is necessarily beset with gender-bending irregularities. When a high-ranking white woman enters the larger sphere of political and social reform, she is still circumscribed, if subtly, by a sort of domestic function. Her proper role is to "mother" the movement, to provide the "higher" sentiments of cultural, spiritual, and social guidance rather than the rough-and-tumble masculine attributes of political savvy, business acumen, corporate experience, or entrepreneurial know-how. Although black and white women displayed such masculine patronizing skills, their contributions in doing so were seen as exceptional and tended to be reduced anyway to the image of "mothering." By exploring further Ovington's efforts at race patronage and black men's views of her efforts, we can observe how black men's claims to racial self-reform were necessarily placed in competition with white women's professional and political aspirations, even a major black female "patron" such as Wells-Barnett could view black men and white women in an erotically tinged conspiracy. It also helps to keep in mind that this rivalry between black men and white women within cross-racial uplift organizations was being enacted during the 1910s and 1920s, that transitional moment when white women were achieving their long struggle for the franchise at the same time that most black men were still barred from voting and other markers of full citizenship, despite the passage of the Fifteenth Amendment to the Constitution more than fifty years earlier. It may be that the black male–white female rivalry was intensified by the prospect of the New (White) Woman, most tangibly represented by her newly won right to vote. Just as doling out voting rights as a scarce commodity during the struggle over the Fifteenth Amendment in the 1860s had pitted prominent white suffragists, who had supported the black freedom cause, against black men, who had generally supported women's suffrage, so in this Jim Crow moment the system of white male privilege exploits racial uplift patronage as a scarce resource that naturally divides the ambitions of white women from the ambitions of black men.[27]

As a socialist woman, Mary White Ovington seems much more aware of the politics of class and sex in race work than her fellow patron, Villard. In her memoirs, *Black and White Sat Down Together,* and even more in her personal history of the NAACP, *The Walls Came Tumbling Down,* Ovington goes out of her way to resist the patronizing habits that routinely characterize cross-racial political patronage after Reconstruction and before the Civil Rights period. She tellingly suggests that "philanthropy and justice often stand apart. The very recognition of the need of philanthropy denies justice" (*Walls* 168). Although Ovington herself may have been able to resist some of the most apparent patronizing habits in her work and writing, as we have seen in the Committee of Forty controversy, the machinery of personal politics operates both within and against the work to which she devotes most of her adult life. As Carolyn Wedin points out in her afterword to the 1995 reprint of *Black and White Sat Down Together,* Ovington's reminiscences are even more reticent about self-assertion and self-revelation than the very reticent autobiographies of contemporary women reformers like Jane Addams. Wedin also remarks that Ovington unfortunately has fallen between the cracks of histories in both African American studies and women's studies (*Black and White* 159–160). Given that until Wedin's 1998 biography so little was written about her in historical, literary, or sociological studies, it is not surprising that most commentary on her life remains in the realm of the heavenly crusader (with the exception of Wells-Barnett's critical comments, which should not be overlooked). On the surface, it may appear that, unlike Wells-Barnett or Du Bois, both of whom had to trumpet their worthiness for race patronage, Ovington could avoid such self-promotion. Yet, as we examine the link between her patronage status and the black men whom she deigns to aid, we discover a more complicated relationship to black male patronage than such feminine modesty would allow. What the white female would-be patron and the black male would-be patron say about each other reveals a great deal about the sexual machinery of race patronage.

This remarkable woman who decided against marriage and devoted her life to social and economic reform is frequently represented as a twentieth-century embodiment of Du Bois's angelic Yankee schoolmarm. In Walter White's foreword to *The Walls Came Tumbling Down,* he calls her a "Fighting Saint." In his unpublished version of the introduction he sets forth a physical description that calls up the menacing, unfeminine figure of the monstrous Yankee schoolmarm in order to dispute it:

Her delicately pale blue eyes, her placid and sensitive face, and her beautifully tailored pastel clothes leave breathless and defenseless those who meet her for the first time after becoming angered because of her views. When, instead of the grubbily dressed, fanatic-eyed loose-moralled [sic] female which neurotic enemies always picture in their minds as typical of those who speak out for minorities, such visitors to Miss Ovington's office find her quite different, it is usually some time before they can gather their wits together enough to launch the planned attack. When her cool and incisive wit and wisdom [are?] brought into the discussion, Miss Ovington's erstwhile foes are changed into friends.[28]

In linking Ovington's virtue to her physical appeal—and its capacity to captivate the unsuspecting observer—White ironically hinges the effective agency of this female reformer not on her intellectual or verbal skills, nor on her ideological commitment, but on her physical attributes. Furthermore, he constructs her captivating beauty noticeably on the quintessential aesthetic standards of white femininity—delicacy, pale blue eyes, calm, sensitivity that can be immediately read in the face, and subdued clothing. Adding "her cool and incisive wit and wisdom" to her physical features, White's portrait falls into a cliché of the refined, civilized, urbane white woman—the nemesis of Nella Larsen's character Helga Crane, who feels like a savage in donning loud clothes (discussed in chapter 7). Furthermore, White's tribute unwittingly replicates Wells-Barnett's scene of the college-bred black man so rapt in adoration of the upper-class white woman that he is distracted from the actual political objective of her presence. By insisting that "Miss Ovington" is not the ugly harpy that opponents of her agenda would imagine her to be, White unintentionally reinforces this stereotype of the female reformer by making Ovington a rare specimen of real feminine beauty, implying that where other, less conventionally attractive women would fail, she succeeds in converting enemies into friends. Ovington's chastity—or at least her unwedded state—contributes to this iconography, in which the most common standards of white feminine beauty are made out to be magnetizing because exceptionally virginal and pure.

As Wedin suggests, Ovington's decision to cut White's material from the published version of the introduction may be attributed to her desire to remain behind the scenes, not bringing attention to herself as a central historical agent even as she enacts this agency to the utmost.[29] However, beyond proper feminine embarrassment and erasure of the ego in sacrifice to a larger community and cause, it may also be that Ovington felt uncomfortable with White's focus on the physical rather than on her mental, ethical, political, and ideological commitments. Ovington herself exploits physicality, that of black men as well as her own, on those occasions in the autobiography when she wants to bring attention to her motivations in being attracted to—as well as *attractive* to—the cause of racial uplift.

Like many of the first generation of college-educated women—black and white—born in the decades of the Civil War and Reconstruction, Ovington relied on social welfare and reform organizations as a way of professionalizing herself and gaining an important role in the political sphere before women possessed the franchise. Thus, the professionalization of white middle-class women might be analogized to that of black middle-class men who exploited sociology as a forum for garnering cultural authority, given the lack of the masculine entitlements to full citizenship. As with some of the most prominent among these women, Ovington's unmarried status provided a certain freedom to pursue sociopolitical activism ironically based in the need (and desire) to earn a living, not so much economically as psychologically. Wedin points out that until 1930, Ovington relied on a modest income provided by the family gift-shop industry, but after the death of her older brother and the Depression, earning money became more of an issue (*Black and White* 148). In this way, Ovington is halfway between African American leaders (both male and female), almost all of whom had no family fortune of any kind to rely on, and her white male colleagues at the NAACP—Villard, Milholland, the Spingarns—all of whom were independently wealthy. Possessing nonetheless an elite New England inheritance of *noblesse oblige* as the descendant of blue-blood abolitionists, Ovington has a "kin" relation to her colored wards (though less patronizing than that of Villard) that still participates in some of the crucial aspects of old-fashioned race patronage.

Ovington characterizes her race work not only as resulting from a deeply felt commitment but also from that greatest apparent resource of upper-class women—leisure: "I was the only one among the white and colored board of the Association who had plenty of leisure and at the same time a conviction that this was the most important work that she could do. So dropping all interest not Negro, I gave time—the one thing Moorfield Storey or Oswald Villard or Hutchins Bishop did not have—to the Association's needs."[30] Self-deprecatingly, Ovington puts herself in the conventional place of the elite white lady with moral integrity and deep conscience, transforming her one resource, leisure, for the benefit of a marginal group. Money, however, crops up repeatedly in *Black and White,* and as Wedin points out, Ovington's lack of wealth is made an advantage (*Black and White* 153). Her need for money, instead of being an embarrassment, is emphasized because it places her in closer empathy with her black colleagues and thus enhances her sympathy for those whom she aids. If Ovington does not exactly seek out the adoration of college-bred black male leaders—that is, if this is not the guiding motivation of her sacrificial work—the sexual and racial effect of her presence nonetheless cannot be separated from elite leisure, desire for professionalization and for earning a living, racial standards of feminine beauty, and the claim to an abolitionist family legacy.

Physical attraction operates in an odd manner in the autobiography, but instead of going from black men as desiring subjects to Ovington as desirable white object, the attraction is directed from desiring white subjects, male and female, toward black objects, male and female. Black men in particular occupy a special niche as objects of white desire in her narrative of discovering her attraction to the Negro problem. In the first chapter, aptly titled "Early Impressions,"[31] Ovington begins with an unidentified upper-class couple on their way to hear Frederick Douglass speak in 1890. She describes the conventionally attractive physical attributes of the couple: "The girl is conspicuously blonde, blue eyes, pink cheeks, golden hair; the man—well, if you want to know what the man looked like, see McMonnies's statue of Nathan Hale in the New York City Hall Park. He posed for it, and it's a perfect likeness" (*Black and White* 3). The couple are arguing "excitedly" over the fact that Douglass has just married a white woman, he "in defense of the dominant race" and she "in defense of the individual." Ovington ascribes the difference in opinion to region, not to sex: "The girl is of New York and Yankee descent. The young man, she realizes for the first time, has roots in Baltimore." As Douglass mounts the platform, his physical presence takes charge of the audience, including the originally dubious male companion:

> He is a strong, powerfully built man, with brown skin and a shock of bushy hair. His eyes gleam with that liveliness to things about him so common to the Negro. He stands at the reading desk, immovable, unsmiling, looking at the applauding audience. The girl leans forward, clapping excitedly. The man leans forward, too, and pays his tribute.
>
> "I don't wonder she married him," he says. "He looks like Aesop." (3–4)

Similar to White's unpublished description of Ovington's physical power of conversion, this scene of adoration depicts the physique of the strong, powerfully built black man as having a magnetism so attractive that it can reform "Baltimore roots," converting the white man from a strict segregationist to a racial liberal—indeed, a miscegenationist—on first glance. This image of the big black man magnetizing a white man and woman to join the racial cause seems to contradict Du Bois's inference that only a little black man can be placed in charge of the race; but this is less a contradiction than merely the other side of the same coin. If the white male companion does not exactly fall in love with Douglass, he does experience what it might be like if he could do so. Instead of directly acknowledging his physical attraction to Douglass's person and personality, he expresses his desire through an identification with Douglass's white wife, empathizing with her desire. Douglass's physical presence contrasts with the "conspicuously blonde" features of the female companion and transcends the statuesqueness of the male companion, for rather than merely posing for a statue of a hero, Douglass is recognized as the living embodiment of a great classic. In his transcendence, however, Douglass still holds true to racial type: "His eyes gleam with that liveliness to things about him so common to the Negro." Even as Ovington through her characters is attracted to Douglass's gigantic stature, she finds a way of diminishing him by reducing his gaze to the racial typology of the shiny-eyed Negro—an act that we see her performing more explicitly in relation to working-class black men.

In the succeeding paragraphs, Ovington drops the third-person perspective, proceeding with an explanation of the encounter in the first person. "I had never seen Frederick Douglass before (I drop the third person not to resume it) and I was never to see him again, but that night was to me a great event. I had come face to face with one of my heroes" (4). Because she knows people of African descent only in imagination, through her reading and through the family legacy, which she describes in the next few paragraphs, she supposedly is able to possess a picture of and relationship to black people different from those of Southerners, who encounter "the Negro" too closely and frequently "in the flesh": "I did not know the Negro in the flesh. My 'mammy' was Irish and quite as devoted, I am sure, as any black woman. We had no Negro servants" (4). This notion of the flesh takes on vital significance in Ovington's reminiscences. Her argument insists that it is only "in the flesh" that the race problem can be solved. The activity of black and white sitting down together constitutes the radical act of racial advancement in and of itself.

Ovington's only physical contact with a black person comes in the form of a repeated patronage incident: "Once a year at Thanksgiving time, an old, blind Negro, led by an attractive boy, came to our church and asked for money for the Howard Orphan Asylum. I think we sent him away pleased. Anyway, he always said so. He was the only Negro with whom I had any contact. Otherwise I knew the race by its heroic deeds" (4). That Ovington had no contact with African Americans is revealing, because she grew up not far from the black middle-class neighborhood in Brooklyn. Contrasting her first encounter with a black hero from her fantasies with her only physical contact with African Americans, we see the difference between the potential and the condition of the race. Against Douglass's gleaming eyes, the eyes of the old, blind beggar do not capture her imagination, but they do breed in her a sense of duty to the race. This bifurcation of the race into the heroic male leader and the pathetic, helpless beggar, representing the downtrodden mass, is sustained throughout the autobiography, and it duplicates the patronage ideology in which exceptional Negro men represent the potential for more equal contact with liberal whites while they serve as a proxy for the interests of the mass of backwards black people, who are kept at a physical, social, and psychological distance in accordance with Jim Crow.

Ovington's "second direct Negro contact" (her first being the encounter with Douglass, not the beggar?) comes, predictably, with the man who supplanted Douglass as leader of the race: Booker T. Washington. By charting her motivation to become a race worker back through these two black *male* patrons of the race, Ovington can frame her own bid to patronage through them, compensating for her patronage deficiency as a woman by identifying with the masculine strength of their heroic blackness. Through this narrative of black male–white female attraction—one is tempted to say *seduction*—she makes it clear that she is predestined to participate in this line of leadership. As a member of the Social Reform Club, who have been reading *Up from Slavery* as it appears in installments in *Outlook* magazine, she chairs the committee responsible for arranging a dinner for Washington. Although Ovington distances herself from Washington—perhaps as one of those "not standing up more for his rights"—she nonetheless repeats the scene of adoration in which a white man is magnetized by the presence of a leading black man:

Booker Washington did not shine particularly that night. Maggie Washington made an interesting speech on her work among Negro mothers. But the person who remains in my memory is the late William H. Baldwin. I can see him now at the speakers' table, leaning forward, looking at Washington, and saying: "I worship that man." (*Black and White* 10)

Baldwin, one of the most important patrons of Tuskegee, seems to submit himself to the black hero—surely a rhetorical flourish rather than an actual relationship, given his power to make or break Tuskegee's, and Washington's, fortunes. Through Baldwin's gaze at Washington, the race leader of the moment, Ovington gives Washington his due; however, for the black audience of the Baltimore *Afro-American* magazine in which the memoir first appeared, she lets it be known that, from the start, her agenda lies not with Washington but with a more radical ideology.

The sexual basis of Ovington's patronage operates subtly, then, from the start of the autobiography. Not only does she initially position the race problem as a sexual dispute (between a white couple and over a black-white couple), but she identifies its solution with the capacity of white men in particular to be attracted to heroic black male leaders. Ovington's shift from socialist patronage of the white working class to devotion solely to the race problem also operates within a gendered social arrangement and psychological evolution based in cross-racial attraction. Ovington's desire to work for the race results not only from what she sees as a greater need on the part of the race but also from a deeper desire to feel needed as an exceptional radical woman. The Negro problem represents this neediness beyond her unsatisfactory commitment to the white poor, who, she points out, were being aided by many other patrons and women reformers. Her early sociological text *Half a Man: The Status of the Negro in New York* (published in 1911 with a foreword by Franz Boas) is the first major product of Ovington's shift from the white working class to the Negro problem. As the title indicates, she examines how racial discrimination diminishes the manhood especially of unskilled male laborers and creates a situation in which disemployment characterizes the mass of black men and an unusually high degree of employment outside the home characterizes black women. Like the Chicago sociologists, Ovington also attempts to explain other patterns—truancy and crime, for instance—by providing a statistical and ethnological portrait of the race in its new urban habitat.

Throughout her career, Ovington was at such great pains to correct the stereotype of the black brute that she countered it with the image of the white brute in the form of the southern white male rapist.[32] Against the stereotype of the black brute, she also offered a different image of the typical black man amid his family:

Paul Laurence Dunbar has painted the Negro father, his "little brown baby wif sparklin' eyes," nestling close in his arms.[33] Working at unusual hours, the colored man often has a part of the day to give to his family, and one sees him wheeling the baby in its carriage, or playing with the older boys and girls.

Negroes seem naturally a gentle, loving people. As you live with them and watch them in their homes, you find some coarseness, but little real brutality. Rarely does a father or mother strike a child. Travellers in Central and West Africa describe them as the most friendly of savage folk, and where, as in our city, they live largely to themselves, they keep something of these characteristics. (*Half a Man* 71–72)

Ovington's initial investment in the Negro problem is motivated by this projection of natural gentleness onto black people, and especially black men, as the essence of their racial temperament, as opposed to her difficulties with the temperament of the white working class. As this temperament is sexualized, it presents the familiar stereotype of the working-class black woman as a natural mammy: "And if the child lavishes affection upon its parent, the mother in turn gives untiringly to her child. She is the 'mammy' of whom we have so often heard, but with her loving care bestowed, as it should be, upon her own offspring" (70). As the reference to Dunbar's dialect poem indicates, Ovington's sociological observations of the migrant people captures them, though in the big city, essentially still tied to the natural ways of the plantation life, along with the stereotypes of that locale. For the black man of the masses, she overlays the familiar folk image of the gentle "uncle" onto the disemployed urban laborer. And as the passage above evinces, lurking not far beneath the surface of this portrait of the "loving" black migrant is the noble savage. The black migrants, however, are in danger of being influenced by their hostile neighbors in the city, the European immigrants: "But it is only a step in New York from Africa into Italy or Ireland; and the step may bring a sad jostling to native friendliness. To hold his own with his white companions on the street or in school, the Negro must become pugnacious, callous to insult, ready to hit back when affronted" (72). Ovington here is addressing the same problem of gender dissonance that Walter White embodies in his protagonist, Dr. Kenneth Harper. Just as White represents southern white men as uncivilized brutes next to Harper's sensitive demeanor but also indicates how this sensitivity subtracts from Harper's capacity for conventional heroics, so Ovington, more unilaterally, casts the white working-class man as a brutal savage and the black working man as gentle—though decidedly not genteel.

The same temperament that makes the Negro migrants seemingly so amenable and attractive for Ovington's patronage objective also makes them vulnerable to the bad influences of the white immigrants whose reform she has abandoned. The "native friendliness" of black migrants is no match for the aggressions of the white immigrants. We can infer that this special vulnerability of the working-class black man—what she calls his "sensitive" nature—requires the kind of guardianship and tutoring for which *Half a Man* is the preparatory casebook.

I have tried to depict the New York colored wage earners as they labor in the city today. They are not a remarkable group, and were they white men, distinguished by some mark of nationality, they would pass without comment. But the Negro is on trial, and witnesses are continually called to tell of his failures and successes. We have seen that both in the attitude of the world about him, and in his own untutored self, there are many obstacles to prevent his advance; and his natural sensitiveness adds to these difficulties. He minds the coarse but often good-natured joke of his fellow laborer, and he remembers with a lasting pain the mortification of an employer's curt refusal of work. Had he the obtuseness of some Americans he would prosper better. (*Half a Man* 102–103)

As we shall see is also the case with Robert E. Park, Ovington needs this romance of the overly sensitive black man to justify her sociological attraction as the basis for her new patronage interest. Although she attributes his diminished manhood to the socioeconomic conditions resulting from racial discrimination, her phrase "half a man" ironically could also refer to the black man's temperamental racial deviation from the masculine norm evident in the more aggressive Italian and Irish immigrants who threaten to coarsen his gentle nature.[34] She sees the black man's diminished power for earning a living as a real problem, but she is also attracted to the masculine deviation that she projects onto him as a kind of sensitive savagery. Is this projection of the sensitive savage so appealing because it alters her own gender relationship to the group she has chosen to patronize—relieving her from merely performing the limited feminine role of the matron, whose job it is to domesticate and sensitize her charges for the gentle rituals of refined civilization? If black men are already natural gentle men and black women natural mammies, she can be relieved from having to perform these tedious domesticating tasks for them. She can then view herself as called to a different, more "masculine" political and economic task.

As we discussed in chapter 2, Taylor Gordon lambastes black men for messing with the superstitions of religion rather than mulling over scientific problems and becoming practical, productive inventors. In effect, he is arguing against the kind of temperamental theory of black men's nature that Ovington holds onto in *Half a Man,* in which native African sensitivity is implicitly contrasted with scientific, mechanical rationality, characterized not only as natively European but also as normatively masculine. "The New York Negro has no position in the mechanical arts," Ovington writes. "It may be that, as we so often hear, the African does not possess mechanical ability. You do not see Negro boys pottering over machinery or making toy inventions of their own" (113). With this characterization, Ovington is presented with a dilemma. She suggests that industrial training is the best avenue for black men to take in advancing their status as a race, but given her suspicion of their mechanical abilities, how effective can they be as skilled laborers? It is this sort of dilemma that drives the sociological observations of *Half a Man* and likewise motivates Ovington's patronage agenda toward a race whose men already possess a sort of feminine sensitivity, which in turn will guarantee both that she is needed to work on their behalf and that she is not needed merely for her femininity.

Perhaps it is difficult to overcome such a dilemma, considering the emphasis placed on social and sexual separation as a basis for racial superiority, and the black man's uncontrollable desire for the white woman as a justification for that separation. Through this logic, by her very presence as a conventionally attractive white woman amid unassaulting black men, Ovington helps disprove the myth of the lascivious intent hidden in black aspirations for racial integration. Ironically, however, her constant appeal to physical attraction as proof of black equality and justification for her race work reminds us of how she, too, cannot escape the sexual undertow of cross-racial identification as magnetic physical attraction.

A large chunk of Ovington's autobiography traces her interest in promoting African American literature and arts in a New Negro Renaissance manner, as least as much as, if not more than, her political contributions to the NAACP. As a sort of renaissance patron, Ovington focuses not on her ability to provide funding for budding artists but rather on her generosity despite humble means, her fine taste, her access to housing in the bohemian districts, and her access to other people's money. As we shall see is also the case with Van Vechten's infamous novel *Nigger Heaven,* Ovington's artistic uplift efforts place the spotlight as much on the chances for the protégé's failure to meet the patron's expectations as on any success, thus reasserting the rigorous standards of high civilization already mastered by the patron. As with Villard's necessary disappointment in the local Negroes who failed to support his Manassas industrial school experiment, the white patrons of the Negro Renaissance cannot help but emphasize the weaknesses of the talented Negroes whom they patronize; otherwise, there would be no rationale for the protégé's neediness and for the patron's being needed. When the weaknesses of the protégé are not being pointed out, the heroic, sacrificial difficulties of the patron's task become the focus. In a chapter on two young black male protégés, Ovington describes how money lent is never returned by one (Didwho Twe), and how the other ends first with abandonment of art for the practical agenda of uplifting the race and then in tragic early death (Richard Lonsdale Brown).[35] In a later chapter, titled "Two of My Girls," she describes the kind of help that she offers two young black female protégées. The rationale for why Ovington genders her arts patronage first through two young black men who fail and then through two young black women who succeed remains obscure; perhaps it accords with her general assumption in her sociological text that the harder path lies in wait for black men. The kind of help she gives the second young woman, Lorenza Jordan Cole, perhaps clarifies the different degree of patronage allowed according to gender, in that she shares an apartment with the young girl. As controversial as this act of integrated living turned out to be, provision of housing would not have been permissible at all as a kind of financial aid to the young men. Certainly, a greater degree of intimacy between patron and protégée is implied with the young women, but it does not seem to be suggested that this greater intimacy allows for their greater success.

In the case of Cole, a pianist at the Cincinnati Conservatory of Music, Ovington casts herself as a "parent" when she agrees to help with the funding for her to attend the Julliard School:

> Impulsively, I told Mrs. Hall [secretary of the Seattle NAACP] that, if she and her friends would raise money to help out for the first half of the year, I would raise it for the second half. Lorenza fell on my neck, and I found myself assuming the responsibilities of a parent. It was the first time, and it looks as though it would be the last time, that I had had means to take up such grave responsibilities. (*Black and White* 109)[36]

Ovington labels her patronage role "parenting"—specifically *not* mothering, perhaps because it is primarily a matter of providing financial means. Equating patronage with parenting raises a number of interesting questions pertinent to the roles taken by male and female, black and white Negro Renaissance patrons. Could Ovington be also assuming or projecting onto the patronage relation an analogy to the blood bond that does not—or cannot—exist, similar to her assumption that the black mammy, who is necessarily not kin, will be devoted to her charges as a blood mother would be? Is money needed for a woman to become this particular sort of patron, rather than merely a society matron? If so, how does money factor into the emotional, psychological, and social implications of a relationship that is supposed to simulate a maternal-filial bond? As is discussed in chapter 5, patronage during the Negro Renaissance movement is frequently expressed as such kin relations, and yet these blood tropes would seem to conflict with the primary "means" through which patronage is established and maintained as a relationship based in cross-racial civilizing contact and monetary contract.

When Rayford Logan says that Ovington is called the "Mother of the New Emancipation, a term she richly deserved" (foreword to *The Walls Came Tumbling Down* I), he extends this trope as a blood relationship between the civilizing matron and the client race as a whole. Likewise, when Claude McKay calls Ovington "the godmother of the N.A.A.C.P." (*Long Way from Home* 113), he is granting her a role similar to that claimed by the leading white female Negro Renaissance matron, Charlotte Osgood Mason, when she demanded that her black protégés call her "godmother." As Wells-Barnett points out in her criticism of the NAACP's treatment of Addams, conceptualizing a female activist as the "mother" of a cause imposes its own constraints. We are more familiar with this notion in terms of the common reference to Rosa Parks as the "Mother of the Civil Rights Movement," an honorific phrase that oddly positions her beyond or above the movement (giving birth to and raising it), rather than as an agent *within* it, effecting it, and shaped by it. Similarly, but perhaps with an even odder metaphorical effect, the phrase "Mother of the New Emancipation" honors Ovington while constraining her within a particular role that limits her agency of and in the new emancipation. The image of the white woman birthing and rearing the New Negro presents an interesting counter to Abraham Lincoln as the father of the old emancipation. Finally, the metaphor positions a white woman in a position that raises questions about black people's role in "parenting" their own movement. If Ovington is the mother of their new emancipation, then what are black women such as Wells-Barnett, Anna Julia Cooper, Mary Church Terrell, and Mary McLeod Bethune to the movement and to her? Also *my* girls? Does this mean that all New Negro men, including contemporaries such as James Weldon Johnson and Du Bois, are her metaphorical sons? Metaphors and honorary titles are rarely meant too be pushed so far, and yet this constant blood troping of the patronage/matronage relations before and during the Negro Renaissance seems to insist on being taken seriously.

Alongside the image of her mothering the race we must set the articles in Ovington's syndicated column, "Book Chat," in which she displays her discriminating cultural taste to chide and encourage the race in its artistic efforts during the emerging Negro cultural renaissance. As an adviser to aspiring Negro writers, Ovington takes on the character of a master of progressive culture, one who has her finger on the pulse of all the most recent developments and thus one who can decide from a superior position the merits and flaws of each effort as well as the whole. Judging African American fiction to be the least impressive of the cultural efforts, Ovington places the black (male?) novelist in a dilemma that is impossible to overcome:

> And each year novels come to me by Negroes, setting forth with some truth the life of the Negro world. I qualify the truthfulness because the educated Negro is afraid of his material. If he writes what he knows intimately, he has to look out of the corner of his eye at his people. "What will they think of me," he asks, "if I ridicule our group?" And out goes a bit of satire.
>
> The race has been laughed at so much, abused so much, that it seems cruel to add to the dark picture; but, after all, colored folk are just as human as white, and the story that refuses to show them as they really are lacks virility. (*Black and White* 121)

As columnist of "Book Chat," Ovington possesses considerable influence over the reception of African American literature and scholarship—or at least this is the way she takes her charge. The number of novels that "come" to her seeking her dispensation confirms the credibility of her mastery and judgment in the field. Her willingness to tell the truth about these books, despite the vulnerability of the race, confirms her capacity to be critical of the race's efforts despite her own sympathy with its cause. Ovington's assumption of the race's sensitive temperament seems to be at work in this assessment of African American (male?) fiction. The sensitivity of the race becomes a typical rationale for why white progressives are needed to shepherd black culture not only as patrons but also as critics. African Americans are still too raw, too exposed, too self-doubting to perform this vital critical role for themselves.

The question of the relationship of racial sensitivity to artistic competence remains enough of a stereotype that Alain Locke counts "self-criticism" as a crucial cultural project as late as 1950.[37] As early as 1921, however, racial oversensitivity is already so salient an issue among cross-racial progressives that Du Bois plays off it in *Darkwater: Voices from within the Veil,* when he begins his essay "Of Beauty and Death" with a dialogue between a blonde woman (Ovington?) and a black speaker (himself?):

> My friend, who is pale and positive, said to me yesterday, as the tired sun was nodding:
> "You are too sensitive."
> I admit, I am—sensitive. I am artificial. I cringe or am bumptious or immobile. I am intellectually dishonest, art-blind, and I lack humor.
> "Why don't you stop all this?" she retorts triumphantly.
> You will not let us.[38]

Du Bois's reading of this charge of oversensitivity unveils its real derivation as a perceived lack within the Negro male leader. Though made as a charge of excess (*oversensitivity*), it is really a charge of masculine deficiency. To be overly sensitive is to be "artificial," cringing, "bumptious," "immobile," "intellectually dishonest," "art-blind," and humorless. The humor in the speaker's response—responding purposively with excessive sensitivity to the woman's statement of what she sees as a fact—does not defeat her accusation but instead reinforces it, giving her a triumphant retort. The teasing flirtation implicit in the brief interchange does not counteract the sobering reality of the speaker's final retort: "You will not let us." Because it is an exchange between a white woman and a black man, Du Bois is also able to highlight the gender aberrance of the accusation; it is usually the man who accuses the woman of being overly sensitive.

In effect, according to Du Bois's pale speaker, and to Ovington, African Americans do not yet possess skin thick enough for hard-hitting realism and self-satire—an odd assessment, given the prevalence of humor and self-satire in black men's writing of 1920s and 1930s (not to mention Washington's self-deprecating humor).[39] African American (male?) fiction too easily risks a lack of "virility," Ovington has decided, because of this excessive vulnerability to racial abuse and ridicule. Her judgment, however, displays confusion in this gendered assessment, for while she asserts that black working-class men are perfectly sensitive for patronizing purposes, she charges that black middle-class men are too sensitive for writing good realistic fiction.

In the end, after her settlement work; after her leadership in the NAACP; after her vast reading in African American literature, history, and sociology; after her personal patronage of individual artistically gifted, "educated Negroes"; after engaging in the fight against *Birth of a Nation* and its propagandizing of the black brute, Ovington rests her own authority and expertise on African American culture with the superiority of ersatz, anachronistic folk expression over the putative "renaissance" embarked on by the black intellectuals of her time. The city Negro is a sham, uprooted figure, heroic only to the extent that *he* struggles against "the white *man.*" Countering the notion that the cityward migration improves culture—a theory made popular by Park and the Chicago sociologists after World War I—Ovington holds out for her reverent belief in dominant American representations of the plantation Negro. Her rejection of the black male as raping brute hinges on her attraction to the gentle savagery of the working-class black man clinging to a folk culture unreconstructed from his plantation past, despite his trek to the big city, and the oversensitivity of the middle-class black man who would become a patron to his own race. It is only through such sexualizing gestures that cut black men in half that Ovington can construct an influential patronage role for herself that both exploits and denies the attraction of her white femininity. It is only by massaging a mutual attraction between the white reformer and her black protégé that she can both exploit and deny her self-conflicting agency as "Mother of the New Emancipation."

Tutoring "the Lady of the Races":
The Ambivalent Attraction of the White Male Patron

Ovington's evasive relationship to patronage as "mothering" clarifies the dodgy sexual predicament of leading black men who would be patrons in biracial activist organizations. Another crucial institutional situation for understanding the gender tenuousness of black men's patronage networks is the prestigious white northern university. By examining the most influential academic race mentor of the early decades of the twentieth century, Robert E. Park (1864–1944), we can begin to illuminate the often obfuscating filial claims made on black male protégés by their white male mentors. When Ralph Ellison speaks of the "unconscious connection between economic interests and philanthropy" mediated by Chicago sociology, he is offering an analysis of race patronage that continues the argument begun by Du Bois. Whereas Du Bois sees the merchant philanthropists of the Progressive Era as supporting Tuskegee and industrial education out of narrow economic and regional self-interest, Ellison suggests that these economic interests are reflected in the rise of Chicago's school of "bourgeois science," with Park as its head tutor.[40] Whereas for both Villard and Ovington race work is inherited along with their family fortunes, for Park it is a wholly new venture, filtered through his interest in newspaper muckraking, philosophy, social science, colonialism in Africa, and the adventuresome "world of men."[41]

After studying at Michigan and Harvard, Park took a job with the Congo Reform Association. Park took with him from this post a keener understanding of the influence of "civilization" on "primitive" cultures. About the Congo mission he writes:

> I discovered what I might have known in advance—that conditions in the Congo were about what one might expect, what they have since become, though not by any means so bad, in Kenya. They were, in short, what they were certain to be whenever a sophisticated people invades the territories of a more primitive people in order to exploit their lands, and incidentally, to uplift and civilize them. I knew enough about civilization even at that time to know that progress as [William] James once remarked, is a terrible thing. It is so destructive and wasteful. (*Race and Culture* vii)

Just as his interest in the Congo was not to change the conditions but to study them in order to understand the progress and waste that sustain the project of civilization, so he went to Tuskegee not as a race "patron," in the old-fashioned sense of that word, but as a student of "race," "culture," and "civilization," with all the residual imperialist implications as well as emerging modern anthropological meanings of these words. In his essay "Culture and Civilization," Park defines these terms as adversarial phenomena. "Culture" means that which is local, parochial, continuously stable (stagnant?), ritualistic, and associated with the mores of traditional agricultural and hunting-based subsistence societies; it is, in other words, what anthropologists of his period call "primitive" or "folk" culture. "Civilization," by contrast, is universalizing, cosmopolitan, ever improving and progressing, secular, and associated with the techniques of utilitarian modern science and high art, literature, history, and philosophy. The farther away one goes from the modern city created from the resources of scientific inquiry, capitalist institutions, and imperial conquest, the closer one is to culture. The closer one is to the metropole, the more one must adapt to a universal, cultureless, technologizing civilization (see *Race and Culture* 18).

In the way Park theorizes the relationship between culture and civilization, racial progress becomes a matter of structural change that naturally (according to a Darwinist paradigm) occurs when an aggressive, restless, mobile group (of men) comes into contact with a more passive group—a notion that reminds us of Pickens's aggressive view of race modernization, discussed in chapter 1.[42] Studying the processes, costs, and benefits of invasion, conquest, adaptation, assimilation, and marginalization, Park helps bring race studies into the age of bourgeois science, just as he helps bring African American students into sociological professionalization as a process of assimilation. In his essay "Politics and 'the Man Farthest Down,'" originally published as an introduction to a 1935 book on Negro politicians, Park identifies Booker T. Washington as the embodiment of the U.S. version of this successful move from culture to civilization; he sees Washington as participating in "the spirit most conspicuously manifest in the personalities, from Benjamin Franklin to Andrew Carnegie, of our so-called self-made men" (*Race and Culture*

175). As the press agent for Washington at Tuskegee from 1905 to 1912, Park became intimate with accommodationist ideas concerning the need for African Americans to stay in the rural South to build a civilization based in individual achievement, private accumulation, and incorporated industries. While he applauds Washington's approach to modernizing the race, he seems to dissent with Washington's idea that progress can be made in a rural setting. Park's idea of the city as a zone of conflict between culture and civilization presents for the Negro Renaissance writers a fertile way of conceptualizing not only the phenomenon of racial passing but also the inner dynamics of social fragmentation and integration occurring within the migrating race and the individual migrant as advancement is sought through urbanward migration.[43] Ironically, Park himself gleaned these insights while at Tuskegee, where he witnessed "firsthand" the disputes between the Washington and Du Bois camps over the proper sites and processes for advancing the race toward civilization.

Looking back on his career, Park writes:

> I believe in firsthand knowledge not as a substitute but as a basis for more formal and systematic investigation. But the reason I profited as much as I did from this experience [at Tuskegee] was due, I am sure, to the fact that I had a long preparation. As a result I was not, as I found later, interested in the Negro problem as that problem is ordinarily conceived. I was interested in the Negro in the South and in the curious and intricate system which had grown up to define his relations with white folk. . . . I became convinced, finally, that I was observing the historical process by which civilization, not merely here but elsewhere, has evolved, drawing into the circle of its influence an ever widening circle of races and peoples. (*Race and Culture* vii–viii)

When Park says that he realized he was "not . . . interested in the Negro problem as that problem is ordinarily conceived," he means that he was not interested in the kinds of missionary patronage as patrimonial *noblesse oblige* that Armstrong, Villard, and Ovington practiced. In another sense, however, Park is more than a kissing cousin to these race patrons. Whereas they felt an activist obligation to reform and refine African Americans so that they could enter the circle of universal civilization, his desire was to observe this process rationally and systematically, firsthand but from the distance of scientific observation. Possessing the liability of urbane civilization, Park could not experience this process of assimilation from culture to civilization for himself. However, he could undergo it *as though* firsthand as a trusted employee of the Tuskegee Machine. In the 1941 essay titled "Methods of Teaching: Impressions and a Verdict," Park clarifies his "firsthand" relation to the "inside" experience of the race. "I was in the unique position of seeing, as it were from the inside, the intricate workings of an important and significant historical process," he says. "At Tuskegee I was, it seemed, at the very center of the Negro world. I had the access to most everything that was likely to throw light on the processes that were slowly but inevitably changing Negro life and the South" (*Race and Culture* 42).

Being a press agent for the Tuskegee Machine carries its own risks for someone as clearly ambitious as Park. In a revealing letter that Park wrote to Washington concerning how to represent his contribution, he set the terms for his own professional recognition: "I should not like to be represented as a professional writer who had helped you to put together the book. Rather I should like it to appear that I had been working at Tuskegee, interested in the school as others who are employed here. I would not want to [be] represented as engaged in any philanthropy or 'unselfish' work." Rolf Lindner writes: "From this letter, it is clear that Park was afraid of appearing as a hired hack."[44] It is also clear that Park does not want to be portrayed as an unpaid race patron. In this sense, as Park developed a career in race work, he participated in the process of retooling social science from advocacy and reform to an academic discipline focused on the objective collection and interpretation of data, a retooling in which the Chicago school of sociology under its first chair, Albion Small, played a crucial role, and to which Park himself contributed significantly after 1914, when he began to teach a full course load at Chicago.[45]

Despite his rejection of unpaid race philanthropy as a way of developing a career and identity, Park, like his patronage predecessors and contemporaries, saw himself as attached to and attracted to African Americans and their folk culture—an attachment with fleshly undertones and an attraction that implicates a sort of erotic yearning, as we discuss below. Park's rationale for this attraction, however, is justified in his sociological theory in terms that see black folk as "a special problem in method." One could go so far to say that his professionalization as a sociologist depended on his ability to transform this erotic curiosity and fleshly attraction to the mysterious other into an abstract problem of sociological method. In his introduction to *The Shadow of the Plantation,* a 1934 book by one of his star students, Charles S. Johnson, Park identified the attraction that the academic race patron possesses for black folk culture. Park's essay quotes his son-in-law Robert Redfield, who, like many other white and black intellectuals of the interwar period, conceptualized African Americans to be "our one principal folk."[46] For these intellectuals, the African American best embodied the moment before that transitional phase from rural peonage to modernity, from orality to literacy, from culture to civilization, out of which a national mythology of native genius could be formulated.

For Park, the plantation Negro of the United States South was the best example of "marginal peoples," those occupying "a place somewhere between the more primitive and tribally organized and the urban populations of our modern cities" (*Race and Culture* 67). Such "folk cultures," especially African American plantation folk, "constitute . . . a special problem in method, but one which is after all fundamental to studies of society and human nature everywhere." Park goes on to suggest that "[t]he difficulty consists in making that culture intelligible; in discovering the meaning and the function of usages, customs, and institutions" (*Race and Culture* 69). As the homegrown primitives of the United States, black plantation folk provide the perfect opportunity for resolving sticky problems in ethnographic methodology. And when placed on the evolutionary continuum alongside the black "proletariat" or "populous" who have migrated to the southern cities, the plantation Negro can enable the social scientist to trace folk culture from its transitional stage among "the mobile and migratory Negro laborers who crowd the slums of southern cities" (68) but are no longer "folk" of the "mind and mood of the plantation Negro," the pure expression of the true folk. In other words, the plantation Negro provides a ground of authenticity against which the processes of adaptation, assimilation, and marginalization into civilization can be precisely, scientifically measured by someone able to get close enough to the "inside" of this culture to observe it intimately. As Park himself becomes the sociologist best able to theorize the sociology of race adaptation because of his "firsthand" experience at Tuskegee, his black male protégés at Chicago become the perfect students for putting this theory into practice in the field. Existing both inside the race by biological temperament and social adaptation and outside it by sociological training, these black male sociologists can combine the firsthand insight needed with the scientific distance required to conduct ethnographic work. If the otherness of primitive black plantation culture presents a problem in sociological method, the sociological training of black men just removed from this culture represents the solution.

Park's attraction to the primitive concept of the Negro does not stop at the methodological attachment that provides a supposedly rational, empirical foundation for his science. The attraction also stems from a more visceral, sensuous appeal. Like the white patrons of the Negro Renaissance, Park is fascinated by what he perceives as a more real physicality in the black plantation *ur*-folk and in the migratory, semi-urbanized demi-folk. In "The Negro and His Plantation Heritage" and other related essays, his sociological observations display an unabashed ideology of race nostalgia: "It has been observed that as long as their social institutions are functioning normally, primitive peoples ordinarily exhibit an extraordinary zest in the life they lead, even when that life, like that of the Eskimo in the frozen North or the pigmies in the steaming forest of Central Africa, seems to be one of constant privation and hardship." In the event of a "catastrophe"—"frequently . . . the sudden advent of a more highly civilized people"—"their natural lust for life . . . deserts them." Relying on climatic assumptions about racial temperament, Park pictures a people tragically doomed to "become completely obsessed by a sense of their own inferiority" and preferring "to identify themselves, as far as they are permitted to do so, with the invading or dominant people" (*Race and Culture* 70). In an infamous 1918 essay, Park depicts the plantation Negro also in terms of the theory of biological temperament, a genetically selected inheritance determining racial "types."[47] Without the ideological assumptions of a natural racial temperament, Park's whole social science begins to deteriorate at the core, and, more to the point, the visceral attraction motivating his ethnographic study of race begins to lose its pull. This sort of attachment can be glimpsed in Park's description of the Negro spirituals: "The words, often striking and suggestive to be sure, represent broken fragments of ideas, thrown up from the depths of the Negroes' consciousness and swept along upon a torrent of wild, weird, and often beautiful melody." These songs, which are "more primitive" than those of any other folk in the world, also result from evolutionary processes: "If it is the plantation melodies that, by a process of natural selection, have been preserved in the traditions of the Negro people, it is probably because in these songs they found a free and natural expression of their unfulfilled desires" (276, 277).

One could say that such racial projections are thrown up from Park's own subliminal unfulfilled desires in relation to his need for a "wild, weird, and often beautiful" primitivism in which to ground his confidence and against which to placate his doubt of the pleasures of expanding European "civilization." In the same essay, he disputes the idea that the spirituals are written predominantly in a minor key, because he needs the happy darky as an essential object of his desire for primitivism:

> There are no other folk-songs, with the exception of those of Finland, of which so large a percentage are in the major mood. And this is interesting as indicating the racial temperament of the Negro. It tends to justify the general impression that the Negro is naturally sunny, cheerful, optimistic. It is true that the slave songs express longing, that they refer to hard trials and great tribulations, but the dominant mood is one of jubilation. (278)

Park is arguing specifically against Du Bois's characterization of the "sorrow songs" in *The Souls of Black Folk*. Against Du Bois's insistence on the African American experience as one of bastardy, mourning, and double consciousness, Park needs the sunny Negro as much as he needs to stipulate that double consciousness applies temperamentally to mulattos as "marginal men," not to full-blooded plantation Negroes.

Park's racial ideology, then, though in conflict with itself, ends up reerecting the idea of the passive, skin-surface "racial type" that New Negroes such as Pickens, Wells, White, Du Bois, Locke, and James Weldon Johnson—as well as Park's own students, Charles Johnson and Frazier—struggle to eviscerate. In fact, Park goes so far as to pin down this racial type to the very kind of externality, bodiliness, and skin-surface materialism that we have seen Locke attacking in his contributions to *The New Negro*. As Matthews remarks, Park's attraction to the idea of the black primitive seems to conflict with his identification of the city as the place of progressive civilization (see *Quest for an American Sociology* 76). Perhaps the inevitability of this process of modernization is what makes Park yearn for the primitive, even as he ultimately values what he calls civilization. Park's view of the Negro temperament would seem, however, to suggest that African Americans must endure greater pain and friction in entering the "arena of modern life," for he attributes to them a ma-terial-external approach to life that seems incompatible with his view of self-con-scious modernity. This is evident in one of his most definitive statements on Negro temperament:

> This temperament, as I conceive it, consists in a few elementary but distinctive characteristics, determined by physical organizations and transmitted biologi-cally. These characteristics manifest themselves in a genial, sunny, and social dis-position, in an interest and attachment to external, physical things rather than to subjective states and objects of introspection; in a disposition for expression rather than enterprise and action. (*Race and Culture* 280)

One project of New Negro–era activists, social scientists, artists, autobiographers, and novelists is exactly to delineate the "subjective states and objects of introspec-tion" that such scientists as Park want to claim are lacking in African American folk. This assessment of the racial character accords with both the need for a grounding folk as a signal of national unity and progress and the desire for a pro-tégé race whose emerging creative expression can be leveraged against the imper-sonal, unfamiliar, alienating, self-conscious, fragmenting aspects of modernity by a patronizing master race wanting to move forward into modernity, but without leaving their nostalgia for premodernity behind.

Nowhere is this more apparent than in Park's division of the racial talents, so that the "Anglo-Saxon" can represent "action" and "enterprise" in relation to the Negro's "expression." In perhaps his most notorious delineation of racial character, Park concludes:

> Everywhere and always it [the Negro racial temperament] has been interested rather in expression than in action; interested in life rather than in its recon-struction and reformation. The Negro is, by natural disposition, neither an intel-lectual nor an idealist, like the Jew; nor a brooding introspective, like the East African; nor a pioneer and frontiersman, like the Anglo-Saxon. He is primarily an artist, loving life for its sake. His *métier* is expression rather than action. He is, so to speak, the lady of the races. (280)

This passage almost eradicates in one rounded phrase Park's other efforts in his so-ciological theory of race. How can the Negro be both interested in expression and not interested in introspection? How can the race be interested in advancing, as Park claims in other passages, but at the same time not interested in enterprise nor in life's "reconstruction and reformation"?[48] The passage on the Negro as the lady of the races accomplishes a neat division of labor within the national economy. Whereas the (male) "Anglo-Saxon" is left free for "action" in the world—for guid-ing the national interests and managing the imperial borders domestically and globally—the Negro race (gendered male) is left to perform the feminine role of accessory artistic expression. In this national division of labor according to the sexual temperament of each race, it is clear that the Anglo-Saxon (male) represents the superman of the races. Park's sexualization of the races results in an odd pronominal syntax in which the Negro race is gendered masculine, according to the logic that men head each race, but the complement identifying the essential character of the race is paradoxically gendered feminine: "*He* is, so to speak, the *lady* of the races." This attribution of a feminine essence to the masculine whole of the race epitomizes its sexual abnormality in the face of the Anglo-Saxon's civilizing aggressions. The syntax imitates the way in which the Negro, as long as he lags in this condition of unselfconscious expression, embodies a deviance from the normal (traditionally masculine) direction of civilizing progress. The qualifying phrase "so to speak," while it acknowledges the paradox of the race's sexual deviance by highlighting the metaphorical nature of the statement, cannot undo the intrinsic deviance of the race's paradoxical sexual status. As the lady of the races, the Negro, we can infer, needs a man of action and enterprise to protect and admire *him*. Or does the Negro lady of the races need, more precisely, a man of chivalry? "Park's descriptive metaphor is so pregnant with mixed motives," Ralph Ellison writes, "as to birth a thousand compromises and indecisions." The lady of the races is certainly not capable of reforming himself. "Imagine the effect such teachings have had upon Negro students alone!"[49]

Instead of trying to pursue the abstract logic of this leap into metaphor in the midst of scientific speculation, we might take another tack in ferreting out the implications of Park's theory for his black academic protégés. In his 1928 essay "The Bases of Race Prejudice," Park adduces the first phase of racial antipathy to be the result of "the spontaneous response of most sentient creatures—including men and dogs—to what is strange and unfamiliar." When individuals of one race first encounter individuals of another, they focus on the apparent differences, but curiosity and fascination may overtake any fear or suspicion:

> The first effect is to provoke in us a state of tension—a more vivid awareness and readiness to act—and with that a certain amount of reserve and self-consciousness which is incident to every effort at self-control. In all this there is so far neither prejudice nor antipathy, but merely expectancy. The strange new creature may prove to be attractive, even fascinating. The reports of the first meetings of primitive peoples with Europeans are instructive on this point. The first Europeans to reach Mexico were received ceremonially and regarded as superior beings. (*Race and Culture* 238)

Just as he attributes racial temperament to biology, so Park also attributes to natural instinct a fascination with and attraction to the racial other—which is why, he says, interracial mixing of blood is the natural outcome of life on racial frontiers, despite strong taboos against interracial sex. In the 1934 essay "Race Relations and Certain Frontiers," he spells out this sort of biological sexual attraction for the racial other:

> Romantic interest invariably attaches to the strange, the distant, and unfamiliar, and the disposition of men to go abroad for wives and of women to welcome these roving strangers is probably part of original nature. Human beings are naturally exogamous. Endogamy, on the contrary, has grown up in the interest of the family, the clan, and the community. (*Race and Culture* 134)

Again we see that "original nature" resides in the "men" who "go abroad for wives," not in those who are content within the narrow boundaries of their own parochial culture. These "roving strangers" are principally European men, Park indicates; he points out that one can gauge the expansion of European frontiers across the globe by the higher incidence of this group's miscegenation with Africans, Asians, South Pacific Islanders, and Native Americans.[50]

We should not be surprised, then, to come across Park's own moment of romantic gazing at the racial other in a private, unpublished manuscript titled "Land of Darkness." Winifred Raushenbush quotes amply from the first page of the manuscript, in which Park explains that it is written upon a trip to "places untouched by the influence of Tuskegee" (quoted in *Robert E. Park* 44). In other words, Park goes on a venture into the heart of darkness, where even the civilizing acts of Tuskegee have not been able to penetrate. Like a good participant-observer ethnographer, Park records his response on encountering a scene that, touched with the illusory ink of literary romanticism, constructs life among the sharecropping poor with a definite patina of nostalgic longing and repressed passion:

> While we were sitting there, tardy laborers from the more distant fields came silently straggling in through the golden moonlight. I noticed that one of the mules bore a young woman, barefooted and in a sunbonnet. A young man walked by her side and led the mule. When the mule reached the house he lifted her carefully down. Some one else took the mule and they wandered away arm in arm down the path that led to the little garden. I didn't see them again until a shrill voice called out in a few minutes: "Heah, you lovers, come in to supper." We had supper in the little kitchen built apart from the house. A gigantic black woman, slim as an athlete and straight as an arrow, her black head cropped in a white turban did the cooking. A couple of young girls served the table. I have rarely seen anything human that impressed me more with a sense of power than this big, primitive, black woman. (*Robert E. Park* 45)[51]

Yearning regret hovers over the portrait, because we know that eventually the black Tuskegee middle-class reformers will be driven to touch, to alter, this scene, just as the white sociologists have been driven by their scientific curiosity to seek it out before it disappears. The final line of the paragraph speaks most revealingly about the ethnologist's own desire, even as it seems to cast our gaze onto this dark earth mother. The incomparable "sense of power" impressed on Park in this moment of vision seems almost inhuman. Just as Park feminizes the race as a way of protecting the naturally enterprising temperament of the Anglo-Saxon male, so he chooses a phallic woman, not a physically slight woman or a black male—for instance, the patriarch farmer described in the preceding paragraph of the manuscript—to embody the overpowering truth of the primordial peasant. In the same way that Du Bois chooses to emphasize White's small stature in order to minimize the other black male's potential rivalry with the black man in charge, so Park chooses subliminally to focus on a phallic black woman, rather than a phallic black man, as the object of his romantic nostalgia. To choose the black man would be too threatening not only to the masculine enterprise of his science but also to the racial construction of his superior status within civilization. The phallic imagery indicates the power of the primitive, while the anatomical sex of the primitive within the vision shields the ethnologist from passivity in the gaze and protects his normative masculinity, evident in his own aggressive gaze. What is supposedly scientific and rational—the modern self-consciousness of Park's stance—hinges on this exchange of power between the primitive woman as overpowering object and the white modern observer as passive aggressor. If Park has "rarely seen anything human that [has] impressed [him] more," it is because the allure of the primitive— its smell, its touch, its power—seems to unnerve his sense of the inevitability of civilizing progress itself.

Finally, however, it is not this overpowering vision of the phallic primitive *woman* but the self-conscious cosmopolitanism of the mixed-blood *man* that Park displays in his race theory and advances through academic patronage. For him, sociology remains a "world of men."[52] In Park's theory of the "marginal man," we can detect another way in which both the professionalization and the sociological study of race are sexualized to suit the needs of a masculine "roving" modernity that both privileges aggressive white masculinity and desires to transcend it through an intimate bond with mulatto protégés. Park's idea of the marginal man is heavily indebted to Du Bois's theory of double consciousness, though he does not cite Du Bois specifically in his discussion of his own concept of marginalization.[53] In his 1923 essay "Negro Race Consciousness as Reflected in Race Literature," Park traces the history of Negro poetry from the spirituals to his time and sees in this literary development a progressive struggle toward citizenship despite the sociopolitical handicap of being Negro. It is in this context that he quotes Du Bois's theory at length (*Race and Culture* 291–292), but only to counter Du Bois's attack on white supremacy with a romanticized "fortunate" view of the Negro as marginal man:

> In some respects, however, it seems to me the Negro, like all the other disinherited peoples, is more fortunate than the dominant races. He is restless, but he

knows what he wants. . . . It is always a source of great power to any people when they feel that their interests, so far from being antagonistic, are actually identified with the interests of the antagonists. We of the dominant, comfortable classes, on the other hand, are steadily driven to something like an obstinate and irrational resistance to the Negro's claims, or we are put in the position of sympathetic spectators, sharing vicariously in his struggles but never really able to make his cause wholeheartedly our own. (300)

As lucid a statement of the ambivalent situation of the white male patron cannot be found elsewhere in the literature of the Jim Crow era. As a "sympathetic spectator" who knows that he cannot ever "wholeheartedly" take the Negro's "cause" as his own, for it would be against his immediate interests, Park identifies the psychic complex that makes the marginal position both romantically alluring and, at the same time, absolutely undesirable. In other words, he reads Du Bois's double consciousness back into his own situation as a race patron, as someone committed to "sharing vicariously" the marginality experienced by the people he studies, but his "irrational resistance" demands that he is "never really able" to vacate his own civilized status as a scientist on the racial frontier, one who observes from the "comfortable" pinnacle of white male privilege.

The real source of hope, in Park's theory, for interracial rapprochement and progressive cooperation resides in the migratory "mixed-blood" Negro man—Du Bois and Washington being the two he mentions most. As the model for both the marginal man and the liberal intellectual, Du Bois's double consciousness gets literalized by Park into the struggle of two competing racial temperaments in a single mulatto individual.[54] Park goes out of his way to discriminate between the mulatto and the Negro as distinct racial types (*Race and Culture* 386–387). "If the mulatto displays intellectual characteristics and personality traits superior to and different from those of the black man," he writes, "it is not because of his biological inheritance *merely*, but rather more, I am inclined to believe because of his more intimate association with the superior cultural group (389, emphasis added). Park's strong support of biracial organizations accords with Villard's rationale for including exceptional Negroes on the NAACP Board of Directors.[55] Park seems to reduce the idea of the Talented Tenth, rejected by Du Bois in the 1930s, to a matter of "blood." Referring to Du Bois's paper, "The Talented Tenth," he writes in a footnote that the plea for higher education of the Talented Tenth "is based on the general conception that the Negro masses can only hope to improve their status as a result of the advances made by the so-called 'talented tenth.' This talented tenth, however, was composed then, as it is now, very largely of mixed bloods."[56]

Because they are one-half civilized and one-half primitive, "mixed bloods" become for Park the embodiment of marginal men. Their "double inheritance" results in a personality that is "often sensitive and self-conscious to an extraordinary degree," and "[o]ne of the consequences of his more intense self-consciousness is that the mulatto lives at a higher tension than the Negro" (387). Just as Park's "roving man" is gendered as an Anglo-Saxon male who spreads his seed in the process of invading, conquering, and almost unwittingly spreading civilization on the racial frontier, so the literal product of his insemination, the marginal man, is gendered prototypically a migrant mixed-blood male, trapped between two worlds. His most lucid definition of this racial/cultural "personality type" comes in his introduction to E. V. Stonequist's 1937 book, *The Marginal Man*:

> The marginal man is a personality type that arises at a time and a place where, out of the conflict of races and cultures, new societies, new peoples and cultures are coming into existence. The fate which condemns him to live, at the same time, in two worlds is the same which compels him to assume, in relation to the worlds in which he lives, the rôle of a cosmopolitan and a stranger. Inevitably he becomes, relatively to his cultural milieu, the individual with the wider horizon, the keener intelligence, the more detached and rational viewpoint. The marginal man is always relatively the more civilized human being. (*Race and Culture* 375–376)

Although he refers to the Jew, "particularly the Jew who has emerged from the provincialism of the ghetto," as "the most civilized of human creatures" (376), it is clear that marginal manliness also manifests itself in the male mulatto. Through his hands-on contact with such halfway men, the sociological ethnographer-adventurer can find a model for his own necessarily ambivalent fusion of distant observation and insider knowledge. Park celebrates the world of men and the manly adventure that supposedly accompany the moment of invasion. However, it is the marginality deriving from imperial dislocations that he endows with an intellectual superiority and a greater access to emancipation:

> When the traditional organization of society breaks down, as a result of contact and collision with a new invading culture, the effect is, so to speak, to emancipate the individual man. Energies that were formerly controlled by custom and tradition are released. The individual is free for new adventures, but he is more or less without direction and control. (350)

From passages like this, we can see the deep ambivalence that haunts Park's project, an ambivalence also evident in the white patrons of the Negro Renaissance and in their African American clients in a different way. While the Anglo-Saxon invades and thus creates civilization through his aggression, it is not this roving manliness that represents for Park the ultimate model of modern restless consciousness aspiring toward civilization while desiring to resist it; it is instead the one invaded, emancipated, forced into cultural collision—whose "energies" are freed "for new adventures" to carry progress forward. The ethnographic scientist metonymically shares with the marginal mulatto this double fate of being invaded as becoming emancipated. Through the white sociologist's intimate tutelage of the mulatto as marginal man, he can imbibe—*almost* firsthand—the adventure of modern home-lessness and the objective detachment from custom, while still having as an object of study that other, archaic world of primitive cultural attachment to family, clan, and ethnic group that the marginal mulatto carries inside himself biologically and culturally. As Lindner points out, Park's theory demands that the sociologist be-come "an *experimental marginal man*,"[57] one who, when he himself is neither Jew nor mulatto migrant, must vicariously take on this persona in his scientific inves-tigations of culture. In the end, then, Park's race theory is a rationalization of how he can have it both ways. He imagines that Du Boisian double consciousness hoards a benefit of self-conscious cosmopolitanism that can be experienced only secondhand by the Anglo-Saxon scientist, and thus, in his resentment, he parlays this benefit to the scientist without the concomitant loss of white male privilege.

On leaving Tuskegee, Park says, "I became, for all intents and purposes, a Negro myself" (quoted in Raushenbush, *Robert E. Park* 49). In his resignation letter to Washington, he writes:

> I want to say, now that I am leaving here, that I have never been so happy in my life as I have since I became associated with you in this work. Some of the best friends I have in the world are at Tuskegee. I feel and shall always feel that I be-long, in a sort of way, to the Negro race and shall continue to share, through good and evil, all its joys and sorrows.[58]

Like the "so to speak" that distances the Negro from *his* temperament as a lady, Park's "in a sort of way" is exactly the ambivalent metonymy that guarantees a foot on each side of the color line: his patronizing status as an objective white male sci-entist can stay put only when it leans on this slippery desire for an identity as a marginal mulatto man. Structurally, Park's patronage position resembles that which Wells-Barnett describes in relation to Ovington: a single white man sur-rounded by a group of educated mulatto men. By preselecting the mulatto as the only type of Negro who can adapt to modern civilization, Park enhances the para-digm of scarcity that justifies the need for white patrons to choose carefully their black protégés from an even more limited number. Furthermore, by singling out mulatto men for the burden of representation, Park is able to claim a racial blood relation to those men whose experiences of marginality become the advance guard of civilization. While keeping hold of his own white male privilege of civilizing guardianship, he makes room for a class of energetic half-breeds in need of tutor-ing by him. As we have already seen with such pupils of Park as Charles S. John-son, such black male patronage derives its influence from this intimate bond with white male mentoring, but at the same time the white patron's longing for a mar-ginal other to gratify his sense of curiosity, adventure, and manly wanderlust cap-tures the black male student in a permanent halfway zone not of his own making: one half masculine subject with whom the white patron can bond, the other half a passive object and objective ready for the white mentor's reformation.

Park's theory of the mulatto as the embodiment of self-conscious, restless, urbane modernity presents a relatively optimistic view of the eventual assimilation of racial cultures into progressive civilization, despite his sense of civilization's record of destruction and his attraction for the supposedly naive, premodern plantation Negro. Yet, although it correlates closely with notions of the New Negro, Park's marginal man as a harbinger of progressive civilization cannot be *equated* with aspirations for New Negro modernity. Park's idealization of marginal manhood derives from the peculiar securities and insecurities of his inhabiting the ascendant position within a national culture seeking world dominance while also being able to see some of the weaknesses attendant upon such domination. His idea of the marginal man projects onto the liabilities of African American manhood the benefits of marginality (double consciousness, creativity, modern self-consciousness, curiosity, empathy, risk, potential for growth) while attempting to retain the contrary benefits of dominant white masculinity, such as confidence in the progressive outcomes of adventuresome aggression, the fraternity of individualism, the marketplace of competition, the mastery of scientific technique, and the forwardness of modernity. New Negro writers and activists challenge the equation between race as a sexed phenomenon and what James Weldon Johnson calls "the spirit of self-assertion."[59] Despite myriad forms of color consciousness operating in African American politics and literature during the Jim Crow era, New Negroes advocate the ability to overcome color through what are seen as universally accessible and applicable attributes of self-assertion, rather than through an exceptional inheritance of Anglo-Saxon aggressiveness coursing specially through the veins of exceptional mulattos. The presence of a mulatto discourse in New Negro writing exists largely as a foil to the dominant New Negro ideal, for in black male discourse the New Negro is cast as someone who has, or is struggling to, overcome not only the color line but also color self-consciousness.[60]

5 Midwifing the Renaissance

Prostitution, Same-Sexuality,
and the Procreative Logic of Patronage

> Jessie Fauset at the *Crisis,* Charles Johnson at *Opportunity,* and Alain Locke
> in Washington, were the three people who midwifed the so-called New
> Negro literature into being. Kind and critical—but not too critical for the
> young—they nursed us along until our books were born.
>
> —Langston Hughes (*The Big Sea* 218)

> Some of these seekers after new sensations go beyond the gay night-clubs;
> they peep in under the more seamy side of things; they nose down into
> lower strata of life.
>
> —James Weldon Johnson (*Black Manhattan* 160)

> No! stand erect and without fear,
> And for our foes let this suffice—
> We've bought a rightful sonship here,
> And we have more than paid the price.
>
> —James Weldon Johnson, "Fifty Years"
> (*Book of American Negro Poetry* 132)

Park's notion of the Negro as the lady of the races carries the implications of a gender deviance endemic to men of the race, due to their peculiar status in the midst
of modernity but not of it. His attraction to the study of African American culture
is motivated partly by a curiosity about this racial/sexual deviation. Although
Park's most stunning moment comes in an unpublished text in which he gazes at
a big black primitive woman, for most white patrons of the period it was the urban
exotica that awed and attracted them. In his 1930 study of the rise of Harlem,
James Weldon Johnson refers obliquely to the "seamy" experiences in the "lower
strata of life," experiences that attract "some of these seekers after new sensations"
to Harlem during the renaissance. He attributes these "lower strata" to Harlem's
cosmopolitan edge: "Harlem has its sophisticated, fast sets, initiates in all the wis-

dom of worldliness. And Harlem has, too, its underworld, its world of pimps and prostitutes, of gamblers and thieves, of illicit love and illicit liquor, of red sins and dark crimes. In a word, Harlem possesses in some degree all of the elements of a cosmopolitan centre" (*Black Manhattan* 169).

Characteristically turning the handicap of an underworld into a sophisticated worldliness, Johnson is more generous than most commentators in acknowledging any relationship between the "fast sets" and the underworld. "Illicit love" is as close as he comes to acknowledging the relationship between the performance of worldly sophistication and the cultural influence of the sexual "underworld" of prostitution, homosexuality, and interracial sex, which in Harlem and other African American urban communities, could be very much above ground. Despite the logic fundamentally linking the sexual fast set to the artistic avant-garde, Johnson nonetheless, like many other commentators on the renaissance, attempts to keep separate the high aspirations of Harlem New Negroes from the lower strata and their fast attractions of exotic, cross-racial eroticism. This chapter examines the various ways in which figurations of sexual deviance—particularly prostitution, interracial intimacy, and same-gender desire—shape Negro Renaissance cultural patronage as a conflictingly gendered racial institution.

Tropes of Affiliation:
Theorizing the Sexual Subtexts of Renaissance Patronage

Prostitution, same-sexuality, and other "deviant" practices are frequently addressed in the fiction of the renaissance period, as we shall see in Part 3. In the criticism, history, and sociology related to the movement, however, writers were more circumspect in linking high renaissance aspirations and these sexual practices. Prostitution crops up repeatedly in the criticism and history, but usually as a metaphor for the exploitation of black talent by white patrons or the notion of black patrons selling out the race for profit and attention among influential whites. Homosexuality is usually mentioned only in the most oblique ways, even as it was seen as intimately linked to prostitution in the "vice" districts that were often located in black urban neighborhoods.[1] Even the most "objective" New Negro sociological studies (discussed in chapter 3) tend not to mention the issue of same-sexuality while seeking to expose the prevalence of deviant sexual practices among some black migrants. A signal exception can be found in Drake and Cayton's *Black Metropolis*, in which they list the kinds of deviant behavior evident in "the world of the lower class": "These centers of lower-class congregation and festivity often become points of contact between the purveyors of pleasure 'on the illegit' and their clientele—casual prostitutes, bootleggers, reefer peddlers, 'pimps,' and 'freaks.' Some of these places are merely 'fronts' and 'blinds' for the organized underworld" (610). Drake and Cayton define "freak shows" in a footnote as "pornographic exhibitions by sexual perverts" (610)—in other words, homosexual drag balls.[2] Drake and Cayton point out that in Bronzeville, the lines separating the aspiring respectable from the unrespectable lower class are "fluid and shifting," sometimes coexisting in the same household (*Black Metropolis* 600); one could say, often existing in the same individual. As Drake and Cayton note, the response of the black middle class to the wide range of deviating behaviors, sexual and otherwise, frequently entails their attempts to mediate the *appearance* of African American life for the consumption of dominant United States society. Given the visible and relatively integrated experience of same-sexuality amid black neighborhoods, the reticence on the part of black male sociologists, critics, and historians on the subject cannot easily derive from their ignorance of it.

There is one significant instance of a leading black male renaissance patron who claims to be oblivious to the lives of freaks, faggots, and bull-daggers so evident in black urban folk culture. Given his status also as the "father" of African American urban sociology, Du Bois's assertion of ignorance is especially revealing. In his 1968 autobiography, Du Bois, after a short paragraph describing his "married life," explains that he has had no comprehension of homosexuality:

> In the midst of my career there burst on me a new and undreamed of aspect of sex. A young man, long my disciple and student, then my co-helper and successor to part of my work, was suddenly arrested for molesting men in public places. I had before that time no conception of homosexuality. I had never understood the tragedy of an Oscar Wilde. I dismissed my co-worker forthwith, and spent heavy days regretting my act. (*Autobiography of W.E.B. Du Bois* 282)

One of the reasons Du Bois mentions this episode is to assert his unusual shyness and isolation, as well as his unusual puritan innocence about all things sexual—unusual, that is, for an African American. "When I went South [to study at Fisk]," he writes, "my fellow students being much older and reared in a region of loose sexual customs regarded me as liar or freak when I asserted my innocence. I liked girls and sought their company, but my wildest exploits were kissing them" (280). Ironically, Du Bois uses the word *freak* according to its wholly negative usage in dominant culture—a freak of sexual nature—apparently ignorant of its more positive popular usage among African Americans. His New England uptightness about sexuality serves to indicate here his *alienation* from the ordinary mass of African Americans, who in 1885, when he first arrives at Fisk, are "reared in a region of loose sexual customs." (Could it be possible that Du Bois was totally unaware of the sexual disposition of Countee Cullen, whose brief marriage to Du Bois's daughter lasted for six months in 1928 and whose sexuality was very much an "open secret" among the Harlem elite of the 1920s?) Du Bois's "heavy days" of regret for having dismissed Augustus Granville Dill (1881–1956) complete the picture of his absent relationship to such "freaks."[3] The chilly distance that so many others identify in Du Bois operates as a marker of this self-alienation from the freakish excesses of the race, even as it also serves to mark his exceptional leadership as a man whose unimpeachable integrity fuels his compassion for the race.

More to the point, Du Bois's public silence on the topic of same-sexuality after the firing incident bespeaks a central dilemma of the double burden afflicting black male patronage. On the one hand, the would-be patron is expected to know about the inner workings of "his people," including their most freakish behaviors, and to epitomize that behavior as its representative exemplar. On the other hand, he must keep himself clean of any imputation of freakishness himself; otherwise, his claim to the masculine rights and rites of patronage become deeply suspicious in dominant culture. Du Bois's autobiographical passage, then, serves also as a cautionary tale concerning the sexual risks of taking on the role of race patron. In choosing Dill as his "disciple and student, then my co-helper and successor," Du Bois, putatively unknowingly, embarked on a charge of reforming a sexual pervert into normality alongside his self-conscious task of reforming a young black man into a race leader. In actuality, race patronage always implies sexual reform of some sort, as it also tends to repress or suppress the potential same-sex perversion that haunts the intimacy between the patron as solicitous master and the protégé as adoring disciple. Race patronage marks itself as such by claiming to be something other than sexual intimacy between men. The moment that sexual attraction exposes itself even as mere potential, the normalizing function of patronage as an act of reforming black men for proper citizenship is put in jeopardy. When race patronage places an interested white man over an adoring black protégé not in the proper Jim Crow role of master or boss-man, the intimacy of cross-racial affiliation carries the threat of gender as well as racial deviance, for it skirts the protocol whereby normal white masculinity is defined by its authority over, distance above, and lack of regard for the inferior black male. As we shall see, race patrons can exploit the anti–Jim Crow agenda as the perfect cover for a covert interest in cross-racial sexuality. In other words, white patrons' advocacy of physical intimacy between the races during the Jim Crow era cannot be seen as a totally sexually unmotivated agenda. Physical intimacy between the races always raises the specter of cross-racial lust, either explicitly (especially for the Jim Crow advocates, who readily label white liberals "nigger lovers") or subliminally.

As a result of the ways in which sexual deviance haunts race patronage, black male patronage of the renaissance relied on a double strategy: (1) a policing of artistic production in order to keep patrons and practitioners clean, which often meant accusing *other* individuals of "prostituting" the movement in one way or another; and (2) a process of networking that affirmed the "blood" intimacy of the black patron in relation to his protégé, the mass black body, other leading participants of the movement, and beneficent white patrons. By insisting on the familial nature of patronage as a relation of proper fathers and their sons, godmothers and spiritual wards, brothers across or in racial difference, the improper taint of a sexual interest is purged. Negro Renaissance patronage therefore was conceived and expressed through two complementary, contrary paradigms with an embedded sexual logic: prostitution (usually heterosexual and interracial) and affiliation (usually patriarchal and familial).

Interracial prostitution was used as a guiding metaphor to indict those aspects of the renaissance in which white benefactors exacted various forms of profit—psychic, cultural, social, ideological, sexual, and monetary—as compensation for bringing attention to black achievement. As a metaphor, prostitution operates to highlight the role of capitalist exchange as degrading to the body of the race—how an established white elite can exploit black talent for its own benefit while claiming to advance black civilization. Critics used prostitution to condemn the motivating forces of a sensationally commodified black sensuality, everything from literal prostitution to prurient interest in African American dance, music, art, worship, and housing arrangements as titillating primitive spectacles. The metaphor usually indicts the black movers of the renaissance along with the white shapers. According to this line of thinking, black talent is inevitably prostituted in the process of white patronage, in that black intellectuals and artists have to give up something precious (usually racial and/or artistic integrity) in order to gain something specious (recognition, money, influence in the larger society). Black talent is also exploited in disregard to or even against the self-interest of the black masses, who stand to gain little beyond a smattering of service jobs in the Harlem cabarets and more good-paying customers for pimps, hustlers, bootleggers, and streetwalkers. Finally, although prostitution is used metaphorically, it is grounded in the actual practices in which black communities become exotic sites of prostituting exchange for white patrons of vice.

If prostitution is used negatively to image the base sexual exchange that brings many affluent white "patrons" to Harlem streets, indicting the whole renaissance transaction, then figures of patriarchal and familial kinship are frequently used positively, to vindicate some aspect of the movement. Critics, historians, and renaissance participants themselves routinely refer to relations between white patrons and their protégés and between black intermediaries and their black clients through images of blood affiliation, because friendship, acquaintanceship, collegiality, professional courtesy, and philanthropy are not intense enough to connote the entangled generosity, indebtedness, intimacy, and codependency characterizing patronage relations. Writers during the renaissance and after often resort to claims of paternity, maternity, fraternity, "sonship" (to use James Weldon Johnson's phrase), and adoption—though rarely sorority or daughterliness—as metaphors for the transference of a white patron's interest onto the black race's development, or of the black mediator's interest onto artistic individuals who come to represent the race's political development. Yet, patrilineal images of blood kinship used in a wholly recuperative manner would seem to cover over exactly what the prostitution metaphor attempts to unveil. Whereas the prostitution trope spreads the logic of interracial sexual traffic and exchange across the whole renaissance endeavor, the blood affiliation metaphor tends to hide the unequal racial, monetary, consumer, class, and sexual implications implicit in renaissance transactions.

The national fiction of the Jim Crow era is that blacks and whites cannot be blood kin, even when they literally are descended from the same forebears, because the two races are separate species by nature, science, morality, and the law of the land. The opposing fiction created by the renaissance and reproduced in these figures of kinship is that, in the moment of the renaissance, exceptional individuals are able to come together as adopted family across the color line to put the lie to Jim Crow strictures. Cross-racial patronage seems to trespass against Jim Crow mores by insisting on familial intimacy between elite whites and talented blacks in the interest of a progressively unified United States national culture. However, the metaphor of patriarchal kinship across race—with its appeals to the dominant sexual, social, and moral norm—also seeks to purify the erotic, sexual, and monetary entanglements actually structuring renaissance patronage practices from top to bottom. Just beneath the surface of high-minded arts patronage we find the subterfuge of sexually charged interracial transactions that focus on the prurient attractions of black culture in the flesh. Like the open secret of the master's intercourse with his captives as a sign of his mastery during slavery, these interracial dalliances between white patrons and black "natives" do not so much threaten the mores of Jim Crow as reaffirm the socioeconomic hierarchy segregating white patriarchal respectability from black sexual looseness. At the same time, even as the reality of illicit sexual exchange permeates the renaissance movement as an underground challenge to patriarchal, masculine, and heterosexual norms, the image of a patriarchal family across race more tightly binds black men's reform to those dominant norms. On the one hand, to become a successful black patron or artist is to reaffirm conventional masculine norms by adopting and adapting to the dominant culture of patriarchal, heterosexualized patronage. On the other hand, to become entangled with white renaissance patronage is to become sexually exploited, racially prostituted, and potentially emasculated.

The question of racial prostitution has operated at some level in many accounts of the renaissance, especially when the writer reckons the movement as a failure. Such critical and historical accounts of the renaissance—from the 1920s to the present—actually take their cues from the paradigms used in renaissance texts and practices, and therefore they often help perpetuate the gender and sexual assumptions already at work in renaissance patronage. In his famously scathing 1967 critique of Harlem politics in *The Crisis of the Negro Intellectual,* Harold Cruse uses an incident concerning prostitution to indicate the ways in which the ideal of "black economic nationalism" (18) was sidetracked in the 1920s and continued to undermine the cultural ambitions of leading Harlemites through the 1950s. For instance, instead of expending so much energy in attempting to force the white owners of the Apollo Theater to present a "higher" (i.e., white) form of theater with parts for African American actors, the Harlem intellectuals and activists should have focused on mounting their own indigenous black-written drama on black topics in black-owned and -operated theaters. In commenting on one of these misdirected protests against the Apollo management in 1950, Cruse exploits the prostitution image:

> [T]he Apollo Theater became an issue in the Harlem press over a controversy in-spired by a stage joke that was interpreted as a slur against Negro women, specif-ically the prostitutes who frequented the neighborhood near the Apollo. The in-cident took place at the very time certain members of the Harlem theater move-ment were trying to convince the Apollo management to permit the presentation of some legitimate drama. The Apollo had responded by presenting Negro ver-sions of *Rain* and *Detective Story,* both of which were box-office failures. The Apollo went back to its usual variety entertainment, and then came the stage joke: A white ventriloquist had his dummy say that he was having a hard time with women lately, whereupon the ventriloquist replied that "just around the corner, women are a dime a dozen." A Harlem Women's Group protested and the Apollo management was chastised in the press which was still smarting over being re-buffed by the Apollo on "legitimate drama." (16)

The ventriloquist's joke encapsulates what Cruse is saying about the situation of African American intellectuals in their own "cultural Mecca." Prostitution is a thriving business in the Harlem of 1950, as in 1925, even if black theater is not, and the protest of the Women's Group and the black press does nothing to change that situation. Of course, the ventriloquist's joke plays off of a long tradition of slum-ming, in which African American bodies, male and female, are put on display—and on sale—for any white dummy with a dime. Cruse is suggesting that because African Americans have abandoned black economic autonomy for biracial cooper-ation, they make themselves susceptible to the sort of exploitation, sexual and oth-erwise, attendant on white men gratifying their desires and whims. For Cruse, the price of this bargain is "too high a cost to pay," for it can only deliver goods grati-fying to white domination and unfair to collective African American needs.

Cruse judges the renaissance through an implicit logic that links black cultural autonomy to masculine strength and conversely links economic and cultural de-pendency first to a "prostituted" movement and then to racial emasculation, each implying the other. "A cultural renaissance that engenders barriers to the emer-gence of the creative writer is a contradiction in terms, an emasculated move-ment," Cruse writes. "For the creative edge of the movement has been dulled, the ability of the movement to foment revolutionary ideas about culture and society has been smothered" (37). Cruse's "emasculated movement" begins to look some-thing like James Weldon Johnson's protagonist-narrator, the ex-colored man: the Harlem New Negroes have sold their "birthright for a mess of pottage" (*Autobiog-raphy of an Ex-Coloured Man* 211). Running through Cruse's language is an appeal to the natural, native, original, indigenous collective body that becomes corrupted by white patronage. Courting and pampering the black artists, the white patrons treat them like children or like whores, using them to satisfy their needs and then moving on to the project of United States nationalist reproduction through respectable white society, and the black artists react by allowing their oppressors to "dictate cultural standards to them" (*Crisis of the Negro Intellectual* 52). Deep within this logic, Cruse's charge of emasculation harbors a same-sexual subtext. Prostituted and thus emasculated on their own native ground, the black artists and intellectuals are cut off from their phallic capacity for creating "a gushing spring" of cultural production for future generations. Instead of procreating the future of the race as manly men, they can only reproduce (like concubines) the bastardized offspring desired by their white patrons. Cruse's narrative of the Harlem Renaissance figures it as an il/legitimate paternity, but one lacking the subversive potential that Hortense Spillers theorizes in such a gap in the patriarchal logic.

Although influential historian Nathan Huggins stands at the opposite pole from Cruse's black cultural nationalism, his humanist outlook resorts to a similar logic, seeing the renaissance as prostituted and thus incapable of reproducing the proper kind of cultural progeny. Whereas the logic of sexual barter operates subtly in the figurative register of Cruse's language, in *Harlem Renaissance*, Huggins takes the (hetero)sexual dynamic of cross-racial patronage as the explicit target of his erudite wit. In a chapter aptly titled "Heart of Darkness," Huggins details the racial, social, historical, psychological, and economic impulses that lure avant-garde whites to Harlem after World War I, and in turn lure leading African American thinkers and artists into accepting begrudgingly their various forms of patronage:

> White Americans got much out of blacks in Harlem, but there was a price. The money that fed the joints and cabarets, that kept Harlem flowing with bootleg liquor, that kept the successful pimps dressed and fed, that made Harlem jump, came from whites following a sex lust, or escape, or bindings for their inner wounds. Their money let Harlem Negroes, square and hip, live. Yet some whites paid more than money. Few were injured or lost their lives, but many discovered the narcotic that Harlem could be to the wounded soul. For while guilt might fly in the arms of a black whore, necessarily callous and indifferent, she could hardly have the gentle hands to make a man really whole. Sex, furtive and fugitive, could nurture another kind of guilt. Some whites, pulled into the black vortex, paid the ultimate price of their identity. They defected, became apostates; they became Negroes. (*Harlem Renaissance* 93)

The ethos of prostitution as an act of erotic-economic exchange, Huggins suggests, operates at every level of the patronage relation. Huggins treats this exchange with an even hand, understanding that there are ennobling and demeaning motives and results for both races, yet also understanding that, because there is not an equation between the races, the exchange itself cannot be equal.[4] Explaining the New Negro Renaissance through this paradigm, however, genders the phenomenon in conventional heterosexual and masculine terms. In a sense, the black race becomes not the lady but the whore of the races, "the black vortex," offering to give up artistic integrity for a price. This whore of the races, however, has never guaranteed to assuage white (male) guilt, and the exchange ends up nurturing "another kind of guilt." Unlike Cruse, Huggins believes that the white patron-client pays a price as much as the black whore and pimp. That price is the failure of a nationally unified humanist culture.

Huggins touches on this unequal erotic-economic exchange in discussing three of the most influential (commercially successful) novels of the period: Van Vechten's *Nigger Heaven* and two novels Huggins reads as responses to Van Vechten, Rudolph Fisher's *Walls of Jericho* and Claude McKay's *Home to Harlem* (both published in 1928). Huggins recognizes a link between Van Vechten's earlier decadent novels and his compulsion for Harlem. At work in the earlier fiction, he says, "was a deliberate dislocation of conventional moral sensibilities, such that each novel, in some way, demanded of the reader some inversion of accepted values" (95). Not wanting to spell out too clearly the same-sexual (not to say freakish) interest spurring Van Vechten's "Negrotarian" patronage, Huggins allows "inversion" to stand here as a thinly veiled code for a more specific fascination with "sexual inversion"—the homosexuality and sadomasochism that haunt and hover around all of Van Vechten's work. Huggins may be reversing cause and effect, implying that white renaissance writers such as Van Vechten are interested in sexual inversion because of a more general concern with sociomoral inversion (109), rather than the other way around. He also short-circuits the question of why a writer like Van Vechten would turn to Harlem when seeking to (un)mask the realities and fantasies of inversion, given an underground culture of white sexual/moral inverts at hand much closer to home: the quite visible networks of fairies and queers clustered in downtown and midtown Manhattan. As the work of George Chauncey demonstrates, these had been on display as a titillating scene for white middle-class men and women, who occasionally went slumming in these working-class areas to view the fairies, as early as the 1890s (see *Gay New York*, especially 33–45). This culture of inverts would seem to be the perfect theater for Van Vechten's interest in an "inversion of accepted values," but its place in his novels, before and after *Nigger Heaven*, is most significant in its absence. What does it mean for "sex, furtive and fugitive," to be seen as a primary motivating undercurrent for white participation in the renaissance? Why would not furtive, fugitive, and exotic sex already available in European Americans' own backyard suffice?

Far from inverting middle-class procreative norms of sex and sexuality, *Nigger Heaven* promotes a rather conventional—and dull—cautionary morality.[5] Like the structure of cross-racial patronage, the novel's structure fuses (and perhaps confuses) a high-minded attempt to reform black men in order to make them capable of manning the race with a titillating and vicarious peek into the deviant sexual practices that lure respectable white patrons to marginalized black culture. Ironically, Van Vechten and his readers must claim to reform the racial deviance that attracts them in the first place. To some extent, Huggins is right to emphasize the novel as a failed apologia revealing that black people are, after all, human beings. Whatever Van Vechten's intentions, however, the novel is not primarily devoted to showing that *all* Negroes are "much like other people" (*Harlem Renaissance* 111).[6] It is, instead, trying to show how, despite most Negroes' difference from "other" people—a difference lodged solely in their nonchalant attitude toward sexual "perversion"—the most seriously refined Negroes, the New Negroes, are becoming too much like "other" people to be considered either new or Negro. Huggins's humanism promotes integration in the common figure of the United States nation as a family culturally unified across race—a notion that marginalizes the deviant social and sexual practices central to the renaissance by turning them into forbidden subterfuge. He can carry his analysis no further because the term *inversion* means little without linking it explicitly to sexual inversion—that is, to experiences of same-sexuality in African American communities and homosexuality in dominant white middle-class society.

Unlike the white homosexual underground, where most individuals are forced to lead a double life of normality in public and homosexual risk in private, the "defection" of the black-identified white patron appears aboveground. The double life of homosexuals creates a potential bond with United States blacks, whom W.E.B. Du Bois theorized as possessing double consciousness, but to a large extent this bond is illusory and inoperative, for segregation and racial oppression impose different strictures from the kind of underground existence enforced by the repression of variant sexualities.[7] Just as white patrons—whether reactionary or progressive—need an oppressed race to tighten their hold on the meaning of high European American culture and cosmopolitan broadmindedness in the country's ascent to world dominance, so white homosexuals of the time turn to the black race seeking a platform for articulating and lifting their abject sexual status with United States society. In the case of both the white patron and the white homosexual, however, overinvestment in blackness invites its own dangers, which can feed a current of racial aversion running beneath acts of generosity, affection, and defection into Negroness. The flight away from dominant culture through black community can easily boomerang into its contrary, becoming a flight away from a fearful black identification, which swerves the white patron or homosexual back toward the United States cultural norm.

As the leading white patron of Harlem, one who also happens to be homosexual, Van Vechten predicted his own swerve away from African American culture after a brief flirtation with it. In an offhand comment made in a 1925 letter to another important patron, H. L. Mencken, he remarked: "Jazz, the blues, Negro spirituals, all stimulate me enormously for the moment. Doubtless, I shall discard them too in time." The next year he told Mencken that once he had finished with the Negro, he would take up the Chinese and the Jews. Immediately after the publication of *Nigger Heaven,* he wrote to another friend, "Now that I have thoroughly explored Harlem, I think I shall take up the Chinese."[8] Although Van Vechten's prediction proved wrong—for he never totally gave up this interest—his expectation is revealing. The white (homosexual) patron sees how some aspects of African American culture deviate from dominant mores and assumes that in that deviation license beckons. This projection of license onto the black body of the race encourages the white (homosexual) patron to become attracted to the idea of defection, but the ingrained habits of white superiority and the knowledge of African American oppression are likely to fashion that attraction in the fleeting and seductive form of a flirtation.

Huggins sees the renaissance as a failure because, enmeshed in the didacticism of racial progress and illusions of an "ethnic province," it fails to produce great art. White patronage prevents New Negro artists from seeing themselves—their authentic "nativity"—clearly enough to break the bonds of provincialism.[9] "Whatever that provincialism may contribute to identity and sociology, it will constrict the vision, limiting the possibilities of personality. Needless to say, that will produce a crippled art" (*Harlem Renaissance* 308). For Huggins, true art must rise above the ethnic province to participate in the national arena of one's birthright.

> The truth was (and is) that black men and American culture have been one—such a seamless web that it is impossible to calibrate the Negro within it or to ravel him from it. . . . At least the decade of the 1920s seems to have been too early for Negroes to have felt the certainty about native culture that would have freed them from crippling self-doubt. I think that is why the art of the renaissance was so problematic, feckless, not fresh, not real. The lesson it leaves us is that the true Negro renaissance awaits Afro-Americans' claiming their *patria,* their nativity. (309)

Huggins embraces the dominant nationalist standards for art that Cruse so consciously aligns with particular economic, social, and political ideologies. Beneath Huggins's critique of failure, then, is a deeper narrative of nationalist affiliation and destiny unifying black and white in "a seamless web" of culture. The *patria* that naturally links Afro-Americans to their nativity also links them to their white patrons through this common nationalism. Such a unified national inheritance can be imagined only through a deeper bond of metaphorical blood kinship, tying black and white *men* together as brothers—or at least as kissing cousins—under the natural tutelage of the fatherland. What role "inversion"—sexual, moral, social, or otherwise—can take in such a vision is difficult to know.

David Levering Lewis's justly celebrated history *When Harlem Was in Vogue* (1979) makes its case for New Negro Renaissance failure not only on the basis of the prostituted talent of a black elite seeking its own class interest at the expense of the working body of the race but also on the notion of a well-intentioned Talented Tenth fatefully and thus excusably stuck in its own ineffectual ideology. The working and disemployed masses, reaping no profit from the renaissance movement, become frustrated and at times titilated observers of this drama, even as they are also the spectacular objects of the vogue that brings white patrons to gaze at them. Accordingly, then, Lewis makes the concluding event of the renaissance decade the Harlem uprising of 1935, a moment in which the masses explode the elitist, gradualist myth of racial acceptance through artistic genius.

The salon hopping of the Talented Tenth is placed against the backdrop of Harlem's development as a slum. In contrast to the high-minded biracial affairs and trendy, voyeuristic cabarets, Lewis points out, the favored form of entertainment of the working masses was the rent party. "Rent parties were a function first of economics," he writes, "whatever their overlay of camaraderie, sex, and music" (*When Harlem Was in Vogue* 108). Such activities are associated exactly with the kinds of behavior that Drake and Cayton say become an embarrassment to most of the aspiring respectable middle class. About the rent parties and buffet flats, Lewis writes:

> Their very existence was avoided or barely acknowledged by most Harlem writers, like that other rare and intriguing institution, the buffet flat, where varied and often perverse sexual pleasures were offered cafeteria-style. With the exception of Langston Hughes and Wallace Thurman, almost no one—at least no one who recited poetry and conversed in French at Jessie Fauset's—admitted attending a rent party. (107)

With an unusual frankness about the presence of variant sexualities in the ethos of the renaissance, *When Harlem Was in Vogue* nonetheless does not follow through with an interrogation of how diverse sexualities helped shape the renaissance, its structure, practice, and historical representation. Might, for instance, Hughes and Thurman have had a greater affinity for rent parties partly because of their own sexual dispositions? That is, might they have felt more at ease with their own sexual variance when not hedged in by the more conventional attitudes toward sexuality so clearly expressed by many in the black middle class, with its obsessive concern about how the race would appear to dominant society? Lewis directly and routinely relates the open secret kept by Harlemites of Countee Cullen's homosexuality and his father's rumored sexual predilections (see 76). In a single sentence, he makes a compelling judgment about the potential effect of Cullen's shame on his work: "Like his lowly birth and orphanage, Cullen's homosexuality was to be a source of shame he never fully succeeded in turning into a creative strength" (77).[10] In discussing Cullen's career and work in the larger context of the renaissance, however, these insights fall out of sight. How might Cullen's sense of himself and sense of his duty as the "poet laureate," and how might Harlem's open secrecy about him, have shaped the sense of his status as leading poet, as ward for white patronage? We could ask similar questions about Hughes, Locke, McKay, Van Vechten, and many others, including those who expressed heterosexual orientations.

Like that of the participants themselves, Lewis's conception of the renaissance is strongly shaped by patriarchal constructions of manly camaraderie, competition, and mastery. Sensitive to the unequal exchange and not wholly altruistic motives of the white Negrotarians,[11] Lewis instructively reads the biracial spirit of renaissance patronage as an alliance of mismatching psychic needs, one that not surprisingly creates a sort of codependence on the part of black and white patrons. He captures the resulting intimate affection of these biracial relationships in tropes of kin affiliation. About Van Vechten's bond with Johnson, for instance, he writes: "He developed a filial affection for James Weldon Johnson, with whom he shared a birthdate" (182). Like many of the renaissance's participants, historians, and critics, Lewis speaks of patronage relations as a family affair between the races. If it was inevitable that the renaissance would fail because of the "chasm of culture" (305) between the Talented Tenth and the masses, it was likewise inevitable that white patrons and their black colleagues and clients would develop such deep bonds of individual commitment. Although for Lewis the renaissance is a total loss as a social reform movement, he still holds out these relationships as authentic experiences, despite their inauthentic context. Like Huggins's conclusion that black and white are American brothers of a single *patria,* Lewis, in a much subtler way, retains the genuineness of these relations as a signal of commonality amid his trenchant fatalism about the "Tree of Hope" (306) spawned in "the margin of a rigidly divided, racist society" (305).

A crucial figure of blood filiation emerges in the debate over who "midwifed" the renaissance, with Carl Van Vechten, Alain Locke, Charles S. Johnson, James Weldon Johnson, Walter White, and Jessie Fauset (the lone female) vying for this honor in the scholarship.[12] Hughes helped to initiate this way of thinking about the period. "Jessie Fauset at the *Crisis,* Charles Johnson at *Opportunity,* and Alain Locke in Washington, were the three people who midwifed the so-called New Negro literature into being," he wrote in his autobiography, *The Big Sea.* "Kind and critical—but not too critical for the young—they nursed us along until our books were born" (218). The question of who midwifed the renaissance carries with it a network of assumptions about artistic production as procreation and how it is nurtured and managed. Behind the midwife figure is the vernacular image of the woman who exploits folk wisdom to nurse the mother and fetus along to a successful delivery in the comfort of the home-ground; this figure contrasts with the professional obstetrician (usually male) who uses modern medical science to monitor birthing in the alien clinical setting of a hospital. The midwife is one who possesses the genius of the particular time and place in which a folk culture is ready to be brought into the process of advancing civilization on its own native ground. Also behind the midwife figure is Plato's concept of the Socratic midwife, the mature male philosopher who delivers truth out of the dark ignorance of youth through a process of rigorous interrogation. Ironically, although the figure of midwifing seems to gender the process of renaissance productivity as feminine, the Socratic meaning tends to subsume this impulse toward notions of patrilineal bonding, insemination, and dissemination.

Furthermore, the image of Socratic midwifing heterosexualizes the structure and practice of renaissance patronage by suppressing the pederasty entailed in actual Socratic midwifing—the same way that dominant culture celebrates Socrates as father of Western philosophy by suppressing Socrates as "corrupter of boys." In a 1959 sketch of Locke, Eugene C. Holmes refers to the sexually purified image when he claims that Locke "did more to shape the attitudes and the thinking of a generation of Negro youth than any other educator of his time." According to Holmes, Locke refers to himself in similar terms: Locke "was best known for his espousal and fathering of the 'New Negro Movement,' and becoming as he himself said, 'more of a philosophical midwife to a generation of younger Negro poets, writers and artists than a professional philosopher.'"[13] Placing Locke in a conventionally masculine position of cultural mastery as metaphorical husband and father as well as the gender-bending status of midwife to the renaissance, Holmes gives him an especially seminal status, both inseminating the seed that grows a new civilization and nursing the processes of birthing labor and delivery (cultural nurturance and guidance). In actuality, fathering and midwifing are quite similar in metaphorical terms, connoting a superior position of causative influence in the birthing process intimate enough to partake in the process but far enough above it not to be the female body through which reproduction is enacted. The midwife figure serves as a foundational concept in renaissance memoirs and scholarship partly because it bodies forth filiation as a positive cause of renaissance creativity. The midwife may not be a member of the patriarchal family exactly, but she more importantly is the vehicle who brings the family into productive being through patient management of the processes of reproductivity.

In *Black Culture and the Harlem Renaissance,* Cary D. Wintz has conducted the most extensive study of the personal dimension of patronage relations during the period. Like Cruse, Huggins, and Lewis, he judiciously disentangles the varying motives for patronage, but toward the aim of exonerating the renaissance as a successful step in black cultural achievement. Significantly, racial prostitution does not figure much in his analysis, but patterns of patrilineal affiliation do, especially the parental-filial and coterie-companionate (brotherly) sort. In making the case for the cultural, as opposed to the economic, success of the renaissance for black people, Wintz emphasizes the robust, cordial, and sanguine bonds tying publishers, editors, patrons, and other promoters to renaissance participants as intimate friends and symbolic family. To argue for the success of the renaissance, he must separate economic from cultural effects. Spotlighting the positive dimension of intraracial and cross-racial affiliation enables him to accomplish this separation. Against Cruse's relentless indictment of the literary revival as a white-controlled enterprise for profit, Wintz portrays the black intelligentsia as the guiding force of the movement (*Black Culture and the Harlem Renaissance* 102). About James Weldon

Johnson he writes: "He was far more of a father figure (or perhaps a friendly uncle) to the younger writers than a colleague or an intimate friend" (110). And if Johnson was a father figure to these writers, then "Jessie Fauset was their older sister" (128).

Accordingly, Wintz ascribes miscarriages of intraracial patronage to deep-seated temperamental differences between the patron/midwife and the expectant artist/protégé—like the rifts that might occur among family members. For instance, in discussing Alain Locke's troubled relations with his protégés, Wintz writes: "Perhaps even more than any overt action on Locke's part, his personality and style offended many black writers (and offended them in a way that James Weldon Johnson's aloofness did not). Most observers described Locke as a small, fastidious, and even dapper man who openly cultivated the polish usually associated with a Harvard Ph.D. and Rhodes scholar" (118). Instructively, Wintz suggests that Locke's manner made him a perfect target toward which the younger members of the movement could express their anxieties over their own class and educational privilege. "In a sense they resented Locke because he reminded them too much of themselves and reflected many of the problems and inherent contradictions of the Renaissance" (118). Though "personality," "style," and a sort of oedipal strife doubtless help explain Locke's uneasy relation to his protégés, we have to wonder to what extent his protégés were also responding, in varying, complicated ways, to Locke's effeminacy and sexual orientation. The homosexual who refuses a familial procreative function and positions himself as a guardian of advanced culture exploits the inverse relation between aesthetic purity and the procreative middle-class values of husbandry, breadwinning, manly role modeling, and other socially prescribed masculine disciplines. Wintz appropriately dubs Locke an aesthete, an identity constructed by and for Locke through his manner, clothing, vocation, travel habits, marital status, and attitude toward art. Because aberrant masculinity, if not deviant sexuality, is already strongly associated with the aesthete's pose, Locke's role as midwife to the renaissance must be placed in the context of this association if we are to understand the repeated references in renaissance memoirs to Locke's mannerisms, diminutive physical features, and irritating habit of overstepping his boundaries.

In his article "Dr. Johnson's Friends," David Levering Lewis alludes to this overreaching aestheticist, decadent representation of the professor: "A small, dapper man, Locke was ceremonious to the point of prissiness. His Edwardian manners occasionally failed to conceal his dislike for the opposite sex" (504). Locke's infamous misogyny becomes entangled with his decadence, which in turn is entangled with his sexual orientation. Decadence stems from a trivializing, irresponsible philosophy that places conventionally feminine concerns of art, beauty, and style above the masculine obligations of political ambition, moneymaking, and other forms of cultural procreation, including fathering children, heading a family, and building national institutions. Locke's dislike of women situates him in a sort of envious feminine cultural sphere in which he is competing with women for the attentions of men and the reproduction of feminine culture. This attitude toward Locke is most wittily captured in 1924 by the satirist George Schuyler, who, writing in the black socialist journal, *The Messenger,* calls him a "high priest of the intellectual snobbocracy" and awards him the journal's monthly award, an "elegantly embossed and beautifully lacquered dill pickle."[14] Through his aestheticism, Locke turns the power of the phallus, Schuyler suggests, into a useless decorative object, just as he turns his penis to unproductive pleasures that deny its natural function in procreation. Although the midwife trope usually indicates patronage as positive affiliation, we can see in Schuyler's attack how it can also be exploited to indicate effeminization of the renaissance movement—in which case the midwife begins to look like the prostitute, a bastardizing effect that smothers the normal masculine procreativity expected of Negro cultural leadership.

The unproductivity of pandered or exploited sexuality in the figure of the renaissance as the prostituted body of the race more frequently is overridden by the notion of the midwife. As it personifies the procreative conception of cultural production assumed in texts written during and about the renaissance, midwifing operates positively as a foil to prostitution and as a "nursemaid" to masculine filiation.[15] Whether the renaissance is judged as failing or succeeding frequently amounts to whether it is prostituted as an illegitimate exchange or procreatively reproduced as a familiar family. Prostitution reduces the renaissance to a failed intimate relationship, an aborted (family) romance; filiation hypes the renaissance as the productive consummation of a star-crossed racial bond, whose offspring is often the triumph of national modernism, representing the fateful triumph of a unified United States culture emerging into its global dominance. In either case, the long-standing representation of the movement elides the significant function of variant sexual practices beyond the patriarchal norms, which are indicated by pure (nonsexual) masculine bonding at one end and impure heterosexual prostitution at the other. These conventional metaphors of masculine affiliation (master, father, son, brother, best pal) and masculine conquest and feminine impurity (heterosexual prostitution) obscure the explicit influence of same-sexuality and thus prevent us from understanding the complications of male desire and ambition in renaissance tutelage and creativity. By exploring the specific ways in which male renaissance participants represented their own relations to patrons, both black and white and male and female, we can understand the erotic binds that hold together the social bonds of racial patronage, and that constantly threaten to undo the "stamp of virility" promised by patronage itself.[16]

The False(tto) Accent of White Bohemianism: McKay's Patronage Attack

As a reluctant participant in the renaissance, Claude McKay (1889–1948) identified with many of its aims while ending up a controversial target for older renaissance promoters such as James Weldon Johnson, Du Bois, and Benjamin Brawley—all of whom saw him as a glaring instance of what was going wrong among the more "bohemian" writers of the renaissance movement. A Jamaican immigrant who spent more of his time in the bohemian and socialist circles in downtown Manhattan and in the expatriate enclaves of Europe and North Africa than in Harlem itself, McKay outwardly expressed a deeply ambivalent attitude toward the social and class strictures of the dominant idea of renaissance respectability. Especially in the publication of his steamy novel *Home to Harlem* in 1928, McKay became not only a lightning rod over the question of how the Negro should be portrayed in the movement but also the prime example of a black male elder encouraging the corruption of the "the younger Negro Artists," a generational concept articulated by Hughes's influential 1926 *Nation* essay "The Negro Artist and the Racial Mountain," and followed up with the bohemian efforts of the one-issue journal *Fire!!* (1926).

Although not explicitly mentioned by critics such as Du Bois and Brawley, the experimental literary expression of same-sexuality significantly marks the bohemianism of both *Home to Harlem* and *Fire!!* and links McKay to the younger group of renaissance writers, such as Thurman (who served as chief editor of the journal), Hughes, Richard Bruce Nugent, Aaron Douglas, Gwendolyn Bennett, Arna Bontemps, Countee Cullen, Helene Johnson, and Arthur Huff Fauset.[17] In Brawley's 1927 essay "The Negro Literary Renaissance," he attacks the morals of this younger generation as he warns that the contents of *Fire!!* are so objectionable, the journal will be subject to the censorship authority of the state: "If Uncle Sam ever finds out about it, it will be debarred from the mails."[18] As Lewis notes, some of the writing in *Fire!!* is clearly "calculated to scandalize Professor Brawley" (*When Harlem Was in Vogue* 196). Without a doubt, Brawley's warning of state censorship refers especially to Bruce Nugent's modernist prose poem "Smoke, Lillies and Jade," whose stream-of-consciousness style hints at themes of cross-racial homosexuality, androgyny, and pederasty. Going even beyond Van Vechten, one of the silent patrons who paid for the single-issue journal, Nugent's prose poem raises the specter of Van Vechten's homosexuality and pederasty—and his particular interest in African American call boys—in a way that never shows up explicitly in Van Vechten's own published work.[19] Understanding that to name these taboo sexual practices out loud would be to risk sinking to *Fire!!*'s level, Brawley instead employs the typical puritan euphemisms.

Similarly, in his 1937 treatise *The Negro Genius: A New Appraisal of the Achievement of the American Negro in Literature and the Fine Arts*, Brawley links the patron Van Vechten, the elder McKay, and the younger generation of "New Realists" in an assault that reveals his moral dismay while hiding its ultimate source in artistic expressions of same-sexual deviance. While praising McKay's earlier work, the protest and sentimental poetry, and identifying it with the more respectable precursors from the pre–World War I generation, Brawley changes his tone altogether in describing McKay's shift to fiction, a downward trend to the gutter that is initiated with McKay's first novel, *Home to Harlem*, and that to Brawley indicates the writer's moral decline and corrupting influence on the younger generation:

To turn from the poems of Claude McKay to the novels he has written is to be aware of something very close to a tragedy. For years he had been writing exquisite or dynamic verse, and the favor of the public, judged at least by commercial standards, was but luke-warm. Now there was a change of tone and emphasis. It is impossible for him to write incompetently; on everything he puts the stamp of virility. After the success of Mr. Van Vechten's *Nigger Heaven,* however, he and some other authors seemed to realize that it was not the poem or story of fine touch that the public desired, but metal of a baser hue; and he decided to give what was wanted. The result was a novel, *Home to Harlem,* that sold thousands of copies but that with its emphasis on certain degraded aspects of life hardly did justice to the gifts of the writer. (*Negro Genius* 245)

As a black cultural arbiter, Brawley attacks McKay by implying that he has compromised his art for the sake of reaching a titillated crossover audience—the charge of "prostituting the race." We can also see here how such artistic prostitution is intimately connected to Brawley's sense of sexually inappropriate subject matter within the fiction. Brawley's assertion that McKay is able to put "the stamp of virility" on whatever he writes—whether "poem or story of fine touch" or "metal of baser hue"—maintains some distance between McKay and the younger male writers, whom Brawley blasts more unambiguously. As we shall see, McKay himself went to great lengths to protect his "stamp of virility," even as he took forays into what Brawley labels the "forbidden" (233), the complex of sexual deviances expressed in his novels as sexually transmitted disease, extramarital bonding, sweetbacking, female prostitution, sadomasochism, and same-sexuality.

Even though McKay is frequently figured as a leading proponent of sexual exoticism and primitivism among the Harlem writers, in *A Long Way from Home: An Autobiography* (1937) he figures himself as a lone race gadfly who learns more from his white American and European socialist fellow travelers than from any New Negro patrons or peers. McKay pictures himself as something of a wide-eyed, virile ingénue—though distinctly *not* a primitive—among his white worldly colleagues, as he learns about the primitive that he is supposed to be from their own attempts at sophisticated social and sexual liberation.[20] In contrast to *Home to Harlem,* in which McKay couches homosexual deviance overtly and inextricably within the narrative of class liberation, in *A Long Way from Home* he carefully desexes his own narrative of liberation, so much so that we would be hard pressed to find a homoerotic subtext underlying his own relationships with the myriad white male mentors that populate the autobiography. As Rhonda Cobham has pointed out in a superb article on McKay's homoerotic relationship with Walter Jekyll, as revisioned through his 1933 novel, *Banana Bottom*:

McKay's need to shield himself from the prurience and emotional violence of white patronage undoubtedly contributed to [his] ambivalence about representing his own sexuality in his writing, although he so fully identified with Jekyll's view that the ambiguity of sexual repression, which led to the displacement of the erotic from the body to the mind, was precisely the "problem" of modern society.[21]

McKay's autobiography desexes the patronage intentions and practices of Jekyll, the effete upper-class white English dandy who took an interest in McKay as a rural boy in his native Jamaica. This does not mean, however, that McKay abandons his interest in "the ambiguity of sexual repression." Instead, in the autobiography, the sexual interest is projected onto McKay's white patrons and onto other people of color, while he attempts to keep himself clean of such implications. McKay viscerally lashes out at those he calls the "Negroid élite" (314) and "the conventional Negro moralists" (318–319) who manage the renaissance from Harlem. More circuitously, he also challenges the liberating intentions of bohemian white patrons. As he blasts both groups for their repressive behavior, however, he ironically exploits the same kind of puritan euphemisms employed by James Weldon Johnson, Du Bois, and Brawley when referring to the role of same-sexual deviance in these cross-racial transactions. Resisting his own need to censor (and censure) these homoerotic proclivities while desiring to censure their patronizing, exploitative usage among the white bohemians, McKay is put in the position of heterosexualizing his narrative while providing occasional hints of the role that same-sexuality plays in these patronage relations.

By making intriguing connections between neoimperialist oppression and modernist sexual repression, McKay comments on the hypocrisy of European male bohemians who celebrate their attraction to colored women from the colonies as proof of their interest in political liberation. Sardonically, McKay sides with the old-fashioned bold imperialists and slave traders in the age of exploration over their hypocritical descendants in the modern age of sexual experimentation:

> I am a little tired of hearing precious bohemian white men protesting their admiration and love for Negro women and the rest. Yet many of them are shocked at the idea of intimacy between a black man and a white woman, because of their confused ideas of erotic attraction. Perhaps I am hypercritical in detecting a false accent in their enthusiasm. But it strikes me as being neither idealistic nor realistic. I know it is a different thing from the sympathy and friendship that the humane and tolerant members of one group or nation or race of people feel for the members of another. And I know it is different from that blind urge of sexual desire which compelled white men to black women during the age of black slavery in the Occident (and perhaps in Africa today), and created an interesting new type of humanity. The performance of such men was not actuated by false and puerile theories of sex. I have a certain respect for them. But these nice modern faddists—they give me a feeling of white lice crawling on black bodies. (*Long Way from Home* 336–337)

This is McKay's most direct and trenchant attack on the sexual self-deceptions of progressive European patronage. While claiming a post-Freudian, liberating view of sex between the races, these men are hypocritical not only because their claims for liberated desire only go in one direction—from white men to black women—but also because their desire itself is self-deceiving. In fact, it is worse than the "blind urge of sexual desire" that caused marauding male Europeans to rape the dark women whose land they were in the process of pillaging and colonizing. This "urge" had the virtue at least of not being rationalized by putatively liberated but actually "false and puerile theories of sex." Also, it is in its own manly way productive and innovative: it produces mulatto progeny. McKay implies that the modern bohemians talk too much about their sexual alliances with dark women, so that the stamp of virility (in the form of mulatto children) is lacking. McKay further suggests that these "nice modern faddists" enact a sort of psychic damage, on the oppressed and on themselves, by substituting ersatz sexual license for genuine political liberation. Relayed through the disgustingly graphic image of "white lice crawling on black bodies," this psychic damage might seem benign because invisible in its operation, but it insinuates itself into the flesh, blood, and nerves of black bodies in a way much more difficult to overcome than savage acts of sexual/colonial conquest.

Contrasting such old-fashioned, potent male sexual conquest with the new-fangled psychic experiments of progressive but impotent white male liberals, McKay's narrative seems on the surface to accept the heterosexual logic of his overt critique and imagery. However, he cues us circuitously to another, hidden logic of homoerotic attraction, more repressed and thus operating more repressively to actuate this sort of neoimperialism while pretending heterosexually to liberate everyone's desire: "Perhaps I am hypercritical," he writes, "in detecting a false accent in their enthusiasm." Although the "false accent" would appear merely to be the racial hypocrisy that prevents the white male bohemians from embracing sexual relations between black men and white women, something more is at stake in their self-deception. An "accent" is hard to decipher because so nuanced to an outsider used to bold, direct manly actions. Of course, it is the job of a writer to be expert in the nuance of accents, but McKay has already made it clear that he prefers aggressive men of up-front action to "precious" men who "protest" too much in their subtle codes of talk. Just before this diatribe on the psychic costs of white male bohemians' neoimperialist patronage, McKay presents a breathing example of one of these men in the person of the famous French modernist photographer Henri Cartier-Bresson (b. 1908). If we pay too much attention to the colored concubine that Cartier-Bresson brandishes before McKay's eyes, we might easily overlook the "false accent" in his cross-racial liaison:

An interesting couple of visitors from Paris was Monsieur Cartier-Bresson, and his friend, an American colored woman. He was a Norman, and a painter and photographer. He had studied at Oxford and had a suggestion of upper-class English something about him. He had a falsetto voice which was not unpleasant, but it wasn't so pleasant to listen to it reiterating that its possessor could fancy only Negro women because he preferred the primitive. That falsetto voice just did not sound authentic and convincing to me.

And if a white man is fond of black women, why should he be declaring his liking to *me!* (335)

Cartier-Bresson, having studied at Oxford, has brought with him his American Negro woman to visit McKay in Morocco, as a retreat from the bohemian expatriate artist colony surrounding Gertrude Stein in Paris. Instead of *seeing* an authentic progressive, modernist man fulfilling his unrepressed desire against the grain of stultifying technological Western society, what McKay *hears* in Cartier-Bresson's accents are false tones. The inauthentic and unconvincing "falsetto voice" could indicate a man who has simply put on too many layers of polyglot postcolonial culture: the native French tongue jangling against Oxford English; the smooth Harlem lingo that he has learned from his Negro girlfriend dissonant within the hard Parisian phrasings. More repressively, however, the falsetto insinuates another sort of layering, the multiple repressions of neoimperialist lust in the guise of liberating intentions. This is a man playing a role, desiring to dominate his primitive sophisticated woman while pretending to desire her. Even more distressing, however, beneath the heterosexual layers, we might detect the insinuation of homosexual deviance as a paradigm of the neoimperialist desire to dominate the black male other through a feigned rivalry over a black female. The most subliminal source of Cartier-Bresson's falsetto is the practiced intention of alerting McKay to the white man's own ambiguous sexual availability to the black male primitive. One of the ways in which men of this period signal their desire for other men is through the assumption of a queer voice, the falsetto of the castrato, whose muted larynx comes to represent the sexual mutilation of homosexual deviance, as Wayne Koestenbaum has compellingly theorized.[22] As we saw in chapter 2, Van Vechten projects onto Taylor Gordon such a falsetto voice as a way of signaling the black primitive's availability to him as a vulnerable male protégé in need of a patron-master. Similarly, McKay reads in Cartier-Bresson's falsetto accent the contorted homoerotic attraction lurking beneath the white bohemian's heterosexually displayed desire. "And if a white man is fond of black women, why should he be declaring his liking to *me!*"

Lest this subtext seem farfetched, consider the episode that follows McKay's diatribe against neoimperialist white male bohemianism. McKay frames his heterosexualized account with falsely accented, obliquely insinuated homoeroticism. Like Cartier-Bresson, Charles Henri Ford also travels from the Gertrude Stein expatriate colony to search out McKay in his "primitive" hangout in Morocco, a region synonymous with homoerotic abandon in European homosexual underground cultures since at least the time of Lord Byron.[23] As surely as the mention of Stein

serves to mark the same-sexual practices rampant in her modernist coterie in supposedly sophisticated, liberated Paris, the encounter with Ford marks the covert
puritan repressions lurking behind avant-garde polish:

> The most interesting visitor of them all was the American writer and protégé of
> Gertrude Stein, Charles Henri Ford, who published a queer book of adolescence
> in Paris under the rather puritan title of *The Young and Evil*. Young Mr. Ford sud-
> denly dropped in upon me one day when a group of tribesmen were killing a steer
> in my garden. They cooked the liver in the yard and roasted some of the meat on
> skewers and invited him to join us in the feast. He was like a rare lily squatting in
> among the bearded and bournoused natives, and he enjoyed it. When he left in
> the evening I gave him a chunk of meat from what had been given to me.
>
> He had been in Italy with a Cuban girl. When they came to Madrid she found
> a young Spanish lover and the three of them came on to Tangier. He came to see
> me soon again and I invited some of the younger Moors and a few fatmahs to
> meet him. They all rather liked him. They said he looked wonderfully like the cin-
> ema portraits of Marlene Dietrich. (337–338)

Ford's 1933 novella was published in Paris because the subject matter was too
risqué for puritan American readers, and includes the obligatory scene of a Harlem
drag ball; yet, like other homosexually themed jazz age American novels, *The Young
and Evil*, as McKay points out through the title, retains a telltale residue of the U.S.
puritanism out of which its upper-class, rebellious bohemianism grows.[24] Attempting to move beyond both the homosexually suppressed aestheticism of Van
Vechten's novels and moralizing novels of homosexual apology such as Blair
Niles's *Strange Brother* (1931), Ford's fairy tale/novella, influenced by Stein's and
Djuna Barnes's experimental modernism, places homosexuality and cross-dressing
in the foreground in the very first paragraphs:

> There before him stood a fairy prince and one of those mythological creatures
> known as Lesbians. Won't you join our table? they said in sweet chorus.
>   . . .
>   A little girl with hair over one ear got up close and said I hope you won't be of-
> fended but why *don't* you dress in girls' clothes?
>   The Lesbian said yes your face is so exquisite we thought you were a Lesbian
> in drag when we first saw you and for two long hours they insisted that he would
> do better for himself as a girl. (*Young and Evil* 11)

The Young and Evil attempts to move in a world outside of morality, sentiment, and
political ideology—a luxury afforded only to those who can claim to desire nothing worth protesting, as in the case of Van Vechten's novels. Even the penniless
hunger of the characters is taken as a luxury that enhances their sensory deprivation and encourages the purely aesthetic suffering of their passion and poetry. As

McKay well understands, the "evil" of the title indicates the residue of an ethical system that supposedly no longer applies to these homosexual aesthetes. The only time the word *evil* is used in the novella, it is willfully divorced from its abstract moral meaning so as to refer to a mysterious expression on a young man's face, which evokes in the onlooker a momentary pang of intense desire. Linking the "young Mr. Ford" to "young" in the title of his novel, McKay is able to invoke the whole panorama of deviant sexuality elicited by this "queer book of adolescence," but only for those lucky few in the United States who might have made a trip to France—given that the novella was fully censored in the States.

McKay refers obliquely to the homosexual content of the novella through the subtle cross-dressing and inverted sexuality alluded to in his own scene of meat skewering. His female Cuban lover having taken a Spanish lover of her own, Ford becomes the queer, uncoupled third term in a scene of double triangulated desire that is worthy of *The Young and Evil,* at the heart of which is an incident in which Julian goes to bed with the salon patroness Mrs. (Mabel?) Dodge and her male Mexican lover only to get rid of another jealous female live-in lover whom he neither loves nor desires. Amid the masculine ritual of slaughter in McKay's Moroccan garden, Ford is a pale flower of civilization, desired by and desirable to the squatting dark Muslims in their burnooses. Their flowing cloaks would mark them as men cross-dressing in the modern West, but their self-confident "bearded" manliness only accentuates Ford as a vulnerable feminine presence available to the legendary lusts of the sex-segregated Muslim men of North Africa. They see Ford as Marlene Dietrich, the possessible and yet unpossessible image of white femininity made more desirable by the fact that she is seductively dressed in a man's costume. McKay almost absents himself from this scene of perversely averted desire; his only gesture is the ritual sharing of a "chunk of meat," which has been passed to him by the "natives" in this mythic scene of homoracial male bonding. It is not the peasant-poet McKay who disturbs the masculine routineness of the scene but the young Ford, the white colonial master refigured into the cinematic image of inviting white femininity ripe for sodomistic violation.

By framing his attack on white patronage practices with these coded scenes of same-gender desire and repression, McKay reminds us subliminally of how, skirting the accepted and routine narratives of imperialist conquest and postcolonial reconciliation, sexual deviance helps define these narratives through an undercurrent of continuing censorship and repression. Despite its circuitous nature, McKay's attack is lucid. Just as the imperialist master's sexual conquest of dark women becomes a metonym for his conquest of black men's land, so the white male bohemian's desire for dark women can serve as a metonym for his desire to possess the primitive potency of phallic dark men. Whether the white bohemian voyeur is Ford, Cartier-Bresson, or Van Vechten, desire for the dark engorged phallus—whether embodied in African "fetishes" or African male bodies—does *not* necessarily equate with a liberated homosexuality. If metropolitan culture were not so deeply repressed, the white bohemian homosexual would not find himself always traveling to the dark fringes, so inexplicably attracted to obfuscating acts of erotic violation behind the color curtain of Morocco and Harlem. For the white patron to be violated by the black phallus does not indicate his liberation from racial/sexual hierarchies and conformities; it merely enables him to exploit his greater access to wealth, resources, and freedom of travel in order to find a way of getting what he lusts after, without giving up his white male status, privilege, and ideology as a mastering patron in dominant, colonizing culture.

Like the respectable critic Brawley, McKay exploits (homo)sexual innuendo to attack a particular element affiliated with the Negro Renaissance, in this case the male members of the Stein enclave. At the same time, McKay strives to protect his "stamp of virility" while still claiming his intimate affiliation with the white avant-garde bohemians; after all, they trek to Morocco to see him. Although he exempts himself from the network of triangulated deviant desire passing from the white bohemians through women of color to the Moroccan natives, McKay remains at the vital center of that network as a judge of others' cultural procreativity. This is especially significant given the charge made against McKay, from his day to our own, that his representation of black culture in *Home to Harlem* prostitutes the promise of the renaissance by mimicking Van Vechten's *Nigger Heaven*. McKay handles the charge of race betrayal with the same kind of manly aplomb. When an uplifting Negro journalist visiting Paris insists that McKay, in publishing *Home to Harlem*, "had exploited Negroes to please the white reading public" (*Long Way from Home* 316), McKay's retort is sharp: "I said I did not think the Negro could be betrayed by any real work of art" (317).

The journalist recoils at *Home to Harlem* because it is "obscene," a word that carries with it the implication of the need for state censorship, as in the case of Brawley's assessment of *Fire!!* Proving that he is not afraid of the charge, McKay defends obscenity itself: "I have often wondered if it is possible to establish a really intelligent standard to determine obscenity—a standard by which one could actually measure the obscene act and define the obscene thought" (315). When he is in dire need of money, an Italian advises him to work as "an occasional attendant in a special *bains de vapeur*." . . . I could not. The very idea of the thing turned me dead cold. My individual morale was all I possessed. I felt that if I sacrificed it to make a little extra money, I would become personally obscene. . . . I preferred a menial job" (316).[25] Yet, setting the limits on what he himself would do, McKay wants to make it clear that this does not lead him to judge what others do as obscene: "Yet I don't think I would call another man obscene who could do what I was asked to do without having any personal feeling of revulsion against it" (316). His laissez-faire approach to obscenity not only affirms his faith in the strength of individuality over collective judgment; it also suggests how his brawny self-sufficiency embraces the right for others to do what they please. Perhaps thinking of a writer like Rimbaud, whom he admires, McKay claims himself a broad-minded cosmopolite, but in a way significantly different from James Weldon Johnson's more genteel pose. He is a burly man of the world whose heft does not leave room for the moral niceties of a bourgeoisie unfamiliar with passions of hunger and the necessities of menial labor.

McKay's debunking of obscenity as a moral category does not mean that he wants to be identified with the particular sort of obscenity associated with Van Vechten and *Nigger Heaven*. In fact, his discourse on obscenity operates to pinpoint the substantial difference between himself and the white homosexual patron, whose messy decadence threatens McKay's own sense of his strapping peasant earthiness. McKay tries to disaffiliate himself from *Nigger Heaven* on a class basis:

> Some of them [Van Vechten's black critics] said that Harlemites should thank their lucky stars that *Nigger Heaven* had soft-pedaled some of the actually wilder Harlem scenes. While the conventional Negro moralists gave the book a hostile reception because of its hectic bohemianism, the leaders of the Negro intelligentsia showed a marked liking for it. In comparing it with *Home to Harlem*, James Weldon Johnson said that I had shown a contempt for the Negro bourgeoisie. But I could not be contemptuous of a Negro bourgeoisie which simply does not exist as a class or a group in America. Because I made the protagonist of my novel a lusty black worker, it does not follow that I am unsympathetic to a refined or wealthy Negro. (318–319)

What the Negro moralists and intelligentsia have in common with Van Vechten is class status, or at least the desire to share an elite social status within United States dominant culture.

McKay then goes on to offer a cryptic but telling class critique of *Nigger Heaven*— a critique that makes it clear that "the Negro friends and foes" of the novel do not understand its patronage politics:

> My attitude toward *Nigger Heaven* was quite different from that of its Negro friends and foes. I was more interested in the implications of the book. It puzzled me a little that the author, who is generally regarded as a discoverer and sponsor of promising young Negro writers, gave Lascar [*sic*], the ruthless Negro prostitute, the victory over Byron, the young Negro writer, whom he left, when the novel ends, in the hands of the police, destined for the death house in Sing Sing. (319)

McKay implicitly attacks the white patron while appearing not to—in an almost passive-aggressive manner. His reading of the black hero's fate connects Van Vechten's patronage ambitions to his hero's protégé failure. In other words, Van Vechten needs a weak-kneed, upwardly aspiring black male hero to reform in order to assert his own authority and social status as a "discoverer and sponsor of promising young Negro writers." Who exactly is corrupting whom? McKay seems to be asking. As opposed to the frontal cutting attack on the Negro admirers and critics of Van Vechten's novel, McKay's deflation of Van Vechten is subtle, wryly dismissive through back-handed applause: "I thought it would be a new experience to meet a white who was subtly patronizing to a black; the majority of them were so naïvely crude about it" (319). By identifying himself with the "lusty black worker" over Van Vechten's defeated black male hero, McKay separates himself from the white bohemian who is supposedly his literary father to provide a more wholesome and muscular provenance through his peasant Jamaican roots for such words as *bohemian, decadent, obscene, corrupt,* and *forbidden.*

Unlike Hughes, who figures himself as a rebellious son of the renaissance and as a perfectly pitched sounding board for the race, McKay establishes his virility through a loner pose that is reminiscent of Pickens in *Bursting Bonds* and Gordon in *Born to Be.* Accordingly, McKay casts himself in *Long Way from Home* as alienated from the renaissance participants and mystified by the racial strategies put forward by the leaders.[26] "I was an older man and not regarded as a member of the renaissance," he writes, "but more as a forerunner. Indeed, some of them had aired their resentment of my intrusion from abroad into the renaissance set-up. They had thought that I had committed literary suicide because I went to Russia" (321). Highlighting his class origins and political activism on the global stage, McKay sets himself up as a worldly observer not prone to fall in line with the parochial notions of renaissance being tested in Harlem. "For my part I was deeply stirred by the idea of a real Negro renaissance," he says, implying that what is happening in Harlem is false (one might even say "falsetto"). "The Arabian cultural renaissance and the great European renaissance had provided some of my most fascinating reading. The Russian literary renaissance and also the Irish had absorbed my interest" (321). Against these celebrated models, formative in his own broadly traveled experience, the Negro Renaissance makes little sense to him:

> The Negroes were under the delusion that when a lady from Park Avenue or from Fifth Avenue, or a titled European, became interested in Negro art and invited Negro artists to her home, that was a token of Negroes breaking into upper-class white society. I don't think that it ever occurred to them that perhaps such white individuals were searching for a social and artistic significance in Negro art which they could not find in their own society, and that the radical nature and subject of their interest operated against the possibility of their introducing Negroes further than their own particular homes in coveted white society. (321–322)

Taking a patronizing stance similar to Gordon's attitude toward the race, if not so extreme, McKay allies himself more with the "modernistic white groups" (321) than with the deluded black reformers. Sapping the renaissance idea of its implicit political objectives by converting uplift into status seeking, McKay's deflation depends on the naïveté and superficiality of the renaissance leaders. Ironically, the man who is frequently seen as the most offending instance of prostituted talent exonerates himself by accusing the others of the same flaw.

The whole narrative of *A Long Way from Home* is devoted to this distancing. Whereas many chapters announce McKay's intimacy with white contacts through such titles as "A Great Editor," "Other Editors," "White Friends," "Another White Friend," "Adventuring in Search of George Bernard Shaw," and "A Look at H. G. Wells," he devotes only two chapters to his black contacts, one titled "Back in Harlem," another called "The Negro in Paris." In the former chapter, he credits Du Bois with shaping his outlook with *Souls of Black Folk,* a book that "shook me like an earthquake" (110). He also has some kind words for James Weldon Johnson, White, and Fauset. But the final impression he leaves of Harlem is one of stilted pretense, so different from his earlier experience of the place: "Where formerly in saloons and cabarets and along the streets I received impressions like arrows piercing my nerves and distilled poetry from them, now I was often pointed out as an author. I lost the rare feeling of a vagabond feeding upon secret music singing in me" (114). The rise of Harlem to class ambitions alienates McKay, the roving husky peasant-poet, from the cultivated rituals of fame and uplift obligation. Leaving us with a diatribe against the penchant for dress formality plaguing the new Harlem, McKay again places himself with the laboring poor over against the status-seeking New Negroes:

> But ever since I had to tog myself out in a dress suit every evening when I worked as a butler, I have abhorred that damnable uniform. God only knows why it was invented. My esthetic sense must be pretty bad, for I can find no beauty in it, either for white or colored persons. I admire women in bright evening clothes. But men! Blacks in stiff-starched white façades and black uniforms like a flock of crows, imagining they are elegant—oh no! (115)

Drawing a firm line between his mastery of aesthetics as a poet and the high-toned style of formal dress, McKay reaffirms his virility through his disdain for men in fancy formal wear. Such evening wear is "falsetto." He can admire women "in bright evening clothes," but the man who admires himself decked out in elegant formality has truly lost touch with earthy manliness. It has taken the Harlem Renaissance of such men to ruin the "secret music" of Harlem for McKay.

In contrast to his passive-aggression toward the Oscar Wilde–Van Vechten tradition of queer decadence and his utter contempt for would-be black renaissance patrons, McKay offers the macho socialist Frank Harris, "a great editor," as a patron to be admired but, significantly, also to be rivaled and surpassed. McKay looks on Harris, before their meeting, as a man who can put muscle and bone into him and his writing, enabling him to rise to the status of the great adventuring male writers of the real world: "Frank Harris appeared to me then as the embodiment of my idea of a romantic luminary of the writing world. He stirred me sometimes like Byron and Heine, Victor Hugo and Rimbaud" (9). As the qualifying "then" in this sentence indicates, McKay needs Harris as the great white patron-father mainly to move beyond him, not in the firmly patronizing manner that he distances himself from Locke but more subtly and cagily.

On McKay's first arrival at Harris's house, they see Mrs. Harris decked out and going to the opera. "She adores it but I don't care a rap about the opera. Of all the arts of the theater it is the tinseliest. A spectacle mainly for women," Harris carps. Harris's attitude toward opera looks suspiciously similar to McKay's attitude toward men in formal wear. However, McKay's response on this occasion is quite different: "I said I liked the opera rather well, such of it as I had seen, especially the chorus and the dancing. Frank Harris said he was surprised that I should, because the art of the opera was the most highly artificial of the civilized arts" (10). McKay's response does not make him any more artificial, overly "civilized," or inclined to "falsetto," like spectacle-adoring opera men; instead, it serves to place him outside the pigeonholes of racial types in which Harris wants to trap him. McKay catches Harris staring at him on their first meeting, only to discover that Harris "was speculating whether I reminded him of any special African type, for he had traveled in South Africa, West Africa, East Africa and the Soudan" (10). In the midst of their long conversation, Harris decides that McKay is unusually sensitive for a man of African descent. Wondering aloud whether McKay's sensitivity is "hereditary or acquired" (23), Harris answers himself: "What I mean is, the stock from which you stem—your people—are not sensitive. I saw them at close range, you know. . . . They have plenty of the instinct of the senses, much of which we have lost. But the attitude toward life is different; they are not sensitive about human life as we are. Life is cheap in Africa . . . " (23–24). Meeting this comment with absolute silence, McKay quickly moves from idolizing this great editor to allowing the reader to judge the white patron against the black peasant-author himself. Able to combine "acquired" sensitivity and discretion with manly judgment, McKay grows in size as Harris's racist indiscretions and false hyperboles diminish him before our eyes.

It is not that McKay totally humiliates Harris in order to firm up his own virility. In the "Back to Harlem" chapter, for instance, he pictures Harris as rightly whipping him into shame over having excised "If We Must Die" from *Spring in New Hampshire* on the advice of a weak-kneed English editor:

> "You are a bloody traitor to your race, sir!" Frank Harris shouted. "A damned traitor to your own integrity. That's what the English and civilization have done to your people. Emasculated them. Deprived them of their guts. Better you were a head-hunting, blood-drinking cannibal of the jungle than a civilized coward. You were bolder in America. The English make obscene sycophants of their subject peoples. I am Irish and I know." (98)

This scene of a white (and self-identified Irish) editor humiliating his black protégé to whip him into shape is especially interesting, given how similar it is to the scene in Van Vechten's *Nigger Heaven*, which McKay attacks as a back-handed mode of patronage. In both scenes, the white editor-patron teaches the black writer-protégé a lesson that can make or break him. Needless to say, whereas the colored hero of

Nigger Heaven is broken by the whipping and becomes a sexual masochist who commits a murder over his mastering female lover, McKay takes the whipping like a man, not like a slave:

> Frank Harris's words cut like a whip into my hide, and I was glad to get out of his uncomfortable presence. Yet I felt relieved after his castigation. The excision of the poem had been like a nerve cut out of me, leaving a wound which would not heal. And it hurt more every time I saw the damned book of verse. I resolved to plug hard for the publication of an American edition, which would include the omitted poem. "A traitor," Frank Harris had said, "a traitor to my race." But I felt worse for being a traitor to myself. For if a man is not faithful to his own individuality, he cannot be loyal to anything. (98–99)

In contrast to McKay's dismissive response to the black journalist who accuses him of betraying the race in writing *Home to Harlem,* McKay takes Harris's charge seriously. Harris's cutting words do not so much perform a racial castration, as in the case of Van Vechten's fictive editor; instead, due to the strength of McKay's "individuality," he is able to shift the "excision" from his own phallic power as a writer to the literal "wound" left in the book by the wrongful omission of the poem. Harris's words "cut like a whip" into McKay's flesh, but McKay's own error of cutting the poem more significantly becomes "like a nerve cut out of me, leaving a wound which would not heal." Not exactly a homoerotic sadomasochistic scene, like the one inferred by Van Vechten, this whipping enacts a desire for homoracial bonding based in the analogous experience of Irish and Jamaican colonial oppression.

There is no danger, we realize, of McKay turning into "an obscene sycophant," either as the masochist subject of the English masters or as the whipping boy of an aggressive Irish American patron. McKay knows how to deflect the charge of obscenity, and he would certainly find "personal revulsion" in becoming a sycophant, which is necessarily obscene to the manly man. McKay has impressed this on us in the first chapter, "A Great Editor," by showing how he refuses to become the sycophant to Harris himself. Harris's shortcomings are literalized through his size: "I was surprised by his littleness. I knew that he was small of stature, but did not expect him to be as diminutive as he was." Unlike Locke and the other "falsetto" men, Harris is not a mincing minion to his own littleness, as indicated by his big, booming voice; "his voice was great and growling like a friendly lion's with strength and dignity and seemingly made him larger than he actually was" (10). The crude sizing up that dictates McKay's diminution of Locke, examined below, contrasts with the more nuanced and metaphorical sizing up that characterizes his respect for the great white editor.

In the end, McKay rejects Harris—and all other white bohemians—as his patron because McKay is his own man. This is why he corrects Harris's mistaken notion that the omitted poem is a betrayal of the race. As a solid man of the earth, McKay is capable of betraying only his own potential. Accordingly, the first chapter ends not with McKay's reaffirmed discipleship but instead with his observation of discipleship in another, pertinently a white female who has begged to work for Harris. "He said that she had written imploring him to let her come to New York to serve 'the master' in any capacity." Substituting the doting white female secretary for himself, McKay has it both ways. He gives to Harris the right of possessing a devoted disciple; he protects in himself the right of not being that disciple. He cuts Harris down to size in possessing a disciple so willing as a mere literary lady; he builds up his own stature in the eyes of the reader, who understands that McKay has grown larger through his homoracial bonding with the great editor. The final sentence of the chapter captures McKay's growth through Harris's gaining of a female worshiper: "And fortunately he had found in her a perfect disciple" (25).

Godmothering and the Psychic Traps of Race Patronage

McKay's ambivalence toward white patronage as a sexual affair that could prove insidiously compromising to his "stamp of virility" is broadly shared among male Negro Renaissance participants. His image of lice, those tiny white parasites, boring into black bodies captures his attempt both to acknowledge the cultural power of white desires and demands and to diminish its perceived impact on his own procreativity. Asserting such intimate affiliations with white cultural influence, the shapers of the renaissance necessarily subjected themselves to a host of artistic, psychic, and political paralyses—not the least of which concerns their own authority to lead and identify with the mobile black masses.

We can see the gendering of this eroticized patronage economy in the way that Langston Hughes represents his relationship to one of the most notable white female patrons, Charlotte Osgood Mason, who was, in Lewis's vivid words, "an aged, well-preserved white dowager of enormous wealth and influence." Calling herself "Godmother" and requiring all her protégés to do so as well, "[o]n pain of banishment, Godmother demanded that her subjects never mention her name to others without permission" (*When Harlem Was in Vogue* 151). As many scholars have noted, Mason enacted the most dreadful aspects of renaissance patronage. She is thus frequently cited as a negative instance of a self-serving white patron, one who not only tyrannized over her protégés, especially Hughes and Hurston, but also caused destructive rivalry between them.[27] Mason is the nightmare version of Ovington as "Mother of the New Emancipation" and of Van Vechten as the "Abraham Lincoln of Negro Art." She brought to the surface what festered beneath it in the race relations of such "good" patrons. Arnold Rampersad points to the sort of duplicity inherent to such a relationship:

> Sycophantic to her face, Hurston often ridiculed Mrs. Mason behind her back; Locke himself was only more elegant in his deception. Mrs. Mason sensed their manipulation and looked even more fiercely for signs of genuine gratitude. Of the

three godchildren, all neurotically mortgaged to Mrs. Mason, only Hughes was both genuinely in love with her and scrupulous in his dealings.[28]

Rampersad's notion that Hughes was "[d]eeply in love with Mrs. Mason" (169) raises a host of puzzling questions about the impact of Mason's godmothering on the young, struggling poet, who tended to think of himself as almost parentless due to his difficult relationship with his mother and father. In her Hughes biography, Faith Berry opts for the maternal over the erotic: "The poet had accepted her as a surrogate mother, whose interest in him was entirely unselfish and altogether motivated by maternal love." Later, she writes, "Hughes responded to his patron like a doting son" (*Langston Hughes* 93).

What is at stake in these competing images of the erotic (with hints of prostituted talent) versus the maternal (following the pattern of patriarchal blood filiation)? That Mason desired to be called *god*mother rather than mother indicates to what extent she did *not* want to confuse her patronage with an actual blood relationship. A godmother is, in a sense, higher than the blood mother. She is the maternal figure who spiritually adopts a child at the moment of Christian baptism and becomes the child's sponsor, teacher, and advocate in faith. Berry points out that Hurston signed one of her letters with the salutation "Darling My Mother God," (129), indicating Hurston's understanding that Mason's title insinuated the status of divine inspiration more than fleshly reproduction. The title "godmother" was intended as much to create distance between Mason and the mammy's willing flesh as it created expectations of maternal authority and spiritual guardianship on her part and childlike gratitude on the part of her protégés.

When he published the first volume of his autobiography, *The Big Sea* (1940), Hughes recaptured the emotional bind and racial logic linking the disappointed love for his hands-on patron with the disappointing love for his distant father. He moves back and forth ambivalently between bartered eroticism and parental loss. He identifies his paralytic illness after the breakup with Mason as even more unsettling than the experience of refusing his father's way in order to find his own (see *Big Sea* 323–324). "[W]hen I think about it, even now," he writes, "something happens in the pit of my stomach that makes me ill" (325). Ordered out of his Mother God's house of patronage, Hughes appropriately returned to his blood mother's home in Cleveland to nurse his wounds. The breakup between female patron and male protégé seems virtually inevitable, given the adopted son's need to prove his mettle beyond the matron's caretaking surveillance. "I didn't realize that my not writing a while mattered so much to the kind and generous woman who was caring for my welfare," Hughes says. The patronized Negro must perform consistently and constantly in order to retain the good graces of the patron—a form of racial surveillance. The moment his conduct disturbs the projected desire of the patron, he must be called onto the carpet. "'It's not you,' my benefactor said when she had read thus far [in one of Hughes's poems]. 'It's a powerful poem! But it's not you'" (*Big Sea* 323). For his power as native genius to match her power as civilizing benefactor, his conduct must represent a fundamental difference (as primitive or atavistic) while not disturbing the myth of mutual interchange leading to mutual racial reform.

Hughes bluntly labels this a relationship of power, recognizing that such great power can be practiced only when it operates on an inferior whose compelling interest must always be bound to the exigencies of the patron's whim or "vogue." Without denying the influence of her generosity, he embeds it in an absolute assertion of racial and economic power: "Great wealth had given to a woman who meant to be kind the means to power, and a technique of power, of so mighty a strength that I do not believe she herself knew what that force might become. She possessed the power to control people's lives—pick them up and put them down when and where she wished" (324). That Mason's kindness is perverted into a "technique of power" turns on a subtle paradox entailed in the tension between a matron's caretaking kindness and the "mighty strength" that normally derives from a male patron's privilege of masculine access. This is similar to the distinction between "mothering" and "fathering" a cultural movement. Perhaps Hughes has chosen Mason because she is a *female* patron as much as she has chosen him because he is a black *male* in need of a father/mother substitute. As a white *woman,* Mason cannot be quite a proper father, and as a *white* woman, she cannot be quite the proper mother; but her status as patron appropriately confuses fathering with substitute mothering, as it also fuses parental concern with an intensely eroticized affair.

Mason desperately needs Hughes, or others like him. The white patron needs the black protégé to embody a fully souled presence, the satiety that *should* accompany wealth, status, influence, and racial privilege, that *should* accompany the ruling class whose national inheritance is emerging as the dominant global power. "Concerning Negroes," Hughes notes, " . . . [s]he felt that we had a deep well of the spirit within us and that we should keep it pure and deep" (316). Like a man who desires a pure, virginal wife upon which to father his progeny, Godmother Mason desired a black man as a pure, virginal body to give shape to her powerful cultural legacy. Historically, patronage has served to signal the efficaciousness of the patron's rank and influence within larger society. In late-eighteenth-century Europe, it helped foster a myth of the resonant relationship between the natural genius of native peasantry and the rightful inheritance of that genius by a civilized elite, who controlled state institutions as a consummation of the natural continuity and progress binding the native folk to the increasing authority of the state.[29] As upper-class patrons "discovered" peasant poets, they also discovered the natural source of their own national power, a source that enabled them to measure the resonance and distance between an eternally felicitous folk heritage and a promising national-imperial progeny. In effect, the capacity for European patrons to reach so far down into their peasantry and folk past to find there the origins and futurity of a great civilization serves to enunciate and announce their worthiness and destiny to rule primitive peoples around the world.

As discussed above with Villard, Ovington, and Park, the United States cultural elite found themselves in an analogous situation in the 1920s. Whereas European patrons had reached down in a firmly established social hierarchy in order to transcend a class distinction that threatened the natural nativity, unity, and power of their liberal-imperialist nation-state, European Americans could best enact such a gesture by reaching down to the racial bottoms. If the United States elite could raise a former slave people up to a level of civilization without spoiling the native genius harbored in the folk spirit of the race, then clearly they could responsibly manage and tutor their accumulating colonies in the equatorial Atlantic and the South Pacific and their client Caribbean and Central American states in the New World hemisphere.

Such patronizing power derives its "technique" from the psychodynamics of the most deeply transforming, intimate human bonds—erotic-romantic, parental-filial, and coterie-companionate—while basing its structure on an economy of generous exchange, entrepreneurial opportunity, and upward mobility and its rationale on a progressive mandate of racial uplift and democratic expansion. As Hughes's own body reveals in shutting down with the collapse of the patronage relationship, even when such power is consciously resisted by the protégé, it can still achieve its effect by enervating, at least temporarily, the will of the one who is being lifted up through racial reform. How ironic that the very mobility (in every sense) that is sought by the New Negro as a sign of his manhood reform and self-modernization is immobilized by the white patron(ess) who claims to be aiding his climb up the social ladder. "So, in the end," Hughes writes, "it all came back very near to the old impasse of white and Negro again, white and Negro—as do most relationships in America" (*Big Sea* 325). Godmother's patronage—like her love—is destined to disappoint, for it is too entangled with the racial ideology that motivates it for either Mason or her adopted son to transcend its hierarchical, segregating racial logic.

"Pussy-Footing" Dr. Locke:
Masculine Networking as (Homo)Racial Contest

As intensely antagonistic as the relationship between Hughes and Mason may have been at some level, Hughes and the historians and critics after him went out of their way *not* to represent it as a rivalry. In a sense, to locate the relationship either as "unrequited love" or as "maternal" is to downplay rivalry as a key component. As in the relationship between Du Bois's Yankee schoolmarms and their students, or between Ovington and Du Bois, the cultural expectation of some sort of erotic attraction or sacrificial caretaking between white female and black male is so strong that it erases the presence of rivalry. In the relationship between a black male patron and his black male protégé, however, the opposite is true. Renaissance participants—and the historians and critics who have commented on them—exploited images of blood filiation to emphasize how rivalry naturally predicates such intraracial bonding, like the blood feuding between Du Bois and Walter White as chosen sons of NAACP political patronage. Of all the black "midwives," the most attention has been focused on Locke, whose overbearing guidance is represented as potentially effeminizing just as Mason's to Hughes is seen as threateningly *un*-feminine.

McKay doles out some harsh treatment of Locke in his autobiography, *A Long Way from Home*, which Locke reciprocates in his review of the autobiography.[30] McKay's criticism of Locke exploits language that relies on the assumed associations among high aestheticism, unreliability, and lack of manly forthrightness—language that carries the punch of an *ad hominem* attack based on gender deviance:

> Yet I must admit that although Dr. Locke seemed a perfect symbol of the Aframerican rococo in his personality as much as in his prose style, he was doing his utmost to appreciate the new Negro that he had uncovered. He had brought the best examples of their work together in a pioneer book. But from the indication of his appreciation it was evident that he could not lead a Negro Renaissance. His introductory remarks were all so weakly winding round and round and getting nowhere. Probably this results from a kink in Dr. Locke's artistic outlook, perhaps due to its effete European academic quality. (*Long Way from Home* 312–313)

Locke's "rococo" personality and his kinky artistic outlook—flaunted in his "weakly winding," roundabout style—constitute his social deviate tendencies, which are directly connected to his gender deviance (his "effeteness"), which in turn disables him from leading the manly charge in the New Negro Renaissance.

In his competitive repartee with Locke, McKay repeatedly impugns his rival's manliness. When McKay became upset over Locke's handling of his poems in the *Survey Graphic* and *The New Negro* anthologies, he quipped, "I am a man and artist first of all," implying that Locke was neither man nor artist and did not have the potency to balance both roles effectively. This is the downside of being a "midwife" or "nursemaid" in the renaissance without also being an artist who procreates culture. Just as it is possible to be man-loving (bonding intimately with other men sexually and otherwise) and manly, it is possible to be artsy and manly. Locke fails this test; McKay calls him "a dyed in the wool pussy-footing professor" (quoted in Tillery, *Claude McKay* 116). In his autobiography, McKay tells an amusing anecdote about their meeting in Paris: "Commenting upon my appearance, Dr. Locke said, 'Why, you are wearing the same kind of gloves as I am!' 'Yes,' I said, 'but my hand is heavier than yours'" (*Long Way from Home* 312; also see Cooper, *Claude McKay* 261). Depending on its delivery, McKay's retort falls somewhere between the virile aggression of the dozens and the coy insinuation of effeminate camp.[31] In protesting so much over his patron's lack of manliness, McKay may be enacting the sort of oedipal rebellion Cary Wintz suggests—Locke reminding McKay too much of himself and reflecting his own contradictions (his tendency toward high-artistic decadence and his own same-sexual predilections). It is also clear, however, that at stake in this entangled patronage relationship is McKay's attempt to distinguish between Locke's renaissance aesthetics and his own, between the identical gloves worn and how they fit the wearers' hands, between a lightweight and a heavy male appendage.

McKay, then, reproduces the renaissance in the figure of a little man who fancies himself elegant in "stiff-starched white façades and black uniforms." In other words, he figures the renaissance in the image of the "pussy-footing," small-handed Dr. Locke. McKay tells an anecdote of walking in the Berlin *Tiergarten* with Locke, who, enamored with the "statues of the Prussian kings supported by the famous philosopher and poets and composers on either side," remarks that these statues are "the finest ideal and expression of the plastic arts in the world." Characteristic of his treatment of Locke, McKay finds this hyperbolic statement contemptuously amusing, "for I had walked through the same row with George Grosz, who had described the statues as 'the sugar-candy art of Germany.'" Locke's effeminate polish prevents him from possessing a true understanding of the procreative power of cosmopolitan (especially *European*) art. "When I showed Dr. Locke George Grosz's book of drawings, *Ecce Homo*, he recoiled from their brutal realism" (*Long Way from Home* 312). Like a brittle parlor lady recoiling from the brutality of real life, Locke is incapable of becoming the arbiter of iconoclastic modernist taste that he claims to be. Such a task requires the rigorous stamina of observing and participating in the brutality of the real. Most damning for Locke, this impotence in the face of brutal life disqualifies him on the ground where he most needs to stake a flag, in the judgment of African art, with its primitive and brutal vitality: "So it was interesting now to discover that Dr. Locke had become the leading Negro authority on African Negro sculpture. I felt that there was so much more affinity between the art of George Grosz and African sculpture than between the Tiergarten insipid idealization of Nordic kings and artists and the transcending realism of the African artists" (313). By making a white man a better judge of African sculpture than Locke, McKay also makes himself a superior judge of both. Having conquered both European high culture and African primitivism, McKay can thus claim to transcend both the decadent self-deceptions of white bohemianism and the high-minded self-deceptions of New Negro uplifters. As in the case of Pickens's attack on the black college administrators as "little men" and Du Bois's attack on White for his small stature, the would-be black male patron is subject to ridicule both for attempting too close a proximity to a white appearance (in clothing, mannerisms, posture), as well as for failing to achieve a proper (white) masculinity. In other words, the black manhood reformer is damned either way: if he imitates the high culture of white masculinity or if he fails to imitate it well enough.

If Hughes is characteristically both more reticent and more embracing than McKay in his portrait of Locke in *The Big Sea*, it is not due to a difference in how he shapes his artless (i.e., natural) manliness against the pussy-footing doctor of high aesthetics and artificial snobbocracy. Using Locke as a foil is one of the crucial ways in which Hughes is able to construct his own masculinity as ordinary, folk-based, sexually unambiguous, and nonchalantly acquired in the manly wanderings of a sailor's life. In *The Big Sea,* Hughes first introduces Locke as a sort of dainty trespassing meddler in the affairs of real men, one prone to drown if thrown into the big sea with Hughes and his chums. Hughes makes the metaphor literal, as he separates himself from Locke by placing himself on a "haunted ship" anchored in the Hudson River "with eighty or more other dead ships of a similar nature" (*Big Sea* 91). The gothic danger of Hughes's hangout is emphasized through his fantasy of what might happen if Locke were to venture into this men-only no-man's-land:

> Meanwhile, there came to me at the fleet, a letter from a gentleman in Washington named Alain Locke. Written in a very small hand, it commented upon what he felt to be the merits of my poems he had seen in the *Crisis,* and he asked if he might come to Jones Point to see me—evidently thinking I lived in the village. I couldn't picture a distinguished professor from Howard, a Ph.D. at that, clambering over the hundred-odd freight boats that made up our fleet, slipping on the wet decks and balancing himself over precarious runways between rocking old vessels. So I wrote back "No." (92–93)

The selected details of the paragraph add up to more than what the words say outright. Again, the "very small hand" seems to tell Locke's number in a subtler way than McKay's contrast of glove sizes, even though the narrator has never met the man whose penmanship reveals so much. Hughes, too, establishes the difference between himself and Locke in terms of hand size—in this case, between a free, spontaneous, loose, manly script and a cramped, delicate, binding signature of an aesthete. He makes it clear who pursues whom, who desires to set up a patronage relation with whom; for the Hughes narrator, in his free and easy way, is too unbridled to attend closely to the professor's commentary on his poetry, as he humbly fails to provide the laudatory content of the commentary. The poet must be ordained by the folk on the big sea of life, not by the "small hand" of the "distinguished" professor. The passage also prefigures, with great gentle subtlety, how the folk poet will manage to keep his distance, will avoid the pitfalls of an aesthete's kinks and mannerisms. Hughes imagines Locke assuming that the young poet lives "in the village," in the center of decadent, bohemian, deviant white life, when the young poet is instead in the tributary of the big sea's mouth itself. Unlike McKay, who creates elbow room for his masculine pose through nasty innuendo, Hughes, ever the good son, shows Locke all the respect he deserves. Yet, in response to the professor's entreaty—with whatever alliances, advantages, admonitions, attentions, and attractions that entreaty entails—Hughes closes the door with a simple, bare, bold, manly no.

Hughes's recounting of this incident downplays the extended correspondence and networking through such an intermediary as Countee Cullen entailed in this decision not to meet with Locke before setting out on the big sea. Arnold Rampersad characterizes the incident in a different light from Hughes's own account, as he suggests that Cullen put Locke in touch with Hughes explicitly for the purposes of sexual seduction: "Countee took his failure gracefully when Langston, with whom he was clearly interested in having an affair, seemed utterly unconscious of such an interest. Then Cullen decided to help another friend, one more worldly, who might succeed with Hughes where he had failed" (*Life of Langston Hughes, vol. 1* 66). Whereas Hughes characterizes his rejection of Locke as a terse no, Rampersad points out that Hughes immediately started up a correspondence with the professor. After "chattering on" about his dreams, travel, opera, and the theater, Hughes "wrote also about the admirable crew at Jones Point, which he located precisely for Locke" (68). In response to Locke's rather explicit hints at a homosexual liaison, Hughes played dumb while egging Locke on:

> Under such pressure, Hughes's sexual desire, such as it was, became not so much sublimated as vaporized. He governed his sexual desires to an extent rare in a normal adult male; whether his appetite was normal and adult is impossible to say. He understood, however, that Cullen and Locke offered nothing that he wanted, or nothing that promised much for him or his poetry. If certain of his responses to Locke seemed like teasing (a habit Hughes would never quite lose with women or, perhaps, men) they were not therefore signs of sexual desire; more likely, they showed the lack of it. Nor should one infer quickly that Hughes was held back by a greater fear of public exposure as a homosexual than his friends had; of the three men, he was the only one ready, indeed eager, to be perceived as disreputable. (69)

Whether Hughes's "appetite" is "normal" or not, his wavering between hot and cold in his correspondence with Locke contrasts starkly with the pose he takes in *The Big Sea*. The sort of masculine aggression he enacts against Locke in his public account of the event—though gentler in tone and degree than McKay's pose—reveals how the private affair of the correspondence positions him as a naive boy desiring and yet resisting the lascivious advances of an older, more worldly man of higher social rank—the proverbial peasant maiden tempted by the master's flattery. Or, against the grain of Rampersad's interpretation, we could plot Hughes as a practiced flirt, one who takes great erotic pleasure in tempting others and even greater pleasure in remaining unavailable. In either case, I am not persuaded that Hughes's flirtation with Locke suggests a "lack" of sexual desire or that Hughes "governed his sexual desires to an extent rare in a normal adult male." To the contrary, flirtation, especially the compulsive kind described by Rampersad, *is* an expression of sexual desire, at the least of an erotic pleasure taken in toying with another's attraction and in deferring intercourse. Finally, we have no way of knowing to what extent Hughes "governed" his sexual desires in that we have no way of knowing what was going on, for instance, with members of that "admirable crew" aboard ship or offshore. The most we can say is that Hughes knew his attractions and knew how to use them to advantage in the correspondence and how to erase their fuller implications in the autobiography.

Faith Berry, who is much more confident about Hughes's homosexuality, nonetheless reads this correspondence between Locke and Hughes along the axis of filiation rather than sexual teasing.[32] Although Berry uses the familiar filiation trope to characterize this budding relationship, she cuts to the quick of what Hughes stands to gain: "Their friendship in its early stages was sustained through correspondence; and the two men developed a relationship that on Hughes's part seems to have been filial, and that on Locke's part was made the instrument of considerable assistance to the poet's career" (*Langston Hughes* 35). As opposed to Rampersad's implication that Hughes's flirtatious rejection resulted from his being turned off by the prospect of a sexual liaison with Locke, Berry attributes Hughes's "frank, yet polite" refusal to the poet's "shyness" and "self-effacement" (35). Regardless of which explanation might come closer to the truth, it is clear that Hughes handled this black sissy patron in a way dramatically different from the way he later handled Godmother Mason. Along with the differences in race, age, gender, economic worth, and class status of the patrons we must enter homoerotic attraction into the complicated patronage affair with Locke, for Hughes's self-effacement and teasing manipulation suggest an understanding, whether calculated or intuitive, of the costs and benefits entailed in a homosexual or homoerotic liaison with a man of Locke's image and reputation.

Despite Hughes's supposed refusal to engage in a sexual liaison with either Cullen or Locke, and regardless of the macho loner image he propagated in his published writings, he in fact involved himself in a homoerotic coterie by teasing out the correspondence and continuing his tempting association (flirtation?) with both men. Because this scenario does not accord with the more familiar heterosexual love triangle, with its normal closure predicated by the dichotomy of impure fallenness (prostitution) and happy marriage (patriarchal filiation), we have been prone to overlook the degree to which these men's sexuality both constitutes and constrains their friendship and patronage through a triangulated network of erotic attractions and resistances. While pursuing this homoerotic coterie in private, Hughes distances himself from Locke in his public persona, an act that accomplishes two intertwined objectives at once. He dons his mantle as a poet of the African American folk rather than of the effete (Europeanized) elite and displays his worthiness to this title by plotting his development from an innocent boy of immense natural talent to a man of the people who, holding onto the youthful naturalness of that talent, never loses sight of his filial origin and manful destiny. Hughes performs this distancing gesture explicitly through his suggestion that he is unable to imagine someone of Locke's educational status and class background meeting him halfway, whereas the correspondence suggests that he has imagined something much more intimate. Despite the fact that Hughes himself was raised in the middle class and clearly is destined for high educational status, especially relative to the African American masses if not to Locke, he wants to create resonance between himself and his projected black folk reader, achieved by linking himself to this reader against Locke. According to Leonard Harris, "Langston Hughes was Locke's ideal author: urbane, steeped in the traditions of black folk literature, and portraying its contours with a sense of universal value. . . . Locke perceived the artist as a community representative."[33]

Locke's cameo appearances serve to remind us of the effete, arch-sophisticated figure that Hughes is *not* becoming in his donning the mantle of worldly author, even as he enhances his own mastery of high European art through his relationship with Locke. Much more so than James Weldon Johnson in *Along This Way*, but more subtly than McKay in *A Long Way from Home*, Hughes is obsessed with constructing a virile black male authorship while retaining the capacity for a racial sensitivity and an erotic sensibility that can justify his genius for acting as a palimpsest for the joys and sufferings of the race as a whole. Hughes's characteristic gentle humor in the little fantasy about Locke's falling into the sea is sustained in the succeeding paragraph of *The Big Sea*, as he makes obvious his folk resonance through hyperbolic panic over meeting his betters: "I was panic-stricken. I pictured the entire staff of the *Crisis* as very learned Negroes and very rich, in nose glasses and big cars" (93). Operating beneath this explicit image of class panic is implicit gender jockeying, suggesting that (homo)sexual panic gets displaced onto class and race anxiety. Hughes as the narrator, as native son of orphaned black America, can have no kinship with Locke and his network, even as his career advances through the institutions, coteries, discourses, and values he shares with these Talented Tenth Negroes.

While describing two meetings with Locke in Europe, Hughes pursues this class panic with an underlying gender/sexual anxiety. He expresses appropriate gratitude to Locke for showing him the high life, but he soon tires of accompanying the "little, brown man with spats and a cultured accent, and a degree from Oxford" (184):

> But before the week was up, I got a little tired of palaces and churches and famous paintings and English tourists. And I began to wonder if there were no back alleys in Venice and no poor people and no slums and nothing that looked like the districts down by the markets on Woodland Avenue in Cleveland, where the American Italians lived. So I went off by myself a couple of times and wandered around in sections not stressed in the guide books. (189)

Hughes's need to wander off alone into the slums expresses not only a homesickness for the sort of ordinary people he might recognize in his hometown but also a sort of homecoming that Locke, the cosmopolitan traveler comfortable in all the high places, would never understand. In discriminating between Locke's high cosmopolitan mode and his own vagabond worldliness, Hughes is able also to discriminate between their high-artistic poses and his own black folk-based mundaneness. Hughes's alienation from Locke is exactly his comfort and natural *kin-ship* with the common man. His encounter with Locke is sandwiched between two episodes that stress both his naïveté as a commoner and world traveler and his passionate vulnerability as an earthy man and (heterosexual) lover. The first is Hughes's account of a brief love affair with Mary, the daughter of a wealthy businessman from the English "Niggerati." Mary's father forces her to leave Hughes, an unsuitable man for such a catch, and return to marry a man the father has selected. The second is Hughes's account of being robbed while sleeping on a train, an act that leaves him penniless, homeless, and stranded on shore for a while. In both cases, we are reminded not only of Hughes's home within the orphaned class of common folk, without credentials, entitlements, pretenses, or inside connections, but also of the affectionate sympathy that ties him to every man who has loved and lost unfairly. Because he wanders out with open arms, he returns to us not hardened, as unsympathetic men become, nor flabby, as an even less sympathetic coddled man would be, but so seasoned by tough experience that he can afford a sensitive heart. This experiment in what I call *moderated masculinity* we shall see again in the various black urban folk heroes created by other black male writers of the period. Without emasculating or effeminizing his sonship, Hughes wants to indicate the strengths of being vulnerable as a man, a vulnerability that ties him empathetically to the dominated lives of the colored poor around the world.

Hughes's treatment of Locke emphasizes how complicated the figure of kinship becomes in renaissance writing, as he shows how the image of filial-companionate intimacy can work both ways, can be used against patronage as an unnatural process of reining in the free flow of the budding folk artist as well as for a concept of progressive patronage. We should not take Hughes's romantic vision of the development of an artist at face value, but neither should we too quickly accept the purely benign affiliative image of patronage celebrated in some books on the renaissance. George Hutchinson, for instance, views the renaissance as a wholly mutually beneficial "interracial intimacy" that he predictably characterizes through the metaphor of "kinship": "To fully appreciate the links between ostensibly opposite racial traditions—to appreciate a once-acknowledged but long-forgotten and repressed *kinship*—we must first look back to the years before World War I."[34] To emphasize the "kinship" between black and white during the renaissance, Hutchinson must diminish the role of race, as he freely admits, especially as a source for misalliance. This version of the renaissance has the advantage of scripting not only a progressive narrative of United States race relations but also a natural network of cultural brethren whose blood affiliation is deeper than any circumstantial race division. The rush to integrate European American and African American experiences into a singular multicultural modernity has the unfortunate effect of more intensely avoiding disturbing aspects of the patronage system. A salutary fraternity becomes the procreative basis upon which the *patria* reproduces, elaborates, and expands its interest.

The most stunning instance of this tendency can be seen in the attitude toward Van Vechten from the 1920s to the present. Strange bedfellows joined ranks against and for Van Vechten when his controversial *Nigger Heaven* is published. Adversaries such as Marcus Garvey and Du Bois, who applauded Garvey's trial and imprisonment, agreed on the corrupting effects of the Van Vechten tradition, with Garvey calling writers who stoop so low "literary prostitutes."[35] Against this prostitution paradigm we again find the figure of patronistic affiliation. Writers as inimical as the cautious, patrician, renaissance booster James Weldon Johnson and the unsentimental, low-hitting, deflator of renaissance ambitions, George Schuyler, sang Van Vechten's praises. In *Along This Way,* Johnson writes of Van Vechten "his regard for Negroes as a race is so close to being an affectionate one, that he is constantly joked about it by his most intimate friends" (382). How one can claim affection for a race we have begun to see with Hughes's casting himself as a son to the black *patria;* but what does it mean for a white patron to claim affection for the black race, especially given how that affection is necessarily entangled in a lust for black boys? Schuyler waxes even more hyperbolic, going so far as to label the racial interchange of the 1920s the "Van Vechten Revolution," despite the fact that in his 1926 *Nation* diatribe he called the same phenomenon "the Negro-Art Hokum." In a *Phylon* retrospective on Van Vechten in 1950, Schuyler suggests that the white patron "has done more than any single person in this country to create the atmosphere of acceptance of the Negro" ("Van Vechten Revolution" 362). Negotiating these competing narratives of Van Vechten's affection for the Negro, Wintz attempts to give a balanced view of Van Vechten's influence as a testament to the role of white patronage in the renaissance:

> Carl Van Vechten represented white support of black literature at its best—sincere and with unselfish intentions. However, even unselfishness and sincerity could not always prevent misunderstandings between black writers and white patrons, nor could it prevent white support from imposing restrictions, as unintentional as they might be, on black literature. (*Black Culture and the Harlem Renaissance* 188)

What is striking here is how Van Vechten's generosity—representing white patronage as a whole—can turn out to be a reasonably equitable partnership whereby the patron demands few, if any, compensating returns ("unselfish intentions"), even emotional or psychological ones.

Sometimes in subtle, sometimes in overt ways, the specter of sexuality haunts Van Vechten's patronage of Harlem talent—shaping the notion of patronage itself to such a degree that conventional patronage paradigms have prevented us from fully acknowledging and analyzing his role. In describing the factious reaction to *Nigger Heaven,* for instance, David Levering Lewis lists the renaissance men who praise Van Vechten's book by cataloging their relationship to him in terms that not only seem to accept Van Vechten's friendship at face value but also intensify these relations into blood ties:

> But there were his new friends among the Afro-Americans whose affections and expectations had to be considered—James Weldon Johnson, as dear to him as his own father and possessing greater "tact and discretion"; Walter White, with whom he got on "like a house afire" and who was soon to bestow Van Vechten's name on his son; and Langston Hughes, who was like a son and a colleague. Their help with the manuscript and their approval of it also made a commercially promising novel an even surer bet. (*When Harlem Was in Vogue* 188)

There is something curious about Lewis emphasizing the profit motive in Van Vechten's publishing the novel while characterizing these friendships with black men through such settled similes and facsimiles of patriarchal filiation. Given Van Vechten's troubled, rebellious relationship to his own father, in which the father's generosity was always both too much and too little for him, one has to wonder how Van Vechten managed this filial role with Johnson or his godfatherly role with White. How exactly is his godfathering different in psychological and economic structure from Charlotte Osgood Mason's godmothering? Given the great difference between a son and a colleague, how could Hughes smoothly perform both roles?

Nonetheless, the ghostly working of Van Vechten's sexual disposition does influence renaissance scholarship and can occasionally be glimpsed in circuitous, if not downright euphemistic, phrasings arguing for or against the beneficence of his influence on black writers and artists. In *From Du Bois to Van Vechten,* Chidi Ikonné, for instance, wants to downplay both Van Vechten's impact on black writers and *Nigger Heaven*'s novelty as an exposé of unconventional sex among Harlem blacks (see 37). Ikonné connects this charge directly to the issue of prostitution: "Van Vechten's novel is regarded by many critics as a perverter of young, promising, black writers who, after the success of *Nigger Heaven,* allegedly became 'Van Vechtenites' and prostituted their art" (xii). Ikonné never mentions Van Vechten's homosexuality in his study, yet the repetition of the phrase "perverter of young black writers" carries with it an insinuation that Van Vechten's decadent "lifestyle" may have lured black youth into a metaphorical life of (male) prostitution and perverted sexuality. The phrase alludes to the common translation of the crime for which Socrates was executed as a perverter or corrupter of Athenian youth and harbors a common notion of the male homosexual as an entrapper of innocent young boys. Ikonné wants to claim that, despite the proclamations of Van Vechten's influence made by young black writers such as Arna Bontemps, these writers are made of stronger stuff, able to resist Van Vechten's seductions by writing a literature that becomes "the expression of their dark selves" (13)—echoing Hughes's famous phrase in "The Negro Artist and the Racial Mountain" (694). At stake in such characterizations of the Van Vechten influence is whether the renaissance embodies the act of young black (male) writers, and the race they represent, coming into manhood.

If same-sexuality has played a significant but largely silent role in shaping our notion of renaissance patronage—its potency or impotence—how can this knowledge help us rethink the cultural representation of the renaissance itself as a pivotal moment of cross-racial interchange? What does such knowledge suggest about both general and particular patronage relations? What does it mean, for instance, that Van Vechten could offhandedly refer to Hughes, whom he had recently met, as his "Negro boy friend" while using his considerable influence to garner a contract for the unknown young poet (quoted in Lewis, *When Harlem Was in Vogue* 180)? Van Vechten's wish-fulfilling presumption need not be carried out as sexual act to shape the "technique" of his patronage power. I would even go so far as to suggest that the wishful presumption of a mutual sexual attraction serves to enhance Van Vechten's entitlement, for it keeps intact the patron's self-image of his influence as desirable, even if he himself is not exactly (sexually) desired by his protégé. The white patron's relationship to the black protégé is like Virginia Woolf's magical mirror: "Women have served all these centuries as looking-glasses possessing the magic and delicious power of reflecting the figure of man at twice its natural size" (*Room of One's Own* 35). Similarly, when Van Vechten calls Hughes his "Negro boy friend," the white patron is able to feel himself as twice his natural size: a doubly powerful man who can shape his ward's destiny as a father would a son's and at the same time be the subject of his ward's erotic desire. Van Vechten's fantasy of Hughes would seem to unbalance any neat formula of masculine bonding implied in the congenial equivalencies of "colleague" or the affectionate equivocations of "son."

Consider further how Van Vechten's dependence on these black men to correct his account of black urban life both inverts and intensifies the normal patronizing relationship. Does their generosity in reading and improving his manuscript of *Nigger Heaven* match his generosity in sponsoring them and their culture? Does his profiting from an arguably exploitative exposé of black culture justly compensate for the white tourists he brings to Harlem, along with their bulging purses? I am not trying to efface the potentially genuine affection that could exist between these men and their white patron. In fact, I would suggest their affection would have to have been profoundly genuine for them to overlook so generously the insidious racial/sexual/class politics of both *Nigger Heaven* and Van Vechten's penchant for black boys. My concern is with the disquieting complications that lurk beneath the conventionally pat labels of heteronormative male bonding. Do Van Vechten's homosexuality and his curious erotic fascination with black boys have any impact on his bonding with these *particular* black men? In "Carl Van Vechten's Black Renaissance," Bruce Kellner describes more graphically the "seamy" underside of Van Vechten's interest: "In all candor, he devoted an inordinate amount of time to shabby pursuits—getting drunk in speakeasies, collecting Harlem sycophants about him, and having dates with steamy sepia courtesans or assignations with handsome black call boys—that were common knowledge" (27). Immediately after listing these sexual escapades, however, Kellner characteristically tries to separate these "shabby" desires from Van Vechten's "genuine," "serious," "professional," higher "intellectual" influences: "But his intellectual admiration was genuine. His response to black music and writing was firmly grounded in nearly a quarter of a century of serious, professional musical, and literary criticism. Moreover, his desire to share his discoveries resulted in a cultural exchange unique at the time" (27). Segregating these desires in this manner tends to ignore the ways in which Van Vechten's "lower" and "higher" passions for the Negro are inextricably entangled in acts of eroticized patronage that associate the sexual availability of the race's oppressed body with the intellectual availability of the race's folk culture.

Gloria T. Hull is one of the few critics to deal with the question of sexualized patronage patterns head-on, in her discussion of women's exclusion from the inner circles of renaissance patronage. She suggests that male privilege influences women writers' access to cultural institutions in a variety of blatant and subtle ways. She appropriately uses as her examples the black man usually given credit for "fathering" the renaissance from the inside, Alain Locke, and the white man most notorious for sponsoring it from the outside, Van Vechten; but she focuses her example on the black homosexual, not the white one:

> Locke's behavior becomes even more problematic because of his obvious partiality toward young males, to whom he was sexually attracted. Locke, in fact, functioned within a homosexual coterie of friendship and patronage that suggests that literary events were, in more than a few instances, tied to "bedroom politics" and "sexual croneyism"—as they no doubt may have been in the heterosexual world also. The point here, though, is that women were definitely excluded from Locke's beneficence and this particular sphere of favoritism. (*Color, Sex, and Poetry* 8)

It is not clear what Hull is suggesting about the role of same-sexuality in these male-male patronage relations. Is the fact of Locke's and Van Vechten's homosexuality coincidental or axiomatic? Does their homosexuality intensify the patriarchal logic of women's exclusion, or does it point to complications in that logic? It is not the purpose of Hull's study to answer such questions, but by focusing on two homosexual men, she leaves the problematic impression that the misogyny operating in renaissance patronage is of a particularly virulent sort when accompanied by homosexuality. This overlooks the complications and difficulties posed by a patronage relationship based on homosexual liaison. Not only does homosexualized patronage potentially duplicate the insidious conditions of sexual/economic traffic practiced by powerful men on women in patriarchal culture, but it also carries with it the complications of homosexuality's stigma in dominant culture. Just as it would be a mistake to equate the female networks of mutual aid that Hull discusses

Figure 5.1. Carl Van Vechten in Paris; photograph by Man Ray. Courtesy of the Man Ray Trust. © Man Ray Trust/ADAGP/Telimage, 2003.

with the patriarchal network of male power and privilege, so it would be a mistake to equate a homosexualized network such as Locke's coterie with heterosexual male bonding or homosociality.[36] As we can see in Wallace Thurman's *Infants of the Spring,* though the homosexual coterie may borrow its structure and technique from homosocial networks of patriarchal power, such a borrowing may serve to ensnare homosexual men further in a self-destructive net of internalized homophobia while ironically seeming to promote their advance in a masculine system of privilege.

One of the complications brought to the surface by focusing on the sexuality of male bonding is a curious fusion, or confusion, between cross-racial identification and same-sex orientation. Miguel Covarrubias's caricature of Van Vechten, titled "A Prediction," graphically depicts a joke that has become common in contemporary gay lingo: the white man who sexually and/or socially prefers black men to his own kind will ultimately defect into blackness. Such men are derogatorily labeled "dinge queens."[37] Part of the joke in Covarrubias's caricature is a contrast between

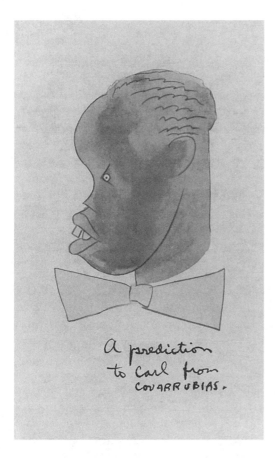

Figure 5.2. Carl Van Vechten—A Prediction; caricature by Miguel Covarrubias. Courtesy of the Beinecke Library, Yale University.

what we know to be Van Vechten's undeniably Caucasian features and the exaggerated Negroid features of the sketch (Figures 5.1 and 5.2). A more subtle aspect of the joke entails inside camp humor. The huge, cartoonish bowtie represents Van Vechten's celebrated exaggeration of civilized style to the point of "inversion" and "decadence." The head rests securely on top of the big bowtie, inverting the relation between substance (the head as deep character) and form (the bowtie as superficial style). The sketch could not claim the outrageousness of its humor, however, without alluding to the atavism or "mongolism" of black physiognomy. Popular science books such as that by F. G. Crookshank, M.D., *The Mongol in Our Midst: A Study of Man and His Three Faces,* which went through three printings between August 1924 and April 1925, give insight into the long tradition of such profile portraiture. Crookshank argues with meticulous scientific logic and method that individuals with Downs syndrome, known as "mongols" due to their putative resemblance to "racial Mongolians," are really atavistic freaks of nature resulting from whites intermixing downward with nonwhites. The regressive "mongol idiot" disproves single-origin theories of human descent and conversely proves the triple-origin theory and its hierarchy of the three races (the "white" race from chimpanzees, the "yellow" race from orangutans, the "black" race from gorillas). For scientists of the time, the proof is in the profile, as the pictures included in Crookshank's study indicate (see Figure 5.3). Such "scientific" experiments conducted during the 1920s base their "objective" findings of the physical and moral inferiority of the African race on measurements of the cranium and brain, as well as on the older science of phrenology, whereby moral character could be accurately determined by interpreting the shape of the head and facial features.[38] These sketches and photographs, based on the most modern scientific research, are supposed to display the specific facial features that determine not only racial and sexual inferiority but also the tendency toward criminality, including sexual depravity.

The brilliance of Covarrubias's sketch, like all camp humor, is that it says so much by saying so little in an exacting tone: Van Vechten's quest for inverted style has taken him beyond decadence, past a postcivilized sophistication, back full circle to humanity's primitive Negroid roots, which, according to scientists like Crookshank, rank even below the "mongoloid imbeciles." In turn, Van Vechten makes those roots modish in the manner of postcivilizing decadence—he remakes the unrefined Negro into the overly refined image of himself, or in Crookshank's terms, the image of the clever, curious, outgoing chimp. The caricature is an apt, if whimsical, commentary on the ideological seams woven into the urbane fabric of *Nigger Heaven*. Likewise, when his good friend and fellow aesthete Avery Hopwood teases Van Vechten about his imaginary Negro inheritance, more is at stake than a little joke about so Nordic a person being secretly tainted (or energized) by black blood: "I am explaining . . . that you really see little of Harlem, these days, but that you saw a great deal of it before you *passed*. They are all so surprised to hear about your Negro strain, but I tell them that your best friends *always knew*."[39] The arch code usually reserved for private banter between homosexual friends here gets interpolated into a mode of racial secrecy translated as matters of passing and hidden blood. It is as if the form of camp communication between two homosexual friends is retained while the content of a doubling homosexual life is displaced by racial doubling. This is the double-crossing form of Van Vechten's *Nigger Heaven*, picked up by Hopwood and wittily quipped in a short note. The intrigue of Van Vechten's novel is ultimately the mystery of why an elite white sexual invert, whose career as a novelist has been staked on saying nothing of moral value, would desire to mimic the sufferings and moral dilemmas of painfully bourgeois Harlem Negroes.

Such fantastic double crossing of racial, sexual, and class identities also receives serious treatment during the time from the other direction: writers explicitly interested in sexual inversion borrow Harlem's tolerance for sexual variance as a didactic backdrop for homosexual pleading and moral conversion in an agenda of liberal national progress. In *Strange Brother* (1931), Blair Niles exploits African

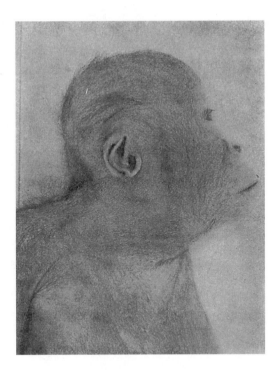

Figure 5.3. Scientific Profiles: Plate VI; from Crookshank, *The Mongol in Our Midst.* Photo courtesy of the University of Virginia Library.

American urban folk culture and its seemingly successful renaissance patronage in an attempt to piggyback her plea for homosexual tolerance among white Americans on the newfound Negro vogue. In a sense, her white homosexual protagonist flirts with what Huggins calls the "ultimate price of [white] identity": defection into Negrohood (*Harlem Renaissance* 93). As Niles's novel suggests, even for those whites who could not totally succumb to the Harlem addiction by becoming Negroes, the prospect of a chance cultural or sexual encounter could risk their own identity, making them more or less secure in their racial privilege, serving further to veil or unveil their stake in a mythic norm. More bluntly put, whites who felt out of place sexually in their own society could enact their deviant fantasies in Harlem while hiding those fantasies behind Harlem's color curtain. At the same time, in enacting those fantasies, they jeopardized the security of their color and entertained, at various levels, the possibility of becoming real sexual/racial outcasts, if not racial regressives, as the interchange between sexual invert and racial revert was conflated. It might even be that the projection of a freer black sexual life and the actuality of less restriction on homosexuals in African American urban communities combined to render the search for a liberated homosexuality across racial and class lines the paradigmatic patronizing experience. Thus, it may not be coincidence that the most controversial black nursemaid to the renaissance is an overly cultured pussy-footing professor with very small hands, and the most *visible* white patron an excessively (decadently) cultured, secretly homosexual man who exploits his privilege to forge the Negro Renaissance and who is willing to entertain, however playfully, the loss of his white identity—the fantastic possibility of becoming an outcast to dominant culture and a revert from his race—in order to explore his erotic fascination with black boys through his patronage of a New Negro culture.

Part III   "A City Jungle This"

Footloose Desire and the
Sexual Underworlds of Harlem Renaissance Fiction

A city jungle this, if ever there was one, peopled largely by untamed creatures that live and die for the moment only. Accordingly, here strides melodrama, naked and unashamed.   —Rudolph Fisher (*Walls of Jericho* 4)

A . . . result of the dominant mood was a preference for sordid, unpleasant, or forbidden themes; and close to this was a certain blatant quality, a striving for effect, that gave an impression of artificiality. In general the writers were closer to the heart of the folk . . . , but while Uncle Tom and Uncle Remus were outmoded, there was now a fondness for the vagabond or roustabout, so that one might ask if after all the new types were an improvement on the old.   —Benjamin Brawley (*Negro Genius* 233–234)

Automatically the effort to view country life through Black eyes produced visions of lynchings, share croppers, slavery, and all the fear and facts of Black life in America. An effort to view the city through those same eyes dredges up Blacks who may roam, but never walk—the violence of the powerless coupled with a kind of stylized adroitness, cunning, and subterranean rip-off tactics.   —Toni Morrison ("City Limits, Village Values" 39)

In a 1929 retrospective essay reviewing three of the novels that would become touchstones of the Harlem Renaissance, Locke laments the year as representing "probably the floodtide of the present Negrophile movement" ("1928: A Retrospective Review" 8). Usually put in the position of championing the youthful rebellions and perceived excesses of the Harlem movement, Locke finds himself wishing for an abatement of whites' interest in Negro art. Acknowledging that "[m]ore aspects of Negro life have been treated than were ever even dreamed of," Locke nevertheless goes on to hope for (and predict) a waning appetite on the Negro topic that might in turn lead to a less inflated, more substantial artistic product. "We shall not fully realize it until the inevitable reaction comes; when as the popular interest flags, the movement will lose thousands of supporters who are now under its spell, but who tomorrow would be equally hypnotized by the next craze" (8). Presciently analogizing the coming loss of interest to a stock market crash, Locke reaffirms his trust in the potential of the Harlem Renaissance in a moment when many others have lost faith, due largely to what they see as the intrusion of white writers taking up sensational Negro topics as a distracting fad. In the end, Locke believes that "the stock-brokers and real productive talents" will stick around to survive the crashing interest. "The real significance and potential power of the Negro renaissance may not reveal itself until after this reaction, and the entire top-soil of contemporary Negro expression may need to be ploughed completely under for a second hardier and richer crop" (8). Accompanying (and competing with) the analogy to stock market investment, the metaphor of planting and cultivation runs throughout Locke's retrospective as he attempts to image the Negro Renaissance as a natural phenomenon whose growth to maturity and stature is unstoppable.

Refusing to fall into Du Bois-style moralistic assaults concerning the negative political implications of the progeny of *Nigger Heaven* and other primitivist white material on black culture, Locke finds ways of praising even the most maligned novel of 1928, Claude McKay's *Home to Harlem*. Touting the novel for its "reflection of the vital rhythms of Negro life," Locke notes the divergence between it and Rudolph Fisher's *Walls of Jericho,* which employs the contrary "art of social analysis"; but he does so in order to praise *both* novels for their differences. "*Home to Harlem* will stand as a challenging answer to a still too prevalent idea that the Negro can only be creatively spontaneous in music and poetry, just as Mr. Fisher's book must stand as the answer to the charge that the Negro artist is not yet ripe for social criticism or balanced in social perspective" (8). While criticizing Du Bois's 1928 novel *Dark Princess* for falling "an artistic victim to its own propagandist ambushes," Locke discriminates between McKay and Van Vechten, on the one hand, and those who, like Du Bois, want to throw all such novels into the same camp, on the other: "Those who read *Home to Harlem* superficially will see only a more authentic '*Nigger Heaven*', posterity will see the peculiar and persistent quality of Negro peasant life transposed to the city and the modern mode, but still vibrant with a clean folkiness of the soil instead of the decadent muck of the city-gutter" (8). The charge of decadence, as we have already seen, serves as code for a whole range of sociosexual practices, with the expression of same-gender sexuality occupying the extreme end of dominant culture's idea of degeneracy. Reconnecting McKay's folk back to the wholesome soil from which they have migrated, Locke ironically insinuates that any dirtiness projected onto these characters must be in the superficial reader's mind, not in the "clean," though "still vibrant," "folkiness" of the novel—a truth to be redeemed by posterity. With the photographs of the three younger black novelists—Nella Larsen, McKay, and Fisher—facing us from the pages of the retrospective essay, we are given a visual frame for Locke's reading of the year 1928. Whereas Du Bois's propagandistic effort will be forgotten, and whereas those white novelists attempting to profit by joining the Negrophile fad will disappear into the obscurity of history, posterity will build on the offerings made by these three.

In his 1965 interview "A Very Stern Discipline" (published in 1967), Ralph Ellison coined his famous phrase characterizing the renaissance as a "decadent baby":

> The Negro writers who appeared during the 1920s wished to protest discrimination; some wished to show off their high regard for respectability; they wished to express their new awareness of their African background; and as Americans trying to win a place as writers, they were drawn to the going style of literary decadence represented by Carl Van Vechten's work. This was an extremely ironic development for a group whose written literature was still in its infancy—as incongruous as the notion of a decadent baby. (In *Collected Essays* 731)

Holding to Locke's metaphor of the natural process of quickened maturation, Ellison turns Locke's praise on its head with the image of the literary movement as a decadent infant. The other objectives of the renaissance—protesting racism, gaining mainstream respectability, and exploring African heritage—are swamped, in Ellison's view, by a people whose literary immaturity is wedded to the bohemian degeneracy of a Van Vechten. As Ellison is aware, Van Vechten in the 1920s was generally seen as the leading proponent of adapting this decadent legacy of Oscar Wilde to American literature. In his important essay titled "Patterns of the Harlem Renaissance," George Kent sets out to rescue the renaissance movement from what Locke vividly calls "the decadent muck of the city-gutter." Yet, even as Kent exonerates the poetry of the period from such a charge, he seems to accept Ellison's— and by extension Du Bois's—accusation of decadence: "It must be admitted that all charges are supportable, in varying degrees, but that some seem more applicable to a part of the Renaissance than to the whole. As a single example, Ellison's charge of decadence, is more applicable to certain novels and stories than to poetry" (*Blackness and the Adventure of Western Culture* 34). With their emphasis on depicting realistically the whole gamut of the social scene, it should not be surprising that Negro Renaissance novelists' endeavors would come under such moralizing scrutiny and be found lacking.[1]

More crucial than the division between poetry and fiction in this debate has been that between the so-called genteel or old-school uplift writers of the renaissance and the generally younger, more socially daring ones. In his 1937 history, Benjamin Brawley codifies this division when he devises two contrary chapters, "Protest and Vindication" and "The New Realists," with the former representing writers such as Du Bois—who, Brawley suggests, "gave to [his people] a new sense of literary values and scholarly achievement, and, so doing, he became an inspiration to many younger men" (*Negro Genius* 202). The high moral praise that Brawley gives to Du Bois, William Stanley Braithwaite, James Weldon Johnson, Alice Dunbar Nelson, Georgia Douglas Johnson, Walter White, and others is reversed when he characterizes the "new realists," who unfortunately do not follow the ennobling lead set by their elders and peers. Describing the social background of the 1920s, Brawley writes:

> In subject-matter there was influence from some writers who were not of the race and who were disposed to exploit it. Harlem began to be attractive, also anything suggesting the primitive. The popular demand for the exotic and exciting was met by a strident form of music originating in Negro slums and known as jazz. Along with this was a mood that was of the essence of hedonism and paganism. Introspection and self-pity ran riot, and the result was a kind of song known as the "blues." (232)

Recognizing a "more serious side" to this "new temper," Brawley praises the New Negro collections edited by Charles S. Johnson and Locke, who is noticeably categorized in Brawley's previous chapter on "Protest and Vindication": "These were of immense help in freeing the genius of the Negro" (233). Despite the classy efforts of Johnson and Locke, however, the hedonism and paganism running riot in the "slums" infect the literary arts. "At the same time in the new day there were some deterrent factors. The first was a lack of regard for any accepted standards whatsoever. Young writers were led to believe that they did not need any training in technique" (233). Freeing up the genius in this atmosphere of slummy jazz, blues, and pagan immorality leads to all sorts of contaminating license. Associating the new realists with "deterrent factors," Brawley, like Ellison after him, issues moralistic dismay over the subject matter of these writings under the cover of a concern for their lack of stylistic technique and artistic standards. Revealingly, Brawley includes both Jessie Fauset and Nella Larsen in the respectable "Protest and Vindication" chapter (as well as Countee Cullen), not in the succeeding licentious "New Realists" chapter, where McKay, Hughes, Fisher, Wallace Thurman, Bontemps, and Hurston are discussed.

Brawley's moralistic take on the descent from Du Bois's sublime to McKay's gutter is not limited to this period, when critics were more prone to view their calling in terms of a moral pedagogy of humanism. Writing fifty years after Brawley, Amritjit Singh approvingly recapitulates this now familiar division of Negro Renaissance texts, as he also embraces its familiar moral judgments:

> The first trend is defined by such black writing which, like much writing on the subject by white contemporaries (although with significant minor variations), presents black life as exotic and primitivistic. One thinks, for example, of novels such as Arna Bontemps's *God Sends Sunday* (1931), Claude McKay's *Home to Harlem* (1928) and *Banjo* (1929) and poems such as Countee Cullen's "Heritage" and Waring Cuney's "No Images." On the other hand were works by writers who with equal force and terror attempted to show that the black American was different from his white counterpart only in the shade of his skin. These writers

found it expedient to plead their case by presenting black middle-class characters and situations in their fictional works in order to demolish the prevailing stereotype. Among such works one may mention the novels by Jessie Fauset, Walter White, Nella Larsen and W.E.B. Du Bois. However, the primitivistic mode had such wide and deep appeal among their readership that white publishers often hesitated to publish their works.[2]

As discussed in chapter 5, the notion of prostituting art for the sake of profit and fame undergirds this division. Even though a common characteristic of these novels is that they scale the range of socioeconomic classes in African American culture, this traditional division also takes its axis supposedly according to the "class" of the characters depicted. In actuality, this usually means that the social status of the protagonist becomes the class of the novel as a whole. The two women novelists of the period, Fauset and Larsen, are routinely included in the respectable uplift group whose characters represent the striving middle class. Until the recent work of black cultural feminists such as Deborah McDowell, Cheryl Wall, Gloria T. Hull, Thadious Davis, and Ann duCille, the issues of sex and sexuality that loom large in Fauset's and Larsen's work have tended to be overlooked. As these critics have amply demonstrated, gender has operated silently as a basis for the classification and judgment of these writers. Larsen and Fauset have been strictly segregated from McKay, Fisher, Bontemps, Thurman, and Hughes as their work has been tied to the higher, purer mode of tragic mulatta fiction and the European novel of manners. As Mary Helen Washington points out, "during the 1920s, Larsen's novels were perceived as 'uplift novels,' novels that proved that blacks were intelligent, refined, morally upright—and therefore equal to whites."[3] It is as if reviewers and readers refuse to allow Larsen's literary similarity to the more daring male writers because of the feared imputation of feminine sexual looseness such a connection entails. Even Locke keeps Larsen distinctly separate from Fisher and McKay in his 1928 retrospective, instead comparing her favorably to Du Bois and binding her work to the more respectable passing tradition in praising her modernization of the form (9). Viewing Larsen's work solely in this line of development, rather than as more closely "akin" to the men's sexually scandalized novels, these male critics shield, with no small degree of unconscious chivalry, the chastity of the middle-class colored female, particularly so that her writing does not become impurified by intimacy with Van Vechten's salacious penetration of the African American literary market.[4]

Ironically, much more than any of the licentious "new realists," Larsen considers herself an intimate friend of Van Vechten, confides in him about the progress and frustrations of her novel, and requests that he read and criticize the manuscript of *Quicksand*.[5] Her work clearly engages with *Nigger Heaven* as much as that of her male contemporaries. Published in the same year as *Home to Harlem* and *Walls of Jericho*, Larsen's first novel is hard to distinguish from the men's stories in terms of both subject matter and narrative structure. In fact, the secret that plagues Larsen's heroine, Helga Crane, but that she advertises herself in moments of crisis, is the dubious sources of her class background, with the implication that she is not only a mulatta but also *a bastard*—the latter detail being crucial to her social identity but generally overlooked in the rush to view the novel as a parable of "protest and vindication" in line with high-minded Du Boisian principles. Helga scurries from city to city almost like a roustabout, is literally tossed in a Harlem gutter by natural force, finagles to commit adultery with her best friend's husband, and *does* commit fornication with a country preacher. It seems ironic that Larsen's protagonist has been so facilely separated from McKay and his supposed model, Van Vechten, whose heroine in *Nigger Heaven* is a paragon of saintly virtue. Given that a woman's social status in the period is normally determined by the marriage she makes, Helga is decidedly downwardly mobile, and in fact has hit rock bottom at the close, no longer able to maintain her urbane air or even to assume social superiority over her husband's female parishioners, from among whom he has choice pickings to commit adultery. A negligent mother and incompetent housewife, Helga is busy dreaming an escape before the narrative closes. My point here is not to reread Helga as a lascivious, immoral character whom Larsen fashions as a didactic model, positive or negative, for women's uplift. Rather, it is that evidently some factor other than thematic treatment or narrative structure is at stake in the long-standing moral judgment of these novels, and in the case of Larsen, gender cannot be dismissed as the other factor.

It would be erroneous to underestimate the effect of Van Vechten and the "Negrophile fad" on *all* the Negro Renaissance novels that succeed his, from the late 1920s to the mid-1930s. To understand the implications of "decadence" on their work, we must examine the ways in which all these novelists engage the sensational fad of depicting black urban sexuality. What we discover is a set of novelists concerned with how black manhood, womanhood, and gender relations are reconstituted under the conditions of modern urbanity as a site of racial oppression. As they take the Van Vechten trend as one inescapable aspect of the representation of black sexuality that must be contended with as a consequence of African Americans' coming under the whiter spotlight of modern urban markets and media, these Negro Renaissance novelists also challenge this prurience as they revise and argue with Van Vechten, as well as with one another. Furthermore, in emphasizing Van Vechten's influence on the male writers, or the assumed lack thereof on Fauset and Larsen, traditional literary critics have grossly underplayed the formative influence of three African American–authored novels: Johnson's *Autobiography of an Ex-Coloured Man* (1912; 1927), Fauset's *There Is Confusion* (1924), and White's *Flight* (1926)—all three published *before* Van Vechten's *Nigger Heaven,* and all treating similar subjects, using a similar narrative method and viewpoint.[6] Responding as much to these African American precedents as to the Van Vechten Negrophile fad, the "new realists," including Larsen, nonetheless take the fad more fundamentally as an opportunity to build on the genre fashioned by Johnson, Fauset, and White to fit what they perceive as the peculiar sociosexual issues of black national progress stemming from the rise of African American migration.

This section examines this genre: the black urban folk novel. As such, it explores the contest and mutual influence that occur between black and white writers, as well as the dissent and dialogue that occur among African American writers as they fashion these controversial literary constructions of African American urban manhood and sexuality. By focusing on the resonances and dissonances between novels with male heroes (in chapter 6) and those with female protagonists (in chapter 7), we also discover the entangled purposes and counterpurposes at stake in foregrounding male-protagonist novels as primarily sensationalized and corrupting while ignoring the give-and-take dialectic at work between chaste and unchaste manhood and womanhood in all the novels. Just as black urban manhood cannot be formulated and re-formed in male-protagonist novels without some ramifications to the representation of black urban womanhood, so the formulation of an urban black womanhood in the female-protagonist novels helps shed light on the sensationally sexualized scandal surrounding black urban manhood throughout the period. The representations of either manhood or womanhood in these novels, to borrow a phrase from Ann duCille, "depend, in varying degrees, on the intimate interactions of men and women" (*Coupling Convention* 83).

White patrons—and sometimes African American patrons as well—wanted to view the New Negro as naturally predisposed toward the creation of poetry as a result of his racial temperament. Whether this predisposition for poetry derived from the full-blooded Negro's primitive emotional exuberance and "sunny" nature (as Park labels it) or from the mulatto's overly sensitive nature (as Ovington would have it), this view—based in the scientific fact of the race's Darwinian place in the race of the races—tended to diminish African American efforts in fiction at a moment when "the great American novel" was taken as the objective of every white writer who hoped to reach the apex of the national canon and to propel U.S. culture to world dominion. It is thus not surprising that so many New Negroes turned to the novel as the medium of choice during the 1920s and 1930s, nor that they turned to realistic subjects that trespassed into daring themes. Blending this realism with a range of humor, from gentle irony to cutting satire, as well as lamentation on the racial state of things, and resexing the image of the race in sophisticated narratives of sexual experimentation, these novelists intended to challenge the dominant notion of black folk's essentially poetic character as "the lady of the races" while resisting any imputation that the fictional depiction of variant sexualities among the folk necessarily defined the race as temperamentally deviant. Thus, by focusing on the emergence of the urban folk novel, this section continues the discussion of how racialized institutions are gendered. Like the new-century race tracts and albums, Jim Crow personal narratives, and sociological studies examined in Part 1, these novels seek to stage the progress or reversion of the race by plotting the race of the races onto individual male and female characters, as well as onto networks of characters bound together by racial struggle. We also find at work on and in these novels the particular kinds of racial and sexual patronage practices examined in Part 2. Perhaps most important for these novels, and least discussed in the scholarship, is the novelists' attempt to survey the inner life of the race—what Locke called the "inner mastery of mood and spirit" (*The New Negro* 48). Like the New Negro sociologists, these novelists are concerned to analyze the social and psychic dynamics of the race in its fast-moving migratory patterns. Foremost in their concerns are matters of gender conflict and violence, class stratification, intraracial and interracial territoriality, and the spotlighted display of the race in modern media.

In chapter 6, we examine how male novelists of the Harlem Renaissance struggle to remake the masculine notion of heroism, based on their perceptions of the manly relations constructed in black urban folk culture. As we see in the case of Rudolph Fisher's *Walls of Jericho* and McKay's *Home to Harlem,* the urban folk novel seeks reciprocity and consolidation within the race by binding the hero to best pals who are erotically "queer." At the same time, it resists making such sexual variance a spectacle to be eyed pruriently by middle-class white readers excited by Carl Van Vechten's depictions of black exotic erotica in *Nigger Heaven.* These novelists want to reform the racial obsessions and sexual appetites of their readers as much as those of their male protagonists. In chapter 7, we see how the representation of black manhood in Harlem Renaissance fiction cannot be understood outside its relationship to black female heroines, whose search for a fit New Negro womanhood both supports and unsettles the search for a black manhood identity that can consolidate, uplift, and advance the race. Depicting the tenuousness of notions of upward mobility among the itinerant masses, these novels seek instead the stabilities of black consolidation at the bottom. Suspicious of the rampant individualism characteristic of the heroic personal narratives represented in chapter 2, the urban folk novel instead pursues the bonded intimacies of black men with one another and with black women. Satirizing the cross-racial uplift agencies controlled by whites, it instead offers viable, if tentative, notions of black self-reform amid the deprivations of the marginal underworld.

6 Waging Urban Warfare

Violence, Fraternity, and Eroticism in Black Men's Urban Folk Narrative

Civilization is fundamentally a territorial affair.
—Robert E. Park (*Race and Culture* 16)

The cities of the North, stern, impersonal and enchanting, needed men of the brawny muscles, which Europe, suddenly flaming with war, had ceased to supply, when the black hordes came on from the South like a silent, encroaching shadow.
—Charles S. Johnson ("New Frontage on American Life" 278)

In migrant folklore, every poor person who moved North had one great advantage and one great disadvantage: the advantage was that there were plenty of jobs for people who knew how to work hard, which all the migrants did; the disadvantage was the constant temptation to fall into the wild life that was there . . . for those who wanted it.
—Nicholas Lemann (*The Promised Land* 65)

Spurred by the urbanization of black culture, novelists during the Harlem Renaissance took up the challenge of recording, interpreting, and critiquing the quickly emergent mass urbanity through a New Negro genre, the black urban folk narrative.[1] In *The Afro-American Novel and Its Tradition*, Bernard W. Bell identifies a similar genre, which he calls "folk romance" or "Afro-American pastoral." In defining this genre, Bell has articulated some important aspects of urban folk narrative:

Rather than pursue Van Vechten's notion of primitivism, it is more illuminating to describe this romantic phase of development in the tradition of the Afro-American novel as a form of pastoralism or, more distinctively, ancestralism. . . . Their passion was to reconcile the urban present and future with the rural, occasionally distant and strange, past. And their immediate dilemma was to free themselves from the well-meaning but pernicious influence of whites encouraging them to emphasize the exotic aspects of Harlem life, and from the equally well-meaning but misguided counsel of the black elite criticizing them for literary pandering and for not using their talents to portray the intellectual and social parity of the race. (113)[2]

Bell's analysis adopts the prostitution figure (discussed in Part 2) as a way of making a distinction between the "committed" artists and those who engage in what their elite critics call "literary pandering," due to their succumbing to "commercial temptation." I would not care to follow through with such a distinction, given that each work of this post–*Nigger Heaven* period negotiates the problem of "pernicious influence" in a different way that does not easily allow us to judge such a matter. Bell's insight that each writer works to "free" him- or herself from the dictates of Van Vechten's popular novel is important, however. Furthermore, his idea that these novels are negotiating racial identity through a synthesis of a folk past with an urban present is compelling. Although these novels do adopt "pastoralism" or "romance" as a key mode, the sharp edge of satire is always close by. Whether the romantic or satiric wins out in the end is a delicate, almost arbitrary matter in the machinations of the plot. In all these novels, the "pastoralism" is so utterly revised by urbanity that even when the protagonist ends up in a rural setting—as in the case of Larsen's *Quicksand*—the rural is harshly judged as insufficient.

These narratives tend to suspect the kind of racial Manifest Destiny upon which United States white supremacy is based, even as they advance the idea of the race as an invading army intent on making opportunities out of the accidents that accompany mass existence in a crowded, mobile, cosmopolitan urban setting. Uplift reform—the putative objective of these narratives—is itself often their satirical object as well. This does not mean that they renounce the notion of uplift as an end, only that they challenge the prescriptive formulas being set by a self-proclaimed exceptional elite, even when they happen to be members of that elite. In this genre, writers seek to exploit the folk legacy to position black people as a highly mobile but grounded folk mass on which national progress hinges, but at the same time they use the notion of folkhood to challenge the assimilationist logic of progress on which the mainstream efforts of reform organizations such as the NAACP and the Urban League are based. Mobility in these narratives, though it includes the prospect of class mobility, refers more definitely to geographic, sexual, and racial mobility, the necessity and desire for moving freely back and forth across boundaries outside and within the race while maintaining the priorities of racial consolidation and advancement from below. Thus, these narratives extend the debates over bodily, geographic, and social mobility stimulated by the new-century polemics and albums, New Negro personal narratives, and black male sociology (discussed in Part 1).

As opposed to black urban folk narratives, Van Vechten constructs urban blackness as a site bounded by the racial borders of Harlem as well as by class notions that restrict black individuals from any meaningful crossing to common paths.

When Byron Kasson, the hero of *Nigger Heaven,* crosses those borders either to find menial work on the elevator crew or to aspire toward authorship in his submission to the white editor, he ends up being fiercely disciplined and punished, quickly returning uptown more out of desperation than out of attraction to Harlem as a Mecca. Despite Van Vechten's excitement over Harlem as the Mecca of the black American, he pictures it as a claustrophobic space that eventually emasculates the aspiring New Negro male. (The novel that comes closest to this vision is apparently Larsen's *Quicksand,* but for reasons rather different from *Nigger Heaven.*) The black urban folk narratives that follow in the wake of *Nigger Heaven* tell very different stories, in which openings to other spaces of racial contact and bonding are found or made even under the most racially oppressive conditions.

Black male writers are more freely positioned in the social system to exploit the core themes nurtured by the dominant assumptions surrounding folk urbanization: muscular labor, earthy humor, outlaw behavior, the roving life, sexual promiscuity and deviance, sexual violence, street fighting, and tricksterism.[3] Black men's narratives frequently rely on male narrators and/or protagonists who can traverse and sample the urban panorama, and as we have already seen in the autobiographical narratives of Pickens, Gordon, and others, the protagonist's identity is constituted largely through his ability to travel across this social spectrum with consummate ease. However, against the European-derived sense of aristocratic, chivalrous gentility adapted by these previous writers, urban folk narrative seeks to forge a gentle manliness from the resources immediately available from black folk culture thriving at the bottom of the "city jungle," to borrow a phrase from Rudolph Fisher. As with New Negro trespassing narratives discussed in chapter 2, male urban folk novelists also tend to forecast a New Negrodom that takes racial trespassing as a positive attribute of the race's modernization, but unlike them, urban folk narrative problematizes the idea of the isolated loner lifting the race through the singular strength and exceptional individualism of his or her will. Instead, urban folk novelists tend to explore the tight bond between their protagonists and the folk mass, including the range of social behavior from the concerted organization of collective reform to eruptions of violence.

In an eloquent essay written for *Survey Graphic* after the Harlem "race riot" of 1935, Locke acknowledges the limitations of cultural and artistic endeavors for the black urban mass in a view similar to that expressed by urban folk narratives:

For no cultural advance is safe without some sound economic underpinning, the foundation of a decent and reasonably secure average standard of living; and no emerging élite—artistic, professional or mercantile—can suspend itself in thin air over the abyss of a mass of unemployed stranded in an over-expensive, disease- and crime-ridden slum. It is easier to dally over black Bohemia or revel in the hardy survivals of Negro art and culture than to contemplate this dark Harlem of semi-starvation, mass exploitation and seething unrest. But turn we must. ("Harlem" 457–458)

The black urban folk novelists had already turned "to contemplate this dark Harlem" a decade before the Harlem riot, and some novelists, such as Fisher, anticipated this mass disorder by thematizing the positive potential for riot as central to the social psychology of the male characters. All these novelists, in different ways, interconnect the frustration stemming from unjust racial boundaries with questions of sexual violence operating in the psychologies of racial oppression. Their interest in sexual license and violence is not merely prurient but derives from the larger concerns of the violence of oppression and how it can or cannot be escaped or resisted in an emerging mass adapting to an urban environment.

Unlike the definiteness of Van Vechten's closure, in which the hero's impotence in both upper and lower spheres is demanded, black male urban folk narrative tends, like Johnson's *Along This Way,* to construct a more complicated view of opportunities and constrictions, openings and vulnerabilities. And writing against the grain of the black urban sociologists, there is a shift in emphasis away from the urbanized mass as passive, disorderly, deviant, and regressive to a more positive portrait of the urban folk as aggressive, naturally rambunctious, honestly desirous, and potentially progressive.[4] Although this rambunctious energy can sometimes be represented as causing violent masculine disorder, the male writers tend to view such seemingly unregulated behavior as the natural offshoot of healthy growing pains. For most New Negro male writers of the period, urban dislocation and "demoralization" frequently signal a necessary resistance to dominant social and moral values, even though the aberrance suggested by the rejection of United States norms does not necessarily lead to individual or collective racial empowerment. Both sexual desire and social ambition tend to be unsettling, and the city becomes a "colony" where boundaries can be tested, constantly resettled and reset, according to the changing fortunes of the race itself.

Like White's *Fire in the Flint,* the urban folk narratives tend to foreground the potential for demoralization—a matter suppressed from the New Negro trespassing narratives of Pickens, Wells, Gordon, and Johnson. Demoralization in these narratives, however, is more a matter of the political-military tactics of maintaining a people's morale than of policing inappropriate sociosexual behavior according to narrow perceptions of dominant morality. Conventional morality is no solution to demoralization, for the narratives also foreground the hypocrisy of normative morality as contributing to demoralized conditions in the first place, given how white supremacy as a political and legal system overly determines conventional social norms. Unlike the new-century polemical texts examined in chapter 1, urban folk narratives are not prone to script normative marriage as a civilizing solution to racial discrimination and as a vehicle for uplift. Even when marriage does resolve the problem of demoralization, it does so in the context of conjugal relations modified by racial experience so as to present a challenge to normative domesticity. Contrary to the rhetoric of dominant culture, marriage cannot protect black people from racism and its demoralizing effects, and for Larsen, the marital bond itself may embody the worst racial/sexual barriers to individual and collective liberation.

Against Du Bois's mourning of his lost son as synecdoche for the tragically bastardized status of an il/legitimate race in *Souls of Black Folk,* the urban folk novelists figure this bastard status as an ambivalent condition. It enables African American subjects, seeing through the hypocrisies of false United States norms, to enjoy illicit pleasures with less guilt, even as they recognize that the ability to partake of such pleasures marks them as an illegitimate people and seems to strand them in moral ghettos corresponding to their segregated social, economic, and political estate. The characters in these narratives, then, seek to expand the black colony as much to legitimate themselves by claiming a right to live amid their "betters" as to have more elbow room in which to test and broaden their pleasures and ambitions—in other words, to live more freely and authentically among themselves.

Going against the grain of both the martial and marital conventions of a national culture defined by the moral disciplines of Jim Crow, the question these novels raise is whether there are intimate contacts (of romance and friendship) so deep within the self or community that not even Jim Crow social strictures and lynching violence can mar their essentially healing nature. Themes of sexual license, bar fights, itinerant movement, street life, and sociosexual deviance bear more scrutiny as forms of cultural critique that expose larger questions about the ethics of sexual desire and social ambition in a racially segregated society whose morality is based in white supremacy. To question the normativity of sexual norms necessarily means to question the deeper values implicit in a commitment to dominant notions of civilization, modernity, upward mobility, assimilation, and racial progress. Just as these folk-oriented male writers cannot ignore altogether the diversity of sexual behavior that the urbanized folk feel free to display to themselves in the relative security of their new environs, so they cannot ignore altogether the conflicting avant-garde fantasies and middle-class moralities of the European American patrons and audiences who control the institutions of highest culture and finance. Thus, the convergence of urbanization with folk self-determination offers both an opportunity and a curse, an advantage and a temptation. It represents the opportunity to awaken and call forth a more heroic image of black manhood (and less frequently womanhood), symbolizing the emerging modernity of a previously indentured peasant people embarked on an unprecedented cultural experiment. At the same time, it presents the jeopardy of a falsified folk consciousness. What if the black mass turns out to be merely rural Jim Crows parading in the garb of urban titans? What if the upward-lifting New Negro turns out to be merely an urban decadent in blackface—mimicking the fantasies and anxieties of the white elites he can never truly become one of without the infrastructure of white power and privilege? What if the spectacle of folk empowerment turns out to be but another nigger heaven?

Writing at the height of the New Negro Renaissance, and despite his own success in the 1925 *Crisis* essay contest, Gustavus Adolphus Steward presents the renaissance as such a ruse, insisting that it is no more than "bunk."[5] In his 1928 essay "The New Negro Hokum," Steward takes the renaissance as a scam perpetrated by a select group of middle-class African Americans on willing white patrons, to the profit of both. In a fiercely satirical tone, he lambastes the virile images of aggression and chivalry that the New Negro attempts to promote:

> In the first place and according to his gospel, he is a real, honest-to-God he-man, keen-eyed, keen-minded, virile, red-blooded, two-fisted and challenging. He is at one and the same time both champion and despiser of the weak among his dark-skinned compatriots, the novel knight who resents and redresses all insults heaped upon the poverty-stricken, the widows and orphans, the Negro's latter day savior from the damnation of American race prejudice. (438)

Following the prostitution paradigm, Steward views renaissance promoters as ersatz men donning the guise of either "a real, honest-to-God he-man" or a "novel knight"—primitive brutality or elite chivalry. He further sets up the New Negro as a foil to the real men of the common people who fight the real battles:

> But who fights these battles? The New Negro? At least some of those for civil rights were begun and successfully terminated before his heaven-sent appearance. Moreover, it has been more than once remarked that it is the hoodlum element—the street lounger, the poolroom habitue, expert in knife juggling and bullet dodging, to whom fighting is an exhilerating [sic] avocation—who strikes back so effectively when the city mob gathers to "teach the nigger a lesson." And it has also been said that it is the much touted New Negro who, after "the tumult and the shouting dies," comes in for surveys and conferences and interracial backscratching and ponderous tomes, all to explain how the "criminal misunderstanding and great catastrophe" might have been avoided. (440)

This attack on the manhood of the New Negro associates "interracial backscratching" with unmanly cowardice, and it especially seems to cast aspersion on the kind of effort made by Charles S. Johnson and the Chicago Urban League at the conclusion of the 1919 Chicago riots, whose "ponderous tomes" catapulted Johnson into the New Negro limelight. Because the New Negro has not addressed the real problem of the race's role as "the nation's industrial pariah" (441), in the end he is "dependent upon whatever crumbs he may be able to capture in a deadly scramble with his preferred and more powerful white brother" (441). Instead of creating something new, the New Negro, in Steward's eyes, "puts over" on white profiteers "the unique creation of the hooted 'old' Negro" as his own achievement. Even blues and jazz derive from old Negro spirituals and ragtime (444).

Despite Steward's puncturing of the New Negro man, he himself relies on some of the key strategies of New Negro narrative in his essay, including suspicion of New Negro uplifters, affiliation with the working poor as a consolidated urban folk, suspicion of dominant masculine values while still admiring folk aggressions, and suspicion of interracial backscratching while addressing a biracial audience.[6] Steward's attack alerts us to the self-consciousness about such gender poses operating among those participating in the New Negro Renaissance. Like most of the male writers of urban folk narrative, Steward assumes that New Negrodom is a search for fit manliness, and he senses that New Negro manhood does not accord with traditional masculine postures, even though there is cross-fertilization with these dominant images. If the New Negro does not fit easily with either the street-smart fighter or with the chivalrous gentleman, then what constitutes his new manliness? The failures in consolidation and mobility in these novels are represented as resulting from too heavy a reliance on the dominant norms of gender (especially masculine) behavior. By focusing on two of these novels, we can understand how urban folk narrative negotiates these questions of urbanity and folklore, linear progress and trespassing mobility, cross-racial patronage and intraracial attraction, marriage and "illegitimate" bonds, racial warfare and peaceful reciprocity within the race. These novelists find ways of challenging normative masculinity without giving up on "manhood" itself as a privileged category of the heroic. Fisher's *Walls of Jericho* and McKay's *Home to Harlem,* perhaps the most paradigmatic male-focused instances of the genre, exploit a conventional romance structure (manly adventure melded to sexual intrigue) to fashion male protagonists who reject both the chivalrously genteel and the aggressively violent poses of dominant masculinity, while still offering a heroic take on manhood among the masses.

Rudolph Fisher's Moderated Manhood

In his first novel, Rudolph Fisher (1897–1934) presents characters who invert the ways of the male protagonists of *Autobiography of an Ex-Coloured Man* and *Nigger Heaven.*[7] The hero, Joshua Jones, known to his friends as "Shine," is clearly an idealized embodiment of the manhood of the folk. Unlike the ex-colored man or Van Vechten's mulatto hero Byron Kasson, Shine stands out not because he self-consciously differs from the folk but because he shines as one of them. Significantly, our first sighting of Shine occurs in a place that for Harlem men "was supremely the neighborhood's social center, where you met real regular guys and rubbed elbows with authority," Henry Patmore's Pool Parlor. Even more significant, Shine's first words in the novel intervene in a verbal contest between two friends, Jinx Jenkins and Bubber Brown, who seem on the verge of a bar brawl that ensues over the question of whether there will be a "possible riot in Harlem, a popular topic among these men who loved battle" (*Walls of Jericho* 5). Interrupting this contest that has progressed to the climax of "slippin',"[8] Shine immediately halts the battle between Jinx and Bubber:

> But now this newcomer spoke and his words, soft and low though they were, commanded immediate attention.
> "Winner belongs to me."

Everybody looked—spectators holding their drinks, Bubber with his blank black face, Jinx with his murderous scowl. They saw a man at one end of the bar counter, one foot raised upon the brass rail, one elbow resting on the mahogany ledge; a young man so tall that, though he bent forward from the hips in a posture of easy nonchalance, he could still see over every intervening head between himself and the two opponents, and yet so broad that his height was not of itself noticeable; a supremely tranquil young Titan, with a face of bronze, hard, metallic, lustrous, profoundly serene. (12–13)

On hearing Shine's words, the men "limply lost interest in their quarrel" (13). Shine serves as a unifying, pacifying force throughout the novel, not because he shrinks from battle or believes in back-scratching to solve problems but because he faces the battle head on with the pragmatism of a practiced warrior. Knowing that Jinx and Bubber's game is little more than that, he reminds them of the serious work to be done. He is their supervisor in a furniture-moving business, and he will not risk needing to break in rookies to do their next moving job over the prospect of their being hurt in a bar brawl. Emphasizing Shine's size and muscularity, Fisher places his metallic, titanic hero physically above the rest but otherwise makes him a man in their spitting image—a true "cool" embodiment of what they desire to be. Shine's "posture of easy nonchalance"—his "supremely tranquil" and "profoundly serene" demeanor—captures this bond between him and them. As an uncommon commoner, Shine represents the hardened muscularity resulting from labor at the bottom of the United States economy.

Fisher's hero contradicts Van Vechten's Anatole Longfellow, the sweetbacking dandy whose salacious description opens *Nigger Heaven*. Van Vechten trains his readers' eyes onto the seductively exotic, sensual body of Longfellow, whose fancy urbane clothing cannot mask the behavior of an unsophisticated plantation darky. *Nigger Heaven* seeks to debunk the myth of black urbanization by splitting the image of black manliness between figures like Longfellow, whose erotic attraction stems from the primitive impulse lurking beneath the city attire, and Byron Kasson, the aspiring mulatto hero whose primitive regression is exposed in the end through his participation in a vulgar bar brawl with Longfellow over a woman. By reducing his middle-class hero to the condition of a violent, lust-driven primitive, Van Vechten implies the unfeasibility of adapting black men's behavior from its authentic tropical temperament into an urbane, civilized future. Instead of hearkening back to the nineteenth-century literary traditions of the plantation darky and the tragic mulatto as rescripted by Johnson's ex-colored man and Van Vechten's Kasson, Fisher molds his protagonist on three celebrated heroic figures of black folklore: John Henry, *Titanic* Shine, and Jericho's Joshua.

Joshua "Shine" Jones resembles the legendary black railroad tunnel builder and steel driver, John Henry, whose feats of labor often end in death from physical exhaustion. As Lawrence W. Levine has pointed out, John Henry embodies the idea of the black laborer's collective will of steel in the face of dehumanizing industrial machinery and dangerous, often fatal, working conditions.[9] In many ways, John Henry is sociomorally a conventional hero, one who masters machinery and works harder than anyone else, though to no economic avail; one whose loyal wife mourns him when he dies and whose macho bravura celebrates traditional masculine attributes of uncompromising hardness.[10]

The opposite of the soft, loose-limbed, slack-jawed, docile plantation primitive, John Henry's steel driving serves as a metonym for his own muscular character, a man with a determined, strong, immovable will. Against the notion spread by plantation owners and white supremacists that African American men were *not* naturally predisposed to master industrial machinery—a notion we have seen even northern liberals such as Mary White Ovington and Oswald Garrison Villard repeating—the John Henry legend spreads through popular song the word of black men's expertise and contribution in the industrial development spurred by the building of the intercontinental railroad. John Henry's tendency to die from hard labor, however, distinguishes him to the extent that these dominant values can seem futile in the face of an equally uncompromising economy of racial oppression. The same thing that makes John Henry heroic—his undaunted muscular labor and triumph over the white man's machinery—murders him. Contrary to his legendary model, Joshua "Shine" Jones is a survivor, more like his other two namesakes: Joshua of the Old Testament, whose legendary status in black rural culture is spread through spirituals and folk preaching, and Shine, the stoker who survives the sinking of the *Titanic* in the toasting rituals of urban black folklore. Through the intermixing of these popular heroes, Fisher melds the rural folk past (Joshua) with the mass urban future (Shine) through the assertion of the black man's mastery of industrial machinery and labor on the frontier (John Henry).

The Shine of black folklore survives because he understands white men's technology, in this case the *Titanic*, better than they, having to stoke coals in the belly of the doomed ship. The first to know that the ship will sink, he jumps overboard. Because of his wits, revealed in his verbal assaults, Shine is able to resist the fatal enticements offered by the rich whites on the sinking ship and is also able to escape natural dangers, such as sharks lurking in the ocean. Shine swims as fleetly as he speaks, an adept body-mind coordination that associates him with traditional trickster figures and proves that he can transform the derogatory intent of his name, originally applied to black men during enslavement, into a sign of his capacity for brilliant escape from the drudgery of white technology and the machinations of those who would reenslave him in the ruse of technological advances.[11]

Fisher's Shine, too, accepts the implications of his name in the context of African American resistance. He is named not for the fact that as a young man he works as a shoeshine "boy," making ten dollars a week, but from a revelation foisted on him by the head barber, who sees that when he stoops over to shine shoes, "his heels is higher 'n head," and announces that he is too "husky" for such a job: "Great big husky . . . like you—it's a shame. You oughter be movin' pianos 'stead o' whippin' shoe-leather" (*Walls of Jericho* 21). Shine proves himself worthy of the nickname when he refuses to be called this name by a white man whose shoes he has shined:

> "How do you get to the subway from here, Shine, my boy?" he asked, paying his bill.
>
> Shine looked him up and down, and after a moment inquired, "How'd you know my name was Shine?"
>
> "Guessed it," smiled the patron.
>
> "Guess how to get to the subway, then."
>
> The patron stared, gaped and departed mystified at so sudden hostility. (22)

Shine's snap-witted retort to the white patron indicates that, like the folkloric Shine, he is a natural-born race man. "Nobody called him Shine . . . but Negroes" (22), because he understands the usage of the name in the opposed racial contexts. Joshua's hardness toward whites and those in his own race who aspire to be like them further associates him with the folkloric Shine figure, who would prefer to let the bosses sink even if it means giving up immediate profit to himself. In the long run, folkloric Shine believes that the ship of whiteness will sink, and regardless of how long that takes, he casts his lot, and himself, into the shark-infested sea—a humorous take on the captive Africans who acted similarly in the face of kidnapping enslavement during the Middle Passage. Contrary to Bernard Bell's conclusion that Fisher "undercuts his hero's intelligence" (*Afro-American Novel and Its Tradition* 139), Fisher's Shine has constant flashes of his namesake's wit, demonstrated in his ability to handle others with words, such as the way he affectionately deals with Jinx and Bubber in the first exchange of the novel and the way he cuts down the white shoeshine patron with his razor-sharp hostility. That he so frequently resorts to language as a weapon highlights the fact that, given his size, he could easily employ his fists instead, if he were so inclined.

In addition to Shine and John Henry, the characterization of Joshua "Shine" Jones most obviously borrows from the African Americanized biblical hero of the spiritual "Joshua Fit the Battle of Jericho." Like biblical Joshua, Joshua Jones uses not just the physicality of soldiering but all the collective and individual resources at his command. In contrast to Moses, the biblical hero with whom historically African Americans have most identified as the one who leads the Israelites out of slavery, Joshua is the commander who takes over after Moses dies, just before entering the promised land of freedom. Joshua is an appropriate hero for a people who have left the sites of their long enslavement for the new freedoms promised by the urban North. After he has brought his people over the threshold of Jordan, Joshua's biggest burden entails fighting for the expanding property rights to the promised land. He is thus also a fitting hero for a novel about racial turf warfare over the real estate being expanded by the swelling army of black migrants into the promised land of Harlem. Known for his strength and resoluteness, as well as his tactical brilliance, the biblical Joshua is that warrior-leader who takes the enemy's city by encircling it with unrelenting violence. Although committed to encircling the enemy from without, biblical Joshua also learns from hard experience that most frequently the enemy is within, as his defeat of Jericho relies on spies who enter the city and win over a prostitute, and as Israel's security after winning Jericho is jeopardized by traitors who seek to profit on the forbidden booty of the enemy. Fisher implies that his hero will be no less resolute in his tactical invasion of the enemy's walled fortress, but as we shall see, he is more interested in the internal racial turmoil that jeopardizes black consolidation in Harlem and in Joshua's growing self-awareness of his own, inner disloyalties.

Although Joshua Jones's work involves the seemingly menial task of moving heavy furniture, it is as spiritually treacherous as biblical Joshua's battles in enemy territory. This work tests the hero's mental preparedness in the dangerous belly of the enemy, like Shine in the *Titanic,* and it demands physical and moral stamina amid a modern mobility as murderous as John Henry's railroad construction. Whereas John Henry builds rails through dynamited tunnels for a transportation system that will keep him chained to its tracks as a roving laborer, Joshua "Shine" Jones's moving job symbolizes the "footloose" mobility of the disinherited folk mass—not only the constant influx of migrants from the South and from other cities in the North but also the frenzied movement within upper Manhattan of a people always on the lookout for better lodging in segregated neighborhoods, where rents are exploitative. Like biblical Joshua's constant expanding of Israel into enemy territory by treaty and warfare, the constant testing and expanding of Harlem's segregated boundaries by alliance and violence within and across color lines constitutes a principal concern of the novel.

Whereas Joshua, Shine, and John Henry are all concerned with horizontal territorial crossings or expansions, Fisher's Joshua Jones must also be attentive to another sort of mobility, the social and spatial verticality of the modern city. The urbaneness of Joshua Jones's job is encapsulated in his expertise in moving pianos to the upper stories of tall buildings. For Booker T. Washington, the piano had represented an eager desire for the trappings of upward mobility by a rural people who did not yet have the economic and educational resources to sustain such decorative signs of advanced civilization. Fisher brings a very different reading to the piano in black folk culture. For Shine, it is a dangerous object, the most difficult piece of furniture to move because it requires both the greatest strength and the nicest delicacy at once:

A tight kid makes a hard man—two hundred and twenty pounds of hardness in this case, wrestling daily with pianos; pianos equally hard and four times as heavy; two hundred and twenty pounds of strength; not the mere strength of stevedores hooking cotton bales on a wharf; you can't hurt a bale of cotton—it can't hurt you; tumble it, hook it, kick it—what the hell? But pianos—even swaddled in quilting—pianos must be handled like glass. Not mere strength do they require, but delicacy and strength; not muscles driving out or yanking in with abandoned force, but muscles held taut, precisely controlled under however great tension, released or restrained at will. You are protecting not only the instrument but yourself and your partner at the other end. (*Walls of Jericho* 22–23)

Unlike Byron Kasson, who fails to learn how to operate the ups and downs of the elevator, Fisher's hero exemplifies the kind of intelligence beyond sheer strength required to master the moving job. Like John Henry and folkloric Shine, Fisher's Shine is dealing with a "malicious" foe, the piano: "[I]t loves to slip out of your grip and snap at your toes, with an evil chuckle inside. Push up its lip and see it sneer; touch it and hear it rumble or whine. Ponderous, spiteful, treacherous live thing—a single spirit in a thousand bodies, one of which will crush you soon or late" (23). Like John Henry, Fisher's Shine loves his work: "It was work that Shine loved because of the challenge it presented to his personal strength and skill. He took charge, accepted responsibility, helped execute the orders he gave" (45). His work, however, constitutes a sort of displacement in which mastery over work sublimates the desire for frustrated racial empowerment, which directly would mean the ability to master the white bosses who enforce this oppressive labor on him. In his own mind, this sublimation takes the form of a concerted battle with the personified piano as an instrument that endangers labor: "Pianos indeed, were his particular prey, his almost living archenemies. He personified them, and out of controlling them, handling them, directing them helpless through midair, he derived a satisfaction comparable to that of a tamer of beasts" (46). The piano is both the enemy he labors against and the precious object of his labor, both his ability to master through labor and the frustration of being mastered in labor.

Despite these continuities with rural black labor, Fisher wants to contrast his hero's labor with the fabled frontier work of John Henry ("not muscles driving out or yanking in with abandoned force") and the old-fashioned southern labor of "stevedores hooking cotton bales on a wharf" (23). It is "precisely controlled" muscularity that Fisher emphasizes, for this moderated muscularity indicates Shine's superior sexual and social restraint as an urbane man—his vulnerability to the larger needs of the race if it is to succeed in the racial warfare of the city. His muscles must be taught the limits of their strength. The mastery of piano moving is a parable of migrant mobility itself, of mastering the urbane culture of the white city from the bottom up. Managing this dangerous mobility, our hero must protect not only the instrument but also "yourself and your partner at the other end." The collective nature of piano moving is emphasized when Fisher describes a time when the hooks holding the instrument crumble under its weight. Reaching through the window, Shine grabs hold of the piano and keeps it suspended until Jinx and Bubber are able to help him haul it in (24–25). Shine's self-endangering strength protects not only Jinx and Bubber but also any hypothetical passerby.

Fisher tempers Shine's muscularity so that, unlike John Henry's, it does not tend toward an unrelenting hardness, a fatalistic work ethic and sexuality that isolate the hero as a self-made superman, a natural genius of manly self-destruction. Ironically, it is through Shine's muscular labor that his vulnerability to and for others in the race is most viscerally expressed. Shine's necessarily hard manhood is intentionally softened, and his progress in the novel records a growing self-awareness of his access to his own vulnerability in relation to others in the race. This softness is inherent from the outset, however, in the velvet smoothness of his bronze voice: "The voice, too, was like bronze, heavy, rich in tone, uncompromisingly solid, with a surface shadowy and smooth as velvet save for an occasional ironic glint" (13). In contrast to Van Vechten's castration of Taylor Gordon's tenor voice and McKay's derogatory attribution of a falsetto to Locke, Fisher's Shine has a distinctly manly voice, but one not devoid of velvety vulnerability. Against Gustavus Adolphus Steward's suggestion that the New Negro of the renaissance images himself as an uncompromising he-man, Fisher is most concerned with the negative racial consequences of unrelenting masculinity. As much as Fisher's New Negro narrative is about the re-forming of the race into a mobile urbanity, it is also about the reform of black manhood and sexuality into an urbane mobility that can meet the city's peculiar racial challenges.

Shine's growing self-awareness of the weakness hidden in his supermasculine strength not surprisingly derives from his falling in love with Linda Young, a beautiful young "K.M.," or "kitchen mechanic," whom he encounters while moving furniture to the house of Fred Merrit, a wealthy mulatto lawyer who has decided to move onto an all-white street to provoke a riotous reaction from whites. As the similarity in the names indicates, Linda Young is an answer to Van Vechten's mulatta heroine, Mary Love. Like Mary, Linda is a chaste, aspiring woman of color who tries to make the hero a perfect match for her social aspiration by tutoring him in the manners of respectable uplift. However, Fisher declasses his heroine so that Mary's and Byron's elite literary aspirations are reviewed through the lens of Linda's and Shine's working-class desires. In wanting to become a secretary, Linda aspires to a modicum of the education and status that Mary already possesses as a professional librarian, though it is clear that Mary desires more than what she already has in wanting to lift up the reading habits of Harlem Negroes.

Mary's danger in possibly choosing the wrong suitor (one not upwardly mobile enough) is put into perspective by the sexual danger lurking in Linda's class status and the necessity of doing menial work in others' homes.[12] Linda is immediately sexualized as a lone black woman walking to work on a white street in view of the four men staring at her: Bubber and Jinx, who hyperbolically are "rapturizing" her attractions, and Merrit and Shine, who silently appraise her. Going to work for the rich racist Agatha Cramp, who lives two doors past the house into which Merrit is moving, Linda is sexualized by these men *despite* her display of chastity (see 52–53). Contrasted with Bubber and Jinx voicing their enthusiasm in her earshot, Shine's more circumspect appraisal immediately enables him to imagine himself as a rival to the rich, white-appearing lawyer, Merrit: "Figgerin' on a jive already—the doggone dickty hound. Why the hell dickties can't stick to their own women 'thout messin' around honest workin' girls" (54). Shine's prejudgment of Merrit because of his "dickty" class also reveals his prejudgment of Linda as honest because she is a "working girl." To Bubber's loud insinuations about Linda, he replies: "You jes' a damn liar. . . . She walks like what she is, a lady—and you talk like what you is, a rat" (54). This reply startles Bubber and Jinx, for "[h]ere was indeed something new, Shine championing a woman" (55).

Fisher also highlights Linda's sexual endangerment by reworking the *ménage à quatre* that Van Vechten insinuates in *Nigger Heaven,* when the latter involves Kasson, Longfellow, and Randolph Pettijohn, the Bolito King, in a deadly bar brawl. Initially, Shine fears that he has two rivals for Linda's hand, Merrit and Henry Patmore—though the initial projected rivalry can hardly be seen in terms of the respectable cliché of "winning a lady's hand" through the rituals of courtship and marriage. Shine's chivalry is new to his experience because, as befitting a man of steel, he has before this preferred his moving van, whom he calls Bess, to women: "Bess, the great van, became a willing mistress, and from her he derived a sort of unconfessed consolation" (216). Just as he personifies the piano as a spiteful foe, Shine sees his van as a mistress who eagerly yields to his mastery. The overblown sadomasochism of Van Vechten's novel is subtly reinvested in Fisher's description of Shine's relationships to these objects, but to different effect. The violence implicit in Shine's handling of Bess not only contrasts with his gentle devotion to Linda but also accentuates the potential violence in his relationship to women *before* he falls in love with Linda. Pressing the issue of Shine's potential sexual violence, Fisher contrasts Shine with his other would-be rival, Patmore (called "Pat"), the shady pool-parlor proprietor who is clearly a revision of Van Vechten's Pettijohn, the petty gangster who profits on vice schemes among the black masses. In Shine's eyes, Patmore is but a seedier version of Merrit, for both are seen as treacherous to ordinary African Americans—Merrit through his dickty desire to live among whites, Patmore through his scheming exploitation of the blacks among whom he lives. Just as Van Vechten creates triple alter egos in Byron, Longfellow, and Pettijohn, so Fisher fuses Shine, Merrit, and Patmore in this triangulated rivalry. Without denying the social, economic, and sexual ties that bind these men racially, the novel rejects the logic of *Nigger Heaven,* in which the triplet is reduced to a shoot-out of senseless sexual violence. Although both Shine and Pat have "boundless choice" among Harlem's "diversity" of women, Pat sees women as "legitimate prey" to his coarse desires (79–80). The manipulation and force that Pat puts into stalking women and money, without regard to the il/legitimacy of his actions, Shine puts into his mastery of moving pianos (see 80–81).

If neither quite chivalrous nor egalitarian, Shine's attitude toward women before his reform is at least not lasciviously exploitative. Just as he easily could exploit his physical attractions and size to intimidate other men, so he could exploit his attractions and size for the kind of deceptive manipulation and violent abuse of women that Patmore attempts on Linda. But in both cases, Shine refuses to do so. To him, Patmore's reputation is "nothing to brag about. Indeed, this reputation of Pat's was one of the things about him that Shine most disliked. It summed Pat up as less of a man to be so much of a sap" (81–82). And yet, Shine's attitude toward women contains the potential for Pat's conduct, just as his treatment of the pianos and moving van could slip over to his sexual relations, given his clichéd belief that women "don't mean a man no good" because they "[a]lways got they hands out" (81).

Shine sees Linda the second time halfway through the novel, at the General Improvement Association (GIA) ball—obviously a parody of the NAACP affair with which Van Vechten concludes his novel. Transferring to a pivotal place in the rising action of *Walls of Jericho* the concluding incident that dooms Kasson-Pettijohn-Longfellow in Van Vechten's novel, Fisher also recasts the triangulated rivalry so that his hero can be saved from Kasson's fate. Not realizing that Linda has agreed to dance with Pat only because he has deceived her into thinking that he is a judge of a costume contest, Shine attempts to compete with Pat on his own turf, thinking confusedly that since Linda is not chaste, he may as well have her on the same terms that Pat is negotiating: a "conquest of ordinarily inaccessible prey" (78). "If Henry Patmore had so easily picked up the girl, why should not he pick her up also? Or—why should he?" (90). After Shine manages to insult her by awkwardly apologizing for his intention, she in turn insults him by telling him that Patmore has called him a dirty rat. Further enraged when he sees Pat grab Linda, Shine advances toward them through the crowd on the dance floor.

At this moment in the impending public brawl, Fisher interrupts the action by shifting to Merrit's devious courtship of his new white neighbor, Agatha Cramp, in the upper boxes of the hall where the elite cross-racial patrons are seated. Ironically, while Patmore has been deceiving Linda by passing for a black race patron on the dance floor, Merrit has been passing as a white race patron with Cramp, who has come to the ball out of curiosity and a newfound interest in helping the poor Negroes. Pretending to agree with her patronizing ideas about black people, Merrit is luring her into desiring him only to foist on her that he, her new neighbor, is indeed African American. Through this juxtaposition between the lower and upper conversations, Fisher reveals how the verbal arguments and deceptions, the cross-racial attractions and misalliances, that are occurring in the elite upper boxes are invested with the same sexual violence impending among the lower class on the dance floor. The racial entanglements of the upper boxes also reveal how race is silently at work in a sexual triangle that, from the view of the dance floor, looks merely like another working-class bar brawl between two black men lusting after the same loose Negro woman. In other words, Fisher satirizes not only Van Vechten's spectacle of racial violence but the whole project of racial uplift through the intimate contact of a white elite patronizing a black Talented Tenth toward the disciplining of the footloose black folk migrants.

Fisher accentuates the complicit nature of the impending sexual violence as a racial spectacle constructed between an observing cross-racial elite, including Merrit and Cramp, and an observed black lower class. Because we know the circumstances behind this spectacle and the merits and weaknesses of the actors in the sexual triangle, our viewpoint as observing readers is quite different from the desire for sexually violent titillation that focuses the attention of the cross-racial patrons on the primitive actions of Shine, Linda, and Pat. In this way, Fisher attempts to distance us as readers from the likely desires of the white patron-readers who would purchase his novel to engage in the prurient projections of sexual violence, sadomasochism, and exotic primitivism promulgated by *Nigger Heaven*. When a Van Vechten–type climax is avoided, the patrons' expectations are deflated:

> Then those who from above focused attention on the little crowd of dancers around Patmore and Linda, saw Shine succeed in breaking through to meet Linda as she endeavored to escape; saw Patmore look up, draw back, shrink, stand for a moment uncertain, as if both eager and loath to flee; saw Shine and Linda halt, facing each other, the girl distressed and surprised, the man grim and tense, saw her then fling herself impulsively toward him, uttering an inaudible but obvious plea; saw him catch her, thrust her behind him, and turn back—to find Patmore gone; saw Patmore, already out of the crowd, moving with surreptitious speed toward one of the lateral exits. (131–132)

Disappointing the patrons' (and readers') prurient desire, Fisher scripts a pantomime (we can see the action but cannot hear the actors) that unwrites the sadomasochistic triangle that makes Kasson the alter ego of both Longfellow and Pettijohn, the lower-class rivals who bring him down to his rightful level in *Nigger Heaven*'s concluding shoot-out. Fisher throws this desire for sexual violence back onto the readers as he encourages them to reform their salacious expectations of the black characters. At the same time, by briefly doubling Shine with Patmore in their lascivious expectations of Linda, Fisher acknowledges the operation of sexual violence in relation to the particular racial and class conditions of his Harlem subjects. Just as he reforms his readers' desires to project sexual violence onto African American culture, he suggests that his hero, too, needs to reform the sexual violence impending in his racial desires, even in this moment of his chivalrous gesture of protecting Linda. In this moment of excitement, we may desire to see Shine standing at the ready to commit violence on a dastardly Patmore, but by the end, we shall be as disappointed as Shine in our adulation of aggressively violent masculinity.

Through his narration of black male rivalry, Fisher implicitly offers a critique of the kinds of homoracial behaviors that we analyzed in Part 2, whereby the system of Jim Crow encourages African American men to scramble for the scraps the white elite offers by turning on one another—and on black women—in the hope of becoming the exceptional protégé-token deemed worthy of entering white men's inner parlors. Although Shine no longer sees Patmore as a rival after Shine and Linda begin to date, he continues to project rivalry onto Merrit, which prevents him from assessing Merrit, Linda, Patmore, or himself correctly in the sexualized race war that is silently raging within him. When Linda becomes a housekeeper for Merrit, Shine sees it "as a mere gesture of defiance, as a matter rather complimentary and encouraging" (215) to his courtship, instead of, more accurately, an opportunity for her to make a better salary and have some time off for pursuing her education.

Fisher explores the sexual ramifications of racial violence, and vice versa, as he links Shine's passion for Linda to his suspicion of Merrit's racial integrity. Instead of celebrating aggression as a weapon against the color line, which we see active in New Negro personal narrative, Fisher posits that such aggression can easily backfire, as it implies a potential aggression against other African Americans. Thinking only about his own desires, Shine continues to nurse "his own futile resentment," which renders "him daily more and more violent. He worked harder and played harder and knew that nothing ailed him" (215). At first, his love for Linda does not diminish his potential for sexual violence; rather, it intensifies his aggression, causing him to displace it onto the feminine object of the moving van. Bubber humorously recognizes this displacement when Shine almost gets them killed in his reckless binge of self-destructive driving: Bubber "asserted that it just wasn't good arithmetic for no three men to commit suicide over one woman" (216). Shine, however, can no longer pretend that forcefully manipulating Bess will suffice: "But the zest with which Shine drove Bess did not give him sufficient relief, left him still unsatisfied, like the deep but ineffectual breathing of a man suffering acute airhunger" (216). Distracted in love, he again almost gets himself killed when he lets a piano fall from the third floor of a building, grazing his forehead over one eye as it plummets. "The piano lay half supine in a grotesque angular posture, its row of white keys gleaming like teeth, the lid of its keyboard sprung back and fixed, like the retracted upper lip of a creature that has died in agony" (230). The death of the piano symbolizes the healthful wounding of Shine's supermasculine ego. Before this, "Shine had so far gone without a scratch, had never been caught off guard," a fact that has enabled him to remain encased in his male fortress (see 223–224). When Linda asks him to go to the hospital even though he feels fine, he gives in: "Shine, the disciple of hardness, would not in any imaginable situation have been guilty of a surrender like that" (232). His capacity to recognize himself as vulnerable to physical wounding is the first step toward his ability to recognize the strength of embracing his own sexual, social, and spiritual vulnerabilities as a reformed New Negro man.

As Bell remarks, Shine's "surface toughness conceals a compassionate heart, which is sympathetically revealed through the agency of his girlfriend" (*Afro-American Novel and Its Tradition* 139). Fisher borrows from the situation in Walter White's *Fire in the Flint* in which Jane tutors Kenneth into racial leadership, but he makes some significant revisions. On the surface, Linda seems to be conventionally domesticating Shine's fiercer (more uncivilized?) impulses to make him suitable for upward mobility in the city, whereas Jane has the task of making Kenneth behave in a more conventionally masculine way by pumping him up to command others in the rural South. Whereas Linda must make Joshua realize his own sensitivity to his wounds, Jane's verbal spanking of Kenneth is supposed to toughen him up. Whereas Jane's action sacrifices her own talent for exemplary leadership of the race to open a bigger space for Kenneth, Linda pacifies Shine to help enlarge her own sphere for mobility, conduct, and labor beyond the constraints of a jealously prying lover. Fisher bypasses the racial/sexual self-mutilations that necessarily plague in different ways the protagonists of White's, Van Vechten's, and James Weldon Johnson's novels. He instead imagines a working-class couple capable of self-patronage and yet needing support of the others who surround them.

Linda's ambition is not to replace her housework in others' homes with her own middle-class homemaking. In other words, Fisher does not want to portray Van Vechten's sort of New Negrodom, in which the leading characters are most concerned with assimilation into the banal security of white middle-class domesticity. It is misleading to think of Linda's reform of Shine merely as conventional domestication, which ultimately reaffirms dominant gender roles by temporarily reining in the male's aggressive desire to sublimate it toward the ends of marriage, work, and imperialist civilization. Fisher instead seems to be moderating Shine's "surface toughness" to prepare him not just for respectable marriage but, more important, for enterprising, egalitarian intraracial alliances with his female companion and his male mates. Fisher attempts to exploit and enhance the utopian elements that always lurk, but usually get repressed, in the conventional romance plot. Just as the New Negro personal narratives of chapter 2 demote the romance plot to spotlight the heroic aggressions of cowboying loners, so, conversely, the urban folk novel tends to reinscribe the romance plot to emphasize the centrality of intimate bonds—between men and women and among men—in the construction of communities consolidated despite or against larger Jim Crow humiliations. At first, *Walls of Jericho* appears to be a story about the black conquest of white territory, the invasion of white property rights through the traditional settling down of a titanic man who acquires the legal rights and sexual rites to a devoted wife. Instead, it turns out to be an altogether more complicated narrative, exploring the limits of masculine conquest as a manifestation of the marital and martial rights/rites of masculine territoriality.

This is why Fisher reconstructs the conventional exegesis of the Joshua story. As Israel's strong man and battle tactician, Joshua enacts the seminal feats of adding larger and larger tracts of territory while bolstering the internal national security (stoning the traitors within) of a people not long ago suffering under the lash of slavery in the Egyptian empire. When Shine goes to church with Linda, he hears Tod Bruce, the preacher, deliver a novel interpretation of the Joshua fable. Calling it a "Hebrew fairy-tale," Bruce dismisses its literal objective meaning—its celebration of national, martial, and imperialist values in the name of obedience to a strong-arming God—for a subjective, internal, "spiritual value" (184). The walls of Jericho become not some external object of conquest. "Do you know what that blank wall is?" the preacher asks. "It is the self-illusion which circumstance has thrown around a man's own self" (184). The preacher continues: "No man knows himself till he comes to an impasse; to some strange set of conditions that reveals to him his ignorance of the workings of his spirit; to some disrupting impact that shatters the wall of self-illusion. This, I believe, is the greatest spiritual battle of a man's life, the battle with his own idea of himself" (185–186). Although Tod Bruce's lesson is not explicitly about sexual and racial self-knowledge, its sexual impact is borne out in the tutoring that Linda provides for Shine when he fails to grasp the spiritual point. "There's a wall around you. A thick stone wall," she tells him. "You're outside, looking. You think you see yourself. You don't. You only see the wall. Hard guy—that's the wall. Never give in, never turn loose. Always get the other guy. That's the wall" (255–256). When Linda informs Shine toward the end of the novel that he is not hard, mean, and tough but "scared" (256), she reveals the part of him that he has hidden.

Beyond Linda's gendering of the Reverend Bruce's lesson, the structure of the novel itself brings this point home, in both sexual and racial terms. Earlier in the novel, Shine discovers that someone has attempted to assault Linda sexually while she has been housekeeping in Merrit's home. This sexual assault has come just before an apparent racial assault on Merrit's house, which is dynamited. The sexual and the racial feed each other surreptitiously in the novel. Shine erroneously blames the sexual assault on the lawyer, and with "unquestionable intent to kill in his eyes and the whole attitude of his body," he goes after Merrit. When he reaches the house, however, he finds out that it has been blown up. He discovers Merrit amid the ruins slumped, violently weeping, with a burned-out picture frame grasped in his hand. "Shine belabored his brain to catch an elusive memory of that frame, till it broke upon him that this was the one that had contained the likeness of Merrit's mother; the one about which Mrs. Fuller had warned, 'He'd die if he ever lost it'" (249). We know that Merrit's mother symbolizes for him "sexual martyrdom, a bearer of the cross, as he put it, which fair manhood universally placed on dark womanhood's shoulders" (38). Through the burned-out picture of the dead mother, then, Fisher further connects the sexual violence committed by white men against black women to the two kinds of ruination in this episode: the dynamited house of a trespassing and passing mulatto and the assaulted chastity of an honest working-class girl. Stunned by this vision of vulnerability, Shine is unable to carry out his plan of revenge, and he quietly leaves without disturbing Merrit's feminine grief.

It is not Merrit but Merrit's enemy Patmore who has attacked Linda. When Shine realizes this during a poker game in Patmore's pool parlor, he also recognizes that Patmore, not the whites, dynamited Merrit's house. The revelation gathers his violent impulses into one last burst of intensified hatred:

And it seemed that all the hatred he had ever felt for anybody welled up within him to be concentrated now on Henry Patmore alone: his hatred of the asylum superintendent, of the fay who had called him Shine, of all fays, of the evil thing he'd escaped in pianos, of dickties in general and the blameless dicty Merrit in particular—all these now gathered in one single wave, advanced in one tidal on-rush. And all that he knew and felt gleamed in his bronze face. (270)

The racial warfare that has been provoked and anticipated throughout the novel finally erupts, but not in the form of a retaliatory riot enacted by blacks against whites. Instead, the outburst erupts in the factions created by the central battle between Patmore and Shine. Patmore's sexual attack on Linda, Shine finally realizes, correlates with the bar owner's use of racial animosity to shield his attack on Merrit. Patmore is the traitor within, the man who harbors the forbidden treasures of Jericho not for the profit of the emancipated Israelites but for his own secret gain.

In the opportune moment of unassailable victory over the traitor, Shine refuses to strike the final blow expected from the warrior-hero of such a narrative:

The crash and jangle of the falling glass wall was all that snatched Shine out of madness. The sound transfixed him as if all the walls of the place had tumbled instead of just one. He stood set, motionless, blinked once or twice and stared a long moment at Pat.

Only then, perhaps, did he actually see him, on his knees, gasping, helpless. Presently the poised, retracted arm began to relax; the tension went out of Shine's frame. His head sank a little forward, and his good arm slowly dropped to his side, as limp as its useless fellow. (275–276)

This climactic scene is loaded with irony. The mirror wall that crumbles does not indicate an enemy conquered, a territory annexed. Instead, it literally acts to snap Shine out of the "madness" of masculine conquest. As Tod Bruce and Linda have explained to him, the walls of Jericho represent a fractured, and thus distorted, mirror on the self; so it is appropriate that Shine's clearer vision is signaled by the literal breaking of the mirror behind the bar. Furthermore, the ability to see the self hinges on a clearer racial vision of the supposed internal enemy. In this case, when Shine "actually" sees Patmore's true helplessness, he also sees that Patmore's gasping for air *is* his own suffocation. His right arm having been hit by Pat's bullet, Shine at last allows this fighting arm to go limp. Shine's resistance to his own muscular power enables him to recognize the gasping helplessness of the man who would be his foe. In this moment, Shine's education into moderated manhood is effected, if not completed. Without recognizing the true vulnerability in his foe, he could not fully see his own wounding and capacity for wounding others. Without recognizing this capacity, he could not find the more healing alliances with Linda and Merrit that open up in the final chapter.

I am not suggesting that, in moderating Shine's hard muscularity, Fisher is insisting on a wholly vulnerable, pacifist manhood for his hero. Probing the vulnerability within the titan does not mean that Fisher has abandoned altogether a concept of heroic black manhood. Instead, he tries to fashion some terms in which such manhood can be enacted without replicating the imperialist masculine thinking that justifies concepts of civilized advancement as territorial and sexual/racial conquest. Other writers exploring this genre exploit different methods to achieve similar goals. Some writers give their heroes a distinguishing physical characteristic that makes them visually vulnerable despite their tough masculine behavior. In *One Way to Heaven,* for instance, Countee Cullen's protagonist, Sam Lucas, is a con man who travels from Black Belt to Black Belt, duping churchgoers out of their money by pretending to be a sinner in need of their salvation. What helps him in this nefarious enterprise is the mystery and sympathy elicited by the fact of his missing left arm, cut off years before upon a misstep when jumping a freight car. Sam turns the disadvantage of his missing arm into a benefit, eliciting sympathy and religious passion. Like Shine's damaged arm at the end of *Walls of Jericho,* Sam's missing arm indicates the potential for vulnerability and reform. At the same time, it also represents Sam's cynical duping of the communities through which he travels, and thus his hardened masculinity, which gets in the way of his struggle to love and be loved.

Similarly, in Arna Bontemps's *God Sends Sunday,* his roving hero, Little Augie, from the start is distinguished by his small size. This handicap, however, is compensated by his being born with a caul, "a mysterious veil with which he had entered the world" (3), which in African American southern culture signifies great luck. In the novels of Bontemps and Cullen, the protagonists are physically diminished, and this diminishment, a synecdoche for their social handicap, makes them, like Shine, open to manhood reform. Little Augie's childhood experience could stand for the kind of masculine difference that often characterizes these heroes: "Set apart from his mates by these circumstances, Little Augie soon grew to be miserable. In his heart he felt inferior to the strong, healthy children who worked alongside the grown-ups in the fields. He became timid in the presence of unfamiliar people and fell into the habit of stuttering when he tried to talk" (4). A loner on the surface, Little Augie yearns for comradeship, which he finds, to some extent, in his relationship to horses, confirming his lucky nature when he becomes a successful jockey. As is often the case in these novels, however, Little Augie's luck is not reliable. As whites take over the jockey profession, the feeling of being set apart as a member of a lucrative, manly profession turns into the negative sense of being set apart again. Shine's massive size, Sam Lucas's missing arm, and Little Augie's pint size and stutter are all devices that enable the writers to explore through a handicap that ends up liberating the protagonists from the most negative aspects of conventional masculinity the psychic and social constitution of manliness as a characteristic influenced by, but not determined by, the conditions of racial oppression.

Some of the narratives trace the development of their protagonists from boyhood as a way of accentuating the process of self-awareness into moderated manhood, as in Johnson's *Autobiography of an Ex-Coloured Man,* a case of masculine difference that leads to manhood failure, and *Along This Way*, a case of successfully moderated manhood. Hughes's first novel, *Not without Laughter*, and George Wylie Henderson's second, *Jule*, follow this pattern, and both, like *God Sends Sunday*, also plot the movement from rural boyishness, and the naïveté it so frequently implies, to urban manhood, with its unsettling compensations. Hughes's hero, Sandy, is named for the texture and color of his hair, representing also his skin color as the son of a high-yellow man and a dark woman. Sandy and Henderson's hero, Little Jule, are not so much missing something physically as missing something paternally. Both have fathers who are oversized in their imaginations because they are either missing or derelict. Depending primarily on women for their gender identity, these boys develop a subtle orientation to the world that strands them between feminine and masculine as conventionally opposed principles of experience and outlook. In *Go Tell It on the Mountain*, Baldwin combines many of these strategies, not only making his hero, John, diminished in size, very dark in color, and bug-eyed but also highlighting his alienation to the masculine by making him a bastard in his own home. Baldwin makes explicit the interest in "sissyness" that is much subtler in Hughes's and Henderson's earlier novels, just as he intensifies the exploration into masculine difference by strongly insinuating John's sexual interest in males—as if to underscore the question of gender/sexual deviance already interwoven into the tradition of urban folk novels written by African American men, from Johnson onward. For all these novelists, a degree of masculine deviance is a necessary condition of racial difference for their male protagonists, and each exploits this degree of deviance to challenge the assumptions of dominant masculinity as a code for measuring male heroism.

Reforming Martial and Marital Values of Manhood in McKay's *Home to Harlem*

Of all the black urban folk narratives, *Home to Harlem* is the one that has been most criticized for depicting African American culture as an underworld of gender/sexual deviance. In attending so much to the question of whether McKay's "primitivism" distorts and exploits African American culture, critics have overlooked the larger question of how McKay's narratives manipulate supposedly unconventional behaviors to understand and critique racial and sexual norms.[13] In this novel, published the same year as *Walls of Jericho*, the Jamaican American writer constructs a protagonist in some ways quite different from Shine, but with the same easygoing, winning attractiveness to ordinary men and women. McKay also introduces the notion of martial rites as a test of manhood, though more literally than Fisher, by making Jake a deserter from the so-called Great War. In other words, McKay inverts White's strategy in *Fire in the Flint* by making his hero experience disgust not at the senseless carnage of World War I but at his exclusion from participating in it because of his race. From the first chapter, the question of the hero's failed soldiering is connected to his racial ambition and sexual competence: "Jake was disappointed.

He had enlisted to fight. For what else had he been sticking a bayonet into the guts of a stuffed man and aiming bullets straight into a bull's-eye? Toting planks and getting into rows with his white comrades at the Bal Musette were not adventure" (*Home to Harlem* 4). Jake's desertion leads him back to a roving life, as we find him shacking up with an Englishwoman in London and going the rounds of rowdy bars. Because the military has prevented black men from being true soldiers—that is, from killing enemy soldiers—Jake Brown has already begun, at the beginning of the novel, to question the specific kinds of martial values propagated by dominant masculinity.

Jake must lay low to avoid charges of military desertion, and McKay exploits this as a way of highlighting both the "underworld" nature of his life and its daily sense of living on the edge of survival. Living and loving from day to day, Jake "was used to the lowest and hardest sort of life" (2). Going a bit lower on the social scale for his hero than Fisher, McKay makes Jake one of the "footloose" male migrants who scurries from job to job, city to city, and woman to woman—comfortable in the cabarets, gambling houses, buffet flats, and black tenderloins that present to the New Negro sociologists a nightmare vision of black folk urbanity. While arguably romanticizing this life, McKay, like Fisher, is interested in probing the social and psychological agencies and limitations operating within this marginalized racial existence on the bottoms.

McKay's plot is episodic rather than a progression, but like Fisher's, it plumbs the utopian element awaiting in a resexed romance plot. Likewise, McKay moderates the calculated sexual diffidence of his hero not so much by reforming him as by constantly altering his circumstances so that Jake can test varying manhood behaviors until the optimal behavior is hit upon. Jake keeps moving on until he finds those circumstances that satisfy his psychic needs, which in turn represent the collective needs of a people marginalized by race, class, gender, and history. More fundamentally, his footloose practices keep him out of reach of the kind of disciplinary punishments that are the bane of working-class subjects such as Linda and Shine. Through sporadic labor, rather than commitment to a laboring "career" or vocation, Jake and his friends are able to avoid, for long stretches of time, the murdering discipline of work that Linda and Shine subscribe to as enterprising laborers. As we shall see, this avoidance of disciplinary labor is enabled partly by the sexual practice of sweetbacking, which can protect men at the bottom from the racial humiliations of work in the way that normally middle-class women are supposed to be protected by husband-providers. McKay searches the limits of the United States system of legal, economic, and military surveillance to understand how people at the bottom construct their own sense of coherence in matters of love, friendship, sex, and gender identity.

Jake does not develop or evolve into moderated manhood per se; he stumbles into a situation that enables him to practice it as he intuitively recognizes its benefits. Although McKay indicates this in many ways, we can see it through one example. McKay contrasts an episode at the beginning of the novel, when Jake is living with Congo Rose, a cabaret singer, with the concluding episode in which Jake finds the woman who suits his needs best and whom he suits best—at least for the duration. Like Fisher, McKay organizes the novel so that it appears to duplicate Van Vechten's movement toward climactic intraracial sexual violence. Like Fisher, too, he decidedly disappoints this expectation, but he does so by repeatedly hyping and deflating such violence within each episode. Not long after returning to Harlem, Jake is offered the "job" of being a sweetman for Congo Rose, just as his best "chappie" of the moment, Zeddy Plummer, inspired by Jake, takes up as a sweetman with Gin-head Susy. Zeddy's relationship is short-lived, though, because against his romantic anticipation of the sweet life, he discovers its sour side (see 82). After Zeddy's friends tease him about "his lady riding him with a cruel bit" and call him a "skirt-man" (87), he attempts to prove his independence from Susy, only to be thrown out of the house. McKay explores the complications of the sweet life for kept men and their female keepers. As Helen Pyne-Timothy has pointed out, this sex-role reversal can be seen as McKay's putting the male's survival on the working woman's shoulders.[14]

McKay constantly finds himself balancing the benefits of sexual experimentation—or at least what appears as such in the eyes of dominant culture—against its downfalls for both sexes, although he emphasizes its effects on male characters more. On the one hand, these men desire the sweet life as evidence of their sexual competence, of their attractiveness to women; on the other hand, the sweet life can easily be perceived as emasculation when the woman appears too visibly domineering. The sweet life, furthermore, can bring pluses and minuses for the woman as much as for the man. She has a significant say in determining her role against the dominant expectations of patriarchal marriage, yet this does not mean that the alternative heterosexual arrangement does not have its own protocols. Just as in a conventional marriage, there may be strict roles to be played in the sweet life. On the surface, Susy is the one who is granted the upper hand: "To have an aggressive type like Zeddy at her beck and call considerably increased Susy's prestige and clucking pride" (84). No longer ruler of the roost, a sweetman must be willing to submit to his lady and to take ribbing from his friends for the sake of being kept; but Zeddy is not so willing. He fails to negotiate his own masculine pride with Susy's "clucking pride." In the structure of the novel, this is seen not as a gain for Zeddy's manhood but as a palpable failure for both partners. We see Zeddy at Susy's doorstep pleading to be let back in. And by the end of the novel, we realize that Zeddy never truly recovers and, as a result, becomes the loose cannon who jeopardizes a happy ending for the heroic couple.

Almost as quick as Zeddy's rise and fall as a sweetman, Jake experiences similar relationship woes, but his stem from *not* playing the role of sweetman for a woman who desires such a contract. Revealingly, McKay has his hero categorically reject the sweet life, not as a judgment against others but as a circumstance incompatible with his own desire—similar to McKay's explanation of his own attitude toward obscenity (discussed in chapter 5). Congo Rose proposes to Jake: "'If you'll be mah man always, you won't have to work,' she said." His refusal is firm: "'Me?' responded Jake. 'I've never been a sweetman yet. Never lived off no womens and never will. I always works'" (40). Congo Rose's proposal insists on an inequality in the relationship that Jake refuses. Jake knows that he does not love Congo Rose, as he goes in search of Felice, "the little lost maroon-brown," whom he has met earlier (41). His refusal to play the sweetman clearly has nothing to do with puritan sexual morality; after all, he does live with Rose without any sense of being nagged by moral scruples. Later, when he finds Felice, he takes up with her in the same makeshift way—that is, without sanction of church or state. Jake's rejection of the sweet life, however, does help to define his heroism, just as Zeddy's giving in to it and failing in it define his antagonistic supporting role in the novel. Jake's determination to provide for himself casts him as having more respect for Congo Rose than Zeddy has for Susy: "He never took money from her. If he gambled away his own and was short, he borrowed from Nije Gridley, the longshoreman broker" (42). Actually, however, Jake's manly code of ethics, his insistence on financial self-sufficiency, reveals how the novel is fundamentally rooted in a man's world of trust, loyalty, and comradeship, despite McKay's efforts at constructing a utopian, egalitarian relationship between Jake and Felice. Jake prefers to take money from a loan shark because that loan shark is a man. He keeps his financial matters between men, protecting himself from Rose's clutches as much as protecting her from his potential exploitation of her.

McKay seems to suggest that Jake respects Rose more than she respects herself. We see this when he refuses to play rooster of the nest, even though this is what Congo Rose desires of her sweetmen. The contrast in the two relationships, Zeddy and Susy and Jake and Rose, indicates the vast variations within alternative sexual contracts, demonstrating how the sweet life itself functions as a way of testing variant—and, in the eyes of dominant society, deviant—heterosexual practices to meet the conditions of a socially marginalized existence. Rose demands to be dominated much in the way that Lasca commands Byron to dominate her in *Nigger Heaven*. "As Jake was not brutally domineering, she cooled off from him perceptibly" (114). Rose begins to take other lovers when Jake is not around, expecting him to make her submit, and significantly, she brings a white man to the house to provoke Jake. In the midst of a row concerning her being "free in her ways" (113), Rose scratches at Jake's face, and he for the first time strikes back: "Jake gave her two savage slaps full in her face and she dropped moaning at his feet" (116). For Rose, this incident begins to redeem him as a lover: "[I]t's the first time I ever felt his real strength. A hefty-looking one like him, always acting so nice and proper. I almost thought he was getting sissy. But he's a *ma-an* all right" (117). Jake's response, however, is immediate shame and a decision to get out of the relationship. Rose's idea of sissyness correlates with the conventional notion of a man's role in a heterosexual relationship: the man who fails to be in total control must be sissy, just as for Zeddy's friends, the man who gives in too willingly to a woman's domination must be a "skirt."

Jake's gentle sexual expectations are explicitly articulated: "Walking down the street, he looked at his palms. 'Ahm shame o' you, hands,' he murmured" (116). Clearly commenting on the sadomasochistic scene between Byron and Lasca, McKay examines the variances of sexual desire in the tenderloin but resists defining his hero's wants according to sexual violence, even when the woman who desires to keep him in the sweet life begs for it. In the structure of the novel, sexual violence is not exotic as it is in Van Vechten; instead, it is all-too-common an aspect of the structure of sexual desire. McKay's point seems to be, however, to provide a critical vantage whereby readers can discern the larger social and psychic implications of such violence and can resist taking prurient pleasure in the expectations set up by Van Vechten and by the racial history of sexuality in the United States.

In discussing the difference between how McKay and Fisher respond to Van Vechten, Huggins suggests that Fisher, unlike McKay, holds onto a moral center: "So, while *The Walls of Jericho* exploited the commercial interest in Harlem exotica, it reserved a kind of gentility and propriety that was absent from *Nigger Heaven*" (*Harlem Renaissance* 121). Although I agree that McKay's novel pushes the limits further than Fisher's, the two may be closer in spirit than Huggins judges. It is certainly the case that, in order to subvert "a stable sense of moral order" (121), McKay has to experiment with sexual topics that his audience would immediately associate with decadence, sensationalism, and primitivism. McKay seems to want to find particular kinds of collective agency in the various psychosocial practices of the footloose, but he wants to distinguish their approach to life from Van Vechten's treatment of these topics. Instead of merely pandering to commercial tastes or conforming to a primitivist vogue, McKay has a genuine interest in the sociopolitical potential of these unconventional sexual relationships.

Although the underworld in which his characters move may lack "a stable sense of moral order," this does not mean the characters lack a stable sense of ethical behavior. *Home to Harlem* attempts to move beyond morality's conventional prescriptions and proscriptions while retaining a commitment to human reciprocity—respectful sexual relations, comradeship, decency to strangers, and fairness to foes—that betokens values, however makeshift, deeper than the hypocritical disciplines enforced in a society devoted to white racial supremacy and proprietary relationships, whether whites possessing and dominating blacks or men possessing and dominating women. Though not exactly intended as a model of manhood behavior like Fisher's Joshua, McKay's Jake nonetheless embodies a critical stance against masculine conventions, a stance that he develops through intuition, feeling, experience, and upbringing. His mother has told him, "Nevah hit no woman" (*Home to Harlem* 116). Despite the fact that Rose experiences being hit as acceptable—indeed, desirable—behavior, and despite the fact that some sweetmen and pimps make it standard practice, Jake rejects both behaviors. And yet, this rejection does not stem from the conventional justification of chivalry toward the "weaker sex." As Zeddy's relationship with Susy indicates, strength is a relative matter and not necessarily gender-determined. McKay's characters form bonds based on economic need as much as on love—a fact that does not in itself distinguish these relationships from ones in dominant culture, where economics are a major factor in courtship and marriage. However, the unsanctioned nature of these makeshift bonds does call attention to the circumstantial nature of desire. People form desires based in their circumstances, and this means that negative circumstances can lead to negative formations of desire. As Pyne-Timothy notes, "Apparently Congo Rose has managed to match the violence of her environment by responding to masochism" ("Perceptions of the Black Woman" 158). When Zeddy attempts to possess Felice through violence, he is enacting behavior that helps determine the kind of masochism that Rose thinks she desires as much as he is responding unresistingly to the violent insecurity of his own circumstances.

Like Fisher, in the final episode McKay builds up to a Van Vechten–like climax of a public brawl resulting from a sexual rivalry that pits the hero against his alter ego, in this case Zeddy; and like Fisher, McKay dashes our expectations. The triangle embroils Jake with Zeddy and Felice, the woman he has fallen for after one sexual encounter early in the novel, and who shows up serendipitously toward the end. By coincidence, Felice, unbeknownst to Jake, has had a brief relationship with Zeddy while Jake has been away from Harlem working as a waiter on a Pullman car. When Zeddy sees Felice with Jake, Zeddy moves upon him "like a terrible bear with open razor." In contrast to Fisher's framing of the public brawl through the elite's prurient spectatorship, McKay disperses the elite *before* the public spectacle: "All the fashionable folk had already fled." The moment the fight gets underway with a woman's shriek, "there was a general stampede for the exit" (*Home to Harlem* 326). The fleeing crowds indicate a realistic check on the pleasure of watching actual violence: the fear of one's own harm. Like the "adventure" of the Great War (the word that Jake uses at the beginning), the ugly reality of violence undercuts its romance as exotic adventure. Any reader predisposed to expect pleasure in such danger is thus doubly disappointed, for McKay also disperses the violence itself almost as soon as it commences. Jake pulls a gun that stops Zeddy "like a cowed brute in his tracks" (326). What ensues is not a *physically* violent episode but instead language so hurtful that it stops the show of weaponry and leads instead to a more sinister *verbal* danger.

In an act that makes him analogous to Fisher's Patmore as a figure of race treachery, Zeddy accuses Jake of having deserted the military out of cowardice: "You kain kill me, nigger, ef you wanta. You come gunning at me, but you didn't go gunning after the Germans. Nosah! You was scared and runned away from the army." Zeddy's statement is a threat worse than physical violence because it endangers Jake's safety with the authorities. Someone, if not Zeddy himself, might well spread the gossip to the wrong quarters. More sickening to Jake, however, are the implications of this sort of race treachery. "Jake looked bewildered, sick. He was hurt now to his heart and he was dumb. The waiters and a few rough customers that the gun did not frighten away looked strangely at him" (327). Zeddy's act reveals the violence enacted not only in men's sexual rivalries over women and in men's bonds among themselves but also within themselves psychologically. Through Zeddy's accusation, Jake is stunned into self-reflection. In a meditation that contradicts those who suggest that Jake is pure primitive physicality and emotion, he connects the kinds of violence—martial, sexual, racial—that have circumscribed his experience throughout the narrative:[15]

> These miserable cock-fights, beastly, tigerish, bloody. They had always sickened, saddened, unmanned him. The wild, shrieking mad woman that is sex seemed jeering at him. Why should love create terror? Love should be joy lifting man out of the humdrum ways of life. He had always managed to delight in love and yet steer clear of the hate and violence that govern it in his world. His love nature was generous and warm without any vestige of the diabolical or sadistic.
>
> Yet here he was caught in the thing that he despised so thoroughly. . . . Brest, London, and his America. Their vivid brutality tortured his imagination. Oh, he was infinitely disgusted with himself to think that he had just been moved by the same savage emotions as those vile, vicious, villainous white men who, like hyenas and rattlers, had fought, murdered, and clawed the entrails out of black men over the common, commercial flesh of women. . . . (328)

Following the same track as Fisher in revising Van Vechten and attempting to redefine the strength of black manhood away from dominant masculinity, McKay pits the generous and warm nature of his hero against the violence that has become stereotypical of working-class and black men in much United States literature and in United States culture more generally. By suggesting that such violence "unmans" him, Jake explicitly rejects even his own initial "daydreams of going over the top" in combat as a way of proving his manhood. When his other pal, Billy Biasse, earlier offered him the gun that stops Zeddy in his tracks, Jake at first rejected it outright, saying, "I don't carry no weapons nonetall, but mah two long hands" (287). Jake's vision of accepting the gun is one of "a regular gun-toting army of us up here in the haht of the white man's city" (286). Perhaps the gun has saved Jake's life, but his response to the incident indicates that it is too high a cost to pay for a miserable survival, as his words unwittingly echo those of Thomas Hobbes in describing life in a state of nature: "beastly, tigerish, bloody."

Finally, McKay enacts one more deflation of the impulse toward sexual violence as definitive of black manhood rights by bringing Zeddy back for a heartfelt apology. Having reflected, like Jake, on the meaning of the incident for men's fraternal and sexual bonds, Zeddy returns to apologize:

> I done think it ovah and said to mah inner man: Why, you fool fellah, whasmat with you? Ef Zeddy slit his buddy's thwoat for a gal, that won't give back the gal to Zeddy. . . . So I jest had to come and tell it to you and ast you pahdon.[. . .] You was always a good man-to-man buddy and nevah did wears you face behind

you.[. . .] What you done was all right, Jakey, and I woulda did it mahself ef I'd a
had the guts to. (334)

Ironically, the violent episode between the men precipitates a crisis in their relationship that motivates this change of heart on Zeddy's part. Here we see how
McKay has a tendency to reform the manhood of his male characters but to leave
his female characters more static, for Congo Rose is never afforded such an opportunity for self-reflection and rapprochement with Jake. This converting crisis is
very different from Rose's habitual engagement in violence as a mode of sexual
pleasure.

Duly accepted, Zeddy's apology mends the friendship but cannot undo the
damage. Leaving for Chicago at the end of the novel, Jake and Felice represent a
very different image from that of Shine and Linda riding away in Bessy to prepare
for another moving job. With a less definite utopian ending than *Walls of Jericho*,
McKay's novel leaves open the possibility that Jake and Felice will not make it together. As Richard Priebe writes, "Even though Felice does come back we know that
Jake will find neither the relationship to work that he needs nor the relationship
with Felice that he wants."[16] Although Priebe interprets this rightly as Jake's alienation, we have to place this alienated aspect alongside the potential of liberating
desire and resistance to dominant culture's values of routine menial work, episodic
warmongering, and rigid marital vows for the laboring poor. Both couples, Jake and
Felice and Shine and Linda, the footloose and the firmly rooted, represent the will
to mobility as a collective act of racial advancement. What makes both types of mobility possible is the prospect for another kind of manhood. The kind of movement
in both novels is more lateral than upward, more rejection of assimilationist values than uplift, more leveling than aspiring toward Talented Tenth exceptionality.
Nonetheless, the mobility in these narratives is *not* resignation to the place that
dominant culture has deemed appropriate for poor people of African descent. In
individual stories and as a genre, the black urban folk narrative attempts to challenge the pleasure of sexual license and violence without falling back into normative modes of sexuality and masculinity, which function to determine the oppressive marginality of urban black folk in the first place.

Pals and Lovers:
Companions and Men-loving Men in the Urban Folk Novel

Heterosexual romance is only one way in which these novels experiment with a
New Negro manhood altered by the mobility of urban folk life. Urban folk narrative devotes a great deal of attention to varying expressions of male-male camaraderie and sexuality—setting a precedent in the history of African American men's
literature. Before the urban folk novel, black men's writing tended to focus on constructing black manhood in terms of legitimate paternity, loyal sonship, and exceptional individuality for racial leadership.[17] As a significant cultural-historical

event, this new trend in black men's writing tells us as much about the changing public construction of gender in the push toward black urban modernity as it tells us about particular kinds of self-aware male subjectivity of the men who composed these stories. Just as they tend to challenge the norms of masculine romance as imperial conquest while exploiting those norms to mark the heroic manhood of their male protagonists (men who *could* perform such conventional behavior if they so desired), so these narratives also tend to challenge—sometimes subtly and sometimes explicitly—the purely or ideally heterosexual basis of male-male companionate bonds in dominant United States culture.

Jerry H. Bryant has noted the emphasis on intraracial violence in these Harlem Renaissance novels and seems to suggest that these kinds of violence—"knifings, shootings, razor fights between men, hair-pulling fights between women"—negatively replace the more powerful social critique of lynching common to the previous generations of black novelists.[18] To the contrary, the representations of male camaraderie in these texts frequently attack the kinds of rivalry that define supposedly normal masculine identity, while also investigating the wide range of passionate bonds among men that are seen as sexually deviant in terms of dominant homosociality. Shine's reclamation of a manly vulnerability makes him available for deepened alliances with men as well as with his female partner, without necessarily suggesting that the racial war is won. While admitting the ongoing race war, *Walls of Jericho* simply attempts to redefine the ways in which battles are fought *within* the African American community by exposing the potentially negative reverberations of unrelenting martial conquest.

In a novel with its title, we should not be surprised that *Walls of Jericho* explores the psychology of warfare and the fraternity of warriors as an aspect of blacks' "invasion" of the urban North. As we have seen in Steward's essay, northward migration and New Negrodom are frequently articulated in terms of martial imagery, with race men conceived as the front line of soldiers. In *Black Manhattan,* James Weldon Johnson describes the urban skirmish that ensues between the black "colony" and their white neighbors as African American migrants jockey for more territory and more economic and social opportunities in uptown Manhattan: "The situation now resolved itself into an actual contest. But the Negro pressure continued constant. . . . Then, in the eyes of the whites who were antagonistic, the whole movement took on the aspect of an 'invasion'—an invasion of both their economic and their social rights" (149–150). The prospect of a prosperous African American colony in the midst of America's most influential city calls for policing action, the conspiracy of red-liners who work to keep blacks contained in inferior neighborhoods. Fisher plays off of this sort of masculine martial imagery, but ironically, he adapts it to suggest that the immediate battle is being fought within the self and within the African American colony itself. Like Walter White's *Fire in the Flint, Walls of Jericho* is deeply suspicious of the lone heroism of racial leadership based in unrelenting combative aggression, depicted in different ways in the writing of both Talented Tenth and Bookerite advocates. Thus, one of the ways in which Fisher moderates manhood is through the constitutive social, psychic, and economic dependencies on other men of which Shine himself at first is not fully aware.

In commentary on urban folk narratives, it is frequently the minor or "background" characters, such as Jinx Jenkins and Bubber Brown, who come under the most virulent attack for their simple-mindedness, minstrel stereotyping, and social (and implicitly sexual) deviance. An otherwise laudatory *Crisis* review of *Walls of Jericho* by Du Bois has helped set the terms of the debate:

> For the main story of a piano mover and a housemaid is a well done and sincere bit of psychology. It is finely worked out with a delicate knowledge of human reactions. If the background were as sincere as the main picture, the novel would be a masterpiece. But the background is a shade too sophisticated and unreal. Mr. Fisher likes his two characters, Jinx and Bubber, and lingers over them; but somehow, to the ordinary reader, they are only moderately funny, a little smutty and certainly not humanly convincing. Their conversation has some undoubted marks of authenticity, for this kind of keen repartee is often heard among Negro laborers. But neither of these characters seems human like Shine. ("Browsing Reader" [Nov. 1928] 374)

Jinx and Bubber have been rather solidly fixed as the element aimed at what Bernard Bell calls "the exotic appeal of Harlem for . . . white readers." "This is apparent," he writes, "in the minstrel antics and coarse wit of Jinx and Bubber."[19] We cannot deny that Jinx and Bubber play primarily a comic role bordering on a sort of minstrelsy. As is often the case with such minstrelsy in African American culture, however, Fisher exploits it to mask a more serious undercurrent that examines male bonding and sexuality in black working-class culture. Bell hints at this: "By interpreting the verbal insults and aggression between Jinx and Bubber as an effort to suppress the mutual affection that their class considers unmanly and unnatural, Fisher reinforces the ironic thrust of the plot and characters while simultaneously revealing his ambivalence toward the comic pair" (*Afro-American Novel and Its Tradition* 140). I think the "ambivalence" resides more in Jinx and Bubber than in either Fisher's handling of them or some putatively objective sociological determination of the attitude held by 1920s black working-class men toward male same-sexuality. If the "verbal insults and aggression" mask a deep "mutual affection" between these two men, it is also the case that their buffoonery masks the importance of their presence as problematizing symbols of the masculine rivalries and physical aggressions that are considered perfectly manly in dominant culture. Although not a *homosexual* couple in the sense in which this word has come to be used, Jinx and Bubber are clearly plotted *as a couple* passionately, erotically bonded. Fisher goes as far as he can in suggesting, without actually spelling it out, the couple's sexual involvement with each other, given the demands of the propriety to which he has decided, or more probably his white publishers have decided, to adhere.[20] When Fisher's casting of this couple is examined beyond the buffoonery, we discover the subtle significance of their erotic bond for the larger themes of moderated manhood.

The novel begins with an argument between Jinx and Bubber concerning the warfare between black and white. As one takes the side that blacks will riot and the other that they will not, the characters replicate the larger theme of internalized racial warfare when their argument over interracial combat devolves into the dozens and a potential intraracial bar fight. The verbal aggression between Jinx and Bubber in one sense is a ruse—as Bell has pointed out—but in another sense it is not. The ruse is that, despite their fighting words, the two men really prefer *not* to fight. In fact, their fighting words forestall actual combat more than they provoke it. In this way, Jinx and Bubber are no different from any other two black buddies in a bar who use the dozens to display their rough masculinity in accordance with just one of the rituals that serve to mark manhood in their cultural environment. Most such verbal games are exactly that—games that dance around the possibility of actual physical aggression. The novel explores the ways in which the markers of manhood are self-conflicting. The dozens can signal readiness for combat, but it more generally enacts manly camaraderie, a bond stemming from the play of aggression. In terms of their *gender* identification, Jinx and Bubber are represented as typical, for their verbal aggression toward each other constructs them as black working-class men who perform their affection through this ruse of aggression.

Their sexual orientation, however, problematizes this typicality, pointing up the constructed nature of this stereotype by underlining how such aggression *must* be a ruse. They can be seen as enacting masculine rituals compulsively as overcompensatory behavior, to hide their desire from others and/or to hide it from themselves. Ironically, this behavior equates them with the "straight" men in the pool joint, for their overcompensation highlights how these other men also routinely use horseplay to ensure their putatively natural conformity to heterosexual masculinity.

In this sense, Jinx and Bubber represent the "perversion" of overcompensatory behavior that provokes "straight" men, black and white, to trust physical strength and sexual coercion as effective weapons of race war and sexual conquest. This perverse, overcompensating behavior is a difficult cycle to break, especially within an oppressed group in which able young men may experience the traditional burden of constituting a front line to protect the women, children, weak, and elderly from the oppressors. *Walls of Jericho* raises the issue of this cycle at the outset. Before the piano movers go into enemy territory—to move furniture into Merrit's new house in the white neighborhood—Shine feels compelled to remind Bubber and Jinx that he is relying on them "in case of crisis." Shine informs them that other African Americans who have attempted to move into this neighborhood have been dynamited, and he asks them if he should hire extra hands for the job, as Merrit has advised. Beneath their banter about whose hips will move faster if there is trouble on Court Avenue (a humorous spin on the theme of racial mobility in the novel),

Shine understands that they are pledging to stand by him, to brave an exploding white mob or their hidden dynamite, if necessary:

> To Shine this banter was merely pledge of allegiance in case of crisis, assurance that the hiring of extra hands would in no event be necessary. Beneath the jests, the avowed fear, the merriment, was a characteristic irony, a typical disavowal of fact and repudiation of reality, a markedly racial tendency to make light of what actually was grave—a tendency stressed in Jinx and Bubber by the habitual perversion of their own conduct toward each other. (*Walls of Jericho* 29)

As overcompensation, Jinx and Bubber's horseplay perverts their true feeling—in this case, their deep affection for Shine and their desire to stand next to him. At the same time, however, the overcompensation of a surface masculine diffidence seems to protect their fragile inner selves from the unpredictable bombardment coming at them in the midst of an ongoing race war, in the same way that it protects them from the taunts and humiliations of their peers if they were to "flaunt" their sexual attraction for each other unconventionally. Just as their erotic involvement is hidden behind typical horseplay, their bravery and allegiance to others are hidden behind minstrel cowardice and self-protection.

Fisher's use of perversion here is revealing. The "habitual perversion" is not their giving in to sexual deviance but their habitual denial of their affection through masculine rituals of verbal aggression. In an earlier passage, Fisher is even more explicit in his bringing attention to the "inverting" intent of his terminology. Whereas in the passage above he uses the word *perversion,* a common synonym for homosexuality during the time, in this passage he applies another common euphemism for same-sexuality, an "inverted" order of life:

> As a matter of fact, the habitual dissension between these two was the symptom of a deep affection which neither, on question, would have admitted. Neither Jinx and Bubber nor any of their associates had ever heard of Damon and Pythias, and frank regard between two men would have been considered questionable to say the least. Their fellows would neither have understood nor tolerated it; would have killed it by derisions, conjectures, suggestions, comments banishing the association to some realm beyond normal manhood. Accordingly their own expression of this affection had to take an ironic turn. They themselves must deride it first, must hide their mutual inclination in a garment of constant ridicule and contention, the irritation of which rose into their consciousness as hostility. Words and gestures which in a different order of life would have required no suppression became with them necessarily inverted, found issue only by assuming a precisely opposite aspect, concealed a profound attachment by exposing an extravagant enmity. And this was a distortion of behavior so completely imposed upon them by their traditions and society that even they themselves did not know they were masquerading. (11)

There is nowhere in United States literature a more insightful articulation of the effects of compulsory gender identification among men who think they have a stake in "normal manhood." Although Bubber and Jinx might not know of the classical Greek model of Damon and Pythias's passionate same-gender love, Fisher's readers—especially formally educated homosexual ones—certainly would.[21] As soldiers whose erotic devotion for each other inflames greater bravery on the battlefield, Damon and Pythias would seem to code a heroic—even epic—analogy unmasking the silent heroism behind Bubber and Jinx's bumbling minstrelsy. As obfuscated as their erotic attachment to each other may be, Jinx and Bubber represent not only the utmost bravery in the racial war but also the utmost ideal of commitment to a fraternity of warriors, but with a vital difference: that commitment is based in a deeply felt passion rather than in the "extravagant enmity" of masculine rivalry over the conquest of women.

So different in nature from white novels of homosexual apology such as Blair Niles's *Strange Brother,* in which Harlem itself represents optimal tolerance for homosexuality because black folk are already sexually deviant, Fisher's investigation of same-sexuality in Harlem attempts to capture the curious arrangement in which two male lovers can run with the hardest of men as long as their outward behavior conforms to the dictates of normative masculinity. Whereas in Niles's depiction of African American tolerance for homosexuality, the homosexual remains a spectacle of sexual deviance whose presence elicits patronizing sympathy from readers, Fisher brings attention to ways in which same-sexuality can be subtly interwoven into the fabric of black folk life. Just as he offers a stunning critique of the kind of sadomasochistic spectacle that whets Van Vechten's appetite for exposing black male flesh, so Fisher comments on the heterosexist assumptions that always scandalize self-affirming same-sexuality as a flagrant—Fisher might use the word *extravagant*—spectacle of easily categorizable behavior. The spectacle staged in Fisher's novel is not queer sexuality but the masculine "masquerade" or minstrelsy that attempts to conceal sexual difference behind an "extravagant enmity." Moving beyond the appeal to pity or sympathy that becomes characteristic of fiction of homosexual apology, Fisher's strategy is to demonstrate the complex and sometimes obscure operation of sexual deviance within the very protocols of heterosexual conformity. His representation of Jinx and Bubber also demonstrates how macho "banter" is double-edged. It perverts and inverts the range of genuine affections experienced among men by reducing the public face of such affections to a narrow expression of horseplay. At the same time, this diffident minstrelsy of macho behavior serves to cement these men together to survive the white hostility that, at any moment, can put them in the situation of having to fight for one another, and literally for their lives. The question is to what extent they can abandon the negative perversion of their affections without also abandoning the need for battle readiness in the jungle of white supremacy, where manhood is so narrowly defined, where only the fierce survive, and where only the reckless can advance. In Fisher's subtle analysis of the manhood risks entailed in this "city jungle" that white men call advancing civilization, we see, then, the unlayering of the kinds of confusions that haunt Park's theory of being both civilized and manly.

Although most critics seem to come away with the combative image of Bubber and Jinx in their minds, Fisher as frequently implants an image of mutual affection. If their exaggeration of horseplay is to be lamented, their devotion to each other is set apart in the novel as a sign of what Shine himself is initially missing: the capacity to be fully vulnerable to others in the privacy of the self, if not in public. We cannot know exactly how Bubber and Jinx treat each other in private, but Fisher provides glimpses of their love even in the masculine public sphere of Patmore's pool parlor:

> Joshua Jones, whom his fellows called Shine, came out of his reverie, to observe the return of Jinx and Bubber, arm in arm and quite happily drunk.
>
> "This yeh freckle-face giraffe, he's a good boogy," Bubber declared. "Good boogy—yassuh. He's my boy. Ain't you my boy, biggy?"
>
> "No lie," Jinx agreed. (26)

The couple can exhibit their erotic affection under the pretext of being "happily drunk." Using the lingo of running buddies still common among African American men today, each claims the other as his "boy."[22] As a racially derogatory term whose application was coined by southern slave owners for the purposes of emasculation, the men's deployment of "boy" turns it against its racist usage in an outward gesture of conventional male camaraderie as a fraternity of warriors, just like the use of "Shine" as a nickname. In Jinx and Bubber's private usage, it also becomes a pun that suggests a deeper erotic bond between two men-loving men. In the 1920s, "boy" was common usage among black men-loving men as a term denoting an actual or prospective male sexual partner. It was so common for a male sexual partner in a same-sexual exchange that it also came to refer to hustlers. Revealingly, in another usage "boy" also indicated the members of a street gang, another sort of fraternity of warriors.[23]

At the one moment in the novel in which Bubber and Jinx actually come to blows as a result of their verbal sparring, the customers in Pat's place at first cannot believe what is happening, because at some level they understand the erotic bond between these two men. Even Jinx is taken aback by Bubber's "blow to the midriff": "Not quite certain whether this was serious or make-believe, Jinx reached mechanically forward and gathered Bubber's neck and shoulders in an embrace usually reserved for pianos" (204). Fisher's depiction of Jinx's "embrace" captures the doubleness of this violent episode, reminding us of Shine's ambivalent relation to the piano as a beloved object to be protected and an enemy to be wrestled down. Concerned for any damage that might be done to his establishment, Pat sends the couple down to the basement and locks the door behind them, so that they can duke it out in the privacy and safety of the cellar. "The bystanders crowded about the door, listening. Pat, grinning, kept his hand on the knob, his ear against the panel. The others pressed forward . . . [by yet] a dozen others, all surging forward, all listening with arched brows or grins of relish" (206–207). Again we have an ironic scene of spectatorship, but this time the spectators literally cannot see the violence, much less the true (sexual) motivations provoking it. As becomes the case with the final bar brawl, Fisher deflates this one, as the bystanders wait first in anticipation, then in suspense, then in fear when all is silent in the cellar. Afraid the fight has ended fatally, Pat unlocks the door, with the crowd surging behind him, only to discover that the couple, instead of fighting themselves to death, have found a case of liquor to imbibe together. "Bubber was heard to murmur stupidly, 'Ain' nuthin' to fight about, boogy. Ain't you my boy?'" Through this parody of a bar fight, Fisher prepares us for the outcome of the actual fight that later stuns Shine into his vision of the senselessness of such violence. However their drunken affection has been expressed in the privacy of the cellar, we are not privy to it. We cannot help but recognize, however, that even a public "blow to the midriff" cannot bring Bubber and Jinx to blows beyond the voyeuristic public eye that attempts to survey and discipline men's passionate interactions.

As if to exonerate Jinx and Bubber from any potential taint of cowardice in conventional terms, Fisher emphasizes the role that they play in the climactic bar fight between Shine and Patmore, and at the same time he reminds us of the allegiance that binds them to Shine in moments of crisis. Jinx saves Shine's life by diverting Pat's gun in the nick of time (270). Both Jinx and Bubber have refused to flee the scene and instead enter the fray on Shine's behalf (272). The couple's cheerful and wily defense of their partner stresses the alliance that has been silently formed among them beyond the highly cooperative venture required in their moving labor. It also demonstrates that the couple's avoidance of fighting each other has nothing to do with fear of combat and everything to do with their devotion to each other.

If Shine's reaffirmed relationship with Bubber and Jinx represents an alliance *downward* within the race, his discovery of a partnership with Merrit in the end represents his intraracial alliance *upward,* enabling him to overcome his hatred of all dickties. Throughout the novel, Merrit and his class are self-segregated from Shine and his. Against the tendencies we examined in Parts 1 and 2, in which the exceptional male leader must emphasize his distance from the black masses even as he claims to be their representative voice, the urban folk novel stresses the intimate bonds necessary to racial mobilization and self-protection. A sort of class segregation is emphasized in the first chapters when Fisher juxtaposes the debate about race rioting that ensues among the "rats" in Pat's place with a similar debate among the dickties who have formed a club, calling themselves the "Little Rats," who meet informally in the house of their president. Except for their dialect, which is in the language of the formally educated, the elite colored men's club covers exactly the same ground as Shine's friends do in the pool joint. Thus, although the two groups of men segregate in mutual hostility toward each other, they share the same concerns in the same way.

Against his fellow dickties, who argue that the Harlem "colony" should "extend itself naturally and gradually rather than by violence and bloodshed," Tod Bruce, the preacher, sparks nostalgia for the good old days when African Americans were more prone to engage in combat with their white enemies:

> Harlem began its growth by riots. I remember when I was a youngster, I used to be scared to stay out after dark. It was pretty bad then—either a crowd of fay boys would catch a jig and beat him up or else a crowd of jigs would get a fay boy and teach him the fear of the Lord. In either case the thing would be the first skirmish of a pitched battle somewhere on the frontier. (40)

Placing these "comical" times in the context of the "tragedy" of imperialist conquest on the frontier, Bruce quickly retracts his nostalgic take on the racial war, but Fred Merrit resists this tragic shift:

> "It's the old, old story," said Bruce. "War—conquest of territory. But our side of the thing isn't all there is to it. The fays have a side too, you know."
>
> "I know," Merrit protested, like the lawyer he was, "but we aren't supposed to see that."
>
> "Well, I don't know. It's easy to laugh now. But the fact is, it was tragedy. Black triumph is always white tragedy. We won—we won territory. . . . How do you suppose they felt about it?"
>
> "Best thing that ever happened to 'em," grinned Fred. (41–42)

Merrit's refusal to grant the viewpoint of the other side—a trick learned from his legal vocation—means he also fails to see the tragedy that reverberates in his own community. Practicing his "passive conquest" (43) by buying into a white neighborhood in the hope of provoking a violent reaction, Merrit learns the truth of what Bruce is saying only after he has experienced his own tragedy of having his house dynamited, with the consequence of losing the irreplaceable keepsake of his mother. Like Shine's, Merrit's smart retorts and tough exterior mask a denial of the battle waging within himself and within his own community. He is so focused on retaliating against the whites for the crime perpetrated on his assaulted foremothers that he becomes blind to the consequences of his own combative actions.

The enmity between black and white is mirrored in the novel as this segregated awareness between the lower-class rats and the upper-echelon dickties, a mirroring Fisher captures at the dance:

> So swept the scene from black to white through all the shadows and shades. Ordinary Negroes and rats below, dickties and fays above, the floor beneath the feet of the one constituting the roof over the heads of the other. . . . Out on the dance floor, everyone, dicky and rat, rubbed joyous elbows, laughing, mingling,

forgetting differences. But whenever the music stopped everyone immediately sought his own level. (74)

Inverting Van Vechten's "nigger heaven," in which the dark ones are in the balconies of theaters (and in the upper streets of Manhattan) while the light-skinned ones are on the floor, Fisher also changes the outlook of this arrangement, with the bottom becoming the floor that supports the top. Bottom and top may momentarily rub elbows on the dance floor, but they always seek out their own level after the music stops. Fisher's satire on the do-gooding patrons at the GIA ball splits the race along the color line and thus topples Van Vechten's drawing of that line more strictly along a racial divide between the observed exotic primitivism of all black people and the sophisticated titillation of observing white readers.

Despite being on opposite sides of the color/class line, Shine and Merrit find themselves companions on the same side of the race war. This heroic doubling again inverts Van Vechten's use of the Kasson-Pettijohn rivalry to bring Kasson down to the level of Anatole Longfellow. Instead, Fisher brings Shine and Merrit to common "middle" ground against the obvious white foes, and eventually against Patmore, the hidden traitor within. Even before Shine meets Merrit in person, he is confronted with the temptation of such treachery—a temptation that would have some pull, given his hatred of all dickties, except that he despises backstabbers even more than dickties. When Patmore tries to interest him in a supposed bootlegging business by asking Shine to sneak some liquor into Merrit's house for the purpose of infiltrating the dickties and becoming their supplier, Shine immediately smells a rat and refuses, telling him to "[u]nscheme yo' scheme, boogy" (33). Patmore admits his desire to move into a white neighborhood like Merrit, and believes he could already have done so if the lawyer had not supposedly bilked him out of some money. Not guessing the extent of Patmore's plan of revenge on Merrit, Shine nonetheless refuses the prospect of what appears to be a lucrative business deal: "Wise guy. Aimin' to choke Merrit and throw the blame on me" (34). This failed business partnership anticipates, as a foil, the successful one between Merrit and Shine in the novel's closure. Patmore misreads Shine's hatred of dickties and thus his racial ambition. Rather than an overreaching desire to get ahead by exploiting the dickties, Shine's ambition, unlike Pat's, is not motivated by envy, spite, revenge, and a desire to manipulate and subordinate others within the race.

If Patmore's prejudice proves wrong about Shine, Shine's proves equally wrong about Merrit. Upon first encountering Merrit on their moving job to his house, Shine, Jinx, and Bubber are thrown off balance by the man's forthright egalitarianism, so uncharacteristic of dickties in their experience (see 48). Merrit's genuine lack of snobbery at first heightens the men's prejudice rather than allaying it, just as Shine had rightly suspected Patmore's attempt at chumminess earlier. Merrit must want something from them beyond what they owe him in labor. Between Shine and Merrit, however, the "air of nonchalance" creates an unspoken and at first unrecognized bond. When Merrit confides in Shine that he has received a threatening note, they both accept that it has been sent by white neighbors, and the common enemy enables a fleeting moment of tactical coalition: "'Humph,' said Shine. 'Jes' let 'em start sump'm while we're here, that's all.' And because he disliked dickties and wanted no talk with any one of them, he changed the subject rudely" (49). Shine cannot help but begin to admire Merrit, however, as the man's egalitarian air persists:

> Shine came around to lend a hand, and Merrit moved along the curb to a position such that he could observe them. Now he indulged in another astonishing speech.
>
> "Don't be too damn careful about these things. Flat didn't have anything but junk in it, anyway. Good stuff's in the country—won't move it in till fall. Just chuck this stuff in and let it lay."
>
> What manner of dicky was this? He greeted you like an equal, casually shared his troubles with you, and did not seem to care in the least what the devil you did with his furniture. (51)

At first Merrit seems to be asserting his right to survey and discipline the men working for him; as it turns out that he instead is making their work easier, observing them out of sympathy instead of spying on them out of dominating efficiency, Jinx and Bubber remain suspicious but Shine's shell begins to crack: "Shine said to himself, 'If this bird wasn't a dicky he'd be o.k. But they never was a dicky worth a damn'" (51). As we have already seen, in a moment when the tables are turned, and Shine witnesses Merrit in the latter man's crisis after his house has been dynamited, Shine cannot avoid outright sympathy with Merrit. When Fisher turns Shine's quest for vengeance into a spectacle of supposedly unmanly tears, he reroutes Van Vechten's urban folk romance toward manhood reform. The pathos of Merrit's hysterical weeping unnerves Shine and softens him so much that he goes away in silence—a silence that counters the noisy violence expected between opposed black men in this city jungle.

Equally important to Shine's embrace of Linda on her own terms is his partnership with Merrit at the end. When the two men see their common interest in entering into the moving business, we understand, as do they, that more is at stake than profits. Even the profits, however, are to be shared "fifty-fifty" and, crucially, "with an option [for Shine] to purchase outright in due time" (282). On the surface, this concluding exchange could look suspiciously similar to Bookerite self-help, as the pointed moral of Merrit's proposition makes clear:

> That's what we Negroes need, a business class, an economic backbone. What kind of a social structure can anybody have with nothing but the extremes—bootblacks on one end and doctors on the other. Nothing in between. No substance. Everybody wants to quit waiting table and start writing prescriptions right away.

Well, here's a chance for you and a good investment for me. Race proposition, too. How 'bout it? (282–283)

Merrit's "race proposition" is literally a bid to construct "the middle" as a substantial buffer for the opposing extremes of top and bottom. Mixing the language of egalitarianism with Washington's conviction that African Americans must play the game that white men have perfected—advanced capitalist enterprise—Fisher combines uplift with a discourse of socioeconomic leveling. The objective in rising is to grow in "substance," to consolidate the race's gains and spread them as widely as possible.

Also undercutting Merrit's quasi-Bookerite proposition is his own utopian stance of observation in the final paragraph of the novel. As he watches Shine and Linda drive away in the moving van, Merrit redirects our sight one final time away from Van Vechten's spectacle of the race's violent self-defeat in the crucible of urban civilization:

> He stood and watched and smiled. The road led up and over a crest beyond which spread sunrise like a promise. Away for a time, then up moved Bess, straight into the kindling sky. With distance the engine roar grew dim and the van seemed to stand and shrink. Against that far background of light he saw it hang black and still a moment—then drop abruptly out of vision, into another land. (293)

As Fisher directs romance toward a utopian purpose, we also find him rethinking the heroic nature of black manhood, the gender relations that tie the central protagonist to women and other men. In the end, this means he also offers an implicit critique of the solitary, central role of the mulatto—Park's "marginal man"—in the city jungle of advancing civilization. Like Park's mulatto, Merrit is the victim on the frontier, the man caught between the native mores of a conquered race and the spreading civilization of aggressive white invaders and conquerors. Merrit hates that he has "white" blood running in his veins as much as he sanctifies the light-skinned mother who bore him to this miscegenated fate. Fisher radically revises this frontier vision, however. Merrit is not the central, solitary mulatto who, due to his marginality, can bring about a sensitive assimilation while keeping one foot in the securities of a discrete community. Absolutely rejecting Park's binary of the assimilating mulatto versus the conquered pure-blooded primitive, Fisher places transformative power in the hands of the collective efforts of Merrit, Shine, and Linda—none of them defined, in the end, as marginal mulattos. Just as the explosion of the maternal keepsake represents the purgation of Merrit's (self-)hatred for whiteness, the business contract between Shine and Merrit symbolizes the redirection of their energies, Shine's away from hating light-skinned dickties, Merrit's away from hating whiteness, for these hatreds have previously clouded their bonds to each other. By insisting that Merrit and Shine can choose their alliances while exploiting the technology of civilization—that they can become urban capitalists without becoming "civilized" and thus distracted by whiteness—Fisher risks his own fictional capital on black consolidation. The race's future lies in this sort of consolidation for progress, rather than in merely switching places with the white conquerors by invading white Manhattan from the frontier outpost of black Harlem. The "black" thing that hangs silent on the horizon in the final paragraph betokens the future promise of the darkening race, and it beckons the novel's readers to share in it not as prurient spectators but as reformed participants.

Uncannily, McKay's *Home to Harlem* concludes with a similar gesture, as Zeddy gives his blessing to Jake and Felice, who have determined to move on into "another land," Chicago. There are significant differences, however, in how McKay achieves moderated manhood through the male protagonist's relationships with male comrades. We know that Jake and Felice will encounter similar problems, no matter to which northern city jungle that they move. McKay's more radical giving in to mobility—to a footloose desire for changing the circumstances until the right ones are found—provides a much less stable closure for his couple than Fisher's does for Shine and Linda.

Footloose mobility is represented in McKay's novel not only through the couple's need to leave Zeddy behind but also through the parting that occurs between Jake and another pal, Raymond, the educated, middle-class Haitian whom Jake has befriended while they worked as Pullman-car waiters. The bond between Raymond and Jake symbolizes the crossing of the class line as well as the coming together of the African diaspora for tactical alliances. Such alliances *are* tactical—effectual, though temporary—because conditions at the bottom do not allow for settling down into a permanent coalition in Fisher's "middle." Consolidation occurs not through the establishment of a literal working-class/middle-class coalition of enterprise, as in *Walls of Jericho*, but instead through the fleeting contacts that heal, soften, and bind beyond geographic contiguity. Raymond, in one of his characteristic melancholic moods, captures this problem as he observes the other staff on the Pullman car:

> These men claimed kinship with him. They were black like him. Man and nature had put them in the same race. He ought to love them and feel them (if they felt anything). He ought to if he had a shred of social morality in him. They were all chain-ganged together and he was counted as one link. Yet he loathed every soul in that great barrack-room, except Jake. Race. . . . Why should he have and love a race?
>
> Races and nations were things like skunks, whose smells poisoned the air of life. Yet civilized mankind reposed its faith and future in their ancient, silted channels. Great races and big nations! There must be something mighty inspiriting in being the citizen of a great strong nation. To be the white citizen of a nation that can say bold, challenging things like a strong man. Something very different from the keen ecstatic joy a man feels in the romance of being black. (*Home to Harlem* 153–154)

Home to Harlem ironically does not offer a home to any of its characters. What it does offer is resistance to the "ancient, silted channels" that settle "great races and big nations" into deep, narrow identities. Instead of being dominated by these oppressive burdens of races and nations, which try to tie the feet of the oppressed to an immobile place at the bottom while raising others into masculine dominance, McKay's characters resist through constant movement across geographic, national, racial, and sexual boundaries. Just as Jake gets up and leaves when the military no longer suits his purposes, just as he and Felice decide to move when New York authorities pose a threat, so Ray, too, learns the footloose life as he chooses to leave America to vagabond around the Old World.[24]

Although read from his day to ours as a "romance of being black" at the bottom, McKay's novel cannot be so easily typed with such celebration of black primitivism—a strain that does enter the novel in complex ways, especially through Ray's point of view. The constant moving in and out of deepened contacts is a wounding process, as we understand when contact between Ray and Jake, or between Zeddy and Jake, must be lost. McKay plots a pathos-laden scene between Jake and Ray (271–275) as Ray determines to leave Harlem. Ray *does* romanticize Jake and his life as pure "animal" sensation: "Ray felt more and his range was wider and he could not be satisfied with the easy, simple things that sufficed for Jake. . . . But he drank in more of life than he could distill into active animal living. Maybe that was why he felt he had to write" (265). But Jake is as desirous of Ray's greater formal knowledge and the security it seems to bring as Ray is wistful for Jake's supposed living in the moment without intellectualizing (273). Neither character, it turns out, is exactly right about the other, for Ray is not as secure as Jake speculates, nor is Jake lacking in intellect and forethought as Ray speculates. Neither character, moreover, is complete in himself, and though they help inform and reform each other, neither can fully satiate the other's needs. Yet the cross-currents of Jake and Ray's wanderings position them as sharing a deepened contact that not even their class, national, linguistic, and educational differences can dissipate.[25] As they touch each other and move on, each deepens the other's desire for a common identity deeper than race or gender.

Like Fisher, McKay inserts the question of gendered spectatorship into the pathos of Ray and Jake's leave-taking. Another of Jake's pals, Billy Biasse, is drinking with them and seems to undercut their maudlin scene of departure. When Jake begins to wish that he and Ray could "settle down and make money like edjucated people do, instead a you gwine off to throw you'self away on some lousy dinghy and me chasing around all the time lak a hungry dawg" (273), Billy interjects the kind of deflating humor associated with Jinx and Bubber in Fisher's novel: "'Oh, you heart-breaking, slobbering nigger!' cried Billy Biasse. 'That's the stuff youse got tuck away there under your tough black hide.'" When Jake retorts, "Sure Ise human. I ain't no lonesome wolf lak you is," Billy pridefully stakes his claim to a wolfish identity: "A wolf is all right ef he knows the jungle" (273–274).

Billy's feigned criticism of the passionate relationship between Jake and Ray is layered with multiple ironies, for Billy loves Jake with the same sort of heartbreaking devotion that Jake displays in this moment of drunken frankness toward Ray. Like Bubber and Jinx, Billy Biasse is the man-loving man interwoven into rough manhood; but instead of employing a couple whose eroticism is playfully masked, McKay provides signals that Billy's erotic interests in men are in the open, without it negatively affecting his tight bonds with his "straight" buddies. Billy calls himself, and others label him, a *wolf,* a word with a slippery meaning in the novel.[26] According to Clarence Major, a "wolf" denotes "an extremely aggressive male who is constantly attempting to seduce women; male on the make" (*Juba to Jive* 513). The wolf is a lone predator who avoids intimate contact with other males and devours females sexually but has no desire to settle down with one. In this sense, Billy is clearly a foil to Zeddy and Jake, who constantly experiment with ways to couple beyond sexual escapades. But Billy is a foil in a more important sense. He does not fit the prevailing idea of a wolf. He is not interested in women, nor is he a loner, as he himself freely admits throughout the novel. As he teases Zeddy toward the beginning about being "Susy's skirt," he boasts that "Black women, or the whole diversified world of the sex were all the same to him." When Zeddy retorts by suggesting that being a "skirt-man" is at least better than being a wolf, Billy replies: "'Ise a wolf, all right, but I ain't a lone one. . . . I guess Ise the happiest, well-feddest wolf in Harlem. Oh, boy!'" (88). Later, when Jake is bed-ridden with a sexually transmitted disease, Billy comes to visit him and has to put up with the preaching of Jake's landlady of the moment:

> "All you younger generation in Harlem don't know no God," she accused Billy and indicted Young Harlem. "All you know is cabarets and movies and the young gals them exposing them legs a theirs in them jumper frocks."
>
> "I wouldn't know 'bout that," said Billy.
>
> "You all ought to know, though, and think of God Almighty before the trumpet sound and it's too late foh black sinners." (220)

The landlady's earnest retort suggests that she fails to grasp Billy's pun, which reveals that he knows nothing of sex *with women,* but which the old landlady takes to mean that he knows nothing about the terrible final consequences of Harlem sinfulness. She also fails to grasp her own pun, when she says that he *should* know about what's going on between men and women in Harlem. Billy is confident in his wolfish ways, but his wolfing has nothing to do with sexual conquest of females. Billy is a wolf because he happily goes his own way, keeping himself well fed with Harlem "boys," in the same-sexual sense defined above.

Just after Billy announces to Zeddy that he is a wolf but not a lone wolf, implying that he'll take his own kind of wolfing any day over Zeddy's skirting, McKay presents the sort of exotic spectacle of sexual variance that Van Vechten incorporates into *Nigger Heaven* and that Niles will later incorporate more apologetically into *Strange Brother*. Amid the revelers in Congo Rose's cabaret, where "Gin-head" Susy is about to encounter her Zeddy with another woman, we come across Billy in company with a group different from Jake's circle:

> Billy Biasse was there at a neighboring table with a longshoreman and a straw-colored boy who was a striking advertisement of the Ambrozine Palace of Beauty. The boy was made up with high-brown powder, his eyebrows were elongated and blackened up, his lips streaked with the dark rouge so popular in Harlem, and his carefully-straightened hair lay plastered and glossy under Madame Walker's absinthe-colored salve "for milady of fashion and color." (91)

When Zeddy's date asks him why they call Billy "the Wolf," Zeddy responds, "'Causen he eats his own kind" (92). Billy, this night drinking at a table "with his own kind," seems to inhabit two distinct but intermingled worlds, the one with his "straight" buddies, the other with his sexual partners; but neither seems to contradict the other. This coming together of the two worlds in perfect symmetry is represented by the dance. Rose and her dancing partner, the "straw-colored boy," perform a sensual dance for the all-black patrons of the Congo:

> They danced, Rose and the boy. Oh, they danced! An exercise of rhythmical exactness for two. There was no motion she made that he did not imitate. They reared and pranced together, smacking palm against palm, working knee between knee, grinning with real joy. They shimmied, breast to breast, bent themselves far back and shimmied again. Lifting high her short skirt and showing her green bloomers, Rose kicked. And in his tight nigger-brown suit, the boy kicked even with her. They were right there together, neither going beyond the other. . . . (93)

In *Strange Brother*, Niles places black sexual deviants such as Sylvia, the performer in the Lobster Pot, center-stage to plead for whites' acceptance of the authenticity of a white homosexual man's desire on par with the way it is already accepted in the black underworld, which is in turn equated with the (white) fairy underworld. Sylvia and her female lover become a mirror image of heterosexuality, their desire normalized in structure, if not in moral and social import. Niles does not question the heterosexual structure of Sylvia's same-sexual desire because her real concern is how to exploit these black characters in order to imagine how her white, upper-class protagonists, June and Mark, can fit back into, and thus enjoy the privileges of, dominant white society despite any deviance lurking in their desire. The bulldyker Sylvia is presented as a natural manifestation of deviant desire, not only in that her community accepts her as she accepts herself but also in that, unlike the white fairies with the marcelled hair and carmined lips who visit the Lobster Pot, her performance on stage is supposed to embody an un-made-up, authentic self.

Like Fisher, McKay seems much more interested in the ways that variant sexualities (of both "straight" and queer) are publicly performed amid the constraints of sexual normativity and racial oppression than in pleading for some sort of acceptance based in a logic of natural desire. Despite the novel's overtures toward "primitivism," it places sexual desire solidly in the realm of circumstance, makeshift, and accident. Thus, the staging of same-sexual desire in these novels is more self-consciously suggestive and ironic—even playful—than pleading and apologetic. Against the lurid, serious exoticism of Van Vechten's black mass and the Byron-Lasca sadomasochism scenes, McKay presents deviance that is both a parody of Van Vechten and a parody of normative sexuality along the axis of playfully self-conscious sexual deviance.[27] McKay highlights the sensuality of the dance in the Congo club to show the extent to which it is a self-conscious, playfully parodic performance of heterosexual pleasure before a crowd who know something of the sexual predilections of the two dancers: the boy's gender deviance is displayed in his clothes and makeup, and Rose makes no secret of her bisexuality.[28] As with Jinx and Bubber's performance of stereotypical black masculinity, this sexualized dance is another way of bracketing gender roles that are supposed to be natural but come under question ironically through the dancers' self-conscious conformity to heterosexual pairing in the dance. As the dancers imitate a heterosexual couple, they also invert that coupling as the man-loving boy follows the lead of the bisexual woman's steps. As deviance is staged paradoxically as compulsive heterosexual performance, the spectators partake of these ironies, taking pleasure in the form of the dance itself as indistinguishable from them. If the Congo were invaded by earnest whites, like June and Mark of *Strange Brother*, seeking sexual enlightenment from the authentic desire of the natives, this spectatorship would take on a different tenor, as Jake acknowledges when Rose points out that the cabaret has hired the "straw-colored boy" as a new dancer: "And the ofays will soon be nosing it out. Then we'll have to take a back seat" (91). The presence of prying whites would immediately put a different spin on the symbolic construction of sexual variance, the pleasure one can take from observing its display, as well as on the literal seating arrangements.

Like Jinx and Bubber, Billy Biasse represents the innocuous integration of same-sexuality into Harlem life, and at the same time its acknowledged variance from the sexual norm. After explaining to one of his Pullman coworkers that a lesbian is "what we call bulldyker in Harlem," Jake hums a blues song that sums it up: "And there is two things in Harlem I don't understan' / It is a bulldyking woman and a faggoty man."[29] Jake could have composed the words himself. His erotic passion is decidedly for women, so much so that he would doubtless have a difficult time understanding why any man or woman would choose his or her own gender. But just as crucially, the song places the "bulldyking woman" and "faggoty man" as a visible, even prominent presence *within* the community. Jake's befriending of Billy Biasse indicates his more general tolerance (in the truest sense of the word) for what he does not understand. After all, in the eyes of dominant culture, Jake's own desire—his failed sweetbacking with Rose and his egalitarian extramarital arrangement on the road with Felice—is anathema.

The irony is that Billy, with his sexual appetite and rough manly ways, serves as a foil to Jake's moderated manhood. Billy lives for the hunt and the conquest, only his object of affection is other males, rather than women. But Billy is also a man's man, not a "boy" in any sense of the word, for "[h]e loved to indulge in naked man–stuff talk, which would be too raw even for Felice's ears" (324). Just as Bubber and Jinx save Shine's life in the bar fight, it is Billy the Wolf who insists that Jake carry a concealed gun to protect himself, an act that probably saves his life, as Jake himself points out to Felice. "Billy is a good friend, eh?" Felice asks. "You bet he is," Jake responds. "Nevah gets mixed up with—in scraps like that [which Jake has just had with Zeddy]" (330). Jake almost says that Billy never gets mixed up with women, who are seen as the cause of these scraps. In fact, we come to understand that "Billy was a better pal for Jake than Zeddy. . . . They made a good team. Their intimate interests never clashed" (268). In other words, Billy's lack of sexual interest in women frees him from the sort of life-risking rivalry that Jake has with Zeddy. Thus, Billy's more conventional masculinity is both heightened and undercut by his sexuality, which makes him available for a kind of manly bonding with Jake that deviates from the dominant homosocial norm, and in turn allows Jake to be the gentle, open, passionate sort of hero and lover that he is.

As with *Walls of Jericho*'s man-loving couple, *Home to Harlem* exploits the boy-loving minor male character to accentuate and balance the male hero's racial and sexual commitments. Without their queer best pals, Shine and Jake could be neither the "cool" New Negro pacifists that they are nor the egalitarian-leaning lovers that they learn to become. In the hands of Fisher and McKay, the urban folk novel seeks reciprocity and consolidation within the race by binding their heroic men to sexually variant companions. At the same time, they resist making such variance a spectacle of exotic deviance to be eyed lasciviously and deplored hypocritically by their middle-class and white readers; they seek to reform the racial obsessions and sexual appetites of their readers as much as those of their male protagonists. In contrast to Du Bois's distancing act when he discovers that one of his male protégés is a "freak" who has been arrested in a men's room, Fisher and McKay tighten the bonds between the women-loving and men-loving men. For them, the reform of black manhood cannot be the sort of squeamish affair that causes one to fear and ostracize what dominant society turns into taboo. Instead, the reform of black manhood occurs on the ground *inside* the social experiences, sexual habits, and intimate bonds already practiced among ordinary African Americans. If black manhood is culturally transformed, as it constantly is, this happens not from the stance of some prying black male sociologist or some curious white slumming patron-novelist but through the changing practices of the black folk themselves.

**Female Protagonists and the
Resistance to Dominant Masculinity**

> Men's got a whole lot of women in their nature, I tell you.
> —Lavinia Curdy to Gin-head Susy (Claude McKay, *Home to Harlem* 85)

Hazel Carby points out how the sexual policing of African American women mi-grants during the Great Migration comes to represent the more general attempt of both black and white social agencies and other authorities to control the formation of an ambitious new urban group that brings its own culture to the city with it. Carby demonstrates how white and black middle-class social welfare authorities take it upon themselves to propagate an image of the migrant mass as an unso-phisticated horde that needs to be tutored in the urban ways of self-initiative and wage labor—a phenomenon we have already seen in chapter 3 of this study with the emergence of urban sociology as an uplifting discipline that separates the pro-fessionalization of middle-class black men from the footloose ways of the folk mass. She further explores how women migrants are presented as dangerous, based on the logic that if they fall morally, there must be even less hope for their fathers, husbands, suitors, sons, and brothers. According to Carby, black women, some of them having risen from the lower migrant class, sometimes enforce these policies themselves, creating narratives of moral transformation that contain what she calls "moral panic" over the threat to and of the women who do not seem to conform to dominant sociosexual practices. Actually, the ideological intent of these policies and narratives is to confirm these women "in their subordinate, working-class sta-tus as female domestics."[1]

Citing Van Vechten's *Nigger Heaven* and McKay's *Home to Harlem,* Carby argues that in the fiction of the New Negro Renaissance period, "moral panic" over black women's sexuality helps determine the constitution of an appropriate urban mas-culinity for black heroes:

> In each text representations of urban black women are used as both the means by which male protagonists will achieve or will fail to achieve social mobility and as signs of various possible threats to the emergence of the wholesome black masculinity necessary for the establishment of an acceptable black male citizenship in the American social order. ("Policing the Black Woman's Body" 747)

Carby's brief readings of Van Vechten's Mary Love and Lasca Sartoris and of McKay's Felice bring out the ways in which issues surrounding black urban manhood rely heavily on the representation of black female sexuality in these novels. Her interpretation of McKay's use of women to bolster Jake's sense of manhood development is especially provocative:

> The assumption of the novel is that male love and desire could not be generated for, or be sustained by, a woman like Rose, who is characterized as bisexual because she lacks the acceptable feminine qualities. . . . Indeed, Rose's sexual ambiguity is positioned as a threat to the very existence of black masculinity, reducing Jake to the role of a "big, good slave." . . . Jake's refusal to beat Rose is a triumph of wholesome masculinity over the degenerate female element and allows Jake to proceed on his journey to become a man. (750)

Carby rightly brings attention to how Jake's manhood relies on a rejection of Rose's desire as appropriate femininity. I think, however, that McKay complicates this perspective by pointing to the conflict that occurs between individual desire and normative expectations in different ways for both women and men. One way McKay does this is by providing Susy and Zeddy's relationship as an inverted foil. According to Zeddy's pals, he is being dominated by Susy, but the difference between Susy's desire for a man to boss around and Rose's desire for a man who will beat her indicates the inequity between men and women already implicit in normative heterosexual relations. A symmetrical contrast would obviously be a Susy who desired literally to brutalize Zeddy as a match for Rose's desire to be brutalized. Zeddy is willing to enact fatal violence on Jake in order to prove his total control of Felice— a violence that we can easily imagine as being eventually directed at Felice if she were to consent to a relationship with Zeddy. Has Rose's desire become illegitimate in the ethical frame of the novel, or is Jake's rejection of her more narrowly a matter of circumstantial ethics, in which Rose's desire is not inappropriate *for her* but is inappropriate for Jake *in relation to her?*

I do not believe these issues are—or can be—worked out in the novel, given the decentering of normative sexuality that McKay is attempting. What is clear, however, is that the women characters in these men's urban folk novels tend to lack the dynamic development toward a moderated womanhood commensurate with the male protagonists' movement toward sexual and racial reform. Jake moves on to the next woman when one does not suffice, a behavior that could easily look like old-fashioned sexual exploitation and philandering. Or as George Kent has pointed out, "The reader can admire the superiority of Jake and Felice's natural normality, but cannot forget that the real test comes when Jake has given hostages to fortune in the form of a wife and children, a situation in which the vibrations of the black man's condition in Western culture are not so easily brushed aside."[2] Fisher's Linda Young has a different set of problems. She already knows what Shine has to learn, fitting into the role that Carby refers to as "a figure of virginal purity" in reference to Van Vechten's Mary Love (747). In other words, other, more difficult issues concerning the reproduction and raising of children are conveniently left out of these novels, enabling McKay and Fisher to glide over what the black sociologists of their time—and ours—obsess about: the question of the socioeconomic impact of these alternative sexual arrangements on children's welfare and the prospects for productive community institutions.

If these novels are able to work toward a moderated manhood only at the expense of urban womanhood, does this mean that male-protagonist urban folk fiction is an intrinsically masculine genre that ends up embracing the kinds of sexual subordination and conquest that I have been arguing Fisher and McKay wrestle against? We find these questions addressed directly in the realm of urban folk novels with female protagonists.

Mobile Heroines:
The Female-centered Precursors of Urban Folk Fiction

The best way to answer this question is to examine novels with themes and plots similar to those of McKay and Fisher that stage the development of mobile female protagonists across the urban environment and up and down the social scale. The fact that such novels exist indicates that however much male protagonists dominate the genre, the genre itself is not necessarily intrinsically masculine. Before Van Vechten, Fisher, and McKay received such a sensational reception with their male-focused novels, Jessie Fauset (1882/1884?–1961) published her first novel, *There Is Confusion* (1924) and Walter White his second, *Flight* (1926). Both novels, though less evidently treating questions of urban folk mobility, do so through crucial contacts experienced by their middle-class female protagonists in relation to characters from the urban folk bottoms.

Fauset's Joanna Marshall makes a grave error when she writes a letter to Maggie Ellersly, a lower-class girl befriended by the family, in order to persuade Maggie to break her engagement to Joanna's brother. Joanna's manipulative intervention, stemming from class snobbery, sets in motion a subplot that plunges Maggie into an abusive marriage with a violent, shady figure named Henderson Neal, a character on whom Van Vechten's Randolph Pettijohn and Fisher's Henry Patmore are based, and who eventually attempts to murder Maggie when she refuses to return to him. Like the later novels with male protagonists, *There Is Confusion* is interested in how sexual violence intersects with a typical mode of masculinity (for Neal is the most aggressively masculine character in the novel), a mode that in turn has racial implications. Neal's violence results from a racial and class desperation that also characterizes Maggie's decision to marry him in the first place. Fauset brings Joanna face to face with the consequence of this violence when she enters Maggie's apartment to find her lying on the floor, bloodied by a knife wound. Joanna herself experiences this violence only through Maggie, so that the novel shields her while enabling her to confront the reality of the violence and her own culpability. The narrative implies through Joanna's saving of Maggie at the end that the heroine is also, at the same time, helping to rectify the error she has made at the beginning. Through this saving action, Fauset interconnects the heroine's middle-class plot with Maggie's lower-class subplot in such a way that neither story can be satisfactorily told without the other.[3]

Like the novels that it influences, *There Is Confusion* also foregrounds the vertigo that results from a female character's incessant, desperate mobility, both geographic and social. Maggie moves restlessly from city to city, and because she has so little control over her social status, her plot line is characterized by an up-down-up-down-up motion. She rises when she gets Philip Marshall as a fiancé, only to fall precipitously upon receiving Joanna's letter; she rises again, or at least she thinks so at first, after the marriage to the apparently well-heeled Neal, until she realizes that, because of Neal's shady dealings, she actually has fallen socially and is ostracized; she rises one more time when Joanna's lover, Peter, in a moment of frustration with Joanna, asks Maggie to marry him, then falls yet again with the violent encounter with Neal, only to rise again in the end when she receives a wounded Philip in marriage. Joanna, too, represents a constant mobility in her vocation as a singer and dancer. Not only does her work take her away from the comforts and securities of her middle-class home into the harsh world of racial and sexual discrimination, across the United States and to Europe; it also jeopardizes her future with the man she loves. The Jane Austen–like marriages that close the novel try to redeem the messiness, confusion, and desperate mobility throughout, but despite the excessively tidy romantic marriage knots made in homage to the British novel of manners, Fauset manages to relay—for instance, through Neal's suicide and Philip's early death from his wartime wounds—the unpredictable, sometimes violent disruption that shatters the "coupling conventions," to use Ann duCille's apt phrase, of heterosexual romance.[4]

Flight seems to start out as a novel of "mulatta" manners, in which the proper heroine steers her way toward marriage (or tragedy) through the social barriers that confront morally circumspect women of color in a society where their sexuality is always suspect, their skin color already inscribing them as flagrant products of someone's sexual indiscretion. Wavering between the romantic novel of manners and a footloose folk novel, White seems to take Fauset's interjection of the Maggie subplot a step further in *Flight*. When his heroine, Mimi Daquin, becomes pregnant and refuses to conform to the sexual dictates of her social status and gender, the novel takes a turn into urban folk narrative, as she is forced into transmigrations sexually, socially, and geographically. White depicts Mimi as a highly principled and independent young woman in her refusal to accede either to an abortion, as requested by her lover, Carl Hunter, or to marriage for the sake of appearing respectable. In other words, her own sexual indiscretion becomes the crisis that shows her mettle. In having Mimi reject Carl after his parents force him to do the "gentlemanly" thing by proposing, White sets up a contrast between mature womanhood and immature manhood under the conditions of middle-class blacks, who have a modicum of social privilege under racial oppression. Carl's failure at school, as well as his alcoholism and sexual looseness, can be blamed on the corroding pressures of racism, but his treatment of Mimi seems to indict him as having exploited the reality of racial pressures as an excuse for un/manly behavior, which, in turn, casts him as a man whose gender status pampers rather than mans him. Whereas Kenneth Harper's escapism in *Fire in the Flint* locates him as a sissy attempting to do a heroic job by leaning on the strength of the woman he loves, Carl's escapist behavior in *Flight* brands him as a womanizer who uses the bohemian pose of a tortured artistic soul to cover his dissipation into lethargy, alcohol, sponging, and bartered sex.

White hinges Mimi's development—her geographic mobility and search for womanly maturity—on Carl's manhood failure. Finding him even more unacceptable after he has bowed to his parents' wishes by agreeing to turn respectable in order not to be disowned, Mimi decides that it is better to brave the world alone, pregnant, and without apparent marketable skills than to end up chained to Carl and the conformities of bourgeois marriage. Just as Fisher's and McKay's heterosexual romance of manhood reform depends on women who are either sexually inappropriate or statically already awaiting the hero's arrival, so White's mobile heroine depends on highlighting the excesses of sexually inappropriate men. We shall see that Wallace Thurman and Nella Larsen construct a similar bargain, as their heroines are motivated into mature womanhood through the serial failures of (un)suitable black men.

Flight transits from Mimi's relatively secure condition in Atlanta—at least in terms of her father's protection, her finances, and her social status—to the obscure poverty, single motherhood, and the dangers that await a woman who must go into others' homes to make a living in Philadelphia. She becomes like the migrant women Carby describes, but her once-elite status further alienates her from this lowly experience. Having given his mulatta heroine all the social problems usually identified with working-class black migrant women in this period, White relatively quickly proceeds to reposition her as an upper-class mulatta, after she settles in Harlem and has her son placed in a white boarding school. When her identity is revealed and Harlem gossip threatens to ruin her again, she begins to pass for white. Without child, she can pursue a career in fashion design and take on the problems suitable to the mulatta novel of manners. Like her passable color, Mimi's success in the fashion industry provides her with easy access to leisurely productive travel, as opposed to coerced and desperate mobility, and also to suitable men again (apparently honorable men of her own status). While on a business trip in

Paris, she falls in love with Jimmie Forrester, a wealthy white New Yorker, and marries him against her better judgment. The dynamism—a bit of inconsistency—in Mimi's character results from the shifting plot formulas, foregrounding the various kinds of limitations in Mimi's options: first as middle-class mulatta woman in a seemingly secure bourgeois world (though even here a race riot can interrupt her security and threaten her life); then as a penniless black migrant mother; then as a passing, childless professional woman, whose accessible identity in the black community risks her security in the white professional world; and penultimately as a securely married white woman, whose wealth and status exempt her from both working-class and professional labor.

This penultimate position of white upper-class womanhood seems as close as she can come to returning to her shielded status before the pregnancy. However, marriage, instead of becoming a safe harbor, turns out to be torture, as she discovers the extent of her husband's racism and the extent of her own yearning for community among the historically kindred racial group. The converse of Carl, Jimmie Forrester represents the insecurity of the marital state consummated by true love, a state that usually constitutes the final objective of conventional heterosexual romance. Just as Carl sets loose the cowardly conformity lurking in the pampered colored gentleman who uses racism to excuse his own un/manly failure, so Jimmie embodies the barriers erected for white upper-class women by a dominating masculinity, as fierce in its aggression and conformity as it is polite in its chivalrous manners. Mimi's absence of family background, history, and network of friends is no problem; in fact, it adds to her mysterious allure, given Jimmie's expectation that she will simply adopt and accept his own priorities, acquaintances, and identities. Jimmie always assumes his wife to be what he projects onto her, a sort of masculine arrogance that Carl cannot afford. Despite the wealth she has achieved through her own talent and effort, Mimi is reduced again to a state of dependence, loneliness, self-denial, and identity denial that she finally cannot accept.

White passes Mimi from the mulatta novel of manners to the passing novel—two plot lines so deeply interrelated in African American literary history that they frequently occupy the same narrative—a passing so complete in *Flight* that it almost becomes a "white" novel of manners.[5] This movement from mulatta plot to passing plot, however, passes through the urban folk episode in Philadelphia and Harlem, and it is this transitional episode that ultimately beckons Mimi back to Harlem, despite the external horrors of racism and the internal pressures of race. The novel concludes with Mimi's hopeful but uncertain return to blackness, including her decision to retrieve her son, who has throughout been relegated to others' care, out of her white husband's sight. Leaving Jimmie behind to reclaim her son is both the same as and different from leaving Carl behind to affirm her right to single motherhood—a gesture that seems to equate the two as failed men. White seems to imply that Mimi's experience will serve her well in returning to Harlem, just as her inexperience had threatened to ruin her in Philadelphia. All along, however, Mimi is innocent, even when she is most culpable in conventional moral terms: getting pregnant outside of marriage, allowing her child to be raised by others, and lying about her racial identification in order to get ahead professionally, socially, and romantically. White refuses to finish off Mimi's development by marrying her happily to the colored gentleman of similar color, status, and ambition (Carl)—a gesture that would complete the mulatta novel of manners. He similarly refuses to complete the passing novel by leaving her married to the white man—a gesture that would simulate the closure of Johnson's *Autobiography of an Ex-Coloured Man*. Being handmaiden to the colored man's chivalry (like Jane in *Fire in the Flint*) would mean that the heroine rests her fate insecurely on the tissue of race-inflicted masculine anxieties. Becoming the pedestaled lady of the white gentleman's chivalrous devotion turns out to be a nightmare of jealousy, denial, mastery, and racist psychological abuse.

In this sense, White's novel resists the inclination toward a moderated (hetero)sexual romance that becomes the dominant pattern set by Fisher and McKay in urban folk narrative. Although it is certainly the case that by moderating their heterosexual protagonists with the same-gender passions of their best buddies, Fisher's and McKay's heterosexual heroes resist the dominant patterns of heterosexual romance in another way not contemplated in *Flight*, even though it is hinted at in the sissy protagonist of *Fire in the Flint*. Yet the closure to *Flight* is a sort of romance. White insists that in fleeing—first the conformities of her middle-class colored family, then the vulnerabilities of impoverished single black motherhood, then the indignities of a double passing professional life, and finally the objectifying banalities of white upper-class femininity—his heroine can find herself racially and sexually. Mimi's mobility almost magically changes her options and evolves her character. Despite the fact that they romantically have each other, Felice and Jake have no greater social, economic, or racial options. Racial bonding is not the reward Fisher's and McKay's characters receive for surviving racism; it is the process that enables them to survive it.

Mimi is ready for racial bonding only once she has given up on her marital bonds. Radically for a man writing in his time, White has Mimi sacrifice heterosexual romance *in order to find happiness* rather than as tragic closure. Unfortunately, perhaps even more than Fisher and McKay, White seems to replace heterosexual romance with a "romance of being black," as McKay has Raymond label it (*Home to Harlem* 154): "'Free! Free! Free!' She whispered exultantly as with firm tread she went down the steps. '*Petit* Jean—my own people—and happiness!' was the song in her heart as she happily strode through the dawn, the rays of the morning sun dancing lightly upon the more brilliant gold of her hair" (*Flight* 300). Given the lack of any sense of how racial consolidation can occur for Mimi in her return, the plot does seem to lead into racial romance.[6] Given that "*petit* Jean," her son named after her saintly father, has lived his whole life as a white child among whites, the rebinding of Mimi to the race cannot occur without disruption and adaptation, the cost of which the closure itself refuses to reckon. Seeming to rewrite Johnson's *Autobiography of an Ex-Coloured Man*, which would be republished the following year, as well as the bleak conclusion of his first novel, White makes Mimi's negotiation of racial and sexual economies, her adaptation to and of migratory womanhood, a more flexible matter than do these earlier stories; yet this hopeful closure for Mimi leaves the figure of black manhood as stranded and static as McKay and Fisher leave black womanhood in their first novels.

White's move from a tragic male-focused novel in 1924 to a triumphant female protagonist in 1926 indicates how he is investigating gender constructions as the differential consequences of racism for the two sexes. This gender dichotomy in White's novels also indicates how all the urban folk narratives of this era seem capable of conceptualizing dynamic development for only one sex at a time, and much less capable of imagining an integrated, commensurate development of reformed sexual identity across the gender divide. While all these novels to some extent recognize the fluidity and artificiality of sexual categories, even these recognitions tend to be expressed through sexual differentiation, as in the case of the statement by McKay's character Miss Lavinia Curdy: "Men's got a whole lot of women in their nature, I tell you" (Home to Harlem 85). Even as men's "nature" naturally crosses over into women's, the differing natures of the sexes are reaffirmed. White seems to be making a similar statement by experimenting with the sexual exploration of a female protagonist who has as much in common with Theodore Dreiser's protagonist in Sister Carrie (1900) as with Dr. Kenneth Harper or with White himself.[7] By placing autobiographical elements into the narrative, such as Mimi's encounter with a race riot in Atlanta at a young age, White seems to be exploring his own experience from the viewpoint of a female character with peculiarly feminine problems (such as pregnancy and sexual harassment while working as a domestic). In one letter White writes: "Mimi is, so far as I consciously know, wholly a creation. She is modelled upon no person I have ever known."[8] He wants to attribute to this character a universal application, much in the way that, as a black author, he wants his stories about racial prejudice to transcend race, as is also evident in the letter: "In telling her story, I sought to solve no problem, to write no treatise upon race or any other question. I sought simply to create a character or, better, to put down on paper a character who had been created within me" (quoted in Waldron, Walter White and the Harlem Renaissance 94). Despite White's rhetoric of universalism, Flight's coherence and confusion both derive from his attempt to project himself into a woman in the belief that "men's got a whole lot of women in their nature," and vice versa. "In telling of Mimi, I revealed, I now realize, a great deal more of myself than I knew at the time of writing" (94). In this sense, in writing across gender identity, White challenges men's "nature," as it is conventionally known, and at the same time delineates the particular social difficulties that women like Mimi face in a sexually differentiated culture of race. Men and women may have a lot of each other in their natures, but under the circumstances of a sexually differentiated culture, sexual differences cannot go unheeded.

Salvaging Mimi from the awful fate of the ex-colored man in the nick of time, White sets a precedent for black urban folk narrative; but, interestingly, it is a precedent that not only Fisher and McKay refuse to follow, when they place male protagonists center stage, but also Nella Larsen and Wallace Thurman turn down, even when they do follow up with footloose female protagonists. While motivating a dynamic, moderated urban heroism, Fisher and McKay keep White's insistence on a consolidated racial romance. Nella Larsen and Wallace Thurman, however, find it more compelling to decline romance altogether—both of the racial and the heterosexual kind, as they fiercely interconnect the pitfalls of heterosexual romance with the failures of racial consolidation. Larsen's *Quicksand* (1928) and Thurman's *The Blacker the Berry* (1929) seem almost to chastise White for his happy ending, suggesting that race cannot provide such an easy escape from the stultifying banalities and violent bindings of heterosexual coupling, while also suggesting—contrary to Fisher and McKay—that such coupling cannot go far enough to overcome the dreadful class inequities and racial compromises weighing down and helping to uphold the gender conventions of heterosexual romance.

Perhaps because the novels respectively come from the perspective of a woman with an unconventional sexual inheritance as the African American daughter of a white-identified family and of a queer-identified man, *Quicksand* and *Blacker the Berry* also call into question Fisher's and McKay's positioning of the possibility of racial consolidation through manhood reform within the comfort zone of, as well as from the vantage of, male companionship. When Fisher and McKay supplement and undercut their heroes through companionship with men-loving men and through a scathing critique of the intraracial sexual violence lurking within laudatory images of combative fraternity and masculine conquest, do they leave intact the sufficiency—if clearly not the self-sufficiency—of masculine rites by leaving intact conventional femininity as a secondary concern of manhood reform? The contrary narratives of Larsen and Thurman seem to suggest that they do.

The Quicksand of Black Feminine Desire

Larsen uses a structure similar to *Flight*'s, insofar as she takes her heroine through a series of drastically different social conditions in relation to men who seem to offer some hope of rescue but fail her, each in his own way. Understandably not taking as much license as her male contemporary and friend, Larsen makes Helga Crane a less risqué character than White's Mimi Daquin. Mimi's giving in to Carl toward the beginning of *Flight* contrasts with Helga's resistance to the men who court her. It is not until the end that Helga experiences sexual intercourse, and immediately afterward she assents to a desperate marriage. Through a horrifying vision of humdrum but hypocritical conjugal respectability among southern black peasantry, Larsen charges the normativity of marriage with a malignant burden of inescapable smothering racial and sexual constriction. Even the regenerative hope of reproducing and rearing children becomes not a site for folk uplift and consolidation but instead, like Du Bois's Josie in *Souls of Black Folk*, entrapment in a stagnant, sinking bog. Thus, even though *Quicksand* apparently adheres more closely to the greater circumspection expected of colored middle-class women, it finds a way of engaging with the sexual and social deviations explored by White, Fisher, and McKay while at the same time launching a strategic attack on the American sexual norm of marriageable respectability for such women. As Ann duCille has written, "[f]ar from silent on the topic of sexuality, Fauset and Larsen are more rightly claimed, I believe, as the first black women novelists to depict openly sensual black female subjects, as the first black writers to explore the dialectics of female desire and to address what having children can mean to a woman's physical and mental health, as well as to her independence" (*Coupling Convention* 87).

In addition to being influenced by *There Is Confusion, Quicksand* seems to be rewriting *Flight,* as the opposition in the two titles indicates. A heated quarrel that occurred in the pages of *Opportunity* helps shed light on the convoluted gender politics at work in Larsen's relationship to White's novel. When Frank Horne lambasted *Flight* in his *Opportunity* review, White enlisted Larsen to compose a defense of the novel for the journal.[9] Larsen's coming to White's defense is an especially interesting ploy, given the attempt of White's novel to move beyond New Negro chivalry by depicting an independent, sexually liberated black middle-class heroine. As a middle-class, sophisticated, independent-minded mulatta, Larsen ironically can bestow authenticity on White's authority in having constructed such a female character.

Furthermore, Horne's review of the novel opens with a gesture of chivalry in an anecdote that seems a preemptive strike against any "lady" who might want to challenge his right to criticize the novel:

> Just the other evening, a most charming lady asked me what I thought of this story of Mr. White's. Quite unthinkingly and most abruptly my answer came:— "It seems to me a good story gone wrong." She perceptibly disliked my remark and went on to say that she thought "Flight" a distinct advance over "The Fire in the Flint." And in the way of weak critics with charming ladies, I limited my discourse to those elements upon which we were in agreement; but here, alone at my desk I shall say what I jolly well please. It may be that I feel so strongly about this book, because I had hoped to do such a story some day myself—there are so many elements contained that are problems of my life, so many experiences that are my experiences, that I feel less than a man if I withhold the honesty of my opinion.[10]

Chivalrously dismissing the critical judgment of this "most charming lady," Horne effectively recasts the rivalry as one between men, between the male author and the male critic over the properties of a fictive black lady's experience. Horne would "feel less than a man" if he did not engage with White directly and forcefully. Ironically, in writing the lady out of the conversation, Horne also reveals the risky sort of sexual politics silently at work in White's decision to focus on a black *heroine.* Horne claims his turf not only by dismissing the lady's experience; he also claims that the experience White has depicted through a female character actually belongs to Horne. Like Van Vechten's ability to rationalize his hero's failure in *Nigger Heaven* as a way of claiming his own superior authority over African American experience, Horne is clearly attempting to wrest White's subject matter from his hands in order to clear ground for his own future novel with a male hero—himself—authorizing African American migratory experience. Although the gender of the interlocutors never comes up explicitly in the series of counterattacks that follow Horne's review, the gendered construction of African American identity through Harlem Renaissance fiction is at the center of the controversy.

Significantly, a major volley in Horne's explosive attack aims at White's ending:

> And so the climax meant to be so intense and sweeping, strikes a hollow, blatant note. Then, too, we must conjecture that he [White] has left this girl [Mimi] at the most critical stage of her career. She leaves a white world, with all its advantages of body and spirit, a position of eminence which she has developed out of the soul-sweat of her spirit, to go back to "her people." How then to be received?—how to adjust on a lower, cramped scale a life that had become so full?—how to compensate for the intense freedom of "being white"? Truly, has Mimi been left in the lurch! ("Correspondence" 227)

While declaring that "the ruggedness and power" (227) to be found in White's first novel is lacking in *Flight,* Horne targets exactly the problem of closure that Larsen will also criticize implicitly in the way she chooses to close *Quicksand.* In her response to Horne, however, she is given the task of defending this happy ending.

Larsen applauds the "thesis" of the novel as being carried out by its closure: "Surely, the thesis of 'Flight' is 'What shall it profit a man if he gain the whole world and lose his own soul?'"[11] Appropriately, this thesis seems in accord with the lesson the ex-colored man in James Weldon Johnson's novel takes from his experience, when he utters in the final sentence: "I cannot repress the thought that, after all, I have chosen the lesser part, that I have sold my birthright for a mess of pottage" (*Autobiography of an Ex-Coloured Man* 211). Despite her effective defense of *Flight,* Larsen in her own novel seems to offer a critique of White's closure, as well as of Johnson's novel, when she places her heroine in a position similar to that of Mimi and the ex-colored man but effectuates a drastically different ending. Instead of passing into a safe whiteness like the ex-colored man, Helga flees into what she thinks will be the safety of rural southern blackness, with the prospect of a life of simple self-sacrifice to "her people." Supposedly, this sort of sacrifice is what the ex-colored man *should* have done, and it is what he planned to do in traveling to the South; but at the sight of a lynching he fled north again and into white security. Similar to Mimi, who joyfully returns to "her people" after passing in a white marriage more torturous than that of the ex-colored man's, Helga escapes to white Denmark, but only to find herself terribly disillusioned. Whereas Mimi gives in and marries a white man, having to deny her racial history in order to do so, Helga categorically rejects an offer of marriage from a white Danish aristocrat, as she realizes the racial quicksand such a marriage would make. Having rejected whiteness, again like Mimi, Helga returns to the black folk with an image of consolidated race work in her head. The utopian vision of racial consolidation for which the ex-colored man wistfully yearns amid the comforts of his whiteness, and toward which Mimi moves in flight from her deadening white marriage, Helga experiences as a hellish lowering and cramping of the self amid the discomforts of the black peasantry. Thus, Larsen's defense of White's ending seems to contradict the ending of her own novel.

As Edward Waldron points out, Larsen resorts to an *ad hominem* attack on Horne (105) as she accuses him of being blind to the racial implications of the novel—a charge that implies Horne's own tendency toward racial betrayal. Quoting Horne's own words, she turns them against him in a hard-hitting way improper for any charming lady:

> "There is in her travail the lonely vicissitudes of a lost race . . . " What "lost" race? It is here that your reviewer stumbles and falls. It is here that we detect his blindness. It is here that we become aware that he fails to realize that this is the heart of the whole tale. A lost race. Yes. But I suspect that he refers to the black race, while Mr. White obviously means that it is the white race which is lost, doomed to destruction by its own mechanical gods. How *could* your reviewer have missed this dominant note, this thing which permeates the whole book? (Larsen, "Correspondence" 295)

By attributing *Flight*'s "dominant note" to race, Larsen seems to suppress the sexual agenda of White's novel, as well as Horne's surreptitious exploitation of that agenda in his review.[12] Given the way that the correspondence proceeds through charges and countercharges of racial blindness,[13] we could easily forget how Mimi's experience of race is filtered through her gender predicament, more precisely the act of her becoming pregnant out of wedlock and going against her elders' wishes in refusing to marry—the defiant gesture that motivates the novel's flighty plot. Ironically, this theme of the sexual construction of race is repressed in exactly the same way that the masculine rivalry, conducted through Larsen's intercession, between black male author and black male reviewer supplants the question of the black woman's frame of racial reference.

In *Quicksand,* Larsen rethinks the sexual frame of racial reference by appearing to agree with Horne. Helga does feel lowered and cramped as a result of sinking into the heart of Negro life, a feeling inextricable from her gender trouble. Helga's flight leaves her stranded in quicksand. In thus stranding her female protagonist, Larsen seems to be challenging the idea, proffered at the end of *Flight,* that a woman of Mimi's color, status, ambitions, and experience *can* return to the folk as an objective of personal fulfillment. The harsh reality of poverty at the bottom that White depicts in Mimi's Philadelphia adventure Larsen brings back intensified at the end of *Quicksand,* like the return of the repressed. Thus, in both its class and sexual politics, the closure of *Quicksand* seems disillusioning not only of *Flight* but also of utopian solutions offered by Fisher and McKay. Larsen highlights the sacrifice of femininity (how the feminine is defined by sacrifice) and the femininity of sacrifice (how men's heroic sacrifice is silently coded by the supplementary, unheroic sacrifice of and by women) at work in Fisher and McKay by leaving her heroine sinking in a dreadful marriage from which we cannot imagine she can extricate herself.

As Larsen illustrates this middle-class black woman's descent, she also presents the case of Helga's three black male suitors (and one white), each representing a different sort of manhood reform. By tracing Helga's involvement with her suitors, we can discern the modes of masculine control that she struggles against and why Larsen insists—against the optimism of White, Fisher, and McKay—on the heroine's unheroic downfall in this struggle.

Like Mimi's, Helga's story begins with her dissatisfaction in being forced to live in a provincial southern environment in which social obligations—here, those of Naxos, an uplifting Bookerite institution—demand strict conformity to a code of restrained feminine conduct. Although Helga's sphere of sacrificial race work seems far from Mimi's social world of teas, dances, and middle-class feminine idleness, the two settings share an obligatory mimicry of white bourgeois respectability, fostered through caretaking ladies whose chaste conduct and demure demeanor help signal the worthiness of the race—or of their group within the race—for national inclusion. With a sensitivity that betokens their rightful belonging to their cultivated status but a roving personal ambition that unfits them to their feminine roles, Mimi and Helga desire greater freedom to enact a greater purpose. No doubt modeled on her Fisk and Tuskegee experiences, Larsen's Naxos, as Deborah McDowell has pointed out, encourages a misplaced devotion to a mythical ideal of superior Anglo-Saxon civilization.[14]

The character of Helga thus provides us with a belated vantage from which to understand the idealized Yankee schoolmarms examined in chapter 1, for Helga is supposed to be both a product and an exemplar of their great influence in schools like Fisk and Tuskegee. From the outset, Larsen connects obligatory femininity, with its emphasis on ladylike propriety, to racial subordination, with its emphasis on racial propriety for those Negroes lucky enough to become formally educated in institutions largely funded by wealthy white northern patrons. Helga experiences this interconnection when she goes to chapel—itself a racial obligation—to hear "one of the renowned white preachers of the state" flatter Naxos conduct with "patronizing" and "insulting remarks" (*Quicksand* 2):

And he said that if all Negroes would only take a leaf out of the book of Naxos and conduct themselves in the manner of the Naxos products, there would be no race problem, because Naxos Negroes knew what was expected of them. They had good sense and they had good taste. They knew enough to stay in their places and that, said the preacher, showed good taste. He spoke of his great admiration for the Negro race, no other race in so short a time had made so much progress, but he had urgently besought them to know when and where to stop. (3)

Propriety, whether racial or feminine, means knowing when and where to stop without having to be told. If racial propriety is explicitly enforced by Jim Crow, sexual propriety is explicitly enforced by the gender codes of the early twentieth century. Larsen's point, however, is that Jim Crow enforces codes of *sexual* propriety among and between the races as much as the gender code enforces racial proprieties between and among the sexes. This dual system of sexual/racial propriety enforced by both the racial and gender codes is the internalization of the particular limits set for each group by the proper and propertied class, for themselves and those beneath them.

Revealingly, Helga's provocation at this racially condescending sermon results in her exceeding the limits of racial propriety, expressing ingratitude to a superior white patron, which in turn causes her to exceed the limits of feminine propriety. Shut away in her room, she feels first "a surge of hot anger and seething resentment" at the preacher, then hatred at the black listeners who obediently applaud the sermon (3). Her disillusion with the institution's achievement, which "she had ardently desired to share in, to be a part of this monument to one man's genius and vision" (3), leads her to a violent outburst, ominously not against those whom she disdains but against the objects in her own room:

> At last she stirred, uncertainly, but with an overpowering desire for action of some sort. . . . Next she made a quick nervous tour to the end of the long room, paused a moment before the old bow-legged secretary that held with almost articulate protest her school-teacher paraphernalia of drab books and papers. Frantically Helga Crane clutched at the lot and then flung them violently, scornfully toward the wastebasket. It received a part, allowing the rest to spill untidily over the floor. The girl smiled ironically, seeing in the mess a simile of her own earnest endeavor to inculcate knowledge into her indifferent students. (4)

In contrast to the violence that explodes in Fisher's and McKay's novels, Helga's seems aptly indirect.[15] As repressed an assault on her demure racial/sexual role as it is, this private outburst nonetheless explodes the decorum of feminine self-sacrifice: patience, selflessness, silence, physical restraint, lack of desire, and submission to authority and tedious labor without irony or scorn.

This outburst also predicts her inability to remain engaged to James Vayle, a fellow teacher, as a correlate of her refusal to bury herself in the mindless conformities of Naxos. James ironically embodies all the attributes that Helga should possess as a proper lady, but in the register of a Bookerite male disciple whose manhood is determined by his appearance of racial/sexual passivity. We can read

James's facile conformity, timidity in courtship, selfless sacrifice, and avoidance of confrontation as a sort of unmanning posture, like that of White's Dr. Kenneth Harper, or we can more precisely link it to the fluidity of gender identifications required of Bookerite achievement, as in the case of Washington himself or of Washington's successor, Moton (whom Larsen knew personally). Analogous to Congo Rose's attitude toward Jake, but much more polite and subtle, Helga finds James to be too submissive, not emotionally and intellectually forceful enough. Fearing the consequences of her own willful nonconformity, Helga thinks that she needs a man who can inspire her obedience and self-sacrifice toward a passionately directed cause. By observing the similarity between Congo Rose's masochistic desire to be beaten by her sweetman and Helga's masochistic desire to be forcefully inspired by her fiancé, we can better understand how the sexual psychology of race operates across class economies. Helga's mental masochism may be masked by the politeness of its terms: feminine self-sacrifice to a larger cause and greater man. Likewise, Rose's more brutal physical masochism masks the ways in which her desire is not merely personal but also determined by her gender and racial circumstances.

Because James Vayle does not or cannot direct Helga's energy, she associates him with her own "frigidity," a term whose sexual connotation is submerged in favor of its nonsexual denotation: "Returning to James Vayle, her thoughts took on the frigidity of complete determination. Her resolution to end her stay in Naxos would of course inevitably end her engagement to James" (7). As with Mimi's Carl, James's lack of aggressive action stemming from passionate conviction enables Helga more easily to take the initiative on her own behalf. "Frigidity" here suggests her resoluteness to act with "complete determination," not a more familiar meaning of inability to respond sexually out of nervous fear. Ironically, however, her frigid determination to act also derives from this sexual meaning—lack of passionate response. Her cold determination to leave James and Naxos results from her coldness toward him sexually. Helga's frigidity is also connected to the social background that James comes from, and which she lacks. "Negro society, she had learned, was as complicated and as rigid in its ramifications as the highest strata of white society. If you couldn't prove your ancestry and connections, you were tolerated, but you didn't 'belong'" (8). Thus, as Deborah McDowell has pointed out, the novel charts Helga's ongoing retreat from her own sexual feelings until these desires, "pent-up throughout the novel, finally explode in Helga's primitive, passionate religious conversion" ("*Changing Same*" 84–85). Her violence toward the objects in her room bespeak a repressed violence within the self that can be directed either sadistically outward, toward her male suitors, or masochistically and self-destructively inward.

In disfavor with the Vayle family and with Naxos, Helga realizes that what is expected of her is a machine-like performance of duty consonant with the values of these conformist, sexually repressed (rigid *and* frigid) institutions, the haughty blue-vein family and the high-minded uplift school. Helga sees the school as just such a machine: "This great community, she thought, was no longer a school. It had grown into a machine. It was now a show place in the black belt, exemplification of the white man's magnanimity, refutation of the black man's inefficiency" (*Quicksand* 4). The meaning of "machine" here links Du Bois's idea of corrupt patronage, discussed in chapter 4, with the idea of becoming unthinking, mechanized instruments of others' (men's) will—Helga's fear throughout the novel. Although Helga's womanhood reform would seem to be a personal matter, in actuality it is directly linked to the reform of racial institutions on which she depends for a living and a legitimate social identity. Helga is at a loss, for she wants to belong but does not want to conform; "[s]he could neither conform, nor be happy in her unconformity" (7). James's own conformity to these institutions makes him f/rigid as well. It prevents him from sweeping her off her feet, from displaying a passion that might overcome her doubts. He too quickly gives his "ready assent" to her suggestion that they postpone their marriage due to his fear of her "maladjustment" (7). Larsen is able to insinuate the familiar meaning of sexual frigidity when she has Helga consider the potential nature of James's desire and her own response to such masculine f/rigidity:

> She knew too that a something held him, a something against which he was powerless. The idea that she was in but one nameless way necessary to him filled her with a sensation amounting almost to shame. And yet his mute helplessness against that ancient appeal by which she held him pleased her and fed her vanity—gave her a feeling of power. At the same time she shrank away from it, subtly aware of possibilities she herself couldn't predict. (7–8)

Is his "nameless" desire romantic passion, or is it a savage lust repressed by their environment to a chivalrously expressed courtship?[16] Cheryl Wall points to the subtle way in which Larsen through this scene implies "an incipient realization that sexuality is political; it is 'power'" (*Women of the Harlem Renaissance* 97). Helga's vision of their romance is one of f/rigidity on both sides, he helplessly mute and powerless in the face of his repressed passion or lust, she filled with shame and shrinking from the "possibilities." At the same time, his helplessness attracts her to him because of the "feeling of power" it provides. Her pleasure in the idea of dominating him belies her own notion that what she really wants is a man who will overpower her. Wall writes that "Helga mistakenly assumes" that this realization of sexual power "is hers to wield. Actually, she is trapped by the need to repress sexuality, to assume the ornamental, acquiescent role of 'lady,' which not only Vayle but the entire Naxos community expects" (97). This scene of subtle sadomasochism, always at work to some extent when sexual frigidity is at stake, aligns Helga with both Congo Rose and Gin-head Susy in a way that represses physical violence into modes of social and mental manipulation—a kind of manipulation that comes back to haunt Helga in her relationships with prospective male lovers and female friends. What she refuses to pursue in her imagination—the power over James she might wield—she also refuses to pursue in the flesh, because she, too, has the capacity for feeling totally disempowered, in case his great passion to possess her should have the opportunity to be sexually expressed rather than chivalrously repressed into a timid, patient, self-abnegating pose of helpless desire. In other words, she resists both her power over him and, given their long engagement, the authority he, as a man, can claim over her.

We do not see an encounter with James Vayle until the latter part of the narrative. Instead of introducing us to James, as might be expected, in a scene in which Helga would inform him of her decision to leave him and Naxos, Larsen introduces another suitor in a scene of Mimi-like abandonment. Dr. Robert Anderson is a man to whom Helga *does* feel that she could submit herself totally, and one who ends up intensifying her misplaced desire for feminine/racial submission by his principled rejection of her toward the end of the novella. As principal of Naxos, Dr. Anderson represents a much more forceful, seductive (i.e., manipulative) version of black manhood than James. Like James, he is committed to racial uplift as a member of the Talented Tenth, but it is clear from the start that Dr. Anderson's demand for a lady's submission to service has a much more commanding appeal for Helga. It is in an interview with him, not with the more timid James Vayle, that she must struggle to hold to her purpose of leaving the school to find and fulfill her own ambitions.

Dr. Anderson's almost passive-aggressive wooing of Helga to stay seems to rewrite Carl's forced proposal to Mimi in *Flight,* replacing Mimi's obligation to family and maternity with Helga's racial obligation to the institution and its students. Upon her announcement that she hates the school, Dr. Anderson seems to retreat into a safe nonchalance. He asks why she hates it, his question "detached, too detached." To enact her desire to wound the imposing Dr. Anderson, Helga would have to rise to a greater level of self-control, as well as a greater knowledge of how to manipulate another whose identity as self-confident manly authority gives him an undeniable advantage. "In the girl blazed a desire to wound. There he sat, staring dreamily out of the window, blatantly unconcerned with her or her answer" (*Quicksand* 19). After further questioning, however, he tries to win her over, telling her that "[s]ervice is like clean white linen, even the tiniest speck shows," and appealing to her by "explaining, amplifying, pleading" (20). The irony of his comment about purity is that Helga's hatred for the hypocrisies of the institution derives from her own feeling of status insecurity and social impurity, her fear that she comes from an illegitimate racial/sexual line. In shame, and in anger over her shame, she confesses to being probably a bastard whose father, a gambler, deserted her mother, and then abruptly leaves the room with her decision made. Her self-righteous outburst against Naxos hypocrisies results as much from her feeling that she is not worthy to conform to their codes of gentility as from her condescension to those codes. Prior to Dr. Anderson's stating that she should stay because "[y]ou're a lady," a statement that prompts her declaration and abrupt exit (21), she had given in to his seductive pleading:

> Helga Crane was silent, feeling a mystifying yearning which sang and throbbed in her. She felt again that urge for service, not now for her people, but for this man who was talking so earnestly of his work, his plans, his hopes. An insistent need to be a part of them sprang in her. With compunction tweaking at her heart for even having entertained the notion of deserting him, she resolved not only to remain until June, but to return next year. She was shamed, yet stirred. It was not sacrifice she felt now, but actual desire to stay, and to come back next year. (20)

Helga thinks that she wants a strong man to motivate her submission, one so worthy that his mastery can justify the subordination of her own will through a sexual desire that is so bound to racial service that it rises to purity.

Brilliantly, Larsen interlinks Helga's desire for racial "service" to her desire for Dr. Anderson. Again, it is not clear to what extent her "mystifying yearning" is lust or romantic passion or racial identification, the three being as intertwined as desire and sacrifice become when she throbs to be part of "*his* work, *his* plans, *his* hopes." It seems at this moment that Helga can, like the mythical pure Yankee schoolmarm, sublimate a willful passion into selfless sacrificial service. Turning sacrifice into desire, or more precisely, desire into sacrifice, means accepting the conformity to feminine (and racial) conduct that she has already confessed to despising. Unlike James, Dr. Anderson seems to have the power to bring about this subordination to his work in the guise of *her* belonging. Leaving Naxos becomes a wife's desertion of her husband or a mother's of her children. It takes very little, however, for this feminine submission to revert to f/rigid self-determination. The unqualified assertion of her gentility, which should be taken as a compliment in the value system of Naxos and of genteel families like the Vayles, turns out to be an insult. When Helga says that she was "born in a Chicago slum," Anderson replies: "That doesn't at all matter, Miss Crane. Financial, economic circumstances can't destroy tendencies inherited from good stock. You yourself prove that!" (21). Helga's insecure pride prevents her from hearing "the import of his words" as her "angry thoughts" scurry "here and there like trapped rats" (21). In a sense, however, she *has* heard the import of his words, for if she were to stay in Naxos, she would become trapped, not the least by his seductive flattery and self-assured mastery. Refusing to be flattered, Helga takes the risk of moving on; despite a lack of resources and objectives, she chooses the risk of mobility over the risk of being trapped. Of course, this desire to flee into submission as an escape from the risks of the willful self *does* trap her in a quagmire of southern servility—feminine and racial—in the end.

Returning to her native city on the Jim Crow car, Helga realizes how alone she is, and this aloneness is accentuated by a memory of James and by the pressing reality of the railcar. She realizes that she could never have married James Vayle, even if she had remained in Naxos. "Gradually, too, there stole into her thoughts of him a curious sensation of repugnance, for which she was at a loss to account" (24). This repugnance mounts as she remembers his timid but persistent desire:

> Acute nausea rose in her as she recalled the slight quivering of his lips sometimes when her hands had unexpectedly touched his; the throbbing vein in his forehead on a gay day when they had wandered off alone across the low hills and she had allowed him frequent kisses under the shelter of some low-hanging willows. Now she shivered a little, even in the hot train, as if she had suddenly come out from a warm scented place into cool, clear air. (24)

She again becomes aware of the smells and noises and grime in the Jim Crow car, of the white man who passes through and spits into the receptacle of drinking water, of the baby crying and the soiled floor. Her desire to flee the peasant excesses of the railcar matches her desire to flee the elite constrictions of Naxos: the image of James's quivering lips, his attempt to restrain his desire, is associated with its inverse, the flagrantly crude unrestraint of the lower-class black migrants, some of them smacking their lips on fried chicken. In a sense, Larsen is exploring the missing link of the middle ground that Fisher cultivates in *Walls of Jericho*—the constitution of a medium sensibility connecting the mobile mass and the established elite in a shared sense of racial purpose. Given Helga's peculiar class situation, she would be a prime candidate for such an intermediary; but this is not to be, for the class anxiety produced by her awkward social status is exactly what causes her to react with such repugnance to both Talented Tenth sensibilities and the crudity of the abject mass.

By bringing attention to the smells and sounds on the Jim Crow car, Larsen provides another view of Charles S. Johnson's notion that one cause of racial rioting might be the smell of black working bodies offending cleaner white workers, as discussed in chapter 3. Helga's nausea is caused both by her present sensations of smelling and hearing the black migrants and by her daydreaming about the quivering lips of a Talented Tenth man. The black body's invasiveness can be expressed even when those bodies are literally passive, consenting to be seated on a Jim Crow car with all its physical, social, and sexual humiliations and offenses. Indeed, perhaps it is when the black body *is* passive, assenting to rather than confronting the color line, that racial nausea is most pronounced. The black migrants' coerced consent to such conditions makes Helga retch in self-contempt. Analogously, Helga's contempt for her rejected fiancé is also a form of self-contempt. She despises him for not being more manfully active—aggressing against racial conscriptions as well as sexual proprieties—just as she despises herself for consenting to marry such a sexually and racially passive man. In this way, Larsen demonstrates how the reform of black manhood is a matter not only of instilling racial leadership into men deprived of manhood rights/rites in larger society but also of interrogating the relationship between racial timidity and sexual passivity.

Larsen poses this question again in a different way when we witness Helga's relationship to a manly female racial reformer. In her most desperate moment in Chicago, when she has gone the round of employment agencies to meet only with arrogance and dismissal, she is referred as a suitable traveling companion and secretary for Mrs. Hayes-Rore, a race woman and widow of independent means who uses her money and time in the cause of uplift. Mrs. Hayes-Rore has managed to rise above her low circumstances by exploiting the wealth of her late husband, who passed away "hurriedly and unexpectedly and a little mysteriously, and somewhat before the whole of his suddenly acquired wealth had had time to vanish" (37). More concerned with the uplift cause than with conventional social conduct, Mrs. Hayes-Rore exploits the independence she gains from wealth and widowhood to gain a voice as a New Negro spokeswoman without having to bow to the kinds of hypocrisy and subservience that Helga's colleague, Margaret, happily accepts at Naxos. The race woman's nonconformity is indicated by her poor grooming, ill-fitting clothes, aggressive gaze, and "tart" no-nonsense personality:

> Mrs. Hayes-Rore proved to be a plump lemon-colored woman with badly straightened hair and dirty finger-nails. Her direct, penetrating gaze was somewhat formidable. Notebook in hand, she gave Helga the impression of having risen early for consultation with other harassed authorities on the race problem, and having been in conference on the subject all day. Evidently, she had had little time or thought for the careful donning of the five-years-behind-the-mode garments which covered her, and which even in their youth could hardly have fitted or suited her. She had a tart personality, and prying. (35–36)

Despite her nonconforming independence, Mrs. Hayes-Rore can hardly serve as a model for Helga, with the latter's lack of financial means and obsession with style. In fact, Mrs. Hayes-Rore helps demonstrate the limits of Helga's independence, for the young woman *does* care what others think about her in such superficial matters as appearance. A different version of feminine sacrifice, Mrs. Hayes-Rore is able to find self-fulfillment in "service to the race," but she can do so only because her service accords more closely with a masculine pose of heroic sacrifice to a cause. Unimpeded by a husband or any other man, she turns the lady's traditional role of decorous philanthropy into an imposing vocation that meshes with her direct, penetrating, formidable bearing.

On the train to New York, Mrs. Hayes-Rore attempts to gain the confidence of Helga, as she sees immediately that the young woman has a mystery in her background. So different from the kind of confidante Margaret could be, Mrs. Hayes-Rore can only relate to Helga as a cause, for she is "interested in girls." This attempt at patronage provokes the same response in Helga as Robert's attempt at flattery, pointing to the similar logic of these modes of interaction when directed at a young woman without means, kin, or male authorities to protect her. In need of the job that Mrs. Hayes-Rore is providing, and perhaps also desiring to end her isolation by opening herself to a sympathetic (and dominating) other, Helga relates the story of her family. "But as she went on, again she had that sore sensation of revolt, and again the torment which she had gone through loomed before her as something brutal and undeserved. Passionately, tearfully, incoherently, the final words tumbled from her quivering petulant lips" (39). The "quivering" lips place Helga in relation to Mrs. Hayes-Rore in the same dynamic in which James was placed in relation to Helga. Because Helga is unable to play this vulnerable, submitting role well, any potential bond between these two women is snapped as quickly as it has formed.

In both Larsen's and Thurman's novels, female friendship occupies a position analogous to that of male fraternity in Fisher's and McKay's. However, in contrast to *Walls of Jericho* and *Home to Harlem,* in which male camaraderie is silently deepened, complicated, and eroticized in order to moderate the hero's manhood and sustain his partnership with male and female others, in *Quicksand* and *Blacker the Berry,* female friendships help the heroines survive and grow only to disintegrate finally under the strain of competitive undercurrents and sexual rivalries over men. At the risk of stereotyping women's relationships with each other, Larsen and Thurman probe the underside of intimate heterosexual female attachments in order to isolate their heroines in the world and strengthen their wills to find themselves despite, or because of, their sense of self-reckoning through isolation.

Helga's relationship with Anne Grey, the sophisticated young race woman with whom she boards in Harlem, is haunted by the latter's more secure social status; similarly, Thurman's protagonist, Emma Lou Morgan, eventually finds a best friend in a more sophisticated, self-confident race woman, Gwendolyn Johnson. Both Anne and Gwendolyn are race protesters—though not so effective as Mrs. Hayes-Rore—whose constant sermonizing on race leads to friction with Helga and Emma Lou, respectively. Just as Gwendolyn can afford to be adamant about her negative attitude toward mulattos due to their color prejudice because she herself is not as dark as Emma Lou, similarly Anne can afford her hard line on the race question because of her higher status in the race—at least, in Helga's eyes. Anne "revel[s] in this orgy of protest" so much so that it distresses Helga, because Anne's obsession feeds Helga's own (48). Helga's contradictions over class identification as a form of racial failure are mirrored by Anne's contradictions over racial identification as a form of class failure. Anne obsesses over a rhetoric of black superiority while, actually, she despises the low folk as much as Helga does (see 48). Behind Anne's sophisticated self-confidence in race work lies a racial insecurity as nagging as Helga's anxieties over her social background, and this insecurity that they share, and its capacity for being provoked into violent outbursts, creates friction in their friendship instead of greater intimacy and mutual self-knowledge.

This friction is intensified when Robert Anderson, frustrated with Naxos, moves to New York to conduct social welfare work for a large manufacturer employing hundreds of Negro men. Thus, we see Larsen bringing explicitly into the urban folk novel the black male sociologist we examined in chapter 3. By having Anderson move from a Bookerite black institution to a white industry intent on disciplining its black workers with such ease, Larsen seems to be linking Washington's self-help apologetics to Du Boisian academic sociology, often perceived as its contrary. Anne's relentless protest and Robert's uplift mobility push Helga in the other direction, so that she ends up basically as contemptuous of the Harlem protesters as she had been of the Naxos conformists (52). By bringing Robert to Harlem, Larsen presents a very different use of triangulated sexual desire from Fisher and McKay, for *Quicksand* exploits the sexual triangle not to motivate greater racial consolidation and reformed gender relations but instead to demonstrate the intractable quagmire that can operate to pull down friends and lovers in a culture of sexually repressed racial oppression.

Amid the urban cynicism of the sophisticated Harlemites (to whom Anne already belongs and whom Robert quickly joins), Helga displays even greater contempt, not only of the earnest, trembling conformity of a James Vayle but also of the more aggressive Du Boisian–type race protest embodied in Anne and Robert. In other words, her initial fascination with the aggressive openness of the mass black invasion of upper Manhattan devolves into a hostility as palpable as her racial/class claustrophobia in the Jim Crow car out of Alabama. Having lost Robert to Anne, Helga begins to recognize, if not readily to admit, her desire (lust? passion? love?) for a man no longer available to her—at least, not without enacting sexual manipulation, adultery, and betrayal of a friend. Hidden in the doubling relation between Robert Anderson and James Vayle is another sexual triangle, one that even more blatantly brings out the *emotional* violence at work in Helga's racially self-destructive relation to sexual power. The racial aggression that Helga experiences before leaving Harlem gets sublimated into sexual aggression upon her return, just as sexual frustration at Naxos was expressed as racial claustrophobia.

As Hortense Thornton remarks, upon returning to Harlem from Copenhagen "Helga assumes a new role of aggressor, or manipulator of events" ("Sexism as Quagmire" 299). After Anne and Robert's marriage, Helga encounters James, who has come to New York on business for Naxos. Unchanged except that he has been promoted to an assistant principal of the school, James is no match for an even more jaded Helga, who angers him with her flaunted knowledge of the cross-racial entanglements of the smart set at an integrated party. As she argues against his simplistic notion that people like them are obligated to marry and produce children for the good of the race, he becomes more agitated. "Marriage—that means children, to me," she says flippantly, reminding him that a woman's burden in marriage is not the same as a man's. "And why add more suffering to the world? Why add any more unwanted, tortured Negroes to America? Why *do* Negroes have children? Surely it must be sinful" (*Quicksand* 103). Playing with what she takes to be James's naïveté, Helga provokes him to venture all in a clumsy marriage proposal that takes her by surprise. Later, she literally stumbles into Robert's arms and, without speaking, they kiss passionately. "She fought against him with all her might. Then, strangely, all power seemed to ebb away, and a long-hidden, half-understood desire welled up in her with the suddenness of a dream" (104). Unattainable, Robert becomes most desirable to her, just as she comes to yearn for black Harlem only after she has abandoned it for white Copenhagen.

Bringing home the contrast between James and Robert in Helga's mind, Larsen exposes the treachery of Helga's desire as the negotiation of the sexual power that she fears others have over her, and that she can have over others. Her treatment of James comes back to haunt her when she offers herself to Robert and he refuses. She proves herself willing to risk the opprobrium of Harlem society, but she underestimates Robert's kinship to James, both men being bound to a principle of heterosexual conformity that seems a trap to her:

> She had ruined everything. Ruined it because she had been so silly as to close her eyes to all indications that pointed to the fact that no matter what the intensity of his feelings or desires might be, he was not the sort of man who would for any reason give up one particle of his own good opinion of himself. Not even for her. Not even though he knew that she had wanted so terribly something special from him. (108)

Though lacking the physical manifestations of sadomasochistic violence present in Fisher's and McKay's characters, Helga is plagued by the violence that frequently lurks in the repression of intense passion. "For days, for weeks, voluptuous visions had haunted her. Desire had burned in her flesh with uncontrollable violence. The wish to give herself had been so intense that Dr. Anderson's surprising, trivial apology loomed as a direct refusal of the offering" (109). She now feels victimized by Robert as the result of her inopportune, naive venture in the same way that James must feel victimized by her. She is as green as James in matters of the heart and libido. The disastrous psychic impact of these double triangulations leads her to stereotypical hysteria, a total loss of faith in her own self-will as a woman, a state that finally causes her to submit to a man whose crude lowliness and apparent sexual appetite make him the polar opposite of painfully chivalrous James and annoyingly coy Robert.

Helga punishes herself by giving in to the first seemingly masterful man she comes across, the Reverend Mr. Pleasant Green, a visiting preacher from a tiny Alabama town where he pastors "a scattered and primitive flock" (118). More directly and paradoxically, preacher Green is foil to the suitor who pursues her in Copenhagen, Axel Olsen, a bohemian painter from one of Denmark's most aristocratic families and thus one whom Helga's Danish aunt and uncle deem a splendid catch. Whereas Green turns her into a subservient housewife and baby machine in the "primitive" Alabama backwoods, painter Olsen turns her into an exotic work of bohemian art. In the end, these two men—so seemingly opposite socially, culturally, and temperamentally—are the same, or have the same effect on her. When Axel proposes to her, he does so in the habit of a ruling male aristocrat who is used to getting what he wants. In the alienating whiteness of the Copenhagen elite, she realizes that the form of what he says is not the substance of what he wants. Insightfully, Larsen positions Helga in a place that she has previously imagined as gratifying, the quintessence of style, grace, and desire beyond race. She discovers, however, the racial trap of this sexual category, as she realizes the travesty of being desired for her blackness is as sexually demeaning as being despised for it.

Helga rejects Olsen only to fall into the arms of preacher Green after the disastrous episodes with James and Robert. As she stumbles into a storefront church, after literally being "tossed . . . into the swollen gutter" by a storm (110), she is mistaken by the congregation for a "scarlet 'oman," a "pore los' Jezebel" (112). The "Bacchic vehemence" of the congregation over having found a fallen woman to save is so overwhelming to Helga in her hysteria that she finds it easy to get lost in the role that they project onto her. She submits to the "echo of the weird orgy" resounding within her and feels "possessed by the same madness" (113). The sexual connotations of this scene of resignation and self-loss as salvation anticipate her submission to the preacher, who walks her home after the service. "Larsen dramatizes the fine line between sexual and religious ecstasy, often said to be characteristic of fundamentalist religious sects," McDowell writes, "further underscoring the ambiguity of Helga's motives in her marriage to the Rev. Green."[17]

Like Axel, Green is used to getting what he wants, a characteristic that at first enables Helga to believe she can settle down to a life of simple service committed to *his* work. Nonetheless, despite herself she remains willful, desiring something that has nothing to do with preacher Green's sense of his calling; she wants to lift the people up by teaching them about beauty, that is, by civilizing them. Failing to see that she is doing to them what Axel Olsen attempted with her, she fantasizes a life of racial service in terms of her ability to transform her husband's backwoods parishioners and their environment into aestheticized objects worthy of her labor:

> Her young joy and zest for the uplifting of her fellow men came back to her. She meant to subdue the cleanly scrubbed ugliness of her own surroundings to soft inoffensive beauty, and to help the other women to do likewise. Too, she would help them with their clothes, tactfully point out that sunbonnets, no matter how gay, and aprons, no matter how frilly, were not quite the proper things for Sunday church wear. . . . She visualized herself instructing the children, who seemed most of the time to run wild, in ways of gentler deportment. (119)

Trying to turn Washington's cleanly scrubbed humble people of the earth into more sophisticated beings "according to her ideas of beauty" (119), Helga embarks on a futile enterprise that makes Washington's hygiene project look sanely egalitarian. Bringing her back to rural Alabama where she started, only this time in a much lowlier position, the narrative intensifies her commitment to racial uplift while ironically creating an even greater disparity between her sense of propriety and the actual conditions in which she finds herself. What she fails to recognize is that her married state is not a secure place from which to enact such racial reform.

Helga fails to learn the lesson that Chesnutt's Uncle Wellington comes to understand when he is forced to return south to his former-slave wife. To reform the black peasants under her husband's pastoral care, Helga would beforehand or simultaneously have to reform her husband as well. An aristocrat among his flock, the Reverend Green has his pick of the women, who gladly tend to his needs when Helga, in her frigidity, finds it impossible to fulfill his voracious sexual appetite. Burdened with the menial obligations of a rural pastor's wife and with relentless childbirthing and childrearing, Helga's vision of religious and racial duty through feminine submission turns out to be not that different from the nightmare of being subjected to the lascivious claims of masculine domination anticipated from Axel Olsen. Whereas Axel's name symbolizes the cold, pale, heartless, polished machinations of high European culture, the Reverend Mr. Pleasant Green's name indicates the idyllic romance of happy green pastures that supposedly awaits Helga in rural Alabama.[18] Of course, the name is ironic. Instead of the imposing phallic black earth mother that Park fantasized when he saw a "primitive" farmer's wife in backwoods Alabama, Helga shrivels into a frail, pale lady, exhausted by housework, birthing labor, and the repugnant duties of sexual intercourse with her coarse, lusty husband.

In the final paragraphs, Helga fantasizes fleeing yet again, but this time flight seems impossible: "And hardly had she left her bed and become able to walk again without pain, hardly had the children returned from the homes of the neighbors, when she began to have her fifth child" (135). Unlike Mimi, whose return to the folk leaves us with the hope of a nonconforming middle-class African American woman's ability to combine sexual freedom and racial consolidation, attendant upon self-knowledge and risky experience, Helga seems to symbolize the impossible dilemmas such a woman faces regardless of the race, status, or temperament of the man who promises her self-fulfillment. "The novel closes with a representation of 'the folk,'" Carby writes, "but they were not represented as a positive alternative to the black urban elite" (*Reconstructing Womanhood* 174). And in contrast to the utopian closures of heterosexual reform administered by Fisher and McKay, Larsen seems to suggest that as long as the high-minded colored heroine is boxed in by the demands of heterosexual femininity, she will find herself bogged down in the sexual quicksand of unbearable racial burdens. If the novel offers no solution for integrating positive desire with black middle-class femininity, it also challenges the New Negro notion that black manhood can be reformed and thus help transform the whole of the race through its reformation.

Same-Sexuality, Sadomasochism, and Feminine Rebellion in Thurman's *Blacker the Berry*

In creating his heroine, Emma Lou Morgan, Wallace Thurman seems to make a point similar to Larsen's, but by inverting the tragic mulatta tradition that she exploits and revises. Emma Lou has all the characteristics of a classic mulatta heroine—status, education, good family background, sophistication, ambition, chastity—except for the key attribute of light skin color and thus the perception of beauty among the black middle class. Thurman's novel also engages with earlier narratives of color flight and racial urban mobility in the African American tradition—especially Johnson's *Autobiography of an Ex-Coloured Man* and White's *Flight*—as well as with the two manly urban folk novels published only one year before, *Walls of Jericho* and *Home to Harlem*. Thurman crosses over the gender line to stage the psychic development of a female protagonist who struggles not only with her dark color but also with gender discriminations and the sexual entanglements of racial dissension. By placing the emphasis on color *within* the race, Thurman amplifies the themes of racial consolidation and sexual rivalry, same-gender friendship and sexuality, and internecine racial warfare operating in the novels of his contemporaries. Because Thurman is rather publicly a queer-identified man, attending to his gender crossing and his use of same-sexual desire in *Blacker the Berry* opens up an especially fertile exploration of the uses of black sexual diversity. Like Thurman himself, Emma Lou is born and raised in the western United States (Boise, Idaho), moves to Los Angeles to attend the University of Southern California (USC) without completing her degree, and then makes the trek to Harlem in search of like-minded others. But I am more interested here in Thurman's cross-gender revision of urban folk narrative as cultural critique of the varieties of black manhood than in the precise implications of any biographical resonances between his heroine and himself.[19]

Following the lead of African American women novelists especially, Thurman examines how an aesthetics of color functions in the racial politics of sexual discrimination for middle-class women whose ability is overshadowed by questions of their sexual attractiveness and conformity. In many New Negro texts, especially by men, diversity of color is celebrated as an index of the New Negro's arrival into urban civilization (whether Harlem or Chicago, or even James Weldon Johnson's celebration of the diverse colors of women at Atlanta University in *Along This Way*). Although the burden of color easily takes on a negative slant when these texts explore the binary of black versus white, or the upsetting of this binary in racial passing, the varieties of colors to be found on a city street come to represent the self-confidence, freedom, and promise of a manly New Negro urbanity. As we have glimpsed in Van Vechten, Johnson, and others, but as is most self-consciously evident in novels by the two most prominent women writers of the 1920s, Larsen and Fauset, the choice of color in a black person's (especially a black woman's) clothing and accessories codes her relation not only to urbane sophistication but also to the purifying chastity of European civilization, as opposed to the primitive lewdness of African heritage. When Larsen's Helga attempts to flee racial and sexual discrimination by going to Copenhagen, she allows her Danish aunt and uncle to refashion her according to their dream of blackness. Helga has trained herself to wear dark, dull colors, recognizing that flashy clothes and jewelry are indexes for both sexual transgression and racial typecasting in women. When Helga has to decide what to wear to tea, she restrains her desire for color, "glancing at her aunt's dark purple dress and bringing forth a severely plain blue *crepe* frock":

> "Too sober," pronounced Fru Dahl. "Haven't you something lively, something bright?"
>
> And, noting Helga's puzzled glance at her own subdued costume, she explained laughingly: "Oh, I'm an old married lady, and a Dane. But you, you're young. And you're a foreigner, and different. You must have bright things to set off the color of your lovely brown skin. Striking things, exotic things. You must make an impression." (*Quicksand* 68)

At first Helga resists: "Left alone, Helga began to wonder. She was dubious, too, and not a little resentful. Certainly she loved color with a passion that perhaps only Negroes and Gypsies know. But she had a deep faith in the perfection of her own taste, and no mind to be bedecked in flaunting flashy things" (69). Seduced by the attention and by her own "primitive" love of color, however, Helga gives in, even though she "felt like a veritable savage" (69). When Helga returns to Harlem after having grown frustrated over the European fascination with her, a sign of her seeming self-confidence and self-development is that she continues to wear these flashy colors in New York.

Likewise, in Fauset's *There Is Confusion*, Joanna Marshall's willingness to break racial boundaries in claiming her own talent as a diva is signaled by the bold colors she wears onstage and off, clothes designed by her sister Sylvia, who scorns the so-called sophisticated look—dull gray and brown shades—dictated by blue-veined mulatta matrons copying the blueblood white society women (see *There Is Confusion* 225). "Isn't she a genius?" Joanna says about her sister. "Through me she certainly is teaching these colored people how to dress. We will not wear these conventional colors—grays, taupe, beige. . . . They're all right for these palefaces. But colored people need color, life, vividness" (132). The burden of aesthetics that bears down more heavily on women than on men places a different emphasis on the meaning of color diversity in these novels. Or as Ann E. Hostetler phrases it in her discussion of *Quicksand*, "the emphasis on color advances a thematics of race" intersecting with gender.[20] "Although Helga begins to see past the monotone construction of race to a vision of subtly colored multiplicity" when she comes into a Harlem jazz club, Hostetler writes, "she refuses to reflect on or interpret her experience, for she is again preparing to 'fly'" ("Aesthetics of Race and Gender" 41). For Helga, this swirl of color represents sexual danger more than the creative potential of alternative modes of sexual expression. She experiences a characteristic vertigo: "For a moment everything seems to be spinning round; even she felt that she was circling aimlessly (*Quicksand* 58–59), as though swirling in the emotional quicksand that seems to swallow her by the end. Instead of representing the broad range of colored female beauties accompanying the greater license and mixed population in an urban environment, in these women's novels the choice of color more frequently indicates the attempt to fashion a meaningful life of romance and vocation not hemmed in by predetermined limitations of racialized femininity.

In *Blacker the Berry*, color aesthetics as a burden of sexual discrimination limits Emma Lou's options from the outset, partly because of its impact on her self-concept. The narrative starts with a self-conscious donning of her white robe at her high school graduation ceremony:

> Why had she allowed them to place her in the center of the first row, and why had they insisted upon her dressing entirely in white so that surrounded as she was by similarly attired pale-faced fellow graduates she resembled, not at all remotely, that comic picture her Uncle Joe had hung in his bedroom? The picture wherein the black, kinky head of a little red-lipped pickaninny lay like a fly in a pan of milk amid a white expanse of bedclothes. (4)

Emma Lou's obsessive fear of being perceived—of *being*—a pickaninny, rather than the legitimate progeny of high-minded blue-veins, is similar to Helga's fear of being a mulatta bastard in a respectable white family. Without this class complex, Emma Lou could more tolerably confront the limitations that society imposes on her as a result of color. Thurman is interested, however, in exploring Emma Lou's flight from herself, the complicated denials of her own desire, which result in her repeated submission to masculine coercion—that is, in her masochistic tendencies—as well as in her eventual attempt to manipulate sexually men whose color or class makes them putatively her inferior. Like the mental manipulation and emotional violence lurking in the friendships and heterosexual relationships of *Quicksand*, Emma Lou's relationships repeatedly trap her in an extreme manifestation of heterosexual feminine submission until, in the end, she hits bottom, where she finds that she can reassemble herself only after refusing—at least temporarily—the temptations of heterosexual romance. By examining the men whom Emma Lou attempts to manipulate in order to make space for some self-determination of her own gender/racial identity, we can see how Thurman, like Larsen, challenges the New Negro notion that the progress of the whole race will result from the reform of individual men as proper leaders of the race.

The psychic disequilibrium created in Emma Lou by her color complex makes her vulnerable to a series of imbalanced sexual relationships that restrict her sexuality to a norm as suffocating as Helga's marriage to preacher Green. While attending university in Los Angeles for one year, she discovers that color intolerance is not limited to provincial Boise. Dashed in her expectations of finding a more color-tolerant environment in the leading West Coast city, she finds herself subjected to ridicule, dismissal, and flagrant scorn by the young men of the university. It is only among the more marginalized lower middle class that she finds men willing to date her, but she has no desire for them. In her condescending treatment of Hazel Mason—a dark loud girl from the rural South whose father has struck oil and thus been able to send her to university—Emma Lou asserts her own affiliation with those who oppress her. Even more pointed than the obvious hypocrisy of her attitude, the psychic mechanisms whereby female friendships can be constituted through masculine domination are revealed in Thurman's narrative. Thurman emphasizes how relationships among the college women, whose role is largely defined by the men they catch, can be subject to the desires of the college men:

> It was not the girls in the school who were prejudiced—they had no reason to be, but they knew full well that the boys with whom they wished to associate, their future husbands, could not tolerate a dark girl unless she had, like Verne, many things to compensate for her dark skin. Thus they did not encourage a friendship with some one whom they knew didn't belong. (48)

This scene rewrites and unwrites the scenario celebrated by James Weldon Johnson's autobiography, where he peruses the various colors of black women at Atlanta University as a signal of the cosmopolitanism awaiting within the race. For Thurman, color within the race, too, has its vicious sexual hierarchy, and one that enables gender coercion in no less a way than the sexual strictures of color segregation in the Jim Crow regime.

Scarred by her experience at USC, Emma Lou, upon returning home for summer recess, takes up with Weldon Taylor, a dark brown medical student from the East who has come west to make money to complete his schooling. Thurman explores the risk that Emma Lou is willing to take when she has sex with Weldon on their first meeting, under the romantic spell of a summer picnic:

> She loved this man. She had submitted herself to him, had gladly suffered momentary physical pain in order to be introduced into a new and incomparably satisfying paradise.
>
> Not for one moment did Emma Lou consider regretting the loss of her virtue, not once did any of her mother's and grandmother's warnings and solicitations revive themselves and cause her conscience to plague her. She had finally found herself a mate; she had finally come to know the man she should love. (51–52)

Setting a pattern for later relationships, Emma Lou is oblivious to the sexual uses she is being put to by Weldon. He has decided to give up medical school to make a living as a Pullman porter, for through his experience with Emma Lou and other women, he has discovered the easy pickings in the towns he travels through for his work. Even after she realizes that she has been used, she does not understand that her own color has not played a factor in his sexual exploitation: "Emma Lou did not understand that Weldon was just a selfish normal man and not a color prejudiced one, at least not while he was resident in a community where the girls were few, and there were none of his college friends about to tease him for liking 'dark meat'" (57). In fact, it is Emma Lou who has been more concerned with *his* color, deciding that she can love him despite the fact that his skin is dark brown (50).

Thus, Emma Lou's pattern of feminine subordination necessarily induces its incipient opposite, a desire to dominate those dark or otherwise unworthy men whose attraction for her seems stronger than hers for them. The varieties of sexual choices celebrated as the license of an urban mobility in the manly tales of Fisher and McKay become for Thurman's heroine, as for Larsen's Helga and Fauset's Maggie, a self-destructive bent. The sadomasochism evident in relationships like those between Jake and Rose, Zeddy and Susy, or, more subtly, Shine and various women before Linda becomes a more deeply sinister mode of sexual (self-)mutilation for the women in these heroine-focused novels.

Thurman continues the investigation of the East/West axis of black migration that we examined in the texts of earlier chapters. Like the autobiographical narrator of Gordon's *Born to Be,* Emma Lou searches for self-determination and social empowerment beyond color by seeking the supposedly more sophisticated seats of power in the East, the home of the New Negro, only to discover that color typecasting is a *national,* rather than merely a regional, preoccupation. Thus, Thurman's west-to-east axis can also serve as a critique of Gordon's celebration of the notion of a raceless West. By fleeing eastward, his heroine calls into question not only the American ideal of Manifest Destiny but also the African American desire to exploit migration as a way of escaping racial strictures. At the beginning of the novel, Thurman satirically points out how pioneers took their color-class snobbery with them onto the western frontier. Similarly, Emma Lou takes her color/gender insecurities with her to New York. Having made her way to the East, supposedly "where life was more cosmopolitan and people were more civilized" (58), Emma Lou repeats the naive expectations she had experienced in moving from Boise to Los Angeles. As with Helga, the repetitiveness of these movements helps emphasize how New Negro racial mobility itself can create a false sense of progress, for both men and women.

Almost as revenge for her treatment at the hands of Weldon, she immediately takes up with a dark-skinned man whom she does not love, John, in order to take pleasure in punishing him. She tells him immediately after sex that she does not want to see him again. "Mischievously, she wished now that she could have seen the expression on his face, when, after seeming moments of mutual ecstasy, she had made this cold, manifesto-like announcement. But the room had been dark, and so was John. Ugh!" (64). The sadism that creeps into her relationship with John gives Emma Lou a false sense of being more experienced, more sophisticated, more cynical than John, and thus of being in control of the sexual situation. Control, however, is a tricky thing in a sexually rigged society where men tend to have the upper hand in even the most fleeting sexual exchange. Immediately after taking pleasure in punishing John sexually, Emma Lou experiences a slight panic over money, which has supposedly been absent from the sexual exchange either as the respectable idea of marriage or as the unrespectable prospect of prostitution. "She had only thirty-five dollars left in the bank, and, unless it was replenished, she might have to rescind her avowals to John in order to get her room rent paid" (65).

Emma Lou's financial vulnerability necessarily brings money back into the lop-sided equation, but in such a way that *she* is the one potentially dependent on John, not the other way around. Her intention to use John sexually to reap some financial security places her unknowingly in a prostituted position. Innocently, she would choose to become a proto-whore in order to avoid becoming wife to a man whose color and working-class status she abhors. Of course, to marry John for the sake of financial security would place her in no less a condition of proto-prostitu-tion. The fact is that Emma Lou is not in control, even after she has exploited John for crucial knowledge of urban life as much as for sex: "[H]e had attempted to give her all the 'inside dope' on Harlem, had told her of the 'rent parties,' of the 'num-bers,' of 'hot' men, of 'sweetbacks,' and other local phenomena" (89). Emma Lou erroneously believes that her class status protects her from these putatively unre-spectable "local phenomena." She can thus exploit John sexually without realizing that she has already initiated herself into these sociosexual practices, which are so disparaged by the dickties and white dominant society that she desires to emulate.

Emma Lou soon enough finds herself deeply invested—emotionally and eco-nomically—in such deviant sexual practices, even as she continues to deny it to herself. But in her relationship with Alva, she is the one being used for financial se-curity. She is attracted to Alva partly because of his "exotic" look (his "mother had been an American mulatto, his father a Filipino" [97]) and partly because of his so-phisticated ways. His golden skin, self-assured ways, "oval" face, and "features more oriental than Negroid" (97) together seduce her into a sweetbacking experi-ence with him. As his blue-vein Boston roommate, Braxton, makes clear, Emma Lou is totally unacceptable, but once Alva indicates that he is seeing her for one reason only, Braxton stops his teasing. Using Emma Lou to support his alcoholism and aversion to hard labor, Alva seems to be Thurman's indictment of the way of life that McKay represents as a form of manly race resistance. The sweetbacking life can easily be romanticized as a mode of resistance to humiliating conditions of dis-employment among black men, and thus as an alternative progressive sexual-eco-nomic arrangement within urban black communities. But as we see clearly in Thur-man's novel, sweetbacking raises serious questions about an economic-sexual sys-tem in which black women can be doubly exploited, first through the limitations of domestic labor enforced by dominant society and then by sweetbacking men within black communities.

Thurman's indictment comes, however, not so much in simple moral judg-ment of Alva, who is tragically trapped in his own self-destructive bent stemming from racial and sexual oppressions, as an identification of the kinds of oppres-sions afflicting Emma Lou's status as a dark-skinned character trapped in a plot historically designed for mulatta heroines. If Emma Lou is a mulatta character in a dark-skinned woman's body, then Alva is the underside of Fisher's and McKay's integrated, benign portrayals of manly mobility (sexual and geographic) and male same-sexuality. From Thurman's own experience he understands the sinister en-trapment, the deeply embedded taboos that stigmatize nontraditional sexual desires. Having himself been entrapped while enacting such sexual practices, having himself attempted to use the heterosexual structure of marriage to overcome the social stigma of homosexuality, Thurman might be less prone to romanticize sexual deviance as a complement to or supplement of a reconstituted urban manhood. In his later novel, *Infants of the Spring,* he explores more directly the psychic entrapments of the stigma against same-sexuality among a bohemian enclave who seem to be above society's irrational sexual prejudices, but in *Blacker the Berry,* he interestingly opts to explore a similar dynamic in the risks attending the supposed virtues of feminine innocence. Rather than seeing Thurman's treatment of sexual deviance as an indictment of the practices themselves, we should understand that he is attempting to depict realistically the dangers cast onto such deviance, and thus the dangers they truly pose in the mind of a young woman whose character has been informed and deformed by the dominant sexual ideology of race.

Clinging to this racial ideology of sexual chastity even after her sexual knowledge with Weldon and John, Emma Lou projects onto Alva a sort of chivalry. Because in the dominant racial/sexual system she does not have access to the purest form of sexual chastity, which is saved for an idealized notion of upper-class white femininity, Emma Lou projects onto Alva this masculine ideal of sexual high-mindedness wed to sexual experience. Emma Lou desires in her mulatto man this mixture of macho protection, courtesy, solicitousness, and fidelity enhanced by sexual sophistication because she believes that such a man attracted to her reflects back onto her this sexual attractiveness as a feminine object of desire:

> Emma Lou had never met any one in her life who was as loving and kind to her as Alva. He seemed to anticipate her every mood and desire, and he was the most soothing and satisfying person with whom she had ever come into contact. He seldom riled her—seldom ruffled her feelings. He seemed to give in to her on every occasion, and was the most chivalrous escort imaginable. He was always courteous, polite and thoughtful of her comfort. (159)

Alva appears to be a lower-class replica of Larsen's chivalrous James Vayle, but with the added advantage of a more forthright sexual passion. Alva fulfills the need that Emma Lou wrongly believes she possesses for a sexual patron, a man who will put her on a pedestal while requiring nothing in return.

We realize here how much the acts of cross-racial patronage examined in Part 2 have in common with notions of chivalry as a system that makes upper-class men proper patrons of chaste womanhood. Both Larsen and Thurman remind us that racial patronage—the pretensions of uplift reform—is intricately linked to sexual patronage. Insightfully, however, Thurman makes Emma Lou a foil to Helga. Whereas Helga despises the hypocrisy of this sort of patronizing race uplift and condescending male chivalry, Emma Lou thinks that she desires both, because supposedly they put the lie to her being unattractive and thus unsuitable as a proper woman of a leading race man. Whereas Helga thinks she desires a forceful man who will direct and subject her willful desire to a higher purpose, Emma Lou thinks that she desires a polite, attentive, self-abnegating man who will submit his desire to her in a conventional act of romantic fealty. Of course, neither woman wants either of these options, but their blindness to other options results from how effectively they—and their male suitors—have been shut off from reconstructing their relationships toward other possibilities. Just as Helga's marriage turns out to be a nightmare version of her idealized bond, so Emma Lou's ideal relationship turns out ironically to be a snare of masculine tyranny. Like Axel Olsen's chivalrous suggestion of Helga's predisposition to be sexually bartered, Alva's chivalry assumes his sexual superiority. In effect, he assumes that he can continue to dupe her into believing that he is giving her what she wants while, actually, he is getting most what he wants from her.

Not only does the successful operation of chivalry depend on the deceptive submergence of the man's dominance in rituals of politesse, but the successful operation of sweetbacking can depend on the fantasy that the man is simply giving the woman what she wants by reversing the traditional roles of provider and sexual object. Alva is not Emma Lou's patron, in any sense of that word. She, in fact, is the paying customer:

> As yet she had been unable to become angry with him. Alva never argued or protested unduly. Although Emma Lou didn't realize it, he used more subtle methods. His means of remaining master of all situations were both tactful and sophisticated; for example, Emma Lou never realized just how she had first begun giving him money. Surely he hadn't asked her for it. It had just seemed the natural thing to do after a while, and she had done it, willingly and without question. The ethical side of their relationship never worried her. She was content and she was happy—at least she was in possession of something that seemed to bring her happiness. (159–160)

Ironically, Alva's behavior assumes the qualities associated with kept women, while Emma Lou begins to behave like a jealous male lover unable to keep the woman he pays to possess. Such a simple sexual inversion, however, is not possible. Although Alva can accrue the benefits of a kept woman along with his gender privilege of sexual supremacy in the relationship, Emma Lou does not accrue any benefit from being the one with the purse strings. Although Emma Lou is paying for Alva's sexual expertise, she is receiving neither the male partner's patronizing guardianship (chivalry) nor his sexual subordination (sweetbacking) in return.

Like McKay, Thurman is interested in the ethics of these alternative relationships, but, less optimistic than his precursor, he cannot see his way clear to the utopian potential residing in mobility through these experiences. Instead, these relationships seem as prone to the negative consequences of sexual inequality as conventional marriage, given the manipulative fantasies that can reside as much in sexual inversions as in sexual conformities. Thurman brings this point home when he has Emma Lou begin to want the legitimacy of a conventional bond. "Once she had suggested marriage, and had been shocked when Alva told her that to him the marriage ceremony seemed a waste of time. He had already been married twice, and he hadn't even bothered to obtain a divorce from his first wife before acquiring number two" (160). Intuitively, Emma Lou recognizes that marriage, with all its inequalities, *can* be a sort of protection for the woman, at least assuring a semblance or modicum of clearly set legal boundaries, even if giving the male the upper hand legally, socially, and psychically. Alva's suave dismissal of her innocent proposal fools her into thinking that his sophistication enhances him as a good catch. In the end, she is in the worst possible situation without knowing it yet, having most of the disadvantages of conventional marriage with none of the advantages that sweetbacking might give to the woman.

Alva's decadence, degeneracy, and incipient deviance are suggested by his attempt to impress Emma Lou by introducing her to his bohemian acquaintances in the hope of retaining his sweetbacking power over her. Erroneously, he thinks she will be impressed by these New Negro Renaissance artists, who talk about the race problem boldly in front of whites and make outrageous statements for the sake of ultrasophisticated, *outré* argument. It is only after she has discovered that Alva is still seeing another woman, Geraldine, that she determines to give him up for good. As she begins to develop closer ties with the right set after getting a job as a teacher and meeting Gwendolyn Johnson, she finds herself sinking not into degeneracy but into a dull respectability, dating a high-yellow college man, Benson Brown, who has every intention of marrying her and going to work to support her. "At last she had met the 'right sort of people' and found them to be quite wrong" (208). Given the choice between Benson's dull respectability and Alva's unrespectable decadence, she decides to choose the latter. Ironically, as Emma Lou has been discovering her dissatisfaction with a respectable life among the "right sort of people," and even her disappointing attractiveness to the high-yellow Benson—who unfortunately also happens to be quite ugly and dull—Alva has been discovering the hardships of virtual marriage and fatherhood. Not legally married to Geraldine, he nonetheless finds himself in an obligated bond that simulates marriage. Through the Alva-Geraldine subplot, Thurman is able to redirect the tendency of urban folk fiction to repress the question of children and child raising. Although children are thoroughly missing in the novels of Van Vechten, Fisher, and McKay, the heroine-based novels at least raise the specter of children as a complicating factor for urban mobility, sexual independence, and race uplift.

Thurman's intervention in the Alva-Geraldine subplot intensifies the role that pregnancy and children play in White's *Flight,* in which the child is disposed of while Mimi rises to fame and fortune, and in Larsen's *Quicksand,* in which the quick production of four children and a fifth pregnancy serves to confirm the heroine's tragic immobility among the abject folk in the final pages. After Geraldine gives birth to Alva Jr., she moves in with Alva and they settle down to domestic obligations, or at least to the semblance of such. Even before the birth, the violence implicit in the relationship between Alva and Geraldine is potentially transferred onto the fetus. Upon Geraldine's first telling him of her pregnancy, Alva responds: "'But,' he began after a moment, 'can't you—can't you . . . ?' 'I've tried everything and now it's too late. There's nothing to do but have it'" (187). The cutting omission of Alva's ellipses symbolizes the fact that in 1929, abortion is both illegal and socially viewed as a form of murder—infanticide. Geraldine's cryptic "everything" also refers to a whole range of possible enactments of violence against the fetus, and necessarily also against herself, such as poisoning, illegal operations in dark unclean rooms, enforced miscarriage, and other practices dangerously available to women in a system that outlaws abortion. Likewise, Geraldine's "nothing" represents the blank emptiness of a future tying both of them to an expensive, unwanted child, who will make her employment difficult and his more necessary.

Adding injury to this nothingness, the baby is born a "sickly, little 'ball of tainted suet,' as Alva calls it. It had a shrunken left arm and a deformed left foot. . . . Alva declared that it looked like an idiot" (198–199). Alva and Geraldine's alienation from "it" is indicated by this deformity. Ironically, the putative beauty that Emma Lou sees in the light skin color of both parents becomes in the offspring a sign of monstrosity for the parents themselves. Geraldine's mother gives a pointed, predictable interpretation to the baby's idiocy and deformity: had the parents "not lived in sin, this would not be. Had they married and lived respectably, God would not have punished them in this manner. According to her, the mere possession of a marriage license and an official religious sanction of their mating would have assured them of a bouncing, healthy, normal child" (199–200). The novel does not confirm this "pious" logic, in fact mildly satirizing it; nonetheless, its power operates on Geraldine: "There was no denying to her that had she mated with some one else, she might have given birth to a normal child" (199). Thurman is insinuating here the "scientific" findings of his era concerning "mongolism," the idea of defective genealogy resulting from the mixture of races and resulting in regressive offspring that putatively looks like ethnic Mongolians (the racist derivation of "mongoloid" for those with Downs syndrome), as examined in Van Vecthen's playful racial reversions in chapter 5. What Emma Lou appreciates in Alva's Asiatic eyes and "oval" face in the offspring becomes monstrous to Alva, Geraldine, and her "pious" mother:

> The baby now a year old was assuredly an idiot. It neither talked nor walked. Its head had grown out of all proportion to its body, and Geraldine felt that she could have stood its shrivelled arm and deformed foot, had it not been for its insanely large and vacant eyes which seemed never to close, and for the thick grinning lips, which always remained half open and through which came no translatable sounds. (199)

Through these subtle references to a potential third race, the Asiatic, as a way of interrupting the binary logic of black/white, light skin/dark skin, Thurman ironically also undercuts the kind of racial triangulation practiced by New Negro writers such as Chesnutt, Du Bois, Pickens, Wells, and others. Instead of the Asiatic serving as a hinge outside the black/white binary to leverage a new perspective and practice of race, Thurman's novel demonstrates how the racism operating against the intermediating race only intensifies the racism operating against and within a black identity. The category of the Asiatic can do nothing to salvage the bottom status of blackness, for the same racist logic operates to construct both identities as inferior. As the "parchment gray conquered the yellow in his skin and gave him a death-like pallor" (200), Alva begins to look like the "suet" color of his baby, both being overcome by the "mongolism" of their regressed circumstances. Thurman makes it clear, however, that it is not racial biology at work here but socially oppressive circumstances and the actions that result from them. Alva's alcoholism and carousing debilitate him and turn him into a walking corpse, and once Emma Lou takes over care of the baby—oiling, nursing, and exercising him according to the doctor's orders—Alva Jr. begins to take on a much more healthy tone and stature.

The virtual marriage created by this child dooms the relationship between Alva and Geraldine, as it brings out the worst desire for flight in each. From the outset, "Geraldine had a struggle with herself, trying to keep from smothering it [the baby]. She couldn't see why such a monstrosity should live" (199). Alva becomes more footloose, staying away from home, quitting work and lying about it, and, as we discover later, entering into hustling relationships with dissipated young queers. The only option in ridding themselves of Alva Jr. is one neither has the courage to do alone (201). Both of them start devising ways to flee and to abandon the other with care of the child—a feat Geraldine manages before Alva. Thus, Thurman interjects into the sexual violence and footloose mobility of urban folk fiction this idea of the degeneration of abuse, as the violence that deforms a sexual relationship is necessarily transferred to abuse of its progeny, and as the prospect of flight takes on the implications of abusive neglect.

After two years of dull respectability, Emma Lou returns to Alva, committing herself to taking care not only of him but also of the deformed baby that he and Geraldine have produced. Emma Lou's "love" for Alva, so infuriating to Gwendolyn that it ends their friendship, causes her to submit to his drunkenness, carousing, inattention, and other forms of disrespect common in an abusive relationship. In effect, she becomes both provider to him and mother to his child, though not legally so. In fact, she becomes not a mother but a black mammy: "And now when he came home with some of his boy friends, he always introduced her as Alva Junior's mammy. That's what she was, Alva Junior's mammy, and a typical black mammy at that" (221). Despite her conviction that after a professional career enabling "economic independence, everything else would come," she "found herself more enslaved and more miserable than ever" (221). Mistakenly, Emma Lou believes that getting out of this situation necessarily means finding a man who can lift her up, and as a matter of course, she goes to the other pole of a man she can dominate—Benson. Thurman here recalls the scene in *Quicksand* in which Helga discovers the engagement between her best friend and the man she loves. After realizing her abused condition with Alva, Emma Lou decides to reconcile with Gwendolyn in order to make contact with Benson. Upon calling Gwendolyn, she finds out that her former best friend and boyfriend are now engaged, despite Gwendolyn's previous ridicule of Benson's mulatto color (223).

Caught between the impossible options of sexual subjection and domination, Emma Lou's situation replicates that of Mimi and Helga. Although both Mimi and Helga are trapped in marriages at the opposite end of the social/racial scale, they serve as a foil to Emma Lou's desperate desire for further flight: "She had once fled to Los Angeles to escape Boise, then fled to Harlem to escape Los Angeles, but these mere geographical flights had not solved her problems in the past, and a further flight back to where her life had begun, although facile of accomplishment, was too futile to merit consideration" (225). Although Thurman gives Emma Lou an option out of the relationship, he does not want to duplicate the closure of *Flight*. Despite Emma Lou's escape of Alva in the end, the shock that pushes her and the reality she faces in black Harlem dispel any sense of racial romance that may be lurking in Mimi's final flight back to her race. The unsettling uprootings and dilemmas at the end of the *Blacker the Berry* make it feel more like the despair of *Quicksand* than the uplifting progress of *Flight*. This is accentuated by the limited nature of the lesson that Emma Lou grasps to shield herself from replicating her present predicament:

> She could strive for a change of mental attitudes later. What she needed to do now was to accept her black skin as being real and unchangeable, to realize that certain things were, had been, and would be, and with this in mind begin life anew, always fighting, not so much for acceptance by other people, but for acceptance of herself by herself. In the future she would be eminently selfish. If people came into her life—well and good. If they didn't—she would live anyway, seeking to find herself and achieving meanwhile economic and mental independence. (226–227)

Having learned the necessity of being "selfish"—that is, of accepting and protecting the self above all else—in order to survive, Emma Lou is presented with a challenge she can certainly master. Whether its mastery leads to something more than survival, however, remains very much to be seen in a future the novel refuses to narrate. The dangers lurking in a belief in solitary self-achievement may be as damaging as the dangers of waffling between psychosexual feminine dependence on men and manipulative domination over them.

The shock that wakes Emma Lou up to the dangers of Alva comes in the form of his sexual relationships with boys. Earlier in the novel, when Emma Lou has been kicked out of her apartment because her landlady sees her come in late, drunk, in Alva's arms, she is desperately searching for a new place. As Alva has refused the idea of their moving in together, she goes it alone, determined to be self-sufficient. She comes to the last rental listing, in which the "landlady was the spinster type, garrulous and friendly. She had a high forehead, keen intellectual eyes, and a sharp profile" (116). Thurman is painting the stereotype of the lesbian as a way of signaling female ways of life so alien to Emma Lou that she can only express shock and disgust at the proposition that the spinster landlady evidently makes:

> *Miss* Carrington had learned the history of Emma Lou's experiences in Harlem. Satisfied of her ground, she grew more familiar, placed her hand on Emma Lou's knee, then finally put her arm around her waist. Emma Lou felt uncomfortable. This sudden and unexpected intimacy disturbed her. The room was close and hot. Damask covering seemed to be everywhere. Damask coverings and dull red draperies and mauve walls. (116)

Emma Lou's suffocation in Miss Carrington's embrace presents a portrait of the innocent heroine potentially seduced or raped by the sinister, fearful same-sexuality lurking in the dark shadows of the spinster's closeted rooms. However low Emma Lou thinks that she has fallen, there are always lower depths at the bottom and margins of a darkly segregated African American culture.

Emma Lou escapes this encounter with female same-sexuality only to be confronted with it more forcefully when she finds that Alva's "boy friends" have become exactly that. Indecisive about leaving Alva, she returns to his apartment one final time after the phone call to Gwendolyn:

> [S]he subdued her flight impulse and without knocking threw open the door and walked into the room. She saw the usual and expected sight: Alva, face a death mask, sitting on the bed embracing an effeminate boy whom she knew as Bobbie, and who drew hurriedly away from Alva as he saw her. There were four other boys in the room, all in varied states of drunkenness—all laughing boisterously at some obscene witticism. (229)

Alva's descent into same-sexual liaisons can represent ambiguously either the enactment of a desire that has been repressed all along or the opportune shift to same-sexual hustling when he can no longer attract women like Emma Lou due to his emaciated state, the illness evident in his face from his relentless alcoholism. In either case, he duplicates with Bobbie the same manipulation that he has been practicing with Emma Lou, except that the violence so hidden in his chivalry with Emma Lou displays itself as a lack of self-possession in drunkenness. When Bobbie, embarrassed, attempts to slip away with the other boys, Alva is enraged:

"What the hell's the matter with you," he shouted up at Bobbie, and without waiting for an answer reached out for Bobbie's arm and jerked him back down on the bed.

"Now stay there till I tell you to get up." (230)

Struggling with her "immense compassion for him" and her "difficulty in stifling an unwelcome urge to take him into her arms," Emma Lou is forced to see her own degraded relationship with Alva as a mirror image of the stigmatized samesexual abusive relationship between him and Bobbie. "Then once more she saw Alva, not as he had been, but as he was now, a drunken, drooling libertine, struggling to keep the embarrassed Bobbie in a vile embrace" (231). Emma Lou's being "snapped" into greater self-determination in face of this "vile" scene seems to suggest that she has witnessed the worst, that she no longer can assume an innocence that corrodes the self as surely as those actions considered most vile by the socially respectable. Shocking Emma Lou into self-recognition through this stigmatic scene of male same-sexuality, Wallace Thurman ironically exploits manly eroticism in a way that both Fisher and McKay have studiously avoided. Regardless of the implications of McKay's reputed bisexuality or Fisher's reputed heterosexuality, their attempts to rethink black manhood contribute to sympathetic emplotments of male same-sexuality, as they benignly encode this as relatively integrated into the urban life of the black bottoms. Deeply suspicious of the appeal to manhood innocence being salvaged by such benign representations of same-sexuality in folk urban narratives, Thurman instead depicts the debilitating consequences that can flow from the enactment of desires deeply stigmatized and extremely marginalized by dominant culture. Thurman seems to insist that true sexual self-knowledge is found neither in fleeing the darkest reality of a stigmatized sexuality nor in benignly representing that sexuality as innocuously integrated into the mainstream of life, even on the bottoms. For Thurman, unexamined feminine innocence and unexamined masculine depravity are but opposite sides of the same interchange. As long as women like Emma Lou are oppressed by their internalization of feminine submission, men like Alva will be oppressed by the masculine violence that they perpetrate on others and on themselves. As long as men like Alva oppress themselves by doing violence to women, such men will also seek advantage in stigmatized enclaves of same-sexuality, whose continued repression in turn distorts and devalues everyone's desire.

Like Larsen's *Quicksand,* Thurman's *Blacker the Berry* offers a trenchant critique of the common belief that by reforming black men, the whole of the race can be transformed; and both novels challenge the notion underwriting earlier black urban folk fiction that alternative sexual arrangements offer some relief from racial and sexual domination. These heroine-focused novels are cynical about racial uplift through such mechanisms of sexual reform because they are attuned to the subtle interactions binding dominant heterosexual norms to deviant conduct, even among the most marginalized groups at the bottom of United States society. Para-doxically, the reform of black men depends, to some undecipherable extent, on the reform of United States society more largely, just as the racial reform of American society cannot occur without reforming black men *and* women. Sensitive to this impossible dilemma, Larsen and Thurman refuse the easier option of a gratifying closure in which reformed and reforming black men get what they need by being matched with the right women. Instead, their fiction leaves us with heroines on the verge of leaving the men who have abused them. Although the chances of their finding full gratification—sexual, social, companionate—under current racial cir-cumstances are not good, we can at least know that in leaving they resist their own racial oppression and the sexual subordination that helps authorize it.

Whether they promote or subvert the utopian dream of a reformed New Negro, these urban folk novelists continue the tradition of probing the role that sexuality and gender play in prospects for racial reformation evident in many of the works of the Jim Crow era. As these novelists, activists, and social scientists struggle to overcome the racial conditions of Jim Crow, they repeatedly discover—and seek to explode—the sexual dilemmas presented by their particular racial situation.

Epilogue

By concluding this study with an analysis of black heroines who fail to reform the men upon whose patronage their own reform depends, I hope to emphasize how the identity formation and subject status of black manhood accrue meaning only in the context of black women's experiences and representations. In a profound sense, Thurman's Emma Lou and Larsen's Helga "fail" to reform black men because the racial system intentionally keeps these men unmanned. Both women desire real men who will either command or patronize them—or both—only to realize that the black men they desire are all too like real white men, insofar they have the potential to be almost as sexually abusive as white slave masters were according to the dictates of enslavement. This double paradox of Jim Crow disentitlement is fittingly summed up in these heroine-centered black urban folk narratives. The more black men attempt to man the race through a fit masculinity patterned on dominant gender norms, the more they risk emulating the white ruling men whose Jim Crow racial/sexual codes unmans them. At the same time, the more that African American men resist the gender norms set up by the Jim Crow color line, the more they seem to lack the resources of manhood power and influence to man the race for a defeat of the very Jim Crow regime that unmans them.

As this study demonstrates in a variety of ways, this double bind has a violent sexual impact on African Americans beyond the familiar lynching savageries of Jim Crow. In Part 2, we saw the psychological violence experienced from putatively kind acts of racial patronage, and in Part 3, we saw the sexual violence that operates as sadomasochism in figures as diverse as the "underworld" character Congo Rose and the striving middle-class character Helga Crane. As the male-focused urban folk narratives suggest, however, African American social relations—from same-gender friendship to cross-sexual intimacy—are not totally determined by Jim Crow, even when they are shaped by its violent racial strictures. Both Fisher and McKay, in very different ways, are eager to explore how African American men create their own sense of manhood agency, whose mobile subjects are too "foot-loose" for the racial codes that attempt to arrest their movement. Such urban folk narratives also indicate how the project of reforming black manhood under the aegis of and against the tenor of Jim Crow in the end dictates the reformation of American notions of manliness more broadly, beyond the gender construction of white men's sexual superiority.

Across the Jim Crow era, this project of manhood reform calls forth a variety of ideologically competing, and sometimes conflicting, strategies. Just as the "pecu-liar institution" of slavery has been understood to perpetuate particular gender forms ensuing from practices of what Hortense Spillers calls "twice-fathering," so the just as peculiar institution of Jim Crow necessitates a variety of responses to black men's circumstance of possessing "emancipated" manly obligations without full access to manhood rights and privileges. As explored in chapter 1, the "New Negro" phenomenon that emerges at the turn of the nineteenth century seeks to answer this challenge either by surreptitiously asserting manliness in the Booker T. Washington mode of obediently managing the racial household like a political boss or by aggressively displaying manliness in the manner of William Pickens's racial trespassing. It is in this period that New Negro personal narrative—fiction and autobiography—is developed to stake a claim to self-making identity beyond the slave narrative, by a generation born with no firsthand knowledge of slavery, reared under the more liberal agenda of Reconstruction, and coming into adult-hood under the worst assaults of the Jim Crow regime. As examined in chapter 2, these narratives are less concerned with proving their humanity against the past condition of enslavement and more focused on assaulting the color line as a threshold of brash self-making. It is also in this period that urban sociology, ex-plored in chapter 3, is forged as a field in which black men can stake a claim to pro-fessionalization as cultural authorities on the race, by promising to police the rest-less migrations of the black mass. The emergence of black urban sociology demon-strates the sorts of accommodation that sometimes characterize the effective negotiation of an influential black manhood identity, for black male sociologists find themselves needing to distance themselves from the black masses in order to create a professional coterie of capable black male leaders. The birth of the New Negro movement, the emergence of anti–Jim Crow personal narratives by the first generation born after emancipation, and the development of black urban sociol-ogy constitute three different but interrelated discourses wherein black men work through their desire to prove their manliness by reforming their own sense of agency and leadership. As New Negroes stage the race by showcasing black men's alert geographic and social mobility in a plethora of visual media and discursive modes, they constantly seek ways to disrupt the binary logic of Jim Crow (black/white, masculine/feminine), often by triangulating their relationship to white masculinity through the mobilization of other racial and ethnic groups ei-ther to demonstrate their more advanced position in the race of the races or to sub-vert the notion of evolutionary competition altogether.

In addition to staging the geographic and social mobility of black men as a sign of their fast pace toward self-modernization, New Negroes are also concerned with how to circulate easily within the national institutions established to further their own emancipation, despite strong racial/sexual taboos restricting such circulation. Along with the new-century discourses formed around the turn of the nineteenth century, the Jim Crow period witnesses the development of biracial institutions aimed at defeating racial segregation, violence, and disenfranchisement, in part by tutoring black men for leadership of the race. Part 2 examined the sexual politics of manhood reform at work in three of these new biracial sites: the NAACP, the Chicago School of sociology, and the New Negro renaissance patronage system. As chapters 4 and 5 argued, these anti–Jim Crow institutions are supposed to show-case how intimate physical contact across racial lines can benefit national progress; yet each of these racial uplift sites seeks to exclude black men from becoming rivals with white male racial patrons while appearing to position exceptional black males as tokens deserving of tutelage. Using the theory of homoraciality, we have seen how such patronage institutions necessarily beget various modes of rivalry across and within races, across and within sexes. The repressed sexual rivalry between black and white men frequently explodes into eroticized contests between women and black men. These chapters have shown how black manhood, as the object of biracial tutelage, is an embattled site, structurally akin to the secondary condition of women by the explicit exclusion of black men from white men's networks of masculine power and influence.

In addition to new discourses of manhood self-making and new sites of cross-racial patronage, the Jim Crow era witnesses the emergence of a new literary form, the urban folk novel, which spotlights the significance of geographic and social mobility in the making of a modern black mass. Like the anti–Jim Crow personal narratives, urban folk fiction is obsessed with defining the basis upon which free movement can be asserted despite or against the barriers of Jim Crow, but unlike these personal narratives, urban folk fiction resists the myth of the lone cowboy-warrior, with its implications of a macho Manifest Destiny. Whether centered on a male or female protagonist, these narratives satirize the biracial institutions exam-ined in Part 2 as they explore the everyday experience of black manhood reform by depicting how ordinary African Americans circulating among themselves pursue their passions, ambitions, vocations, and dreams without being defined exclusively by the color line that seems to characterize their historical condition as blacks of one sex or the other. The study shows how, for the first time in literary history, the rich panoply of black males' relations with each other—including violent rivalry, fraternal labor, devoted companionship, same-gender eroticism, and cross-class coalition building—are complexly imaged in fiction. Across these genres, social practices, and political agendas we can see how African American men, writing and acting under the most trying circumstances, are able to rethink fit manliness on the run. In these polemical essays, race albums, autobiographies, novels, sociological tracts, social agencies, and political organizations, we find that African American men have self-consciously theorized the too-familiar notion of normative masculinity from their positions of decided alienation from it, and hence their efforts can provide insights into our own attempts to understand the construction of diverse masculinities. These men have been forced to take the notion of manhood seriously, even as they have remodeled, reformed, satirized, critiqued, and unraveled it from its sources of empowerment.

Finally, it is far too easy in our culture *not* to take black manhood seriously. I have encountered amusement among some colleagues that I should devote so many years and pages to dissecting a subject that putatively could be taken care of in one essay. An academic can spend a whole career dissecting the complexity of a single white male author—a Shakespeare or a Melville—and be rewarded with the greatest applause for much-needed labor. Despite some mild trendiness in the topic of African American masculinity, exactly the opposite expectation predominates, for however little has been written on the subject, that little is always already too much. Indeed, the tendency to see an interest in black manhood as a trend indicates that it should be merely a passing matter, something to catch our attention when some crisis of the black male problem flares into the mass media but not a subject worthy of permanent, sustained intellectual analysis. Both in academe and in the larger world of mass culture, we already presume that we know "the black man" in a single glimpse of a police mug shot or in the most facile epithets projecting clichés such as "emasculation" and "hypermasculinity" onto lives and histories denied the most rudimentary assumptions of human conflictedness, intricacy, subtlety, and richness. By insisting on the complexity, intricacy, subtlety, and richness of black manhood's cultural history, I hope—at the least—that this book also resists this long-standing tendency to reduce black manhood identity to the shock of the latest fad in clothing or the prurience of the most recent racial scandal.

Notes

Notes to the Introduction

1. See, for instance, the essays by these theorists collected in Wall, *Changing Our Own Words*, as well as Christian, *Black Women Novelists;* Spillers, "Mama's Baby, Papa's Maybe" and "Hateful Passion, Lost Love"; McDowell, *"Changing Same";* Wall, *Women of the Harlem Renaissance;* Tate, *Domestic Allegories of Political Desire* and *Psychoanalysis and Black Novels;* Hull, *Color, Sex, and Poetry;* Davis, *Women, Race and Class* and *Blues Legacies and Black Feminism;* Carby, *Reconstructing Womanhood;* and duCille, *Coupling Convention* and *Skin Trade.*

2. See Carby, *Race Men* (1–6).

3. For a fuller answer to this question, see my review of Carby's *Race Men.*

4. In focusing on the boundaries and borders, my approach is also indebted to the work being done in Chicano/a studies, particularly Gloria Anzaldúa, *Borderlands/La Frontera;* Tomás Almáguer, *Racial Fault Lines;* Carl Gutiérrez-Jones, *Rethinking the Borderlands.*

5. Wiegman, *American Anatomies* (3, 31); also see Winthrop D. Jordan, *White over Black* (259–265).

6. "Permanent Obliquity of an In(pha)llibly Straight" (129).

7. The debates over the nature of men's sexuality emerged in the men's movement in the 1970s and also dialectically out of feminism in men's studies in the 1980s. More precisely, it should be considered a subfield of whiteness studies insofar as its key theoretical texts have focused primarily on *white* masculinity as the *gender* norm, often underanalyzing its racial construction. See, for instance, Eve Sedgwick, *Between Men;* Harry Brod, ed., *Making of Masculinities;* and Peter F. Murphy, ed., *Fictions of Masculinity;* for one account treating the racial makeup of white maleness, see Fred Pfeil, *White Guys.*

8. For an elaboration of this critique, see my essay "Race, Rape, Castration."

9. For Awkward's important contributions to black manhood studies, see *Negotiating Difference,* particularly chaps. 2, 4, 6, and 7.

10. My approach more closely approximates that of Wallace, whose brilliant study moves from the Revolutionary period to the present; but whereas his *Constructing the Black Masculine* spotlights pivotal topics and moments in each major historical era, *Manning the Race* attempts a continuous, layered account of the trajectory of Jim Crow conceptualized as one long historical era, the 1890s through the 1930s.

11. Lemelle looks to literature—Richard Wright, Ralph Ellison, and James Baldwin in particular—and to literary theory and cultural studies to bolster his sociological theories of the role of deviance in the construction of black masculinity.

12. In *Sweet Home,* Charles Scruggs has dealt rather extensively with the relationship between sociology and African American literature in the earlier decades of the twentieth century (1–67), as well as sociology in relation to post–World War II black male fiction. The forthcoming companion volume to *Manning the Race,* titled *The Color of Manhood,* will continue the treatment of this subject, which, as Scruggs points out, can be comprehended fully only by charting what transpires between sociological and black literature in the middle decades of the century.

13. Fortunately, black queer theorists have begun to interrogate such binaries, often through personal inquiries. See recent compelling instances in Phillip Brian Harper's *Private Affairs* and Robert F. Reid-Pharr's *Black Gay Man*. In a rare instance where a major queer white theorist takes race seriously for understanding sexuality, Lee Edelman's *Homographesis* devotes a full chapter to the question (42–75). While I admire some of the subtleties Edelman offers of homophobia as a racialized concept, he still tends toward a binarized approach to black men's sexuality through a Baldwin tokenized to represent a marginal, tenuous black gay identity and a Fanon exploited to represent hypermasculine black male assimilation of homophobia.

14. I'm thinking here of the work that sex and sexuality do in Harriet Brent Jacobs's *Incidents in the Life of a Slave Girl* and in Martin Robison Delany's *Blake*.

15. See Donna Haraway, *Simians, Cyborgs, and Women* (210); Marilyn French, *Beyond Power* (97–122); and Gerda Lerner, *Creation of Patriarchy*.

16. Because only men held full citizenship rights when former male slaves were enfranchised in the 1870s, the question of how to count African American citizenship was rhetorically a matter of how to manage the franchise for African American *men;* but in reality, as Elsa Barkley Brown has pointed out, it was also a matter of how to limit the very active influence of women, including African American women, in the masculine forum of institutional politics. See her "Negotiating and Transforming the Public Sphere" (especially 121–124); and Glenda Elizabeth Gilmore, *Gender and Jim Crow* (17–19, 124–126).

17. As Winthrop D. Jordan explains: "Ever since the days of confrontation in Africa the sexual connection between Negro and ape had served to express the deep-seated feeling that the Negro was more animal—and accordingly more sexual—than the white man" (*White over Black* 491).

18. Sedgwick, *Between Men.*

19. See Brown, "Considering the Social Identities of Africanamerican Men"; and Grandison, "Landscapes of Terror" and "Negotiated Space."

20. The scholarship on romantic friendship among middle-class white women has set the terms for such work on men; see, for instance, Lillian Faderman, Carol Smith-Rosenberg, and Martha Vicinus. Some work has been done on romantic friendship among white men in the nineteenth century, when such relations were accepted as a normal aspect of homosocial bonds: Rotundo (75–91); John W. Crowley; Jeffery Richards; and Jonathan Katz (667–679). Donald Yacovone's work on the friendships among white abolitionists is instructive but unfortunately does not consider how these intense friendships are triangulated around the enchained bodies of black captives. Robert K. Martin, elaborating on the work of Leslie Fiedler (see esp. 182–214, 367–390), has pointed out in a rare analysis of racially bonded men that white male writers "located their erotic fantasies" with "noble savages" in "exotic lands" that "provided sexual excitement and cultural difference"; see "Knights-Errant and Gothic Seducers" (171); as well as Martin's monograph *Hero, Captain, Stranger* (esp. 28–39, 66–84); and Wiegman on the function of race in Hollywood buddy films (149–178).

21. The "homo" prefix in "homosocial" (meaning "the same" in Greek) denotes the strong social attachments between men in patriarchy but is frequently confused with homoeroticism, when in fact homosociality is instead decidedly homophobic and heterosexist. See Diana Fuss (111) and Christopher Newfield (29–30).

Notes to Chapter 1

1. James D. Corrothers's new-century autobiography, published in 1916, captures this logic perfectly in its title, *In Spite of the Handicap.*

2. Judith Butler, *Bodies That Matter* (95).

3. Performance theory works better for understanding the unselfconscious aspects of maintaining the normativity of whiteness or masculinity or heterosexuality than it does for oppressed identities, but in any case, it tends to diminish the *collective* politics of identity and to *dehistoricize* the processes of identification. Butler, for instance, attempts to rethink performativity to account for "what must be excluded from discourse in order for political signifiers to become rallying points," but she overlooks the problem of the theory's ahistorical tendencies (*Bodies That Matter*, 187–222). For a more extended discussion of the need to account for temporal and historical change in the process of racial/gender identification, see my essay "Camping the Dirty Dozens."

For a compelling application of performance theory in tune with the dilemmas of historical change, see Saidiya V. Hartman (esp. 49–78).

4. To complicate the dominant focus on the North-South axis in African American scholarship and culture more generally, I discuss here both remigration (moving back and forth across regions) and the westward narrative as crucial components of staging the race's progress, but I do not want to supplant the former with the latter.

5. Obviously, representations of interactions among women are also important. Although this falls outside the purview of this study, I occasionally point to the importance of such interactions.

6. "Policing the Black Woman's Body in an Urban Context," rpt. in *Cultures in Babylon* (23).

7. See Frances R. Keller in *American Crusade* (102) and Kenneth L. Kusmer's *Ghetto Takes Shape* (10).

8. The negative epithet "uncle" when applied to black men during slavery seems especially ironic given the honored place of the uncle relationship in many West African cultures.

9. Wallace's work tends to emphasize black freemasonry as a racially assimilative performance that imitates dominant white masculinity (see part 2 of *Constructing the Black Masculine*), and Walker's work tends to emphasize the adaptive productivity of an indigenous culture of black manhood (see his dissertation "The Freemasonry of the Race"). Both would agree, however, that the fraternal order is a key site for understanding black manhood as a whole.

10. In the journal that he kept while a young man, Chesnutt copied passages from Samuel Robert Wells's *A Handbook for Home Improvement*, published around 1857, focusing on entries concerning "The Daily Bath," "The Feet," "Change of Linen," etc. Chesnutt, who was trained in a freedmen's school, was teaching himself the hygiene curriculum that white patrons of newly established black schools, such as Samuel Armstrong's Hampton Institute, placed at the forefront of racial uplift strategies. Wellington's argument against the apparent rationality of such hygiene presents an interesting counterpoint to an ideology of cleanliness that during the time became virtually unquestioned in dominant discourse. See Richard H. Brodhead, ed., *The Journals of Charles W. Chesnutt* (40–41).

11. As Eric Lott and others have persuasively shown, Irish immigrants in nineteenth-century U.S. culture had to struggle to overcome their racialized subordinate status and did so partly by adopting a distancing relation to blacks through performing minstrelsy, participating in exclusive fraternal organizations, organizing racially segregated unions, and other such activities. See Lott, *Love and Theft* (esp. 91–100); Michael Rogin, *Blackface, White Noise* (56–58); David R. Roediger, *Wages of Whiteness* (115–163); and Theodore W. Allen, *Invention of the White Race* (136–158).

12. As Myles Raymond Hurd points out, Chesnutt exploits prejudice against the Irish immigrant to clarify racial prejudice against African Americans (see "Booker T., Blacks, and Brogues"). Chesnutt is doing the converse of Washington's tutelage of Native Americans while at Hampton, examined below, and James Weldon Johnson's exploitation of American native peoples in his autobiography, *Along This Way*, by showing how the logic of the color line also precludes working-class immigrants, especially women, from possessing legitimate sexuality and citizenship.

13. Washington was the only black man invited by the Board of Directors, "composed of [white] men who represented the best and most progressive element in the South," to speak on the opening day of the Atlanta Cotton States and International Exposition. "I was asked now to speak to an audience composed of the wealth and culture of the white South, the representatives of my former masters. I knew, too, that while the greater part of my audience would be composed of Southern people, yet there would be present a large number of Northern whites, as well as a great many men and women of my own race" (*Up from Slavery* 210–211).

14. An immediate spark for Chesnutt's essays was Washington's 1899 tract *The Future of the American Negro*, which Chesnutt reviewed for the *Saturday Evening Post* January 1900 issue. Chesnutt's proposal of race erasure is, of course, diametrically opposed to Washington's accommodationist, almost separatist policies, though the similarities between amalgamation and accommodation are interesting in that both on the surface appear to accept white racial supremacy for the short run.

15. On the historical vagaries of race as a concept, see Laura Doyle, *Bordering on the Body* (esp. 35–40) and "Racial Sublime" (15–39); Kenan Malik, *Meaning of Race* (esp. 71–100); and Roediger (esp. 43–64, 95–114). For a slightly different view, where the development of "race" is seen as related to but more distinct from the Western development of class ideology, see Oliver C. Cox, *Caste, Class, and Race* (esp. 317–352).

16. As David J. Hellwig has explained, some African Americans throughout the nineteenth and early twentieth century tried to exploit nativism against itself and for the purposes of uplift ("Strangers in Their Own Land").

17. For the opposing arguments made by Ferguson in "Chesnutt's Genuine Blacks and Future Americans" and Elder in "'Future American Race,'" see the *MELUS* 15.3 (1988) forum on Chesnutt's trilogy. Dickson D. Bruce Jr. makes an assessment similar to Elder's (*Black American Writing from the Nadir* 173). These opposed readings indicate to what extent Chesnutt himself may have had conflicting impulses concerning the uplift advantages of the black race's consolidation.

18. An excellent analysis of the European treatment of native sexual practices can be found in Jonathan Goldberg's *Sodometries*, chap. 6, "Discovering America" (179–222).

19. In this way, Chesnutt anticipates the arguments being made in the emerging field of African American/Native American studies, in which scholars are pointing to the ways in which the blending of Negroes and Indians through intermarriage, political and military alliance, and cultural hybridity has been a constant threat to the black/white and black/red binaries of racial subordination. See, for example, Daniel F. Littlefield Jr., *Africans and Seminoles*; Murray R. Wickett, *Contested Territory*; Bruce Edward Twyman, *The Black Seminole Legacy and North American Politics*; William Loren Katz, *Black Indians*; Katja May, *African Americans and Native Americans in the Creek and Cherokee Nations*; and especially the essays in James F. Brooks, ed., *Confounding the Color Line*.

20. Chesnutt, "The Courts and the Negro," reprinted in *Plessy v. Ferguson: A Brief History with Documents*, ed. Brook Thomas (156).

21. In *A Ghetto Takes Shape*, Kusmer provides a helpful thumbnail sketch of the relatively integrated life of the small black elite in Cleveland before World War 1. See chaps. 5 and 6, esp. 126–130.

22. Chesnutt, too, explores this idea in his later fiction, especially *The Marrow of Tradition* (1901) and *The Colonel's Dream* (1905).

23. For details of Pickens's life, see Sheldon Avery's biography, *Up from Washington* (25–34).

24. Rotundo instructively points out that this image of the competitive workplace is partly myth, given the extent to which the work of middle-class white male managers of the capitalist economy depended on business contacts, male sociability, loyalty, conviviality, and trust (*American Manhood* 196–205).

25. The scholarship on pederasty in classical Greece is extensive. See, for instance, Michel Foucault's *The Use of Pleasure* (187–254); David M. Halperin's *One Hundred Years of Homosexuality* (54–71); Eva C. Keuls's *The Reign of the Phallus* (274–299); and William Armstrong Percy III's *Pederasty and Pedagogy in Archaic Greece* (98–121).

26. Carole Marks, *Farewell—We're Good and Gone* (30).

27. Moton's diatribe against the migration North cannot be taken too much at face value, however. The rhetoric is surely aimed at least partly at sustaining the kinds of alliances within the South that enabled Washington to build Tuskegee in the first place. Only four years earlier in his contribution to Alain Locke's anthology *The New Negro*, Moton celebrated both the migration and Tuskegee's part in it. See "Hampton-Tuskegee: Missioners of the Masses" (324).

28. Recent scholarship on black migration has suggested that much of the migration was from rural to urban South, and Carole Marks argues that many of the northern migrants were from southern cities, not rural areas (*Farewell—We're Good and Gone* 32–44). Nonetheless, in New Negro discourses the South is pretty consistently figured as rural, the North as urban, and the movement from rural to urban as migration northward. On migration from rural to urban South, also see the essays collected in Joe William Trotter, Jr. *The Great Migration in Historical Perspective*.

29. For a history of this concept, see Arthur O. Lovejoy's still-definitive book *The Great Chain of Being* (esp. 183–207 and 227–287); for its implications on the historical construction of race and racial superiority, see Winthrop D. Jordan, *White over Black* (216–252 and 482–506).

30. On the theoretical relation between word and image, I have been influenced by the work of W.J.T. Mitchell, especially his *Iconology* and *Picture Theory*, as well as by Richard C. Sha's *Visual and Verbal Sketch in British Romanticism* (1–21).

31. According to Kwame Anthony Appiah, "there is an astonishing consistency in [Du Bois's] position [on race] throughout the years" (*In My Father's House* 28). This may be the case in regard to his struggle over how to account for and discount the claims of a biological basis for racial differentiation, as Appiah persuasively argues. The way that Du Bois makes his case for a distinctively African contribution to world civilization, however, does change.

32. Tate, introduction to *Dark Princess* (xx–xxi). According to David Levering Lewis, *Star of Ethiopia* was originally presented in 1913 as part of New York's commemoration of the fiftieth anniversary of the Emancipation Proclamation. Du Bois "transformed *The Star of Ethiopia* into a three-hour extravaganza in six episodes, featuring a thousand creamy-complexioned young women and tawny, well-built men, and flocks of schoolchildren marching through history" (*W.E.B. Du Bois: Biography of a Race* 459–460).

33. See David Levering Lewis, *W.E.B. Du Bois: The Fight for Equality and the American Century* (441).

34. As Thomas Holt explains, "*Souls of Black Folk* marks Du Bois's conscious turn toward active political engagement" through "a sustained attack both on the sterile and pusillanimous leadership of Booker T. Washington and the materialist ethos of U.S. capitalism to which Washington's philosophy was indebted." See "Political Uses of Alienation" (303).

35. As we see in chapter 4, Mary White Ovington, later to become Du Bois's close friend and colleague at the NAACP, shares a similar ideology of the transformative role of cross-racial physical contact, perhaps because she is influenced by Du Bois.

36. Dickson Bruce comments on *Souls*: "Du Bois identified the key mark of black distinctiveness in spirituality" over against "white materialism" (206). "When Du Bois developed his attack, he did not simply condemn Washington for open accommodationism. He also attacked him for New South vulgarism, for advocating a merely material solution to what were also spiritual problems" (207). Du Bois's anti-materialist bent is carried in a different direction by Alain Locke's later attack on Bookerite materialism in *The New Negro*, discussed below.

37. Various scholars have mentioned Du Bois's early Hegelianism and gradual shift toward Marxism. Shamoon Zamir deals extensively with this in *Dark Voices* (esp. 11–14, 113–153, 199–206). On Du Bois's gradual turn to socialism and on his racial revision of Marxist theory, see Holt, "Political Uses of Alienation," as well as Manning Marable, *W.E.B. Du Bois* (83–113 and 145–146); and Joseph P. DeMarco, *The Social Thought of W.E.B. Du Bois* (68–84, 105–132).

38. Suzanne C. Carson quotes a letter from Samuel Chapman Armstrong's father, who was a leading missionary and adviser to the king of Hawaii, in which he expostulates on the importance of this trilogy to civilizing the Hawaiian "savages": "'My general plan,' he wrote, 'is to aim at the improvement of the *heart*, the *head* & the *body* at once. This is a lazy people & if they are ever to be made industrious the work must begin with the young. So I am making strenuous efforts to have some sort of manual labour connected with every school & teachers are paid as much for going out to work on the land with the boys as they are for teaching" (quoted in "Samuel Chapman Armstrong: Missionary to the South" [20]). In an effort that became popular in the middle decades of the nineteenth century, Armstrong's father put this manual education theory to work in Hawaii in a school that Armstrong himself attended until matriculating at Williams College.

39. This scenario presents real difficulties for Du Bois. He has to distance himself from redemptionist historians, who argue that Reconstruction was a mistake and a crime against the South because it gave the spoils of Civil War to know-nothing blacks and unscrupulous Northerners while robbing the genteel former slave owners of their rightful patrimonial inheritance. Du Bois's idealized portrait of cross-patronage is intended to counter this reading.

40. "But for recognition proper there is needed the moment that what the master does to the other he should also do to himself, and what the bondsman does to himself, he should do to the other also" (G.W.F. Hegel, *Phenomenology of Mind* [236]).

41. *Black Atlantic* (135–136). Gilroy cites a series of images across Du Bois's career, including "the woman's body he used to personify black cultural creativity in his 1938 book *Black Reconstruction in America*." Gilroy goes on to indicate a conflict between Du Bois's fiction and nonfiction: "The idealised figuration of racial culture and community through the bodies of black women in Du Bois's non-fiction has to contend with the rather less celebratory images of African-American womanhood that appeared in his novels" (136). I see similar ambiguities in the nonfiction.

42. This is not to detract from Du Bois's genuine feminist impulse. Yet, even in an essay such as "The Damnation of Women," in which he makes it clear that he is a strong supporter of women's vocational, educational, domestic, political, and economic emancipation, he tends to emphasize maternity as a sort of sacred trust and duty; see *Darkwater* (163–186).

43. Maurice Wallace points out that Washington's autobiography contains ambivalences in relation to outdoor work (as field hand) and indoor work (as house servant): "Washington belongs exclusively to neither side of this grand division but slips in and out of both discursive universes comfortably, and—for the moment—unproblematically. It is only later, when the slaveboy reaches liminality, finally confident that he can manage outdoors, that he is called preemptorially away from his station to domestic work in the 'big house'" ("Constructing the Black Masculine" 258). Though I agree that in maturity Washington must have some ambivalence about the indoor labor, it has to be remembered that white rulers also work indoors; the "big house," like the White House, represents the polished feminine household and the white male ruler's domain.

44. On the reform movement in the Progressive Era, see Nell Painter's *Standing at Armageddon* (253–282); Alan Trachtenberg's *Incorporation of America* (161–181); Robert H. Wiebe's *Search for Order, 1877–1920* (164–195); and Howard Mumford Jones's *The Age of Energy* (155–178).

45. "Miss Nancy," of course, imputes a homosexual tendency, as well as gender disorder and sissy cowardliness.

46. Forbes, *Africans and Native Americans* (esp. 2–5).

47. See Lindsey, *Indians at Hampton Institute* (96–97).

48. These articles appear from September 1880 to May 1881 and are reprinted in *The Booker T. Washington Papers*, vol. 2, ed. Louis Harlan et al. (78–132).

49. On Washington's mixed report to the government concerning his colonial charges at Tuskegee, see Harlan, *Booker T. Washington: Making of a Black Leader* (283–284).

50. Gilroy's influential *Black Atlantic* tends to attribute a nationalist parochialism to African American identity and studies before the advent of Richard Wright as "the first black writer to be put forward as a major figure in world literature" (146). In Gilroy's geography, the Atlantic becomes the pond joining Europe and America—so much so that he discounts the trans-Atlantic as the ocean linking Africa with the West Indies and the Americas by dismissing the centrality of Africa in the formation of African American identities, not only in 1960s–1970s black nationalism but over the long course of the history of "New World" people of African descent.

51. For an analysis of Pickens's critique of the white American European traveler, see my essay "Trespassing the Colorline" (62–64).

52. The anthology does point out that "in the distribution of military honors the President was extremely generous to the whites of the South," and this goes far to explain the "enthusiasm" of the Southerners (*A New Negro* 26).

53. Actually, the race analysis in Sedgwick's theory is lacking but can be inferred. See her *Between Men* (esp. 8–11).

54. Washington's chapter on "Afro-American Education" (chap. 6) focuses on the coalition between black and white patrons as "pioneers in the work of education," with their "splendid army of emulators" (79–80). The masculine-identified language of frontiersmanship and warfare thus infiltrates even those aspects of the homoracial enterprise that could easily be seen in terms of feminized, domesticated, bureaucratic chores.

55. The strict gender segregation of the photographs is mirrored in the verbal discourse of the volume. In chapter 6, Washington mentions without an accompanying sketch Mary Peake, the former captive who had started the first school for freedmen in the South; but, interestingly, her name appears in a passage he quotes from Samuel Chapman Armstrong (see *A New Negro* 82). The procession of black men's pictures continues through "Fathers to the Race," with a sketch of Frederick Douglass (335) heading the chapter.

56. There are two exceptions: one photo of the first colored female dentist (*A New Negro* 412) and the other of a nurse pursuing a medical degree (413).

57. In a post-Reconstruction precursor to *A New Negro for a New Century* we can see a similar visual logic at work. The Reverend William J. Simmons's biographical dictionary of prominent black men, *Men of Mark* (1887), also places great store in the photographs and sketches of its subjects: "The illustrations are many, and have been presented so that the reader may see the characters face to face," Simmons writes (9).

58. In his 1920 book *Progress of a Race*, John William Gibson extends the photographic strategy used in *A New Negro*, following through with the injunction to update the Negro's progress perpetually. In addition to portraits similar to those in *A New Negro*, *Progress of a Race* includes contextual photographs intended to display more concretely the material wealth being accumulated by New Negroes. For a fuller discussion, see my article "New Negro Displayed."

59. Not much more than this is known about John Henry Adams Jr. According to Wayne Martin Mellinger, he was probably born around 1880, but the date of his death is unknown. About the magazine, *Voice of the Negro*, edited by John W. E. Bowen and Max Barber, Mellinger writes that it "openly criticized the accommodationist views of Booker T. Washington. Contributors included W.E.B. Du Bois, Fannie Barrier Williams, Benjamin Brawley, Kelly Miller, Pauline Hopkins and Mary Church Terrell. After the Atlanta riot of September 22, 1906, the magazine, now called *The Voice*, moved to Chicago. The editors were seriously injured and feared being lynched by the next angry white mob" ("John Henry Adams and the Image of the 'New Negro'" [29]).

60. These professions are mentioned in the captions describing the six New Negro men whose sketches, executed by Adams, complement the essay.

61. For biographical information on Locke, see Leonard Harris, "Rendering the Text," in *Philoso-*

phy of Alain Locke (3–8); Eugene C. Holmes, "Alain Leroy Locke: A Sketch"; William M. Brewer, "Alain Leroy Locke"; and Jeffrey C. Stewart, *Critical Temper of Alain Locke* (3).

62. Concerning the influence of Jung and Freud on Locke, see Johnny Washington, *Journey into the Philosophy of Alain Locke* (34, 131–134).

63. Robert E. Park and his associates, for instance, saw Chicago as their great laboratory for studying and measuring the progress of this assimilating process; see Martin Bulmer, *Chicago School of Sociology* (12–27, 89–93).

64. See Herskovits, "Negro's Americanism," in *New Negro* (353–360). Whereas Herskovits makes the case for the Negro's essentially American heritage in his *New Negro* contribution, by 1941 he is championing the idea of the Negro's African "retentions" and "carry-overs," arguing for the continuing influence of African culture on African American identity (see *Myth of the Negro Past*). On Locke's cultural pluralism, see his essays in *Philosophy of Alain Locke*, ed. Harris (esp. "The Contribution of Race to Culture" 201–208); also see William B. Harvey, "Philosophical Anthropology of Alain Locke"; Rutledge M. Dennis, "Relativism and Pluralism in the Social Thought of Alain Locke"; and Johnny Washington, *Alain Locke and Philosophy* (esp. 53–57).

65. Locke's insistence on African Americans' readiness to compete intellectually, artistically, and culturally without being overly sensitive to injury may also be directed against a common stereotype of the Negro advanced at various points by white patrons such as Mary White Ovington, Robert E. Park, and Carl Van Vechten, and examined in Part 2.

66. Washington, *Alain Locke and Philosophy* (168); for another superb reading of Locke's ambivalence toward the black mass in his ideal of the urban racial community, see Charles Scruggs, *The Sage in Harlem* (92–102). In *Sweet Home,* Scruggs notes that Locke's idea of the city is strongly influenced by the work of Park, whose theory displays a similar ambivalence toward the urban mass, and that in Wallace Thurman's novel, *Infants of the Spring,* Locke's character is called Dr. Parkes (1, 50–53).

67. This bourgeois aesthetic of exuberant accumulation and comfort can still be glimpsed in Washington's house, the Oaks, on the campus of Tuskegee University, especially in how Washington displayed in his study the furniture, pictures, paintings, books, and gifts from famous patrons.

68. Locke, "Unity through Diversity: A Baha'i Principle" and "Contribution of Race to Culture," both in *Philosophy of Alain Locke*, ed. Harris (134–138 and 202–206).

69. Washington himself had argued over the inclusion of photographs depicting the "savage" types of naked Africans and "Negroes of the older type" in the U.S. South when one influential explorer-anthropologist, Sir Harry Johnston, published *The Negro in the New World* in 1910. For a discussion of this, see my "New Negro Displayed."

70. Reiss was the art editor of the *Survey Graphic* magazine, and as such was responsible for the expressionist designs of the special issue "Harlem: Mecca of the New Negro" (March 1, 1925), out of which Locke's *New Negro* grew.

71. Actually, Reiss's drawing "The Brown Madonna," discussed below, presides over the volume.

72. The drawing of Hayes was used as the cover of the Harlem special issue of the *Survey Graphic* magazine.

73. Ancestral: A Type Study" breaks with this pattern by representing an anonymous woman against the background of a colorful African print cloth. This portrait has more in common with Reiss's renderings of Blackfeet Indians, in which the Fauvist-influenced bright tones highlight the red tint in their skin color, but here the colors provide more of a foil.

74. Locke does not see his New Negro theory as an ideology or dogma but rather as a flexible, pluralistic frame for what he calls "self-criticism," the capacity to determine how well one has engaged the developing self with political and cultural history. See his "Self-Criticism" (391–394).

75. This essay, "Propaganda—or Poetry," is published in the first volume of the journal *Race: Devoted to Social, Political and Economic Equality,* which was started in the winter of 1935 to try to push analysis of African American culture beyond the New Negro concept for a newer generation. E. Franklin Frazier's brash attack on Du Bois, "The Du Bois Program in the Present *Crisis,*" signals the sort of aggressive agenda set for the journal.

76. Chapter 5 examines further the popular metaphor of the midwife and other images of blood reproduction in reference to effective patronage of the New Negro.

77. In addition to "The Negro: 'New' or Newer?" this assessment is based on my reading of the following retrospective reviews: "Of Native Sons: Real and Otherwise," parts 1 and 2 (1940); "Reason and Race: A Review of the Literature of the Negro for 1946"; "A Critical Retrospect of the Literature of the Negro for 1947"; "Dawn Patrol: A Review of the Literature of the Negro for 1948," parts 1 and 2; "Wisdom *de Profundis:* The Literature of the Negro, 1949," parts 1 and 2; "Inventory at Mid-Century: A Review of the Literature of the Negro for 1950," parts 1 and 2; "The High Price of Integration: A Review of the Literature of the Negro for 1951"; and "From *Native Son* to *Invisible Man:* A Review of the Literature of the Negro for 1952." All these essays are also reprinted in Stewart, *Critical Temper of Alain Locke,* but my citations here are from the original publications.

78. See Ross, "Beyond the Fragmented Word."

79. Wall, *Women of the Harlem Renaissance* (4).

80. In addition to Locke and Hayes, these include Charles S. Johnson (facing 278), James Weldon Johnson (facing 306), Robert Russa Moton (facing 324), Elise J. McDougald (facing 370), and Mary McLeod Bethune (facing 378).

Notes to Chapter 2

1. William Loren Katz points out that scholarship treating African Americans on the frontier has been ongoing since the 1880s but began to receive attention and validation in the 1960s. As is evident in Katz's own language, most of the material devoted to blacks on the frontier and black cowboys displays an ambivalence toward its mythology, wanting to debunk it while celebrating it at the same time (*Black West* xi–xvii). See also Philip Durham and Everett L. Jones for a discussion of the cowboy "as the conquering white man, . . . the noble Nordic" (*Negro Cowboys,* 220–230).

2. The general influence of Washington's *Up from Slavery* on Pickens's *Bursting Bonds* was recognized early in what little scholarship there is on the latter autobiography. See, for instance, Rebecca Chalmers Barton, *Witnesses for Freedom* (27); and Avery (*Up from Washington*).

3. *Manliness and Civilization* (185–186); also Rotundo's *American Manhood* (247–283) and Kimmel's *Manhood in America* (157–188).

4. See Painter's vivid portrayal of this struggle within the working population and the symbolic use of that struggle to promote a fear of workers as disorderly threats to civilization (*Standing at Armageddon* 36–71).

5. Pickens's attitude toward the Yankee schoolmarm movement may be more complicated than *Bursting Bonds* alone would suggest. Maxine D. Jones and Joe M. Richardson claim, for instance, that he "believed that many of the new generation of white teachers lacked the missionary spirit of earlier ones and that they impeded rather than promoted black progress" (*Talladega College* 85).

6. On Councill's competition with Washington, see Harlan, *Booker T. Washington: Making of a Black Leader* 168–171.

7. When White becomes executive secretary, he also becomes Du Bois's boss, and his relations with Du Bois are as troubled as those with Pickens. This kind of masculine bickering over racial leadership status is examined in detail in chapter 4.

8. Some scholars have suggested that White rivals Locke, James Weldon Johnson, Charles S. Johnson, and Van Vechten as a patron of the Renaissance. See, for instance, Charles F. Cooney, "Walter White and the Harlem Renaissance"; Charles W. Scruggs, "Alain Locke and Walter White"; Edward E. Waldron, *Walter White and the Harlem Renaissance* (23–40, 113–166); and David Levering Lewis, *When Harlem Was in Vogue* (130–143). Others give him a less vital role as a patron. For instance, see Cary D. Wintz, *Black Culture and the Harlem Renaissance* (129); and Nathan Irvin Huggins, *Harlem Renaissance* (99).

9. Pickens does try his hand at fiction writing in his novella, *Vengeance of the Gods: And Three Other Stories of Real American Color Line Life* (1922).

10. The hero of *Fire in the Flint* may have been based on Dr. Louis T. Wright, one of White's mentors and one of two persons who encouraged him to take the NAACP job in New York (the other was his father). White describes Wright as "the brilliant surgeon . . . who had only recently returned to Atlanta to practice medicine after a spectacular career at the Harvard Medical School. Bluntly he told me, 'You'd be a damned fool to stay here in Atlanta. Go to New York by all means. Life will mean much, much more to you when you are fighting for a cause than it possibly can if you stay here just to make money. You'll stagnate and eventually die mentally'" (*A Man Called White* 37).

11. Chesnutt's 1901 novel *The Marrow of Tradition* portrays a similar situation through the character Dr. Miller, who attempts to establish a Bookerite hospital in his hometown, only for it to be destroyed by a white mob (a fictionalization of the 1898 Wilmington, North Carolina, riots). Given Chesnutt's own frustrations in North Carolina as a schoolteacher and principal, and his ambivalent attitude toward black southerners, it is not surprising to find his novel anticipating

White's by two decades. More precisely, White's novel is an updating and rewriting of Chesnutt's. Cheryl Wall notes that White's *Fire in the Flint* is also a revision of the 1922 novel *Birthright,* by the white author T. S. Stribling, who similarly depicts a Harvard-trained black doctor returning south only to be defeated. As Wall points out: "in Stribling's text, the tragedy inheres in the hero's black ancestry, which prevents him from achieving the noble ambition to which his 'white blood' causes him to aspire" (*Women of the Harlem Renaissance* 65). In this sense Stribling's hero is similar to the "marginal man" embodied in the mulatto "personality type" theorized and given scientific validity in the social science of Robert E. Park and his followers.

12. New Negro narrative displays a constant conflation between actual geographic-demographic regions and mental-psychic frames of reference that represent these regions. The question is whether leaving these regions necessarily means leaving the frames of reference associated with them.

13. Waldron, *Walter White and the Harlem Renaissance* (46). This uneasy, fascinating tension between romance and protest—the subversive quality of its sentimentalism—may be one reason that the novel is usually ranked low and his second novel, *Flight* (1926), discussed in Part 3, is preferred.

14. See, for instance, Angela Davis's "Rape, Racism and the Myth of the Black Rapist," in *Women, Race, and Class* (191); Sandra Gunning's *Race, Rape, and Lynching* (78–81); and Elsa Barkley Brown's "Imaging Lynching."

15. Wells-Barnett started work on her autobiography in 1928, but it was not published until 1970, almost forty years after her death. See Alfreda M. Duster's introduction in *Crusade for Justice* (xxx–xxxi). Although it is customary to refer to Wells by a combination of her surname and married name (Wells-Barnett), because most of my discussion concerns Wells before she married, and because of the title of her autobiography, I refer to Wells by her birth name.

16. See, for instance, Patricia A. Schechter's recent biography *Ida B. Wells-Barnett and American Reform.*

17. In her account of Wells's contributions to the anti-lynching and women's club movements, Paula Giddings briefly mentions Davidson as an instance of someone with a more "traditional" attitude toward women's uplift role. She quotes Davidson: "[W]hen, in speaking about the need for women to become 'stronger intellectually,' she demurred, 'I would not have you think, especially you, my brother teachers, that we are asking to find out how we can produce more strong-minded women as that term is used in the objectionable sense'" (*When and Where I Enter* 109).

18. In *Black Women Writing Autobiography,* Joanne M. Braxton offers a different take on Wells's treatment of domesticity in *Crusade for Justice:* "Wells's autobiographical reticence about her private experiences in marriage reinforces the public nature of her narrative, as well as its authenticating structure" (133). I agree but also would suggest that the public focus of the autobiography ambivalently imitates masculine self-making narratives while subtly critiquing them. Wells's later focus on motherhood, as Braxton points out, emphasizes the difficulties of achieving domestic and political tasks at the same time.

19. Charles Richard Johnson, "Phenomenology of the Black Body" (129).

20. See Dudley Randall, *The Black Poets* (63). For a history of the poem's publication and reception, see Wayne Cooper's *Claude McKay* (98–101, 140) and Tyrone Tillery's *Claude McKay* (33–37).

21. Shaw, *What a Woman Ought to Be and to Do* (111).

22. For an instructive biographical sketch of the post-1929 part of Gordon's life and his unpublished sequel to *Born to Be* and a novel, see Robert Hemenway's introduction to the 1975 reprint of the autobiography.

23. Van Vechten's comment can be found on p. vi.

24. On the gendering of the falsetto voice and castrati, see Wayne Koestenbaum's fascinating cultural history in *The Queen's Throat* (158–169).

25. I don't mean to imply that African Americans were not heavily involved in what Arna Bontemps calls "lateral East-to-West migration" (Arna Bontemps and Jack Conroy, *Anyplace but Here* 2). My point is that the literary, political, and religious discourse has focused much more on the North/South axis, such that the idea of African American frontier migration is shaped by the ideological priorities of trespassing the Mason-Dixon line. For wonderful accounts of the ideological complications of black frontier experiences, see the vignettes in Bontemps and Conroy's *Anyplace but Here,* as well as Nell Irvin Painter's *Exodusters.*

26. Another instance of an African American narrative that figures the East/West axis and cowboying to advance a myth of total freedom from racial stricture is *The Life and Adventures of Nat*

Love: Better Known in the Cattle Country as "Deadwood Dick"—By Himself, published in 1907. A former captive's liberation narrative reworked through the mythology of western romance, *The Life and Adventures of Nat Love* (130, 155) captures the same equation of the West with absolute manhood freedom as *Born to Be*.

27. I do not mean that cowboying is a white phenomenon; we know that African Americans, Mexican Americans, and Native Americans created much of cowboy culture, although the dominant iconography still colors the experience white. Gordon likes to emphasize how his was the only black family in his hometown, and thus how he had no consciousness of race, despite the fact that his autobiography casually mentions nonwhites coming through town. If we take his own characterization at its word, we would have to say that he learned cowboying from the town's white men.

28. Gaines calls this "the youthful trauma of racial rejection" (see *Uplifting the Race* 47–51); and Hemenway, introduction to 1975 reprint of *Born to Be* (xxxi).

29. See Countee Cullen, ed., *Caroling Dusk* (8).

30. Beavers, *Wrestling Angels into Song* (11–12).

Notes to Chapter 3

1. Will Alexander, a leading white southern patron in Atlanta, made this statement in supporting E. Franklin Frazier for a scholarship in a letter to the executive director of the Rockefeller Foundation. Because Frazier had been fired and attacked for his anti-segregation views by the Atlanta School of Social Work, the Rockefeller Foundation was questioning whether Frazier was an appropriate recipient for a Rockefeller scholarship.

2. Sociology was articulated as an academic field and professional discipline in the same period as the Great Migration. This professionalization emerged especially around 1892, when the University of Chicago instituted the first department of sociology. Elliott Rudwick points out that "during the early twentieth century the most important studies of American blacks . . . were all explicitly directed toward providing knowledge for social work programs" ("W.E.B. Du Bois as Sociologist" 26). Likewise, Charles U. Smith and Lewis Killian note that "the values of the nascent sociological community at the turn of the century were humanitarian and philanthropic as much as they were scientific" ("Black Sociologists and Social Protest" 194). Although sociology was originally indistinguishable from the social work, social reform, and philanthropic race-patronage movements that were shaped significantly by middle-class urban women at the end of the nineteenth century, as sociologists attempted to establish their work as a prestigious professional discipline rooted in scientific method after World War I it became strongly male-identified. Historically, African American sociology has also been a man's field (see Jacquelyne Johnson Jackson's "Black Female Sociologists").

3. Carter G. Woodson's *Century of Negro Migration* is an exception that proves the rule in the voluminous material on black migration and urban studies. Unlike most of these studies, he diminishes the difference between the black upper class and the masses, suggesting that the Talented Tenth, whom he says constitutes a large percentage of pre–World War I migrants, and the folk masses both are remarkably law-abiding, churchgoing, and family-oriented, despite conditions of discrimination and job insecurity found in the new urban neighborhoods (see esp. 187–189). As a result, he minimizes the role of diverse sexual behaviors in the race. Nevertheless, Woodson, too, clearly uses sexual conformity as a code for asserting the continuity between these migrants and the dominant race.

4. For a concise discussion of the role of sexuality in white attitudes toward blacks in the rural South and the efforts of social scientists to document sexual patterns among blacks and to correct such attitudes, see Nicholas Lemann's *Promised Land* (24–38).

5. On the anti-immigration policies of this period, see Robert H. Wiebe's *Search for Order* (288–292) and Howard Mumford Jones's *Age of Energy* (5).

6. William Henry Baldwin Jr. was the chair of the executive committee of Tuskegee's board of trustees and the man responsible for building a railroad to bring northern philanthropists comfortably to the remote, inaccessible Alabama campus by private Pullman car. David Levering Lewis notes: "Nervous, impatient, intolerant of contrary opinions, and decisively convinced of African-American inferiority, Baldwin saw the solution to the South's race problem in salvation through work and rights after obedience. There had been too much pious nonsense about equality spouted by misguided Yankee idealists, his own ancestors included" (*W.E.B. Du Bois: Biography of a Race* 241). Pouring herself even more into race work after her husband's death in 1905, Ruth

Baldwin, in founding and funding the National Urban League, continued the focus on moral discipline and economic self-help for the black masses.

7. Charles S. Johnson also uses the term *lodger evil* in *The Negro in Chicago,* which much more systematically achieves a semblance of scientific objectivity than Haynes's report (158). Johnson writes: "Where there were children and lodgers together, a considerable number of instances were found which suggest probable injury to health or morals, and sometimes both. Even where lodgers are relatives, impairment of health and morals is threatened in certain circumstances, especially if overcrowding is flagrant" (160). By associating lodging with immorality, Haynes and Johnson reaffirm their assumption that "adaptation" to "civilization" must mean enforcing the concept of the nuclear family on the migrants.

8. Smith and Killian, "Black Sociologists and Social Protest" (199–202). As the teacher of E. Franklin Frazier, Charles S. Johnson, St. Clair Drake, and other black sociologists, Park exerts his influence directly through his theories and work on race relations, as well as indirectly through his students' use and revision of his work and through his hands-on nurturing of African American students in a fashion similar to Franz Boas at Columbia (see Stanley H. Smith, "Sociological Research and Fisk University" [164–190]). Park is discussed in chapter 4.

9. Burgess, "Social Planning and Race Relations" (17).

10. For this analysis of the cultural-historical construction of the ethnographic observer, see the essays in *Writing Culture,* ed. James Clifford and George E. Marcus, especially Clifford's "Introduction: Partial Truths" (1–26).

11. On Johnson's biography, see Richard Robbins, "Charles S. Johnson." On the Fisk Machine, see August Meier, "Black Sociologists in White America" (263–265); Butler A. Jones, "Tradition of Sociology Teaching in the Black Colleges" (136–137); and Anthony M. Platt, *E. Franklin Frazier Reconsidered* (98).

12. On Johnson's primary authorship of the report, see Robbins, "Charles S. Johnson" (60). However, according to Arthur I. Waskow, who has done the most extensive study of the report, it was drafted jointly by staff and reviewed by members of the commission, as well as the governor of Illinois, who suggested changes—thus a true bureaucratic collaborative effort. See his *From Race Riot to Sit-in* (87–90); also "Chicago: The Riot Studied" (140–142). For the sake of simplicity, I refer to the report alternately as Johnson's or the commission's, with the understanding that there is no way of knowing exactly how much of the report Johnson drafted.

13. The disparity between Taylor and Johnson was clearly reflected in their salaries: Taylor's at $5,500 to Johnson's $3,500. See Martin Bulmer, "Charles S. Johnson, Robert E. Park, and the Research Methods of the Chicago Commission on Race Relations" (293). Waskow further points out that before hiring Taylor and Johnson the commission "was unsure how to equalize racial status in its staff," an ideal evidently abandoned in hiring the two men so unequally (see *From Race Riot to Sit-in* [72] or "Chicago: The Riot Studied" [129]).

14. Waskow points out that *The Negro in Chicago* lacks any analysis of the municipal power structure in relation to racial politics (*From Race Riot to Sit-in* [97–99] or "Chicago: The Riot Studied" [147–148]).

15. Bulmer, "Charles S. Johnson, Robert E. Park, and the Research Methods of the Chicago Commission on Race Relations" (304). Francis W. Shephardson helped establish the commission, served as acting director briefly and as an *ex officio* member of its executive board, and in 1921, through his close relationship with Rosenwald, became the director of the Rosenwald Fund, which later dispensed a great many funds to Fisk during its million-dollar endowment campaign of the 1930s.

16. John Bracey, August Meier, and Elliott Rudwick, "Black Sociologists" (15).

17. Waskow, *From Race Riot to Sit-in* (93); also "Chicago: The Riot Studied" (144).

18. This is also a good example of how Johnson reshapes the methods and themes he borrows from the Chicago School. Park, who started his career as a newspaper man and became interested in the role of the press in modern culture, encouraged his students to use newspapers as a sociological source on a par with ethnographic information. Instead of merely assessing what influence the black newspapers might have on the migrants, Johnson exploits the newspaper sources to affirm their rightful capacity to discipline the migrant masses.

19. Kelley, *Race Rebels* (55–75).

20. In addition to Robbins, see Meier, "Black Sociologists in White America" (262–267); and Bracey, Meier, and Rudwick, "Black Sociologists" (13–22).

21. On Frazier's controversial career, see G. Franklin Edwards, "E. Franklin Frazier"; and Platt, *E. Franklin Frazier Reconsidered.*

22. On Frazier's biography, see Edwards, "E. Franklin Frazier" (85–117); and Platt, *E. Franklin Frazier Reconsidered* (11–108).

23. Meier suggests that "the greatness of the major monographs produced by Du Bois, Frazier, and St. Clair Drake was in large part actually rooted in the creative tension between their scholarship and their social commitment" ("Black Sociologists in White America" 260). The insight in their sociological work is more precisely the creative tension between their trusting to sociological discourse and their determination to polemicize for their social commitment within the constraints of the discourse.

24. Among the members of the commission were Oswald Garrison Villard, Countee Cullen, and A. Philip Randolph. At least three of the commissioners did not sign the report. See Platt, *Politics of Riot Commissions* (161). Waskow points out that the Chicago commission for the 1919 riots tended to trust the social elites—black and white—rather than the black people on the street most affected by the rioting. As a result, "[m]any Negroes in Chicago made clear by word and deed that they were thoroughly suspicious of the commission's efforts" (see *From Race Riot to Sit-in* [81–82, 101–102] or "Chicago: The Riot Studied" [136, 150]).

25. For instance, see Stow Persons, *Ethnic Studies at Chicago* (135).

26. In his 1920 book *Darkwater: Voices from the Veil*, Du Bois speaks of unattached women and men in his essay "The Damnation of Women": "The Negroes are put in a peculiarly difficult position, because the wage of the male breadwinner is below the standard, while the openings for colored women in certain lines of domestic work, and now in industries, are many. Thus while toil holds the father and brother in country and town at low wages, the sisters and mothers are called to the city. As a result the Negro women outnumber the men nine or ten to eight in many cities" (180–181). Although Du Bois's essay strongly advocates in favor of women's independence, suffrage, and rights, he retains this nervousness of unattached women: "God send us a world with woman's freedom and married motherhood inextricably wed, but until He sends it I see more of future promise in the betrayed girl-mother of the black belt than in the childless wives of the white North, and I have more respect for the colored servant who yields to her frank longing for motherhood than for her white sister who offers up children for clothes" (184).

27. As Gaines notes, many among the black elite adopted this notion during the early twentieth century (*Uplifting the Race* 45).

28. I do not want to suggest that the study is styleless. Actually, it is a spirited, witty text in many subtle ways. Nonetheless, the range of emotion expressed explicitly by the authors is narrow and dispassionate, which is what I mean by "stylistic monotone." Bracey, Meier, and Rudwick suggest that *Black Metropolis* is not strictly in the Chicago sociology tradition ("Black Sociologists" 20), but I think there is enough commonality both in method and in outlook to classify the text in this tradition, given especially that sociology and anthropology at Chicago (Drake was an anthropologist) were closely linked at the time. More important for my purposes here, the text fits the tradition of black male social scientists from Du Bois to Johnson and Frazier to Drake and Cayton.

29. In chapter 9 of *Black Bourgeoisie*, "Behind the Mask," Frazier writes: "Since the black bourgeoisie live largely in a world of make-believe, the masks which they wear to play their sorry roles conceal the feelings of inferiority and of insecurity and the frustrations that haunt their inner lives Despite their attempt to escape from real identification with the masses of Negroes, they cannot escape the mark of oppression any more than their less favored kinsmen" (213).

30. In chapter 19, "Style of Living—Upper Class," Drake and Cayton point out that such slang is used by all social levels to describe the upper class: "The general tone of upper-class life is conveyed by phrases used when people are explaining what they mean by 'dicties,' 'hincties,' 'muckti-mucks'—i.e., 'upper-class' people" (*Black Metropolis* 526).

Notes to Chapter 4

1. See *W.E.B. Du Bois: Biography of a Race* (317–318).

2. Du Bois, quoted by Harlan, *Booker T. Washington: Wizard of Tuskegee* (363). Harlan describes in some detail Washington's relations with some of the major Tuskegee donors in chap. 6, "Other People's Money" (128–142).

3. *Autobiography of W.E.B. Du Bois* (262).

4. Washington's own representation of his relationship with his donors, especially Samuel Chapman Armstrong, is much more complex than what Du Bois allows in his critique. Washington needed to claim intimacy with his donors as a way of publicly displaying his trustworthiness as head of the race while also needing to display his proper respect and distance from them as a sign of his submission to Jim Crow taboos against intimate *social* contact. When he overplays his hand and appears to attempt too much physical proximity, it backfires, as is the case when Washington dines with Teddy Roosevelt in the White House, along with the Roosevelt family. The reaction among whites in Alabama was intensely negative, leading to attacks in the press, anti-Washington popular songs, and other forms of verbal racial assault.

5. I am referring here to the railroad missions of Robert C. Ogden (of the Wanamaker's department store fortune) and Julius Rosenwald (the Sears, Roebuck and Company fortune). "Ogden's Special," a private Pullman car, took northern philanthropist-businessmen south from New York every April from 1901 to 1909 to do patronage prospecting and to assess the true educational needs of the South. Railroad tracks had to be specially built to the Tuskegee campus, given that it was so isolated from the railroad lines. For a school to be on the schedule of the Ogden Special was almost a certain assurance of receiving some financial aid from the well-heeled Southern Education Board. Rosenwald chartered a similar Pullman car, filled with wealthy Chicagoans, for the sole purpose of drumming up support for Tuskegee. On the Ogden Special, see David Levering Lewis, *W.E.B. Du Bois: Biography of a Race* (270–272); on Rosenwald, see Harlan, *Booker T. Washington: Wizard of Tuskegee* (140–142). In his autobiography, Villard provides an inside view of a trip on the Ogden Special and of the mentality of the Tuskegee patrons (*Fighting Years* 172–175).

6. Ovington (1865–1951) was an independently wealthy social worker, descendent of abolitionists, and one of the original founders of the organization. She became briefly its acting executive director, then chair of its board of directors from 1919 to 1932, and then its treasurer to 1947. She is sometimes considered the most influential white leader of the organization. The sexual implications of her race patronage are discussed below.

7. Wells-Barnett, *Crusade for Justice* (327–328); also see Paula Giddings, *When and Where I Enter* (181).

8. Kellogg, *NAACP* (92).

9. On Ovington as "Mother of the New Emancipation," see Rayford W. Logan, prologue to Ovington, *The Walls Came Tumbling Down* (I). In describing the relationship between Du Bois and Ovington, David Levering Lewis writes, "A role Ovington would find herself reluctantly having to assume in numerous crucial situations was that of stern schoolmistress to the sulking star pupil Du Bois" (*W.E.B. Du Bois: Biography of a Race* 350). This observation is especially interesting in light of our discussion in chapter 1 of Du Bois's attitude toward the Reconstruction Yankee schoolmistresses as inverted mammies. The tendency to maternalize women's roles in race work is discussed further below.

10. Ovington, *Black and White Sat Down Together: The Reminiscences of an NAACP Founder* (60), originally printed in the Baltimore *Afro-American*, September 1932–February 1933; hereafter cited as *Black and White*. Ovington's account of the event in her history of the NAACP is even more cryptic; see *The Walls Came Tumbling Down* (106). David Levering Lewis provides yet another take on this episode, seeming to suggest that Du Bois's role on the nominating committee and Ovington's applause of the attempt illegally to place Wells-Barnett back on the Committee of Forty indicate their relative innocence, and that Villard, who "arbitrarily added and deleted names during the week following the conference," may be the real source of the controversy (see *W.E.B. Du Bois: Biography of a Race* 396). Kellogg attributes this "internal strife" to the fact that "Negro leaders were inclined to be as temperamental as prima donnas, each seeking his own place in the limelight," because "there were few places of privilege open to Negroes, and the rivalry for status was keen"; further, "the rank and file tended to be apathetic, indolent, and supine" (*NAACP* 92, 93), a point of view that seems to mirror Villard's frame of reference. Disappointingly, Carolyn Wedin does not shed any new light on this controversy between Ovington and Wells-Barnett, nor does she discuss Ovington's relationship with Wells-Barnett and Jessie Redmon Fauset, black women with early influence on the NAACP, both of whom seemed to have had some tension with Ovington in their NAACP work (see *Inheritors of the Spirit* [111 and 314 n. 23]). In her earlier biography, *Jessie Redmon Fauset, Black American Writer*, Carolyn Wedin (Sylvander) explains that Ovington also did not like Fauset, and she notes that Ovington also may have had a hand in preventing Fauset's nomination for secretary of the organization from going forward in 1916 (41).

11. Villard uses the term *merchant philanthropist* (*Fighting Years* 172) to describe the work of the Wanamaker's department store owner and head of the Southern Education Committee, Robert C. Ogden.

12. Wreszin, *Oswald Garrison Villard* (10); also see Dollena Joy Humes, *Oswald Garrison Villard, Liberal of the 1920s*, chap. 4, "*Noblesse Oblige:* A Liberal Interpretation" (esp. 76–83).

13. See Du Bois's 1920 collection of essays, *Darkwater: Voices from within the Veil,* where he proudly stakes his claim to a New England inheritance alongside the fact of his foreparents' captivity and Africanness (5–7).

14. Kellogg, *NAACP* (21); also see Villard, "Need of Organization," in *Proceedings of the National Negro Conference* (205).

15. For a slightly different version of the contest between Du Bois and Villard, and one a bit less sympathetic toward Du Bois, see Elliott M. Rudwick, *W.E.B. Du Bois: Propagandist of the Negro Protest* (158–183). For an excellent discussion of the boxing metaphor, see Gerald Early, "The Black Intellectual and the Sport of Prizefighting," (5–45), as well as the essays in *Tuxedo Junction.*

16. Also ironically, Du Bois originally intended to write a biography of Frederick Douglass, but the publisher gave the commission to Washington instead. When Du Bois suggested substituting a biography of Nat Turner, the publisher, indicating that Turner was an obscure figure, asked him to do one on John Brown instead. See Lewis, *W.E.B. Du Bois: Biography of a Race* (356–357).

17. Villard, "Harper's Ferry and Gettysburg" (405).

18. Villard, "Need of Organization," in *Proceedings of the National Negro Conference* (199). I discuss the "enlightened" stance on race of the English aristocrat Sir Harry Johnston on the occasion of the dispute between him and Washington in my essay "The New Negro Displayed." Given Johnston's overt racism, we can see that Villard's standard for European racial enlightenment is set pretty low.

19. This mythology also operates currently in the post–civil rights era, in which the socioeconomic system creates a scarcity of blacks for upper-level positions in industry, education, and government, then exploits this invented scarcity as a natural condition afflicting the black race. There are always too few African Americans for the best positions because the system is rigged to exclude African Americans from the best positions. Du Bois's situation in the early years of the NAACP has implications for contemporary affirmative action disputes.

20. There are notable exceptions. Mary Church Terrell, who was ambivalently involved with the NAACP, had the wealth of her millionaire father and the resources of her professional husband on which to rely, if she so desired, while carrying out her race work. Once Wells-Barnett married a professional man and could rely on his employment, she acquired a position more akin to Ovington's than to Du Bois's, but before this, her reliance on her newspaper for employment put her in a position similar to Du Bois, though perhaps more economically independent because she owned an interest in the newspaper along with her African American colleagues.

21. We could read these skirmishes over Du Bois's role on the board and over which African Americans to let onto the Committee of Forty as anticipatory parables of "affirmative action" politics, because the latter policies set up similar parables of natural economic scarcity, lack of black talent, and excess supply of white skills in terms of employment. Of course, using the term would be anachronistic.

22. In his 1963 book *Why We Can't Wait,* Martin Luther King Jr. offers a critique of tokenism that hints at its economic logic when he points out the etymology of the word *token:* "A piece of metal used in place of a coin, as for paying carfare on conveyances operated by those who sell the tokens" (30). He proceeds to argue that the person who accepts the token as the true value of the coin will come up short: "But he who sells you the token instead of the coin always retains the power to revoke its worth, and to command you to get off the bus before you have reached your destination. Tokenism is a promise to pay. Democracy, in its finest sense, is payment" (31). A more thoroughgoing economic critique of tokenism is presented as an attack on "captive leaders" in Kwame Ture and Charles V. Hamilton's 1967 book *Black Power* (13–15).

23. Wedin, *Inheritors of the Spirit* (232–233).

24. Wedin, *Inheritors of the Spirit* (233). Wedin's reading of how Ovington spotlights Johnson and demotes and diminishes Du Bois in her 1927 book, *Portraits in Color,* is instructive on this count (233–235). It is also clear that Ovington played Johnson and Du Bois off each other to maintain authority as a woman amid men on the executive board. A book like *Portraits in Color*—listing, applauding, and sanctifying African American leaders—represents the gesture of a patronage gift, but beneath the gesture is the patronizing act of Ovington setting herself up as judge and jury of the work being done within and beyond her purview.

25. On Jack Johnson's wrapping his penis to make a more threatening impact in the boxing ring, see Randy Roberts, *Papa Jack* (74, 140).

26. Washington to T. Thomas Fortune, 20 Jan. 1911, in *Booker T. Washington Papers,* ed. Harlan et al., vol. 10 (555); Fortune to Washington, 23 Jan. 1911, in *Booker T. Washington Papers,* vol. 10 (556); also see Harlan, *Booker T. Washington: Wizard of Tuskegee* (376).

27. On the tensions between black men and white women over the Fifteenth Amendment and women's suffrage, see Giddings, *When and Where I Enter* (64–74, 119–129); and Gilmore, *Gender and Jim Crow* (204–224).

28. Quoted in Wedin, *Inheritors of the Spirit* (298). According to Wedin, Ovington herself edited out this passage.

29. Wedin, "Afterword," in *Black and White* (152–153). Because Ovington had financial reasons for writing the autobiography, her desire to do so need not be explained solely in terms of a desire for attention; also see *Inheritors of the Spirit* (298).

30. Quoted in Wedin, "Afterword" to *Black and White* (156).

31. It is clear that Jane Addams's best-selling autobiography, *Twenty Years at Hull-House*, whose first chapter is titled "Earliest Impressions," served as a model for Ovington's. Lincoln and the Civil War play the same role in Addams's book that Douglass and abolition play in Ovington's.

32. She published a short story on this topic titled "The White Brute," in *The Masses*, in 1915 (reprinted in *Half a Man* 88–99).

33. Ovington is quoting from one of the Dunbar "dialect" poems, "Little Brown Baby," in which a father washes and readies his son for the pallet while telling him a "bugguh-man" story and soothing him (see *Complete Poems of Paul Laurence Dunbar* 134–135).

34. Because Ovington goes back and forth between using the masculine pronoun generically to refer to the Negro as a collective group and using it gender-specifically to refer to the particular problems of African American men, it is difficult sometimes to know which she means. It seems, however, given the context of this passage, that she is referring here specifically to black men, and at the same time to their representativeness as heads of the race.

35. On Brown, also see *The Walls Came Tumbling Down* (118–121).

36. In *The Walls Came Tumbling Down*, Ovington describes her relationship to Lorenza Cole in slightly different terms, using very explicit Negro Renaissance patronage terms: "Lorenza fell upon my neck and I became a patron of the arts—the first and only time I have had the means to occupy this position" (215). Through the substitution of "parent" for "patron," an equation seems to be made between the two.

37. See his essay "Self-Criticism: The Third Dimension in Culture," published in 1950. The oversensitivity of black people on issues of race remains today a standard way of deflecting charges of racism. If racism is merely a personal matter, one that wounds sensitive individuals, it need not be dealt with as a systemic, institutional issue beyond moralistic, individualized behaviors. Although the accusation of oversensitivity is exploited for a different end in early-twentieth-century progressive discourse, it achieves a similar effect of placing the white person in authority over the collectively historical and individually felt experiences of black people.

38. "Of Beauty and Death," in *Darkwater* (221–222).

39. A history of African American literary satire would have to go further back than the 1920s, as we have already seen with Chesnutt's fiction. During Ovington's own time, African American male writers often took a satirical bent—to name just a few examples, James David Corrothers, George Schuyler, Rudolph Fisher, and Wallace Thurman.

40. Ellison, "*An American Dilemma: A Review*," in *Collected Essays* (331).

41. Park, "Autobiographical Note," in *Race and Culture* (vi).

42. The Darwinist logic of Park's theory of civilization becomes clearer in other essays; see, for instance, *Race and Culture* (85, 265). On the influence of social Darwinism on Park, see Lyman, *Black American in Sociological Thought* (28). It is likely that Pickens's *New Negro* polemic has been influenced by Park, or that each has influenced the other.

43. Charles Scruggs notes in passing the probable influence of Park on the Negro Renaissance writers; see *Sweet Home* (52).

44. Quoted in Rolf Lindner, *Reportage of Urban Culture* (47).

45. In "Sociology and the Rise of Corporate Capitalism," Dusky Lee Smith outlines the links between the industrialists and the leading U.S. social-science departments in the late nineteenth century. See especially his comments on Albion Small, the man responsible for hiring Park in 1913 (68–84, esp. 75–77). The history of this conflict between social reform and scientific discipline is more broadly traced in Mary O. Furner, *Advocacy and Objectivity*. Furner points out that the patron industrialists of research universities like Chicago made it clear that they would not support radical activism in social science and insisted on firing scholars (in economics and sociology especially) who did not conform to the dictates of what Ellison labels, and Furner's history confirms to be, "bourgeois science" (see esp. chaps. 7 and 8 [143–204]). See also Lindner, *Reportage* *of Urban Culture* (197–204). For a detailed description of how Park managed the career shift to Chicago from Tuskegee, see F. H. Matthews, *Quest for an American Sociology* (57, 82–87); and Winifred Raushenbush, *Robert E. Park* (63–78).

46. Redfield, *Tepoztlán, a Mexican Village* (4); also quoted in Park, "The Negro and His Plantation Heritage," in *Race and Culture* (68). Du Bois, Chesnutt, Washington, and James Weldon Johnson had already been suggesting this in their different ways.

47. Park, "Education in Its Relation to the Conflict and Fusion of Cultures," in *Race and Culture* (264); in the same essay he writes: "[T]he Negro, when he landed in the United States, left behind him almost everything but his dark complexion and his tropical temperament" (267). In *The Romance of Culture in an Urban Civilization*, Barbara Ballis Lal claims, "Actually, Park's discussion of 'racial temperament' is of little consequence. This theme is mentioned in very few of his publications" (154), suggesting that the quotations about temperament are taken from the infamous early 1918 essay. Matthews tries to diminish the significance of temperament by suggesting that "it was logically separate from the fresher interactional theories which his students would carry forward." He also writes: "However, Park's belief in distinctive 'racial temperaments' was shared by militant Negroes of the early twentieth century, including W.E.B. Du Bois" (*Quest for an American Sociology* 171–172). For a similarly apologist stance, see Stow Persons, *Ethnic Studies at Chicago* (80–84, 111). If racial temperament had been a minor or marginal aspect of the theory of Park and Chicago sociology more generally, E. Franklin Frazier would not have felt compelled to attack it so trenchantly in his 1927 essay "Racial Self-Expression" (in Charles Johnson's collection *Ebony and Topaz* 120–121). See the critique of Park and his colleagues that started to take focus in sociological theory concerning race in Gunnar Myrdal's 1944 *An American Dilemma* (11049–1051) and Ellison's review of Myrdal's book (in *Collected Essays*)—a critique that became more hostile with the black liberation and other radical sociologists from the early 1970s on. These sociological critics include: Oliver C. Cox, *Caste, Class and Race* (463–476); T. L. Philpott, *Slum and Ghetto* (esp. 140–228); Lyman, *Black American in Sociological Thought* (41–43); and among the essays in Joyce A. Ladner, ed., *Death of White Sociology*, see especially Bracey, Meier, and Rudwick, "Black Sociologists" (10–15); Abd-l Hakimu Ibn Alkalimat, "Ideology of Black Social Science" (177–181); Dennis Forsythe, "Radical Sociology and Blacks" (220–221); and Joseph Scott, "Black Science and Nation-building" (295–296).

48. In 1918, to suggest that African Americans were not interested in "reconstruction" seems to side with the southern apologists, who were arguing that Reconstruction was a colossal error. As Lyman points out, Park "seems to have accepted uncritically the picture of antebellum plantation life as painted by pro-slavery historians, and so he assumed that the relations between master and slave—and especially between master and house servants—were amicable and intimate" (*Black American in Sociological Thought* 38).

49. Ellison, "An American Dilemma: A Review," in *Collected Essays* (332). Also see Wahneema Lubiano's brief commentary on the lady metaphor in "'But Compared to What?'" (195).

50. Park's attribution of a biological "romantic interest" to so-called primitive women upon seeing white men for the first time falls into the tradition that George M. Fredrickson labels *romantic racialist*. Rolf Lindner also labels this aspect of Park and Chicago sociology "romantic" and identifies it as a cultural historical penchant evident in the estranged intellectual elite who comprise the first wave of modernity in the first quarter of the century. Although I disagree with Lindner that these intellectuals were able to avoid "a patronising attitude," the rest of his description seems apt (*Reportage of Urban Culture* 202–203).

51. In his 1941 retrospective essay "Methods of Teaching: Impressions and a Verdict," Park admits that most of his contact during his stay at Tuskegee was with the black elite, not with the so-called primitives: "I gained very little knowledge, except indirectly, about that nether world of Negro life with which white men, particularly if they grew up on a southern plantation, knew a great deal" (41). Ironically, Park's sociological theory of race is based on little "firsthand" experience of African Americans as a folk mass.

52. Lindner points out that Park was eager to segregate sociology as a discipline from the social welfare work that was closely associated with the leadership of women reformers such as Jane Addams and Frances E. Willard, his contemporaries and colleagues in Chicago (*Reportage of Urban Culture* 92–93).

53. He does cite Du Bois's *Souls of Black Folk* in his discussion of the "sorrow songs" (*Race and Culture* 278, 298), and he names Du Bois alone as a founder of one of the new civil rights organizations "eventually taken up by the emerging Negro intelligentsia" (172). Shamoon Zamir points out that "fragmented consciousness and the divided self were ubiquitous in the 1880s and 1890s not only in psychology but also in literature" (*Dark Voices* 116); also see Arnold Rampersad, *Art and Imagination of W.E.B. Du Bois* (74).

54. On Du Bois's being trapped by a biological concept of race in philosophical terms, see Kwame Anthony Appiah, "Illusions of Race," in *In My Father's House* (28–46); and in historical terms, see Keith E. Byerman, *Seizing the Word* (81–99). Nonetheless, Park's reductionism seems quite different from Du Bois's struggle to move beyond biological thinking.

55. On Park's support of such organizations, see Barbara Ballis Lal, *Romance of Culture in an Urban Civilization* (146–147); and Ernest W. Burgess, "Social Planning and Race Relations" (17–19). Park served as the first president of the Chicago Urban League from 1916 to 1918.

56. "Mentality of Racial Hybrids," in *Race and Culture* (387 n. 19). Later, Park states that the "degree of intelligence" displayed by "mixed bloods" evinces an intelligence "of which their parents were apparently quite incapable"—citing especially the cases of "the two most eminent leaders of their race," Frederick Douglass and Booker T. Washington (390).

57. Lindner, *Reportage of Urban Culture* (160).

58. Quoted in Matthews, *Quest for an American Sociology* (83).

59. Johnson, *Black Manhattan* (128).

60. Although I think this is true for the representation of both men and women of African descent, it may be more accurate for the representation of men. Because of the stronger association of lighter skin color with vulnerable femininity as a desirable attribute according to dominant culture as well as among many African Americans during the time, the self-conscious female mulatto presents more complications to the New Negro project of overcoming color consciousness as a sign of rightful self-assertion. This problem is analyzed in the discussion of Nella Larsen's *Quicksand* in chapter 7.

Notes to Chapter 5

1. Although Adrienne Rich's concept of "compulsory heterosexuality" helps explain the marked reticence on the part of writers on the renaissance to address the role of same-sexuality (see "Compulsory Heterosexuality and Lesbian Existence"), the historical construction of academic disciplines also must be considered as a factor. That scholarship on the Harlem Renaissance begins to blossom at the same point that gay liberation becomes a controversial topic cannot be overlooked. In the early 1970s, when black studies was being institutionalized as an academic discipline, black studies scholars were certainly aware of the risks entailed in broaching the topic of same-sexuality. Such an exploration could easily damage the chances of legitimating black studies as a discipline, and also could easily be misinterpreted both by individuals in the black community and by scholars outside the discipline. Concerning another topic, Houston Baker Jr. has suggested that this kind of disarming gesture characterizes too much African Americanist scholarship (*Modernism and the Harlem Renaissance* xvii). Darlene Clark Hine more recently has pointed out the historical disciplinary conservatism of black studies ("Black Studies" 25). Of course, the "conservatism" of black scholarship in the 1970s and early 1980s is a highly relative matter, for this scholarship was pushing the academy toward "radical" questions concerning race, economics, political inclusiveness, social and cultural values, and scientific objectivity. Furthermore, beneath the surface of corroborative liberation movements during the 1970s lurks a rivalry that eventually enables the pitting of the gay (largely male) "ghetto" against the black "inner city," creating an identity crisis that separates blackness from queerness in a way that would not have been imaginable in the 1920s, a period in which liberated sexuality for queers was intimately associated with a freer attitude toward sexuality in black urban communities.

2. Clarence Major traces the word *freak* as a noun to the 1920s, when it means "in jazz, a musician who possesses the skill to play high brass notes for an impressive length of time." He traces the African American adjective *freakish* to the 1940s, meaning "weird or homosexual; describing oral or anal sex." During the same time *freakology* in African American culture comes to mean "the 'study' of being unusual, of being homosexual, or different." In the 1950s, Major says, the noun *freak* could signify "a person who obviously enjoys sex" or "homosexual," a double meaning that it still carries in African American lingo today (*Juba to Jive* 181–182). There is a slippage that occurs in the etymology between a sexual practice regardless of sexual orientation and a decided sexual preference for someone of the same gender, just as there is a slippage between "freak" meaning anyone who enjoys sex immensely and only those who enjoy it same-sexually. To be black in United States society is to be treated as a freak or weird person; therefore freakology, the practice of learning how to enhance weirdness, cannot be a wholly bad thing.

3. On Augustus Granville Dill, see *The Dictionary of American Negro Biography*, and James E. Coleman Jr.'s criticism of the biographic entry on Dill in the *Dictionary* ("No Gay Blacks? *Dictionary of American Negro Biography* Notes No Homosexuals!" 5). On the Dill episode, see Lewis, *W.E.B. Du Bois: Fight for Equality* (204–205).

4. In emphasizing the unity and common interest between black and white in the renaissance, some recent writers not only must underplay the inequity in the relationship but also assume the beneficence of the United States nationalist project that ultimately motivates whites' interest in black folk materials. See, for instance, George Hutchinson, *Harlem Renaissance in Black and White;* Ann Douglas, *Terrible Honesty;* Susan Gubar, *Race Changes* (95–168); Eric Sundquist's ambivalent response to this trend in his review essay "Red, White, Black, and Blue"; and Jeffrey C. Stewart's more critical response in his exhibition catalog essay "Paul Robeson and the Problem of Modernism."

5. As James de Jongh notes, "[m]ost of Van Vechten's novel is guided by a didactic imperative, skillfully integrated with the fictional necessities of the story" (*Vicious Modernism* 28).

6. Cary D. Wintz also reads Van Vechten's "portrait of blacks" in this way: "[H]e insisted that blacks were just people—people who differed very little from other people of similar social and economic background" (*Black Culture and the Harlem Renaissance* 97). In his laudatory *Opportunity* review of *Nigger Heaven*, James Weldon Johnson initiates this sort of commentary: "If the book has a thesis it is: Negroes are people; they have the same emotions, the same passions, the same shortcomings, the same aspirations, the same graduations of social strata as other people" ("Romance and Tragedy in Harlem—A Review" 330).

7. See Chauncey's discussion of the double life (*Gay New York* 6–7, 271–291).

8. *Letters of Carl Van Vechten* (78 and 88); Lewis, *When Harlem Was in Vogue* (188) and "Dr. Johnson's Friends" (511).

9. In this sense, Huggins's critique continues a way of thinking about the ideal of African American arts as the aspiration for cosmopolitanism in the context of a parochial United States culture, an ideal proffered in the New Negro movement itself, as we have seen in Walter White's *Fire in the Flint* and James Weldon Johnson's writing and career, and as we shall see is also the case for Langston Hughes.

10. Contrast Lewis's greater frankness with Huggins's oblique treatment of Cullen's sexuality: "[N]one of the Harlem writers was more formally schooled, none more genteel in inclination and taste, none indeed more prissy than Cullen" (*Harlem Renaissance* 161). The implication of gender deviance runs throughout and shapes Huggins's negative assessment of Cullen's poetic output. "There is a prettiness here that wants to live in all of Cullen's work," he writes. "He liked softness and liquid sounds. Seldom did he write anything harsh" (213).

11. Lewis borrows this wonderfully descriptive word from Zora Neale Hurston. For Lewis's most detailed analysis of the Negrotarians' motives, see *When Harlem Was in Vogue* 89–103.

12. Gloria Hull, Thadious Davis, and Cheryl Wall have brought attention to the ways in which Jessie Redmon Fauset's role in the Harlem Renaissance has been slighted historically by critics and historians, due to gender assumptions operating in patronage; see, respectively, *Color, Sex, and Poetry* (5–11); *Nella Larsen* (157–162); and *Women of the Harlem Renaissance* (5–9, 34–37). In addition to these more frequently mentioned names, Charles Scruggs makes a case for H. L. Mencken as a midwife of the renaissance; see *The Sage in Harlem* (4). Most recently, in her biography, Carolyn Wedin positions Mary White Ovington as a "catalyst to the Harlem Renaissance" for her editing of a Negro high school reader in 1920 and her column "Book Chat," distributed to black newspapers; see *Inheritors of the Spirit* (199–228).

13. Holmes, "Alain Leroy Locke" (84–85). Holmes does not provide a citation for this quotation, and I have not been able to locate it. Johnny Washington similarly calls Locke a "Socratic midwife" (*Journey into the Philosophy of Alain Locke* 30).

14. This satirical barb against Locke appears in the column "Shafts and Darts" (183), co-authored by George Schuyler and Theophilus Lewis. Also see David Levering Lewis, "Dr. Johnson's Friends" (517–518). Given what happened to Augustus Dill, Du Bois's homosexual disciple, a couple years after Schuyler's barb, one has to wonder whether the satirist is punning on Dill's name here.

15. Arna Bontemps refers to the black patrons of the renaissance as "nursemaids" (*One Hundred Years of Negro Freedom* 229); also see Patrick J. Gilpin, "Charles S. Johnson" (215–216).

16. Fortunately, excellent work has already been initiated on the question of how gender influenced the renaissance. See, for instance, Mary Helen Washington, *Invented Lives* (164–166); Hull, *Color, Sex, and Poetry* (1–31); Wall, *Women of the Harlem Renaissance* (esp. 1–32); Davis, *Nella Larsen* (esp. 156–162 and 172–186); and Deborah McDowell, *"The Changing Same"* (61–77).

17. In "Insolent Racing, Rough Narrative," Michael Cobb points out how homosexuality figures in the self-construction of the second-generation renaissance movement, especially around the bohemian figure of Richard Bruce Nugent, and how this figuration tends to be suppressed by later critics.

18. Brawley, "Negro Literary Renaissance" (184); Lewis, *When Harlem Was in Vogue* (194). Benjamin Brawley (1882–1939), the most influential Negro academic critic of the period, was a professor at Howard University. He held conventional aesthetic/moral views on art, but like Du Bois, James Weldon Johnson, and Charles S. Johnson, he saw social and political uplift as a major objective for the renaissance. The gender implications of Brawley's aesthetic judgments are discussed in greater detail in the next chapter.

19. In *Nigger Heaven,* for instance, Van Vechten focuses on heterosexual sadomasochism between his colored hero and his bohemian colored lover, Lasca Sartoris. Van Vechten also depicts a "black mass" in which the sadomasochism in Catholic religious ritual is highlighted, a blasphemous gesture that Nugent makes more explicit in "Smoke, Lillies and Jade" when he intertwines the singing of a spiritual with homosexual imagery of what Lewis aptly calls "pointillistic soft pornography" (*When Harlem Was in Vogue* [197]). The fact that "Smoke, Lillies and Jade" was reprinted as a foundational black gay male text in the 1983 anthology *Black Men/White Men,* along with three poems on homosexual themes by Hughes, indicates how, although these texts have fallen out of the African American literary canon, they have achieved an underground life among black and white gay readers interested in homosexualizing the Harlem Renaissance.

20. I use the feminine *ingénue* next to the adjective *virile* intentionally, to suggest how McKay positions himself structurally in the feminine position of an innocent abroad while paradoxically retaining his posture of bold, roving selfconfidence as a curious, quick-witted, self-sufficient, earthy man of peasant stock.

21. Rhonda Cobham, "Jekyll and Claude" (63).

22. Wayne Koestenbaum, *Queen's Throat* (158–169).

23. Wayne F. Cooper remarks, "One of the attractions of Tangier for McKay must have been its tolerance of homosexuals, though as usual he remained circumspect. Ford remembered that parties in McKay's home included native musicians, good food, and hashish. McKay, he recalled, always appeared reserved at such gatherings" (*Claude McKay* [277]). On Byron's homosexual encounters with boys in the southern Mediterranean, see Louis Crompton, *Byron and Greek Love.*

24. For rare commentary on this novella, see James Levin, *Gay Novel in America* (36–38); on the circumstances of this novella's composition and publication, see Roger Austen, *Playing the Game* (59–62).

25. It is possible that what the Italian has suggested is not merely prostitution but sexual favors for other men.

26. McKay's views on racial uplift through assimilation and consolidation are contradictory and changing, as Liliane Blary points out in "Claude McKay and Black Nationalist Ideologies" (especially 214–216).

27. Many scholars have focused on the patronage of "Godmother" and its damaging consequence to Hughes and Hurston. For instance, see Huggins, *Harlem Renaissance* (129–136); Lewis, *When Harlem Was in Vogue* (151–155, 256–261); Robert Hemenway, *Zora Neale Hurston* (104–157); bell hooks, *Yearning* (135–143); Faith Berry, *Langston Hughes* (92–133); Arnold Rampersad, *Life of Langston Hughes,* vol. 1 (156–181); and Ralph D. Story, "Patronage and the Harlem Renaissance." Sometimes Godmother is used as a foil to demonstrate the sincerity and generosity of other patrons, as Bruce Kellner tends to do in implicitly contrasting her with Van Vechten (see "'Refined Racism'" [93–106]). In *Pocahontas's Daughters,* Mary V. Dearborn mounts an implausible defense of Mason's patronage, taking the "mother" part of godmother seriously by suggesting that Mason became a substitute mother (a white mammy?) for Hurston (64–69).

28. Arnold Rampersad, *Life of Langston Hughes,* vol. 1 (168). Huggins views the relationship in a similar fashion: "There was something in the arrangement Langston Hughes could not stand. . . . His description of the episode is filled with compassion and the pain of unrequited love" (*Harlem Renaissance* 133).

29. I make this argument more extensively in "Romancing the Nation-State" and in "Authority and Authenticity." On the history and theory of European patronage, see Michael Brennan, *Literary Patronage in the English Renaissance* (esp. 1–11); A. S. Collins, *Profession of Letters;* and especially Dustin H. Griffin, who nicely theorizes the "cultural economics" and politics of obligation exacted from the protégé upon the acceptance of the patron's generosity (*Literary Patronage in*

England 13–69). On the gendering of patronage in U.S. letters, see Shirley Marchalonis, *Patrons and Protégées.*

30. On the feuds between McKay and Locke, see Wintz, *Black Culture and the Harlem Renaissance* (116–118); Lewis, *When Harlem Was in Vogue* (153–155); Tyrone Tillery, *Claude McKay* (115–120 and 153–155); and Wayne Cooper, *Claude McKay* (261 and 319–321). Both Tillery (12–30) and Cooper (23–34) have commented on McKay's different treatment of white and black patrons, as has Cobham, "Jekyll and Claude."

31. On the cultural-historical relation between the dozens and camp, see my essay "Camping the Dirty Dozens."

32. About Countee Cullen's sending Hughes the sensual poem, "To a Brown Boy," which he had dedicated to "L.H.," Berry writes: "Hughes surely sensed the nuances in the poem. By then he knew, too, that there was between him and Locke and Cullen an attraction to their own sex" (*Langston Hughes* 43).

33. Leonard Harris, "Rendering the Text," in *Philosophy of Alain Locke,* ed. Harris (6).

34. George Hutchinson, *Harlem Renaissance in Black and White* (25, 31). For other examples, see Bruce Kellner, *Carl Van Vechten and the Irreverent Decades* (esp. 252–288); Edward Lueders, *Carl Van Vechten and the Twenties* (124–126); Jervis Anderson, *This Was Harlem* (214–216); Leon Coleman, "Carl Van Vechten Presents the New Negro" (107–125); and Ann Douglas, *Terrible Honesty* (esp. 82–83).

35. See Tony Martin, *Literary Garveyism* (137); John Runcie, "Marcus Garvey and the Harlem Renaissance" (8, 22); and Adam Lively, "Continuity and Radicalism in American Black Nationalist Thought" (230–231).

36. A common confusion seems to operate, as here in Hull's argument, whereby homosociality and homosexuality are equated. More accurately, for homosociality to achieve its power as patriarchal institution, it must repress homosexuality psychologically and seek to purge it culturally. It could even be said that homosociality is the contrary of homosexuality. Of course, this does not mean that, as men, individual homosexuals cannot exploit their privilege over women or that white homosexuals cannot exploit their racial privilege over blacks.

37. The converse figure is called a "snow queen"; see Clarence Major, *Juba to Jive* on the "snow queen" (431–432). Interestingly, Major has no entry for "dinge queen," though he does include "dinge."

38. See Stephen Jay Gould, *Mismeasure of Man;* and Elazar Barkan, *Retreat of Scientific Racism* (16, 76–89, 104–108, 115–119, 162–168).

39. Quoted in Bruce Kellner, *Carl Van Vechten and the Irreverent Decades* (220). In *Race Changes,* Susan Gubar briefly discusses both the Covarrubias cartoon and the Hopwood comment (154–155), but she comments on neither the context of homosexual coterie nor the scientific context.

Notes to Part III

1. Despite Kent's claim, the poetry of the renaissance has also been subjected to such scrutiny and such charges. On the accusation of sensationalism in the black press reviews of Hughes's *The Weary Blues* (1926) and *Fine Clothes to the Jew* (1927), see Faith Berry *Langston Hughes* (70–71 and 83–85); also Arnold Rampersad, *Life of Langston Hughes,* vol. 1 (129 and 139–142).

2. Amritjit Singh, "Black-White Symbiosis" (37). For other examples of this gender division silently at work, see Margaret Just Butcher, *Negro in American Culture* (175); Robert Bone, *Negro Novel in America,* where Fauset and Larsen are placed with Du Bois and White in a chapter called "The Rear Guard," instead of with "The Harlem School" (65–107); Scruggs, *Sage in Harlem* (15); Hiroko Sato, "Under the Harlem Shadow" (esp. 69–72, 81–82); Huggins, *Harlem Renaissance* (236–238). In his monograph *Novels of the Harlem Renaissance* (1976), Singh attempts to exonerate McKay as he suggests that "[i]n retrospect, we can take McKay's word that *Home to Harlem* was not written to exploit the market created by *Nigger Heaven*" (47), even though he continues to use the primitivist-versus-genteel division in focusing on a contrast between the class sympathies of McKay and Fauset (46).

3. Mary Helen Washington, *Invented Lives* (160). In one of the earliest essays to bring careful attention to the gender politics of Larsen's *Quicksand,* Hortense Thorton provides a brief reception history of Larsen criticism as she points out the tendency to reduce the novel to the "tragic-mulatto motif." Unfortunately, Thorton then takes the reading of Larsen too far in the other direction, downplaying the racial implications of *Quicksand* based on the idea "that Helga's tragedy was perhaps more a result of sexism than of racism"; see "Sexism as Quagmire" (288, 290–293). Also see Wall, *Women of the Harlem Renaissance* (117–120); and Priscilla Ramsey, "Freeze the Day" (28–31).

4. In *"The Changing Same,"* Deborah E. McDowell offers a similar critique of Fauset's reception (62). In *The Coupling Convention,* Ann duCille has identified a similar tendency in the construction of blues as the basis for African American cultural identity (68–69).

5. On Larsen's friendship with and seeking advice from Van Vechten, see Thadious M. Davis, *Nella Larsen, Novelist of the Harlem Renaissance* (156, 212–222, 232, 285–288). Davis also points out that Van Vechten's character Mary Love was modeled partly on Larsen (212) and that Larsen's genuine affection for Van Vechten does not exclude the possibility of her exploiting their friendship for developing inroads into the publishing industry (210–211). Also see Wall, *Women of the Harlem Renaissance* (95–96).

6. According to Edward E. Waldron, White completed the manuscript of *Flight* by early September 1925, was preparing the galleys in January 1926, and on March 16 the publisher sent out its announcement of an April 19 publication date (*Walter White and the Harlem Renaissance* [82, 96]). *Nigger Heaven* was published in August 1926. Given that Van Vechten had a hand in getting White's novel published, and Johnson's republished with his own introduction, it is clear that both novels influenced *Nigger Heaven.*

Notes to Chapter 6

1. In addition to Johnson's *Autobiography of an Ex-Coloured Man* (1912, 1927) and *Along This Way* (1933) as texts in intimate dialogue with urban folk narrative, I include the following male-pro-tagonist narratives: Rudolph Fisher, *The Walls of Jericho* (1928) and *The Conjure Man Dies* (1932); Claude McKay, *Home to Harlem* (1928), *Banjo* (1929), and *A Long Way from Home* (1937); Langston Hughes, *Not without Laughter* (1930) and *The Big Sea* (1940); Taylor Gordon, *Born to Be* (1929); Arna Bontemps, *God Sends Sunday* (1931); Countee Cullen, *One Way to Heaven* (1932); George Wylie Henderson, *Jule* (1946); and James Baldwin, *Go Tell It on the Mountain* (1952). Also in this genre, but with the revealing differences made by female protagonists, I include: Jessie Redmon Fauset, *There Is Confusion* (1924) and *Plum Bun* (1929); Walter White, *Flight* (1926); Nella Larsen, *Quicksand* (1928); Wallace Thurman, *The Blacker the Berry* (1929); and Dorothy West, *The Living Is Easy* (1948).

2. More recently, Farah Jasmine Griffin has brought our attention to what she calls the "migration narrative" in her book *"Who Set You Flowin'?* Griffin is especially insightful in pointing out the ways in which migration narratives shift from a focus on the body to a focus on the psyche when the North is the setting (see esp. 52). Also see Robert Bone's discussion of the pastoral mode in these novels in *Down Home* (113–138); and Renoir W. Gaither, "Moment of Revision" (82–85).

3. Hurston presents an interesting exception in this regard. It could be argued that she is exploring the same issues but through the nostalgic vehicle of a putatively dying rural black folk culture. In "Primitivism as a Therapeutic Pursuit," Robert A. Coles and Diane Isaacs remark on this gender difference in relation to the use of the primitive (6–11). Wall points out that the blueswomen of the Harlem Renaissance—generally of lower socioeconomic status—were bolder in their engagement with "raunchy" issues, and that Hurston's literature has much in common with them (*Women of the Harlem Renaissance* 18–28). Also see Hazel V. Carby, *Reconstructing Womanhood* (166–168); Deborah McDowell, *"Changing Same"* (72–77, 80–83); and Ann duCille, *Coupling Convention* (66–85).

4. This is a matter of emphasis, for as Kevin Gaines shows, the positive potential of folk energy can be glimpsed in such prewar writers as Paul Laurence Dunbar, James D. Corrothers, and James Weldon Johnson (*Uplifting the Race* 179–208).

5. This essay by Gustavus Adolphus Steward (b. 1881) is clearly influenced by the more famous one by George Schuyler (1895–1977), "The Negro-Art Hokum," published in *The Nation* in 1926. Steward was the winner of the third prize for essays in the 1925 *Crisis* literary contests. *The Crisis* for March 1926 printed his prize-winning essay, "Salvation," on varieties of religious experience among migrating African Americans, along with this brief biographical insert. Steward's name is misspelled "Stewart" in the byline of the "New Negro Hokum" essay.

6. Published by the University of North Carolina beginning in 1922, *Social Forces,* the journal in which Steward's essay appears, was founded to advance social science as both an objective science of society and a force for progressive social change.

7. Published to generally positive reviews in 1928, *Walls of Jericho* was reputedly "written on a

wager that such a book couldn't be done" (see Dewey R. Jones, "The Bookshelf" 2:1). Unfortunately, there is very little scholarship on Fisher's work, which deserves much more attention in literary and cultural studies.

8. At the back of the novel, Fisher, like Van Vechten, includes a dictionary of slang, "Introduction to Contemporary Harlemese, Expurgated and Abridged," in which he defines *slip:* "1. To kid. 2. *To slip in the dozens, to disparage one's family*" (305).

9. Lawrence W. Levine, *Black Culture and Black Consciousness* (427). Levine also points out that John Henry's hardness sometimes refers to his sexual prowess, and that sometimes his death results not from overexertion but from an unbearably large erection (422–423). The dominant characteristic of Fisher's Shine is not loss of control to a hard-on but ability to master his muscularity and thus his ambitious labor and sexual desire. In this sense, Shine is both more optimistic and more respectable than the most graphic versions of the John Henry legend.

10. In one version of the ballad, John Henry's wife, Polly, "drove steel like a man," and in another, he names his hammer after his wife, Lucy; see Guy B. Johnson, *John Henry* (2, 92). At the end of Johnson's book (published in 1929), he urges: "I marvel that some of the 'new' Negroes with an artistic bent do not exploit the wealth of John Henry lore. Here is material for an epic poem, for a play, for an opera, for a Negro symphony. What more tragic theme than the theme of John Henry's martyrdom?" (150).

11. What John W. Roberts writes about the traditional trickster under slavery applies also to the legendary Shine, as well as to Fisher's hero: "Although the trickster tale tradition functioned primarily as a normative mode of heroic action for securing the material means of survival under the restrictive and repressive conditions of slavery, it was also a tradition in which the central figure's actions were motivated primarily by the socio-political oppression of those who celebrated his action as those of a folk hero" (*From Trickster to Badman* 185).

12. Fisher defines "K.M." to indicate the sympathetic condescension in the tone of the men who use the term: "Kitchen mechanic, i.e., cook, girl, scullion, menial" (*Walls of Jericho* 302). Of course, as the most common vocation available to African American and many immigrant women, domestic labor is both the job most pursued and that most desirable to move beyond. As such, it represents both the temporary stepping-stone to something better and the stone around the neck that prevents young women from finding an avenue into middle-class status and other kinds of personal fulfillment. On the respectability and sexual dangers of black women's housekeeping vocations, see Elizabeth Clark-Lewis, *Living In, Living Out* (esp. 48–49 and 99–113); Jacqueline Jones, *Labor of Love, Labor of Sorrow* (164–166); and Tera W. Hunter, *To 'Joy My Freedom* (11–12, 105–108).

13. See, for instance, contemporary reviews of *Home to Harlem* and *Walls of Jericho:* W.E.B. Du Bois, "Browsing Reader" *The Crisis* 35.6 (June 1928) 374 and 35.11 (November 1928) 202; Dewey R. Jones, "The Book Shelf" 2.1; Aubrey Bowser, "Nearing the Big Day" 16. Earlier, Bowser had issued an ambivalent defense of *Home to Harlem* as "dirt for art's sake" ("Dirt for Art's Sake" 20). Among more recent commentators on McKay, see Bell, *Afro-American Novel and Its Tradition* (116–117); Michael B. Stoff, "Claude McKay and the Cult of Primitivism" (130–135); Stephen H. Bronz, *Roots of Negro Racial Consciousness* (80–82); Adam Lively, "Continuity and Radicalism in American Black Nationalist Thought" (231); Lewis, *When Harlem Was in Vogue* (229); and Singh, *Novels of the Harlem Renaissance* (50).

14. Helen Pyne-Timothy, "Perceptions of the Black Woman in the Work of Claude McKay" (157). For Hazel Carby's much more critical view of McKay's female characters, see the discussion below.

15. For instance, in his review of the novel, John R. Chamberlain writes: "Jake is a naturally happy man, and a black man unworried by any philosophical preoccupation with the race question" ("When Spring Comes to Harlem" [5]). Bell allegorizes the novel so that Jake becomes the "man of instinct" and his formally educated Haitian friend, Ray, becomes "intellect" (*Afro-American Novel and Its Tradition* [117]).

16. Richard Priebe, "Search for Community in the Novels of Claude McKay" (24). Priebe further points out that when we encounter Jake in McKay's succeeding novel, *Banjo*, he is alone and back on the road again.

17. We see glimpses of a concern for black male friendship in Martin Robison Delany's *Blake; or the Huts of America*, not known at the time of the New Negro Renaissance. Unlike the urban folk novelists, who are interested in both the personal and the sociopolitical implications of the psychic and sexual networks of male camaraderie, Delany is more narrowly interested in the political aspect of men's alliances with women and other men.

18. Jerry Bryant concludes: "Such violence was the yeast that vitalized the dancing, gaming, drinking, and loving that went on among the carefree blacks" (*Victims and Heroes* [143]). Bryant's judgement repeats the dichotomy between uplifting and gutter novels observed traditionally in criticism on the Negro Renaissance.

19. Bell, *Afro-American Novel and Its Tradition* (140); also see the anonymous review "*The Walls of Jericho* and Other New Works of Fiction" (3.6). Amritjit Singh says that instead of Damon and Pythias, Jinx and Bubber remind "early reviewers more of Miller and Lyles, or the vaudeville team of Glenn and Jenkins" (*Novels of the Harlem Renaissance* 84).

20. Given the high visibility of same-sexuality, along with other modes of sexual deviance, tolerated in African American urban communities during this period, it does not make sense to suggest that it is the ambivalence of the working class toward such behavior that is Fisher's utmost concern. More likely, he is concerned about the propriety of his own black middle class, in their obsessive anxiety over presenting a respectable face to the white world. In this sense, Du Bois's response to Jinx and Bubber as a "little smutty" is symptomatic. In "Love and Sex in the Afro-American Novel," Gloria Naylor argues that "Hughes, together with Arna Bontemps and Wallace Thurman, did not openly explore his own sexuality in his work. . . . Like the homosexual woman, the homosexual man was the victim of a double consciousness, a double standard. Obviously, fear or shame, within their own community and in the world outside it, held these newer voices back from full creative expression—expression, that is, of their whole selves" (24). Though containing an element of truth, Naylor's statement needs to be revised in light of the prominence of representations of same-sexuality throughout African American men's literature in terms "open" but not necessarily self-evident. In the cases of Hughes and Thurman (as well as Chester Himes, William Attaway, John Edgar Wideman, and many others of various sexual dispositions), they *did* explore same-sexuality openly, though not necessarily by identifying *themselves* openly as homosexual or bisexual. What constitutes "open" same-sexuality is not a historically fixed or culturally uniform matter.

21. Another instance of this sort of coded reference to same-sexuality occurs in Arna Bontemps's reminiscence of the Renaissance, "The Awakening: A Memoir," included in his 1972 anthology, *The Harlem Renaissance Remembered*. He writes: "Harold Jackman became Countee Cullen's closest friend. They were the David and Jonathan of the Harlem twenties."(12). Although in dominant culture David and Jonathan represent the prototype for idealized deeply passionate homosocial friendship, in homosexual networks the two biblical figures have long represented the ideal of devoted same-sexual love.

22. In today's parlance, "boy" is short for "homeboy." "My niggah" is used in a similar way in Hip Hop lingo.

23. On the meanings of "boy" in African American usage, Clarence Major points out that calling heroin "boy" in the 1920s to 1940s derived either from female speakers or from male homosexuals; heroin "was so called because of the sexual sensation it gives" (*Juba to Jive* 60). Also see his next entry, "boys" (60). The usage of "punk" has a similar etymology. Starting out as a derogatory term for a homosexual or the "passive" partner in male same-sexual intercourse (not necessarily "homosexual" intercourse, because the "active" partner could identify as "straight"), it comes to indicate any weak man or "sissy." To punk served as a verb denoting the performance of anal intercourse, whether intragender or not, and most famously it has been used among black men in prison culture (migrating outward to larger prison terminology) since at least the 1940s to refer to any male, regardless of an identifiable sexual orientation, who accepts or is coerced into anal intercourse (see Major, *Juba to Jive* 367–368). Again, the perpetual slippage of such words into or out of specific same-sexual meanings and out of or into more general non-same-sexual applications indicates the curious ways in which same-sexuality has historically been ambivalently interwoven into larger African American culture since at least the first decades of the twentieth century.

24. McKay's succeeding novel, *Banjo: A Story without a Plot* (1929), continues with Ray's story by following him in his vagabond adventures.

25. McKay's treatment of Ray is ambivalent. On the one hand, he shows up the contrast between what Ray feels and thinks about Jake's life and the reality of Jake's life. On the other hand, McKay seems to identify himself with Ray as a sensitive writer whose "misfit" status prevents him from experiencing what he perceives as Jake's completeness. Adam Lively recognizes the paradox: "But ironically, Ray's education gives him a deeper notion of the primitive than Jake can attain intuitively, since the impulse to the primitive is a protest—a product of reflection upon the blacks' condition in America. Ray's dilemma feeds upon itself. His visions of the primitive (often drug induced) are precisely that—artificial and transitory. The often ugly realities of Harlem life form a

bitter back-drop" ("Continuity and Radicalism in American Black Nationalist Thought" [231]). In Elmer Lueth's defense of the novel, he accepts the tendency toward animalistic stereotype of the lower-class blacks as savages, but he argues that Ray's contradictions as a sensitive savage educate Jake and thus undercut the typical primitivism of which the novel is accused. This reading, however, relies on an educated, middle-class character to raise the tone and purpose—a solution I find unsatisfactory ("Scope of Black Life in Claude McKay's *Home to Harlem*").

26. McKay does not provide a dictionary of African American usage, an intentional move to distance the facile expectations of white readers who think they can gain access to black primitivism vicariously.

27. In *Vicious Modernism*, James de Jongh also remarks on McKay's parodic relationship to *Nigger Heaven*. As de Jongh points out, McKay also insisted that "early drafts of *Home to Harlem* antedated *Nigger Heaven*" (31).

28. "Rose had her friends of both sexes and was quite free in her ways" (*Home to Harlem* 113).

29. Traditional blues song, quoted in McKay, *Home to Harlem* (36, 129).

Notes to Chapter 7

1. Hazel V. Carby, "Policing the Black Woman's Body in an Urban Context" (747).

2. George Kent, *Blackness and the Adventure of Western Culture* (48). Nathan Huggins makes a similar point: "For the purpose of ethnic identity, primitivism is peculiarly limited. It is especially a male fantasy. It is easier to imagine men as roustabouts, vagabonds, bums, and heroes, harder to draw sympathetic females whose whole existence is their bodies and instinct. It is also difficult to create the illusion of development and generation; there are no children anywhere in these works" (*Harlem Renaissance* 188–189). In *Black Women Novelists*, Barbara Christian concurs (40) but points out that Fauset's use of conventional middle-class characters and their values "posed a serious threat to the New Negro Philosophy. If blacks were culturally no different from whites except when downtrodden, how could anyone posit a unique Negro genius, a specifically different culture?" (47). Also see Amritjit Singh, *Novels of the Harlem Renaissance* (55–57).

3. Though formally a subplot, Maggie's story takes up almost half of the novel, as Fauset interweaves the two stories throughout.

4. What Ann duCille says about *Comedy: American Style* and *Plum Bun* seem to apply, if in a less pointed way, to *There Is Confusion*: "Fauset draws on the romantic form and traditional social and literary conventions to explore racial and class ideology and to critique the ways in which the sentimental romance idealizes love, marriage, and family" (*Coupling Convention* 93). Deborah McDowell makes a similar point about *Plum Bun* in "Changing Same" (64–65).

5. Barbara Christian explores this relationship between the passing novel and the mulatta novel of manners in *Black Women Novelists* (44–53); also see Missy Dehn Kubitschek, *Claiming the Heritage* (93–94).

6. Phillip Brian Harper insightfully points out how this closure gives Mimi a sort of personal possession of racial identity, a possession that can be read as returning her to feminine domesticity after all (*Are We Not Men?* [118]).

7. On Dreiser's influence on White and other Harlem Renaissance novelists, see Charles Scruggs, *Sage in Harlem* (16).

8. Quoted in Edward E. Waldron, *Walter White and the Harlem Renaissance* (94).

9. For discussion of Larsen's involvement in the *Opportunity* controversy over *Flight*, see Waldron, *Walter White and the Harlem Renaissance* (100–107); and Thadious M. Davis, *Nella Larsen* (200–207).

10. Frank Horne, "Our Book Shelf" (227). Horne continues this surreptitious gendering of the argument in the guise of chivalry in his response to Larsen's response, although he ends up admitting her to the fray on the merits of her aggressive spirit: "When I first read Nella Imes' answer to my criticism of Walter White's *Flight*, it had been my intention to let the matter drop there, else we be accused of creating much ado about nothing. But the realization of this charmingly energetic partizanship [*sic*] in a literary matter within my own group, aroused by my own controversial review, so tickled my innate and unpardonable vanity, that words fairly bubble from my pen in reply. Perhaps when we are more critically mature and colder of blood, neither Mrs. Imes nor myself will bother to express our opinions in so open and positive a manner. But now, I welcome her into the lists of critical controversy"; see Horne, "Correspondence" (326).

11. Nella [Larsen] Imes, "Correspondence" (295).

12. Interestingly, though, Larsen seems obliquely to respond to Horne's gender condescension when she calls into question his chivalry by implying, in the final sentence of her response, that he cannot detect charm when it stares him in the face: "It may be that your reviewer read the book hastily, superficially, and so missed both its meaning and its charm" ("Correspondence" 295).

13. Walter White's own final word in the debate also takes up this issue of Horne's missing the racial meaning; see White, "Correspondence" (397).

14. McDowell, *"Changing Same"* (83); and Davis, *Nella Larsen* (106).

15. Thadious Davis also comments on this violent aspect when she writes: *"Quicksand* is comparable to a 'discharge of violence,' an expression of anger usually suppressed and restrained" (*Nella Larsen* [255]).

16. This ambiguity is also symbolically represented in James's name. As Thadious Davis notes, Vayle, "suggestive of the veil within which people of color functioned, according to Du Bois, is at once a lure and a repulse" (*Nella Larsen* [261]); Kubitschek also comments on the punning name (*Claiming the Heritage* 102).

17. McDowell, *"Changing Same"* (85). In *"Who Set You Flowin'?"* Farah Jasmine Griffin also remarks on the interchange between religion and sexuality in this scene: "Sexuality is linked to religion, because the latter allows her [Helga] to act upon her sexual desires within the confines of marriage. Sexual ecstasy becomes conflated with Helga's own sense of religious ecstasy. When her sexual activity leads to the misery of childbirth, she immediately begins to reject religion" (159). Kubitschek cleverly reads Naxos, the island home of the god Dionysus in Greek mythology (or the Roman god Bacchus), as a symbol of the conflict between orgiastic desire and patriarchal subjection (see *Claiming the Heritage* [102–103]).

18. Cheryl Wall also points to the aptness of Rev. Green's name, which she identifies with the "chimera" of a "retreat" in *Women of the Harlem Renaissance* (114).

19. Thurman (1902–1934) was born and raised in Salt Lake City, Utah, and, like Emma Lou's, his father deserted the family when Thurman was a small boy. He moved to Harlem in 1925 after studying briefly at the University of Utah and then the University of Southern California as a pre-medical student, without taking a degree, and working at a post office in Los Angeles with Arna Bontemps. Just as Countee Cullen briefly married Nina Yolande Du Bois, Thurman was married to Louise Thompson in 1928—an event that shocked his friends, who knew about his same-sex disposition, since he was arrested in a subway restroom shortly after arriving in New York. Thompson cited incompatibility stemming from Thurman's homosexuality in the divorce proceedings. Thurman's desire for marriage indicates the inordinate pressure to conform to middle-class expectations even for someone with his nonconformist, bohemian pose. On Thurman's biography see Mae Henderson, "Portrait of Wallace Thurman" (147–170).

20. Hostetler, "Aesthetics of Race and Gender in Nella Larsen's *Quicksand*" (35); also see Wall, *Women of the Harlem Renaissance* (100).

Works Cited

Abel, Annie Heloise. *The American Indian in the Civil War, 1862–1865*. Lincoln: University of Nebraska Press, 1992.

Adams, John Henry. "Rough Sketches: The New Negro Man." *Voice of the Negro* 1.10 (Oct. 1904): 447–452.

———. "Rough Sketches: A Study of the Features of the New Negro Woman." *Voice of the Negro* 1.8 (Aug. 1904): 323–326.

Addams, Jane. *Twenty Years at Hull-House with Autobiographical Notes*. 1910. Introduced by James Hart. Urbana: University of Illinois, 1990.

Allen, Theodore W. *The Invention of the White Race*. Vol. 1. London: Verso, 1994.

Almáguer, Tomás. *Racial Fault Lines: The Historical Origins of White Supremacy in California*. Berkeley: University of California Press, 1994.

Anderson, Elijah. *Streetwise: Race, Class, and Change in an Urban Community*. Chicago: University of Chicago Press, 1990.

Anderson, Jervis. *This Was Harlem: A Cultural Portrait, 1900–1950*. New York: Farrar, Straus, Giroux, 1981.

Andrews, William L. Introduction. In *Bursting Bonds: The Autobiography of a "New Negro,"* by William Pickens, xi–xxviii.

———. *The Literary Career of Charles W. Chesnutt*. Baton Rouge: Louisiana State University Press, 1980.

Anzaldúa, Gloria. *Borderlands/La Frontera: The New Mestiza*. San Francisco: Spinsters/Aunt Lute, 1987.

Appiah, Kwame Anthony. *In My Father's House: Africa in the Philosophy of Culture*. New York: Oxford University Press, 1992.

Aptheker, Herbert. *The Literary Legacy of W.E.B. Du Bois*. White Plains, NY: Kraw International Publications, 1989.

Austen, Roger. *Playing the Game: The Homosexual Novel in America*. Indianapolis: Bobbs-Merrill Co., 1977.

Avery, Sheldon. *Up from Washington: William Pickens and the Negro Struggle for Equality, 1900–1954*. Newark: University of Delaware Press, 1989.

Awkward, Michael. *Negotiating Difference: Race, Gender, and the Politics of Positionality*. Chicago: University of Chicago Press, 1995.

Baker, Houston A. Jr. *Long Black Song: Essays in Black American Literature and Culture*. Charlottesville: University of Virginia Press, 1972.

———. *Modernism and the Harlem Renaissance*. Chicago: University of Chicago Press, 1987.

Baldwin, James. *Go Tell It on the Mountain*. New York: Dell, 1953.

Barkan, Elazar. *The Retreat of Scientific Racism: Changing Concepts of Race in Britain and the United States*. Cambridge: Cambridge University Press, 1992.

Barrett, Lindon. *Blackness and Value: Seeing Double*. Cambridge: Cambridge University Press, 1999.

Barton, Rebecca Chalmers. *Witnesses for Freedom: Negro Americans in Autobiography.* New York: Harper, 1948.

Beavers, Herman. *Wrestling Angels into Song: The Fictions of Ernest J. Gaines and James Alan McPherson.* Philadelphia: University of Pennsylvania Press, 1995.

Bederman, Gail. *Manliness and Civilization: A Cultural History of Gender and Race in the United States, 1880–1917.* Chicago: University of Chicago Press, 1995.

Bell, Bernard W. *The Afro-American Novel and Its Tradition.* Amherst: University of Massachusetts Press, 1987.

Berry, Faith. *Langston Hughes: Before and Beyond Harlem.* Westport, CT: Lawrence Hill and Co., 1983.

Blackwell, James E., and Morris Janowitz, eds. *Black Sociologists: Historical and Contemporary Perspectives.* Chicago: University of Chicago Press, 1974.

Blary, Liliane. "Claude McKay and Black Nationalist Ideologies (1934–1948)." In *Myth and Ideology in American Culture,* edited by Regis Durand, 211–231. Villeneuve d'Ascq: University de Lille III, 1976.

Blount, Marcellus, and George P. Cunningham, eds. *Representing Black Men.* New York: Routledge, 1996.

Bone, Robert. *Down Home: Origin of the Afro-American Short Story.* 1975. New York: Columbia University Press, 1988.

———. *The Negro Novel in America.* 1958. Rev. ed. New Haven: Yale University Press, 1965.

Bontemps, Arna. "The Awakening: A Memoir." In *The Harlem Renaissance Remembered,* edited by Arna Bontemps, 1–26.

———. *God Sends Sunday.* New York: Harcourt, Brace and Co., 1931.

———. *One Hundred Years of Negro Freedom.* New York: Dodd, Mead and Co., 1961.

———, ed. *The Harlem Renaissance Remembered.* New York: Dodd, Mead and Co., 1972.

Bontemps, Arna, and Jack Conroy. *Anyplace but Here.* New York: Hill and Wang, 1966.

Boone, Joseph A., and Michael Cadden, eds. *Engendering Men: The Question of Male Feminist Criticism.* New York: Routledge, 1990.

Bowser, Audrey. "Dirt for Art's Sake." *New York Amsterdam News,* 21 March 1928, 20.

———. "Nearing the Big Day." *New York Amsterdam News,* 8 August 1928, 16.

Boykin, Keith. *One More River to Cross: Black and Gay in America.* New York: Anchor Books/Doubleday, 1996.

Bracey, John, August Meier, and Elliott Rudwick. "The Black Sociologists: The First Half Century." In *The Death of White Sociology,* edited by Joyce A. Ladner, 3–22.

Brawley, Benjamin. *Early Black American Writers: Selections with Biographical and Critical Introductions.* 1935. New York: Dover, 1992.

———. *The Negro Genius: A New Appraisal of the Achievement of the American Negro in Literature and the Fine Arts.* New York: Dodd, Mead and Co., 1937.

———. "The Negro Literary Renaissance." *Southern Workman* 56.4 (April 1927): 177–184.

———. *A Social History of the American Negro, Being a History of the Negro Problem in the United States, Including a History and Study of the Republic of Liberia.* Introduction by Eric Lincoln. 1921. London: Collier Books, 1970.

Braxton, Joanne M. *Black Women Writing Autobiography: A Tradition within a Tradition.* Philadelphia: Temple University Press, 1989.

Brennan, Michael. *Literary Patronage in the English Renaissance: The Pembroke Family.* London: Routledge, 1988.

Brewer, William. "Alain Leroy Locke." *Negro History Bulletin* 18 (November 1954): 26, 32.

Brodhead, Richard H., ed. *The Journals of Charles W. Chesnutt.* Durham: Duke University Press, 1993.

Brod, Harry, ed. *The Making of Masculinities: The New Men's Studies.* Boston: Unwin and Hyman, 1987.

Bronz, Stephen H. *Roots of Negro Racial Consciousness; the 1920s: Three Harlem Renaissance Authors.* New York: Libra, 1964.

Brooks, James F. ed. *Confounding the Color Line: The Indian-Black Experience in North America.* Lincoln: University of Nebraska Press, 2002.

Brown, Elsa Barkley. "Considering the Social Identities of Africanamerican Men: The World of Edward McConnell Drummond." Unpublished manuscript.

———. "Imaging Lynching: African American Women, Communities of Struggle, and Collective

Memory." In *African American Women Speak Out on Anita Hill–Clarence Thomas,* edited by Geneva Smitherman. Detroit: Wayne State University Press, 1995. 100–124.

———. "Negotiating and Transforming the Public Sphere: African American Political Life in the Transition from Slavery to Freedom." *Public Culture* 7 (1994): 107–146.

Bruce, Dickson D. Jr. *Black American Writing from the Nadir: The Evolution of a Literary Tradition, 1877–1915.* Baton Rouge: Louisiana State University Press, 1989.

Bryant, Jerry H. *Victims and Heroes: Racial Violence in the African American Novel.* Amherst: University of Massachusetts Press, 1997.

Bulmer, Martin. "Charles S. Johnson, Robert E. Park, and the Research Methods of the Chicago Commission on Race Relations, 1919–1922: An Early Experiment in Applied Social Research." *Ethnic and Racial Studies* 4 (1981): 289–306.

———. *The Chicago School of Sociology.* Chicago: University of Chicago Press, 1984.

Burgess, Ernest W. "Social Planning and Race Relations." In *Race Relations, Problems, and Theory: Essays in Honor of Robert E. Park,* edited by Jitsuichi Masuoka and Preston Valien, 13–25. Chapel Hill: University of North Carolina Press, 1961. 13–25.

Butcher, Margaret Just. *The Negro in American Culture, Based on Materials by Alain Locke.* New York: New American Library, 1956.

Butler, Judith. *Bodies That Matter: On the Discursive Limits of "Sex."* New York: Routledge, 1993.

———. *Gender Trouble: Feminism and the Subversion of Identity.* New York: Routledge, 1990.

Byerman, Keith E. *Seizing the Word: History, Art, and Self in the Work of W.E.B. Du Bois.* Athens: University of Georgia Press, 1994.

Carby, Hazel V. *Cultures in Babylon: Black Britain and African America.* London and New York: Verso, 1999.

———. "'On the Threshold of Woman's Era': Lynching, Empire, and Sexuality in Black Feminist Theory." In *"Race," Writing, and Difference,* edited by Henry Louis Gates Jr., 301–316. Chicago: University of Chicago Press, 1986.

———. "Policing the Black Woman's Body in an Urban Context." *Critical Inquiry* 18 (Summer 1992): 738–755. Reprinted in *Cultures in Babylon,* 22–39.

———. *Race Men.* Cambridge: Harvard University Press, 1998.

———. *Reconstructing Womanhood: The Emergence of the Afro-American Woman Novelist.* New York: Oxford University Press, 1987.

Carson [Lowitt], Suzanne C. "Samuel Chapman Armstrong: Missionary to the South." Ph.D. diss., Johns Hopkins University, 1952.

Chamberlain, John R. "When Spring Comes to Harlem: Claude McKay's Novel Gives a Glowing Picture of the Negro Quarter." *New York Times Book Review,* 11 March 1928, part 4, 5.

Chambers, Ross. *Room for Maneuver: Reading Oppositional Narrative.* Chicago: University of Chicago Press, 1991.

Chauncey, George. *Gay New York: Gender, Urban Culture, and the Making of the Gay Male World, 1890–1940.* New York: Basic Books, 1994.

Chesnutt, Charles Waddell. *The Colonel's Dream.* 1905. Upper Saddle River, NJ: Gregg Press, 1968.

———. "The Future American: A Complete Race-Amalgamation Likely to Occur." *Boston Evening Transcript* 1 Sept. 1900: 24.

———. "The Future American: A Stream of Dark Blood in the Veins of Southern Whites." *Boston Evening Transcript* 25 Aug. 1900: 15.

———. "The Future American: What the Race Is Likely to Become in the Process of Time." *Boston Evening Transcript* 18 Aug. 1900: 20.

———. "The March of Progress." *Century* 61.3 (Jan. 1901): 422–428.

———. *The Marrow of Tradition.* Edited by Nancy Bentley and Sandra Gunning. 1901. Boston: Bedford/St. Martin's Press, 2002.

———. *The Wife of His Youth, and Other Stories of the Color Line.* 1899. Ann Arbor: University of Michigan Press, 1968.

Christian, Barbara. *Black Women Novelists: The Development of a Tradition, 1892–1976.* Westport, CT: Greenwood Press, 1980.

Clark, Kenneth B. *Dark Ghetto: Dilemmas of Social Power.* New York: Harper and Row, 1965.

Clark-Lewis, Elizabeth. *Living In, Living Out: African American Domestics and the Great Migration.* New York: Kodansha International, 1994.

Clifford, James, and George E. Marcus. *Writing Culture: The Poetics and Politics of Ethnography.* Berkeley: University of California Press, 1986.

Cobb, Michael. "Insolent Racing, Rough Narrative: The Harlem Renaissance's Impolite Queers." *Callaloo* 23.1 (2000): 328–351.

Cobham, Rhonda. "Jekyll and Claude: The Erotics of Patronage in McKay's *Banana Bottom.*" *Caribbean Quarterly* 38.1 (March 1992): 35–78.

Coleman, James E. Jr. "No Gay Blacks? *Dictionary of American Negro Biography* Notes No Homosexuals!" *The Gay Review* 1.1 (December 1990): 5–8.

Coleman, Leon. "Carl Van Vechten Presents the New Negro." In *The Harlem Renaissance Re-examined,* edited by Victor A. Kramer, 107–127.

Coles, Robert A., and Diane Isaacs. "Primitivism as a Therapeutic Pursuit: Notes toward a Reassessment of Harlem Renaissance Literature." In *The Harlem Renaissance,* edited by Amritjit Singh, William S. Shiver, and Stanley Brodwin, 3–12.

Collins, Arthur Simms. *The Profession of Letters: A Study of the Relation of Author to Patron, Publishers, and Public, 1780–1832.* London: Routledge, 1928.

"Complete Riot Report Bared: Report Mayor Hid Complete in this Issue; Amsterdam News Is First to Publish Harlem Study." *Amsterdam News,* July 18, 1936, 1, 6–9, 20, 24.

Cooney, Charles F. "Walter White and the Harlem Renaissance." *Journal of Negro History* 57 (1972): 231–240.

Cooper, Wayne F. *Claude McKay: Rebel Sojourner in the Harlem Renaissance.* New York: Schocken Books, 1987.

Corrothers, James David. *The Black Cat Club: Negro Humor and Folklore.* Illustrated by J. K. Bryans. New York: Funk and Wagnalls Co., 1902.

———. *In Spite of the Handicap: An Autobiography.* New York: George H. Doran Co., 1916.

Cox, Oliver C. *Caste, Class and Race: A Study in Social Dynamics.* 1948. New York: Modern Reader Paperbacks, 1970.

Crookshank, F. G. *The Mongol in Our Midst: A Study of Man and His Three Faces.* New York: Dutton, 1924.

Crompton, Louis. *Byron and Greek Love: Homophobia in 19th-Century England.* Berkeley: University of California Press, 1985.

Crowley, John W. "Howells, Stoddard, and Male Homosocial Attachment in Victorian America." In *The Making of Masculinities: The New Men's Studies,* edited by Harry Brod, 301–324.

Cruse, Harold. *The Crisis of the Negro Intellectual: A Historical Analysis of the Failure of Black Leadership.* 1967. New York: Quill, 1984.

Cullen, Countee, *One Way to Heaven.* New York: Harper and Brothers, 1932.

———, ed. *Caroling Dusk: An Anthology of Verse by Black Poets.* 1927. New York: Citadel Press, 1995.

Davis, Angela Y. *Blues Legacies and Black Feminism.* New York: Vintage, 1999.

———. *Women, Race and Class.* New York: Vintage, 1983.

Davis, Arthur P. *From the Dark Tower: Afro-American Writers, 1900–1960.* Washington, D.C.: Howard University Press, 1974.

Davis, Thadious M. *Nella Larsen, Novelist of the Harlem Renaissance: A Woman's Life Unveiled.* Baton Rouge: Louisiana State University Press, 1994.

Dearborn, Mary V. *Pocahontas's Daughters: Gender and Ethnicity in American Culture.* New York: Oxford University Press, 1986.

De Armond, Fred. "A Note on the Sociology Negro Literature." *Opportunity* 3 (1925): 369–371.

de Jongh, James. *Vicious Modernism: Black Harlem and the Literary Imagination.* Cambridge: Cambridge University Press, 1990.

Delany, Martin Robison. *Blake; or, The Huts of America.* Edited by Floyd J. Miller. 1861–1862. Boston: Beacon, 1970.

DeMarco, Joseph. *The Social Thought of W.E.B. Du Bois.* Lanham, MD: University Press of America, 1983

Dennis, Rutledge M. "Relativism and Pluralism in the Social Thought of Alain Locke." In *Alain Locke,* edited by Russell J. Linnemann, 29–49.

The Dictionary of American Negro Biography. Edited by Rayford Logan. New York: W. W. Norton, 1982.

Douglas, Ann. *Terrible Honesty: Mongrel Manhattan in the 1920s.* New York: Farrar, Straus, and Giroux, 1995.

Doyle, Laura. *Bordering on the Body: The Racial Matrix of Modern Fiction and Culture.* New York: Oxford University Press, 1994.

———. "The Racial Sublime." In *Romanticism, Race, and Imperial Culture, 1780–1834,* edited by Alan Richardson and Sonia Hofkosh, 15–39. Bloomington: Indiana University Press, 1996.

Drake, St. Clair, and Horace R. Cayton. *Black Metropolis: A Study of Negro Life in a Northern City.* 1945. Rev. and enlarged ed. Introduction by Richard Wright. Foreword by William Julius Wilson. Chicago: University of Chicago Press, 1993.

Duberman, Martin Bauml, Martha Vicinus, and George Chauncey Jr., eds. *Hidden from History: Reclaiming the Gay and Lesbian Past.* New York: New American Library, 1989.

Du Bois, W.E.B. *The Autobiography of W.E.B. Du Bois: A Soliloquy on Viewing My Life from the Last Decade of Its First Century.* New York: International Publishers, 1968.

———. *Black Reconstruction in America.* 1935. New York: Russell and Russell, 1968.

———. "The Browsing Reader." *The Crisis* 35.6 (June 1928): 202, 211.

———. "The Browsing Reader." Rev. of *Born to Be. The Crisis* 37.4 (Apr. 1930): 129.

———. "The Browsing Reader." Rev. of *The Walls of Jericho,* by Rudolph Fisher. *The Crisis* 35.11 (Nov. 1928): 374.

———. *Darkwater: Voices from within the Veil.* Introduction by Herbert Aptheker. 1920. Millwood, NY: Kraus-Thompson Organization, Ltd., 1975.

———. *Dusk of Dawn: An Essay toward an Autobiography of a Race Concept.* 1940. New Brunswick: Transaction Publishers, 1984.

———. *The Philadelphia Negro.* Philadelphia: University of Pennsylvania Press, 1899.

———. *The Souls of Black Folk.* 1903. New York: Penguin Books, 1989.

duCille, Ann. *The Coupling Convention: Sex, Text, and Tradition in Black Women's Fiction.* New York: Oxford University Press, 1993.

———. "The Occult of True Black Womanhood." In *Skin Trade,* 81–119. Cambridge: Harvard University Press, 1996.

Dudley, David L. *My Father's Shadow: Intergenerational Conflict in African American Men's Autobiography.* Philadelphia: University of Pennsylvania Press, 1991.

Dunbar, Paul Laurence. *The Complete Poems of Paul Laurence Dunbar.* 1895. New York: Dodd, Mead and Co., 1980.

———. *Sport of the Gods.* New York: Dodd, Mead, & Co., 1902.

Duneier, Mitchell. *Slim's Table: Race, Respectability, and Masculinity.* Chicago: University of Chicago Press, 1992.

Durham, Philip, and Everett L. Jones. *The Negro Cowboys.* New York: Dodd, Mead, and Co., 1965.

Early, Gerald. "The Black Intellectual and the Sport of Prizefighting." In *The Culture of Bruising: Essays on Prizefighting, Literature, and Modern American Culture,* 5–45. Hopewell, NJ: Ecco, 1994.

———. *Tuxedo Junction: Essays on American Culture.* Hopewell, NJ: Ecco Press, 1989.

Edelman, Lee. *Homographesis: Essays in Gay Literary and Cultural Theory.* New York: Routledge, 1994.

Edwards, G. Franklin. "E. Franklin Frazier." In *Black Sociologists: Historical and Contemporary Perspectives,* edited by James E. Blackwell and Morris Janowitz, 85–117.

Elder, Arlene A. "'The Future American Race': Charles W. Chesnutt's Utopian Illusion." *MELUS* 15.3 (Fall 1988): 121–129.

Ellison, Ralph. *The Collected Essays of Ralph Ellison.* Edited by John J. Callahan. New York: Modern Library, 1995.

Faderman, Lillian. *Surpassing the Love of Men: Romantic Friendship and Love between Women from the Renaissance to the Present.* New York: Morrow, 1981.

Fauset, Jessie Redmon. *Plum Bun: A Novel without a Moral.* Introduction by Deborah McDowell. 1928. Boston: Pandora Press, 1985.

———. *There Is Confusion.* Foreword by Thadious Davis. 1924. Boston: Northeastern University Press, 1989.

Ferguson, SallyAnn. "Charles W. Chesnutt's 'Future American.'" *MELUS* 15.3 (Fall 1988): 95–107.

Fielder, Leslie. *Love and Death in the American Novel.* 1960. New York: Anchor Books, 1992.

Fisher, Rudolph. *The Conjure Man Dies: A Mystery Tale of Dark Harlem.* 1932. Ann Arbor: University of Michigan Press, 1992.

———. *The Walls of Jericho.* 1928. Ann Arbor: University of Michigan Press, 1994.

Forbes, Jack D. *Africans and Native Americans: The Language of Red-Black Peoples.* 2d ed. Urbana: University of Illinois Press, 1993.

Ford, Charles Henri, and Parker Tyler. *The Young and Evil.* Paris, 1933. Reprint, New York: Arno Press, 1975.

Foucault, Michel. *The Use of Pleasure.* Vol. 2 of *The History of Sexuality.* Translated by Robert Hurley. 3 vols. New York: Vintage, 1980–1986.

Fowler, Arlen L. *The Black Infantry in the West, 1869–1891.* Westport, CT: Greenwood, 1971.

Frazier, E. Franklin. *The Black Bourgeoisie: The Rise of a New Middle Class.* 1957. New York: Free Press/Macmillan, 1965.

——. "The Du Bois Program in the Present *Crisis." Race: Devoted to Social, Political and Economic Equality* 1.1 (Winter 1935–36): 11–13.

——. "The Failure of the Negro Intellectual." *Negro Digest* 11 (February 1962): 26–36.

——. *The Negro Family in Chicago.* Chicago: University of Chicago Press, 1932.

——. *The Negro Family in the United States.* Chicago: University of Chicago Press, 1939.

——. "The Negro in Harlem: A Report on the Social and Economic Conditions Responsible for the Outbreak of March 19, 1935." In *Amsterdam News,* July 18, 1936, 6–9, 20, 24.

——. "New Currents of Thought among the Colored People of America." Master's thesis, Clark University, Worcester, MA, 1920.

——. "Racial Self-Expression." In *Ebony and Topaz: A Collectanea,* edited by Charles S. Johnson, 119–121. Freeport, NY: Books for Libraries Press, 1971.

French, Marilyn. *Beyond Power: On Women, Men, and Morals.* New York: Ballantine Books, 1985.

Furner, Mary O. *Advocacy and Objectivity: A Crisis in the Professionalization of American Social Science, 1865–1905.* Lexington: University Press of Kentucky, 1975.

Fuss, Diana. *Essentially Speaking: Feminism, Nature, and Difference.* New York: Routledge, 1989.

Gaines, Kevin K. *Uplifting the Race: Black Leadership, Politics, and Culture in the Twentieth Century.* Chapel Hill: University of North Carolina Press, 1996.

Gaither, Renoir W. "The Moment of Revision: A Reappraisal of Wallace Thurman's Aesthetics in *The Blacker the Berry* and *Infants of the Spring." CLA Journal* 37.1 (1993): 81–93.

Gates, Henry Louis Jr. "The Trope of the New Negro and the Reconstruction of the Image of the Black." *Representations* 24 (Fall 1988): 129–155.

Gibson, John William. *Progress of a Race, or the Remarkable Advancement of the American Negro, from the Bondage of Slavery, Ignorance, and Poverty to the Freedom of Citizenship, Intelligence, Affluence, Honor, and Trust.* 1920. Edited by J. L. Nichols and William H. Crogman. Rev. ed. Washington, D.C.: A. Jenkins, 1925.

Giddings, Paula. *When and Where I Enter: The Impact of Black Women on Race and Sex in America.* New York: Bantam Books, 1984.

Giles, J. R. "Religious Alienation and 'Homosexual Consciousness' in *City of Night* and *Go Tell It on the Mountain.*" Special issue of *College English,* "The Homosexual Imagination," edited by Louie Crew and Rictor Norton, 36.3 (1974): 369–380.

Gilmore, Glenda Elizabeth. *Gender and Jim Crow: Women and the Politics of White Supremacy in North Carolina, 1896–1920.* Chapel Hill: University of North Carolina Press, 1996.

Gilpin, Patrick J. "Charles S. Johnson: Entrepreneur of the Harlem Renaissance." In *The Harlem Renaissance Remembered,* edited by Arna Bontemps. 215–246.

Gilroy, Paul. *The Black Atlantic: Modernity and Double Consciousness.* Cambridge: Harvard University Press, 1993.

Goldberg, Jonathan. *Sodometries: Renaissance Texts, Modern Sexualities.* Stanford: Stanford University Press, 1992.

Gordon, Eugene. Review of *Born to Be. Opportunity* 8 (January 1930): 22–23.

Gordon, Taylor. *Born to Be.* With an introduction by Muriel Draper and foreword by Carl Van Vechten. Illustrated by Miguel Covarrubias. New York: Covici-Friede, 1929.

Gould, Stephen Jay. *The Mismeasure of Man.* New York: W. W. Norton, 1981.

Grandison, Kenrick Ian. "Landscapes of Terror: A Reading of Tuskegee's Historic Campus, 1881–1915." In *The Geography of Identity,* edited by Patricia Yaeger, 334–367. Ann Arbor: University of Michigan Press, 1996.

——. "Negotiated Space: The Black College Campus as a Cultural Record of Postbellum America." *American Quarterly* 51.3 (1999): 529–579.

Griffin, Dustin H. *Literary Patronage in England, 1650–1800.* Cambridge: Cambridge University Press, 1996.

Griffin, Farah Jasmine. *"Who Set You Flowin'?": The African American Migration Narrative.* New York: Oxford University Press, 1995.

Gubar, Susan. *Race Changes: White Skin, Black Face in American Culture.* New York: Oxford University Press, 1997.

Gunning, Sandra. *Race, Rape, and Lynching: The Red Record of American Literature, 1890–1912.* New York: Oxford University Press, 1996.

Gutiérrez-Jones, Carl Scott. *Rethinking the Borderlands: Between Chicano Culture and Legal Discourse.* Berkeley: University of California Press, 1995.

Hall, George. "Alain Locke and the Honest Propaganda of Truth and Beauty." In *Alain Locke,* edited by Russell J. Linnemann, 91–99.

Halperin, David M. *One Hundred Years of Homosexuality and Other Essays on Greek Love.* New York: Routledge, 1990.

Haraway, Donna J. *Simians, Cyborgs, and Women: The Reinvention of Nature.* New York: Routledge, 1991.

Harlan, Louis R., et al., eds. *The Booker T. Washington Papers.* Vol. 2: 1860–1869 and vol. 10: 1901–1911. Urbana: University of Illinois Press, 1981.

Harlan, Louis R. *Booker T. Washington: The Making of a Black Leader, 1856–1901.* New York: Oxford University Press, 1972.

———. *Booker T. Washington: The Wizard of Tuskegee, 1901–1915.* New York: Oxford University Press, 1983.

Harper, Phillip Brian. *Are We Not Men? Masculine Anxiety and the Problem of African-American Identity.* New York: Oxford University Press, 1996.

———. *Private Affairs: Critical Ventures in the Culture of Social Relations.* New York: New York University Press, 1999.

Harris, Leonard, ed. *The Philosophy of Alain Locke: Harlem Renaissance and Beyond.* Philadelphia: Temple University Press, 1989.

Hartman, Saidiya V. *Scenes of Subjection: Terror, Slavery, and Self-Making in Nineteenth-Century America.* New York: Oxford University Press, 1997.

Harvey, William B. "The Philosophical Anthropology of Alain Locke." In *Alain Locke,* edited by Russell J. Linnemann, 17–28.

Haynes, George Edmund. *Negro Newcomers in Detroit.* Home Missions Council, 1918. New York: Arno Press and the *New York Times,* 1969.

Hegel, G.W.F. *The Phenomenology of Mind.* 1807. Translated by J. B. Baillie. New York: Harper and Row, 1967.

Hellwig, David J. "Strangers in Their Own Land: Patterns of Black Nativism, 1830–1930." *American Studies* 23 (1982): 85–98.

Hemenway, Robert. Introduction. Reprint of *Born to Be,* by Taylor Gordon, ix–xliv. Seattle: University of Washington Press, 1975.

———. *Zora Neale Hurston: A Literary Biography.* Urbana: University of Illinois Press, 1979.

Hemingway, John Hylan. "An Immigrant Artist Captured the Faces of the New World." *Smithsonian* 20, Nov. 1989; 172–183.

Henderson, George Wylie. *Jule.* Introduction by J. Lee Greene. 1946. Tuscaloosa: University of Alabama Press, 1989.

Henderson, Mae. "Portrait of Wallace Thurman." In *The Harlem Renaissance Remembered,* edited by Arna Bontemps, 147–170.

Herskovits, Melville J. *The Myth of the Negro Past.* 1941. Boston: Beacon, 1964.

———. "The Negro's Americanism." In *The New Negro: An Interpretation,* edited by Alain Locke, 353–360.

Hine, Darlene Clark. "Black Studies: An Overview." In *Three Essays: Black Studies in the United States.* With Robert L. Harris Jr. and Nellie McKay. New York: Ford Foundation, 1990.

Holmes, Eugene C. "Alain Leroy Locke: A Sketch." *Phylon* 20.1 (Spring 1959): 82–89.

Holt, Thomas C. "The Political Uses of Alienation: W.E.B. Du Bois on Politics, Race, and Culture, 1903–1940." *American Quarterly* 42 (June 1990): 301–323.

hooks, bell (Gloria Watkins). *Yearning: Race, Gender, and Cultural Politics.* Boston: South End Press, 1990.

Hopkins, Pauline. *Contending Forces: A Romance Illustrative of Negro Life North and South.* 1900. New York: Oxford University Press, 1988.

Horne, Frank. "Correspondence." *Opportunity* 4 (Oct. 1926): 326.

———. "Our Book Shelf." *Opportunity* 4 (July 1926): 227.

Hostetler, Anne E. "The Aesthetics of Race and Gender in Nella Larsen's *Quicksand*." *PMLA* 105.1 (1990): 35–46.

Huggins, Nathan. *Harlem Renaissance.* London: Oxford University Press, 1971.

Hughes, Langston. *Arna Bontemps/Langston Hughes Letters, 1925–1967.* Selected and edited by Charles H. Nichols. New York: Paragon House, 1990.

———. *The Big Sea.* Introduction by Arnold Rampersad. 1940. New York: Hill and Wang/Farrar, Straus and Giroux, 1993.

——. "The Negro Artist and the Racial Mountain." In *African American Literary Theory: A Reader,* edited by Winston Napier, 27–30. New York: New York University Press, 2000.

——. *Not without Laughter.* Introduction by Arna Bontemps. 1930. New York: Macmillan, 1969.

Hull, Gloria T. *Color, Sex, and Poetry: The Women Writers of the Harlem Renaissance.* Bloomington: Indiana University Press, 1987.

Humes, Dollena Joy. *Oswald Garrison Villard, Liberal of the 1920s.* Syracuse: Syracuse University Press, 1960.

Hunter, Tera W. *To 'Joy My Freedom: Southern Black Women's Lives and Labors after the Civil War.* Cambridge: Harvard University Press, 1997.

Hurd, Myles Raymond. "Booker T., Blacks, and Brogues: Chesnutt's Sociohistorical Links to Realism in 'Uncle Wellington's Wives.'" *American Literary Realism* 26.2 (Winter 1994): 19–29.

Hurston, Zora Neale. *Dust Tracks on a Road.* 1942. New York: HarperCollins, 1991.

——. *Their Eyes Were Watching God.* Foreword by Mary Helen Washington. 1937. New York: Harper and Row, 1990.

Hutchinson, George. *The Harlem Renaissance in Black and White.* Cambridge: Harvard University Press, 1995.

Ikonné, Chidi. *From Du Bois to Van Vechten: The Early New Negro Literature, 1903–1926.* Westport, CT: Greenwood Press, 1981.

Imes, Nella. See Larsen, Nella.

Jackson, Jacquelyne Johnson. "Black Female Sociologists." In *Black Sociologists: Historical and Contemporary Perspectives,* edited by James E. Blackwell and Morris Janowitz, 267–295.

Jacobs, Harriet. *Incidents in the Life of a Slave Girl.* Edited by Nell Irvin Painter. 1861. New York: Penguin, 2000.

James, Joy. *Transcending the Talented Tenth: Black Leaders and American Intellectuals.* New York: Routledge, 1977.

Johnson, Charles Richard. "A Phenomenology of the Black Body." In *The Male Body: Features, Destinies, Exposures,* edited by Laurence Goldstein, 599–614. Ann Arbor: University of Michigan Press, 1994.

Johnson, Charles S. "The New Frontage on American Life." In *The New Negro: An Interpretation,* edited by Alain Locke, 278–298.

——, ed. *Ebony and Topaz: A Collectanea.* 1927. Freeport, NY: Books for Libraries, 1971.

Johnson, Charles S., and the Chicago Commission on Race Relations. *The Negro in Chicago.* Chicago: University of Chicago Press, 1922.

Johnson, Guy B. *John Henry: Tracking Down a Negro Legend.* Chapel Hill: University of North Carolina Press, 1929.

Johnson, James Weldon. *Along This Way: The Autobiography of James Weldon Johnson.* 1933. Introduction by Sondra Kathryn Wilson. New York: Penguin Books, 1990.

——. *The Autobiography of an Ex-Coloured Man.* 1912, 1927. Introduction by Henry Louis Gates Jr. New York: Vintage, 1989.

——. *Black Manhattan.* 1930. New York: DaCapo, 1991.

——. *The Book of American Negro Poetry.* New York: Harcourt, Brace, and Co., 1931.

——. "Harlem: The Culture Capital." In *The New Negro: An Interpretation,* edited by Alain Locke, 301–311.

——. "Race Prejudice and the Negro Artist." *Harper's,* November 1928, 769–770.

——. "Romance and Tragedy in Harlem—A Review." Review of *Nigger Heaven* by Carl Van Vechten. *Opportunity* 4 (1926): 316–317, 330.

Johnston, Sir Harry H. *The Negro in the New World.* London: Methuen, 1910.

Jones, Butler A. "The Tradition of Sociology Teaching in the Black Colleges: The Unheralded Professionals." In *Black Sociologists: Historical and Contemporary Perspectives,* edited by James E. Blackwell and Morris Janowitz, 121–163.

Jones, Dewey R. "The Book Shelf: More 'Nigger Heaven.'" *Chicago Defender,* 17 March 1928, 2.1

——. "The Bookshelf: The Walls Come Tumbling Down." *Chicago Defender,* 11 August 1928, 2.1.

Jones, Howard Mumford. *The Age of Energy: Varieties of American Experience, 1865–1915.* New York: Viking, 1971.

Jones, Jacqueline. *Labor of Love, Labor of Sorrow: Black Women, Work and the Family, from Slavery to the Present.* 1985. New York: Vintage/Random House, 1995.

Jones, Maxine D., and Joe M. Richardson. *Talladega College: The First Century.* Tuscaloosa: University of Alabama Press, 1990.

Jordan, Winthrop D. *White over Black: American Attitudes toward the Negro, 1550–1812*. New York: W. W. Norton, 1968.

Katz, Jonathan. *Gay American History: Lesbians and Gay Men in the U.S.A.* New York: Discus/Avon Books, 1976.

Katz, William Loren. *Black Indians: A Hidden Heritage*. 1986. New York: Aladdin, 1997.

———. *The Black West: A Documentary and Pictorial History of the African American Role in the West-ward Expansion of the United States*. 1987. New York: Touchstone/Simon and Schuster, 1996.

Keller, Frances Richardson. *An American Crusade: The Life of Charles Waddell Chesnutt*. Provo, UT: Brigham Young University Press, 1978.

Kelley, Robin D. G. *Race Rebels: Culture, Politics, and the Black Working Class*. New York: Free Press, 1994.

Kellner, Bruce. *Carl Van Vechten and the Irreverent Decades*. Norman: University of Oklahoma Press, 1968.

———. "Carl Van Vechten's Black Renaissance." In *The Harlem Renaissance: Revaluations,* edited by Amritjit Singh, William S. Shiver, and Stanley Brodwin, 23–33.

———. "'Refined Racism': White Patronage in the Harlem Renaissance." In *The Harlem Renais-sance Re-examined,* edited by Victor A. Kramer, 93–106.

———, ed. *Letters of Carl Van Vechten*. New Haven: Yale University Press, 1987.

Kellogg, Charles Flint. *NAACP: A History of the National Association for the Advancement of Colored People*. Vol. 1: *1909–1920*. Baltimore: Johns Hopkins University Press, 1967.

Kent, George. *Blackness and the Adventure of Western Culture*. Chicago: Third World Press, 1972.

Keuls, Eva C. *The Reign of the Phallus: Sexual Politics in Ancient Athens*. New York: Harper, 1985.

Kimmel, Michael. *Manhood in America: A Cultural History*. New York: Free Press, 1996.

King, Martin Luther Jr. *Why We Can't Wait*. New York: Penguin, 1963.

Koestenbaum, Wayne. *The Queen's Throat: Opera, Homosexuality, and the Mystery of Desire*. New York: Poseidon, 1993.

Kramer, Victor A., ed. *The Harlem Renaissance Re-examined*. New York: AMS Press, 1987.

Kubitschek, Missy Dehn. *Claiming the Heritage: African-American Women Novelists and History*. Jack-son: University of Mississippi Press, 1991.

Kusmer, Kenneth L. *A Ghetto Takes Shape: Black Cleveland, 1870–1930*. Urbana: University of Illi-nois Press, 1976.

Ladner, Joyce, ed. *The Death of White Sociology*. New York: Random House, 1973.

Lal, Barbara Ballis. *The Romance of Culture in an Urban Civilization: Robert E. Park on Race and Eth-nic Relations in Cities*. London: Routledge, 1990.

Larsen, Nella. "Correspondence." *Opportunity* 4 (October 1926): 295.

———. *Quicksand* and *Passing*. Edited by Deborah E. McDowell. 1928, 1929. New Brunswick: Rut-gers University Press, 1986.

Lemann, Nicholas. *The Promised Land: The Great Black Migration and How It Changed America*. New York: Vintage/Random House, 1991.

Lemelle, Anthony J. Jr. *Black Male Deviance*. Westport, CT: Praeger, 1995.

Lerner, Gerda. *The Creation of Patriarchy*. New York: Oxford University Press, 1986.

Levin, James. *The Gay Novel in America*. New York: Garland Publishing, 1991.

Levine, Lawrence W. *Black Culture and Black Consciousness: Afro-American Folk Thought from Slav-ery to Freedom*. New York: Oxford University Press, 1977.

Levy, Eugene. *James Weldon Johnson: Black Leader, Black Voice*. Chicago: University of Chicago Press, 1973.

Lewis, David Levering. "Dr. Johnson's Friends: Civil Rights by Copyright during Harlem's Mid-Twenties." *Massachusetts Review* 20 (1979): 501–519.

———. *W.E.B. Du Bois: The Fight for Equality and the American Century, 1919–1963*. New York: Henry Holt and Co., 2000.

———. *W.E.B. Du Bois: Biography of a Race, 1868–1919*. New York: Henry Holt and Co., 1993.

———. *When Harlem Was in Vogue*. New York: Oxford University Press, 1979.

Liebow, Elliot. *Tally's Corner: A Study of Negro Streetcorner Men*. Boston: Little, Brown and Co., 1967.

Linder, Rolf. *The Reportage of Urban Culture: Robert Park and the Chicago School*. Translated by Adrian Morris. Cambridge: University of Cambridge Press, 1996.

Lindsey, Donal F. *Indians at Hampton Institute, 1877–1923*. Urbana: University of Illinois Press, 1995.

Linnemann, Russell J., ed. *Alain Locke: Reflections on a Modern Renaissance Man*. Baton Rouge: Louisiana State University Press, 1982.

Littlefield, Daniel F. Jr. *Africans and Seminoles: From Removal to Emancipation.* 1977. Jackson: University Press of Mississippi, 2001.

Lively, Adam. "Continuity and Radicalism in American Black Nationalist Thought, 1914–1929." *Journal of American Studies* 18.2 (1984): 207–235.

Locke, Alain. "1928: A Retrospective Review." *Opportunity* 7.1 (Jan. 1929): 8–11.

———. "The Contribution of Race to Culture." Reprinted in *The Philosophy of Alain Locke: Harlem Renaissance and Beyond,* edited by Leonard Harris, 202–206.

———. "A Critical Retrospect of the Literature of the Negro for 1947." *Phylon* 9 (1948): 3–13.

———. *The Critical Temper of Alain Locke: A Selection of His Essays on Art and Culture.* Edited by Jeffrey C. Stewart. New York: Garland, 1983.

———. "Dawn Patrol: A Review of the Literature of the Negro for 1948." *Phylon* 10 (1949): 5–14, 167–172.

———. "From *Native Son* to *Invisible Man:* A Review of the Literature of the Negro for 1952." *Phylon* 14 (1953): 34–44.

———. "Harlem: Dark Weather-Vane." *Survey Graphic* 25 (August 1936): 457–462.

———. "The High Price of Integration: A Review of the Literature of the Negro for 1951." *Phylon* 13 (1952): 7–18.

———. "Inventory at Mid-Century: A Review of the Literature of the Negro for 1950." *Phylon* 12 (1951): 5–12, 185–190.

———. "The Legacy of the Ancestral Arts." In *The New Negro: An Interpretation,* edited by Locke, 254–267.

———. "The Negro: 'New' or Newer? A Retrospective Review of the Literature of the Negro for 1938." *Opportunity* 17 (January–February 1939): 4–10, 36–42.

———. "The Negro Spirituals." In *The New Negro: An Interpretation,* edited by Locke, 199–213.

———. "Negro Youth Speaks." In *The New Negro: An Interpretation,* edited by Locke, 47–53.

———. "The New Negro." Introduction. In *The New Negro: An Interpretation,* edited by Locke, 3–16.

———. "Of Native Sons: Real and Otherwise." *Opportunity* 18 (January–February 1941): 4–9, 48–52.

———. "Propaganda—or Poetry." *Race: Devoted to Social, Political, and Economic Equality* (Summer 1936): 70–77, 87.

———. "Reason and Race: A Review of the Literature of the Negro for 1946." *Phylon* 8 (1947): 17–27.

———. "Self-Criticism: The Third Dimension in Culture." *Phylon* 11 (1950): 391–394.

———. Unity through Diversity: A Baha'i Principle." Reprinted in *The Philosophy of Alain Locke: Harlem Renaissance and Beyond,* edited by Leonard Harris, 134–138.

———. "Who and What Is Negro?" Reprinted in *The Philosophy of Alain Locke: Harlem Renaissance and Beyond,* edited by Leonard Harris, 207–228.

———. "Wisdom *de Profundis:* The Literature of the Negro, 1949." *Phylon* 11 (1950): 5–15, 171–175.

———, ed. *The New Negro: An Interpretation.* New York: Albert and Charles Boni, 1925.

Logan, Rayford. *The Betrayal of the Negro from Rutherford B. Hayes to Woodrow Wilson.* 1965. 2d ed. New York: Da Capo Press, 1997. Reprint of *The Negro in American Life and Thought: The Nadir, 1877–1901.* 1954.

———. "James Weldon Johnson and Haiti." *Phylon* 32 (1971): 396–402.

Lorde, Audre. *Sister/Outsider: Essays and Speeches.* Freedom, CA: Crossing Press, 1984.

Lott, Eric. *Love and Theft: Blackface Minstrelsy and the American Working Class.* New York: Oxford University Press, 1993.

Love, Nat. *The Life and Adventures of Nat Love: Better Known in the Cattle Country as "Deadwood Dick"—By Himself.* 1907. New York: Arno, 1968.

Lovejoy, Arthur O. *The Great Chain of Being.* Cambridge: Harvard University Press, 1936.

Lubiano, Wahneema. "'But Compared to What?': Reading Realism, Representation, and Essentialism in *School Daze, Do the Right Thing,* and the Spike Lee Discourse." In *Representing Black Men,* edited by Marcellus Blount and George P. Cunningham, 173–204.

Lueders, Edward. *Carl Van Vechten and the Twenties.* Albuquerque: University of New Mexico Press, 1955.

Lueth, Elmer. "The Scope of Black Life in Claude McKay's *Home to Harlem.*" *Obsidian II: Black Literature in Review* 5.3 (1990): 43–52.

Lyman, Stanford M. *The Black American in Sociological Thought: A Failure of Perspective*. New York: Capricorn Books, 1973.

Major, Clarence. *Juba to Jive: A Dictionary of African-American Slang*. 1970. New York: Penguin Books, 1994.

Majors, Richard, and Janet Mancini Billson. *Cool Pose: The Dilemmas of Black Manhood in America*. New York: Simon and Schuster, 1992.

Malik, Kenan. *The Meaning of Race: Race, History and Culture in Western Society*. New York: New York University Press, 1996.

Marable, Manning. *W.E.B. Du Bois: Black Radical Democrat*. Boston: G. K. Hare, 1986.

Marchalonis, Shirley. *Patrons and Protegées: Gender, Friendship, and Writing in Nineteenth-Century America*. New Brunswick: Rutgers University Press, 1988.

Marks, Carole. *Farewell—We're Good and Gone: The Great Black Migration*. Bloomington: Indiana University Press, 1989.

Martin, Robert K. *Hero, Captain, Stranger: Male Friendship, Social Critique, and Literary Form in the Sea Novels of Herman Melville*. Chapel Hill: University of North Carolina Press, 1986.

———. "Knights Errant and Gothic Seducers: The Representation of Male Friendship in Mid-Nineteenth-Century America." In *Hidden from History: Reclaiming the Gay and Lesbian Past*, edited by Martin Bauml Duberman, Martha Vicinus, and George Chauncey Jr., 169–182.

Martin, Tony. *Literary Garveyism: Garvey, Black Arts, and the Harlem Renaissance*. Dover, MA: Majority Press, 1983.

Matthews, F. H. *Quest for an American Sociology: Robert E. Park and the Chicago School*. Montreal: McGill-Queens University Press, 1977.

May, Katja. *African Americans and Native Americans in the Creek and Cherokee Nations, 1830s to 1920s: Collision and Collusion*. New York: Garland, 1996.

McDowell, Deborah. *"The Changing Same": Black Women's Literature, Criticism, and Theory*. Bloomington: Indiana University Press, 1995.

McKay, Claude. *Banana Bottom*. 1933. New York: Harcourt, Brace, Jovanovich, 1961.

———. *Banjo: A Story without a Plot*. 1929. New York: Harcourt, Brace, Jovanovich, 1970.

———. *Home to Harlem*. 1928. Boston: Northeastern University Press, 1987.

———. *A Long Way from Home: An Autobiography*. 1937. Introduction by St. Clair Drake. New York: Harcourt, Brace, Jovanovich, 1970.

Meier, August. "Black Sociologists in White America." *Social Forces* 56 (1977): 259–270.

Mellinger, Wayne Martin. "John Henry Adams and the Image of the 'New Negro.'" *International Review of African American Art* 14 (1997): 29–33.

Mercer, Kobena. *Welcome to the Jungle: New Positions in Black Cultural Studies*. New York: Routledge, 1994.

Mitchell, W.J.T. *Iconology: Image, Text, Ideology*. Chicago: University of Chicago Press, 1986.

———. *Picture Theory: Essays on Verbal and Visual Representation*. Chicago: University of Chicago Press, 1994.

Morrison, Toni. "City Limits, Village Values: Concepts of the Neighborhood in Black Fiction." In *Literature and the Urban Experience: Essays on the City and Literature*, edited by Michael C. Jaye and Ann Chalmers Watts, 35–43. New Brunswick: Rutgers University Press, 1981.

———. *Playing in the Dark: Whiteness and the Literary Imagination*. New York: Vintage/Random House, 1993.

Moton, Robert Russa. "Hampton-Tuskegee: Missioners of the Masses." In *The New Negro: An Interpretation*, edited by Alain Locke, 323–332.

———. *What the Negro Thinks*. Garden City, NY: Doubleday, 1929.

Mumford, Lewis. *Brown Decades: A Study of the Arts of America, 1865–1895*. New York: Harcourt, Brace, Jovanovich, 1931.

Murphy, Peter, ed. *Fictions of Masculinity: Crossing Cultures, Crossing Sexualities*. New York: New York University Press, 1994.

Myrdal, Gunnar. *An American Dilemma: The Negro Problem and Modern Democracy*. 1944. New York: Harper and Row, 1962.

Naylor, Gloria. "Love and Sex in the Afro-American Novel." *Yale Review* 78.1 (1988): 19–31.

Newfield, Christopher. "Democracy and Male Homoeroticism." *Yale Journal of Criticism* 6.2 (1993): 29–62.

Nichols, Charles H., ed. *Arna Bontemps–Langston Hughes Letters, 1925–1967*. New York: Paragon, 1980.

Niles, Blair. *Strange Brother.* 1931. London: GMP, 1991.

Nugent, Richard Bruce. "Smoke, Lillies, and Jade." *Fire!!* 1.1 (1926): 33–39.

Ovington, Mary White. *Black and White Sat Down Together: The Reminiscences of an NAACP Founder.* New York: Feminist Press at CUNY, 1995.

———. *Half a Man: The Status of the Negro in New York.* Foreword by Franz Boas. New York: Longman, Green and Co., 1911.

———. *Portraits in Color.* New York: Viking, 1927.

———. *The Walls Came Tumbling Down.* New York: Harcourt, Brace, Jovanovich, 1947.

Painter, Nell Irvin. *Exodusters: Black Migration to Kansas after Reconstruction.* New York: Alfred A. Knopf, 1976.

———. *Standing at Armageddon: The United States, 1877–1919.* New York: W. W. Norton, 1987.

Park, Robert E. "Methods of Teaching: Impressions and a Verdict." *Social Forces* 20 (Oct. 1941): 36–46.

———. *Race and Culture: Essays in the Sociology of Contemporary Man.* Glencoe, NY: Free Press, 1950.

Percy, William Armstrong III. *Pederasty and Pedagogy in Archaic Greece.* Urbana and Chicago: University of Illinois Press, 1996.

Persons, S. *Ethnic Studies at Chicago, 1905–1945.* Urbana: University of Illinois Press, 1987.

Pfeil, Fred. *White Guys: Studies in Postmodern Domination and Difference.* London: Verso, 1995.

Philpott, T. L. *The Slum and the Ghetto: Neighborhood Deterioration and Middle-Class Reform, Chicago, 1880–1930.* New York: Oxford University Press, 1978.

Pickens, William. *Bursting Bonds: The Autobiography of a "New Negro."* Edited by William L. Andrews. 1923. Bloomington: University of Indiana Press, 1991.

———. *The Heir of Slaves: An Autobiography.* Boston: Pilgrim, 1911.

———. *The New Negro: His Political, Civil, and Mental Status; and Related Essays.* 1916. New York: AMS Press, 1969.

———. *The Vengeance of the Gods, and Three Other Stories of Real American Color Line Life.* 1922. Freeport, NY: Books for Libraries Press, 1972.

Platt, Anthony M. *E. Franklin Frazier Reconsidered.* New Brunswick: Rutgers University Press, 1991.

———, ed. *The Politics of the Riot Commissions, 1917–1970: A Collection of Official Reports and Critical Essays.* New York: Macmillan, 1971.

Priebe, Richard. "The Search for Community in the Novels of Claude McKay." *Studies in Black Literature* 3.2 (1972): 22–30.

Proceedings of the National Negro Conference. New York, 31 May and 1 June 1909.

Pyne-Timothy, Helen. "Perceptions of the Black Woman in the Work of Claude McKay." *CLA Journal* 19 (1975): 152–164.

Rampersad, Arnold. *The Art and Imagination of W.E.B. Du Bois.* 1976. New York: Schocken Books, 1990.

———. Introduction. In *The New Negro: Voices of the Harlem Renaissance,* edited by Alain Locke, ix–xxiii. 1925. New York: Atheneum, 1992.

———. *The Life of Langston Hughes.* 2 vols. New York: Oxford University Press, 1986–1988.

Ramsey, Priscilla. "Freeze the Day: A Feminist Reading of Nella Larsen's *Quicksand* and *Passing.*" *Afro-Americans in New York Life and History* 9 (Jan. 1985): 27–41.

Randall, Dudley. *The Black Poets.* New York: Bantam, 1971.

Raushenbush, Winifred. *Robert E. Park: Biography of a Sociologist.* Durham: Duke University Press, 1979.

Redfield, Robert. *Tepoztlán, a Mexican Village: A Study of Folk Life.* Chicago: University of Chicago Press, 1930.

Reid-Pharr, Robert F. *Black Gay Man: Essays.* With a foreword by Samuel Delaney. New York: New York University Press, 2001.

Rich, Adrienne. "Compulsory Heterosexuality and Lesbian Existence." In *Powers of Desire: The Politics of Sexuality,* edited by Ann Snitow, Christine Stansell, and Sharon Thompson, 177–205. New York: Monthly Review Press, 1983.

Richards, Jeffrey. "Passing the Love of Women: Manly Love and Victorian Society." In *Manliness and Morality: Middle-Class Masculinity in Britain and America, 1800–1940,* edited by J. A. Mangan and J. Walvin, 92–122. New York: St. Martin's Press, 1987.

Robbins, Richard. "Charles S. Johnson." In *Black Sociologists: Historical and Contemporary Perspectives,* edited by James E. Blackwell and Morris Janowitz, 56–84.

Roberts, Dorothy. *Killing the Body: Race, Reproduction, and the Meaning of Liberty.* New York: Pantheon, 1997.

Roberts, John W. *From Trickster to Badman: The Black Folk Hero in Slavery and Freedom.* Philadelphia: University of Pennsylvania Press, 1989.

Roberts, Randy. *Papa Jack: Jack Johnson and the Era of White Hopes.* New York: The Free Press/Macmillan, 1983.

Robinson, Sally. *Marked Men: White Masculinity in Crisis.* New York: Columbia University Press, 2000.

Roediger, David R. *The Wages of Whiteness: Race and the Making of the American Working Class.* London: Verso, 1991.

Rogin, Michael. *Blackface, White Noise: Jewish Immigrants in the Hollywood Melting Pot.* Berkeley: University of California Press, 1996.

Rose, Dan. *Black American Street Life: South Philadelphia, 1969–1971.* Philadelphia: University of Pennsylvania Press, 1987.

Ross, Marlon B. "Authority and Authenticity: Scribbling Authors and the Genius of Print in Eighteenth-Century England." In *The Construction of Authorship: Textual Appropriation in Law and Literature,* edited by Martha Woodmansee and Peter Jaszi, 231–257. Durham: Duke University Press, 1994.

———. "Beyond the Fragmented Word: Keats at the Limits of Language." In *Out of Bounds: Male Writers and Gender(ed) Criticism,* edited by Laura Claridge and Elizabeth Langland, 110–131. Amherst: University of Massachusetts, 1990.

———. "Camping the Dirty Dozens: The Queer Resources of Black Nationalist Invective." *Callaloo* 23.1 (2000): 290–312.

———. "In Search of Black Men's Masculinities." Review essay on Don Belton's *Speak My Name: Black Men on Masculinity and the American Dream;* Phillip Brian Harper's *Are We Not Men? Masculine Anxiety and the Problem of African-American Identity;* Marcellus Blount and George P. Cunningham's *Representing Black Men. Feminist Studies* 24.3 (Fall 1998): 599–626.

———. "The New Negro Displayed: Self-Ownership, Proprietary Sites/Sights, and the Bonds/Bounds of Race." In *Claiming the Stones, Naming the Bones: Cultural Property and the Negotiation of National and Ethnic Identity.* Edited by Elazar Barkan and Ronald Bush, 259–301. Los Angeles: Getty Research Institute, 2002.

———. "Race, Rape, Castration: Feminist Theories of Sexual Violence and Masculine Strategies of Black Protest." In *Masculinity Studies and Feminist Theories: New Directions.* Edited by Judith Kegan Gardiner, 305–343. New York: Columbia University Press, 2002.

———. Review of *Race Men,* by Hazel Carby. *Modernism/Modernity.* 7.2 (April 2000): 313–315.

———. "Romancing the Nation-State: The Politics of Romantic Nationalism." In *Macropolitics of Nineteenth-Century Literature: Nationalism, Exoticism, Imperialism.* Edited by Jonathan Arac and Harriet Ritvo, 56–85. Philadelphia: University of Pennsylvania Press, 1991.

———. "Trespassing the Colorline: Aggressive Mobility and Sexual Transgression in the Construction of New Negro Modernity." In *Modernism, Inc.: Essays on American Modernity.* Edited by Jani Scandura and Michael Thurston, 48–67. New York: New York University Press, 2001.

Rotundo, E. Anthony. *American Manhood: Transformations in Masculinity from the Revolution to the Modern Era.* New York: Basic Books, 1993.

Rudwick, Elliott M. "W.E.B. Du Bois as Sociologist." In *Black Sociologists: Historical and Contemporary Perspectives,* edited by James E. Blackwell and Morris Janowitz, 25–55.

———. *W.E.B. Du Bois: Propagandist of the Negro Protest.* New York: Atheneum, 1986.

Runcie, John. "Marcus Garvey and the Harlem Renaissance." *Afro-Americans in New York Life and History* 10.2 (July 1986): 7–28.

Sato, Hiroko. "Under the Harlem Shadow: A Study of Jessie Fauset and Nella Larsen." In *The Harlem Renaissance Remembered,* edited by Arna Bontemps, 63–89.

Schechter, Patricia A. *Ida B. Wells-Barnett and American Reform, 1880–1930.* Chapel Hill: University of North Carolina Press, 2001.

Schor, Naomi. *Reading in Detail: Aesthetics and the Feminine.* New York: Methuen, 1987.

Schuyler, George S. "The Negro-Art Hokum." *The Nation,* 16 June 1926, 662–663.

———. "The Van Vechten Revolution." *Phylon* 11.4 (1950): 362–368.

Schuyler, George S., and Theophilus Lewis. "Shafts and Darts: A Page of Calumny and Satire." *Messenger* 6.6 (June 1924): 183.

Scott, Emmett J., and Lyman Beecher Stowe. *Booker T. Washington: Builder of a Civilization.* Garden City, NY: Doubleday, Page, and Co., 1916.

Scruggs, Charles W. "Alain Locke and Walter White: Their Struggle for Control of the Harlem Renaissance." *Black American Literature Forum* (1980): 91–99.

————. "Crab Antics and Jacob's Ladder: Aaron Douglas's Two Views of *Nigger Heaven.*" In *The Harlem Renaissance Re-examined,* edited by Victor A. Kramer, 149–181.

————. *The Sage in Harlem: H. L. Mencken and the Black Writers of the 1920s.* Baltimore: Johns Hopkins University Press, 1984.

————. *Sweet Home: Invisible Cities in the Afro-American Novel.* Baltimore: Johns Hopkins University Press, 1993.

Sedgwick, Eve Kosofsky. *Between Men: English Literature and Male Homosocial Desire.* New York: Columbia University Press, 1985.

————. *Epistemology of the Closet.* Berkeley: University of California Press, 1990.

Seymour-Smith, Martin and Andrew C. Kimmens, eds. *World Authors, 1900–1950.* Vol. 3. New York: H. W. Wilson Co., 1996.

Sha, Richard C. *The Visual and Verbal Sketch in British Romanticism.* Philadelphia: University of Pennsylvania Press, 1998.

Shaw, Stephanie J. *What a Woman Ought to Be and to Do: Black Professional Women Workers during the Jim Crow Era.* Chicago: University of Chicago Press, 1996.

Silverman, Kaja. *Male Subjectivity at the Margins.* New York: Routledge, 1992.

Simmons, William Johnson. *Men of Mark: Eminent, Progressive, and Rising.* Cleveland: George M. Rewell and Co., 1887. New York: Arno Press and *New York Times,* 1968.

Singh, Amritjit. "Black-White Symbiosis: Another Look at the Literary History of the 1920s." In *The Harlem Renaissance Re-examined,* edited by Victor A. Kramer, 31–42.

————. *The Novels of the Harlem Renaissance: Twelve Black Writers, 1923–1933.* University Park: Pennsylvania State University Press, 1975.

Singh, Amritjit, William S. Shiver, and Stanley Brodwin, eds. *The Harlem Renaissance: Revaluations.* New York: Garland, 1989.

Smith, Charles U., and Lewis Killian. "Black Sociologists and Social Protest." In *Black Sociologists: Historical and Contemporary Perspectives,* edited by James E. Blackwell and Morris Janowitz, 191–228.

Smith, Dusky Lee. "Sociology and the Rise of Corporate Capitalism." In *The Sociology of Sociology: Analysis and Criticism of the Thought, Research, and Ethical Folkways of Sociology and its Practitioners,* edited by Larry T. Reynolds and Janice M. Reynolds. New York: David McKay, 1970.

Smith, Stanley H. "Sociological Research and Fisk University: A Case Study." In *Black Sociologists: Historical and Contemporary Perspectives,* edited by James E. Blackwell and Morris Janowitz, 164–190.

Smith-Rosenberg, Carol. "The Female World of Love and Ritual: Relations between Women in Nineteenth-Century America." *Signs* 1 (1975): 1–29.

Spillers, Hortense J. "A Hateful Passion, a Lost Love." In *Feminist Issues in Literary Scholarship,* edited by Shari Benstock, 181–207. Bloomington: Indiana University Press, 1987.

————. "Mama's Baby, Papa's Maybe: An American Grammar Book." *Diacritics* 17.2 (Summer 1987): 65–81.

————. "'The Permanent Obliquity of an In(pha)llibly Straight': In the Time of the Daughters and the Fathers." In *Changing Our Own Words,* edited by Cheryl A. Wall, 127–149.

Steward, Gustavus Adolphus. "The New Negro Hokum." *Social Forces* 6 (March 1928): 438–445.

————. "Salvation." *The Crisis* 31.5 (March 1926): 235–238.

Stewart, Jeffrey C. "Paul Robeson and the Problem of Modernism." In *Rhapsodies in Black: Art of the Harlem Renaissance,* 90–101. Berkeley: University of California Press, 1997.

————. *To Color America: Portraits by Winold Reiss.* Washington, D.C.: Smithsonian Institution, 1989.

————, ed. *The Critical Temper of Alain Locke: A Selection of His Essays on Art and Culture.* New York: Garland, 1983.

Stoff, Michael B. "Claude McKay and the Cult of Primitivism." In *The Harlem Renaissance Remembered,* edited by Arna Bontemps, 126–146.

Story, Ralph D. "Patronage and the Harlem Renaissance: You Get What You Pay For." *CLA Journal* 32.3 (March 1989): 284–295.

Sundquist, Eric J. "Red, White, Black, and Blue: The Color of American Modernism." *Transition* 6.2 (1996): 94–115.

Sylvander, Carolyn Wedin. See Wedin, Carolyn.

Talbot, Edith Armstrong. *Samuel Chapman Armstrong: A Biographical Study.* New York: Doubleday, 1904.

Tate, Claudia. *Domestic Allegories of Political Desire: The Black Heroine's Text at the Turn of the Century*. New York: Oxford University Press, 1992.

———. Introduction. In *Dark Princess* (1928), by W.E.B. Du Bois, ix–xxviii. Jackson: University of Mississippi Press, 1995.

———. *Psychoanalysis and Black Novels: Desire and the Protocols of Race*. New York: Oxford University Press, 1998.

Thomas, Brook, ed. *Plessy v. Ferguson: A Brief History with Documents*. Boston: Bedford Books, 1997.

Thorton, Hortense. "Sexism as Quagmire: Nella Larsen's *Quicksand*." *CLA Journal* 16 (1973): 285–301.

Thurman, Wallace. *The Blacker the Berry*. Introduction by Therman B. O'Daniel. 1929. New York: Collier/Macmillan, 1970.

———. *Infants of the Spring*. Foreword by Amritjit Singh. 1932. Boston: Northeastern University Press, 1992.

———, ed. *Fire!!* 1.1 (1926).

Tillery, Tyrone. *Claude McKay: A Black Poet's Struggle for Identity*. Amherst: University of Massachusetts Press, 1992.

Trachtenberg, Alan. *Incorporation of America: Culture and Society in the Gilded Age*. New York: Hill and Wang, 1982.

Trotter, Joe William Jr., ed. *The Great Migration in Historical Perspective: New Dimensions of Race, Class, and Gender*. Bloomington: Indiana University Press, 1991.

Ture, Kwame, and Charles V. Hamilton. *Black Power: The Politics of Liberation*. 1967. New York: Vintage, 1992.

Twyman, Bruce Edward. *The Black Seminole Legacy and North American Politics, 1693–1845*. Washington, D.C.: Howard University Press, 1999.

Van Vechten, Carl. *The Letters of Carl Van Vechten*. Edited by Bruce Kellner. New Haven: Yale University Press, 1987.

———. "The Negro in Art: How Shall We Be Portrayed?" *The Crisis* 31.5 (March 1926): 219–220.

———. *Nigger Heaven*. New York: Alfred A. Knopf, 1926.

Vicinus, Martha. "Distance and Desire: English Boarding School Friendships, 1870–1920." In *Hidden from History: Reclaiming the Gay and Lesbian Past*, edited by Martin Bauml Duberman, Martha Vicinus, and George Chauncey Jr., 129–140.

Villard, Oswald Garrison. *Fighting Years: Memoirs of a Liberal Editor*. New York: Harcourt, Brace, Jovanovich, 1939.

———. "Harper's Ferry and Gettysburg." Review of *John Brown* by W.E.B. Du Bois. *The Nation*, 28 Oct. 1909, 405.

———. "The Need of Organization." *Proceedings of the National Negro Conference*, New York, 31 May and 1 June 1909, 197–206.

Waldron, Edward E. *Walter White and the Harlem Renaissance*. Port Washington, NY: Kennikat Press, 1978.

Walker, Alice. *Meridian*. New York: Simon and Schuster, 1976.

Walker, Corey D. B. "'The Freemasonry of the Race': The Cultural Politics of Ritual, Race, and Place in Postemancipation Virginia." Ph.D. diss., Williamsburg, College of William and Mary, 2001.

Wall, Cheryl A. *Changing Our Own Words: Essays on Criticism, Theory, and Writing by Black Women*. New Brunswick: Rutgers University Press, 1989.

———. *Women of the Harlem Renaissance*. Bloomington: Indiana University Press, 1995.

Wallace, Maurice. *Constructing the Black Masculine: Identity and Ideality in African American Men's Literature and Culture, 1775–1995*. Durham: Duke University Press, 2002.

"*The Walls of Jericho* and Other New Works of Fiction." *New York Times*, 5 August 1928, part 3, 6.

Washington, Booker T. *The Future of the American Negro*. Boston: Small Maynard, 1899.

———. *A New Negro for a New Century: An Accurate and Up-to-Date Record of the Upward Struggles of the Negro Race*. Chicago: American Publishing House, 1900. Reprint, Miami: Mnemosyne Publishing Inc., 1969.

———. *Up from Slavery*. Introduction by Louis Harlan. 1901. New York: Penguin Books, 1986.

Washington, Johnny. *Alain Locke and Philosophy: A Quest for Cultural Pluralism*. Westport, CT: Greenwood, 1986.

———. *A Journey into the Philosophy of Alain Locke*. Westport, CT: Greenwood, 1994.

Washington, Mary Helen. *Invented Lives: Narratives of Black Women, 1860–1960*. New York: Anchor, 1987.

Waskow, Arthur I. "Chicago: The Riot Studied." In *The Politics of the Riot Commissions, 1917–1970: A Collection of Official Reports and Critical Essays,* edited by Anthony M. Platt, 120–157.

———. *From Race Riot to Sit-in: 1919 and the 1960s.* New York: Doubleday, 1966.

Wedin, Carolyn. *Inheritors of the Spirit: Mary White Ovington and the Founding of the NAACP.* New York: Wiley, 1998.

———. *Jessie Redmon Fauset, Black American Writer.* Troy, NY: Whiston, 1981.

Wells-Barnett, Ida B. *Crusade for Justice: The Autobiography of Ida B. Wells.* Edited by Afreda M. Duster. Chicago: University of Chicago Press, 1970.

———. *On Lynchings: Southern Horrors, a Red Record, and Mob Rule in New Orleans.* 1892, 1895, and 1900. Reprint, New York: Arno Press and *New York Times,* 1969.

West, Dorothy. *The Living Is Easy.* Afterword by Adelaide M. Cromwell. 1948. New York: Feminist Press, 1982.

White, Walter. "Correspondence." *Opportunity* 4 (Dec. 1926): 397.

———. *Fire in the Flint.* New York: Alfred A. Knopf, 1924.

———. *Flight.* New York: Alfred A. Knopf, 1926.

———. *A Man Called White: The Autobiography of Walter White.* New York: Viking, 1948.

Whyte, William Hollingsworth Jr. *The Organization Man.* New York: Simon and Schuster, 1956.

Wickett, Murray R. *Contested Territory: Whites, Native Americans, and African Americans in Oklahoma, 1865–1907.* Baton Rouge: Louisiana State University Press, 2000.

Wiebe, Robert H. *The Search for Order, 1877–1920.* New York: Hill and Wang, 1967.

Wiegman, Robyn. *American Anatomies: Theorizing Race and Gender.* Durham: Duke University Press, 1995.

Wintz, Cary D. *Black Culture and the Harlem Renaissance.* Houston: Rice University Press, 1988.

Woodson, Carter G. *A Century of Negro Migration.* Washington, D.C.: Association for the Study of Negro Life and History, 1918.

Woolf, Virginia. *A Room of One's Own.* 1929. New York: Harcourt, Brace and World, 1957.

Wreszin, Michael. *Oswald Garrison Villard: Pacifist at War.* Bloomington: Indiana University Press, 1965.

Wright, Richard. *Twelve Million Black Voices: A Folk History of the Negro in the United States.* New York: Viking, 1941.

Yacovone, Donald. "Abolitionists and the 'Language of Fraternal Love.'" In *Meanings for Manhood: Constructions of Masculinity in Victorian America,* edited by Mark C. Carnes and Clyde Griffen, 85–95. Chicago: University of Chicago Press, 1990.

Zafar, Rafia. "Franklinian Douglass: The Afro-American as the Representative Man." In *Frederick Douglass: New Literary and Historical Essays,* edited by Eric J. Sundquist, 99–117. Cambridge: Cambridge University Press, 1990.

Zamir, Shamoon. *Dark Voices: W.E.B. Du Bois and American Thought, 1888–1903.* Chicago: University of Chicago Press, 1995.

Index

About the Author

Marlon B. Ross is Professor of English and of African-American and African Studies in the Carter G. Woodson Institute at the University of Virginia. He is the author of *The Contours of Masculine Desire: Romanticism and the Rise of Women's Poetry.*